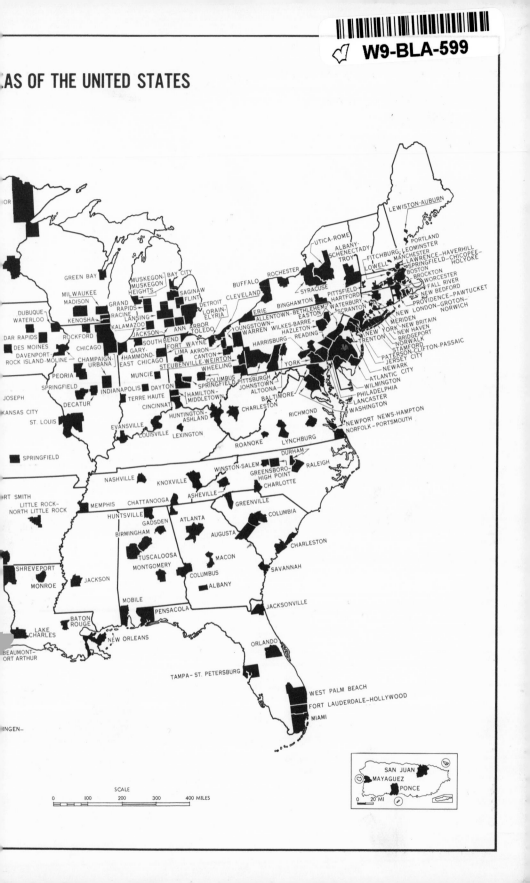

W9-BLA-599

UTICA-ROME
LEWISTON-AUBURN
PORTLAND
ALBANY-
SCHENECTADY-
TROY
FITCHBURG-LEOMINSTER
LAWRENCE-HAVERHILL
LOWELL
MANCHESTER
SPRINGFIELD-CHICOPEE-
HOLYOKE
BOSTON
BROCKTON
WORCESTER
GREEN BAY
BUFFALO
ROCHESTER
FALL RIVER
NEW BEDFORD
MUSKEGON
BAY CITY
PITTSFIELD
HARTFORD
PROVIDENCE-PAWTUCKET
MILWAUKEE
MADISON
MUSKEGON
HEIGHTS
SAGINAW
SYRACUSE
WATERBURY
SCRANTON
NEW LONDON-GROTON-
NORWICH
FLINT
BINGHAMTON
GRAND
RAPIDS
RACINE
DETROIT
CLEVELAND
ERIE
ALLENTOWN-BETHLEHEM-
MERIDEN
NEW BRITAIN
DUBUQUE
WATERLOO
KENOSHA
LANSING
LORAIN-
ELYRIA
EASTON
YOUNGSTOWN-
WARREN
WILKES-BARRE-
HAZLETON
NEW
YORK
NEW HAVEN
BRIDGEPORT
KALAMAZOO
ANN ARBOR
NORWALK
DAR RAPIDS
ROCKFORD
SOUTH BEND
TOLEDO
TRENTON
STAMFORD
PATERSON-CLIFTON-PASSAIC
DES MOINES
CHICAGO
FORT WAYNE
HARRISBURG
READING
JERSEY CITY
DAVENPORT-
ROCK ISLAND-MOLINE
GARY-
HAMMOND-
EAST CHICAGO
LIMA
AKRON
CANTON
NEWARK
ATLANTIC CITY
CHAMPAIGN-
URBANA
STEUBENVILLE-WEIRTON
YORK
WILMINGTON
JOSEPH
PEORIA
MUNCIE
WHEELING
COLUMBUS
PITTSBURGH
PHILADELPHIA
LANCASTER
SPRINGFIELD
INDIANAPOLIS
DAYTON
SPRINGFIELD
JOHNSTOWN
ALTOONA
WASHINGTON
KANSAS CITY
TERRE HAUTE
HAMILTON-
MIDDLETOWN
BALTIMORE
ST. LOUIS
DECATUR
CINCINNATI
CHARLESTON
EVANSVILLE
HUNTINGTON-
ASHLAND
RICHMOND
NEWPORT NEWS-HAMPTON
SPRINGFIELD
LOUISVILLE
LEXINGTON
NORFOLK-PORTSMOUTH
ROANOKE
LYNCHBURG
DURHAM
RT SMITH
NASHVILLE
WINSTON-SALEM
RALEIGH
LITTLE ROCK-
NORTH LITTLE ROCK
KNOXVILLE
GREENSBORO-
HIGH POINT
CHARLOTTE
MEMPHIS
CHATTANOOGA
ASHEVILLE
HUNTSVILLE
GREENVILLE
GADSDEN
COLUMBIA
ATLANTA
BIRMINGHAM
AUGUSTA
CHARLESTON
TUSCALOOSA
MACON
SHREVEPORT
MONTGOMERY
SAVANNAH
MONROE
JACKSON
COLUMBUS
ALBANY
MOBILE
JACKSONVILLE
PENSACOLA
BATON
ROUGE
LAKE
CHARLES
NEW ORLEANS
ORLANDO
BEAUMONT-
ORT ARTHUR
TAMPA-ST. PETERSBURG
WEST PALM BEACH
FORT LAUDERDALE-HOLLYWOOD
INGEN-
MIAMI

SCALE
0   100   200   300   400 MILES

SAN JUAN
MAYAGUEZ
PONCE
0   20 MI

THE METROPOLIS

THE METROPOLIS

ITS PEOPLE, POLITICS, AND ECONOMIC LIFE

JOHN C. BOLLENS

UNIVERSITY OF CALIFORNIA, LOS ANGELES

HENRY J. SCHMANDT

UNIVERSITY OF WISCONSIN, MILWAUKEE

HARPER & ROW, PUBLISHERS

NEW YORK

Library of Congress Catalog Card Number: 65–19489

H-P

CONTENTS

FIGURES

TABLES

PREFACE

THE METROPOLIS—which looms large in the modern world—is a complex phenomenon of many facets. It may be seen as a governmental system, a social organism, an economic unit, a collection of people and buildings, or simply a geographical area. For the political scientist, one set of dimensions seems to predominate; for the sociologist another; and for the planner, the geographer, the economist, the philosopher, and the artist, still others. What the observer or scholar looks for in the urban community depends largely on his point of vantage, his individual interests and tastes, and his objectives.

Our purpose here has been to present a balanced, multidimensional view of the metropolis, with emphasis on process and behavior as well as on form and structure. In doing so, we have been concerned with many of its major phases: social characteristics and trends, economic developments, physical and land use considerations, government and politics, and citizen roles. We have also been concerned with the kinds of problems that metropolitan growth and functioning generate and with the various attempts to solve these difficulties. This focus on the "larger" community and its affairs leads to a more realistic portrayal of contemporary urban life than a compartmentalized treatment of the local community.

The approach throughout has been based on the conception of the metropolis as a functioning and dynamic system of interacting relationships among people, organizations, and institutions. The selection of material and fields of emphasis, although governed by this conception, has been eclectic and the treatment general. However, we have sought to utilize as fully as possible the growing number of empirical investigations into urban phenomena and the relevant theory that has emerged. For this purpose we have relied on the literature of political science, sociology, economics, and other related disciplines, and on our own research. The result, we hope, is a book that will be of interest and value to persons in the social sciences, planning, and other fields and to governmental personnel and other civic-minded citizens.

We are indebted to the many scholars who have written so ably and preceptively on various phases of the metropolitan community. We have also profited from the insights of practitioners in the field, both public officials and private leaders, who have been confronted with the mounting challenges of growth. Special words of appreciation go to Robert C. Wood and James A. Norton, who served as prepublication reviewers.

Los Angeles   JOHN C. BOLLENS
Milwaukee   HENRY J. SCHMANDT

THE METROPOLIS

CHAPTER 1

Metropolitan Backdrop

THROUGHOUT the United States the word "metropolis" and its derivative "metropolitan" have become almost as common as "apple pie." Use of the derivative in the title of the world's largest insurance company and in the name of New York City's new major league baseball team—although it was quickly shortened to "Mets" —are not sufficient reasons for its acceptance into our everyday language, even though both have contributed to public recognition of the word. The reasons are far more extensive and complex and center on one of the great phenomena and challenges of our times, the growth and growing importance and problems of densely settled developments that house most of the people of our nation and which are generally called "metropolitan areas."

The words "metropolis" and "metropolitan" have different meanings to different individuals. To an expanding number of people, they mean a major problem or a series of problems that need solution. To some others they bring forth such epithets of fear as "supergovernment" and "un-American." To others they are only words of idle and polite conversation, current status symbols in our language for those who are "informed," much in the fashion of knowing the latest best selling books, popular plays, or hit records. (One scores a hundred on this social test by knowing the title and the author, actor, or singer.) And to still other people, they are nebulous and at times troublesome words that, like democracy and foreign policy and peace and automation, need to be brought into focus.

THE WAVE OF METROPOLITANISM

We are in a rising tide of interest in metropolitan developments and problems. And the growing awareness is noticeable everywhere —by governmental officials, agencies, and associations and private individuals and groups at the national, state, and local levels, in newspaper stories and series of articles, in television and radio reports and special programs, in conferences and public lectures, in universities and colleges, in scholarly and professional journals and popular magazines and publications, and even in books of fiction. Meeting metropolitan developments in one form or another are daily events for most of us. They have become part of our way of life, although we do not always readily recognize all of them as being of a metropolitan nature.

A selection of only a small number of the almost countless items of recent years, organized into various categories, shows the extremely broad sweep and pervasiveness of matters metropolitan. (The terms "metropolitan," "urban," "regional," and "city" are sometimes used synonymously by speakers, writers, and persons of action—a fact that is evident from some of the following items, all of which relate to metropolitan affairs.)

National

A reorganization plan to establish the Department of Urban Affairs in the national government is defeated. . . . The Housing and Home Finance Agency creates the Office of Metropolitan Development to coordinate agency programs related to metropolitan planning and development. . . . The Urban Renewal Administration appoints an adviser on metropolitan and intergovernmental problems. . . . An Advisory Commission on Intergovernmental Relations is established as a permanent national governmental agency; it makes many studies and recommendations about metropolitan areas. . . . The Senate Subcommittee on Intergovernmental Relations distributes a questionnaire containing many metropolitan inquiries to 6000 state and local officials and other experts. . . . President Johnson advocates in his housing message new programs of federal financial assistance for sound suburban development. . . .

Senator Harrison A. Williams, Jr. of New Jersey says at a National Housing Conference that metropolitan central cities are rapidly becoming ghettos for Negroes and other minorities, and questions whether public officials are facing the problems of racial discrimination, urban planning, city ugliness, and air and water pollution. . . . Secretary of the Interior Stewart L. Udall in a San Francisco speech calls for Californians to take the lead in the "greatest conservation of our generation"—the planning of well-ordered, livable urban areas. . . . The United States Conference of Mayors requests the President to convene a White House Conference on Urban Problems. . . . The Outdoor Recreation Resources Review Commission completes a three-year study; $480 million program to implement its recommendations introduced in Congress. . . . Federal urban transit aid bill passes. . . .

Twenty public and private organizations, most of them nationwide in scope, form a national clearing house, the Conference on Metropolitan Area Problems. . . . The Committee for Economic Development, a private association of businessmen and scholars interested in major economic issues, releases metropolitan policy recommendations of its study groups in *Guiding Metropolitan Growth.* . . . The Ford Foundation through its urban and regional program makes a variety of large grants to stimulate research and action. . . . The United States Department of Agriculture's yearbook, *A Place to Live,* focuses on the effects of urbanization on rural America. . . .

State

The Council of State Governments, the national association of all the states, prepares two studies on the responsibilities of the states in metropolitan and urban regional development; it also prepares much suggested state legislation in this field. . . . Many state governments, including California, Connecticut, Illinois, Michigan, New

York, Oregon, Texas, Washington, and Wisconsin, authorize state-wide metropolitan studies; an increasing amount of legislation relating to metropolitan areas is enacted. . . . Agencies concerned with metropolitan affairs are created or recommended in a number of states. . . .

Local

Seventy-nine general metropolitan surveys and studies, both public and private and mostly of local origin, initiated in the ten-year period from 1948 through 1957; many others are carried on in subsequent years. . . . Many approaches of a limited functional nature are installed. . . . Voters reject most comprehensive plans of reorganization with Dade County (Miami) and Davidson County (Nashville) as exceptions. . . . Metropolitan councils to foster cooperation increase in number. . . . Metropolitan planning agencies in Little Rock, Tulsa, and Wichita and city planning offices in Denver and Fort Worth jointly establish a metropolitan data center project to use electronic data processing equipment for the storage and analysis of information. . . .

Newspapers, Television, and Radio

Newspaper headlines such as "Urban Areas Described as New Frontier for U.S.," "Metropolitan Man Seen Privileged," "Expert Predicts Regional Chaos in 25 Years," "Urban Churches Seek Comeback," "Branch Hospitals Set Up in Suburban Areas," and "Nationwide Department Store Cites Sales Boost in Suburban Branches" appear in abundance. . . . Extensive series of articles on local metropolitan trends and difficulties run in the *Dayton Daily News, Flint Journal, New York Times, Sacramento Bee, Washington Star,* and other newspapers; George Beveridge is awarded the Pulitzer prize in journalism for distinguished local reporting for his series in the *Star.* . . . *Suburbia Today,* a monthly magazine supplement distributed nationally with newspapers in selected suburban communities, begins publication. . . . Metroplex, a series of educational television films, is completed. . . . Numerous radio stations launch regular or special programs that have metropolis, metropolitan, or megalopolis (meaning a cluster of metropolitan areas) in their titles. . . .

Conferences, Public Lectures, and Educational Institutions

The National Association of Counties convenes regular urban county congresses; second one called "The County's Role in Urban America." . . . The National Municipal League holds three consecutive annual conferences under the general title of "The Web of Government"; one major focus is metropolitan areas. . . . "Key Issues in Urban Growth" is the conference theme of the American Society of Planning Officials. . . . The United States Chamber of Commerce sponsors a national conference on metropolitan growth. . . . Statewide metropolitan conferences are held in California, Indiana, Minnesota, Texas, and elsewhere. . . . Lecture series at the Universities of Michigan and Pittsburgh are published. . . . University and college research institutes and bureaus grow in number and in breadth of programs. . . . Syracuse University holds an annual faculty seminar on metropolitan research. . . . Dartmouth's undergraduate program in city planning and urban studies is acclaimed. . . . University of Wisconsin—Milwaukee establishes a Department of Urban Affairs. . . .

Scholarly and Professional Journals; Popular Magazines and Publications

"Metropolis in Ferment" is the title of an entire issue of the *Annals of the American Academy of Political and Social Science.* . . . "The Future Metropolis" fills an issue of *Daedalus,* the journal of the American Academy of Arts and Sciences, and "Urban Research Report" constitutes an issue of the *Journal of Housing.* . . . A symposium on metropolitan regionalism is published in the *University of Pennsylvania Law Review.* . . . Another on problems of urban growth appears in the *Wisconsin Law Review.* . . . The *National Civic Review* carries a regular metropolitan areas section. . . . *Newsweek* runs the New America series on suburbia, exurbia (which lies beyond suburbia), and urbia; "One-third of a Nation, U.S. Suburbia, 1960" appears in *Time,* and the article on "strip cities" (resulting from the coalescing of metropolitan areas from Boston to Washington and in twelve other sections) is in *U.S. News and World Report.* . . . A series on "The Exploding Metropolis" in *Fortune* becomes a paperback book. . . . "Our Urban Revolution" is a series in the *Saturday Evening Post;* also "A Cure for Sick Cities" and "Bombs, Babies, and Bulldozers," in *Saturday Review,* "Life in the Cities" in *Atlantic Monthly*, and "Metropolitan Areas—Problem or Opportunity?" and "The National Government and Urban Affairs," in *Vital Issues*. . . . Entries in the second edition of *Metropolitan Communities: A Bibliography*, covering a period of only two and one-half years, number 2524. . . . Among books of fiction and popular commentary about metropolises are *The Crack in the Picture Window, Whatever You Do Don't Panic, The Fun Couple, This Demi-Paradise, Peaceable Lane, First Family*, and *The Split-Level Trap*.

•   •   •

In a similar vein, many items could be presented to show the international and worldwide scope of metropolitan developments. Two will suffice. In 1962 the United Nations was urged to undertake "a world cities urban research project" because the major population centers share enormous problems. In 1964 the World Health Organization warned that the tremendous expected increase in urban population throughout the world "clearly justifies the warning that, after the question of keeping world peace, metropolitan planning is probably the most serious single problem facing man in the second half of the twentieth century."

DEFINING METROPOLITAN AREAS

This panoramic view has presented a sample of the broadening interest in and pervasiveness of metropolitan developments and problems. Awareness of the metropolis is increasing and its various aspects permeate most of American life. But what is a metropolis or a metropolitan area? Only a general answer, a working definition, will be given here; much of Chapter 2 is devoted to showing in detail what makes an area metropolitan and what measures are used to determine its boundaries.

Basic Characteristics

Each metropolitan area consists of heavily populated land whose central and other portions have a high degree of economic and social interaction. The central portion is generally called the central city (or cities). It is the major population, economic, social, and governmental center of the area, but it is not necessarily central in spatial terms; that is, at the geographical center of the area. The other portions are usually called the suburban or outlying parts.

What welds the central and suburban portions together into an entity or unit known as a metropolitan area? It is their extensive economic and social relationships which result in common needs. A metropolitan area is a unit in an economic and social sense, but not in a governmental one. In other words, no metropolitan area in the United States currently has only a single local government.

Most people and organizations that have studied metropolitan areas agree that these are the basic characteristics. They disagree, however, over what specific criteria should be applied to determine the boundaries of the metropolis. Some indexes that have been utilized are population total or density, newspaper circulation areas, transportation facilities and rates, market characteristics, retail sales, wholesale trade, industrial distribution, manufacturing patterns, and land utilization.

Definition Currently Used by the Census Bureau

Over the years the most widely used definitions of metropolitan areas have been those employed by the Bureau of the Census. The current definition, called the standard metropolitan statistical area (SMSA), was established by the Bureau of the Budget with the advice of a committee of representatives from a number of national governmental statistical agencies. According to this definition, each standard metropolitan statistical area must contain at least one city of not less than 50,000 population (or two contiguous cities constituting, for general economic and social purposes, a single community with a combined minimum population of 50,000). In general, then, the SMSA will include the entire county in which this central city is located (often called the central county) as well as adjacent counties that meet two criteria: they are *metropolitan in character,* and they are *economically and socially integrated* with the county containing the central city. (An adjacent county either adjoins the county containing the largest city or adjoins an intermediate county economically and socially integrated with the central county.)

What are the criteria of metropolitan character that adjacent counties must possess? At least 75 percent of the labor force of the county must be engaged in nonagricultural work. In addition, the county must meet at least one of three other conditions. (1) It must have not less than one-half of its population living in minor civil divisions with a density of at least 150 persons per square mile, in an unbroken chain of minor civil divisions from a central city in the area. (Minor civil divisions are the primary divisions of a county, such as townships and election precincts, used by the Census Bureau for statistical purposes.) (2) Its number of nonagricultural workers must equal at least 10 percent of the number of nonagricultural workers employed in the central county, or the county must be the place of employment of at least 10,000 nonagricultural workers. (3) Its nonagricultural labor force must equal 10 percent or more of the number of nonagricultural workers living in the central county, or the county must be the place of residence of a nonagricultural labor force of 10,000 or more.

What tests of integration with the central county must be met by a neighboring county for it to be part of the same metropolitan area? Satisfying either of two criteria is usually sufficient. First, at least 15 percent of the workers living in the county work in the central county. Second, at least 25 percent of those working in the county live in the central county. Other measures of integration are applied only when the results of these two are inconclusive. They include average monthly telephone calls per subscriber from the county to the central county, audited newspaper circulation reports, extent of use by residents of the county of charge accounts in central city retail stores, delivery service practices of such stores, official traffic counts, the extent of public transportation facilities in operation between the county and the central city, and the extent to which local planning groups and other civic organizations operate jointly.

In New England, the minimum population requirement of 50,000 holds for the central city, but the units comprising a metropolitan area are cities and towns rather than counties. Thus a New England metropolitan area consists of a central city (or cities), plus adjacent cities and towns having a population density of at least 100 persons per square mile.

The difficulty of deciding what indexes to apply in establishing the territorial limits of metropolitan areas is well illustrated by the national government's experience. Various factors initially included in the census of 1910, such as a standard of density for territory adjacent to the central city or a rule on maximum distance of such territory from the central city, were first modified and later eliminated. In preparing for the census of 1930, an effort was made to use criteria of commercial, economic, and social activity, but it was abandoned when the data lacked adequate uniformity.

Central City and Entire County Concepts

In spite of the various changes the national government has adopted over the years, it has consistently retained the concept of a central city with a minimum population (although the figure has varied from 50,000 to 200,000) as a basic part of all its metropolitan definitions. In 1949, it added to the definition the concept of a metropolitan area generally consisting of an entire county or a combination of counties in their entirety. Its decision to do this was based on the conviction that it was desirable for all federal statistical agencies to use the same boundaries in collecting and publishing metropolitan data. The current definition, as was true of its predecessors, has received general acceptance. In part, however, this is due to the fact that agencies of the national government, particularly the Bureau of the Census, are the major fact-collecting organizations in the United States and their tabulations must be used if general comparability of information about numerous metropolitan areas is to be obtained without undue difficulty.

The national government's existing definition of metropolitan areas must be viewed, at best, as furnishing only an approximation of the territorial limits of these entities. And the definition has not gone without criticism. One complaint is that use of the entire county concept at times exaggerates the amount of metropolitan territory. This is certainly true in a number of instances. It is especially pronounced in the case of San Bernardino County, California, a central county of a metropolitan area and the largest county in the United States; it stretches some 180 miles from the eastern border of Los Angeles County to the Nevada and Arizona state lines and consists mostly of sparsely populated or uninhabited desert land. In fact, one can drive from Los Angeles to the gambling and entertainment mecca of Las Vegas over many miles of open desert country in San Bernardino County and Clark County, Nevada (and on certain stretches of highway at speeds that defy even gamblers' odds), without ever having been out of a standard metropolitan statistical area! It should be pointed out, however, that the entire county concept distorts principally in terms of territory rather than population.

The other principal criticism of the definition, made by William A. Robson, a noted British political scientist, and others, is that a population minimum of 50,000 for a central city is too low and robs the word "metropolitan" of any sociological or political significance. Robson urges that in a country as large and highly developed as the United States only areas with a central city of at least 300,000 and a total population of not less than 400,000 should be included. But many experts do not agree with this more rigorous definition. For instance, an international urban research unit at the University of California, Berkeley, in devising a metropolitan area definition for use in international comparisons, decided upon a minimum population of 50,000 for the central city (or continuous urban area) and a total population of not less than 100,000.[1]

URBAN AND METROPOLITAN GROWTH

There is a very basic reason for the increasing concern about metropolitan problems. We in the United States are in the midst, both nationally and internationally, of a continuing and seemingly unending period of urban and metropolitan growth. This is an irrefutable fact despite changes in the definitions of "urban" and "metropolitan" over the years and despite the more stringent definitions applied in a number of other nations.

Until relatively recent years, the United States has been a predominantly rural nation. From 1790, when there were only twenty-four urban places of 2500 or more and urban residents made up only about one-twentieth of our population, until the start of the present century, we grew steadily, although at times very slowly, more urban. In the current century, the rate of urbanization was particularly rapid during the first three decades. Nevertheless, the census of 1920 was the first to reveal that more than half of the American people lived in urban areas. Urbanization came to a virtual halt during the poor economic conditions of the 1930s, but it ac-

[1] William A. Robson (ed.), *Great Cities of the World*, 2nd ed. (New York: Macmillan, 1957), p. 31; International Urban Research, *The World's Metropolitan Areas* (Berkeley and Los Angeles: University of California Press, 1959), pp. 26–27.

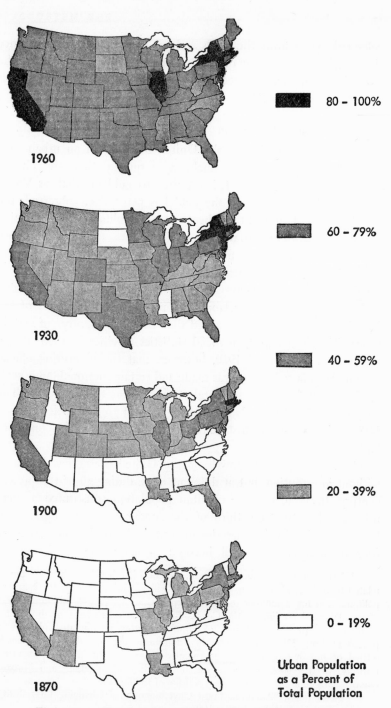

80 – 100%

60 – 79%

40 – 59%

20 – 39%

0 – 19%

**Urban Population
as a Percent of
Total Population**

Figure 1.1   The Growth of Urbanization, by States, 1870–
1960. From John R. Borchert, *The Urbanization of the
Upper Midwest: 1930–1960*, Upper Midwest Economic
Study, Urban Report Number 2, February, 1963, p. 2.

celerated again during the 1940s and has continued to increase since then. In 1960, at the time of the decennial count, 69.9 percent of the nation's population was recorded as urban. And urban growth is expected to continue.[2]

From Urban to Metropolitan

The transformation of the United States from an urban to a metropolitan nation came much more quickly than the change from rural to urban. In fact, it occurred so suddenly that, as Victor Jones, a veteran scholar in the field has perceptively observed, the people of the United States became metropolitan before realizing their change from rural to urban.[3]

The rapidity of the metropolitan development in the United States is evident from the comparative recentness of official use of the designation by the Census Bureau. This governmental agency first took cognizance of the metropolitan phenomenon, in terms of the New York area and what is called the "tributary country" of certain other cities, in a report on social statistics of cities in 1886. It was not until the census of 1910, however, that the pioneering official attempt to define the term was made and certain metropolitan aspects of the population were separately analyzed for the first time. The recentness of 1910 stands in marked contrast to the ancientness of 1790, the time of the first census and the first official defining of "urban."

The metropolitan growth of the United States has increased without interruption, but at different rates, during all of the present century. In 1900, the metropolitan population constituted a small minority—less than one-third of the American people. Forty years later, the minority became the majority; within the short span of four decades America had become primarily metropolitan. The

[2] Although a more inclusive term, urbanization has been a development related to metropolitanization. However, as will be shown in Chapter 2, metropolitanization has a number of distinguishing characteristics in addition to size of population. According to the Census Bureau, the urban areas of the United States consist for the most part of cities and other incorporated places that possess at least 2500 inhabitants. In addition, under this definition, densely settled or heavily populated unincorporated areas also are regarded as urban territory. In this book, we often use the words "metropolitan" and "urban" synonymously to avoid monotonous repetition of the former.

[3] Victor Jones, "American Local Government in a Changing Federalism," *American Review*, II (May, 1962), 108.

population *increase* in metropolitan areas of the decade ending in 1960 exceeded the *total* population living in all such complexes in 1900. By 1960, according to the census, 112,885,178 inhabitants or 62.8 percent of the national total resided in metropolitan areas. Moreover, forecasters agree their expansion will continue.

The United States (and the world, too) has been experiencing a general population growth of major proportions for many years. This nation virtually doubled its number of people in the first fifty years of the current century, from slightly less than 76 million to more than 150 million. In 1960, the official count of our resident population exceeded 179 million. Four years later the national government's estimate was that another approximate 11 million people had already been added. Also in 1964, the Bureau of the Census projected the total by 1975 to a possible range between 218 million to 230 million. The important point here is that during all of the current century the metropolitan population has been increasing faster than the overall national rate, although the difference between the two narrowed temporarily during the 1930s. This development will in all likelihood persist as urban concentrations of medium and large size continue to attract the bulk of the nation's human and material resources.

Metropolitan population growth has been especially impressive. Take, for example, the areas recognized as metropolitan by the Bureau of the Budget in 1960. Now look back at what happened in these areas in the two previous decades. In the 1940s they accounted for about 80 percent of the growth in the United States. And in the 1950s, they made up an even larger proportion—about 85 percent. Consequently, in twenty years these metropolitan areas went up 55 percent in population while the increase for the rest of the country was only 11 percent.

Growth in Number of People and Areas

The metropolitan development, notably in terms of its principal consequences, is high drama at its best and much of it will be portrayed and analyzed in the chapters that follow. At this point, however, some of its dramatic quality can be made readily apparent by considering the comprehensiveness of a few of its significant aspects. The tremendous increase that has been occurring in the number of metropolitan residents is a good starting place. In 1960 the number was up more than 28 million people, a jump of about a third, over their total population ten years before. The same trend is obvious in the number of metropolitan areas. The total went up to 212 in 1960, an addition of twenty-four in ten years.[4] And the addition is largely attributable to formerly non-metropolitan areas growing into metropolitan status.

Metropolitanism is a nationwide rather than a regional or sectional development. Metropolitan areas are located in forty-six of the fifty states as well as the District of Columbia. (There are also three in the Commonwealth of Puerto Rico, but they generally are excluded from consideration in this book.) The only states that have none are Alaska, Idaho, Vermont, and Wyoming. The metropolitan trend, furthermore, has become increasingly widespread or national in recent years in terms of the number of states involved. Three states without such complexes in 1950—Montana, Nevada, and North Dakota—all had certain portions grow enough to be recognized as metropolitan within the next ten years.

METROPOLITAN VARIATIONS

Regional Differences

Although metropolitanism is a national development, its extent and nature vary among regions, states, and individual areas. The Northeast, consisting of the states from Maine through New Jersey and Pennsylvania, is the most highly metropolitan region; metropolitan residents make up about four-fifths of its population. The West, composed of the Mountain and Pacific states, stands second, with about seven-tenths of its people metropolitan. The North Central region (from Michigan and Ohio west through the tier of states extending from North Dakota through Kansas) is third, with a metropolitan population of approximately 60 percent.

Only the South, which is here defined to include Texas, Oklahoma, and Arkansas as well as the "old South," is not a predominantly metropolitan region; slightly less than one-half of its inhabitants lives

[4] The number enlarged to 216 in October 1963, when the Bureau of the Budget, in consultation with the federal statistical committee, determined that four additional areas now satisfied the requirements of the metropolitan definition. However, throughout this book we use the 212 areas of 1960 since the detailed collection of data on population and governmental characteristics by the Bureau of the Census is based on that total.

in metropolitan areas. It is probable, however, that the South also will become largely metropolitan soon; next to the West, it had the biggest percentage increase in metropolitan population between 1950 and 1960. It is probable, too, that the sizable difference in the proportion of population of the Northeast and the South that is metropolitan will lessen over the years; the Northeast had the smallest percentage of increase in metropolitan population of any of the four regions in the 1950–1960 period.

Interstate Differences

Interstate metropolitan differences are also appreciable, and the number of metropolitan areas in a state is one measure of such differences. The range in number is wide, from one to twenty-one. Six states have 10 or more. Texas leads by far with 21, followed by Ohio with 13, Pennsylvania with 12, and California, Massachusetts, and Michigan with 10 each. At the other extreme are nine that have only one apiece. They are Delaware, Hawaii, Maryland, Mississippi, New Hampshire, New Mexico, North Dakota, Rhode Island, and South Dakota.

The number of metropolitan areas in the respective states demonstrates important interstate differences. It should be emphasized, however, that the number may be affected by more than simply the proportion of the state's total population that is metropolitan. Other major factors may be the territorial size of the state and the physical nature of its metropolitan development. Rhode Island or Delaware could not possibly have as many metropolitan areas as Texas, even if they all had about the same degree of metropolitanization; the difference in their territorial size is too great. Similarly, the metropolitan development in one state may be much more compact than in another. What in one is a single area, fanning out over a large amount of land, may in another be several metropolitan areas separated by intervening non-metropolitan territory.

The metropolitan proportion of the population of individual states is a more precise measure of interstate variations than is the number of areas. Here, again, there are extreme differences; the range extends from California, with 86.5 percent of its people metropolitan, to Mississippi, with 8.6 percent (excluding, of course, the four states which have no SMSA's and thus have no degree of metropolitanism).

Twenty-six states, in other words, just slightly more than half, are at least 50 percent metropolitan. And some of these states have a very intense degree of metropolitan development; four are above the 85 percent mark; fourteen others exceed 65 percent. The high

TABLE 1

Metropolitan Proportion of the Population,
by States, 1960

STATE	PERCENTAGE OF POPULATION IN SMSA'S	STATE	PERCENTAGE OF POPULATION IN SMSA'S
California	86.5	Louisiana	50.0
Rhode Island	86.2	Indiana	48.1
New York	85.5	Wisconsin	46.3
Massachusetts	85.2	Georgia	46.0
Hawaii	79.1	Tennessee	45.8
New Jersey	78.9	Oklahoma	43.9
Maryland	78.2	Nebraska	37.6
Pennsylvania	77.9	Kansas	37.4
Connecticut	77.6	Kentucky	34.1
Illinois	76.9	Iowa	33.2
Nevada	74.2	South Carolina	32.2
Michigan	73.1	West Virginia	30.9
Arizona	71.4	New Mexico	27.6
Ohio	69.5	North Carolina	24.6
Delaware	68.9	Montana	22.6
Colorado	68.0	Maine	19.7
Utah	67.5	Arkansas	19.1
Florida	65.6	New Hampshire	17.7
Texas	63.4	South Dakota	12.7
Washington	63.1	North Dakota	10.6
Alabama	63.0	Mississippi	8.6
Missouri	57.9	Alaska	0.0
Minnesota	51.3	Idaho	0.0
Virginia	50.9	Vermont	0.0
Oregon	50.4	Wyoming	0.0

SOURCE: U.S. Bureau of the Census, *Census of Population: 1960,* Vol. I, Parts 2–51 (Washington: 1963).

rank of some states—Hawaii, Nevada, Arizona, and Colorado, for example—may surprise many people. On the other hand, in six states that have metropolitan areas the portion of population that is metropolitan is less than one-fifth of the total. Rhode Island,

Hawaii, and Maryland, each with but a single area, it should be noted, are among the most heavily metropolitan states. In fact, Rhode Island is second only to California.

Contrasts Among Metropolitan Areas

In addition to important regional and state variations, metropolitan areas differ greatly among themselves, a fact well illustrated by several population characteristics. Population size is a good example—and what a tremendous range is involved! Such areas vary

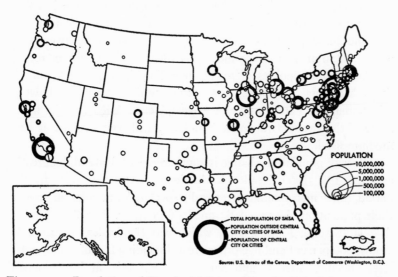

Figure 1.2   Population of Standard Metropolitan Statistical Areas, 1960.

from the New York Standard Metropolitan Statistical Area with a 1960 census total of 10,694,633 to Meriden, Connecticut, with a population of less than 52,000. (It can be argued that the range is even greater. The New York interstate metropolitan area, called the New York Standard Consolidated Area by the Bureau of the Budget, is believed by many people to reflect more realistically the limits of the New York metropolitan area; it had a 1960 population of 14,759,429.)[5]

[5] In recognition of the importance of obtaining very inclusive statistics for New York–Northeastern New Jersey and Chicago–Northwestern Indiana, the Bureau of the Budget designates these two locations as standard consolidated areas. Their territory is specified in footnotes to Table 2. The New York and Chicago SMSA's are defined by the Bureau as intrastate.

Each of four other metropolitan areas—Los Angeles–Long Beach, Chicago, Philadelphia, and Detroit—also has more than 3 million inhabitants. Moreover, there is considerable spread in the middle population range:

			SMSA's
1,000,000	to	3,000,000	19
500,000	to	1,000,000	29
250,000	to	500,000	48
100,000	to	250,000	89

The lowest rung on the population ladder, extending from less than 52,000 up to 100,000 (actually in 1960, the Gadsden, Alabama, area was the most populous with 96,980) is occupied by twenty-two metropolitan areas. For the most part they are the locally or regionally known metropolises of today, including those centering on Billings, Montana; Dubuque, Iowa; Fort Smith, Arkansas; Lawton, Oklahoma; and Laredo and San Angelo, Texas. A few decades hence some of the twenty-two smallest probably will have become at least medium-sized.

Rate of population change is another variant. Rates differ greatly, and the 1950–1960 decade clearly demonstrates this fact. In this period, thirty metropolitan areas had a spectacular population growth; their populations increased by one-half or more. The Fort Lauderdale–Hollywood, Florida, area, which was the leader, increased by almost 300 percent and five other areas, including two of considerable size, Phoenix, Arizona, and San Jose, California, at least doubled their populations in the decade. Five other California areas, including Los Angeles–Long Beach, grew by more than 50 percent. In contrast, eight metropolitan areas, including four in Pennsylvania (Wilkes-Barre–Hazelton, Scranton, Johnstown, and Altoona), had fewer people in 1960 than ten years before. And twenty-three others, including the very populous one of which Pittsburgh is the central city, grew by less than 10 percent. This is substantially less than the nation's population growth, 18.5 percent, during the decade.

Finally, one other general characteristic of the population can be used to show important variations among metropolitan areas. There is a distinct division among them as to which portion, central city or suburban, houses the majority of the residents. In most metropolitan areas, the majority of the people lives in the central city (or cities). This is true in slightly more than three-fifths of them.

But the proportion of metropolitan areas where the suburbs are the more populous section has been constantly increasing. The shifting population balance is even more evident when the relative percentages of the metropolitan population are considered. Reinforcing a long-time trend of faster growth, the suburbs by 1960 had almost equaled the population total of the central cities and had 48.6 percent of the metropolitan residents in the United States. The contrasts in population distribution are startling in individual metropolitan areas. In the San Antonio area, for example, substantially as a result of the central city's ability to absorb adjacent territory through annexation, only about one-seventh of the total population resided outside the central city in 1960. At the other extreme is the Johnstown, Pennsylvania, area which had less than one-fifth of its population within the central city. Also by 1960 the central cities of two of the largest SMSA's, Boston and Pittsburgh, contained only a small portion of the total area population—less than 30 percent.

The variations in metropolitanism that have just been discussed are important. Metropolitan differences by regions, states, and individual metropolitan areas should, of course, be expected in a nation as large and varied as the United States, but they can be easily ignored or lost in generalized statements. On the other hand, although the significance of the diversity of metropolitanism in the United States should be kept in mind, it should not be overplayed. This is to emphasize, then, that metropolitan areas have numerous major characteristics in common, characteristics which weld them together to form a category of phenomena that can be validly called "metropolitan." Some of these common characteristics were discussed earlier in this chapter, particularly in analyzing the metropolitan area definition of the Bureau of the Budget. Others are presented later, notably in Chapter 2.

METROPOLITAN TERRITORY

As we have seen, metropolitan growth in the United States has been occurring in terms of number of residents, proportion of the nation's population that is metropolitan, number of metropolitan areas, and number of states having such areas. And this growth is also shown in the total amount of territory they embrace. In 1960 metropolitan areas contained 310,233 square miles, an increase of about one-half over the 1950 total of 207,583. This gain is due both to the emergence of new metropolitan areas and to the territorial expansion of a number of the older ones. Despite this considerable growth in total territory, the metropolitan areas together contain only 8.7 percent of the nation's land area. Or to put the matter in another perspective, metropolitan residents constitute more than three-fifths of the national population, but they live on only about one-twelfth of the land. Obviously the population density of SMSA's is comparatively high—seventeen times that of the rest of the United States.

Mostly Intracounty

What about the territory included within metropolitan areas? Most of these areas, 133 or slightly more than three-fifths of them, are located in a single county, a fact, which as we will see in Chapter 15, has significant implications for many of these areas when they formulate plans of governmental reorganization. It should be pointed out, however, that the areas of counties differ in the various parts of the country; those in the western states, for example, are much larger than those in the North Central region.

TABLE 2

Interstate Metropolitan Areas

METROPOLITAN AREA	STATES POSSESSING PART OF TERRITORY[a]	NUMBER OF COUNTY AREAS INCLUDED	1960 POPULATION
New York–Northeastern New Jersey[b]	New York, New Jersey	13[c]	14,759,429
Chicago–Northwestern Indiana[d]	Illinois, Indiana	8	6,794,461
Philadelphia	Pennsylvania, New Jersey	8	4,342,897
St. Louis	Missouri, Kansas	6	2,060,103
Washington	D.C., Maryland, Virginia	7	2,001,897
Cincinnati	Ohio, Kentucky	3	1,071,624
Kansas City	Missouri, Kansas	4	1,039,493
Portland	Oregon, Washington	4	821,897
Providence–Pawtucket	Rhode Island, Massachusetts	8	816,148

TABLE 2 (*Continued*)

METROPOLITAN AREA	STATES POSSESSING PART OF TERRITORY[a]	NUMBER OF COUNTY AREAS INCLUDED	1960 POPULATION
Louisville	Kentucky, Indiana	3	725,139
Allentown–Bethlehem–Easton	Pennsylvania, New Jersey	3	492,168
Omaha	Nebraska, Iowa	3	457,873
Wilmington	Delaware, New Jersey	2	366,157
Chattanooga	Tennessee, Georgia	2	283,169
Duluth–Superior	Minnesota, Wisconsin	2	276,596
Davenport–Rock Island–Moline	Iowa, Illinois	2	270,058
Huntington–Ashland	West Virginia, Kentucky, Ohio	4	254,780
Columbus	Georgia, Alabama	3	217,985
Augusta	Georgia, South Carolina	2	216,639
Evansville	Indiana, Kentucky	2	199,313
Wheeling	West Virginia, Ohio	3	190,342
Lawrence–Haverhill	Massachusetts, New Hampshire	2	187,601
Steubenville–Weirton	Ohio, West Virginia	3	167,756
Fall River	Massachusetts, Rhode Island	2	138,156
Fargo–Moorhead	North Dakota, Minnesota	2	106,027
Texarkana	Texas, Arkansas	2	91,657

SOURCE: Adapted from *Standard Metropolitan Statistical Areas*, Executive Office of the President, Bureau of the Budget (Washington: 1961).
[a] The state containing the central city (or the more populous one when there are two such cities) is listed first.
[b] This is a standard consolidated area, which consists of four standard metropolitan statistical areas (New York, Newark, Jersey City, and Paterson–Clifton–Passaic) and Middlesex and Somerset counties, New Jersey.
[c] Counting New York City as a single county area.
[d] This is a standard consolidated area, which consists of two standard metropolitan statistical areas (Chicago and Gary–Hammond–East Chicago).

Although most metropolitan areas thus are intracounty, many are intercounty. They contain from two to eight counties if the standard metropolitan statistical area definition is used exclusively, or they range from two to thirteen counties if the New York Standard Consolidated Area is included. None of these intercounty metropolitan areas, which together have almost three-fourths of the total metropolitan population, is located within the boundaries of a single general-purpose local government.

Interstate and International Areas

Many intercounty metropolitan areas are also interstate in territory. There are twenty-four such areas when the SMSA definition is employed. There are twenty-six if the New York and Chicago standard consolidated areas are included (and certainly it is realistic to regard these two as interstate). Of the twenty-six, seven have more than one million people. The territory of some other metropolitan areas borders but does not cross state lines; these areas are interstate in impact, although not in territory.

Four metropolitan areas of the United States adjoin substantial amounts of urban land that are located in other nations and therefore are in fact international in territorial extent. They are the Detroit, Michigan–Windsor, Canada area, the San Diego, California–Tijuana, Mexico area (these first two are both heavily populated), the El Paso, Texas–Ciudad Juarez, Mexico area, and the Laredo, Texas–Nuevo Laredo, Mexico area. (The United States Census Bureau, on which we must depend for general data, collects information only for the United States portions of these areas.) In each of these four instances the principal city is in the United States; however, Windsor and Ciudad Juarez both have populations over 100,000 and Nuevo Laredo has only about 7000 people fewer than Laredo. In addition, certain other metropolitan areas border international bodies of water, thus involving them in decisions of international importance. In 1964, for instance, representatives from the United States and Canada met to consider how to alleviate the alarmingly low water levels in the Great Lakes, a condition causing severe losses to navigation, industry, water supply systems, marinas, tourism, and conservation.

A WORLDWIDE DEVELOPMENT

Urban and metropolitan population growth, which is so apparent in the United States, is a worldwide phenomenon. One analysis, applying a more rigorous definition (a minimum population of 20,000 to define an area as urban) than that used in the United States by the

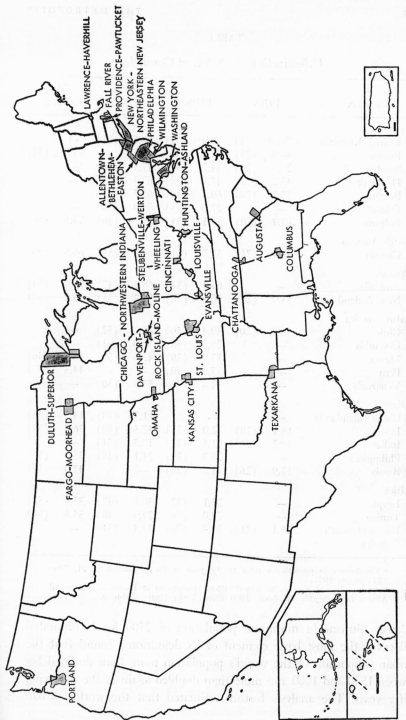

Figure 1.3 Interstate Metropolitan Areas, 1960. The New York interstate metropolitan area consists of the New York, Newark, Jersey City, and Paterson–Clifton–Passaic SMSA's, plus Middlesex and Somerset counties, New Jersey. The Chicago interstate metropolitan area is composed of the Chicago and Gary–Hammond–East Chicago SMSA's. Source: U.S. Bureau of the Census, *Census of Governments: 1962*, Vol. I, p. 22.

TABLE 3

Urbanization, by Selected Countries[a]

REGION	1920s		1930s		ABOUT 1950		1954 OR LATER	
Europe								
United Kingdom	79.3%	(21)	80.0%	(31)	80.8%	(51)	—	
France	46.3	(21)	52.4	(36)	—		55.9%	(54)
Sweden	29.5	(20)	34.2	(35)	47.5	(50)	—	
Denmark	43.2	(21)	44.1	(35)	67.3	(50)	—	
Belgium	57.3	(20)	60.5	(30)	62.7	(47)	—	
Poland	—		27.6	(33)	39.0	(50)	—	
Bulgaria	19.9	(20)	21.4	(34)	24.7	(46)	33.6	(56)
North America								
Canada	49.5	(21)	53.7	(31)	62.9	(51)	66.6	(56)
Oceania								
Australia	—		64.0	(33)	68.9	(47)	78.9	(54)
New Zealand	53.9	(21)	56.8	(36)	55.2	(51)	55.2	(59)
Latin America								
Chile	46.4	(20)	49.4	(30)	60.2	(52)	—	
Colombia	—		29.1	(38)	38.0	(51)	—	
Mexico	—		33.5	(30)	42.6	(50)	44.1	(56)
Peru	—		35.4	(40)	—		44.3	(58)
Venezuela	—		34.8	(36)	53.8	(50)	—	
Asia								
China (mainland)	—		—		11.2	(50)	14.2	(56)
Japan	18.1	(20)	32.9	(35)	37.5	(50)	56.3	(55)
India	10.2	(21)	11.1	(31)	17.3	(51)	—	
Philippines	—		23.3	(39)	24.1	(48)	35.3	(56)
Russia	17.9	(26)	31.7	(39)	—		47.9	(59)
Africa								
Egypt	—		25.1	(37)	30.1	(47)	35.8	(57)
Tunisia	—		27.0	(36)	29.9	(46)	35.6	(56)
Union of South Africa	25.1	(21)	31.4	(36)	42.4	(51)	—	

[a] The figures in parentheses refer to the year of the population count. Thus (21) means 1921.
SOURCE: United Nations Statistical Office, Department of Economic and Social Affairs, *Demographic Yearbook, 1960* (New York: 1960), Table 9.

Census Bureau (a minimum population of 2500 for incorporated places is the most basic element of its definition), found that the urban proportion of the world's population more than doubled between 1850 and 1900 and more than doubled again in the following fifty years. The analysis further estimated that the world's urban population would jump from 20.9 percent in 1950 to 30 percent in 1975.[6]

Urban Trend

A selection of nations by continents, presented in Table 3, also demonstrates the worldwide nature of urbanization. Every country included in the table, except New Zealand, has become more urban in recent decades. Various countries in Asia, Africa, and Latin America, such as Japan, the Union of South Africa, Venezuela, and Russia (which is in both Asia and Europe), have been experiencing high rates of urbanization since the 1920s or 1930s. (The percentages shown in Table 3 are not comparable between nations because they use varying definitions. The figures are valuable, however, in indicating the trends within each nation.)

The Great City

At the world level, the closest widely used concept to metropolitan area is the "great city," which is applied to urban concen-

TABLE 4

Great Cities of the World, 1950–1960

AREA	1950	1960	INCREASE (PERCENT)
World	858	1,116	34.6
North America	140	153	9.3
Latin America	44	68	54.5
Europe (exclusive of Russia)	264	287	9.1
Asia (exclusive of Russia)	263	435	63.5
Russia	100	148	48.0
Oceania	10	11	10.0
Africa	37	64	77.8

SOURCE: United Nations Statistical Office, Department of Economic and Social Affairs, *Demographic Yearbook, 1950* (New York: 1950) and *Demographic Yearbook, 1960* (New York: 1960).

trations of at least 100,000 population. However, it should be noted that different criteria are employed in various countries to determine

[6] Kingsley Davis, "The Origin and Growth of Urbanization in the World," *American Journal of Sociology,* LX (March, 1955), 433–434.

the boundaries of urban concentrations. Data for great cities, therefore, are not fully comparable on a worldwide basis, but they do represent useful information.

That metropolitan growth is worldwide is apparent from the recent increase in the number of great cities of the world. The total increased by more than one-third between 1950 and 1960. A consideration of great cities by specific areas further shows that metropolitanism is gaining on every continent. Moreover, although it is continuing to advance in North America, Europe, and Oceania (the last named largely through developments in Australia), it is realizing its most rapid rates of growth in Latin America, Asia, Africa, and Russia.

ECONOMIC AND INTERNATIONAL SIGNIFICANCE

The importance of the metropolitan areas of the United States has been shown in many ways earlier in this chapter, but two further aspects, the economic and the international, deserve mention here. The significance of metropolitan areas to the economic life of this nation can scarcely be exaggerated. The various phases of the metropolitan economy would be impressive if they simply were similar to the metropolitan proportion of the nation's population—that is, if they approximated 63 percent of the activity in specific economic categories. The accomplishments here are especially impressive, however, because in many economic aspects metropolitan areas outrun that percentage.

Some Economic Measures

Metropolitan areas dominate the national economy. We need only consider various major economic activities of the nation and the portion of the total contributed by these areas to realize that in an economic sense "as metropolitan areas go, so goes the nation."[7]

[7] Computations in the listing that follows are based on U.S. Bureau of the Census, 1958 Census of Business (Washington: 1959) and 1958 Census of Manufactures (Washington: 1959); Federal Reserve System Board of Governors, Distribution of Bank Deposits by Counties and Standard Metropolitan Areas, June 15, 1960 (Washington: 1960); U.S. Treasury Department, Internal Revenue Service, Statistics of Income, 1959: Individual Income Tax Returns for 1959 (Washington: 1961). The subsequent local public finance information is from U.S. Bureau of the Census, 1962 Census of Governments, Vol. V (Washington: 1964).

Wholesale employees payroll	84.9%
Wholesale trade sales value	84.9
Selected service (personal, business and repair, professional and related) trade receipts	79.5
Bank deposits	78.6
Industrial employees payroll	78.2
Retail trade sales value	66.9
Personal income (100 largest metropolitan areas only)	63.1
Value added by manufacture (66 metropolitan areas only)	62.8

The last two items in the above list, it should be noted, involve only a fraction of the total number of metropolitan areas; complete figures are unavailable. Obviously, the respective percentages for these two items in terms of all SMSA's would substantially exceed the metropolitan proportion of the national population.

Similarly, the proportion of local governmental financial activities in metropolitan areas is greater than the metropolitan percentage of the nation's population. Of course, local public financial transactions contribute importantly to the economy as do comparable state and national governmental efforts, which also are on a large scale in metropolitan areas. Metropolitan local governments obtain about two-thirds of all local public revenue and make about two-thirds of all local public expenditure. In addition, they are responsible for about three-fourths of the total local public debt.

Many Resources, Many Problems

Metropolitan areas therefore have most of the people, most of the jobs, and most of the public and private financial resources (as well as most of the debt, it should be added) of the United States. Consequently, they are the primary centers of population, industry, commerce, labor, and government; but they are more, too. They are the major centers of education, art, music, literature, drama, and entertainment. They provide ways of life and ideas that pervade the entire nation. They are the magnets of hope, not alone economic but also social, of many people. They also have most of the critical domestic problems, some governmental and others social or economic. Some involve deficiencies of public services or gross inequities in financing them; others concern the ability of people of different racial, ethnic, educational, and social backgrounds to get along with one another, the ability of newcomers and the metropolitan community to adjust adequately to one another, and the ability of metropolitan areas to prosper in the face of continued growth.

International Phases

What happens in the metropolitan areas of the United States has profound international effects and implications, too. Some are of an economic nature; for example, the status of the economy of metropolitan areas largely determines the health of the national economy which, in turn, has a great impact on the economy of many nations. Other effects and implications relate to national defense and international politics. How strong is the United States in an era of continuing international tension? That question is answered in major part by the strength and condition of the metropolitan areas, because most of the brains and brawn of the nation are found in its metropolitan concentrations.

And what about the battle of ideas in the international arena? Our metropolitan areas are really the showcase of our nation to the world. Their progress, successes, delays, shortcomings, and failures are duly noted by a worldwide audience. Luther H. Gulick, observer and participant in many public affairs, lucidly stated the crux of the situation recently in a university lecture, He first pointed out that the United States is lowered in the eyes of the world by the gap between our dreams and beliefs and our performance, with the chasm being widest in our metropolitan areas. He followed by urging that the most powerful force in the contest for men's minds is distinct progress in solving problems plaguing various metropolitan areas, such as slums, segregation, school congestion, crime, and the breakdown of urban transportation. Our attachment to freedom and human advancement, he then concluded, will be contagious in other nations only if we demonstrate its values at home.[8]

[8] Luther H. Gulick, *The Metropolitan Problem and American Ideas* (New York: Knopf, 1962), pp. 6–8

METROPOLITAN DIMENSIONS

Metropolitan growth has had, and will continue to have, broad implications and repercussions—governmental, political, social, economic, and physical, among others. Many of them will be discussed and analyzed at later places in this book, but a brief statement about some of them is relevant here.

Governmental and Political

To illustrate in governmental terms, metropolitan growth has resulted in large-scale adjustments in existing local governments and in the creation of many new local units, including a wide variety of special districts that individually perform usually only a single service. In part adjustments in old governments and establishment of many new ones have been caused by still another effect of metropolitan expansion—the responses to demands for more intensive levels of traditional public services and for governmental assumption of new functions.

Metropolitan growth also has brought forth in many areas assessments, and frequently one or more reassessments, of the adequacy of their governmental organization, processes, and relationships. And the state and national governments have had to pay increasing attention to such areas, as is evident from the growing number of their programs and volume of assistance; they have had to reappraise, mostly on a piecemeal basis up to this time, the appropriateness and sufficiency of their metropolitan roles.

Metropolitan growth has had major political repercussions as well. The building in some areas of a political "Berlin wall" between central city and suburbs, the reapportionment of state legislatures as the result of national and state court rulings, and the diffused nature of metropolitan public and private political leadership are illustrations.

Social and Economic

The social implications have been tremendous, too; for example, the need for reciprocal adjustment of many metropolitan newcomers and community institutions and the many dire results, some threatening the foundations of our society, that accrue from the frequent failure to accomplish adequate adjustment. (See a daily newspaper in any one of many metropolitan areas for further details about delinquency, violence, exploitation, discrimination, school drop-outs, and other serious matters.) The economic implications of metropolitan growth also have been extensive. Examples are the effects of the intricate system of work specialization that has become a prominent feature of metropolitan economic life, the sensitive interdependence of the various segments of the metropolitan econ-omy, the changes in the central business district, and, in a public finance sense, the sufficiency of the tax base of local governments in the metropolis.

Physical

The physical effects of metropolitanism similarly have been enormous. In fact, metropolitan growth has changed the face of a portion of our land and has brought on a great need for planning and other instruments of guidance and control. More and more rural and agricultural land has been absorbed into the metropolitan caldron, being converted in the process to residential, commercial, and industrial uses. Many corn fields, grazing lands, orchards, and groves of yesterday have become the assembly-line ranch house sub-divisions of today. And the shape of metropolitan America has expanded not only horizontally (as in human beings, this might be considered a sign of growing "maturity"), but also vertically, as illustrated by the increase in tall apartments and commercial build-ings. Hills have been leveled, valleys filled, and water brought great distances as the physical features have been rearranged and supple-mented. Sometimes the topography seems to seek revenge, as with the Los Angeles basin which serves as a natural container for air pollution.

Interrelations Among Dimensions

The metropolis is many-faceted and multidimensional; this is apparent from our small sampling of governmental, political, social, economic, and physical implications. Furthermore, and this is im-portant to note, these different types of major dimensions are inter-related. A few illustrations will point up the significance of this statement. The first is an example of economic-governmental rela-tions. The condition of the economy of a metropolitan area has a direct and major bearing on the ability of its governments to finance their operations and, in turn, the governments of the area through their services and controls affect the prosperity of its economy.

The second is an economic-social-governmental illustration. Work specialization produces a labor force of many diversified types, thus bringing to the metropolis new social values and expectations as well as broadened demands upon its governments. The third involves social-political-governmental relationships. The shifting social composition of central cities often causes changes in the attitudes and positions of both central city and suburban public officials and political leaders; this is frequently evident on a variety of issues, including plans of metropolitan governmental reorganization.

The Intergovernmental Dimension

Another important fact appears from the sampling of the various implications of metropolitan growth. No local government in a metropolitan complex functions in isolation. Instead, the operations of every such unit are greatly affected and conditioned by location in a metropolitan area. The quality of the public services of neighboring communities, the degree to which a city must be a supplier of services and controls for nonresidents who work or play within its boundaries, and the nature of the allocation of the area's financial resources among its governments are all factors that produce intercommunity governmental effects.

And governmental interactions in a metropolitan area are certainly not limited to local units. Both state and national agencies have an increasingly significant impact on the metropolis through a growing number of programs, including in the case of some states the exercise of more vigorous leadership and guidance in technical matters and in the creation of new metropolitan local governments and the adjustment of the boundaries of existing metropolitan local units. Truly, the metropolis is the crossroads of intergovernmental relations, in a sense, a federal republic in miniature.

Obviously, then, more is needed than simply looking at a few disparate slices of metropolitan life or a few governmental fault lines in different formations. The scope, nature, and philosophy of this book have been shaped by our conviction about what is needed for an accurate and meaningful portrayal and analysis of the metropolis —a multidimensional view that considers important relations among and within dimensions.

CHAPTER 2

Nature and
Dimensions of the
Metropolitan
Community

LEWIS MUMFORD begins one of his most recent books, *The City in History*, by asking, "What is the city? How did it come into existence? What process does it further: what function does it perform: what purposes does it fulfill?"[1] A systematic inquiry into the metropolis can also begin by asking a series of similar questions. Mumford's study pointed out that no single definition of the city can apply to all its manifestations or fully describe its nature and role. The same may be said of metropolitan areas, for they, too, are social facts of many dimensions that defy simple analysis or description. As long ago as 1936, a prominent sociologist expressed the conviction of a growing number of social scientists when he observed, "What is happening is the creation by technology of a new population unit— not a city, not a village, not a county. Indeed, there is as yet no name for it. For want of a better designation it is sometimes called

[1] (New York: Harcourt, Brace & World, 1961), p. 3.

a metropolitan area."[2] Despite the passage of many years since then, the subject is still elusive and meanwhile has become increasingly complex. Consider, for example, this comment by a New York state legislative committee:

> Thus the metropolitan areas of the State are different—different in area, population, community attitudes, political complexion, the relative position of the central city, economic characteristics, and different likewise in what is important to the people of these areas. It is questionable whether the word metropolitan means the same thing in the various areas.[3]

Or the statement by the Research and Policy Committee of the Committee for Economic Development:

> The metropolitan area is in effect a new community. Its boundaries often are hard to define. In some instances they change and expand frequently. The area ignores old geographic boundaries, jumping over and around rivers and land masses. It ignores the political lines of districts, villages, towns, cities, counties, and states.[4]

METROPOLITAN CHARACTERISTICS

No precise and universally agreed upon definition of the "metropolis" exists. The term and its derivatives—metropolitan community and metropolitan area—are used interchangeably and in several different ways. Originally metropolis (from the Greek, meaning mother or parent city) referred to the classical city-states of the ancients. Later the word came to be applied to all large urban settlements such as Paris, London, and New York. Within the past century it has acquired a more technical meaning as social scientists have used it as a category or concept to organize and order their data. The SMSA, used by government agencies, is the most common example of this latter application.

Although there is lack of agreement on precisely what a metro-

---

[2] William F. Ogburn, "Technology of Governmental Change," *Journal of Business*, XI (January, 1936), 11.

[3] New York Legislature, Joint Legislative Committee on Metropolitan Areas Study, *1959 Report*, Legislative Document No. 19 (Albany: March 20, 1959), p. 29.

[4] *Guiding Metropolitan Growth* (New York: Committee for Economic Development, 1960), p. 13.

politan area is, there is general consensus on what it is not. Most observers agree that it cannot be defined solely in terms of law, physical geography, or size, or by a combination of these three elements. The metropolis, as is well recognized, does not designate a legally definable entity as a municipality or county does, although metropolitan boundaries might conceivably be coterminous with the territory of a governmental unit. When people speak of Philadelphia, Chicago, or Seattle, they often mean the sociological or economic city, the larger community that extends out beyond the legal limits of the major municipality and embraces the adjacent population and governments. Suburbanites in Boston and Detroit regard the symphony and the Tigers baseball team as part and parcel of their respective communities, even though these institutions are located in the central city.

Population Size

Similarly, size of population is not the only element of metropolitanism. Large cities have existed for over 5000 years, but the metropolis, in the current sense of the term, is a relatively recent phenomenon, dating from less than a century ago. Classical Rome might boast of almost a half million inhabitants at one time—but the Rome of the ancients would not be considered a metropolitan community according to modern concepts discussed later in this chapter. On the other hand, of the 212 urban centers in the United States called metropolitan areas, 188 have populations of less than 1 million. Some may be metropolitan communities only in a very specialized sense and mainly for purposes of statistical tabulation. Vast differences, both qualitative and quantitative, exist among metropolitan areas. Metropolitan New York, for example, with its more than 10.5 million inhabitants bears little resemblance to Metropolitan Terre Haute, population 108,458. Nevertheless, many modern urban communities of vastly different scale have certain common characteristics that distinguish them from the population concentrations of the past and lead us to identify them as metropolitan.

Interdependence

Originally, the metropolitan concept was designed to demarcate the natural boundaries of the "larger" economic and social community. Practical considerations, however, led the Bureau of the

Budget, on the advice of the Federal Committee on Standard Metropolitan Areas, in 1949 to fix the metropolitan area boundary lines as coterminous with the territorial limits of governmental units, mainly counties. This provides an operational definition that is primarily valuable for research purposes. Existence of a standard definition makes it possible for all interested organizations and researchers to utilize the same boundaries (for which comprehensive statistics are periodically collected by various federal agencies) in tabulating data for analyzing metropolitan trends and problems. According to a government spokesman, the latest refinement in the title, changing "standard metropolitan area" to "standard metropolitan statistical area," was made to "describe more accurately the objective of the definition."

Although designed for uniformity in statistical tabulation, the SMSA is based on a general concept that lies at the root of the metropolitan community—that of an economic and social unit which possesses a large population nucleus or center. The criteria for inclusion of an area in this category have been formulated with this concept in mind. The measures of integration employed by the Bureau of the Budget in determining whether two or more counties are in the same metropolitan area thus pertain primarily to the extent of economic and social communication, such as the relation of place of residence to place of work.

This operational view coincides with the thinking of most contemporary social scientists who tend to regard the metropolis as a mosaic of subareas whose inhabitants are highly interdependent on a daily basis in terms of needs, communication, and commutation to and from work. The last characteristic was stressed by R. D. McKenzie in his now famous classic, *The Metropolitan Community*, where he states that the term "metropolitan area" signifies "the territory in which the daily economic and social activities of the local population are carried on through a common system of local institutions. It is essentially the commutation area of the central city."[5] So also a member of the University of Pennsylvania's Institute for Urban Studies commented more recently, "The metropolitan region is not simply an area in which circulation reaches a higher density; it is an area in which a certain type of circulation, the

[5] (New York: McGraw-Hill, 1933), p. 84.

journey to work, is of paramount importance and binds the entire region together."[6]

The interdependence of the parts of the metropolis is pointed to as its key attribute in virtually all current writing on the subject. A moment's reflection should convince even the most skeptical that, regardless of whether this element is the primary factor in defining metropolitan areas, it is indeed a most significant and crucial characteristic. Residential suburbs must rely on other sections of the area for their daily supplies: food, clothing, newspapers, entertainment, hospitalization, and the host of other needs typical of the modern household. So also they must depend on other portions of the area, some of them as far distant as thirty or forty miles, for the employment opportunities necessary to support many of their inhabitants. This dependence on the remainder of the community is precisely what enables such suburbs to specialize in residential development.

Conversely, the central city must rely on the outlying residential areas for a substantial portion of its labor force, including middle and top management. Downtown merchants in all urban centers still look to the entire area for their customers. In New York City 3 million persons daily pour into Manhattan to work, man the executive suites, conduct business, shop, or be entertained. In other SMSA's across the nation, the pattern is the same; only the scale is smaller. The people of the metropolis, in short, share a common spatial area for their daily activities. Within this area, although its limits may be imprecisely defined, an intricate web of business and social interrelationships exists and a high degree of communication and interchange among residents, groups, and firms continually takes place.

Decentralization

The first great expansion of civilization occurred when large numbers of people came together in concentrations that became the large preindustrial cities of the past. In this movement the city served as a container or magnet attracting people of the hinterlands into a centralized urban culture. Security, religious worship, and greater economic and social opportunities were among the factors that drew the isolated villager within the protective walls of the

[6] Britton Harris, "The Economic Aspects of the Metropolitan Region," *University of Pennsylvania Law Review*, 105 (February, 1957), 469.

town. Until well into the nineteenth century most cities were territorially small, highly compact, and largely self-contained. They stood in visible relation and in stark contrast to their surrounding rural environs. Residents of even the largest city could travel on foot from one section or neighborhood to any other within a relatively short time. Market place, temple, work, and kinsfolk were within easy walking distance. Industry was confined to the home or small workshop around which revolved family, religious, and economic activities —all localized in a definable residential district.

In modern times the movement to the urban centers has been greatly accelerated, but now, unlike the compact container of the past, "the city has burst open and scattered its complex organs and organizations over the entire landscape."[7] Under the pressure generated by a rising population the metropolis has expanded territorially, engulfing the agricultural villages and small urban settlements in its path. The resulting scene is familiar to everyone. Long ribbons of development with their gasoline stations, barbecue stands, automobile graveyards, neon signs, and motels stretch out into the countryside and residential subdivisions play leapfrog with the land, spawning in the process new centers of local government and commerce. Historian Oscar Handlin describes it this way:

> Seen from above, the modern city edges imperceptibly out of its setting. There are no clear boundaries. Just now the white trace of the superhighway passes through cultivated fields; now it is lost in an asphalt maze of streets and buildings. As one drives in from the airport or looks out from the train window, clumps of suburban housing, industrial complexes, and occasional green spaces flash by; it is hard to tell where city begins and country ends.[8]

Gertrude Stein expressed it somewhat differently after a visit to one of our typical sprawling metropolises when she was asked how she liked it there. Her response was, "There?—There is no there there."

Jean Gottmann, a French geographer, has summarized the even greater metamorphosis that is taking place in some areas. Writing of "megalopolis," the vast urbanized complex that stretches along the northeastern seaboard of the United States from southern New Hampshire to northern Virginia, he observes:

[7] Mumford, *The City in History*, p. 34.

[8] Oscar Handlin and John Burchard (eds.), *The Historian and the City* (Cambridge: The M.I.T. Press and Harvard University Press, 1963), p. 1.

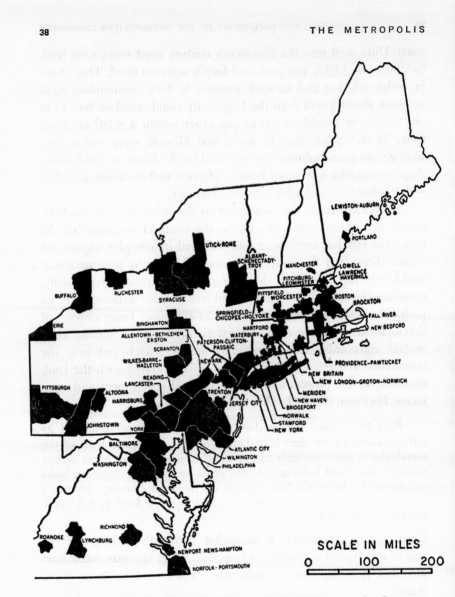

Figure 2.1   Megalopolis of the Eastern United States, 1960. Source:
U.S. Bureau of the Census, *Census of Governments: 1962*, Vol. I, p.
23.

In this area, then, we must abandon the idea of the city as a tightly
settled and organized unit in which people, activities, and riches are
crowded into a very small area clearly separated from its nonurban surroundings. Every city in this region spreads out far and wide around its
original nucleus; it grows amidst an irregularly colloidal mixture of rural
and suburban landscapes; it melts on broad fronts with other mixtures,

of somewhat similar though different texture, belonging to the suburban neighborhoods of other cities.[9]

This combination of centralization and deconcentration—the movement of people into the urban centers and the continuous decentralization within these areas—has resulted largely from the scientific and technological advances of the past century. Mechanization has spurred on the shift from farm to city and freed us from reliance on a predominantly agricultural economy. Since the early days of the Republic, American cities have grown faster than rural areas as surplus agricultural populations have been joined by migrants from foreign countries in the larger centers. The transformation that the nineteenth century witnessed was truly an "urban" revolution. Unlike the past, it meant more than the rise of an occasional New York City or Boston or a modest increase in the size and number of towns and villages. It heralded, instead, the appearance of genuine "urbanization" or the concentration of large masses of people into areas of relatively limited territorial size. This change could not have occurred without the fantastic developments in public health, engineering, transportation, communication, and, most importantly, in the rise of productive activity made possible by the power-operated factory.

The new modes of transportation and communication that emerged from the Industrial Revolution have permitted urban dwellers to settle far beyond the walls of the citadel. First the interurban railway and the horse-drawn tram, later the electric streetcar, and still later the private automobile eliminated the necessity of having home and place of work in close proximity. No longer need the factory be located within walking distance of the worker's hearth or the trolley line. Now a man can spend his working hours in a central business district office or a soot-begrimed plant near the core and retreat in the evenings to the sanctuary of a residential suburb or a semirustic villa many miles away.

The advances in transportation and technology have also influenced factory location. Originally, industry was tied to the waterways and later to the railroads for its access to supplies and markets. (As late as 1910 there were more miles of railroads than high-

[9] Jean Gottmann, *Megalopolis: The Urbanized Northeastern Seaboard of the United States* (New York: Twentieth Century Fund, 1961), p. 5.

ways in the United States.) This dependence has been lessened
as the development of motor truck transportation, the highway
system, and the greater mobility of the labor force have opened
up new locational opportunities. Table 5 shows how these developments have given industry in one metropolitan area a greater
freedom of choice in this matter. Of the 218 plants selecting an
industrial location in Milwaukee County during a recent ten-year
period, 76 percent either chose sites without rail siding or were not
using sidings if they were available.

TABLE 5

Industrial Location as Related to Availability of Rail Siding,
Milwaukee County, 1948–1958

	PLANTS WITH LESS THAN 100 EMPLOYEES	PLANTS WITH 100 OR MORE EMPLOYEES	TOTAL
Available and used	27 (15%)	15 (44%)	42 (19%)
Available but not used	25 (13%)	4 (12%)	29 (13%)
Not available but needed	9 (5%)	1 (3%)	10 (5%)
Not available and not needed	123 (67%)	14 (41%)	137 (63%)
Totals	184 (100%)	34 (100%)	218 (100%)

SOURCE: N. J. Stefaniak, *Industrial Location in Milwaukee County* (Milwaukee:
City of Milwaukee Office of Industrial Development Coordinator, 1959).

In the United States the movement to suburbia began around
a few large cities in the late nineteenth century, but with the
passage of time the outward thrust of urban population also became
characteristic of smaller places.[10] Most cities of 50,000 and over now
exhibit patterns of expansion and diffusion similar to those formerly
found only around the larger municipalities. Graphic proof of this
trend is found in the latest census figures. During the 1950–1960
decennial period, forty-four urban areas acquired metropolitan status;
and these new SMSA's, most of them with populations of less than
100,000, showed an average growth rate of more than 40 percent
in their suburban rings.

[10] Leo F. Schnore, "The Growth of Metropolitan Suburbs," *American
Sociological Review*, 22 (April, 1957), 165.

The decentralization of metropolitan areas, moreover, is not simply an hegira from the core city. Important as this factor is in accounting for ring growth, a portion of this increase is also due to migration from other areas. With high mobility among the managerial ranks of business and industry, the "organization man" frequently moves from the suburb of one metropolis to a similar community in another. White-collar workers in the child-rearing stage who move for one reason or another often follow a similar pattern. Natural increase is a further significant factor since many new suburbanites are young couples beginning the family cycle.

Governmental Fragmentation

The spread of population outward from the core has brought with it a corresponding decentralization of the governmental pattern. When the first great migration waves struck the urban centers, the increased population was absorbed within the cities. Later, as the original boundaries became inadequate to accommodate the newcomers, the corporate limits of the city were expanded by annexing adjacent areas. By the end of the nineteenth century, however, the outward movement had started to outrun the ability of the core city to enlarge its legal boundaries. With the diffusion of population all over the landscape, the metropolis began to look more and more like a formless agglomeration of people and enterprise. New units of local government—cities, towns, villages, school districts, and a wide variety of other special districts—multiplied with astonishing rapidity in the outlying areas. Today, governmental fragmentation is recognized as a major characteristic of the American metropolis.

Specialization

The concentration of people in urban centers, together with technological advancements, has made possible a high degree of specialization. This feature of metropolitanization is reflected in land use as well as commercial and industrial pursuits. With the assistance of planning and zoning, sections of the metropolis have been set aside for various purposes: residential sites, industrial parks, regional shopping centers, and many others. Some suburbs are entirely residential; a much smaller but still significant number are predominantly industrial; and still others contain varied combinations of factories, shops, and homes. Even within the central city, increased specialization of neighborhoods has been under way for a half century or more, stimulated in recent years by urban renewal and redevelopment efforts.

The results of this specialization are evident in both the physical aspects of the metropolis and the spatial distribution of "social classes." The location of various land uses, with their accompanying attributes such as density, property values, and prestige, determine the neighborhoods or areas where different segments of the population will live. Income and racial characteristics are among the significant factors that help to make this distribution. The low-income worker is effectively barred from many suburban communities by zoning and building restrictions that prevent the construction of low-cost homes, while the Negro, and to a lesser extent other minority groups, regardless of income, are kept out by such practices as discrimination in building code enforcement and mortgage lending.

Decentralization and specialization have been made possible by size and technology. The motor vehicle and paved road and new methods of communication have linked the city and its environs in a closer functional relationship. The institutional division of labor which formerly characterized the compact city has been extended to include a wide range of outlying settlement. New subcenters closely linked to the core city have sprung up. These subcenters are seldom complete in their service structure but depend on the core for the more specialized and integrating functions.[11] Yet while they are subject to the dominance or influence of the metropolitan center, they in turn exert a significant influence in their more limited areas. The resulting decentralization of activity has brought urban communities into a new kind of relationship, one marked by a high degree of interdependence between the center and outlying areas and among the latter themselves.

Not only have new subcenters been created by the population "explosion," but the conquering of space by the automobile, telephone, radio, and television has also drawn long-established and formerly semi-independent communities into the orbit of the core city and forged vital links between them and other parts of the metropolitan area. Enveloped in the course of time have been set-

[11] See McKenzie, *The Metropolitan Community*, chap. 6.

tlements, some almost as old as the central city and formerly serving as local trading posts for the adjacent farm areas; industrial satellites which had been established on railroads and waterways some distance from the core; and wealthy residential suburbs peopled by the railroad commuters at the turn of the present century. Virtually without exception, these various territorial segments are under different local public jurisdictions, but this in no way affects the basic interdependence in daily activities that exists among them; it merely makes the process of governing them more difficult.

In summary, no definitive list of criteria for metropolitanism exists. Population size, interdependence, decentralization, governmental fragmentation, and specialization are the most frequently attributed characteristics. If the definition of a metropolitan area employed by the Bureau of the Census (the SMSA definition) is accepted without an understanding of its proper use, any city in an area not previously recognized as metropolitan automatically upon attaining a population of 50,000 becomes part of a metropolis. It would, however, be naive to assume that an area of slightly over 50,000 inhabitants exhibits the same characteristics as one of 5 million. It would be equally naive to believe that by studying the former we would be examining a microcosm or miniature replica of the latter. Size is, of course, a concomitant of metropolitanization, but the point at which an urban area becomes metropolitan cannot be defined merely by numbers of people.

METROPOLIS AS COMMUNITY

The metropolitan area is frequently referred to in writings on urbanism as a "community." The first official recognition of this new phenomenon occurred in a special census report published in 1886. Singling out New York City as an example, the report called attention to the regional ramifications of the area and stated that it seemed ". . . proper, in treating of the vast population occupying the cities of New York, Brooklyn, Jersey City, Newark and Hoboken, to consider them not only as constituting five different municipalities, but as one great metropolitan community. This population has grown from one nucleus—the little trading-post at the Battery—and its separation into different civil divisions is by physical and political lines, which have had little influence on the character of the people, their industries, or their modes of life."[12] Also, at about this time pioneers in the study of American municipal government, Frank J. Goodnow and others, began to refer to the metropolis in their writings; and by 1920 political scientists were describing the metropolitan area as an organic and economic unit. "The simple fact is," as one of them noted, "that the city and suburbs are in reality one community, and no amount of political casuistry can alter that fact."[13]

Community is an ambiguous term with many meanings and connotations. Neighborhoods, suburban municipalities, and central cities, as well as the monastery and the beehive, are spoken of as communities. The sociologically-oriented individual associates the term in a general way with a social group located within certain spatial or territorial limits and organized to satisfy some functional need. The politically-minded person thinks of the term as applying to an organized governmental unit such as a city. But "community" used for the purpose of denoting an easily distinguishable entity has now lost much of its meaning. Some of the newer studies, for example, tend to de-emphasize it as a geographical unit populated by individuals and look upon it as a collection of small and informal social units possessing overlapping memberships that spontaneously generate or foster order in the society. These and similar usages sometimes create confusion, particularly when the fact is overlooked that "community," like many other concepts in social science, can be viewed from different aspects and employed for different purposes.

A Combination of Two Definitions

Despite the broad and varied application of the term and the difficulties of exact definition, a meaning of particular relevance to metropolitan areas can be determined. It is largely a combination of two core definitions that emerge from the literature. One refers to the modes of relationship in which the individuals and families involved share common values and objectives and closely identify themselves with the aggregate population; the other indicates a

[12] U.S. Bureau of the Census, *Tenth Census of the United States, Social Statistics of Cities* (Washington: 1886), Part 1, pp. 531–532.

[13] Chester C. Maxey, *An Outline of Municipal Government* (New York: Doubleday, 1924), p. 120.

spatially defined social unit that has functional significance and reflects the interdependence of individuals and groups.

Community in the first mentioned or classical sense is more applicable to the primary groupings of the past—the village or feudal manor—and seemingly to the early New England town. A community of this kind, as sociologist Scott Greer has pointed out, "disappears under urban conditions; it has no hold over the individual, for its functions are preempted by large specialized organizations in the interest of rational control, while the individual is highly mobile and is isolated in the local area only when he chooses to be. As the functional bases for interaction disappear, communion goes with them."[14]

The second meaning relates essentially to the interdependence that arises among groups as a consequence of large-scale specialization. Here the need for social goods—economic production, employment, public and private services, and the whole network of mutually sustaining activities—requires constant interaction and communication among the residents of an area. The strong sense of communion and shared values characteristic of the first meaning may no longer be present, but the high degree of interdependence in daily activities which the urban system imposes on the aggregation creates a social group with strong ties of mutual interest and concern. These ties are coterminous with—in fact they help to fix— the territorial boundaries of the social collectivity or community.

The close interrelations within a metropolitan area are reflected in many ways other than the work-residence pattern and the territorial division of labor. They are evidenced by the numerous private and semipublic organizations which cross local municipal or city governmental boundaries: the community chest, professional and trade organizations, labor unions, social clubs, and the many other groups that are established and operate on an area-wide basis. They are demonstrated by the privately owned utilities—telephone, electric, gas—which are organized to serve the entire metropolis. They are manifested in the social and cultural fabric of the larger community: the prestigious country club that draws its membership

[14] "Individual Participation in Mass Society," in Roland Young (ed.), *Approaches to the Study of Politics* (Evanston: Northwestern University Press, 1958), p. 338.

from a wide area; the symphony that is supported by central city dweller and suburbanite alike; the urban university that serves the higher educational aspirations of the metropolis; the medical facility that ministers to the specialized health needs of the total population; the civic center that symbolizes the hopes and achievements of the area.

This interdependence is so obvious, so taken for granted, that its significance and implications are commonly overlooked by the metropolitan resident. It is difficult for the average person to identify himself or his primary self-interests with a mosaic of diverse neighborhoods and governmental entities covering many square miles. He may have some vague idea of the interdependence but he seldom relates it to governmental organization and the need for coordinating public policy in matters affecting the metropolis as a whole. The residential suburb can zone out lower-income workers or the central city neighborhood can practice racial segregation with little thought as to how damaging these policies are to the total community. Suburban residents can insist on non-involvement with the social problems of the core city as though escape from their consequences is possible; this reaction is simply to deny the realities.

The low degree of awareness of metropolitan interdependence that is prevalent among many urban dwellers was indicated recently in an attitude survey conducted in the St. Louis City-County area. There a large sample of area residents was asked whether they thought the central city and suburbs shared any major problems. Eighty-one percent answered affirmatively. Yet when they were asked to name the specific problems, one-fourth were unable to cite a single shared difficulty, one-fourth could mention only one, one-fourth recalled two, and only one-fourth listed more than two.[15] These responses may have indicated a vague belief in the natural interdependence of the area, but they showed little public concern or understanding about the nature of the relationship.

METROPOLITAN BOUNDARIES

Delineating the territorial limits of the metropolis is a task that presents further difficulty. The chore is simple if the SMSA defini-

[15] John C. Bollens (ed.), *Exploring the Metropolitan Community* (Berkeley and Los Angeles: University of California Press, 1961), p. 191.

tion employed by the Bureau of the Census is used since county
(or in New England, city and town) boundaries mark the limits.
The process is somewhat more complex if the census-defined "urbanized area" is employed. Here the central city and the surrounding
densely settled area or fringe are included while county lines and
other governmental boundaries are ignored. These areas are similar
to what are called "conurbations" in other countries. Finally, the
task of marking off the spatial extent of the metropolis becomes
exceedingly complex if the criteria of functional interdependence
are applied.

In certain respects the "urbanized area" is more meaningful
than the SMSA for describing the limits of the metropolitan community since it provides a better separation of urban and rural population in the vicinity of the larger cities. The SMSA's inclusion of
entire counties can be misleading unless the nature and objectives
of the definition are kept in mind. The population aggregation of
a contiguous or adjoining county, for example, may be clustered
in sections that border the central county while the major portion
of the outlying county may be entirely rural. Use of the "urbanized
area" definition corrects this deficiency but it compounds the difficulty of working with the data, particularly for comparative purposes, since over a period of time the boundaries of such areas
change more readily than do those of SMSA's. Thus, important
as these two definitions are for statistical purposes, they do not
necessarily mark the territorial limits of the metropolitan community
nor delineate the area for local governmental purposes and mutual
public problems. Other criteria must be employed for these needs.

The Place-of-Work Standard

We have already noted McKenzie's use of the commutation
area of the central city as a key index for delimiting metropolitan
areas. The "place-of-work" question contained for the first time in
the 1960 Census of Population makes work-residence data readily
available to the researcher. Through this test, if accepted as valid,
any doubts about the inclusion or exclusion of particular outlying
sections could be resolved in systematic fashion. However, reliance
on this measure alone would ignore the other factors that generate
areal interdependence, such as those related to the retail trade and
service sectors of the economy.

Economic Base Concepts

A second approach attempts to delineate the metropolitan area by means of economic base concepts. This method utilizes the familiar division of economic activities into basic and non-basic functions. The first pertain to those performed for markets mainly outside a specific area or region; the second to those for consumption principally within such a region. Manufacturing falls predominantly into the first category since most of its products are exported to other areas. On the other hand, retailing and the service functions belong to the latter class because most of their products are locally consumed. Applying this distinction to the metropolis, the boundaries of the community are roughly equated with the primary service areas of its non-basic economic functions because they are the sections embracing the population that is in daily contact with the core city and dependent upon it for many specialized services.[16]

Function-By-Function Approach

A third approach emphasizes the instability of metropolitan boundaries and denies that precise spatial limits can be located. This approach holds essentially that the dimensions of a community vary according to the function under scrutiny. Rejecting the notion that areal limits can be drawn by applying any single criterion as proposed in the other methods, this approach suggests that a community has many boundaries. If the work-residence pattern is the basis, one set of boundaries emerges; if the retail trade area is plotted, another is evident; and if the daily communication network is outlined, there is a third. Fixing the limits of the metropolis for governmental and public service functions presents similar difficulties. The metropolis may embrace one area for purposes of water supply, another for air pollution, another for transportation, and still another for planning. In one case the municipality may constitute an adequate area for administrative or political control; in others it may be the county or even a far broader region.

A recent study of Milwaukee and its hinterland illustrates the varying boundaries of an area when different functions are examined. Distributional data were mapped for forty-two criteria, ranging from

[16] See L. P. Green, "Johannesburg," in William A. Robson (ed.), *Great Cities of the World*, 2nd ed. (New York: Macmillan, 1957), pp. 709–710.

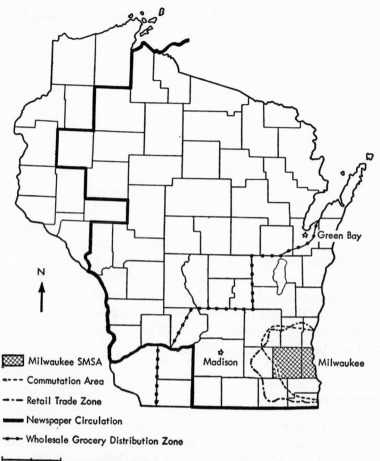

Figure 2.2 Metropolitan Boundaries Based on Four
Measures of Influence, Milwaukee SMSA, 1960. From
Donn K. Haglund, *The Areal Extent of the Milwaukee
Hinterland.*

the commuting area and retail trade zone to newspaper circulation
and the drawing area of the Milwaukee Braves baseball team.[17] The
territorial sphere of influence of each criterion employed in the study
differs. Four of these boundaries are shown in Figure 2.2 to illustrate the broad variances that exist when different criteria are con-

[17] Donn K. Haglund, *The Areal Extent of the Milwaukee Hinterland* (Ann
Arbor: University Microfilms, 1962).

sidered. The commuting and retail trade zones closely correspond to each other, but wholesale grocery distribution and metropolitan newspaper circulation extend farther out into the hinterland. Despite the wide diversity, however, the study also reveals a general grouping of the areal phenomena into a limited number of classes for which composite boundaries might be drawn, each encompassing a progressively larger zone. Other studies have similarly found that distinctions can be made among three or four sets of community boundaries on the basis of various criteria.[18]

These territorial distinctions, vague as they may seem at first glance, serve to illustrate the many factors involved in determining the spatial extent of metropolitan areas. It would be a mistake to assume, however, that the task of defining boundaries in non-legal terms is merely an academic or intellectual pursuit; the existence and location of such boundaries have important implications for the structure and functioning of a metropolitan area. An awareness of the character and extent of areal interdependence—or even of the fact that different functions may have different territorial spheres of dominance or influence—can condition and guide the approach that may be taken to the problems of the metropolis.

SPATIAL PATTERN

Cruising in an airplane over a large urban agglomeration, the traveler is inevitably impressed by the varied pattern of land use stretching far over the countryside. Clusters of large buildings, tightly compressed tenements, concentrations of single-family residences, neatly arranged subdivisions, open spaces, giant industrial areas, an occasional shopping center, and countless roads with their crawling vehicles, all are blended together—sometimes incongruously as though thrown together by happenstance—into a vast web of human settlement. Several ways of describing and analyzing these spatial arrangements have been devised by geographers and sociologists. Those most commonly referred to are concentric zones, sectors, star-shaped configurations, and multiple nuclei. Highly simplified drawings of these four theoretical patterns are presented in Figure 2.3.

[18] See, for example, Amos H. Hawley, *Human Ecology* (New York: Ronald, 1950), chap. 13.

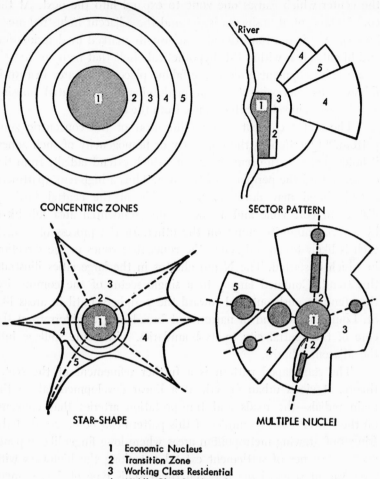

1   Economic Nucleus
2   Transition Zone
3   Working Class Residential
4   Middle Class Residential
5   Upper-Middle and Upper Class Residential
- - Major Traffic Arteries

Figure 2.3   Urban Configurations.

Four Theories of Urban Development

According to the first view, a metropolitan area tends to resemble a series of concentric zones differentiated by type of land
use and structure.[19] Growth proceeds as the result of pressure from

[19] See Ernest W. Burgess' chapter, "Urban Areas," in T. V. Smith and
Leonard D. White (eds.), Chicago: An Experiment in Social Science Research
(Chicago: University of Chicago Press, 1929), pp. 113–138.

the center which causes one zone to expand into the next. At the core is the central business district and the adjacent industrial areas. Surrounding it is a transitional zone usually marked by deterioration and blight. (It is within this hypothetical circle that many of today's urban redevelopment projects are taking place.) This area in turn is followed by successive zones of predominantly residential housing that increases in value with distance from the core.

The sector concept is a modification of the concentric zone pattern.[20] Questioning the symmetry or homogeneity of such zones, it holds that growth occurs in sectors which extend radially from the center toward the periphery of the area. Thus a high-rent apartment neighborhood may develop on one side of the central business district or core zone and a low income residential area inhabited by a racial minority group on the other. In the process of growth each is likely to expand across the concentric zones in the direction in which it started. The Negro ghettos in the large cities illustrate this trend. Confined largely to a single sector of the community, they tend to push outward toward the periphery until in areas like St. Louis they extend in narrow but broadening corridors from the core of the central city to its boundaries, with some spillage into the adjacent suburbs.

The star-shaped pattern is a further refinement of the sector theory. It views urban growth as a linear development along the main radials—the roads and transportation arteries that converge on the central core. Examples of this pattern can be observed at the fringes of growing metropolitan areas where long finger-like append-ages or tongues of settlement extend out along the highways with large vacant spaces lying between them. This type of development was first noticeable along the streetcar routes and the railroad com-muter lines that provided the connecting links between center and periphery. Its vestiges are still evident in the existing land use char-acteristics of most large urban areas. However, with the passage of time, development of the intervening land has created a high degree of circumferential movement and made the pattern less dis-tinguishable.

The fourth method of analyzing the spatial pattern rejects the

[20] For a discussion of this theory, see Homer Hoyt, "The Structure of American Cities in the Post-War Era," *American Journal of Sociology*, XLVIII (January, 1943), 476–477.

notion that the community is uni-centered, as the concentric zonal theory leads one to assume. Pointing out that many phenomena of urban life occur in clusters, it denies that the round of daily life revolves mainly about a single center. As a leading ecologist points out, "Modern forms of communication and transportation have brought into being a sharply etched multi-centered community pattern. Formerly semi-independent communities scattered over the hinterland about a market center were drawn into close contact with one another as well as with the major center, differentiated as to function, and transformed into units in an extensive though highly sensitive local territorial division of labor."[21] Within the principal nucleus—the core or central business district—are concentrated the home or regional offices of business and industry, financial institutions, major governmental agencies, legal and other specialized professional services, the theatre and other cultural facilities, and the shopping point for style merchandise and comparative buying. Clustered about the core throughout the metropolitan area is a constellation of subcenters: neighborhood and regional shopping centers, suburban central business districts, outlying industrial concentrations, and local governmental bureaucracies.

Applying the Theories

These types of urban growth configurations are not likely to be found in their pure form in any existing metropolis. One or the other may be more dominant or noticeable in individual areas, but generally speaking the pattern will embody characteristics of each. In fact, most urban aggregations now resemble great spreading circular and semicircular masses of land and buildings. The Milwaukee SMSA provides a typical illustration of how all these various growth configurations appear to blend together in a single urban complex (see Figure 2.4). The concentric zone pattern is visible although not sharply outlined or symmetrical. Middle- and upper-class residential sectors extend in both directions along most of the lake front. The star-shaped influence is readily observable on the periphery where lines of settlement radiate along the transportation routes like the spokes of a wheel. Finally, various kinds of subcenters or nuclei are distributed around a major core which serves as the integrating

[21] Hawley, *Human Ecology*, p. 270.

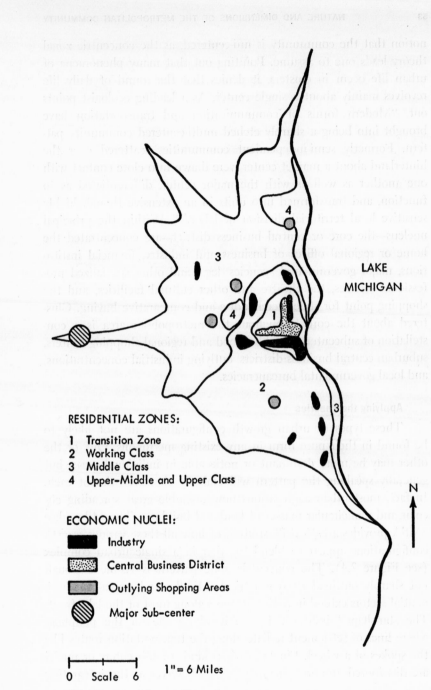

LAKE
MICHIGAN

RESIDENTIAL ZONES:

1 Transition Zone
2 Working Class
3 Middle Class
4 Upper-Middle and Upper Class

ECONOMIC NUCLEI:

Industry
Central Business District
Outlying Shopping Areas
Major Sub-center

N

0   Scale   6   1" = 6 Miles

Figure 2.4   Metropolitan Growth Pattern, Milwaukee SMSA.

point for the area's activities. Many factors including topography, transportation routes, economic base, and the availability of utilities have affected the spatial distribution of activities in the Milwaukee area and helped shape this pattern.

All four theories are useful in analyzing metropolitan growth patterns, although the multicentered concept appears the most meaningful and realistic. It seems obvious that no two large-sized communities follow exactly the same developmental pattern and that each area must be examined individually to identify and understand its characteristics. Yet taking into account topographical and locational differences, metropolitan areas exhibit striking similarities in their spatial compositions. Each has an important central core and many subcenters of activity. Manufacturing establishments are located along the transportation network—rivers, railroads, and highways—while the retail trade and service establishments follow the population. Tall luxury apartments are replacing some of the blighted areas near the downtown section where land costs remain high. The better and newer residential properties are situated in the outlying parts of the central city and in the suburbs. Institutions and activities of different types—medical centers, used car lots, "bright-light" and entertainment districts, wholesale commission rows, publishing houses, garment factories—are huddled together in various sections of the community, determined largely on the basis of their different locational requirements. Areas of segregated family types exist within the residential neighborhoods, the result partly of differences in income and partly of ethnic and racial prejudices. The street and transportation pattern radiates from the center outward with crosstown access usually more difficult. Expressways in increasing numbers are now cutting the metropolis into segments and touching off radical land use changes.

METROPOLIS IN PERSPECTIVE

Whether praised or damned, the metropolis plays a major role in the lives of an ever-growing number of Americans. A giant producer and consumer of goods as well as a center of culture and urbanity, it helps to satisfy many of the deep-seated needs and desires of mankind. At the same time it creates vast public and private problems that challenge the ingenuity of urban America. Dynamic technological, social, political, and economic forces are at work within this complex phenomenon and shape its character, physical form, and institutions. As the crossroads and assembly point for a continuously increasing flow of people, goods, and capital, the metropolis is the modern version of the preindustrial cities which flourished along the great trade routes of Europe and Asia. But now the abacus has given way to the electronic computer and the merchant prince to the organization man.

Variety of choice in all aspects of living and working has come to be regarded by many students of urban affairs as the basic goal of the metropolitan community. Dean John Burchard of the Massachusetts Institute of Technology once put it simply when he said that the only real excuse for the metropolis is that it provides a population large enough to satisfy many diverse interests. It must have enough people, he remarked, so that a particular kind of sausage or special cheese can be found in some store. Participants in a recent symposium viewed it in somewhat more formal terms as "creating fundamental opportunities for high incomes, a greater variety and a wider choice of modes of living, a way of life that could be more stimulating, more enlightened, and more conducive to innovations."[22]

These observations express in a general way the functional role of the metropolitan community in modern society. This role is one of many facets. It relates to the concentration of people and industry that makes possible both a widening variety of consumer goods and a reduction in the costs of producing them. It refers to the social and cultural opportunities that only a large urban complex can offer: the library, theatre, art museum, and music hall. It involves the communications network that permits interpersonal contacts among large numbers of people in business and social transactions. And most importantly, it encompasses the means—the educational, experiential, and employment opportunities—that enable the individual to participate as an active producer and consumer of urban goods and urban culture.

The metropolis represents an accumulation of the human and material resources that make possible the accomplishment of goals undreamed of in a simpler and smaller-scale society. By bringing

[22] Kevin Lynch and Lloyd Rodwin, "A World of Cities," *Daedalus*, 90 (Winter, 1961), 6.

together a variety of personal skills and capital, it fosters specialization and a wide diversity of economic and social activities. It serves as the producer of goods and services and as a market place not alone for its own population but for a larger hinterland. It performs a less tangible but still important function as a symbol of an area's culture, its industrial and commercial might, and its distinctive position in the broader national and international scene. The metropolitan community of today is a way of life, one might even say a civilization. It is the city "writ large."

CHAPTER 3

Metropolitan Models and Types

THE OBJECTIVE of the social scientist is to formulate what is essential for understanding and prediction in the field of social, economic, and political behavior. To this end, he and his colleagues in the physical sciences seek simplicity and order in the world of reality. Confronted with an infinite amount of data, he endeavors to develop a theoretical framework or conceptual scheme to guide him in selecting what is critical and significant from this huge stockpile. Patiently and painstakingly, he strives to determine how he can reduce his data to manageable form, how he can find order in its untold variety, what methods and research tools he can most profitably employ. To assist in this task of conceptualization and analysis, he often attempts to construct models or representations of the real system he is studying. Invariably, for this is one of the basic requisites of the scientific approach, he also attempts to categorize or classify his data so that it can be more easily handled and the relationships ascertained between the variables or factors.

It is not the purpose of this book to describe the scientific method or to examine in detail how metropolitan communities are systematically studied. Yet the nonprofessional but interested observer of metropolitan life can profit from some familiarity with the kinds of approaches that are employed by urban researchers. For after all, the amateur as well as the social scientist is confronted with a bewildering array of data and with incredible complexity when he surveys the metropolitan landscape. He too requires some guidelines and reference points, some conceptual ways of looking at urban phenomena. Passing acquaintance with theory formulation and the methodological tools of contemporary scholars will not, of course, transform the amateur into a scientist nor magically endow him with greater perceptive powers. It may, however, make him a more careful observer and sensitize him to the ways of scientific inquiry. It may also give him greater appreciation of the complexity of the field and the need for examining his own community and its experiences in the light of broader trends and more universal concepts. On the basis of these assumptions and for whatever value the treatment may have for the general reader, we discuss in this chapter two broad categories of research schemes relevant to the study of the metropolis: models and classification.

MODELS

From earliest times man has endeavored to discover order in the universe so that he might better understand its unending flow of data. At first he resorted to myths, but gradually over the centuries these were displaced by concepts, hypotheses, and theories. Whatever his approach to reality, he has invariably sought to explain the mysterious and unfamiliar with images or metaphors constructed from the known and familiar. Thus, among the early nomadic peoples, the universe was viewed as a great tent arching the sky and enclosing the earth. And among the ancient Greek writers the world was explained in terms of a single substance: for some it was water, which took various forms under the pressure of cold or heat; for others it was air, which became fire when rarefied, and wind, water, earth, and stone when condensed; and for still others it was fire, which constantly changed into other forms as a result of the conflicts of opposites. Like his early ancestors, modern man also turns to what is familiar in order to explain what is strange and unknown.

But instead of the cosmological "models" of the past, he uses empirical representations to facilitate his investigation of complex phenomena.

The term "model" is today a fashionable symbol in social science research. Borrowed from the vocabulary of technology (with its miniature replicas of airplanes, automobiles, and buildings), the word is loosely used to include everything from sets of simple propositions to highly sophisticated mathematical formulas. Basically, however, a model rests on analogy. The flow of water through a network of pipes, for instance, might be taken as an analogue of the flow of communications through a large bureaucratic organization. The value of conceptualizing the process in this way is not difficult to see. By examining the first, or the more simple and familiar, the researcher may obtain ideas about the operations of the second, or the more complex and unfamiliar. In other words, one system may serve as a model for another wholly unrelated system if the study of the former is useful for an understanding of the latter. This may be either because the first is less complex or because it has already been carefully investigated and its operations analyzed. The latter case is particularly applicable to the two models of metropolitan political behavior that we will examine here: the international relations or diplomatic model and the economic model.

The International Relations Model

Several students of the contemporary urban scene have suggested that the relations among local governmental units in metropolitan areas can best be described by a theory of international politics. Victor Jones called attention to this possibility some years ago when he observed that the analogy between metropolitan organization and international organization "can serve to remind us that we are dealing with local units of government that are tough organizations with many political and legal protections against annihilation or absorption by another government."[1] He also noted that a study of experiences at the international level might lead to a form of metropolitan reorganization that would enable local governments to function more satisfactorily. More recently, political scientist Matthew Holden has attempted to show in some detail how

[1] "The Organization of a Metropolitan Region," *University of Pennsylvania Law Review*, 105 (February, 1957), 539.

the international model might be used to impose a measure of intellectual rationality upon the study of metropolitan political behavior.[2]

Certainly the governmental structure of the metropolis resembles the international system. Most metropolitan areas are administered by a host of local units, each with jurisdiction over a territorial segment of the whole, each enjoying legal autonomy, and each wary of the intentions of the other. Their actions in many ways are analogous to those of national states. They compete with one another for scarce resources (taxes, industry); they bargain for needed supplies and facilities (water, sewers); they seek to expand their sphere of control (through annexation and consolidation); and they form coalitions for defensive purposes (such as suburban leagues of municipalities). As they interact with each other, they develop an awareness of the problems which grow out of their coexistence and come to recognize the need for creating institutional devices to regulate relations among themselves. In Jones' words, "If local governments in metropolitan areas act toward each other as if they were national states, we should not be surprised to recognize among proposals for reorganizing them counterparts of world government, world federation, functional organization, and bilateral and multilateral compacts."[3] Illustrations of this analogy are readily found in the proposals for consolidation of governments, local federal systems, and functional consolidation, and in the creation of intergovernmental representative bodies such as the Association of Bay Area Governments (ABAG) in the San Francisco Bay area, the Mid-Willamette Valley (Salem, Oregon, area) Council of Governments, the Metropolitan Washington (D.C.) Council of Governments, and the New York Metropolitan Regional Council.

The potential use of the international relations model as an analytical device merits serious attention. Research and theory-formulation in the international field are well advanced over those at the local level. If advantage can be taken of this work and if it can be made applicable to the metropolitan complex, the cause of urban

---

[2] "The Governance of the Metropolis as a Problem in Diplomacy," *Journal of Politics*, 26 (August, 1964), 627–647. See also Philip E. Jacob and James V. Toscano (eds.), *The Integration of Political Communities* (Philadelphia: J. B. Lippincott, 1963).

[3] Jones, "The Organization of a Metropolitan Region," p. 539.

scholarship would be considerably advanced. At the least, it would be possible to derive a set of propositions from international relations theory that could be empirically tested in the operations of metropolitan area governments. Holden takes this approach in exploring the possibilities of the model. Portraying the two systems —metropolitan and supra-national—as analogous, he develops his inquiry around four groups of questions: (1) *What substantive matters make it necessary for governments to interact with each other?* (2) *How nearly equal are the participating governments in status, power, and resources?* (3) *Do conflicts among the governments tend to be prolonged or are they settled in relatively short order?* (4) *What procedures are employed in the interaction situations among the governments?* With these questions as his focal points, he then attempts to relate propositions from the literature of international relations to the behavior of metropolitan area governments.

An illustration of this approach might be helpful. Holden refers to studies of how consensus is arrived at and integrative mechanisms are developed among national states. His purpose is to determine whether experiences on the international plane have relevance at the metropolitan level. Referring to the current emphasis on intergovernmental consultation (as typified in area-wide councils of public officials), he notes that this approach calls for the strategy of first seeking to achieve procedural consensus among the parties— getting them to become more responsive to each other—before tackling issues. The pertinent question here is whether such consultations actually lead to genuine consensus, and, if so, to what degree it will be translatable into substantive policy. As Holden points out, this is precisely the question to which several researchers have addressed themselves in the international field.[4]

Although Holden's efforts are only exploratory, they suggest that the governmental structures and political processes of metropolitan areas bear some analytical similarity to those at the supra-national level. To the extent that they do, the international model can provide a useful analogue for conceptualizing the microcosmic world of the metropolis. We know, of course, that basic differences exist between the two systems as they do between most models and reality. Unlike national states, local governments are creatures of

[4] See, for example, Ernst B. Haas, *Consensus Formation in the Council of Europe* (Berkeley and Los Angeles: University of California Press, 1960).

a higher level of political authority. As such, they are circumscribed in their behavior by constitutional and statutory provisions which define their powers and responsibilities, including the kinds of arrangements, if any, that they can enter into with each other. In addition, they have little control over such crucial elements as economic growth and population expansion. Many of the important decisions affecting their well-being and future are made at the state and national levels—tax allocations, welfare, redevelopment and housing policies, and highway locations, to mention but a few. Hence, the range of significant subject matter about which they can bargain among themselves is relatively narrow. Moreover, they have apparently felt little compulsion to interact extensively with each other even within this limited sphere. As Wallace Sayre and Herbert Kaufman concluded about New York:

> The haphazard character of the relationships between New York City and its neighbors has resulted from their relative independence of each other in the past with respect to all but a few governmental functions. Only occasionally did problems reach a state sufficiently acute to force them to pay close attention to each other and to try to influence each other's actions.[5]

This scene is in decided contrast to that at the international level where interaction among units is continual and negotiation constant.

To point out such differences is not to deny the relevance or usefulness of international relations theory for the study of metropolitan area government; it is to suggest several factors that must be taken into account when seeking to apply it. For despite the differences, the analogy between the two systems appears to be sufficiently strong to warrant full exploration of the model's possibilities. Whatever insight or clues, however small, that might possibly be gained from its application to metropolitan political behavior would be well worth the effort.

The Economic Model

A second model, one derived from economic theory, has also been proposed for the study of metropolitan organization and proc-

[5] *Governing New York City* (New York: Russell Sage Foundation, 1960), p. 596.

esses. Unlike the international relations approach which is based
essentially on political interaction, the economic or municipal-services model rests on the analogue of the market place. It assumes that
a process similar to choice and allocation in the private sector of
the economy underlies the operation of the numerous governments
that comprise the metropolis. Within this framework, the local
units are viewed as competing for the trade of citizen consumers.

Attempts to apply economic models to the study of political
behavior are of recent vintage. The efforts in the main have been
directed toward constructing a theory of government similar to the
theory of markets. As formulated by one economist, the strategies
of political parties to maximize voter support is likened to the efforts
of individuals to maximize their satisfactions or returns in the private
market place.[6] Or as conceived by others, the decision-making process
of individuals in matters of politics is analogous to the determination of the terms of trade in an exchange of goods.[7] Voters theoretically cast their ballots for those candidates who will benefit them
most. So also, they support those public policies which presumably
bring them the greatest returns. The economic approach, in short,
assumes man to be a utility maximizer in his political as well as in
his market activity.

As applied to the metropolitan scene, the so-called municipal-
services market model has received most attention. Basically, this
approach equates the decentralized governmental structure of an
urban community to a "quasi-market" situation.[8] It postulates that
the various agencies producing public goods constitute a municipal-
services industry which can be expected to exhibit patterns of conduct similar to those of private firms. By providing different bundles
or levels of services, the local governments present the citizen con-

[6] Anthony Downs, *An Economic Theory of Democracy* (New York: Harper
& Row, 1957).

[7] James M. Buchanan and Gordon Tullock, *The Calculus of Consent* (Ann
Arbor: University of Michigan Press, 1962).

[8] Discussion of this model is based largely on Vincent Ostrom, Charles
Tiebout, and Robert Warren, "The Organization of Government in Metropolitan
Areas: A Theoretical Inquiry," *American Political Science Review*, LV (Decem-
ber, 1961), 831–842; Robert Warren, "A Municipal-Service Market Model of
Metropolitan Organization," (Paper presented at annual meeting of the American
Political Science Association, Washington, D.C., September, 1962); Charles M.
Tiebout, "A Pure Theory of Local Expenditures," *The Journal of Political
Economy*, LXIV (October, 1956), 416–424.

sumer with a range of alternate choices. If, for instance, he wants high quality education for his children, he can live in that unit which operates a first-rate school system. Or if he is extremely tax conscious and opposed to expanding the public sector, he can choose a community where tax rates are comparatively low and services minimal. Implicit in this model, as in economic theory generally, is the assumption that both the producers (the governmental units) and the consumers (the residents) will act in their own interests to maximize their own values or satisfactions. The public agencies will behave so as to preserve the "establishment," retain and extend their power and influence, and enhance their prestige; the citizens in turn will select the producer that appears to best satisfy their preference patterns at the lowest cost.

Carrying the analogy further, public agencies, like private industries, are forced to compete over the service levels offered in relation to the taxes charged. This competitive situation ideally exists where a number of local units are located in close proximity to each other and where information about the performance of each is publicly available. In such cases, the resident-consumers are presented with the opportunity to compare performance and judge the relative efficiency of the producers. Theoretically, also, competition under such circumstances would motivate desirable self-regulatory tendencies on the part of local agencies, lead to greater responsiveness to citizen demands, and result in more efficient operation. It would furthermore provide residents of a typical metropolitan area possessing many local governments with a greater range of choice than would be available under a monolithic governmental structure.

The validity of the municipal-services model presupposes certain basic conditions: (1) the existence of several producers of similar public goods in the metropolitan area; (2) sufficient differentiation of their products to provide a basis for choice; and (3) awareness by the citizen consumer of the various alternatives and their costs to him. This last condition is the one which causes the most difficulty. The concept of the market place assumes that the buyer is familiar with the range of choices open to him and the price of each. As a rational man he then weighs the alternatives and selects the one which he believes will benefit him most. This kind of knowledge is seldom possessed by the consumer of goods in the public sector of the community. Numerous studies show that he knows relatively little about the operations and costs of the various local governments serving a metropolitan area. Under such circumstances, his choice process is not likely to resemble that of "economic man."

An element of uncertainty, moreover, is present in virtually all governmental transactions. Here, unlike the selection among private goods, no one-to-one correspondence exists between individual choice and the final outcome. When a consumer decides to purchase a Ford in preference to other makes of cars, he knows exactly what he will receive and how much he will pay for it. When he votes for a local official because he wants a better bundle of public services, he has no certainty that his candidate will be elected or, if elected, that he will carry out the promised policies. Similarly, while he recognizes that every public proposal has a cost-benefit ratio, he cannot possibly estimate his own share in the benefits or costs as he can in comparable market choices. (And if he does not exercise his choice, it will be made for him by others.) To move closer to reality, the economic model must take into account this uncertainty and the consequent likelihood that rationality is only approximated by the citizen-consumer in his political decisions. It must also take into account the noneconomic or emotional factors that affect political behavior to a far greater extent than they do private market behavior. Local units are more than producers of goods and services; they are also culture carriers or value systems, control mechanisms, and arbiters among competing interests.

The economic model seeks to provide an analytical framework for exploring metropolitan organization. It proceeds by conceptualizing a local governmental system in which the production of public goods is decentralized and choice is available to the citizens. Operation of the system is simulated by theoretically introducing conditions into the public sector which approximate those of the market place. This conception obviously oversimplifies many aspects of the local governing process and completely ignores others. Yet, like the international relations model, the economic analogue should be utilized for whatever value it may have. In the opinion of its proponents, this value lies in the fact that it provides a theoretical point of departure for re-evaluating traditional assumptions, the nature and development of public organization in metropolitan areas, and the diversity of values that exists among their residents. Beyond this, it potentially has the power to describe the behavior of decision-makers and patterns of conduct that can be expected in a decentralized decision-making system.[9]

To give an illustration of its possible value, the economic model might be of use in the analysis of metropolitan reorganization failures. Presumably, the voter-consumer believes, if his choice is "rational," that the costs of local governmental change will outweigh the net gain to be derived from a reconstituted system. He believes, in other words, that the bargaining and adjustments of a decentralized system among local units formally independent of one another and guided by their own interests can handle the problems of the wider area. Is this decision based on ignorance or lack of information, or is it one based on his own preferences with knowledge of the alternatives and their consequences to him? Reformers have assumed the former, but empirical evidence to answer the question is slight. By conceptualizing the problem in these terms, the economic model could possibly lead to better evaluation of governmental organization in the metropolis and to more meaningful research into certain aspects of its structure and operations.

METROPOLITAN TYPES

It is not easy to capture the essence or flavor of a metropolitan area or to symbolize its distinctive features. Each of us sees a community and its qualities differently. To some, New York City may be the acme of culture and sophistication; to others, an overcrowded and unfriendly Leviathan. Carl Sandburg once described Chicago as:

> Strong, husky, brawling
> City of the big shoulders
> Laughing the stormy, husky, brawling
> laughter of youth.

But some years later the *Chicago Daily News* saw it as:

> Sedate, sedentary, complacent
> City of the big waistline
> That is Chicago today.

In his daily round of working, making a home for his family, and recreating, the urban dweller senses some of the special qualities

[9] Warren, "A Municipal-Service Market Model of Metropolitan Organization," p. 19.

which seem to mark the city or metropolis as a whole. He inevitably attempts to identify and structure this environment, to grasp it sensuously, to give it mental image. He builds up, as Anselm Strauss, a social psychologist, puts it, "a set of associations which prepare him to accept and appreciate a shorthand symbolic characterization of the place."[10]

The social scientist does not enjoy the license of the poet nor the image-making freedom of the citizen-observer. In his role as a scientist, he must seek to discover causal relations among the many variables or dimensions of community life that will enable him to explain urban phenomena. In this work he continuously faces the problem of how to formulate general (and empirically verifiable) statements about metropolitan areas which will be widely applicable despite areal differences in size and other characteristics. He can, of course, limit the statements to relationships which are so general that they apply to all such areas, but this procedure offers little analytical help since it obscures their important quantitative and qualitative differences. It is not likely, for example, that Metropolitan New York is a Metropolitan Abilene, Texas, projected onto a cinematic screen or that a small metropolis of 50,000 will play the political game in the same manner as one of 5,000,000. Nor is it likely that a socially and racially homogeneous community will behave in the same fashion or be confronted with the same spectrum of problems as one of social and racial diversity, even though they are similar in size. A more adequate framework of analysis than impressionistic assumptions is called for if generalizations about metropolitan areas are to achieve greater meaning and accuracy. What we would prefer is a method of grouping together communities which have similar basic characteristics so that general statements could be formulated about each group or type.

Classification implies order and the establishment of categories into which data can be catalogued. It consists, in other words, of grouping objects according to their principal characteristics or properties and applying a designation to each category. Grouping things together in this way not only permits us to organize our data, but also frequently opens the door to the discovery of many more

[10] *Images of the American City* (New York: Free Press, 1961), pp. 5–6. See also Kevin Lynch, *The Image of the City* (Cambridge: The M.I.T. Press and Harvard University Press, 1960).

resemblances than those originally recognized. Classifying books, for example, by size and weight might lead us to find that those in each category have the same kind of binding thread and are assembled in the same way. Or grouping them by their content might result in the discovery of certain other characteristics that are common to each class. The assumption in classification, as in all aspects of science, is that there is an orderliness that is subject to empirical research. The methodological problem is to find ways of organizing and analyzing the data derived from experience and observation.

Ideally, the social scientist would like to develop typologies analogous to those in the natural or physical sciences. Before he can reach this stage, however, he must first ascertain the smallest number of components that will account for the persistent differences in the way the objects of his study behave. To the extent he is successful in this task, he can develop classifications that will permit meaningful comparisons and more rigorous analysis of the phenomena he is investigating. For those studying the metropolis, even a modest accomplishment in this direction would better enable them to inquire into such questions as to why some communities have a higher level of civic participation than others; why some are dynamic, others passive or quiescent; or why some place a higher premium on education and cultural facilities than others.

Single-Dimension Typology

Several approaches might be followed in developing a metropolitan typology that would serve a useful analytical purpose. The simplest way would be to classify the areas on the basis of a single characteristic such as population size or density, a method commonly employed by the United States Bureau of the Census. An example of this approach is found in the *Municipal Year Book: 1963*, in which Victor Jones and his associates classify almost 1700 cities according to their major economic function.[11] Using data from the *1958 Census of Manufactures* and the *1958 Census of Business*, they place each city into one of five major categories: manufacturing, industrial, diversified-manufacturing, diversified-retailing, and retail-

[11] (Chicago: International City Managers' Association, 1963), pp. 85–157. Earlier classifications on a similar basis were contained in the 1953 and 1960 editions of the *Municipal Year Book*.

ing. A manufacturing city is defined as one which has 50 percent or more of its aggregate employment in manufacturing and less than 30 percent in trade. An industrial city also has over 50 percent in manufacturing, but over 30 percent in retail trade. In a diversified-manufacturing community, employment in manufacturing is greater than that in retail but less than 50 percent of the aggregate. Cities

TABLE 6

Percentage Distribution of SMSA's and Their Municipal Units by Economic Function, 1958

ECONOMIC FUNCTION	SMSA'S	CENTRAL CITIES	SUBURBAN CITIES
Manufacturing and industrial	47%	38%	37%
Diverse-manufacturing	24	22	10
Diverse-retailing	21	22	20
Retailing	4	14	26
Other	4	4	7
Total	100%	100%	100%
Number of units	212	258	736

SOURCE: *Municipal Year Book: 1963*, p. 97.

in the diversified-retailing class enjoy greater employment in retailing, but manufacturing constitutes at least 20 percent of the total. Those classified as retailing have less than 20 percent of their employment in manufacturing. A percentage distribution of SMSA's compiled on this basis is shown in Table 6. In Table 7, a numerical breakdown of cities is given, using the same classification but adding an additional dimension or variable, that of regional location.

The value of a typology based on a single characteristic is dubious. Unless the dimension so employed accounts for a substantial portion of the variation in behavior between communities—an unlikely probability in view of their complex nature—the purpose for which it can be used is limited. Jones and his colleagues recognize this fact by presenting data on sixteen other characteristics for each city. In addition to the classification by economic function, the list includes such variables as percentage of non-white residents, median age, percent of elementary school children in private schools, rent levels, percentage of owner-occupied dwellings, and employment-residence ratio. This ambitious undertaking provides a vast amount of raw classification data that may be used, as the compilers note, "for grouping cities in order to study the relationship between communal types and political and other social behaviors." They hypothesize, for illustrative purposes, that political participation and the focus of politics are likely to be different in cities with a high

TABLE 7

Functional Classification of Cities of 10,000 and Over by Region and Number, 1958

ECONOMIC FUNCTION	NORTH-EAST	NORTH CENTRAL	SOUTH	WEST	TOTAL
Manufacturing	234	178	69	33	514
Industrial	26	46	22	2	96
Diversified-manufacturing	53	68	64	27	212
Diversified-retailing	72	104	127	70	373
Retailing	59	86	115	102	362
Other	15	29	39	39	122
Total	459	511	436	273	1679

SOURCE: *Municipal Year Book: 1963*, p. 95.

proportion of upper-income, white-collar, home-owning residents than in communities with opposite characteristics. Few would quarrel with this assumption, but a long jump still exists from the listing of variables by individual cities to the construction of a multidimensional typology that will facilitate investigation of such relationships.

Multidimensional Classification

A second approach to classification is to employ a set of major dimensions on which metropolitan areas differ from one another and then "locate" each area at a particular point along each variable. Thus, if we used population size, median family income, and home ownership as the distinguishing characteristics, we could say that community "A" was in the upper quartile in size, the third quartile in family income, and the lowest quartile in home ownership, and that community "B" was in the third quartile on the first two dimensions and in the second quartile on the last. This would enable us to show how each area ranked on each of the three dimensions in relation to the whole universe of such areas. It would also provide a means for describing the differences between one metropolis and another with respect to their location within the multidimensional field.

Roland L. Warren, a sociologist, utilized a typology of this nature in his study, *The Community in America*.[12] To show the way American communities vary in their structures and functions, he used a set of four dimensions to measure the variations: autonomy, coincidence of service areas, psychological identification with locality, and horizontal pattern. The first indicates the extent to which a locality is dependent on extracommunity units—metropolitan special dis-

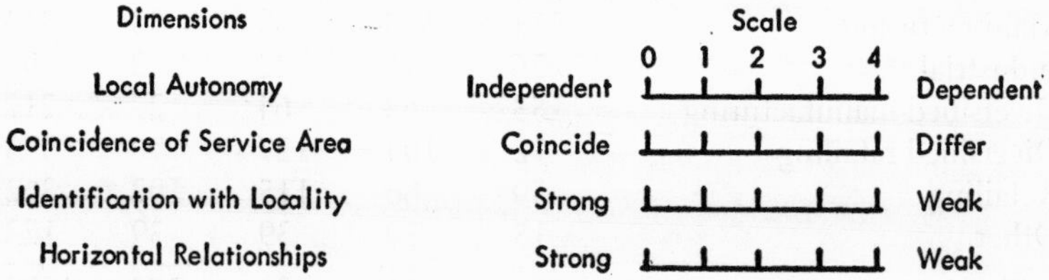

Dimensions		Scale	
		0 1 2 3 4	
Local Autonomy	Independent	⌊—⌊—⌊—⌊—⌊	Dependent
Coincidence of Service Area	Coincide	⌊—⌊—⌊—⌊—⌊	Differ
Identification with Locality	Strong	⌊—⌊—⌊—⌊—⌊	Weak
Horizontal Relationships	Strong	⌊—⌊—⌊—⌊—⌊	Weak

Figure 3.1 Classification Scheme for Differentiating Among Communities. Adapted from Roland L. Warren, *The Community in America*, Rand McNally, 1963, p. 14.

tricts, county government, state and national governmental agencies —in the performance of its major functions. The second involves the extent to which the service areas—stores, churches, schools—coincide with local governmental boundaries. At one end on this scale, all residents are served by institutions within the same community; at the other extreme, an individual may live in one locality, shop in another, attend church in a third, and send his children to school in still another. The third classification concerns the degree to which local inhabitants identify with their community and have a sense of "belonging" to it. The last dimension relates to the strength or weakness of the relationships among the various groups, agencies, and social subsystems within the community.

Figure 3.1 is a graphic diagram of Warren's classification scheme. By locating the communities under study at some point on each

[12] (Chicago: Rand McNally, 1963).

of the lines running from one extreme to the other, the researcher is able to differentiate among his units on all four dimensions. The validity and significance of such differentiation would depend on three factors: (1) the extent to which the selected dimensions represent basic elements of community structure and functioning (if they are only minor or incidental characteristics, a classification constructed on variations among them would tell us little); (2) the relevance of the criteria employed to distinguish each dimension (what, for example, are the indicators of community identification?); and (3) the degree of accuracy with which these criteria can be measured (are they subject to quantitative procedures or only to descriptive and impressionistic assessments?). Warren deals with these questions only in a general fashion and makes no attempt to compile a classification of actual cities or communities on the basis of his typology.

A second example of a multidimensional typology is found in an excellent and highly rigorous study of community characteristics in eighty-eight Ohio counties by sociologist Christen Jonassen.[13] Using United States census data and information gathered by other governmental units, Jonassen devised quantitative measures for eighty-two dimensions ranging from population size to percent of mental illness. He then arrayed the counties from 1 to 88 on each variable, with the county achieving the highest magnitude on a given dimension ranked first and the lowest ranked eighty-eighth or last. Counties ranking 1 to 8 received a score of 11, those ranking 9 to 16 a score of 10, and so on. This method grouped the eighty-eight counties into eleven classes for each dimension. The computation of these scores made it possible to draw a graphic profile for each county showing its position on each dimension relative to the universe of counties. (See Figure 3.2 for an example of such a profile.)

In Table 8, we provide an illustration of this general approach (less the scoring) by showing the rankings of the twenty most populous SMSA's in the United States in respect to six variables or dimensions: population, density, median family income, percent non-whites in the population, median age, and percent white-collar workers. As the table shows, Metropolitan New York, the largest in popu-

[13] *The Measurement of Community Dimensions and Elements* (Columbus: Ohio State University Center for Educational Administration, 1959).

lation size, also ranks first in density and median age but seventh
in percentage of white-collar workers, twelfth in percentage of non-
whites, and thirteenth in median family income. In comparison,
Metropolitan Dallas, the least populous of the twenty, ranks nineteenth in density, twentieth in income, seventh in percentage of non-
whites, eighteenth in median age, and eighth in percentage of white-

Dimension   Standardized Scores
                                           1   2   3   4   5   6   7   8   9   10 11

1   Size

2   Density

3   Urban

4   Population Stability

5   Governmental

6   Heterogeneity

7   Social

8   Economic

9   Newspaper Circulation

10 Productive Population

11 Juvenile Delinquency

12 Welfare

13 Home Ownership

14 Median Family Income

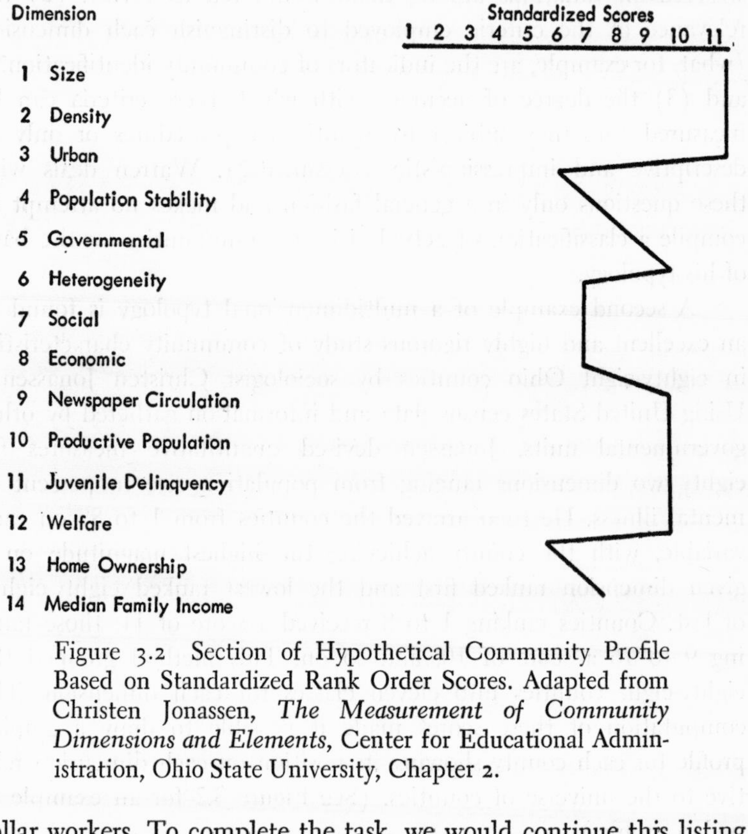

Figure 3.2 Section of Hypothetical Community Profile
Based on Standardized Rank Order Scores. Adapted from
Christen Jonassen, *The Measurement of Community
Dimensions and Elements*, Center for Educational Admin-
istration, Ohio State University, Chapter 2.

collar workers. To complete the task, we would continue this listing
for the remaining SMSA's, group and assign scores for the ranking
on each dimension, and arrive at a set of score categories for each
variable. We would then be in a position to describe a given metropolitan area in terms of its similarities and contrasts to other SMSA's
on these six variables.

It is apparent from this example that the more criteria the
researcher uses, the more complex the process becomes because of all
the possible combinations of variables. Dealing with eighty-two

dimensions for eighty-eight cases, as Jonassen did, produces a complex table which is virtually impossible to categorize or evaluate. On the other hand, if too few dimensions are employed, important differences among communities might be obscured. To overcome

TABLE 8

Ranking of Twenty Largest SMSA's on Six Selected Dimensions,
1960

SMSA	POPU-LATION	DENSITY	MEDIAN FAMILY INCOME	PERCENT NON-WHITE	MEDIAN AGE	PERCENT WHITE-COLLAR WORKERS
New York	1	1	13	12	1	7
Los Angeles	2	9	6	13	10	9
Chicago	3	7	3	6	9	12
Philadelphia	4	11	15	4	7	14
Detroit	5	6	11	5	16	18
San Francisco	6	13	5	11	6	3
Boston	7	3	12	19	5	5
Pittsburgh	8	15	19	14	4	19
St. Louis	9	18	16	9	12	17
Washington, D.C.	10	10	1	1	17	1
Cleveland	11	4	8	8	8	13
Baltimore	12	12	17	2	15	16
Newark	13	5	4	10	2	10
Minn.–St. Paul	14	17	10	20	19	4
Buffalo	15	14	14	15	11	20
Houston	16	16	18	3	20	11
Milwaukee	17	8	7	16	14	15
Paterson, N.J.	18	2	2	18	3	6
Seattle	19	20	9	17	13	2
Dallas	20	19	20	7	18	8

this dilemma, Jonassen sought to determine whether a smaller number of factors could be found that would include or explain all the others. The statistical procedure that he resorted to for this purpose is known as factor analysis.[14] This process involves the clustering of

[14] See Christen T. Jonassen and Sherwood H. Peres, *Interrelationships of Dimensions of Community Systems* (Columbus: Ohio State University Press, 1960); and Christen T. Jonassen, "Functional Unities in Eighty-Eight Community Systems," *American Sociological Review*, 26 (June, 1961), 399–407.

those dimensions which are highly intercorrelated but not related to variables in other clusters. It is based upon the assumption, fundamental to all science, that a large and complex set of phenomena can be organized and understood in terms of a smaller set of concepts. An example in psychological research may illustrate the principle. When the abilities to add, subtract, multiply, and divide were found to be highly interrelated, psychologists were able to reduce these four variables to one factor, that of mathematical ability. And when similar results were found in examining other variables, it became possible to speak of intelligence as consisting of a small number of underlying factors rather than fifty or more different talents or dimensions.

By applying factor analysis to his study of Ohio counties, Jonassen similarly sought to reduce his eighty-two original dimensions to a lesser number that would explain the differences between one community system and another. This method extracted seven factors or clusters into which the eighty-two variables grouped. Jonassen called these urbanism, welfare, influx, poverty, magni-complexity, educational effort, and proletarianism. As he observed, the combinations involved in the interrelationships of the many variables are like the parts of a jigsaw puzzle of thousands of pieces which fit together to present a meaningful picture of community systems. The factor analysis showed, among other things, that differences among communities cannot be explained solely in terms of the degree of urbanization; that there are fundamental differences between small and large urban systems; that educational effort is an important underlying source of community variation; and that the factor designated "welfare" is a strong indicator of the degree to which a community is able to achieve a style of life in accordance with the accepted positive values of middle-class culture.

We need not concern ourselves further with these factors other than to say that they represented the fewest and most basic components of the total community system as revealed by the study. Instead of attempting to describe or to differentiate among the eighty-eight counties on the basis of eighty-two dimensions, Jonassen could now speak in terms of seven factors which explained all the other variables. In this way, the problems of comparability were greatly minimized. Application of a similar technique to metropolitan areas would, of course, be a monumental and costly task, but one that might be extremely revealing.

Composite Index

Reducing the complexity of the metropolitan community to a few factors, as Jonassen did with the counties, would provide us with a more manageable basis for comparison but it still would not completely solve the problem of classification. The possible number of combinations that could result from even this limited number of factors (with each further divided into degrees of magnitude such as high, medium, and low) would remain far too large for practical use. A more ideal typology would be one derived from a single index or score that combines the basic factors. By ranking a score of this kind for each community in numerical order and cutting the array at a limited number of arbitrary points, a corresponding number of classes or types could then be delineated. This procedure, however, would involve the difficult task of devising a satisfactory weighting scheme for combining the factor measurements into a single score. Just as one cannot equate an orange with an automobile, neither can one equate a unit of population with a unit of juvenile delinquency without first ascertaining the relative value of one to the other. In the case of oranges and automobiles, the task would be simple; in the case of social and other complex variables, it might well be impossible. Communities, it must be remembered, are composed of several orders of phenomena—economic, social, political, physical, cultural—and to combine these into a single index is something like trying to mix oil and water. The most that can be hoped for, given the nature of the beast, is a very crude measurement that might provide a modicum of assistance in analyzing metropolitan areas.

One such effort to devise a composite index for cities was made some years ago by E. L. Thorndike, a psychologist.[15] Working with 295 cities, Thorndike ranked them according to an index which he called a "G" or "goodness" score. The components of this index were items such as infant death rate, value of schools, expenditures for cultural facilities, and other miscellaneous social and economic conditions. Although regarded as a pioneer attempt to differentiate

[15] *Your City* (New York: Harcourt, Brace & World, 1939).

among communities by statistical measurement, the range of inquiry was too limited for the index to be used for general comparative purposes.

A similar undertaking was made several years later by the sociologist Robert Angell, who endeavored to devise a moral or social integration index for cities.[16] His index had two major components. First was "welfare effort" based on per capita local expenditures for health and welfare, and the percentage of all spending for such services that was derived from local sources, public and private. The second was "crime" or the number of certain reported offenses per 100,000 population. The first was presumed to be a measure of the local citizenry's determination to achieve worthy social objectives; the second was considered an indication of the extent to which people behave in accordance with norms set forth in the law. The sources of the two components were combined to form the moral integration index.

Angell found a consistent relationship between his index and a substantial number of community variables including home ownership, mobility of the population, racial and cultural differences, support of schools, and number of married women in the labor force. The two most significant associations, both negative, were those with mobility and heterogeneity. The study revealed that these two factors accounted for more of the variation in the index of moral integration among cities than any combination of the others. In other words, the less mobile and heterogeneous the population, the more closely is a community knit together by a common outlook and common aspirations. Angell's index represented the most advanced effort up to that time at the quantitative measurement and differentiation of city characteristics; but, like Thorndike's "G" score, its use was limited since it left many dimensions of the community untouched.

Non-Quantitative Typologies

With the possible exception of Roland Warren's typology, the classification schemes that we have thus far discussed are based

[16] "The Social Integration of American Cities of More Than 100,000 Population," *American Sociological Review*, 12 (June, 1947), 335–342; "The Moral Integration of American Cities," *American Journal of Sociology*, LVII, Part 2, No. 1 (July, 1951).

largely on statistical indexes. It is possible, however, to develop community typologies with little or no reference to quantitative measurements. Although the degree of precision in such cases will be considerably less, nonstatistical classifications can be useful as ordering devices or frames of reference for guiding observation and study. Philosophic-descriptive typologies such as progressive-conservative, static-dynamic, or open-closed communities are essentially of this nature, although some gross measurements of the dimensions may at times be employed.

An example of a non-quantitative typology is found in a recent study of comparative policy-making in four middle-sized American cities.[17] To provide a framework for examining political decisions at the local level, the authors developed a classification scheme based on the "role" of government. Four role types were identified: (1) promoting economic growth; (2) providing life's amenities; (3) maintaining traditional services only; and (4) arbitrating among conflicting interests. Cities in the first category are dominated by the philosophy that the good community is one that grows. Hence, the policies of their governments are directed toward the creation of an image of municipal stability, sound fiscal status, honest government, and friendliness toward business. Those of the second type emphasize the creation and maintenance of a pleasant living environment as the major objective of collective political action. They regard the primary task of local government as one of providing a high level of services designed to increase the comforts of urban living and the attractiveness of the community. Municipalities in the third classification are "caretaker" oriented; that is, they are committed to minimal services and to restriction of the public sector. Their policies are characterized by opposition to planning, zoning, and assumption of new functions by local public agencies. The fourth type views the role of local government as essentially that of arbitrator among conflicting interests. Emphasis here is placed upon the process rather than the substance of public action. In other words, governments in this category are so structured that they do not act directly in terms

[17] Oliver P. Williams and Charles R. Adrian, *Four Cities* (Philadelphia: University of Pennsylvania Press, 1963). Another recent and highly systematic study that employs a typology of power structures in comparing the political systems of four communities is Robert E. Agger, Daniel Goldrich, and Bert E. Swanson, *The Rulers and the Ruled* (New York: Wiley, 1964).

of substantive conceptions of the common good but seek to balance diverse interests and pressures in formulating policy.

Williams and Adrian point to case studies which illustrate each of the four types. They cite *Middletown,* described in the classic work of Robert and Helen Lynd, as primarily concerned with economic growth; Park Forest, in William H. Whyte's best seller, *The Organization Man,* as preoccupied with amenities; Springdale, in Arthur Vidich and Joseph Bensman's *Small Town in Mass Society,* as a caretaker government that opposes the expansion of public functions at the local level by shunting new problems to the private sector and to higher levels of government; and Chicago, in Martin Meyerson and Edward Banfield's *Politics, Planning and the Public Interest,* as an example of an arbitral government. The usefulness of this typology, as the authors admit, depends upon the development of satisfactory criteria to distinguish communities on what might appear to some people as a highly impressionistic basis. Obviously, primary reliance must be placed on descriptive material since the nature of the type does not readily admit of quantitative measurement. The further questions may be raised as to whether the classification is all-inclusive (that is, whether all cities can be placed in one or a combination of the four categories) and whether the classification conceals important differences among communities by restricting the analysis to too narrow a framework.

This type of study cannot be expected to answer questions of this kind, nor do the authors make any such pretense. Their work was exploratory in nature and limited in purpose. They turned their attention to classification as data gathering progressed and as it became evident that the usually employed socioeconomic variables, such as income and education, were inadequate to explain the distinctly varied responses of the communities to similar problems and issues. They found, for example, that the cities they studied, although of similar size and economic base, reacted differently to common problems such as congestion in the central business district and fringe area growth. In the first instance, the responses of the communities ranged from a $15,000,000 downtown rebuilding program to total inactivity, and in the second, from annexation to complete opposition to intervention. To help explain these variations and analyze public policy-making in the four cities, the authors developed the typology we have described. The resulting categories are obviously more difficult to put to scientific use than those based on numerical specifications such as size and per capita income. Yet the study, aside from the validity of its classification scheme, provides an excellent illustration of the formulation and resulting value of typologies in the investigation of urban communities.

THE PATH AHEAD

It is apparent from the foregoing that no universally applicable models or typologies have thus far been discovered in the urban-metropolitan field. It is also evident that none is likely to be found in the immediate future because of the vast complexity of the phenomena. Yet, as this sampling of models and classification schemes demonstrates, urban research, as all scientific inquiry, must proceed on the basis of some theoretical assumptions and some sort of hypotheses, however rudimentary they may be. For without theory the researcher has no way of deciding what kind of facts he will look for in the data confronting him. Nor can he know what kind of typology he should attempt to develop unless he first formulates certain assumptions about the essential nature of the subject matter to be classified.

In the future as at present, the approach to the study of metropolitan areas is not likely to follow any single path or direction. Models will be devised to suit the needs of the particular researcher, theory will be formulated to explain various aspects of the system, new and sophisticated simulation techniques will be developed as means of exploration and verification, and typologies will be constructed to serve different purposes. As Jonassen aptly noted with respect to classification:

It would seem that in any case the basis of classification for communities should be the one most significant and meaningful for the user. Such a classification should take into consideration the community elements and the particular problem or purpose of the classifier. The school administrator, for example, may be interested at a given time in such various aspects of his job as curriculum, community relations, finances, or the passing of a bond issue, the social worker in welfare, the planner in the economic base. In each case the community typology most useful would have a different basis of classification; that is, the combination of factors selected to use in establishing categories and the basis of combinations would probably differ.[18]

[18] Jonassen, *The Measurement of Community Dimensions and Elements*, p. 68.

Our own approach in this book is similarly pragmatic. Although the treatment is broad in scope and purpose, we make no attempt to develop cosmic theories of metropolitan phenomena or construct analytical models that will be sufficient for total coverage of the metropolis. Viewing the metropolis as a functioning system of inter-relationships among people, organizations, and institutions, we endeavor to utilize whatever relevant theory is available for analyzing and explaining its various aspects and operations. The overall picture which emerges is necessarily general but hopefully realistic and suggestive.

CHAPTER 4

The Social Anatomy of the Metropolis

THE METROPOLITAN COMMUNITY is at once a territorial unit of fluid boundaries and a network of human relationships which may be called its social structure. This structure is vastly more complicated than that of the rural village or Sinclair Lewis' classic Zenith. Heterogeneous, constantly changing, fragmented, it presents a mosaic of social worlds arranged spatially in an often confused and seemingly incompatible pattern. "The other side of the tracks" is an expression well known to many small-town dwellers. But in the large population centers there are many "sides of the track." Numerous neighborhoods and suburban groupings of varying social, ethnic, and economic characteristics are scattered throughout the metropolitan complex. The luxury apartment casts its shadow on the tenement houses of workers. The Negro ghetto is ringed by a wall of white neighborhoods. The industrial suburb lies adjacent to the village enclave of the wealthy. Cheap souvenir stalls and penny arcades intermingle with the fashionable department stores and quality gift shops in the central business district. The contrast is strong, the variety infinite.

As society has expanded, diverse groups have been brought together in the same network of social or community control. Shorn of the simplicity of the manor or the rural village and overrun by hordes of newcomers—refugees of a changing technocracy and social world—the twentieth century metropolis offers a troublesome challenge to the practitioners and reformers or medicine men of local government. The massing of people together in relatively small areas—108,000 to the square mile in New York City's Manhattan—has placed new responsibilities and obligations, new stresses and strains, on their governmental (as well as economic and social) systems. Concentration of human and material resources has opened up many new opportunities to society but at the same time it has aggravated the problem of governmental control and service. The task of housing, feeding, and educating the populace, of minimizing and resolving social conflict, of maintaining order, and of providing indispensable public facilities has increased manyfold. And in the process, different values, varied modes of living, and divergent interests must somehow be accommodated to one another. Governing the metropolis is an exercise in social adjustment as well as an object of public administration.

PATTERNS OF SOCIAL DIFFERENTIATION

The many central city neighborhoods and suburban areas that together form the metropolis are socially as well as territorially and physically distinguishable. Families of similar socioeconomic status tend to reside in the same neighborhoods, partly because of the desire to live with their "own kind" and partly because housing in similar price ranges is normally found clustered together. The metropolis offers a wide selection of living facilities to its clientele: from apartments on the "gold coast" and near downtown to semi-rustic dwelling units in the far reaches of the suburbs. For many families, the choice of home and neighborhood is narrowly circumscribed by their fiscal resources. For some, the Negro in particular, it is often less a matter of choice than of enforced segregation.

The pattern of settlement is important to the metropolitan political process. Empirical studies furnish convincing evidence that people who differ in social rank and life style also differ in community participation and political behavior. Hence when people of similar characteristics are grouped together spatially, the resulting homogeneity enhances the political and social importance of the neighborhood as a part of the metropolitan whole. Subareas of high social status, to cite an example, have different expectations and make different demands on their local governments than neighborhoods of low-income and ethnic migrants.

Three Indexes of Social Area Analysis

Sociologists have devised various yardsticks to describe and study the social geography of a community. One such mode of investigation, known as social area analysis, employs three indexes or basic forms of social differentiation: social rank, urbanization, and segregation. Using data organized by census tracts, the first measures the socioeconomic status of the neighborhood as a whole; the second, its life style; and the third, its proportion of Negroes and other segregated populations.[1]

Social rank is a composite index of level of education and kind of occupation. At the low end of the scale are neighborhoods composed predominantly of unskilled laborers and factory workers and of adults with no more than an eighth-grade education. At the other extreme are neighborhoods of business executives, professional personnel, and white-collar workers with high school or college education.

The second index, urbanization, is based on the kind of family and home typical of a particular neighborhood. This index has three components: (1) the ratio of children under five years of age to women of childbearing age (fertility ratio); (2) the proportion of women with jobs outside the home; and (3) the proportion of dwelling units that are single-family and detached. The highly "urban" neighborhood, according to this yardstick, is one of rooming houses and apartment dwellings, of single men and women, and of childless couples with both husband and wife working. The low "urban" area is familistic and is marked by single-family residences, young couples with small children, and few wives in the labor force.

The third index is based on the ethnic composition of the com-

---

[1] These indexes are explained in detail in Eshref Shevky and Wendell Bell, *Social Area Analysis* (Stanford: Stanford University Press, 1954).

munity—the proportion of Negroes and other segregated populations in the neighborhoods compared to the proportion of these populations in the total city or metropolis. Its function is to identify sections of the urban area where there are heavy concentrations of minority groups: Negroes, Mexican-Americans, Puerto Ricans, Orientals, and others. Like the first two measuring instruments, the ethnicity index is useful in plotting the geographic distribution of groups with different social, economic, and racial characteristics.

When we use some method of neighborhood analysis, such as the urban typology or classification described here, the relevance of social geography to metropolitan political and civic behavior becomes more apparent. In areas of low social rank, for example, a large majority of the citizenry participates at only a minimal level in the organizational and political activities of the community.[2] Other evidence indicates a marked distinction in voting patterns on metropolitan reorganization issues between high and low "urban" neighborhoods. Here the home-owning, family-centered voter appears more receptive than the apartment dweller to arguments depicting governmental change as a threat to community autonomy.[3] Still other patterns of participation emerge in neighborhoods where there are barriers against change of residence because of ethnic origin. In such instances segregation blurs residential distinction by social rank and degree of urbanization and produces a different pattern of civic behavior. All of these various factors permeate the organizational structure of the metropolis and influence the manner in which it functions.

SOCIAL GEOGRAPHY

No two metropolitan areas are identical in their social geography. Each has its own distinctive characteristics and its own contour of settlement. One may have many neighborhoods of ethnic groups; another, only a few. In one, the suburbs may be entirely residential; in another, they may contain a substantial number of industrial

[2] John C. Bollens (ed.), *Exploring the Metropolitan Community* (Berkeley and Los Angeles: University of California Press, 1961), chap. 11. Also see *Metropolitan Challenge* (Dayton: Metropolitan Community Studies, 1959), pp. 223–266. Chapter 8 of this book considers many aspects of participation.

[3] Henry J. Schmandt, Paul G. Steinbicker, and George D. Wendel, *Metropolitan Reform in St. Louis* (New York: Holt, Rinehart and Winston, 1961), pp. 51–59.

satellites. Despite the diversity, however, there is enough similarity in urban clusters to permit some generalization.

Overall comparisons of the central city and suburbs tend to obscure the great variations within each as well as the similarities among their parts. The common stereotype of the metropolis depicts a central city of low income and ethnic dimensions and a collection of suburbs of middle and high income. It portrays the flight of the respectable, white, middle-class families to the miniature republics beyond the limits of the core city—and their replacement by the Negro and rural hillbilly. The picture contains enough truth to give it plausibility; but it is a gross and misleading oversimplification. It ignores the fact that the boundary which separates the central city from its suburban dependents is not a social but merely a legal or governmental line. It is a line, moreover, that does not divide the "haves" from the "have nots," the white-collar from the blue-collar neighborhoods, the native American from the migrant, the Republican from the Democrat. A greater proportion of neighborhoods of a particular type may be found in one or the other section; but to assume a rigid social dichotomy between the two sides of the boundary would be highly erroneous. This dichotomy may become more of a reality in the future if present trends continue, but the process is far from completed or certain at the present time.

The lowest status and most highly segregated neighborhoods are usually found in the inner core of the central city adjacent to the downtown business district, the factories, and the warehouses. The oldest homes of the metropolis are located here. Constructed in an era of the horse-drawn trolley car, age, blight, and obsolescence have left them with little that is attractive. Today, these neighborhoods serve as ports of entry for the new migrants: the displaced farmers, the "Oakies," the racial minorities seeking new job opportunities and new freedom. Attempts to "renew" the city through urban redevelopment programs have cleared some of the worst slums in these areas and replaced them with medium and high-priced apartments as well as public housing. One result of these efforts has been the creation of neighborhood islands of higher socioeconomic status in a sea of deterioration and decay.

In the outer reaches of the central city, blight is nonexistent or less prevalent, the homes are newer, their occupants higher on the social scale. Crossing into suburbia, the scene changes little from that in the adjacent areas of the city. It is not until one gets beyond the first tier of suburbs that the lots get noticeably larger, apartment dwellings disappear, and the standardized ranch house—the symbol of middle-class achievement—becomes prevalent. The picture, however, is not one of social and physical uniformity. Nor is the suburbia of today the exclusive domain of the country club set. Increasingly, it is becoming populated by the large middle range of American social class: skilled mechanics, clerks, salesmen, shopkeepers. And scattered here and there over its frequently undulating landscape are neighborhoods of cheap post-World War II homes with faded asbestos siding and small fenced-in yards, the "castles" of working-class families lower on the socioeconomic scale who also aspire to own their little plot of land. Here and there also are the industrial concentrations that are becoming ever more prevalent in the suburban ring.

St. Louis Social Area Analysis

The central city generally contains more neighborhoods of low social rank, high urbanization, and high segregation than the suburbs; but it also includes many sections that resemble its ring counterparts. The conclusions of an extensive and well-documented study in St. Louis City and County are applicable to many metropolitan areas. Researchers there found:

1. The governmental boundary between the central city and its suburbs is nowhere a social boundary between a rural or semirural county and urban city, nor a line between the urban "poor" and the suburban "prosperous." Instead, the St. Louis city limits run through neighborhoods that are essentially similar in social rank on either side of the boundary.
2. Middle-rank neighborhoods contain approximately 70 percent of the population in the city of St. Louis and the suburban county.
3. The neighborhoods in which the other 30 percent resides differ greatly between the central city and the suburbs. Those in the former, which are located primarily in the central portion, are of very low social rank while those in the latter are high on the occupation-education scale.
4. A more consistent difference between the two areas is observable when life style of the neighborhood populations is considered. The suburbs tend to be child- and family-centered, regardless of social rank. The central city is more urban in its characteristics, with more neighborhoods that have apartment dwellers, few children, and many women working outside the home.

5. The segregated populations are mostly in the central city. In St. Louis they are usually Negro, with a few small enclaves of Italians and eastern Europeans. They are found in the older neighborhoods of low social rank. A few small settlements of Negroes are located in various parts of the suburbs, but most of them are of long standing and came into existence before modern means of transportation, to accommodate the household and garden workers of the wealthy commuters.[4]

Figures 4.1 and 4.2 graphically illustrate the spatial distribution of the various neighborhoods in the St. Louis area by the three indexes

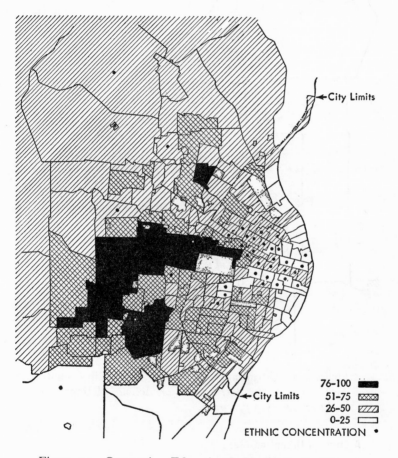

Figure 4.1   Occupation–Education Index, St. Louis City–County Area, 1950. From *Background for Action*, Metropolitan St. Louis Survey, 1957, p. 121.

[4] Bollens (ed.), *Exploring the Metropolitan Community*, pp. 17–18.

that were considered earlier. They show that the social heterogeneity of the central city has been duplicated in large measure in the suburbs and that people of similar socioeconomic characteristics are attracted to common areas.

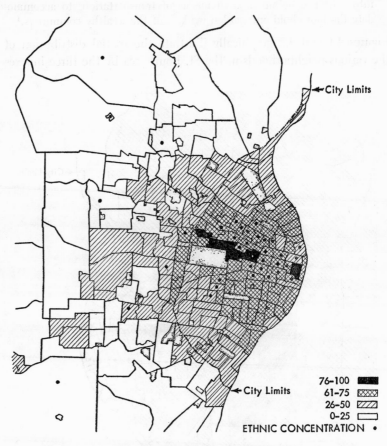

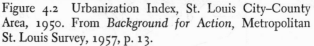

Figure 4.2　Urbanization Index, St. Louis City–County Area, 1950. From *Background for Action*, Metropolitan St. Louis Survey, 1957, p. 13.

A Study of Urbanized Areas

Another recent study, from a somewhat different perspective, throws further light on the relative socioeconomic status of central city and suburb and offers some interesting observations. Employing 1960 census data for 200 urbanized areas, Leo Schnore, a sociologist,

compared core cities and their rings on the basis of income, education, and occupation.[5] His findings demonstrate that the popular
view of city-suburban differentials in social status is derived mainly
from the experience of the larger metropolitan complexes. They show
that although no city of more than 500,000 exceeds its suburbs on
any of the three variables, a clear reversal of this pattern takes place
as one moves down the size range. In the 53 smallest urbanized areas,

TABLE 9

*City-Suburban Income, Educational, and Occupational Differentials
in SMSA's, 1960, by Age of Area*

CENSUS YEAR IN WHICH CENTRAL CITY FIRST REACHED 50,000	MEDIAN FAMILY INCOME		PERCENT WHO COMPLETED HIGH SCHOOL		PERCENT EMPLOYED IN WHITE-COLLAR OCCUPATIONS	
	CITY HIGHER	SUBURBAN FRINGE HIGHER	CITY HIGHER	SUBURBAN FRINGE HIGHER	CITY HIGHER	SUBURBAN FRINGE HIGHER
1800–1860	0	14	0	14	0	14
1870–1880	0	17	0	17	0	17
1890–1900	5	31	9	27	15	21
1910–1920	12	36	12	36	22	26
1930–1940	9	23	14	18	22	10
1950–1960	26	27	28	25	40	13

SOURCE: Adapted from Leo F. Schnore, "The Socio-Economic Status of Cities
and Suburbs." *American Sociological Review,* 28 (February, 1963), 76–85.

those of 50,000 to 100,000, 23 central cities have larger median
family incomes than their suburban rings; 27 of them have a higher
ratio of persons 25 years old or over who completed high school;
and 37 have a higher percentage of employed people in white-collar
occupations.

The study also found that age of the area (measured by the number of decades that have passed since the central city first reached
50,000 inhabitants) is an important determinant of city-suburban
differentials (see Table 9). The common conclusion that high-status
persons live in the suburbs tends to be true of urbanized areas having

[5] Leo F. Schnore, "The Socio-Economic Status of Cities and Suburbs,"
American Sociological Review, 28 (February, 1963), 76–85.

very old core cities, but it is progressively less often true of the newer urban strongholds. In the older areas, suburban fringes consistently register higher median family incomes, higher educational rank, and a greater proportion of white-collar workers. However, in areas that have reached metropolitan status in recent decades, the central cities themselves contain populations that are higher in socioeconomic rank than their adjacent suburbs. Age and population size of the area are, of course, closely related; but statistical analysis showed that even when size is held constant, age of the area continues to exert a substantial influence upon the direction of social differentials between central cities and suburbs.

Leo Schnore speculates that two factors help to account for much of the observed differences based on age. The first is that the housing structures of the older areas are obsolescent and have come to be occupied by groups that have strictly limited housing choices. New residential developments have been concentrated in outlying zones and are occupied by those who can afford home ownership. In contrast, the housing in the central cities of the newer urban areas is not so old or obsolete as to lose its attraction to potential home owners of the expanding middle class. As a second factor, Schnore suggests that the pressures of alternative land uses—particularly non-residential—are less intense in the newer cities than they were in the older urban centers at comparable stages in the past. The automobile and truck have decreased the pressure of industrial and commercial land uses pushing outward from the core. Now they are more likely to be leap-frogging the interior residential zones for new industrial parks and shopping centers at the outer periphery. As a consequence, central residential zones in new cities "may be less likely to undergo the 'succession' or 'sequent occupance' of progressively lower status groups experienced by neighborhoods in the older cities."[6]

Population Distribution and the Governmental System

The relation between geographical distribution of people who have different status and life styles and the governmental system was underscored in recent studies of the Philadelphia SMSA. According to investigations there, persistent conflicts of interest divide

[6] Schnore, "The Socio-Economic Status of Cities and Suburbs," p. 83.

urban subpopulations and these divisions in turn encourage fragmentation of the governmental pattern. A summary of the studies by one of the participants suggests that a decentralized governmental structure is functional to the metropolitan system from the following points of view:

1. It provides a source of social identification for individuals and groups enabling them to relate themselves to the metropolitan system.
2. By reducing the scale of social experience, it curbs feelings of apathy, isolation, and anomie (or loss of meaning of group values and lack of relatedness to society) among individuals and aggregates.
3. It provides an institutional device whereby subpopulations may protect themselves from those whose standards and way of life they do not share.
4. It provides additional institutional settings for the release of individual and group frustration and grievance through public catharsis.
5. It offers the opportunity for a larger number of élites to exercise power.
6. It expands available opportunities for individual participation as a means of contributing to both individuals and public policy.
7. By providing more points of access, pressure, and control, it gives additional insurance that political demands will be heard.
8. It permits minorities to avail themselves of governmental position and power and exert greater influence over policy.[7]

Whether all these factors can be empirically substantiated is questionable. What is important, however, is that they indicate some of the possible political and psychic implications of a social geography in which people of similar incomes, occupations, and styles of life tend to reside in the same neighborhoods.

ETHNIC STRUCTURE

Inscribed at the base of the Statue of Liberty on Bedloe's Island in New York Harbor are the lines:

> . . . Give me your tired, your poor,
> Your huddled masses yearning to breathe free,
> The wretched refuse of your teeming shore,
> Send these, the homeless, tempest-tost to me:
> I lift my lamp beside the golden door.

The invitation, no longer open except on a highly restrictive scale, was eagerly accepted. As a result, generation after generation of

[7] Thomas R. Dye, "Metropolitan Integration by Bargaining Among Sub-Areas," *American Behavioral Scientist*, V (May, 1962), 11.

Americans have been confronted with the task of assimilating strangers. In the half century following the Civil War, 25 million immigrants—over a million during each of six separate years shortly after 1900—came to the shores of the new Canaan. The early arrivals had been mostly from northern and western Europe, but in the several decades before World War I, Italians, Poles, and others of southern and eastern European stock predominated.

The Foreign Born

The majority of those who sought homes in the promised land, particularly the later migrants, settled in the cities. In 1960, there were approximately 9.3 million foreign-born whites in the United States, 87 percent of whom resided in urban areas.[8] Almost half of the total (48 percent) were concentrated in the northeastern states, 90 percent of them in urban areas. The South contained the smallest number, with less than 10 percent of the foreign-born whites residing there; and of these, seven of every ten were urban dwellers. The North Central states had 24 percent and the West 18 percent of the total, with about eight of every ten in both regions living in urban areas.

The number and importance of ethnic groups vary from city to city, with the largest concentrations outside the South. In urban centers such as Boston, New York, San Francisco, Minneapolis, Los Angeles, St. Louis, Milwaukee, Chicago, and Detroit, many different nationalities are represented. Some one group may predominate—in San Francisco, the Italians; in Minneapolis, the Swedes; in Los Angeles, the Mexican-Americans; in St. Louis and Milwaukee, the Germans; in Chicago and Detroit, the Poles—but for the most part the pattern is one of ethnic diversity. As the National Resources Committee noted in 1937:

Never before in the history of the world have great groups of people so diverse in social background been thrown together in such close contacts as in the cities of America. The typical American city, therefore, does not consist of a homogeneous body of citizens, but of human beings with the most diverse cultural backgrounds, often speaking different languages, following a great variety of customs, habituated to different

[8] The Bureau of the Census defines as urban residents all persons living in incorporated and unincorporated places of 2500 or more and in other densely settled unincorporated areas.

modes and standards of living, and sharing only in varying degrees the tastes, the beliefs, and the ideals of their native fellow city dwellers.[9]

Although the process of assimilation has reduced the number and importance of the ethnic colonies and has woven them into the fabric of the large American city, some of them still maintain their distinctive cultures and traditions. The "New Polands," "Little Italys," Jewish ghettos, and Chinatowns bear witness to the continued social reality of the culturally heterogeneous metropolis. And more recently the Negro and Spanish (or Puerto Rican and Mexican-American) harlems have been added to the ethnic enclaves.

The New Migration

The number of foreign born in the United States grew continuously until World War I but since then has steadily declined. The immigration acts of the 1920s slowed the flow of "foreigners" to a trickle; but by this time the new migration within the United States had begun: from South to North and West, from farm to city. The principal participants in the new movement were Negroes, but many rural whites at the bottom of the socioeconomic scale also packed up their meager belongings and headed for the centers of industrial activity. During World War I, Mexicans also began to move into West Coast cities; and by World War II, Puerto Ricans were migrating to New York City in large numbers.

Rapid changes in the racial composition of urban areas have been taking place as a result of the new migration. In 1960, 70 percent of all SMSA's in the nation had a higher percentage of non-white population than they had ten years earlier. In the northeastern region all metropolitan areas showed higher proportions; and in the north central and western states, all but eleven of the eighty-eight SMSA's registered similar increases. The opposite was true in the South. There, about six of every ten metropolitan areas had lower proportions of non-whites in 1960 than in the previous decennial census year, the result of Negro out-migration. However, of the nine southern SMSA's with populations over 500,000, seven showed increases in the proportion of non-whites.[10] These southern

[9] National Resources Committee, *Our Cities: Their Role in the National Economy* (Washington: 1937), p. 10.

[10] Leo F. Schnore and Harry Sharp, "Racial Changes in Metropolitan Areas, 1950–1960," *Social Forces*, 41 (March, 1963), 247–253.

metropolitan areas, where substantial industrial growth is taking place and discrimination is less predominant than in the hinterlands, may well be the first stopping off points for the Negro in his quest for new economic and social opportunities.

Intra-Area Distribution of Migrants

Within the metropolitan area itself, the ethnic colonies are concentrated largely in the central city. Only in some older industrial suburbs which lie outside the larger core cities are such groupings discernible. Chicago, an urban complex of many nationality groups, furnishes a typical example. The latest census shows that of the approximately 600,000 foreign born living in the SMSA, 73 percent reside in the central city. The remainder are dispersed throughout the area, with those from southern and eastern European countries tending to cluster in the industrial and working-class suburbs. In contrast, the majority of foreign born in the wealthier suburban communities, such as Evanston and Wilmette, are of English and German origin. The pattern is similar in the other areas. In the Philadelphia SMSA, 60 percent of the foreign born live in the core city; in Milwaukee, 72 percent; and in San Francisco, 59 percent.

The geographical segregation or distribution of ethnic settlement is even more pronounced when the non-white migrants, predominantly Negroes, are considered.[11] At the turn of the present century, 87 percent of the non-white population was concentrated in the South, mostly on farms. Over the years increasing numbers of these people have left the region, nearly 1.5 million during the 1950s alone. The heaviest movement took place out of the rural areas of Mississippi, Alabama, and South Carolina and into the metropolitan centers of California, New York, and Illinois. Reflecting this shift, the 1960 census found only 56 percent of the total non-white population in the South and increasing proportions in other regions of the nation. As the non-whites have migrated to urban places, they have tended to gravitate into the central cities of metropolitan areas. By 1960 over one-half the non-white popula-

---

[11] The designation "non-white" used by the Bureau of the Census includes Negroes, American Indians, and such far eastern nationality groups as Japanese, Chinese, and Koreans. In 1960, Negroes accounted for 92 percent of this group. Since the 1930 census, Mexican-Americans have been placed in the "white" category.

tion lived in such communities, a gain of 63 percent over 1950. Among the whites, on the other hand, there has been a continual shift from central cities to suburbs with the result that in 1960, 52 percent of the whites in the 212 SMSA's lived outside the central cities compared to 22 percent of the non-whites.[12] In the twelve largest SMSA's, the proportion of whites who live in the central cities has decreased steadily since 1930 while the percentage of non-whites has consistently increased (see Table 10). Between 1950 and

TABLE 10

Percentage of Whites in Central Cities of Twelve Largest SMSA's, 1930–1960

SMSA	1930	1940	1950	1960
New York	95.1	93.6	90.2	85.3
Los Angeles–Long Beach	95.0	94.0	90.2	84.7
Chicago	92.9	91.7	85.9	76.4
Philadelphia	88.6	86.9	81.7	73.3
Detroit	92.2	90.7	83.6	70.8
San Francisco–Oakland	95.1	95.1	88.2	78.9
Boston	97.1	96.7	94.7	90.2
Pittsburgh	91.7	90.7	87.7	83.2
St. Louis	88.5	86.6	82.0	71.2
Washington, D.C.	72.7	71.5	64.6	45.2
Cleveland	91.9	90.3	83.7	71.1
Baltimore	82.3	80.6	76.2	65.0
Total 12 SMSA's	92.4	91.0	86.3	78.6

SOURCE: Adapted from Harry Sharp and Leo F. Schnore, "The Changing Color Composition of Metropolitan Areas," *Land Economics*, XXXVIII (May, 1962), 169–185.

1960 alone, the core cities in these areas lost over 2 million whites while gaining 1.8 million non-whites.[13] In Detroit there are presently over 300,000 fewer whites and 370,000 more non-whites in the core city than in 1930, while comparable figures for Cleveland are approximately 200,000 and 180,000; for St. Louis, 190,000 and 125,000; for Chicago, 400,000 and 600,000; for Philadelphia, 260,000 and

[12] *Our Nonwhite Population and Its Housing* (Washington: Housing and Home Finance Agency, May, 1963), pp. 1–6.

[13] See Harry Sharp and Leo F. Schnore, "The Changing Color Composition of Metropolitan Areas," *Land Economics*, XXXVIII (May, 1962), 174.

310,000; and for Washington, D.C., 8000 and 286,000. In San Francisco, where the white population has remained constant since 1930, the number of non-whites has increased from 3800 to over 100,000.

In contrast to the buildup of non-whites in the core cities, the proportion of non-whites in the suburban rings of these areas has remained fairly constant (see Table 11). Individual suburban communities containing large percentages of Negroes do exist but they

TABLE 11

Percentage of Non-whites in Suburbs of
Twelve Largest SMSA's, 1930–1960

SMSA	1930	1940	1950	1960
New York	3.8	4.6	4.5	4.8
Los Angeles–Long Beach	2.7	2.3	2.7	4.1
Chicago	2.0	2.2	2.9	3.1
Philadelphia	6.7	6.6	6.6	6.3
Detroit	2.9	2.9	5.0	3.8
San Francisco–Oakland	4.1	3.6	6.8	6.8
Boston	1.0	0.9	0.8	1.0
Pittsburgh	3.8	3.6	3.5	3.4
St. Louis	6.1	6.7	7.3	6.3
Washington, D.C.	19.0	13.7	8.7	6.4
Cleveland	1.1	0.9	0.8	0.8
Baltimore	13.8	11.9	10.2	6.9
Total 12 SMSA's	4.0	3.9	4.4	4.4

SOURCE: Adapted from Harry Sharp and Leo F. Schnore, "The Changing Color Composition of Metropolitan Areas," *Land Economics*, XXXVIII (May, 1962), 169–185.

are few in number and are usually found in the highly industrialized centers. East St. Louis, Illinois; River Rouge, Michigan; East Orange, New Jersey; Bessemer, Alabama; and Compton, California, provide illustrations of such suburbs. The implications of this pattern in an age of increasing automation are clear. Negroes are not only segregated within the walls of the central city but they also are concentrated in the kinds of jobs most likely to be abolished by mechanization. Core city residents therefore face the strong possibility of shouldering a disproportionate share of the social burdens resulting from automation.

Population Decline in Central Cities

Along with losses in white population experienced by the large central cities—the result largely of migration to suburbia—many of them are also declining in total population. The 1960 census figures came as a shock to the officials and chambers of commerce of many core cities. Clamors for recounts were heard, but the facts were irrefutable. St. Louis city dropped over 100,000 during the last ten-year census period; Detroit had a net loss of 180,000; Cleveland declined by 39,000; and Washington, D.C., by 38,000. At the same time, the population gains for the SMSA's in which these cities are located showed striking gains because of suburban ring growth: the St. Louis area, 19.8 percent; Detroit, 24.7 percent; Cleveland, 22.6 percent; and Washington, 36.7 percent.

A variety of causes have contributed to this result. Most population losses are taking place in the inner core of the city where homes are oldest and where blight and obsolescence have rendered many of them uninhabitable. Urban renewal projects have cleared out large sections in many of these areas and in the process reduced their density. Expressway construction and industrial development have also removed land from residential use and stricter enforcement of housing codes has eliminated some overcrowding in older structures. Another contributing factor, discussed in the next section, is the changing age structure of the metropolis. Central cities are acquiring a greater proportion of older people as young couples in increasing numbers seek suburban environments for their child rearing. Whether the redevelopment and conservation projects that seek to renew the "worn out" city will reverse the tide remains to be seen. Certainly the rebuilding of cleared areas, many of which are now awaiting development, will recoup some of the population loss for the core city.

THE AGE STRUCTURE OF METROPOLITAN POPULATION

The age structure of a population reflects trends in fertility, mortality, and migration. This structure has considerable social and political significance. A community of predominantly young married couples in the childbearing stage will place different demands on its local governments than will a community of retired workers.

They have different sets of educational, recreational, health, and welfare needs. The young family wants good schools and playgrounds
for its children and modern roads to speed the breadwinner to his
place of work. The elderly couple has specialized health and leisure
requirements that differ from those of young people. As society becomes more complex, the role of government in meeting all these
needs becomes more crucial.

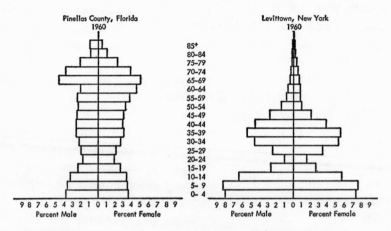

Figure 4.3 Age–Sex Pyramids for Pinellas County,
Florida, and Levittown, New York, 1960. Source: U.S.
Bureau of the Census, U.S. Census of Population: 1960,
General Population Characteristics.

Two Comparisons

The proportion of the population in the economically productive age range is another socially important aspect of the age structure. A community with a large percentage of its residents below
15 and above 65 years of age has greater service needs and less economic potential than a similar area with a high proportion of its
residents in the 15 to 64 age bracket. The local governmental budgets of St. Petersburg, Florida, a popular haven of "senior" citizens,
reflect a different emphasis than that of the Levittowns of New
York and Pennsylvania with their armies of young families. Comparisons of the age-sex pyramids of Pinellas County, Florida, which
includes St. Petersburg, and of Levittown, New York, as shown in
Figure 4.3, illustrate this difference. In the Florida retirement colony
only about 20 percent of the population is under 15 years of age

and almost 30 percent is 65 or over; the comparable figures for Levittown are approximately 44 percent and 3 percent.

A second comparison, made in Figure 4.4, also reveals how urban places of different types vary greatly in their age structure. Here, the age distribution pattern is plotted for three Wisconsin cities: Milwaukee, a central city of a major metropolitan area; Brookfield, a relatively new suburb in the Milwaukee SMSA; and Wau-

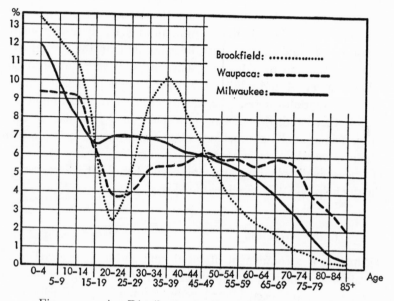

Figure 4.4　Age Distribution for Brookfield, Waupaca, and Milwaukee, Wisconsin, 1960. From Glenn V. Fuguitt, *The Changing Age Structure of Wisconsin's Population,* The University of Wisconsin, Department of Rural Sociology, Population Series No. 3, April 1962, p. 15.

paca, a non-metropolitan city of approximately 4000 in the northwestern part of the state. Brookfield, typical in many ways of the new and rapidly growing suburban communities, has a high concentration of young children and adults in their middle years, but a marked deficiency of older children, young adults, and elderly people. Almost 40 percent of the population is under 15 years of age and less than 4 percent over 65. The situation is quite different in Waupaca, a rural community that showed virtually no population change during the last ten-year census period. Twenty percent of its residents are over 65 years of age and 27 percent under 15. Only 32 percent are in the 15-to-45 age bracket compared to 41 percent in Milwaukee and 44 percent in Brookfield. Milwaukee's age pattern occupies a somewhat intermediate position between the other two places. It has fewer young children and more elderly residents than Brookfield but more young people and fewer older citizens than Waupaca. It also has a greater percentage of residents in the young working years (15 to 30) than the other two.

The national pattern resembles the Wisconsin examples. In large urban areas the suburban communities generally have a higher proportion of children and fewer older people than the central city. Both the core and ring, however, have an increasing proportion of children under 14 and adults over 65, the result of higher fertility and lower mortality rates. The age structure of rural communities, on the other hand, is increasing principally in the higher age categories. Young adults are seeking better opportunities in the metropolitan areas while retired farmers are migrating to the villages or the "pensioner" colonies of the South and Far West where warmer climates help ease the infirmities of old age.

OCCUPATIONAL PATTERNS

Occupation is a component of social rank and a close correlate of education and income; we therefore can learn much about an area by examining the occupational composition of its population. Is it a community or neighborhood where blue-collar workers predominate, or are doctors, lawyers, and businessmen in the majority? What is the proportion of each class to the total population? What is the ratio between those employed in manufacturing and those in the service trades? Is the occupational pattern remaining constant or is it undergoing substantial change? Information of this kind is helpful in analyzing the territorial parts or subcommunities of the metropolis and predicting their social and political behavior.

In tabulating data on employment, the Bureau of the Census classifies workers by major occupational categories, such as professional workers, managers and proprietors, craftsmen, farmers, and laborers. In addition, the bureau reports the number of employed persons in each SMSA, county, and urban place of 10,000 or more by forty industry groups. Included are such classifications as agriculture, manufacturing, wholesale and retail trade, public and private education, personal services, and public administration. Both sets of data are convenient means of examining the occupational structure of a metropolitan area. (Industry groups are discussed in the next chapter.)

At the time of the 1960 census, there were almost 65 million employed individuals, including 21.2 million women, in the nation's labor force. Of the total number, 73 percent were classified as urban residents. The distribution by occupational category is shown in Table 12, which reflects the changes taking place in the occupational structure of urban areas as a result of technological and industrial developments.

TABLE 12

Percentage of Employed Urban Residents in the United States, By Major Occupational Groups and Sex, 1940 and 1960

OCCUPATIONAL GROUPS	1940		1960	
	MALE	FEMALE	MALE	FEMALE
Professional workers	7.4	12.6	12.0	13.2
Farmers	0.4	—	0.4	0.1
Managers, officials, and proprietors	12.4	3.7	11.9	3.7
Clerical and sales workers	18.7	32.5	16.3	40.3
Craftsmen and foremen	18.6	1.1	20.2	1.2
Operatives	22.1	19.6	19.7	14.5
Household workers	0.5	16.4	0.1	7.4
Service workers	9.0	12.1	7.0	13.1
Laborers	9.9	0.9	7.2	0.7
Occupation not reported	1.0	1.1	5.1	5.8

SOURCE: Adapted from U.S. Bureau of the Census, *Census of Population, 1940,* Vol. II, Part 1; *Census of Population, 1960,* Vol. I, Part 1 (Washington: 1943 and 1964).

Upward Occupational Mobility

In the twenty-year period from 1940 to 1960, the proportion of professional workers among employed males in urban areas increased from 7.4 percent to 12 percent. The proportion of skilled workers (craftsmen, foremen) also rose (from 18.6 to 20.2 percent), while the percentage of semi-skilled males (operatives) and laborers declined—from 22.1 to 19.7 in the case of the first and from 9.9 to 7.2

in the latter instance. The category composed of managers, officials, and proprietors showed a slight drop, due in all probability to the continuing mortality among small businesses as the corner grocery store gives way to the national chain and the smaller employer is absorbed by the giant corporation. On the distaff side, the proportions of women who work as household servants and in factories (operatives) have dropped sharply since 1940 (from 16.4 to 7.4 percent and from 19.6 to 14.5 percent, respectively), while the proportion of those in clerical and sales work has grown substantially (from 32.5 to 40.3 percent). These changes reflect in part the upward mobility of the population as automation and other technological developments increase the need for professional and skilled workers and diminish the demand for the unskilled.

Nationwide, the highest concentration of workers in the professional and managerial classes is found in the suburban zones of the metropolitan areas while the central cities contain the largest proportion of persons in blue-collar jobs and the lower paying service trades. However, as Professor Schnore has pointed out, this pattern does not prevail in many areas which have acquired metropolitan status in recent decades. And even in the older SMSA's, numerous residents in each major occupational group can be found in both the core and ring.

THE GROUP MOSAIC IN METROPOLITAN LIFE

The social system of a community is not confined to individuals and families interacting singly with each other. A large portion of modern man's energies is channeled through groups that serve his various needs or act as his alter ego in a wide spectrum of civic matters. Human relations are increasingly finding their way into impersonal, structured, and institutionalized patterns; and human contacts are becoming more generally organized around some activity or cause. The congeries of voluntary associations that are characteristic of contemporary society testify to this trend. Such groups differ greatly in the interests they fulfill and in the number and character of their membership. Their purposes vary from simple social interaction to influencing governmental policy. They also differ markedly in territorial scope, from the strictly neighborhood-based group to one drawing membership from the entire metropolis and even beyond. Because they absorb much of the energy of individuals and serve as coordinating mechanisms or forces—private governments, in fact—for social behavior, they are important to an understanding of metropolitan civic life.

A typology or classification of voluntary associations in a community can be constructed on many different bases, such as size, purpose or function, nature of membership, and territorial scope. Most important from the viewpoint of governing the metropolis are the formal groups that directly, or at least significantly, seek to influence the conduct of local public affairs. Voluntary associations of this type, regardless of how they might be more systematically classified, can be subsumed under three categories: (1) service oriented; (2) economic and professional; and (3) civic. The first deals specifically with community service and welfare problems; the second endeavors to advance the economic and professional interests of its members; and the third has as its major objective the promotion of programs and policies that require governmental action. Political parties might be placed under the third category, although for all intents and purposes they constitute a separate class.

Community Service Organizations

Private organizations in the metropolitan community serve as important adjuncts to the welfare activities of local governments. Family aid societies, the Red Cross, settlement houses, curative workshops, urban leagues, visiting nurse associations, and similar bodies perform functions that otherwise would have to be assumed by public agencies. These private organizations have come to play increasingly important roles in urban areas as society has become more complex and interrelated. Their leadership is largely professionalized and bureaucratic, and "formalized" charity and welfare have come to replace the personalized efforts of ward politicians, neighbors, and friends.

Although organizations of this type are usually preoccupied with their service functions, they occasionally seek to influence local governmental policy when issues of concern to their work or interests are at stake. Thus an urban league may press for an anti-discrimination ordinance or a settlement house may urge municipal officials to establish more playgrounds in a neighborhood. When they enter the political arena, they have ready-made constituencies

—their clientele groups—that can be mobilized to support or oppose the public policy at issue. The lay boards of these agencies, moreover, are commonly made up of community notables, a fact that lends prestige to such organizations and endows them with legitimacy. Similarly, the expertise of their professional staffs enables them to speak with authority when social welfare matters are in question.

The majority of organizations in this category are affiliated with the United Fund or Community Chest and depend for their financial support on the unified fund raising campaign that is conducted annually on an area-wide basis. Many of them also serve a constituency that is confined to no single municipality or section but resides throughout the area. However, since more underprivileged live in the core city than in the suburbs, a larger share of social agency resources—both public and private—are expended there.

Economic Interest Groups

Economic and professional interest groups constitute another large class of organizations functioning on the metropolitan scene. They include chambers of commerce, labor unions, medical and engineering societies, and lawyers' associations. In contrast to the social agencies which serve a nonmember clientele, the business and occupational groups are created to further the interests of their own membership. Thus a labor union exists primarily to look out for the economic concerns of its constituents; a chamber of commerce to promote the cause of the business community; and a medical society to protect the professional interests of its members. These groups also exercise certain controls over the conduct of their members. A labor union may expel or discipline a worker who does not abide by its rules and regulations, or a bar association may cause disbarment of a member who violates the profession's code of ethics.

As is true of the private welfare agencies, the economic interest groups frequently transcend individual governmental boundaries and draw their membership from the entire urban complex. The metropolitan or county medical society, the county bar association, the metropolitan chamber of commerce, the area-wide labor union, and similar associations are common to the total community. Their area-wide organization contributes, at least in minor fashion, to the cohesiveness of the metropolis. It enables them to view local public issues and problems in broader perspective and to consider their relationship to the metropolitan area as a whole. Metropolitan chambers of commerce, for example, have usually supported plans for reorganizing the governmental system of the urban area, while local chambers of commerce in suburban municipalities have generally opposed such action.

Civic Associations

Although community service and economic interest organizations occasionally seek to affect local public policy, such action is peripheral or subsidiary to their major objectives. Conversely, the main function of civic groups is to influence public opinion and stimulate governmental action on community matters. The League of Women Voters, civic alliances, and the various good government groups fall into this category. These organizations operate without the motivation of self-interest that is present in the other types. They must rely for their drawing power on the intangible rewards which they can bestow on their members: prestige, status, and opportunity for civic participation and leadership. However, members of some organizations which might be included under this classification, such as parent-teachers' associations and neighborhood councils, have a more personal stake in the work of the organization.

Some civic groups, the League of Women Voters, for instance, involve themselves in a wide range of governmental problems and policies. Others, such as the "friends of the library," deal only with matters relating to their specific field of interest. Some, particularly the more influential, have area-wide constituencies; others draw their membership and confine their activities to a particular neighborhood or municipality. The civic organizations, like those in the other categories, do not form any cohesive structural pattern. Loose alliances exist among some of them, but these organizations do not constitute a closely linked network that is capable of ordering the sprawling metropolis into an integrated unit. Each group jealously guards its identity and autonomy and each has its own projects and objectives.

SOCIAL PERSPECTIVE

The rapid technological and social changes of the last half century have created a predominantly urban America in which the metropolis is the new frontier. With the passing of the old agricultural order, new vistas and new avenues of opportunity have been opened to a continuously growing society. Urban populations of today find themselves in a process of lively change. Social rank is moving upward, real income is rising, education is becoming more widespread, ways of living are changing.

The transformation has not come easily, however, nor has it been without social costs. The process of adjusting man and his institutions to a rapidly altering environment is no simple or quickly accomplished task. Take, for example, the case of the new migrants to the metropolis, particularly to the central city. Many of them are inadequately equipped for the competitive system into which they are thrust. Often poorly educated and lacking in the skills necessary for an industrial society, many bring social attitudes and ways of living that are ill adapted to their new surroundings. But they are not alone in feeling the effects of contemporary urbanism. Native-born metropolitan dwellers also must make adjustments, some of them radical, to the new system. A large number of them attempt to do so by fleeing the "ugly" specter of the core city after their working day to the refuge of the outlying countryside. Others absorb themselves in their individual pursuits and cease to be active participants in their community and culture. Given such a context, it is not difficult to see how the problem of governing the metropolitan area has been placed in entirely new perspective.

Modern man lives in a dynamic society, and nowhere is this dynamism more manifest than in metropolitan communities. As we have had occasion to see, rapid expansion of population and increasing specialization are only part of the story. To these features must be added the changing social and economic patterns that characterize the contemporary scene. Largely a reflection of the gigantic forces that are transforming the world, these patterns impose new demands on the agencies of social control: from the family, through the voluntary association, to the duly constituted units and agencies of public authority. The nature of the response of these various institutions to the needs and pressures of an expanding urban society is crucially important in determining the kind of metropolitan environment in which most Americans now live and will live in the future.

CHAPTER 5

▷ *The Metropolitan Economy*

THE METROPOLIS is not merely the place of residence for almost two-thirds of the nation's people; it is also the "workshop of American civilization." Vast aggregations of industrial might, scientific and technical skills, and human resources are concentrated within the 212 SMSA's that dominate the economy. These areas produce and consume the preponderant share of American economic wealth. They contain over 65 percent of the nation's labor force, serve as headquarters for most of its large corporate organizations, and enjoy a consistently higher per capita income than the remainder of the country. They also encompass within their territorial limits the majority of the nation's financial institutions and its wholesale and retail establishments. As seats of human activity and organization, they offer the greatest number and variety of opportunities for work and leisure and provide the means for producing and marketing the widest possible range of goods and services.

The characteristics of modern urbanism are largely a result of the changes brought about by industrialization. These changes, such as mass production of goods and increasing specialization, are familiar to all Americans. What is not always recognized is the fact that economic forces are prime determinants of the ecological and physical structures of cities. Directly or indirectly, these factors influence the pattern of living as well as the social and governmental institutions of metropolitan complexes. Changes in the mode of production or of economic organization inevitably find reflection in metropolitan life.

Technological advances, for example, can revolutionize even the spatial pattern of the community. Witness the automobile; in less than a half century it has transformed closely textured cities into sprawling metropolitan areas and has permitted a radical change in life style, from urban to suburban, for many millions of families. The age of technological discovery, moreover, is still in its infancy. Further and probably even more startling transformations can be expected in the future as the peacetime uses of nuclear energy and other scientific resources are exploited. As a consequence, the metropolis of tomorrow will probably be called upon to perform functions quite different from those it is carrying on today.

To speak of the economic structure of metropolitan areas in the singular is not to overlook the differences, many of them substantial, that exist from one to another. We cannot equate the economy of New York with that of Madison, Wisconsin, or of Chicago with Billings, Montana. Size alone would distinguish the economic organization of these communities; but even apart from differences in size, each of the nation's 212 SMSA's has its own distinctive characteristics. One may depend heavily for its livelihood on the manufacture of automobiles, a second on the production of wearing apparel, and a third on the tourist trade. One may be a university town and another a center of government. Great as these variances in scale and functions may be, however, the economic structures of most metropolitan areas have traits in common. The large majority rely primarily on manufacturing for their outside earnings; they provide goods and services for their own residents and an outlying hinterland; they are marked by specialization and an intricate division of labor; and their economic health is highly sensitive to national trends.

THE ECONOMIC PATTERN AND THE GOVERNMENT

The relationship between the economic and social structures of metropolitan areas is generally recognized, at least in vague fashion, by most people. What is often overlooked, however, is that the economic structure, like the social structure, also bears an important relationship to the governmental and political system of the metropolis. As scholars from classical times to the present have pointed out, government and economics cannot be divorced. The urban community, for example, is a workshop and a producer of wealth. The economic activity it generates takes place within an institutional or governmental framework and this framework is naturally of concern to the economic side of urban existence.

On the one hand, industry and business depend on local government for such essential services as water supply, sewage disposal, police and fire protection, roads, schools, and zoning. On the other hand, the character and trend of economic activity affect and, in a sense, even determine the operations of the governmental system. No public body can intelligently plan its service expansion, capital improvement programs, or land use patterns without a knowledge of the community's economic structure and its potential. An area that is expanding in the direction of heavy industry will have a different set of service needs and land use requirements than one which is developing into an electronic research center. A static or declining community will require different governmental treatment than one experiencing explosive growth. Similarly, a large, heterogeneous SMSA will have needs that vary from those of a smaller, homogeneous one. In short, the ability of a metropolitan governmental system to meet the current requirements and to anticipate the direction of change in its economic structure is a critical aspect of the contemporary urban scene.

Many other interconnections could be cited. By way of illustration, one which has important consequences for the administration and financing of government is the daily movement of people throughout the area, a result largely of the wide spatial distribution of jobs and economic activities. The population in some sections of the metropolis, the central business district in particular, increases manyfold during the daytime and then drops sharply at night as workers and shoppers disperse homeward over the countryside. To accommodate this movement, public services in the locations of daytime concentration must be greatly expanded over the requirements of the resident population. Should the pattern of economic activity change so that the downtown or other sections of heavy concentration cease to attract large daytime populations, the impact on local government would be substantial. Not only would the large capital investment in roads and public utilities in these sections be jeopardized and the tax base eroded, but the community would also be faced with the huge task of redesigning its transportation network and its service facilities.

In addition to these fairly obvious relations, the economic pattern has a more indirect and subtle effect on local government. Sociologists and anthropologists have called attention to the fact that the modern urban community tends to create a new structure of social behavior and thought radically different from that which prevailed in a simpler society. The intricate division of labor endows work with a variety of forms and makes the urban labor force a composite of diversified types. These changes in turn give rise to new tastes and values, new manners and life styles, new attitudes toward problems, new expectations, and new concepts of what life ought to be like.[1]

The structure of behavior which results from this transformation finds reflection in the new demands on the social and political institutions of the urban community. Thus we see increased emphasis on educational and training facilities, on cultural and recreational services, on home ownership and better housing, on renewal of the city, and on the elimination of racial and ethnic barriers. And with rising incomes, public goods and activities once considered luxuries have now come to be regarded as indispensable. The metropolitan governmental system, on the other hand, has been slow to react to the modern industrial age, but the pressures which this era generates may in the end give new forms to local government despite deep and inbred resistance.

It is not possible to examine here all the many aspects of metropolitan economic life. Nor is it possible to probe into their interre-

---

[1] See in this connection, Ralph E. Turner, "The Industrial City: Center of Cultural Change," in Caroline F. Ware (ed.), *The Cultural Approach to History* (New York: Columbia University Press, 1940), pp. 228–242.

lations and the many urban activities and institutions which are not themselves part of the economic structure. The most we can do is to direct attention to some of the major features of the economic system and to the general manner in which it functions. With this purpose in mind, we will look at the economic base of the metropolis, the characteristics of the urban labor force, the role of the central business district and other subsectors of the community, and the changes that are taking place in each of these dimensions.[2] These principal facets should give us a general picture of the economic setting in which government and social institutions operate in the metropolis.

ECONOMIC INTERDEPENDENCE

Attention has already been called to the economic interrelatedness of the metropolis in terms of satisfying the daily needs of its inhabitants. A great variety of services and opportunities is required for large numbers of people to live and work together. In a large-scale society, these services and opportunities are widely distributed in space. People reside in one section of the area but rely on another for their livelihood. Factories draw specialized services and supplies as well as their labor force from many parts of the metropolis. The shops, offices, and entertainment facilities of the central business district depend on the larger community for their clientele. Families in pursuit of their daily activities of work and leisure are no longer confined to the boundaries of a single city, town, or village. Now they can look outside their immediate local neighborhood or community to satisfy many of their social, economic, cultural, religious, and recreational needs. As specialization increases in the various geographical sections of the metropolitan community, this web of interdependence becomes more complex and complete.

Impact of a Brewery

A revealing example of economic interrelatedness has been provided in a study of the St. Louis SMSA. To demonstrate the close ties that prevailed in the community, the study traced the impact of a large brewery located in the central city on employment through-

[2] The economy is also of critical importance to governmental financing; but this aspect is treated separately in Chapter 12.

out the area.[3] (Many persons familiar with the summer climate
of the St. Louis area will find more than mere academic interest in
this example.) The brewery in question employed 6000 persons,
4800 of whom lived in the core city, 1100 in suburban St. Louis
County, and the remainder in adjacent counties on the Illinois side
of the Mississippi River. In addition to these workers, the brewery
generated substantial secondary employment in the local plants of
its suppliers. During the course of a year it purchased a large number of beer cans from two St. Louis manufacturing firms that employed a total of 270 central city dwellers, 94 suburbanites, and 11
Illinois residents to fill the orders. It also bought glass from a plant
located in the Illinois portion of the SMSA that required 130 employees to fabricate the goods. Fuel, chemicals, and other supplies
together with business services purchased by the brewery, such as
advertising and auditing, created work for another 1180 area workers.
These direct suppliers, in turn, had to obtain goods and materials
from other manufacturers. The beer cans sold to the brewery, to
cite an instance, required a large amount of tinplate, over a third
of which was purchased from a local steel mill. In all, "tertiary"
employment provided jobs for about 350 SMSA residents.

The impact, moreover, did not stop at this point. Purchases by
the more than 8000 workers who served the brewery either directly
or indirectly generated further employment in grocery stores, furnishing and clothing shops, and service establishments. Altogether,
these workers and their families in their capacity as consumers made
possible the employment of more than 2000 other residents throughout the metropolitan community. In short, a brewery located near
downtown St. Louis provided employment, either directly or indirectly, for approximately 6800 central city dwellers, 2500 suburbanites, and 900 residents of adjacent Illinois counties.

The example of the brewery illustrates in concrete terms what
is commonly referred to as the economic interdependence of the
metropolitan community. It indicates how the fortunes of a business
situated in one section of the metropolis are of concern to the entire
area. It also shows the effects of specialization and their influence
on the spatial distribution of people and economic activities within
the metropolitan complex. Although interdependence as exemplified

[3] *Path of Progress for Metropolitan St. Louis* (University City: Metropolitan
St. Louis Survey, 1957), pp. 25–29.

by this example is generally known, the example shows precisely the magnitude and extent of the economic interrelationships that exist in our metropolitan areas.

ECONOMIC BASE

How does a metropolitan community provide a living for its residents? What particular types of economic activities characterize its operations? What products does it manufacture for its own residents and what goods does it export outside the region? How and to what extent do these activities conform to the pattern in other communities or in the nation as a whole? Questions of this nature refer to the economic structure of an area, which is the productive pattern on which it depends for its material well-being. This structure may be highly diversified as it is when there are many types of industry and business in a community. Or it may be relatively narrow as it is when a single industry, such as airplane manufacturing, or a single group of businesses, such as those serving a tourist trade, dominate the area's economic life. The nature of this base is important since the potential and the rate of development of a community are closely linked to the prospects and fortunes of the key industries that constitute its economic core.

The most important single determinant of future growth in any metropolitan area or region is, of course, the level of production and expansion in the national economy. A rise or decline in the rate of production for the country as a whole will be reflected in varying degrees among its parts. When the nation surges ahead economically, the regions grow vigorously; when the nation lags, so do the regions. The reason is clear: the country in large measure has become a single, highly interdependent economic unit. Major industries produce for a national market; securities markets and money markets have become predominantly nationwide in scope; and psychological attitudes of both business decision-makers and consumers are transmitted throughout the economy.[4]

Changes in the national picture, however, do not affect all areas in the same way. High levels of prosperity, for example, tend to be associated with high levels of durable goods: automobiles, washers,

[4] See Robert C. Turner, "Recent Economic Growth in Seven States," *Iowa Business Digest*, 34 (November, 1963), 3–30.

refrigerators, and the like. An SMSA such as Pittsburgh or Detroit where the economy is strongly oriented toward production of durable goods is therefore particularly sensitive to changes in the rate of national growth. Technological advances may also affect one community differently than another. New discoveries may reduce the relative importance of a particular industry on which one area is dependent while enhancing the potential of other communities. Unless the former has the capability to adjust to the change, it will find itself falling behind in the competitive struggle.

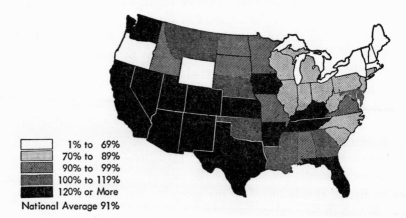

☐	1% to 69%
▒	70% to 89%
▓	90% to 99%
▓	100% to 119%
■	120% or More

National Average 91%

Figure 5.1   Increase in Manufacturing Value Added, by States, 1947–1957/8. From *Metropolitan Economic Study*, Twin Cities Metropolitan Planning Commission, June 1960, p. 7.

Basic and Non-Basic Industries

In analyzing a community's structure and dimensions as a producer of goods and services, economists divide urban economic activities into the two broad categories of basic and non-basic. The first includes the exporting industries or those that bring money into the community from outside. The second covers the non-exporting industries or those that produce goods and services for consumption by people residing within the metropolitan complex. According to this distinction, automobile and steel manufacturing are basic activities since most of the output is destined for external markets. Conversely, the retail trade and service industries are considered non-basic since their output is primarily for the satisfaction of local demands. The level of non-basic activity is closely related to that of the basic industries. Any substantial reduction or layoff of workers in the factories and plants will be reflected in the sales of such retail or service establishments as furniture and clothing stores.

The ascribed importance of specialized production for external markets has prompted some scholars to classify businesses which engage principally in this type of activity as "city-forming," implying that such industries provide the sources of urban growth and the prime reason for the existence of cities as centers of economic enterprise. When this categorization is used, the non-basic activities are referred to as "city-serving." The general assumption underlying these various methods of classification (basic–non-basic, export-import, city forming-city serving) is that most metropolitan areas are self-sufficient with respect to one set of industries and at the same time are specialized producers of certain types of output beyond their own needs.

The standard of living enjoyed by a community depends largely on its basic industries since the revenues derived from external sales enable it to finance the importation of goods and services in which it is deficient. If the community has little to export, it must depend on its own restricted resources to supply its needs. In such a case it resembles the farm family which produces little to sell on the market and therefore finds itself compelled to live on its own limited range of goods. The larger the community, the greater the variety and differentiation of its activities and the more its inhabitants live, to use planner Hans Blumenfeld's expression, "by taking in each other's washing." All relatively large SMSA's now exhibit some activity in each major nonagricultural group of industries, and the overall trend is toward a greater uniformity of industrial structure between the various sections of the country. The traditional economic base study tended to overemphasize the export factor, particularly in the case of the larger metropolises, at the expense of the ever-increasing amount of *intra-area* activity. Modern techniques now permit both aspects to be given due weight.

The Employment Base Method

One method of identifying the basic industries in a community is to compare the structure of local employment with that prevailing nationally. This approach rests on the premises that (1) the country as a whole is relatively self-sufficient and therefore serves as a model for measuring the extent of local self-sufficiency; (2) the output per worker in each industry category is approximately the same in each community; and (3) the extent to which the employment pattern in the community deviates from the national average provides a basis for determining what proportion of the area's various industrial categories is above or below its local requirements. Thus, if 20 percent of the local labor force is engaged in the manufacture of chemicals and drugs in comparison to a national average of 2 percent, we would conclude that the large bulk of its production in this sector is exported. We would assume, in other words, that only about 2 percent of the community's work force was required to supply the chemical and drug needs of its own residents and that the remaining 18 percent was producing for outside markets. The reverse is equally true. If we discovered that less than 1 percent of the local labor force is engaged in food processing as against a national figure of 5 percent, we could justifiably conclude that the area imported a large portion of its food products.[5]

Table 13 illustrates the application of the employment base method to four major sectors of the economy: durable goods manufacturing, non-durable goods manufacturing, personal services, and government or public administration. The percentage of the labor force employed in the four sectors is given for six selected SMSA's and comparisons made with national averages. As the compilation shows, Pittsburgh is far above the national mean in durable goods manufacturing but well below it in non-durable goods production. In the first instance it is a large exporter and in the second an importer. New York exhibits the reverse pattern, standing below the national average in durables but above it in non-durable manufacturing. Such results are hardly surprising since Pittsburgh's economic structure is built principally on steel while New York's manufacturing is oriented more toward printing, publishing, and the production of wearing apparel. In contrast to these two SMSA's, Philadelphia has a more balanced pattern, with approximately the same percentage of its workers employed in each of the two categories.

Unlike Pittsburgh, New York, or Philadelphia, the other three

[5] For a recent study illustrating this method, see Ezra Solomon and Zarko G. Bilbija, *Metropolitan Chicago: An Economic Analysis* (New York: Free Press, 1959).

TABLE 13

Percentage of Labor Force Employed in Selected
Economic Activities in Six SMSA's

SMSA	DURABLE GOODS	NON-DURABLE GOODS	PERSONAL SERVICE	PUBLIC ADMINIS-TRATION
Pittsburgh	30.4	6.6	4.4	3.6
New York	10.2	15.6	5.8	4.7
Philadelphia	17.5	17.5	5.1	4.9
Washington, D.C.	2.8	4.7	6.9	26.9
Sacramento	9.7	6.7	5.9	19.1
Miami	5.4	6.1	11.8	4.4
United States	15.2	11.9	6.0	5.0

SOURCE: *County and City Data Book, 1962* (Washington: 1962).

SMSA's have only a relatively small proportion of their employed residents engaged in either durable or non-durable production. Two of the three, Washington, D.C. and Sacramento, California, are principally exporters of public administration, the first for the nation, the second for an individual state. Compared to a national mean of 5 percent, almost 27 percent of Washington's labor force and 19 percent of Sacramento's are in government service. Miami presents still another picture. Its principal economic activities revolve around the tourist trade, a fact shown by the 11.8 percent of its employment pool (double the national average) that is engaged in personal services such as the operation of hotels. It is evident from these examples that the degree of specialization in an SMSA is inversely related to the national economic structure. The higher the degree of specialization in an area, the more the area will deviate from the national pattern, as the example of Pittsburgh illustrates.

Input-Output Analysis

The use of employment statistics provides a simple means of describing the economic base of a metropolitan area and a framework for observing changes and trends within it. This type of analysis, however, has certain limitations and has been criticized by some

[6] On this point, see the collection of articles dealing with economic base techniques in Ralph W. Pfouts (ed.), *The Techniques of Urban Economic Analysis* (West Trenton, N.J.: Chandler Davis, 1960).

economists.[6] Most importantly, it does not spell out the interrelationships among the various segments of the local structure nor does
it indicate to what extent increases or decreases in one sector of the
economy affect other sectors. If, for example, a 10 percent increase
in steel production is anticipated in the area, how will other local industries, including government, be affected? To provide data of this
kind, a more complex, as well as more costly, method of investigation has recently been put to use in metropolitan economic studies.
Known as input-output analysis, this approach is based on the concept that to produce outputs or goods, such as automobiles and
radios, a set of inputs, such as labor and raw or semiprocessed material, is needed.[7] If increased activity occurs in a particular industry,
additional inputs will be required to meet the new demand. Some
of them will be secured locally and some outside the region. Those
obtained locally will generate activity in other industries and businesses in the community. Thus new sales by a manufacturing firm
will cause increased employment and increased payrolls in the local
economy. These in turn will stimulate additional purchases from
retail firms and additional buying by the retailers from wholesalers.
By tracing this pattern of activity, the total impact of the change
on the economy of the area and on each individual sector can be
predicted. We have observed this principle at work earlier in this
chapter in the case of employment generated by the St. Louis brewery.

Several recent metropolitan surveys, including one in Dayton,
Ohio, have utilized input-output analysis in examining the local
economic structure.[8] The Dayton study, on the basis of information
obtained from consumers and business firms, outlined the effects
of a change in output by one sector upon its purchases from other
sectors of the local metropolitan economy. It showed, for example,
how an increase of $1 in manufacturing sales would ultimately pro-
duce locally an additional 35 cents in retail sales, 49 cents in the
receipts of other businesses, 68 cents in wages, and approximately

[7] For a detailed explanation of this method and its application to metropolitan communities, see John C. Bollens (ed.), *Exploring the Metropolitan Community* (Berkeley and Los Angeles: University of California Press, 1961), chap.
16. Also see Charles M. Tiebout, *The Community Economic Base Study* (New
York: Committee for Economic Development, 1962) for a discussion of the
nature, execution, and uses of economic base studies.

[8] *Metropolitan Challenge* (Dayton: Metropolitan Community Studies,
1959), chap. 13.

TABLE 14

Direct and Indirect Revenue Generation by Sectors, Montgomery County, Ohio

$1 OF SALES BY SECTOR BELOW WILL PRODUCE TOTAL INCREASE SHOWN FOR SECTOR AT THE RIGHT	MANUFAC-TURING, DAYTON	MANUFAC-TURING, REST OF COUNTY	RETAIL, DAYTON	RETAIL, REST OF COUNTY	OTHER BUSINESS, DAYTON	OTHER BUSINESS, REST OF COUNTY	HOUSE-HOLDS, DAYTON	HOUSE-HOLDS, REST OF COUNTY	LOCAL GOVERN-MENTS
Manufacturing, Dayton	$1.1078	$ .0223	$ .2418	$ .1122	$ .4242	$ .0652	$ .3571	$ .3215	$ .0256
Manufacturing, rest of county	.0902	1.0223	.2231	.1238	.3964	.0774	.2986	.3718	.0458
Retail, Dayton	.0588	.0054	1.1691	.0761	.5076	.1061	.2468	.2172	.0211
Retail, rest of county	.1853	.0059	.1803	1.1027	.5303	.0866	.1933	.3183	.0477
Other business, Dayton	.0383	.0045	.1454	.0645	1.1975	.0327	.2154	.1829	.0139
Other business, rest of county	.0753	.0092	.1802	.0974	.4559	1.0473	.2302	.2934	.0412
Households, Dayton	.0598	.0057	.6174	.1161	.5874	.0956	1.2007	.1846	.0320
Households, rest of county	.0791	.0043	.3281	.3598	.5055	.1317	.1739	1.2043	.0524
Local governments	.0492	.0035	.3188	.1715	.4731	.0779	.3343	.5290	1.0289

SOURCE: *Metropolitan Challenge* (Dayton: Metropolitan Community Studies, 1959), p. 157.

three cents for local government in the form of taxes (see Table 14). Part of these increases would occur within the city of Dayton and part in the rest of the county.

The study also traced what would result if there were a 25 percent decrease in payrolls at Wright-Patterson Air Force Base, one of the area's major employers. The immediate effect would be a decrease of $20 million in household income, one-half within the central city and the other one-half in the remainder of the county. Workers removed from the payroll would be forced to cut their purchases from service establishments and retail stores and the latter from wholesale and manufacturing firms. The ultimate effect on Metropolitan Dayton would be a decline of over $27.5 million in wages, $12.7 million in retail receipts, $13.2 million in other business receipts, and $744,000 in local taxes. These figures represent the impact of the wage cutback only. If, as the study points out, the payroll cut was accompanied by a reduction in purchases by the Air Force Base from local manufacturers, the results would be even more drastic.

The Dayton example graphically demonstrates the sensitivity of one sector of the metropolitan economy to changes in another. It also furnishes additional evidence of the high degree of economic interdependence among the geographic divisions of an SMSA. As Table 14 reveals, business and household incomes within the central city are directly affected by the fortunes of an industrial enterprise located in another section of the SMSA. What these figures conclusively demonstrate is that an industry's total impact upon the local economy, particularly on household income, is virtually independent of the plant's geographical location within the metropolitan area. As the study observed, "It makes very little difference where the initial change arises; it will ultimately affect incomes in both Dayton and other parts of the county in approximately the same way."[9] The same statement could be repeated with accuracy for each of the nation's 212 metropolitan communities.

THE LABOR FORCE

The metropolis can be viewed in economic terms as an institution for the creation of wealth and the provision of want-satisfying goods

[9] *Ibid*, p. 156.

and services. Both the private and public sectors of the community are engaged in this broad and continuous task. Many ingredients or inputs, human and otherwise, go into the productive process that characterizes contemporary metropolitan living. In an advanced urban community, the economic structure will be marked by an extensive division of labor and a high degree of occupational differentiation. As a community expands, the number of occupational roles needed to facilitate interaction and maintain a rising level of living becomes greater. We have already touched upon some of these attributes, including the social and occupational composition of the urban population and its spatial distribution within the SMSA. Here we will discuss several features of the metropolitan work force in relation to income and to industrial categories.

The median family income in metropolitan areas is substantially higher than that in the remainder of the nation. In 1959, families residing in the 101 SMSA's of 250,000 or over had a median income of $6439 compared to the national figure of $5660.[10] This difference is not surprising since the bulk of wealth and income-producing facilities is found in the larger urban communities. The differences, however, are not confined to those between metropolitan and non-metropolitan areas; wide variances exist among the SMSA's themselves. Washington, D.C., for example, had a median family income of $7577 in 1959 while that of Tampa–St. Petersburg, Florida was $4490. When the smaller SMSA's are included, the range extends all the way from $8745 in Stamford, Connecticut to $2952 in Laredo, Texas.

Population Size and Regional Location

Two factors are closely correlated with income differentials among metropolitan areas: population size and regional location, both reflections of the degree of industrialization. As Table 15 indicates, median family income tends to increase with size of population. Counties with one million or more residents show median incomes

[10] The percentage of families with annual incomes under $3000—the generally recognized adequate subsistence threshold—is inversely related to the population size of metropolitan areas. In SMSA's with populations of 3 million or more, 13 percent of all families reported incomes under $3000 in 1959; in SMSA's of less than 100,000 residents, the corresponding proportion was 21 percent.

almost $1000 higher than areas in the 100,000 to 250,000 size class
and at least $2400 more than those below 50,000 population. As an
urban area grows larger it becomes more highly industrialized and,
in the process, acquires the means and resources to provide broader
and better employment opportunities. Its increased productive
capacity also enables it to export a larger proportion of its goods and
services and thereby capture a greater share of the regional and
national markets. A higher level of community income is the natural
result of this development.

TABLE 15

Median Family Income by County Population Size, 1959

COUNTY POPULATION SIZE CLASS	MEDIAN FAMILY INCOME
0– 5,000	$3,942
5,000– 15,000	3,622
15,000– 25,000	3,767
25,000– 50,000	4,315
50,000– 100,000	5,115
100,000– 250,000	5,733
250,000– 500,000	6,266
500,000–1,000,000	6,451
1,000,000 and over	6,709

SOURCE: Adapted from G. Ross Stephens and Henry J. Schmandt, "Revenue
Patterns of Local Government," *National Tax Journal*, XV (December, 1962),
436.

The second factor, regional location, is independent of population size in accounting for the wide income differential in metropolitan areas. Most SMSA's in the South have substantially lower
median family incomes than those of similar size in other sections
of the country. Table 16 illustrates the differences among major
geographic regions by reference to several randomly selected SMSA's
in the various size categories. The southern metropolises in each
instance show the lowest income, a result that would be consistently
maintained if all remaining SMSA's were similarly compared. The
variances among the other three regions of the nation are less
marked, although the western and northeastern areas tend to be
higher than their North Central counterpart. A more complete
picture is obtained when median family incomes by region and

TABLE 16

Median Family Income in Selected SMSA's of Similar Population Sizes, by Region, 1959

SIZE CLASS	NORTHEAST		NORTH CENTRAL		SOUTH		WEST	
	SMSA	MEDIAN FAMILY INCOME	SMSA	MEDIAN FAMILY INCOME	SMSA	MEDIAN FAMILY INCOME	SMSA	MEDIAN FAMILY INCOME
Over 1 million	Paterson, N.J.	$7,431	Cincinnati, Ohio–Ky.	$6,318	Dallas, Tex.	$5,925	Seattle, Wash.	$6,896
700,000 to 1 million	Providence, R.I.	5,666	Indianapolis, Ind.	6,609	Miami, Fla.	5,348	Portland, Ore.–Wash.	6,340
500,000 to 700,000	Rochester, N.Y.	7,147	Youngstown, Ohio	6,210	Fort Worth, Tex.	5,617	San Jose, Calif.	7,417
300,000 to 500,000	Springfield, Mass.	6,235	Wichita, Kan.	6,166	Nashville, Tenn.	5,332	Tacoma, Wash.	5,950
200,000 to 300,000	Lancaster, Pa.	5,810	Lansing, Mich.	6,177	Columbia, S.C.	4,540	Bakersfield, Calif.	5,933
100,000 to 200,000	Portland, Me.	5,668	Decatur, Ill.	5,943	Monroe, La.	4,367	Provo, Utah	5,536
Under 100,000	Fitchburg, Mass.	5,866	St. Joseph, Mo.	5,414	Texarkana, Tex.–Ark.	3,817	Great Falls, Mont.	6,032

SOURCE: U.S. Bureau of the Census, *County and City Data Book, 1962* (Washington: 1962).

geographical division are examined in their totality.[11] Here, as Table 17 shows, the Pacific Coast states with $6572 head the list, followed by the East North Central, Middle Atlantic, and New England divisions, all in the neighborhood of $6200. The three southern sections are well below the national median of $5660 and lower than those in all other geographical groupings. The West North Central states are also below the national total while the Mountain states match the overall figure.

TABLE 17

Median Family Income by Region and Division, 1959

REGION AND DIVISION	MEDIAN FAMILY INCOME	PERCENT OF FAMILIES UNDER $3,000	PERCENT OF FAMILIES OVER $10,000
NORTHEAST	$6,191	14.2	17.9
New England	6,128	13.6	16.3
Middle Atlantic	6,211	14.4	18.4
NORTH CENTRAL	$5,892	18.7	15.5
East North Central	6,215	15.9	17.2
West North Central	5,154	25.1	11.5
SOUTH	$4,465	33.0	10.3
South Atlantic	4,713	30.1	11.3
East South Central	3,793	40.7	7.5
West South Central	4,548	32.3	10.6
WEST	$6,348	15.7	19.0
Mountain	5,660	19.3	14.0
Pacific	6,572	14.5	20.5
U.S. TOTAL	$5,660	21.4	15.1

SOURCE: U.S. Bureau of the Census, *County and City Data Book, 1962* (Washington: 1962).

These results make more sense when the percentages of high and low income families in each region are taken into account. In the South, one of every three families had annual incomes under $3000, compared to 14.2 percent in the Northeast, 15.7 percent in the West, and 18.7 percent in the North Central cluster. At the other

[11] It is necessary to utilize the figures for the total population, metropolitan and non-metropolitan, in this connection since the census does not give a regional compilation of median family incomes within SMSA's.

end of the continuum, the South was similarly disadvantaged. Only 10.3 percent of its families showed incomes of over $10,000 as against corresponding figures of 15.5 percent for the North Central region, 17.9 percent for the Northeast, and 19.0 percent for the West.

Income differentials are closely related to the level of industrialization, and hence urbanization, in the various regions. It is not surprising, therefore, to find the South at the bottom of the income scale since it has traditionally lagged far behind in industrial development. Only in recent decades has the situation begun to change with the vigorous efforts of southern states to compete for new business and industry. Before World War II only a relatively few urban areas were able to provide sizable work forces trained in industrial skills. The South was particularly handicapped in this regard. Today, these skills are more widely dispersed so that plants are less restricted in their locational choices.

Worker Distribution Among Economic Sectors

Another relevant aspect in examining the characteristics of the urban labor force is the distribution of workers among the various economic sectors. The occupational pattern of metropolitan residents, previously noted in the discussion of social structure, is based on the nature or level of work performed by the individual. A person who is a physician or lawyer is included in the professional category; a typist or stenographer is in the clerical classification; and machinists or electricians are in the group designated craftsmen. In addition to these occupational features, it is also important to know the relative number of workers, regardless of occupation, that are employed in each of the major industrial groupings. We have just observed how useful this distribution is for conventional economic base studies; it is also valuable for measuring the changes in the economic structure as it responds to community and outside demands.

During the twenty-year period from 1940 to 1960, the nation's employment force increased from 45 million to almost 65 million. Important changes took place in both the size of the labor force and the proportion of workers in the major industrial groupings (see Table 18). The most far-reaching change since 1940 is the sharp decline in the proportion of workers engaged in agricultural pursuits (from 18.9 to 6.7 percent), a reduction in absolute terms of over four million employees. The decrease was greatest in the South, a further sign that the economy there is shifting toward the same industrial distribution as that of the rest of the country. Only two other major categories experienced both relative and absolute losses— mining and private households. The first is due primarily to auto-

TABLE 18

Percentage Distribution of Employed Persons in the United States, by Major Industrial Groups, 1940 and 1960

INDUSTRIAL GROUP	PERCENT OF DISTRIBUTION 1940	PERCENT OF DISTRIBUTION 1960	PERCENT INCREASE IN NUMBER OF EMPLOYEES, 1940 TO 1960
Agriculture	18.9	6.7	−49.6
Mining	2.0	1.0	−28.8
Construction	4.6	5.9	82.8
Manufacturing	23.7	27.1	64.1
Transportation, utilities, and communication	6.9	7.0	58.2
Wholesale and retail	16.6	18.2	57.3
Finance, insurance, and real estate	3.3	4.2	82.7
Business services	0.5	1.2	209.1
Repair services	1.4	1.3	33.3
Private households	5.0	3.0	−14.8
Other personal services	3.7	3.0	17.3
Entertainment and recreation	0.9	0.8	26.8
Education services	3.5	5.2	129.4
Welfare and other professional services	4.0	6.4	129.4
Public administration	3.1	5.0	126.3
Not reported	1.9	4.0	—
Total	100.0	100.0	43.4

SOURCE: Adapted from U.S. Bureau of the Census, *Census of Population, 1960, Characteristics of the Population,* Vol. I, Part 1 (Washington: 1964).

mation, the second to the decreased use of household servants. Although manufacturing added to its share of the labor force, the gains were due largely to the increase in administrative and white-collar personnel. In 1940, production or "blue-collar" workers constituted 82 percent of total employment in manufacturing. By 1960, this figure had dropped to 75 percent, an indication of increased factory productivity and the need for larger office forces to handle the paper work.

The largest percentage gains in the employment distribution pattern as well as in the number of workers occurred in the construction industry and in those sectors which provide consumer services: business, education, welfare and professional, and public administration. These changes are characteristic of a society enjoying increased productivity and rising standards of living. As personal income increases, the demand for consumer services and consumer goods mounts. Women have more to spend at the apparel and beauty shops; more families are able to purchase homes; people have the means to travel more extensively, thus patronizing more motels, resorts, restaurants, and filling stations; local taxpayers are willing to support a broader range of governmental services; and so on. The wealthier a metropolitan area becomes, the more these kinds of demands are reflected in the composition and distribution of its labor force and in the budgets of its local governmental units.

THE CENTRAL BUSINESS DISTRICT

A major topic of concern whenever the economy of metropolitan areas is discussed is the fate of the central business district. As several observers have expressed it, "The CBD is on trial." To many urban planners the future of the metropolis depends on the future of downtown. They regard this core as the heart and soul of the metropolitan community, the focal point around which the activities of the entire area revolve. There can be no prosperous periphery, in their view, without a successful downtown. Destroy or let this hub deteriorate, and the metropolitan area will be sapped of strength and vigor. This view, although widely accepted, is sharply disputed by some observers. Maintaining that the CBD has ceased to serve a useful purpose, the dissidents question the wisdom of spending millions of dollars each year to pump new vitality into what they regard as an obsolete and outmoded appendage. In their eyes, attempts to save the downtown are economically unsound and unrealistic; let its fate be determined by the free play of the market place. Those who take this position would have the community free itself from its long-standing commitment to the preservation of the CBD and devote its resources to the development of alternatives. Others take a more moderate stand and while acknowledging the crucial importance of the downtown section criticize the failure of city planners and administrators to recognize its changing role and to act accordingly.

Regardless of who is right or wrong in this controversy, metropolitan areas—particularly the central cities—have a large stake in their downtown core. Despite any obsolescence, the CBD represents a huge investment of community wealth and an important source of tax revenue for local government. Within its territorial confines is the area's highest concentration of office buildings, department stores, specialty shops, hotels, financial institutions, and governmental agencies. The density of its daytime population greatly exceeds that in any other section of the community. Its land values are by far the highest in the area. It is the center of the community's transportation and communications network. Pick up a map of any large metropolitan area and observe how the expressways, major streets, and mass transit lines gravitate toward the downtown mecca. By almost any test we apply, it would be difficult to ignore the significance of the CBD to the life, economy, and government of the metropolis. And whether it is losing its usefulness or not, it will likely remain a major element of the urban scene for many years.

Changing Characteristics

The character and functions of the CBD have changed materially over time. Until about a half century ago, the downtown was an area of multiple uses—residential, commercial, industrial, and institutional. With the passage of time, overcrowding and obsolescence led first to the decline in residential use and later in manufacturing and wholesaling use. The arrival of the motor vehicle gave the dweller in this core area the mobility to flee from the center and at the same time it broadened the locational freedom of industrial establishments. New methods of fabrication and new techniques for handling materials and goods outmoded the old multistory factory and warehouse buildings and created a demand for single-story space. The high cost of downtown land together with the difficulty of assembling sufficiently large parcels to meet the new space requirements discouraged manufacturing expansion in the core. On the periphery land was far cheaper, traffic and congestion were

much less, and the problem of getting the worker to and from his
job had been solved by the rubber-tired vehicle.

A recent economic study made in Boston tells a story that is
being repeated in many other large metropolitan areas.[12] Between
1947 and 1957, the city's CBD lost 9000 manufacturing jobs but
comparable employment beyond the central city's corporate limits
increased by approximately 35,000 jobs. By 1957 more than 70 percent of all such employment in the Boston SMSA was located in the
suburban environs and only 9 percent in the CBD. It has become
increasingly apparent, as illustrated by the Boston experience, that
not only downtown areas and their surrounding rings but the core
cities as a whole are losing manufacturing jobs to the suburbs. In
many instances these losses are not only relative but also absolute.
During the 1950–1960 decade, manufacturing employment dropped
within the central city in nine of the nation's ten largest SMSA's
(see Table 19). Only Los Angeles showed an increase while older
core cities like Detroit and St. Louis experienced substantial reductions. This migration of factories and plants to the periphery has
continued despite the efforts of central city authorities to retain
them. Today we are witnessing what Robert Wood refers to as the
"cult of municipal mercantilism," as each local government searches
for industry to bolster its property tax base.

A trend, similar to that in manufacturing, has also been taking
place in retail trade. While industrial location is determined by such
factors as space requirements, access to transportation facilities, and
economy in operation, the retail trade pattern is shaped by considerations of convenience for the consumer. As population moves
outward from the center, the shops and stores follow. Prior to 1920
over 90 percent of retail sales were made in the central business
districts. By 1954, this figure for the large metropolitan areas had
dropped to an average of less than 60 percent. One major retailing
chain recently reported that it expects to close 10 to 20 downtown
stores per year as leases expire. At the same time, of 348 new stores
it opened in the past five years, 308 are located in suburban shopping
centers.[13]

[12] Greater Boston Economic Study Committee, A *Report on Downtown
Boston*, Policy Statement, Part 2 (Boston: Associates of the Committee for
Economic Development, May, 1959).

[13] George Sternlieb, "Is Business Abandoning the Big City?" *Harvard
Business Review*, 39 (January–February, 1961), 6–8.

TABLE 19

Number of Persons Employed in Manufacturing in Central Cities
of Ten Largest SMSA's, 1950 and 1960[a]

SMSA	NUMBER EMPLOYED IN CENTRAL CITY, 1950	NUMBER EMPLOYED IN CENTRAL CITY, 1960	PERCENT GAIN OR LOSS, 1950 TO 1960
New York	916,911	870,354	− 5.1
Los Angeles	183,064	271,778	48.5
Chicago	593,086	503,753	−15.1
Philadelphia	291,312	261,924	−10.1
Detroit	348,986	228,806	−34.4
San Francisco	55,864	54,467	− 2.5
Boston	73,831	70,326	− 4.8
Pittsburgh	73,448	57,826	−21.3
Washington, D.C.	27,381	21,145	−22.8
St. Louis	124,432	91,749	−26.3

[a] These figures are somewhat lower than those based on industry and business establishments, as in the *Census of Manufactures*, since the *Census of Population* counts persons employed at more than one job only once.
SOURCE: U.S. Bureau of the Census, *Census of Population, 1950,* Vol. II, *Characteristics of the Population; Census of Population, 1960,* Vol. I, *Characteristics of the Population* (Washington: 1952 and 1963).

Figure 5.2 shows the relative decline of central city trade in the nation's twenty-five largest SMSA's during the short time span between the 1954 and 1958 censuses of business. In all twenty-five areas, the core city's share of the retail market showed a loss. For many downtown areas, the decline represents an absolute loss as well. A Bureau of the Census analysis of CBD's in 109 major cities in 1958 showed that the volume of retail sales in fifty of them had decreased during the preceding four-year period, in some cases as high as 20 percent and in one instance as high as 30 percent.[14] Retail employment in the central city has similarly been affected. Philadelphia, for example, contained 62 percent of the population and 79 percent of the retail jobs in the SMSA in 1930; in 1960, it contained 46 percent of the metropolitan area's residents and 51 percent of its retail jobs.

Huge shopping centers are now a common sight on the metro-

[14] U.S. Bureau of the Census, *1958 Census of Business,* Vol. I, *Retail Trade* (Washington: 1959), p. 13.

% of Total Sales, 1954
% of Total Sales, 1958

SMSA

SMSA	1954	1958
New York	72.9	76.8
Chicago	65.3	70.3
Los Angeles	49.0	49.8
Philadelphia	51.1	57.1
Detroit	51.1	60.5
San Francisco	52.4	58.3
Boston	39.0	42.6
Pittsburgh	37.5	39.9
Washington, D.C.	52.1	59.5
St. Louis	49.1	55.4
Cleveland	62.9	69.4
Newark	30.1	34.2
Baltimore	71.4	76.4
Minneapolis—St. Paul	73.4	80.6
Houston	84.1	86.8
Buffalo	52.2	58.3
Dallas	77.7	79.6
Paterson		32.3
Seattle	66.5	72.8
Kansas City	61.8	65.8
Milwaukee	75.1	76.7
Miami	54.9	63.8
Cincinnati	64.1	67.2
Atlanta	71.5	75.3
Denver	70.4	73.7

Figure 5.2 Central Cities' Declining Proportion of Retail Sales in the Twenty-Five Largest SMSA's, 1954 and 1958. Source: U.S. Bureau of the Census, *1958 Census of Business*, Vol. I, *Retail Trade*, p. 11.

politan periphery. Established downtown department stores have opened outlying branches; major grocery chains have been quick to tap the growing market; and discount houses have emerged on the suburban scene to offer a new form of competition to the merchandising traditionalists. Convenient to the suburban matron and equipped with ample parking facilities, the new centers are luring

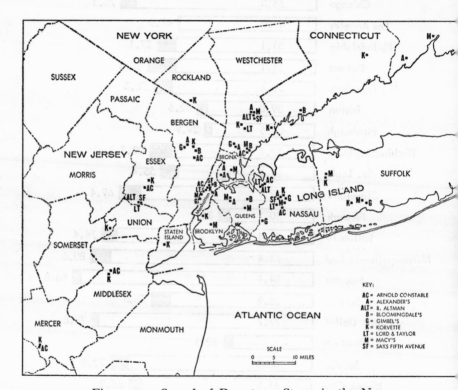

Figure 5.3   Spread of Downtown Stores in the New York Metropolitan Area. Source: Regional Plan Association, Inc., New York City.

shoppers away not only from the core city CBD but also from the business districts of outlying neighborhoods and of the older ring municipalities. These smaller commercial concentrations are especially vulnerable since they have neither the free off-street parking of the new shopping centers nor the wide selection of merchandise of the CBD.

Even the most ardent optimist cannot shrug off the enormity

of the problems that face the CBD. But the picture is not one of unmitigated bleakness. Even though the downtown is losing retail trade and manufacturing to suburbia, it has advantages which no other section of the area can offer. The concentration of office buildings, financial institutions, department stores, and related service facilities provides a business environment that would be difficult to duplicate anywhere else in the metropolitan community. Because of the CBD's unique features, certain activities continue to remain within its special province despite the changing character of urban society and the forces of obsolescence.

Frank Lloyd Wright once proposed the construction of a single mile-high building in the downtown area to house what he identified as the primary functions of the central city: banking and prostitution. We need not accede to Mr. Wright's architectural phantasy nor agree with his delineation of the core city's role to see that what is involved here is the bringing together of certain specialized activities in a central location. These activities, moreover, are metropolitan-oriented and not merely neighborhood-oriented. The banking facilities of the CBD, for example, serve the major needs of business and industry regardless of their location in the SMSA. The same observation applies to the downtown department store since its clientele is area-wide. In contrast, the branches which banks and department stores establish in suburbia can rarely, if ever, lay claim to serving the whole metropolis.

Advantages of the CBD

What then are the activities that fall within the special province of the CBD and for which it offers unique advantages? Three groups of functions are most frequently cited in this regard: (1) furnishing specialized and comparative shopping; (2) providing office facilities for the so-called "confrontation" industries, which are the occupations and activities that depend on face-to-face contact for the conduct of business; and (3) servicing the small businesses and industries that seek the economies which concentration offers. Each of these functional groups contributes to the rationale supporting the continued existence of the CBD and the efforts to preserve it.

Specialized and Comparative Shopping. Until the last few decades, the downtown area of the core city served as the main shopping center for the entire metropolis. In more recent years this function has been badly eroded by the spatial decentralization of retail trade. Whatever viability the CBD now retains in the retail sector is due largely to the opportunities it offers for comparative shopping. Its large aggregation of department stores and specialty shops enables it to provide a depth and variety of merchandise and a range of choice in brand, style, quality, and price that is economically unfeasible to furnish elsewhere. Large numbers of customers are needed to support activity of this type and only the downtown, as the pivotal gathering point of masses of people, satisfies this requirement.

It has been evident for some time that the CBD cannot compete with the outlying centers in standardized goods. The suburban housewife simply will not make the long trip downtown for items that she can readily purchase in her neighborhood or regional shopping district. Only when she wishes to broaden her range of choice or obtain specialized products is she willing to undergo this inconvenience. The development of larger regional centers on the periphery, a tendency that now is emerging, will lessen the advantage of the CBD, even for comparative shopping. On the other hand, the downtown stores can still count on a large clientele of office workers, government employees, and others who are brought into the CBD for purposes other than shopping. A local clientele of some size is also being created in the larger SMSA's as a result of the new luxury apartments which are appearing in or near the core on land made available largely by urban redevelopment projects.

"Confrontation" Industries.   Aside from retailing activities, the downtown area still remains the preferred location for the "confrontation" industries. Financial institutions and business offices, particularly corporate headquarters, tend to group themselves in highly cohesive clusters in the city center. For them the dominant locational need is one of speedy and direct communication. The telephone or letter provides no substitute for the advantages that the managerial élite find in dealing directly with their business associates. As economist Raymond Vernon points out, "The process of negotiation and conferring oftentimes involves subtleties of emphasis and expression too elusive to be imparted by letter, telephone, and even perhaps by closed circuit television."[15] The large office establish-

[15] *The Changing Economic Function of the Central City* (New York: Committee for Economic Development, 1959), p. 30.

ments, moreover, attract to the CBD a host of other activities with which they have linkages. Advertising agencies, accounting firms, office suppliers, and similar service-providing enterprises find it helpful and convenient to be located near the doorsteps of their major clients and customers.

In the past, a downtown location made it easier for a firm with large office needs to recruit clerical personnel. Young women have long held most of the office jobs involving repetitive work. With an employment force of this nature, a location at the hub of the mass transit network was at one time highly advantageous. Today, with automobile commuting commonplace even among young women, this factor has lost much of its appeal. Other features, however, continue to make downtown the preferred place of employment for young female office workers. The opportunities for lunch-hour shopping, for after-hours recreation and entertainment, and for meeting people—including eligible bachelors—are unexcelled in the region. How important these advantages are to the future of the CBD would be difficult to say. Yet they are illustrative of the many intangible factors that assist the downtown in retaining its peculiar drawing powers.

Small Plants and Businesses. The third group of enterprises for which the CBD and its adjacent areas offer locational advantages are the small plants and businesses which are dependent on economies obtainable through the use of "external" facilities or services. The New York Metropolitan Region Study called attention to this feature in noting that size of establishment is closely related to affinity for the central districts. It found that more than half of the New York area's employment in industries having sixty or less workers per plant was in the central city. Because of the limited scale of their operations, these enterprises have to rely on services which their larger competitors provide for themselves. Through clustering, the small plants attempt to overcome the handicap of size by securing externally the economies which the large companies enjoy internally. Thus, as the New York study observed:

To avoid stockpiling their materials in disproportionately large numbers, they [small plants] have clung close to the center of the urban cluster where they can get materials on short notice; to meet the problems of labor force variations or machine breakdowns, they have chosen locations where they can recruit workers for brief periods or on short notice. They have chosen loft space, short run in commitment and flexible in size, in preference to the separate factory building away from the urban center. In sum, the denser areas of the New York Metropolitan Region are acting as a common pool for space, materials, and labor, meeting the inherent uncertainties of the small plants which occupy these areas.[16]

The attractiveness of the core to small industry is, however, diminishing. Clustering can take place in suburbia as well as the CBD if proper facilities become available. The New York study showed, for example, that in recent years Manhattan has suffered an absolute decline in the number of small plants. The study attributed this loss to the spread of external economies to the outlying areas. Rentable manufacturing space is now being offered to smaller plants and businesses in suburban industrial parks, while repairmen and subcontractors are found in increasing numbers throughout the area. At the same time, sewage disposal, water, fire and police protection, and adequate trucking service are becoming available on the periphery. As a result of these developments, "The early city monopolies—their ability uniquely to provide an environment in which small plants may settle—are being broken. And in time small plants will have almost as wide a geographical choice as their larger competitors in selecting a site for their activities in the Region."[17]

The Future of the CBD

It is evident that the CBD is going through a period of change and adjustment, and the same may be said of the central city in general. The CBD's future will depend heavily on its ability to adapt to the new circumstances and to capitalize on those activities which it alone can do, or which it can do better than the remainder of the area. This adaptation may require, as some urban specialists contend, the further enhancement of the CBD's economic efficiency by a displacement of less intensive activities with those of a more specialized nature. Or it may require, as planner and developer Victor Gruen has suggested for Fort Worth, physical changes in which the main downtown streets are made pedestrian malls, with parking garages on the periphery and moving sidewalks to bring shoppers

[16] Edgar M. Hoover and Raymond Vernon, *Anatomy of a Metropolis* (New York: Doubleday, 1962), pp. 48–49.

[17] *Ibid.*, pp. 50–51.

and office workers from their cars to the center of activity. Some observers even feel that many of the CBD's present uses should be marked off as losses, and that efforts should be concentrated on its conversion into a community center dominated by civic monuments, government offices, and cultural and entertainment facilities.

Whatever the future may bring, the CBD's place in contemporary urban society, in the final analysis, will be determined primarily by economic forces. But although the ultimate decisions on business and industrial location and use will continue to be made by private interests on economic grounds, the actions of public authorities and local governments may do much to influence these decisions. Urban renewal projects, rejuvenation of mass transit systems, planning and zoning, capital improvement programs, and other governmental activities may well be deciding factors in determining the future course of the metropolis as well as the fate of the central business district.

THE GOVERNMENT AND ECONOMY OF THE METROPOLIS

In preparing a regional plan for Metropolitan New York in 1927, sponsors of the project observed that "the first thing to be done in making a study of an urban area for the purpose of preparing a plan of physical improvement is to ascertain the composition, volume, distribution, and direction of growth of its principal economic activities."[18] Almost thirty-five years later, the Committee for Economic Development (CED), a group of leading businessmen and educators, issued a comparable policy statement on metropolitan problems and governmental reorganization. Emphasizing the importance of systematic and periodic analyses of the local economy, the statement in part read:

> We believe it important to bear in mind that a metropolitan community is a place for earning a livelihood. The existence of any urban area at a particular place, and its growth or decline, depend on the expansion or contraction of opportunities for employment and investment. If this is understood, a community will usually desire to take the governmental steps which can help maintain and increase such opportunities. . . .
>
> Many areas could benefit from a careful analysis of the economic and demographic forces influencing the volume and pattern of their income-

[18] *Regional Survey of New York and Its Environs* (New York: Committee on Regional Plan of New York and Its Environs, 1927), Vol. I, p. 3.

generating activities. Such knowledge is essential to an understanding of the influence of public policy on the retention, expansion, or attraction of private investment and employment opportunities. Only with such knowledge is it possible to formulate sound master plans to guide community development, to invest wisely in public improvements, and to make the right decisions about urban renewal.[19]

The CED statement sums up well the importance of economic studies for both the practitioner and analyst of government in our metropolitan areas. As a system, the metropolis contains many interdependent and interacting groups which perform specialized functions of various kinds. The ways in which these groups are organized and relate to each other and the ways in which they carry out their social and economic tasks, including the production of goods and services, furnish the raw data for analysis and insight.

Economics as a science is basically concerned with the process by which scarce resources are allocated among competing ends. As a policy-maker, the local governmental official is directly or indirectly involved in this process. The consequences of his actions have repercussions in the economic sphere whether he wills it or not. His decisions on educational, recreational, and other types of governmental expenditures are allocational judgments that help to determine the community tone and environment. To make these allotments intelligently and in the public interest he must be aware, insofar as possible, of the economic and social consequences of alternative courses of action. It is the responsibility of the public official to make the decisions and set the community goals; it is the task of the social scientist to seek understanding of the phenomena of urban processes and change so that rational choices can be made in the public as well as private sector. If urban governments are to provide leadership in metropolitan development and goal formulation and if they are to be positive forces in directing the evolution of the community, those who officially man the helm bear a heavy responsibility.

[19] *Guiding Metropolitan Growth* (New York: Committee for Economic Development, 1960), p. 6.

CHAPTER 6

⟠ *Government in the Metropolis*

No PAUCITY of governments exists in the metropolis. Often invisible to the human eye—but never unknown to the taxpayer's pocketbook —they clutter the landscape in vast number and almost infinite variety. And some types are continuing to become more numerous. The resulting scene is one of many local units, as well as federal and state agencies, functioning in the nation's metropolises and affecting their development and their success or failure in solving particular problems.

Government is of great importance to metropolitan areas, but it nevertheless shapes up as a complex and bewildering pattern. In a general way, many people recognize the significance of public programs to intelligent metropolitan development. In contrast, there is little cognizance of either the abundance of governments operating in these areas (in part because only highly specialized maps show the boundaries of all local units) or the detrimental effects that can grow out of such a fragmented system.

In terms of local governmental units, most metropolitan areas contain numerous municipalities (variously called cities, villages, incorporated towns, and boroughs), one or more counties, a number of school districts, and a variety of non-school special districts.[1] In addition, some of them, particularly in New England, the Middle Atlantic states, and portions of the Midwest, have towns or townships. All these categories of local governments differ tremendously in many respects—in territorial size, powers, financial authority and resources, structure, and ability to adjust capably to metropolitan conditions, to cite some of the more important. Some of these variances often are evident even within the same category or class of local governments; for instance, in various states municipalities differ in structure and substantive powers, special districts differ markedly in features from each other, and county governments are of different types. The variations can be still more pronounced when a metropolis straddles parts of two states, a condition that has become increasingly more common. Each state determines the characteristics of every category of its local units without deliberate regard for comparable actions in adjoining states.

It is important to gain an understanding of the governmental system of the metropolis and its various parts or subsystems. Governments, as we know, represent a very significant dimension of the metropolis and are therefore discussed at various places in this book. At this point we consider them in some detail, looking at their abundance and complexity, considering their historical development, and examining the major criticisms of them. Such an analysis helps in comprehending how the governmental system functions and its capabilities and deficiencies in meeting the challenges of the metropolitan era—subjects that receive further attention in later chapters.

GOVERNMENTS IN ABUNDANCE

The governmental pattern of metropolitan areas resembles a crowded bus or subway. Occupying only one-twelfth of the land, these areas have 18,442 local governments, according to the 1962 *Census of Governments*. This is one-fifth of the national total and a weighty

[1] In this chapter and later ones the term "non-school special districts" is often shortened to the simpler "special districts." Although school districts are a type of special district, they are usually identified separately by the commonly used term "school districts."

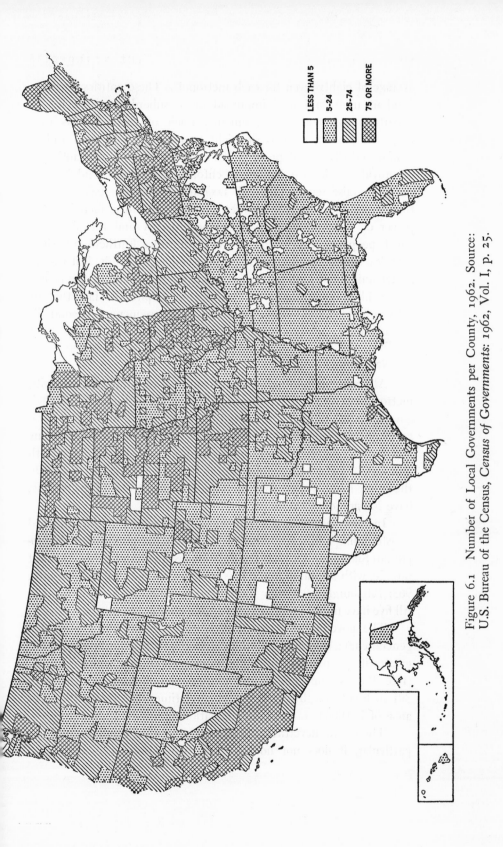

Figure 6.1 Number of Local Governments per County, 1962. Source:
U.S. Bureau of the Census, *Census of Governments: 1962*, Vol. I, p. 25.

LESS THAN 5

5-24

25-74

75 OR MORE

average of eighty-seven for each metropolis. These entities are independent units and not simply adjuncts, subordinate agencies, or departments of other governments. Each of them has its own corporate powers, such as the right to sue and to be sued and to obtain and dispose of property, its own officials, its own authority to provide service (and often to enforce regulations), and its own power to raise revenue through taxation or charges. Each of them thus wears the powerful mantle of public authority, including the power of financial exaction from the citizenry and the ability to affect people's lives beneficially or harmfully. Furthermore, since each is a separate unit and legally independent, it is able, if it wishes, to act unilaterally and without concern for the desires of the people in neighboring jurisdictions. This is true despite the fact that its actions or inactions may have serious consequences beyond its boundaries.

Variations

Although supporting on the average a large array of local units, metropolitan areas differ considerably in the complexity of their governmental systems. A limited number have only a few local governments—from five to twenty. Located chiefly in the South, many in this category have recently experienced extensive population growth that has brought metropolitan status to them for the first time. On the other hand, twenty-four metropolises, about one of every nine, have 200 or more local units.

In some instances, the number of governments can be described as astounding and scarcely believable. The Chicago Standard Metropolitan Statistical Area has the dubious distinction of being the most prolific, with a total of 1060. It is followed by the Philadelphia area, 963; Pittsburgh, 806; New York, 555; and the St. Louis area, 439. All five have more than two million inhabitants.

The governmental organization of these five areas mirrors a general characteristic of government in the metropolis: as a rule, the greater its population, the larger its number of local units. To illustrate, those of one million or more population have an average of 301 such entities; this is more than three times the average (98.5) of areas of 500,000 to one million population.

There are nevertheless exceptions to this generalization. In particular, it does not hold for the two classes of medium-sized metropolises—those of 200,000 to 300,000 and 300,000 to 500,000 population—which have an identical average number (76.6). These two medium-sized classes, however, have a far smaller average than the next most populous group and a far larger one than the less populous classes.

TABLE 20

SMSA's, by Total Number and Average Number of
Local Governments

SMSA SIZE GROUP (1960 POPULATION)	NUMBER OF SMSA'S	NUMBER OF LOCAL GOVERN- MENTS (1962)	AVERAGE NUMBER OF LOCAL GOVERNMENTS
All SMSA's	212	18,442	87.0
1,000,000 or more	24	7,227	301.0
500,000–1,000,000	29	2,857	98.5
300,000–500,000	28	2,146	76.6
200,000–300,000	41	3,141	76.6
100,000–200,000	68	2,540	37.4
50,000–100,000	22	531	24.1

SOURCE: U.S. Bureau of the Census, *Census of Governments: 1962*, Vol. I, *Governmental Organization* (Washington: 1963), p. 11.

Wide discrepancies are also apparent when certain individual metropolitan areas are compared. Metropolitan Baltimore, twelfth largest in the nation with a population of approximately one and three-fourths millions, deviates greatly from the governmental complexity of most large centers; it has only twenty-three local governments. Conversely, the Madison, Wisconsin, area, with about 250,000 residents, has sprouted 178; this is a larger number than that in the nearby Milwaukee area, where the population is more than five times as large. Another important exception is the Portland, Oregon, area; it ranks seventh in number of governments even though containing less than one million inhabitants.

THE COMPLEXITY OF GOVERNMENT

Government in metropolitan areas is complex in part because of their large number of local units. Although a strong case can be made that there are too many local governments of every category in metropolitan areas, the total number continues to increase. The major contributors to this profusion are school districts and special districts; together they constitute about 62 percent of all govern-

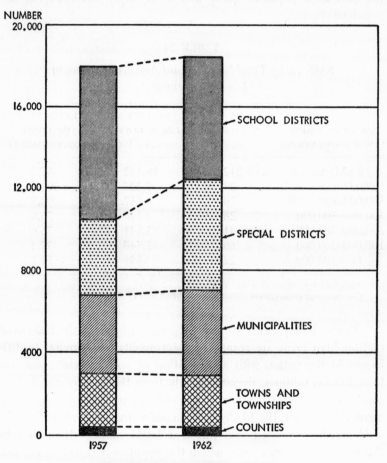

(THE 212 SMSA'S AS DEFINED IN 1962)

Figure 6.2 Local Governments in SMSA's, by Type, 1957 and 1962. Source: U.S. Bureau of the Census, *Census of Governments: 1962*, Vol. I, p. 24.

ments in SMSA's. School districts, however, are noticeably declining, while special districts are still being established at a very rapid rate.

Municipalities make up the third largest number of local

governments in the metropolis. They represent about one-fifth of the total and are continuing to increase, although not so rapidly as special districts. Towns and townships stand next, representing about one-eighth of the total. A major reason for their low rank is that they were never in common use throughout the United States. They operate in twenty-one states, mainly in the New England and Middle Atlantic regions and certain parts of the North Central region. Called "towns" in New England, New York State, and Wisconsin, and "townships" in many North Central states and in New Jersey and Pennsylvania, their number is dropping very slowly, chiefly because of the occasional abolition of a few townships. Counties, which are generally the largest territorial units in the metropolis, are by far the least numerous. They make up less than one-fiftieth of the total and their number remains practically stationary.

TABLE 21

Number of Local Governments in 212 SMSA's,
1962, and Changes in Number, 1957–1962

CLASS OF LOCAL GOVERNMENTS	NUMBER IN SMSA'S, 1962	PERCENTAGE OF SMSA TOTAL	INCREASE OR DECREASE IN NUMBER, 1957–1962	PERCENTAGE CHANGE IN NUMBER, 1957–1962
All local governments	18,442	100.0	458	3
School districts	6,004	32.5	−1,482	−20
Special districts	5,411	29.3	1,675[a]	45
Municipalities	4,142	22.5	298	8
Towns and townships	2,575	14.0	−32	−1
Counties	310	1.7	−1	−0.32

[a] This increase is due partly to the reclassification by the Bureau of the Census of a number of entities, principally municipal authorities in Pennsylvania, considered dependent agencies in 1957 to the status of independent governments in 1962. Much of the growth, however, resulted from the creation of new governments.
SOURCE: U.S. Bureau of the Census, *Census of Governments: 1962*, Vol. I, *Governmental Organization* (Washington: 1963), p. 11.

Small Populations and Areas

A primary contributor to the abundance of local governments in the metropolis is the smallness of many of the units. This characteristic is highly pronounced among many municipalities, school

districts, and non-school special districts, and it is well pointed up
by their population and territorial size. About one-half of the municipalities in SMSA's have fewer than 2500 inhabitants, containing

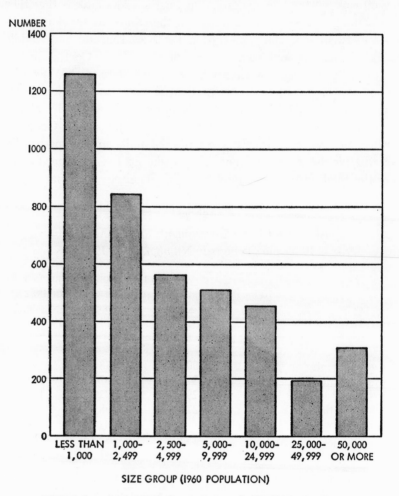

Figure 6.3   Municipal Governments in SMSA's, by Population Size, 1962. Source: U.S. Bureau of the Census,
Census of Governments: 1962, Vol. I, p. 24.

in total less than 2 percent of the metropolitan population. In addition, many of these lightly populated units have territories that cover
less than three square miles and therefore constitute simply minuscule
segments of the metropolitan land. Similarly, many school districts

in the metropolis are small in population and territory. More than
two-fifths of them (2638 or 44 percent) have fewer than 300 students, including more than 100 with as few as fifty students and
about 900 which do not directly provide public education but

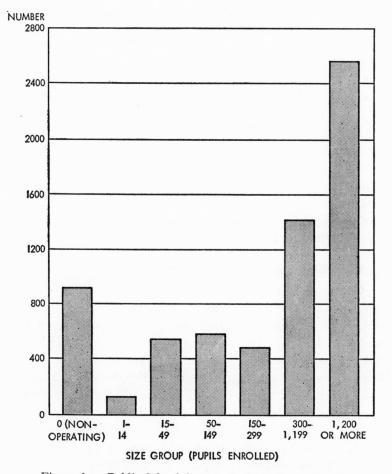

Figure 6.4   Public School Systems in SMSA's, by Enrollment Size, 1962. Public schools systems consist of both
independent school districts and school operations that are
dependent agencies of other local or state governments.
School districts make up almost 97 percent (6004 of 6605)
of the total number of school systems in metropolitan
areas. Source: U.S. Bureau of the Census, *Census of
Governments: 1962*, Vol. I, p. 24.

instead transport students to the schools of other systems. Many school districts have a very small area; in fact, they often cover less land than is contained within municipalities. And the picture is much the same for numerous special districts. Many contain a very small number of residents, less than a hundred in some instances, and an extremely small amount of land, at times as little as a fraction of a square mile.

People frequently think of metropolitan areas as characterized by many forms of giantism. There are, it is true, some giants among their local governments—counties larger in area than certain states, cities of hundreds of thousands or millions of people, of hundreds of square miles of territory, and of annual budgets that range from hundreds of thousands of dollars to more than three billion dollars in New York City, school districts of tens of thousands of students and of areas frequently larger than those of the biggest cities, and special districts that stretch over and beyond entire metropolitan areas. But these big local governments are the exception rather than the rule. Gargantuan governments exist, but standing among them are far more governmental Lilliputians.

Territorial Overlapping

Government in metropolitan areas is also complex because so many units have overlapping boundaries. In most SMSA's a county overlies the boundaries of numerous municipalities. So also in a number of instances, townships spread over municipal limits and represent another layer, a third tier, as it were, of local government. However, the greatest perpetrators of overlapping jurisdictions are school districts and special districts, particularly the latter. No unit of any other class can have part or all of the same territory as any other government of that class. Thus, two municipalities cannot include any of the same territory, although, as we have seen, a municipality can encompass a portion (or in rare cases even all) of the same territory as a county. This mutual territorial exclusiveness is not the situation with school districts and special districts. A school district providing high school education is frequently superimposed upon one or more school districts furnishing elementary education. Similarly, a number of special districts, sometimes as many as five to eight different functional types, are at times piled upon part or all of the territory of one another and of two or more school districts, a county, a city, and even a township.

A section of a metropolitan area, therefore, generally has layer upon layer of local government, anywhere from three to a dozen or so. Its collection of governments is jungle-like in appearance (and frequently as difficult to fathom), resembling not only a crowded bus but also a stack of pancakes. Moreover, the stack is in disarray, as most of these overlapping units do not have coterminous jurisdictions. Customarily their boundaries cover merely a portion of the same land, not all of it. Some have larger territories than others and some have smaller areas; few indeed have identical geographical limits.

Such governmental stacking is repeated in varying degrees in all sections. Since most local governments are small in territorial size, they individually occupy only a minor portion of a metropolitan area. Few of them, most often a county or a special district, encompass the territory of an entire SMSA. In fact, in many metropolitan communities no local government is area-wide. As a result, the governmental pattern of a metropolis typically consists of many adjoining but uneven stacks of overlapping units, with few, if any, local public agencies covering the whole area.

THE ORIGINAL GOVERNMENTAL SYSTEM

The system of local government laid out originally by each state in its constitution and legislation, usually in either the late eighteenth century or the nineteenth century, was fairly simple in design and reasonably understandable. Moreover, each class of local governments in the system was assigned responsibilities wholly or largely unique to it.

Three General Classes

On a national basis, counties, municipalities, and school districts were initially the classes most commonly set up to form the local governmental system of a state. Counties were created to serve two kinds of purposes. They were to aid the state government in carrying out some of its obligations, such as assisting judges of the state court system, conducting elections, and recording legal documents, and they were to provide services to the residents of rural areas, such as building farm roads and keeping the peace. Because of their responsibilities to the state government, the entire state was usually divided into counties.

On the other hand, municipalities were organized to be the suppliers of local services—fire protection, law enforcement, public works, and the like—to the inhabitants of urban settlements. Municipalities therefore were to include only a small portion of the territory of a state. School districts originated as a separate class for a different reason. They were established as independent units mainly because of the strong conviction that public education was so important it should have its own local financing and should be free of the politics of other local governments. (Public schools had been parts of the operations of general local units in colonial America, and today in some states they are not operated or financed by districts but by other governments.) In various states, from the early years of their statehood, school districts were formed in settled portions where youngsters lived. Such units were kept small in territorial size since youngsters of a "bus- and car-free" society had to travel to school on foot or by horse.

Two Regional Classes

The two important regional exceptions to the original commonly established system of local government deserve consideration here. One is the town; the other, the township. The former, most prevalent in New England (and not to be confused with a similarly named type of local government of another class—the town as a type of municipality—existing in a number of other states), originated in colonial days and is still a vigorous government. In the colonial era, settlements in New England, which were called towns, took a compact, small form because the land was densely wooded and represented both a barrier to developing agricultural lands over a large area and a threat to the inhabitants from Indians and animals. Towns grew up around the church, the public meeting place, and the fort or stockade and included the residents' agricultural fields. From the beginning, therefore, these units were natural, real communities, based on social groupings or concentrations of people, conforming to geographical features, and usually containing both urban (initially mostly village centers) and rural territory.

As the population increased and the need for protection declined, other towns were established by dividing old ones or organizing new ones in the recently settled land; eventually towns contained most of the territory of the six New England states. Only occasionally was a heavily populated center detached from a town and organized as a municipality. Boston, Providence, Worcester, Springfield, Bridgeport, and Portland are prominent current examples. Accordingly, as some towns became thickly populated, they took on all the functions handled elsewhere by municipalities. Also, since they included most of the state's territory, towns in New England were assigned many activities carried on by counties in other states. (Counties were established as units of government in New England, but were never significant.)

Townships, most evident in the North Central region, generally followed a different and less successful course of development. From their creation, most of them were highly artificial governmental areas, since their original boundaries were marked out in rectangular fashion by federal surveyors while the land was still part of the national domain. Although attempting to imitate New England towns as institutions of local self-government, many townships were doomed to early oblivion, for several reasons: the aforementioned artificiality of their areas; the early and continued widespread practice of separating both large and small urban centers from the authority of townships, thereby sharply diminishing their financial resources; and the dispersed nature of farm settlement in many states that adopted township organization.

In the early years as well as now, the functions of most townships have been restricted in number and minor in nature and consequently many states never established them as a class of local governments. Generally, however, townships, once created, have tenaciously withstood efforts to eliminate them. Today, obsolete as most of them are, they continue to perform a few functions and to levy taxes in various metropolitan areas.

Few Non-School Special Districts

When the states, even those created during the late nineteenth and early twentieth centuries, formulated their original systems of local government, a present-day significant element was conspicuously absent—non-school special districts. Legal provision certainly seemed to have been made for enough types of local agencies to provide capably for necessary public services. The system, moreover, seemed to be sufficiently adjustable to future needs. Some people may have thought that from time to time unique circumstances might make necessary the occasional formation of a special non-school unit. But no state foresaw the development of a widespread demand for the legal means of establishing a multitude of such districts, which in total would undertake such a broad range of activities. Scattered uses were made of them before the current century—one, for example, being organized in the Philadelphia area as early as 1790. However, the extensive activation of these districts to the point where they became an important part of the nationwide local governmental system is primarily a phenomenon of the twentieth century, particularly since the 1930s.

EVOLUTION OF THE GOVERNMENTAL PATTERN

A tremendous transformation has occurred in the governmental pattern of most areas as they have proceeded from early urbanization to metropolitanization. At the time of the former, they were sparsely populated, compact, and composed of largely self-contained communities. By the time they had become metropolitan (a stage sometimes reached by different areas in widely separated years), they were far more densely populated, considerably larger in territorial size, and each of them had developed highly interdependent and interacting parts. In this transitional span, their governmental system changed from a simple and rational arrangement of relatively few units to a complicated and improvised hodgepodge of numerous units (many having considerable functional similarity) and of much governmental pyramiding.

A portrayal of the evolution of the governmental situation from the era of early urbanization to the age of metropolitanization is revealing. What was the governmental pattern in an area like before it became metropolitan? How did it become more complex? What is it like now? Let us take a typical metropolis of today, look at its governmental pattern in earlier years, and then broadly trace what has happened.

Early Urbanization

In its early years, an area that is now metropolitan contained only a few municipalities (or if in New England a few towns or a combination of a few cities and towns), which were then easily the most important local governments. For the most part these units were separated from one another by large expanses of rural land, ten to twenty miles or more in length. Each municipality, embracing a small amount of territory, was in large measure self-sufficient in its economic, social, and governmental activities. All land development of an urban nature was within municipal (or town) limits. A county government overlaid both the rural and urban portions of the area, furnishing certain services to all residents of the county and certain others to the inhabitants of its rural portions. School districts were the most numerous units, as the drive got under way early to have a separate government for each school. If the area was in the North Central region, it also might have townships performing a few functions, predominantly in the rural sections. Other special districts did not exist or were present in only a few instances.

Period of Growing Urbanization

As urbanization began to intensify, the result of scientific and technological gains and population growth, the governmental pattern began to undergo a metamorphosis, although initially somewhat slowly. For awhile, the local governmental system seemed to be keeping pace with the changes. Many municipalities experienced substantial increases in population and enlarged their territorial size by annexing adjoining land to accommodate the growth. Some new municipalities sprang up through use of the incorporation process, but usually they were not numerous. As these annexation and incorporation developments occurred, the amount of space between incorporated places in the area lessened.

During this period, the county may have been divided into two or more counties in response to the demands for certain services at close range. Even in the Rocky Mountain and far western regions where the original counties were usually much larger in territory than in the eastern and midwestern parts of the nation, counties were frequently divided as the population grew. For instance, California, which was admitted as a state in 1850, promptly established twenty-seven counties. Little more than a half century later it had fifty-eight, counting the city-county of San Francisco, a number that has since remained the same. Towns in New England were exhibiting great durability, partly because they were playing the functional role handled elsewhere by counties. In the North Central region, many townships were declining in importance because some of their sections had become highly urban and had been removed from the township through annexation to an existing municipality or incorporation as a new municipal unit.

Many new schools were built, causing the creation of numerous school districts in recently developed land and the division of many long established districts into separate and independent operations. An increasing number of special districts sprouted. (Special districts are so called because each of them supplies only one or a very limited number of functions, thus serving a special purpose.) They grew as the older general units failed to be sufficiently adaptable, or as supposedly quick and adequate answers to immediate or deeply rooted problems were sought.

The Metropolitan Age

An an area became metropolitan in population and in such social and economic characteristics as interdependence and specialization, its governmental pattern usually exhibited increasing complexity and improvisation.[2] By this time, the pattern bore only slight resemblance to the system as originally conceived in a pre-metropolitan period for non-metropolitan conditions. Although demonstrating some ability to adjust to changing circumstances, the system had not been sufficiently flexible, nor had it been intelligently reformulated in a conscious and comprehensive manner. Its high degree of rigidity had caused odd-looking patches to be added to the governmental quilt. The lack of an intelligent reformulation had resulted in plugs of adjustment being inserted in the metropolitan wall to avoid successive waves of disasters.

Municipalities. With the arrival of the metropolitan age, municipalities greatly increased in number and the boundaries of many of them came to border one another. In brief, this increase was largely the product of policies that deliberately made many state annexation laws more difficult while keeping the incorporation procedures outlandishly easy. As a consequence, long established municipalities often could no longer sufficiently enlarge their territorial limits to encompass all the additional urban population. Concurrently, new municipalities were frequently created, many times at the very

[2] The principal nongovernmental aspects of metropolitan development are considered in the section on metropolitan characteristics in Chapter 2.

borders of the largest city and other major population centers in the area.

The countryside formerly separating cities and villages had become metropolitan in its social and economic characteristics and much of it was carved into a large number of incorporated units. Although metropolitan in nature, not all of this land was within the boundaries of any municipality. A stiffening of annexation laws often left the residents or property owners of a newly developed section free to incorporate the land as a separate municipality or to leave it unincorporated. And many people made and have stood by the latter choice. As a result, municipal governments do not now contain all urban land and population within their jurisdictions; in fact, about one-fourth of all metropolitan residents currently live in unincorporated territory, much of which is distinctly urbanized. Other local governments—for instance, many counties and special districts —have adjusted or have been established to satisfy the most pressing city-type needs of unincorporated urban residents—and both developments have at times met bitter opposition from municipal officials and inhabitants. Furthermore, some types of local governments, again many counties and special districts and even some townships, have become functionally similar to municipalities, thereby destroying the original concept of a system of local governments in which each class was to serve different purposes. Functional as well as territorial overlapping of local units thus became common in the metropolitan period.

A considerable upsurge in municipal annexation has taken place in the post-World War II years. In large part, however, its usefulness has been confined to the absorption of neighboring unincorporated urban fringe areas, many of which had developed serious service and regulatory deficiencies having repercussions both locally and elsewhere in the metropolis. In the meantime, many of the largest cities have become substantially or completely hemmed in by other municipalities and have found annexation to be of little or no value. And there have been few instances where two or more municipalities have consolidated or merged into a single unit.

Counties, Towns, and Townships. In the metropolitan age, the number and consequently the areas of counties have remained virtually unchanged. Similarly, towns, especially in New England,

have shown great staying power; they have changed little in number
or territorial size.

In contrast, townships generally have developed into inconsequential units, performing simply a few minor functions and often
stripped of much of their financial resources through loss of their
wealthier sections as a result of incorporation or annexation. They
have become so unimportant that some of them have been eliminated, but many others still exist although for no justifiable reason.
A countertrend has appeared, however, in the metropolitan areas of
a few states where townships have been assigned some urban functions.

School and Other Districts. The lone important simplification
of the governmental pattern of various areas during their metropolitan period has involved school districts. Abandonment of the
longtime practice in cities of having as many school districts as
schools has contributed substantially to this development. Many
small elementary districts have merged, as have many high school
districts. This has reduced the number of districts and increased
the size of the service areas of the consolidated units. Also, on frequent occasions a number of elementary districts have merged with
a high school district into a unified operation, offering education
from kindergarten through the twelfth grade and at times expanding
the program through the junior college years. Consolidations of this
type have further decreased the number of districts and have made
the service area identical for elementary and secondary instruction
(and for junior college instruction as well when the range of academic
work has been enlarged).

The extent of school district consolidation in metropolitan areas
is encouraging, particularly in view of the fact that no similar development has taken place in any other type of local government.
The magnitude of the movement so far can nevertheless be easily
exaggerated since school districts were so numerous until recent years
that despite the substantial numerical reduction, they still remain
the most prevalent governmental unit in the urban areas. Although
more consolidation is needed in the metropolis, the movement there
continues to lag behind the rate of progress in rural areas. Also, even
though consolidated, a school district frequently still has boundaries
that differ from those of the municipality. In some instances, this
is the result of the consolidation covering an area larger than that

of the municipality in order to bring the residents of unincorporated urban fringe areas into the school system. In other cases, however, the difference in boundaries develops from planned action by professional educators and school board members who apparently fear the eventual merger of school and municipal governments if their boundaries are made coterminous.

Spreading with the swiftness of a brush fire, non-school special districts are largely the product of the metropolitan era. Most of these districts operating in the metropolis cover only a portion, often merely a tiny fraction, of its territory. They may include only a small amount of unincorporated urban land (a very large number are of this type) or simply the area of a municipality (true of many housing authorities) or a combination of parts or all of certain unincorporated land and a municipality. A relatively few encompass the entire SMSA or operate facilities, such as mass transit, airports, or ports, that are vital to the well-being of the metropolitan residents as well as to many people living elsewhere. Because of the scope of the area they serve, districts of this last group often function as the closest approximations to a metropolitan government. Moreover, unlike any other local units, a limited number of districts are interstate in territorial jurisdiction.

GOVERNMENTAL ADJUSTMENTS IN THE METROPOLITAN AGE

How have governments adjusted to the metropolitan age? Has there been much or little adaptation in the functions, organization, and finances of local governments? Have some changed more than others? What roles have been assumed by the state and national governments? Our previous discussion of the evolution of the governmental pattern from early urbanization to metropolitanization dealt chiefly with the expansion or contraction of the number and the territory of the respective local units. But other important adjustments, or the lack of them, have also been apparent and deserve analysis.

Counties

Functions. The most pronounced general change in county governments in the metropolis has been the large-scale expansion of their functions, particularly those normally associated with municipal governments. This enlargement has involved both the performance of some older functions at more intensified levels and the assumption of new activities. Numerous counties in urban areas, for example, have greatly broadened their public health services to combat communicable diseases, epidemics, and unsanitary practices, and their social welfare programs to provide greater assistance to dependent children, the needy, the aged, and the blind. They have also launched into such new activities as developing and maintaining airports, building and operating public hospitals, installing sewers and constructing and operating sewage disposal facilities, and establishing and staffing large park and recreation areas. A number of counties have also grown functionally by making contractual agreements with municipalities to perform certain services for them, such as tax assessment or collection.

The largest proportions of county money are spent on roads and streets, social welfare programs, and hospitals and public health. Occasionally a county in a metropolis provides the local financing of or operates the public schools; when it does, educational activities usually stand first among its expenditures.

Organization. The organizational structure of most county governments in the metropolis has not kept pace with their functional changes. In fact, two basic features have generally remained unaltered since counties were first established. One, most of them still elect a long list of administrative officials, many of whom should logically be appointed because they perform either duties calling for considerable training and skill (the coroner, for example) or duties of a routine and clerical nature (such as the clerk and the recorder or registrar of deeds). Two, few counties have a chief executive, either elective or appointive. Instead, the county governing body, variously called the board of commissioners or supervisors or the county court, has both administrative and legislative responsibilities. The combination of these two organizational features usually results in uncoordinated and undirected performance. Their prevalence constitutes a major stumbling block to public confidence in proposals to bestow increased functional assignments on counties and for the reconstitution of counties into metropolitan governments.

Several important developments in county administration and structure, however, have taken place in recent decades. Generally, as counties have taken on new functions and intensified certain old ones, department heads with professional qualifications have been appointed and made responsible to the county governing body or to a separate board appointed by that body. Public welfare directors and hospital directors are illustrations. Although this procedure does nothing to reduce the large number of elected officials, it does place significant functions and an increased proportion of county activities under the immediate supervision of persons with professional training and experience. Moreover, in some counties employees have been placed under a merit system of appointment and removal. In certain instances, the merit principle has been made applicable only to the public welfare department, an action taken in order to qualify the county for state and federal welfare aid. In others, the principle is in use in many or all departments. When it has been employed extensively, it has done much to wipe out the image of the county government as a center of unsavory politics and the tool of the "courthouse gang," to use the term customarily applied to the dominant clique of county officials.

A limited number of counties have adopted one or both of two other actions that significantly affect the administration and processes of their government and which run counter to the prevailing practices criticized earlier. One is a substantial reduction in the number of elected county officials; the other is the establishment of the position of chief executive. An outstanding example of the former is Los Angeles County, now the most populous in the nation. In 1912 the number of elected officials in the county government, other than the board of supervisors, was reduced to three: the assessor, district attorney, and sheriff. This highly integrated system has remained in effect ever since. Much later, in 1951, Santa Clara County, which is coterminous with the San Jose SMSA, adopted a similar plan. And a few counties (mostly urban) in other states have followed comparable courses of action.

The establishment of a chief executive has taken two directions: election by the voters or appointment by the county governing body. Prominent examples of elected county executives in metropolitan areas are found in Erie County (Buffalo); Nassau, Suffolk, and Westchester counties (all in the New York area); Baltimore County; St. Louis County (Missouri); Milwaukee County; Cook County (Chicago); and Davidson County (Nashville, Tennessee). Practically all elected county executives, or county mayors as they are frequently called, work in metropolitan areas.

Appointed county executives, commonly known as managers, who function in metropolitan counties include those in Dade County

(Miami, Florida); Monroe County (Rochester, New York); Fulton County (Atlanta, Georgia); Sacramento County (Sacramento, California); Santa Clara County (the San Jose, California, area); and Fairfax County, Virginia (the Washington, D.C., area). There are more county managers—a total of twenty-seven—than county mayors, but a larger proportion of the former are in non-metropolitan counties. County managers, as well as most county mayors, have the authority to appoint and remove many department heads.

Appointment and removal power is not granted to another type of management official, who represents a modification of the county manager system. Usually carrying the title of chief administrative officer (CAO) or county administrator, this official is an appointee of the county governing body and its agent in carrying out a number of its responsibilities. To bring about adequate coordination and overall direction, this individual must largely depend upon his role in preparing and administering the proposed budget and his ability to build effective informal working relations with department heads, many of whom are often elected officials. The CAO arrangement has been widely but not exclusively used in California, where in some cases, as in Los Angeles and San Diego counties, it has produced many administrative improvements. In that state virtually every metropolitan county that does not have a county manager has a chief administrative officer.

Finances. A major problem confronting counties is the continued heavy reliance on property levies, largely on real estate such as land, buildings, and other permanent improvements.[3] Property taxes make up more than nine-tenths of all the tax revenue obtained directly by counties and almost one-half of their total revenue. Counties clearly have a very restricted local tax base, a product of often long-standing state legislative and constitutional limitations prohibiting a diversification of county taxation.

The predicament of counties resulting from their extensive dependence on the property tax is further compounded by the fact that most other local governments in the same area also rely on taxing the same property for a significant part of their revenue. The total local property tax therefore is considerable and generally has spiraled upward unceasingly. This development has produced in-

---

[3] Only selected aspects of finances in relation to the degree of adaptation in the metropolitan era are discussed in this chapter. Public finance in the metropolis receives much fuller consideration in Chapter 12.

creased taxpayer discontent about counties and other local units and has caused considerable concern by public officials, who must stand periodically for re-election. Accordingly, even though the total revenue received by counties from various sources, including the property tax, has been advancing in recent years, a continued growth of services by county governments in metropolitan areas will require a broadening of their tax base into non-property fields if trouble is to be averted.

The county in the metropolis frequently faces another problem of finance. It is normally required by state legal provisions to have a uniform rate of property taxation throughout its jurisdiction, and is therefore prevented, except in a small number of states, from setting up special taxing areas in portions of its territory where additional service beyond the substantially uniform countywide level is needed or requested. On the other hand, if a county working under the requirement of financial uniformity does provide some additional service like intensified law enforcement to an unincorporated area, city people may claim this practice results in financial inequity to them. They may say they are taxed twice for municipal services, once by their city government and a second time by the county government to provide municipal-type service to the unincorporated section. In these situations, the county is truly caught on the horns of a dilemma growing out of the financial inflexibility imposed upon it.

In sum, the adjustment of the county to metropolitan growth has primarily involved the expansion of functions. Generally the county has at most insufficiently adjusted its organization, which still is of a ramshackle nature, and it frequently has not modernized its personnel practices to an adequate degree if at all. And finally its finances, both as to local sources and uniformity, plague its efforts to become a more important, or even the most important, local government in the metropolis.

Municipalities

Functions. Municipalities have undergone broader changes than counties in response to metropolitan conditions. Like many counties, a number of them, especially those of large or medium size, have experienced much functional expansion. Sometimes this has involved intensification of older functions: for example, the development of extensive public works systems of streets and street lights, water and sanitary sewers, storm drainage, and traffic signals; the modernization of law enforcement operations; and the enlargement of fire services to include fire prevention as well as fire fighting. In other instances, the expansion of functions has meant the addition of new activities, including airport and auditorium construction and management, purchase and operation of mass transit systems, establishment of recreational facilities and programs for people of all ages, the building and staffing of public hospitals, and urban redevelopment projects. Many older municipal functions have thus moved from a simple to a technical and complex stage while many new services have been added.

But broad functional expansion has not been the pattern in all municipalities. The continued ease of incorporating an area as a city or village has resulted in the creation of many incorporated places in the metropolis that are small in both population and financial resources. The public activities of these units are narrow in range and of an elementary level. A number of them, for instance, do not even have round-the-clock law enforcement nor fire protection except by volunteer fire forces whose members are likely to be found working in other communities in the daytime. Some of them, in fact, have a smaller range and a lower level of services than are received by unincorporated urban areas in other counties. Although the impact, most frequently detrimental in character, of these units on the total area is undeniable, these governments are not in the mainstream of many municipal adjustments characteristic of the metropolitan age.

Municipalities devote the largest proportions of their money to streets, law enforcement, fire protection, sewage and refuse disposal, and public hospitals. A limited number supply the local financing of or manage the local public schools; in many such instances the outlay for education is their top-ranking expenditure.

Organization. Widespread changes have materialized in municipal organization, administration, and processes. Many cities and villages have converted to an integrated structure by reducing the number of elected officials so that the governing body members alone or in combination with the mayor are the only elective officers, decreasing the use of administrative boards or eliminating them entirely, and establishing a strong chief executive. In addition, as municipal activities have become more technical and complex, the

THREE FORMS OF CITY GOVERNMENT

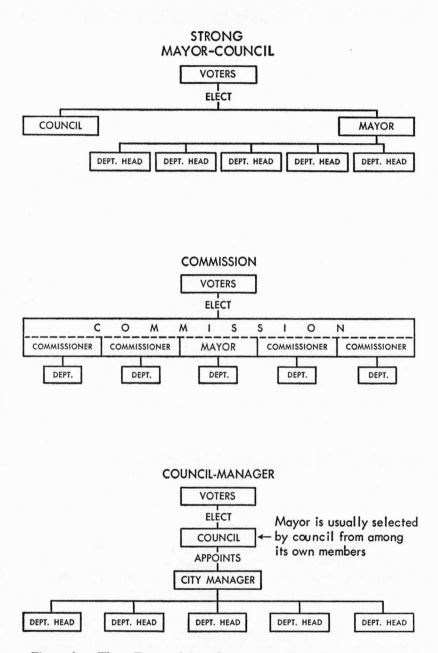

Figure 6.5 Three Forms of City Government. From Peter H. Odegard and Hans H. Baerwald, *The American Republic,* Harper & Row, 1964, p. 654.

personnel staffing them usually has grown in professionalization and has increasingly been placed under a merit system of selection.

In many cities the concept of a strong chief executive has supplanted either of two other systems. One is the long discredited but still frequently used weak mayor-council organization, an arrangement which generally means dominance by the council or by independent administrative boards. The other is the commission plan, which features a small governing board whose members serve collectively as the legislature and individually as heads of the principal departments. This plan experienced considerable popularity—and in some cases overly enthusiastic claims—in the very early decades of the present century, but its use has been constantly declining since 1920. Although offering more integration than the weak mayor-council form, it provided inadequate coordination, insufficient internal control, and amateur direction of administration.

The council-manager plan has been the more widely adopted strong executive form and its two major features have been followed without significant deviation by most municipalities. The first is an elected council of small size, which serves as the legislative body. The second is a manager, appointed by the council, who directs and supervises the administrative departments, appoints and removes their heads, prepares the budget for the council's consideration and administers it after adoption, and makes reports and recommendations to the council at its request or on his own initiative. (Unlike school superintendents in many localities, a manager seldom has a contract, and therefore may be removed by the council at any time.) Generally the mayor in a council-manager community is selected by the council from its own membership and his only additional authority is to preside at council meetings and to sign certain legal papers on behalf of the city.

The city manager idea, first used in Staunton, Virginia, in 1908, received nationwide attention six years later when Dayton, Ohio, became the first sizable city to put the council-manager plan into effect.[4] Subsequently the plan had a steady but not spectacular

---

[4] The distinction of being the first council-manager city is disputed. Staunton was the first to employ the city manager idea and its initial incumbent in the office, Charles E. Ashburner, is recognized as the first city manager in the United States. However, Staunton attached the office of manager to a bicameral council structure. In 1912, Sumter, South Carolina, adopted the council-manager plan in the form that has generally been followed in later years—one featuring a small unicameral council.

growth until after World War II. At that time the councils in many municipalities were confronted with a lengthy list of deferred services and improvements that had backlogged since the depression and recession years of the 1930s. It became increasingly apparent to them that professional assistance was needed for the important tasks at hand. The answer in many cases was adoption of the council-manager form of government, which has grown rapidly since then. The plan has been especially attractive to small and medium-sized localities, many of them suburbs in the metropolis, but it has not generally caught hold in the large cities. Approximately 600 council-manager operations, more than one-third of the national total, are in metropolitan areas, the overwhelming number in the suburbs. The proportion is particularly impressive since many municipalities in the metropolis are extremely small in population and either do not have enough services to feel a need for the plan or have decided they cannot afford the salary of a manager. Some observers contend that two factors have motivated widespread adoption of council-manager government in the suburbs. One, the leaders of the community are from the business world and consider this governmental form analogous to business organization. Two, these leaders want to keep or make their municipal government "non-political" in contrast to their view of the "political" environment of the central city.

Many analysts are convinced that council-manager government usually has improved the tone, quality, and accomplishments of municipal affairs. But increasingly in recent years the criticism of inadequate elective political leadership has been raised and the claim made that many managers have been filling the void left by the council.[5] So far, however, there has been no noticeable groundswell

[5] There is a growing literature on the city manager in relation to policy and political leadership. See, for example, Clarence E. Ridley, *The Role of the City Manager in Policy Formulation* (Chicago: International City Managers' Association, 1958); Gladys M. Kammerer, Charles D. Farris, John M. De Grove, and Alfred B. Clubock, *City Managers in Politics* (Gainesville: University of Florida Social Science Monographs, 1962); John C. Bollens, *Appointed Executive Local Government* (Los Angeles: Haynes Foundation, 1952); C. A. Harrell and D. G. Weiford, "The City Manager and the Policy Process," *Public Administration Review*, 19 (Spring, 1959), 101–107; and Karl A. Bosworth, "The Manager Is a Politician," *Public Administration Review*, 18 (Summer, 1958), 216–222. For appraisals by managers and councilmen of one another, see Jeptha J. Carrell, *The Role of the City Manager: Views of Councilmen and Managers* (Kansas City, Missouri: Community Studies, Inc., 1962).

of interest in adding an independently elected mayor with assigned
policy responsibilities to more council-manager operations or to replacing this governmental form with the strong mayor-council system.

The strong mayor-council plan is the second form that the strong
executive concept has taken. This arrangement is characterized by a
mayor who has significant personnel, financial, and general administrative powers and the authority to veto legislative actions of the
council. He also possesses the means of being a policy-making and
thus political leader as exemplified by his role in enunciating new
or extended municipal programs to the council and to the public
through the mass media and frequently by his stature in a nationwide political party. The strong mayor-council form has firm footing
in many large metropolitan central cities, particularly those of more
than 250,000 population. (However, not all large cities have such
a structure; Los Angeles and Minneapolis are two that fall into the
weak mayor-council category.) Other than occasional outcries in
some cities about political machinations, the principal complaint
against this form has been that despite the mayor's strength in the
policy field, he often is disinterested in and therefore neglectful
of the administrative side of city business. To remedy what was a
genuine defect in various instances, a number of strong mayor-council municipalities have established, notably in the 1950s, a general
management position, variously titled city administrator, city administrative officer, and managing director. The post is staffed by a
professional administrator appointed by and usually accountable
solely to the mayor. His function is to relieve the chief executive
of much administrative detail and to leave him free to devote his
time to policy formulation and political leadership. In contrast, in
council-manager government the manager is appointed by and responsible to the lawmaking body. He generally has a broader grant
of authority than the administrative officer under the mayor.[6]

Finances. Municipalities have the most diversified local tax
base of all local governments. Although deriving considerable money
from property taxes—far more than counties do, for example—they

[6] A clash of views about whether the city administrator idea or the
council-manager plan is more appropriate for large cities is found in Wallace
S. Sayre, "The General Manager Idea for Large Cities," *Public Administration
Review*, 14 (Autumn, 1954), 253–257, and John E. Bebout, "Management for
Large Cities," *Public Administration Review*, 15 (Summer, 1955), 188–195.

depend on this source for a smaller proportion of their tax revenue than does any other type of local unit, a proportion which nevertheless represents more than 70 percent of their locally-derived revenue, thus indicating the burdensome nature of this form of taxation. Cities in various states have obtained adoption of state laws or constitutional amendments that permit them to levy a number of non-property taxes, such as sales and income taxes, but tax diversification has usually come only after a long, hard struggle. As the result of this success, some municipalities can tap a wide range of sources, often at a fairly high rate.

Relatively few metropolitan municipalities are free of financial problems, however. In some states they have not gained a diversified local tax structure, and in others where liberalized legislative and constitutional authorizations exist, many cities and villages consist of residential properties of low value, little or no commercial and industrial development, and low-income residents. Obviously such places have inadequate financial capabilities and should not have been permitted to incorporate as municipalities. Nonetheless, they almost invariably resist attempts to consolidate with other municipal units, or the latter are uninterested in doing so because of the financial burden that would have to be assumed.

Not only the poorer suburbs but many central cities as well encounter financial problems. One reason is that many people who work in the core municipality are not residents and consequently they generally contribute little to its tax revenue despite using its facilities and services. Another reason is that central cities are increasingly becoming the places of residence for persons of low income; while individuals in this category contribute little to municipal revenue, a number of them cause considerable increases in expenditures for various services, including law enforcement and public health. The situation involving the nonresident worker has been partially relieved in some central cities by a payroll tax, but the problem centering on the low-income resident continues to perplex their public and private leaders.

Towns and Townships

New England towns have adjusted to the metropolitan age in two significant ways: taking on a number of municipal-type functions and in many cases appointing a town manager (a development especially widespread in Maine), who as a professional administrator has been assigned management responsibilities. The first trend—increased functions of the municipal type—is also evident in differing degrees in a number of New York and Wisconsin towns and Michigan, New Jersey, and Pennsylvania townships. In many cases, however, the scope and intensity of town and township services are considerably lower than the service levels of municipalities in the same metropolitan areas. As a group, towns and townships in these New England, Middle Atlantic, and North Central states spend the largest shares of their money on roads, law enforcement, sewers and sewage and refuse disposal, and social welfare services. In addition, New England towns operating school systems spend large shares of their money, at times their largest portion, on education. The second trend—establishment of a general management position—is limited among towns and townships outside New England to certain New Jersey and Pennsylvania townships.

Townships in ten other states—Illinois, Indiana, Kansas, Minnesota, Missouri, Nebraska, North Dakota, Ohio, South Dakota, and Washington—are largely useless relics of a bygone day. They perform only a few functions of a highly restricted nature, such as maintaining minor roads and some limited phases of social welfare. They continue to exist in these states because they provide sinecures for various township officials and because residents in some areas cling tenaciously to these units to obviate the need for municipal government. There is an additional factor that entrenches them in certain metropolitan areas in Illinois (as well as in a few other states such as Michigan, New Jersey, and Wisconsin where they are more active units): individuals elected as township supervisors to be members of the township governing body become ex officio members of the county governing body. Since townships therefore are also election areas for county representation, their elimination is even more difficult to obtain.[7] In local taxation, towns and townships are almost universally confined to property taxes.

---

[7] The Wisconsin Supreme Court recently ruled that representation on county governing boards, as in state legislatures, must be apportioned on the basis of population. This decision could do much to reduce further the viability of townships.

School Districts

School districts, which in most states are the exclusive or chief supplier of public education through at least high school, have been undergoing many changes and problems. A continually growing demand for education, caused by a larger birth rate, a lower incidence of infant mortality, and a greater recognition of the value of learning, understanding, and skills in an increasingly complex world, has produced vastly expanded educational offerings and much revision of programs. It has also resulted in shortages of buildings, equipment, teachers, and administrators. And in recent years, school dropouts have become recognized as a critical problem because of society's higher educational standards and the lessening demand for unskilled workers. Many districts also have had to reassess their policies with respect to the provision of equal opportunities for all persons, regardless of racial or ethnic background. Both teaching and administrative personnel have become more professional in training and outlook and an increasing number of school superintendents, the top administrators in the system, have become the highest paid of all local public officials and very powerful forces in the metropolis.

Amid great change school districts have experienced severe financial strains, particularly in terms of local financing. They obtain a larger proportion (almost 99 percent) of their tax revenue and a larger amount of money from the property tax than any other governments. Only in a few states—Pennsylvania is a prominent example—do they have access to significant local non-property tax sources.

The narrow local tax base of school districts has had important repercussions. It has compelled many to turn repeatedly to the local voters for approval of special levies above the state-imposed limits and these proposals have frequently been defeated. Accordingly, a number of them have submitted the same tax proposition two or three times in quick succession, a practice bringing strong protests from opponents of the levy. The same cycle of events has developed in many efforts to obtain popular approval of school construction bond issues, a method used very extensively because a narrow tax base and the amount of need preclude pay-as-you-go financing. Furthermore, since they frequently require an extraordinary majority vote, bond issues are often difficult to pass.

Another important result of the narrow tax base has been increased reliance on state financial assistance. In 1927, for example, state grants and other payments made up less than one-seventh of all local general expenditure for public schools; by 1962, state financial participation amounted to more than one-third of the total. Moreover, numerous states have not limited their interest in school districts and other public school systems to increased financial support. For about thirty years they have imposed a growing volume of state regulation and control over the services, curriculum, and administration of public schools. Also, through school consolidation plans and mandatory reorganization legislation, some state governments have even affected the existence of certain school districts as separate entities. A number of these various actions have been tied into state grants.

Non-School Special Districts

Non-school special districts, which may be called the fifty-seven varieties of government and the new dark continent of American politics, individually are often pygmies, but they add up to a growing and frequently mysterious giant. Separately, they seldom provide more than one function or two closely related services, such as water supply and sewage disposal or water and fire protection. But collectively, they perform a very wide range of functions, one far more extensive than some other governments in the metropolis such as many townships and small municipalities. In addition, even the largest cities and counties undertake few activities that are not also carried out by districts. Basically, however, the responsibility of districts is to supply a service rather than to provide regulation, such as land use control. Thus the most frequent functions of these agencies are fire protection, water supply, sewage disposal, housing, and various phases of protecting natural resources, such as flood control.

Unlike other local governments, many districts do not have the taxing power. In fact, non-school special districts as a group are the only class of local governments not obtaining most of its locally-derived revenue from taxes. More than three-fourths of all such revenue is obtained from service charges, with utility charges ranking first.

Most non-school special districts have been created in the metropolitan era. Underpinning this growth has been a spreading rash of enabling laws by state legislatures which have paid scant attention to three important matters. One is the need for consistency in basic district features such as formation, consolidation, and dissolution procedures. A second is the importance of making all such agencies reasonably accountable to the public; for example, some of their governing board members are appointed by public officials, such as governors and judges, who are not responsible primarily to the people served by the districts, while in some others individuals are board members of one district because they hold similar positions in another. And the third involves the major and often debilitating effects many districts have upon general units of local government.

Principal Reasons for District Growth. The continued rapid growth of these districts demonstrates the high degree of governmental improvisation that has been taking place. As we saw earlier in the chapter, municipalities and non-school special districts currently are the producers of governmental proliferation in the metropolis. We also saw that the combination of easy incorporation procedures and difficult annexation laws has been important to the growth in number of cities and villages, as has been the strictness of consolidation laws permitting the merger of two or more such units. But why has there been so great a proliferation of special districts, a development that has occurred at a much swifter rate than in the case of municipalities? Much of the answer to this question is rooted in the fact that the fast numerical expansion of this type of government is often symptomatic of the insufficient flexibility or the unsuitability of other parts of the local system.

Other local governments may not be suitable in a number of respects: area, financing, functions, administration, or the attitude of those controlling these units.[8] The area whose residents or property owners want a particular function performed may be larger than the territory of a general local unit. But the general local unit may be unable to annex that part of the area lying outside its boundaries or to enter into a service contract with a territorially larger government, such as the county. Usually, however, the latter is also incapable of performing the desired service since, as has been noted

[8] John C. Bollens, *Special District Governments in the United States* (Berkeley and Los Angeles: University of California Press, 1957), pp. 5–14.

previously, it must have a uniform rate of taxation throughout its entire jurisdiction and it meets strong opposition if it provides from general county tax funds a substantially higher level of service to one of its sections than to others. In many of these cases of area inflexibility of municipalities and area and financing inadaptability of counties, the result is the establishment of a special district to perform the function.

Another phase of financing general local governments, which in turn affects their functional ability, also causes the growth of districts. Many general units must operate within state constitutional or legislative tax and debt limits and thus cannot expand functionally when these maximums are reached and are not liberalized. Nevertheless, residents or property owners of the same area frequently are permitted by law to create a special district endowed with the authority to levy taxes or incur debt, or both. In these circumstances, districts are a method of bypassing financial restrictions imposed on general local governments. Furthermore, even when a general unit can exceed its financial limits by obtaining voter consent, it is often easier to win approval for setting up a new government than for increasing the financial ability of an existing one. Sometimes, too, districts are established as a means of pooling the financial resources of an area in which the individual financing ability of existing units is insufficient to take on the function.

Also, at times, the range of functions that may be carried out by established general local governments does not include a service wanted by some people. In some cases this functional deficiency grows out of the reluctance of these governments to press for the necessary legal authority; in others the state legislature refuses to grant the necessary permission. Whichever circumstance holds true, the outcome is often the same—more special districts.

The proliferation of districts may be further caused by the administrative unsuitability of existing local units. Persons seeking a service may oppose vesting it in a government lacking modern administrative organization or processes—for example, one having a diffused structure or a spoils system—because they are suspicious of its ability to perform the desired service properly. Another cause is the attitude of the officials of an existing government: they may be slow to take on the activity or they may exercise it at a lower level than is wanted.

Other reasons may be cited for the continued expansion of these districts. One is the desire for independence by individuals and groups deeply interested in a function. Another is advocacy by existing governments; this may originate from rivalry between local units, each resisting the other's efforts to assume the function, or it may come about through the influence of the functional specialists or aid programs of the state or national governments. Still another reason is simply expediency, that is, the ease and promptness with which a district can be organized, in comparison to more comprehensive alternatives, particularly since such action can be taken without making substantial changes in other governments.

State Governments

The state and national governments also have adjusted and have contributed both beneficially and detrimentally to metropolitan development. Over the years they have become more active in the metropolis with very substantial effects on its local governments. The metropolitan significance and impact of these levels of higher authority are so vast and large-scale as to merit detailed attention in a later chapter, but several matters concerning them should be presented here. First, through provisions in their constitutions and through legislation, which is constantly mounting in volume, the states have always determined the shape and much of the substance of the local governmental systems. If local units in metropolitan areas are deficient in territorial size, organizational structure, functional and regulatory powers, and financial authority, the responsibility rests mainly with the states, primarily with their legislatures. Local governments, it must be remembered, are the creatures of the states, which set their basic ground rules in laws, constitutions, and implementing administrative orders.

The states generally have been slow to respond adequately to metropolitan needs; this has been partly due to rural domination of most state legislatures, a longtime situation now giving way in the face of various court decisions ordering reapportionment of their seats. State participation in metropolitan affairs has greatly increased in very recent years; the activity, however, is devoted almost solely to the provision of more direct services and to increased financial support (often accompanied by expanded state-imposed standards) of services performed by local governments. In contrast, the only

strong hand taken by the states in metropolitan governmental reorganization has involved school districts.

National Government

The national government has emerged as a vast supplier of programs and funds to metropolitan areas. Backed by its huge financial
resources, its actions have often been prompted by the neglect or
sluggish responses of many states to metropolitan problems and by
the growing realization by federal officials of the ever-increasing
importance of the metropolis in national elections.

Highways, urban renewal, public housing, hospitals, aid to the
aging and other needy persons, airports, river and harbor improvement, and sewage treatment facilities are merely some of the functional programs of the national government having broad repercussions in the metropolis. In addition, federal programs of a different
nature have a deep metropolitan impact; for example, the mortgage
financing policies of federal lending agencies have greatly accelerated
suburban development and federal defense contracts with private
firms importantly support the economic life of many metropolitan
areas. Although these various programs have not been used to prompt
governmental reorganization in the metropolis, they have contributed
to its proliferation of local units. To illustrate, federal stimulation
directly produced independent housing authorities, a type of special
district, and federal encouragement of the growth of suburbia
through underwriting liberal mortgage arrangements has made the
national government indirectly responsible for the creation of many
new suburban governments.

Both state and national programs affecting the metropolis have
developed in a piecemeal, uncoordinated way. At times, programs
of the same government have even worked at cross purposes. One
illustration is sufficient at this point. The failure of the federal interstate highway program to provide from its start for relocating
families living in the path of highway construction shows a weakness
in synchronizing this activity with federally-sponsored housing and
urban renewal efforts.

Increasingly, discussions have been held by various federal officials about coordinating their programs, and some state officials have
had similar conferences about state coordination. Recommendations
have followed at the national level to give this responsibility to the

Executive Office of the President, a new coordinating council or committee, or a new department (the last named being proposed by both Presidents Kennedy and Johnson). At the state level placing the assignment in the governor's office or with a new agency has usually been advocated. Nothing of this sort has been accomplished on a seemingly permanent basis in the national government. Meanwhile a few states have set up an office endowed with a limited number of coordinating duties.

EFFECTS OF PROLIFERATION AND INADEQUATE COORDINATION

The proliferation of governments and the lack of adequate coordination of public programs have many important injurious effects on the metropolis. As various types of governments have grown numerically, the volume of personalities and issues on which the voters are expected to make intelligent judgments has also expanded. Conscientious persons have enough difficulty remaining reasonably knowledgeable about several governments—national, state, and local —but the proliferation of local units has made their total task impossible. They would have to devote countless hours to being well informed about their local governments, for the system has come to resemble a circus of many more than the usual three rings. Few individuals have time for this herculean task.

Public Control and Accountability

The frequent consequences are a further decrease in public interest, which even in less complex years was not at a high level, and a resulting decline in public control and accountability. In time, voter turnout becomes lower as public disinterest, cynicism, and alienation mount and as fewer candidates seek certain offices in the wide range of elective possibilities. The scattering of public authority has reached the point in some areas where various incumbent officeholders have called off scheduled elections due to the absence of any opponents filing for the positions and have declared themselves re-elected.

Even the most conscientious citizens, those somehow able to spend enough time on their formidable assignment, meet insurmountable obstacles to adequate public control and accountability. One such impediment occurs when governments are composed entirely of non-elective officials, who might appropriately be called "the untouchables." This situation prevails in those special districts, some handling functions of metropolitan-wide significance, where officials are appointed by officers of other governments. In some instances they are selected by elective officials of other local governments (sometimes these elective officials choose the appointees from their own number), a procedure that furnishes the voters some degree of control, but one that is twice removed from them and thus quite remote. In other cases the authorities of one government charged with selecting the officials of another government are elected by a constituency much larger than the metropolis, or they themselves are appointed. Popular metropolitan control and accountability obviously do not exist at all under such circumstances.

Another obstacle to public control and accountability caused by governmental proliferation and fragmentation is that voters are compartmentalized into many governmental units, customarily small in territory. As a result, their decisions on a matter of general concern—such as improving mass transit or water pollution—are therefore generally binding on only a portion of the metropolitan area. And such compartmentalization breeds political irresponsibility. For example, some nonresidents of a city who work in it exert influence on its government through participation in civic, business, and labor organizations located in the city, but their activities are not tempered by residence in the municipality and the accountability of direct action.

Metropolitan Consensus

The fact that the metropolis is usually not controlled by the metropolitan public but by a host of sub-publics is related to another serious consequence of governmental proliferation: the difficulty, indeed the common impossibility, of arriving at a metropolitan consensus on area-wide matters through formal public means. The dispersion of power among a large number of governmental units makes it legally possible for each of them to reach decisions without concern for their consequences or spillover effects, which may be harmful to other governments and residents of the metropolis. Moreover, such scatteration of authority has produced an increasing number of small formal decision centers, thus generally making it extremely difficult to attain formal metropolitan-wide acceptance of vital proposals. This situation, as pointed out by Robert C. Wood, a discerning analyst of metropolitan affairs, has often led to a coalition of politicians, newspaper editors, businessmen, and labor leaders taking on leadership in area-wide problems, usually on a single-problem basis. Devoid of the elements necessary for effective policy-making—an adequate institutional base, legal authority, direct and regular relationships with the metropolitan constituency, and established processes for considering and resolving issues—this coalition, he concludes, transmits what metropolitan policy it agrees upon to the existing governments, where it receives an uncertain reception and its utilization depends upon voluntary acceptance.[9]

Conflicting Programs

When each government is a king in the fragmented public environment of the urban complex, some major programs undertaken by individual local units tend to work in counteracting rather than synchronized ways and to produce fewer positive area-wide results. And in such circumstances, the state and national governments are destined to assume more active service roles in the metropolis and, as we have seen, often to do so haphazardly, even to the point where agencies of the same government carry out conflicting activities.

Service and Financial Disparities

Governmental proliferation also contributes to wide disparities between service needs and financial resources in different parts of the metropolis and in turn to deficiencies in local public activities. Allowing pockets of wealth to wall themselves off largely from the total community of which they are a part (and for which many of their well-to-do residents may depend for their income) inevitably leads to the emergence of areas of poverty. Consequently, some units are wealthy and can satisfy the comparatively few public needs of their residents at a luxury level and with a low tax rate, while others are poor and have extensive needs they frequently are financially unable to meet. Ironically, the resulting service and regulatory deficiencies in the poor pockets sometimes break out of their confines and cause large-scale problems. Such deficiencies also prompt advocacy of proposals to bring about a degree of area-wide financial equalization (most often advocated in terms of school districts) and

---

[9] Robert C. Wood, *Metropolis Against Itself* (New York: Committee for Economic Development, 1959), p. 38.

increased state and national governmental interest and participation in metropolitan areas.

Area-Wide Problems

A very important result of the fragmented and uncoordinated governmental operations of metropolitan areas is the existence and at times the continued growth of grave area-wide problems of service and regulation. The list of shortcomings is long or brief, according to the particular metropolis, but frequently includes clogged mass and private means of transportation (principally road and commuter rail transportation, but also sometimes involving air, truck, and port facilities), pollution of water and air, disposal of various wastes, dwindling water supplies, insufficient park and recreation areas, declining amounts of needed open spaces, growing ugliness, exploited uses of irreplaceable land, inadequate developmental plans and controls, and others. The metropolitan citizenry occasionally becomes vocal and irritated about one or a few of these area-wide problems (most often transportation, pollution, waste disposal, water, and parks and recreation), but in general its concern about them is slight until a critical condition develops.

THE GOVERNANCE OF THE METROPOLIS

Despite weaknesses in the organization and processes of its governmental system, the metropolis so far has been able to avoid major disasters. This feat has been accomplished by continually adjusting to keep the pressure points from reaching catastrophic levels. Ironically, by averting crisis, these *ad hoc* measures have helped to stifle or defeat most efforts at comprehensive restructuring of the governmental pattern of the metropolis. The process of governing has involved local units, which remain on center stage, other public agencies, and private organizations and individuals. The techniques utilized to sustain the system vary among metropolitan areas, but the process is generally similar.

The Governmental Mix

The governmental mixture usually consists of intergovernmental cooperation, a county government of rising importance, a network of small and large districts, and growing state and national programs.

Contracts betweeen local units, a formal type of cooperation, have been expanding in number. Almost invariably negotiated between two governments, they are always voluntary and usually terminable after notice. Some are mutual aid agreements, which become operative only when a fire, police, or civil defense emergency arises. Others are arrangements whereby a government, such as a county or a city, consents to provide a service to another local unit for a set period of time and a specified amount of money. The time period can be extended upon joint approval and the amount of payment then is also subject to renegotiation. In some instances, too, emergency aid or the use of a service or a facility of one government by another is based on informal understandings between administrators rather than written contracts.

By providing services and facilities through formal and informal means of cooperation with other units, intensifying levels of activity in unincorporated urban areas, and taking on more functions, many county governments have assumed larger roles in the metropolis and have prevented certain problems from becoming more serious. Moreover, a multitude of non-school special districts has been spawned, most of them concerned with small trouble spots and relatively few with individual metropolitan-wide problems.

In addition, the state and national governments have loomed larger on the metropolitan scene. Backed by diversified sources of revenue and staffed by functional specialists, they have plugged certain local and area-wide gaps in the metropolis, usually by offering financial grants that contain stipulations to be met before being awarded. Often these state and federal activities are condemned by local officials as intervention, on the assumption that a stand of this sort is good politics and popular with their constituents. Yet at the same time such efforts by "foreign" governments are widely sought and welcomed as aids in the handling of particular difficulties.

Private Activities

Numerous private organizations and individuals also participate in governing the metropolis. Business and industrial interests, labor unions, political parties, private welfare agencies, civic associations, metropolitan and suburban newspapers, and television and radio stations (which now can take editorial positions) all have important stakes in keeping the metropolitan community operating as a going concern. They possess varying degrees of power and influence (but, as we will see in detail in the next chapter, none to the point of dominating or controlling the community) and they espouse a broad range of objectives. In the process they interact and negotiate with one another and with the elected politicians and professional governmental bureaucrats who make the formal decisions on public policies.

A system of public and private relationships that furnishes a vehicle for decision-making of both a positive and negative nature obviously has always existed in the metropolis; it is a basic necessity for averting crises and for parcelling out some of the rewards of metropolitan life. The system in operation further demonstrates that the proliferated and diffused formal governmental organization of most metropolitan areas is not totally the result of drift; in important part it is the product of deliberate, conscious decisions and actions by numerous governments and private organizations. The multicentered process of governance composed of public and private elements lumbers along by using the techniques of intermittent bargaining and diplomatic maneuvering. In general, the process stands as a formidable barrier to the formation of a governmental institution charged with decision-making on matters of area-wide concern and with the execution of those policies within the framework of the welfare of the total metropolitan community—one providing for appraising the goals of the multicentered forces of interest and influence in the light of the aims and well-being of the entire metropolis.

CHAPTER 7

⊳ *Politics and Power in the Metropolis*

THE IMPRESSION has long prevailed among political and civic reformers that the problems of growing metropolitan areas would be
magically solved if only simple, symmetrical patterns of local government were established. Organizational charts, stereotyped administrative principles, and the rhetoric of economy and efficiency have
constituted the stock in trade of those who have been prominent in
this reorganization movement. Only in recent years have doubts
over this orientation begun to pervade reformist ranks. Political
scientists who traditionally have tended to concentrate on the formal
structure of government are now probing into the informal attributes
of the local political process. By no means rejecting the importance
of form and structure in shaping the political life of the community,
they have become particularly concerned with what takes place within
this institutional framework. How are public policies made and public
problems solved? Who are the key participants and influentials in
this process? What are the critical variables or factors that affect
the operation of the system? These are but a few of the more basic

questions that confront the interested citizen as he observes the functioning of the complex and mystifying aggregation of people and government known as a metropolitan community.

Social scientists view the political system of the metropolis in various ways. Some look upon it as a game in which the contestants compete for the prizes of political action. Others regard it primarily as a service-providing bureaucracy that seeks to satisfy the public needs of its consumer citizens. Still others consider it as a process of interaction among innumerable role-playing actors, institutions, groups, and individuals. None of these views is exclusive; they merge into each other with many combinations and permutations. Even though they may involve basically different theoretical conceptions of the metropolitan system, the pragmatic question in each instance becomes one of focus and emphasis. Is attention to be concentrated on the configurations of power and interest within the community; on the operation of the bureaucracy; on the roles the various participants play; on the imputed pathology of the system? Or is the approach to be one of the shotgun variety in which the elusive target is sprayed with intellectual buckshot in hopes of hitting the crucial variables?

Regardless of arguments over theory and method, one observation seems irrefutable. The metropolitan area, feudal and balkanized as it may be, constitutes a viable social and political system in which interaction takes places among its parts and in which public policy emerges in one fashion or another. This policy may be sufficient or inadequate, sound or unsound, in the public interest or against it. Whatever its quality, the final product results from the accumulated effects of many decisions by many autonomous or semi-independent governments, agencies, interest groups, and individuals. So long as an area-wide authority with general governmental powers is absent, public policy-making in the metropolis can be of no other character.

But (and this point cannot be overemphasized) a metropolitan political system, functioning almost always within a governmentally fragmented structure, does exist here and now. Decisions do get made, local governments continue to operate, services and goods are provided, problems are solved or mitigated, expansion and development take place, and the day-to-day life of the residents goes on. The process may be inefficient and costly and may rationally demand change to maximize output and citizen satisfaction, but these are matters of another ilk. This is not to deny that institutional analysis is relevant or that governmental structure conditions the resolution of issues. It is to note that organization must be dealt with in terms of the resources and strategy it makes available to the various participants in the metropolitan system.

GOVERNMENTAL STRUCTURE: ITS SIGNIFICANCE

The governmental system of virtually all metropolitan areas, as we have already mentioned, is not a unified system of interaction with a centralized agency of control. A creature of quite another breed, it is a loosely knit and disjointed structure of distinct and legally autonomous parts. The functioning of this fragmented system is conditioned and limited by the forces in play in each of the area's territorial subunits that are fenced off by legal boundaries and governed by separate local public agencies. Few would deny that the distinction between a governmentally integrated and governmentally divided structure is of considerable importance; but this distinction must be viewed in a broader context than is usually the case. A metropolis, whether governed by a single local government or many, is composed of diverse parts, each having both functional and territorial characteristics. These parts, whether they are economic and social interests or neighborhoods and ethnic enclaves, have different needs and demands, different orientations, and even different values and goals. Erasing the governmental boundaries will not change the character of these subunits or the forces and pressures which they generate in the metropolitan area. Such reorganization may provide a more effective mechanism of public control and a better means of equitably allocating community resources and values, but such results are by no means assured.

Unionville and Divisiontown

To illustrate this last point, let us examine briefly two hypothetical metropolitan areas of similar social and economic characteristics but with sharply contrasting local governmental systems. The first, which will be referred to as Unionville, has a single general-purpose local government (a city-county government) and a single consolidated school district. The second, called Divisiontown, consists of a central city and a large number of suburban municipalities, school districts, and other special districts. Both are industrial complexes and both have been recipients of large numbers of migrants, mostly Negroes, from the rural South. In each case, the new arrivals have settled in the older sections of the central city where the only low-cost housing in the area is available. This influx of newcomers has been accompanied by a steady outflow of the white and well-to-do residents from the core to the new subdivisions in the suburban ring. In both metropolitan communities the central business district has keenly felt the competition of the outlying shopping centers; blight and deterioration have attacked the older neighborhoods; social problems have increased; and all the other pressures of urban growth and expansion have been experienced. In short, the Unionville and Divisiontown SMSA's resemble each other physically, socially, and economically; only their governmental structures differ fundamentally.

What have been the consequences of this difference in governmental organization? Immediately, we can raise several questions and couch them in terms of the goals usually ascribed to metropolitan government. Has centralized control over land use planning and zoning in Unionville resulted in a more attractive and efficient pattern of urban expansion than in Divisiontown? Has economic development proceeded at a more rapid pace and in more orderly fashion in the governmentally unified area than in the other? Are inequities in education, housing, and job opportunities fewer and racial discrimination less in the former than in the latter? Are public services in Unionville better and more efficiently managed than in Divisiontown? Are residents of the consolidated SMSA better satisfied with their governmental structure and public services and facilities than those in the governmentally fragmented metropolis?

Obviously, one cannot hope to answer these questions in a meaningful way by reference to two fictional communities. Yet an exercise of this kind has certain value. Asking the observer to think in terms of two contrasting systems compels him to consider the possible effects of the distinguishing variable, which in this case is governmental structure. And by asking him to view these urban communities in the light of certain common goals to which each aspires, his attention is directed to the dynamics of the contrasting systems rather than to their formal structures alone. Even imaginary ventures must, of course, be grounded in reality and have some basis in fact if they are to be other than mere flights of fantasy.

Unfortunately, evidence about the relationship between governmental structure and metropolitan functioning is sparse. Rhetoric and *a priori* "truths" rather than empirical research have provided the principal sources of information for speculation in this field. Lacking such data, any conclusions about the questions raised here must perforce be tenuous and largely impressionistic. However, with this acknowledged limitation, we will venture to examine several aspects of the governmental systems in Unionville and Divisiontown as they relate to one of their ascribed goals.

The Planning and Developmental Process. Unplanned and uncoordinated growth is widely recognized as a serious hazard to contemporary urban development. Both Unionville and Divisiontown have been confronted with this problem. In the former, the solution would appear to present no major difficulties. Since the area has a single government responsible for formulating and executing plans, it possesses the institutional means and tools for directing development into a rational pattern. In the Divisiontown SMSA, on the other hand, a radically different situation prevails. Not one but many local units are responsible for planning the area's growth, each having virtually autonomous authority for the kind of development that takes place within its own geographical limits. Order in Unionville and chaos in Divisiontown would seem the logical results of these contrasting systems.

A closer look at the governmental structures and their relation to the physical development in the two communities casts some doubt on the validity of this conclusion. Unionville has managed to formulate a master plan of sorts, the result of a long series of political maneuvers. The various aspects of the plan and the means for its execution, such as the zoning code and capital improvement program, were the end products of many compromises made to satisfy neighborhood and group interests throughout the area. The downtown merchants managed to get a new expressway to the central business district included in the plan in hopes of reviving their diminishing trade; suburban sectors secured high zoning restrictions to keep out "undesirables"; and real estate interests were able to have certain areas designated industrial or commercial for the enhanced value such uses would bring. Later, spot zoning by the council in response to various pressures made a shambles of the original land use plan.

In Divisiontown, the same process went on in each of the individual local governments. Here the bargaining took place largely within each local government and not among the different units. Inherent in this procedure, characteristic of a fragmented governmental system, is the danger that one municipality may adopt zoning ordinances incompatible with those of its neighbor. Thus land may be zoned industrial on one side of a common municipal boundary and residential on the other side. Or the master plan of one unit may call for a four-lane thoroughfare that runs into a two-lane street in an adjacent city or village; but the latter may have neither the intention nor the funds to widen the roadway through its confines. These examples could be multiplied manyfold.

Chaotic as this picture may seem, there are mitigating factors and forces which counteract, at least partially, the anarchy of unilateral action by individual governmental units. These include informal understandings among municipal officials, cooperative agreements between local governments, and county and state action in establishing road systems. More important, the pressures of the market place help to determine the feasibility of land use. A builder normally will not construct high-cost residential housing adjacent to industrially-zoned land nor build low-cost dwelling units in an upper-income neighborhood where the price of land is high. Similarly, a developer will not seek to establish an industrial park in an area that has no access to railroads or major highways or to do so in a predominantly residential enclave where his action would lead to vigorous neighborhood resistance.

What all this is saying is that similar forces and pressures are at work in both Unionville and Divisiontown. Consequently, the planning and zoning and the resulting developmental patterns in these contrasting governmental systems may not vary as much as differences in governmental structure would lead many people to assume. Planning does not take place in a political vacuum. Impressive as the products of the professional city planner may be on the drawing board, their adoption and execution must run the political gamut whether the metropolis is governmentally unified or divided. Unionville, of course, possesses the formal and institutional machinery for guiding growth and development into a rational pattern while Divisiontown must depend largely on chance to achieve this same end.

In the case of Unionville, also, bargaining among local interests is a continuous process in which concessions on one issue can be balanced against gains on another. Intra-metropolitan bargaining in Divisiontown, on the other hand, involves at most intermittent negotiations between two or more governmental units. Hence opportunities for compromise and adjustment among the parties are much less. Devoid of institutional machinery for area-wide decision-making, Divisiontown must rely heavily on *ad hoc* or special arrangements, the pressures of economics, and Dame Fortune to keep the system operative. Whether the actual results differ greatly from those in the governmentally unified metropolis is a matter that merits closer investigation.

Other Functions and Goals. One could continue this hypothetical foray by comparing the handling of other functions and the attainment of other goals in the two communities. Does the Negro, for example, have greater freedom in the choice and location of his housing in Unionville than in Divisiontown? The evidence would probably show that he is as effectively ghettoized in one as in the other. Are educational opportunities more equitably distributed in the consolidated school district than they are among the many autonomous school units of the other metropolis? Probably so; although here again differences in quality and facilities would be found from school to school in both communities. Schools in the high socioeconomic neighborhoods of Unionville are likely to differ in quality from those in the low income and ethnic sections of the same area. Are public services better and more efficiently managed in the governmentally integrated community? The overall answer would undoubtedly be yes. Certainly they would be more uniform throughout the area, although the level of services and efficiency in the long established wealthier suburbs of Divisiontown might equal or exceed that in Unionville. Thus the listing and comparisons could go on. What is important to observe here is that each of these mythical communities provides illustrations of the urban or metropolitan political process as it functions in different institutional settings.

THE PATTERN OF INFLUENCE

The political process, whether at the national, state, or local level, involves the translation of public needs and desires into official policy and action. Politics need not be viewed as a game or as "who gets what, when, and how" to appreciate the fact that power and influence play important roles in the making and execution of law. A zoning ordinance or building code is enacted by an elected body of representatives, a formally constituted arm of government. The formulation of such laws does not take place in a political or social incubator. Those who legitimize and administer public policy—councilmen, mayors, commissions, agencies, departments—are subject to various pressures from the many competing groups and individuals in the community. This pressure may be overt at times, as when a group of property owners protests a zoning change or a downtown business association demands better street lighting in the central business district. Often it will not be so apparent, as when the awarding of a liquor license is at stake or a vacancy on an important public commission is to be filled.

The question is sometimes asked: Who really runs the community? To pose the query in this fashion is to imply that some individual or group of influentials stands behind the scene calling the civic signals. In recent years an increasing number of sociologists and political scientists have taken up this question and have sought to determine the pattern of influence or the so-called power structure of local communities. Their approaches and techniques have differed but their objective has been the same: to discover "how things get done" in the urban polity or community. The resultant studies have aimed at identifying the key actors, those who are the leaders and wielders of power and influence, and tracing the roles they play in the making of public and semipublic decisions. Several such investigations are described here for the light they shed on policy-making at the local level.

Atlanta

The spate of studies about local influentials was touched off by the publication of Floyd Hunter's *Community Power Structure: A Study of Decision Makers* in 1953.[1] Hunter, a sociologist, sought to identify the influentials in Regional City (a pseudonym for Atlanta, Georgia) by first assembling lists of known civic, governmental, and business leaders. These lists were then submitted to a panel of six judges (well-informed individuals active in local civic affairs) who

[1] Chapel Hill: University of North Carolina Press, 1953.

were asked to rate the reputed leaders according to their relative power. From his study, Hunter concluded that key decisions in Regional City are made by a handful of individuals who stand at the top of a stable power hierarchy. Drawn largely from business and industrial circles, these men constitute a strongly entrenched and select group that exercises predominant influence over community policy. With their blessing, projects move ahead; without their express or tacit consent, little of significance can be accomplished. On community-wide issues, policy is channeled through a fluid committee structure down to a lower level bureaucracy where it is executed.

New Haven

A second study made by Robert Dahl, a political scientist, and reported in his provocatively titled book *Who Governs?*, employs a different method and reaches different conclusions than Hunter.[2] Underlying Dahl's approach is the assumption that leaders can best be identified and patterns of influence best determined by observing and analyzing the resolution of various kinds of community issues. His approach, to put it briefly, is based on the study of power in action rather than on opinions of who the leaders are. Turning his analytical insights on New Haven, Connecticut, Dahl examined sixteen major decisions on redevelopment and public education and on the nominations for mayor in both political parties for seven elections.

In contrast to Hunter's highly monolithic and centralized power structure, Dahl found a pluralistic or dispersed system of community power in New Haven. Influence over the course of community affairs is possessed by many individuals in a considerable variety of roles, with each exercising his power only within a fairly limited scope and on certain questions but not others. Thus, if the issue is one of urban renewal, one set of actors will control; if the matter concerns building a new hospital, a different coalition of leaders will be involved. In this pattern, business élites of the type who are said to control Regional City are only one among many influential groups or power clusters. As Dahl states it, "The Economic Notables, far from being a ruling group, are simply one of many

[2] New Haven: Yale University Press, 1961.

groups out of which individuals sporadically emerge to influence the politics and acts of city officials. Almost anything one might say about the influence of the Economic Notables could be said with equal justice about a half dozen other groups in the New Haven community."[3]

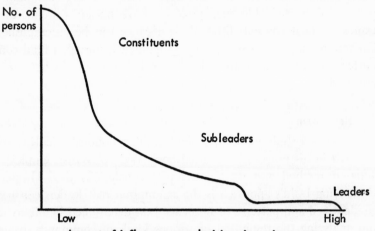

Figure 7.1   A Schematic Diagram of the Distribution of Direct Influence on Decisions. From Robert A. Dahl, *Who Governs? Democracy and Power In an American City*, Yale University Press, 1961, p. 163.

Edgewood and Riverview

A third study of two small New York communities (with populations of 6000 and 8500, respectively) by political scientist Robert Presthus strikes somewhat of a middle ground between Hunter and Dahl.[4] Presthus found that eighty citizens (0.6 percent of the total populations) play the central, active role in initiating and directing major community decisions. He also found two discrete decision-making systems: one political and based on local electoral support; the other economic and based on high formal positions in industry, finance, and business. Influentials in the first category, public officials and other political leaders, generally control "public" issues, those which require the expenditure of public funds or legitimation in the form of referenda. Leaders in the latter category dominate the

[3] *Ibid.*, p. 72.
[4] *Men At the Top* (New York: Oxford University Press, 1964).

"private" types of decisions that entail the use of non-governmental resources. Some sharing of participation in public decisions takes place between the two élite groups, but generally such issues have little saliency for the economic leaders.

According to Presthus, the configuration of power differs in the two communities. In Edgewood where the socioeconomic structure is relatively high, the economic leaders tend to dominate local decision-making primarily because many matters and problems of community import are kept within the private sector. In the less wealthy town of Riverview, on the other hand, the political leaders are more influential largely because the community must look to government for the satisfaction of many of its needs. This difference led Presthus to hypothesize that "in communities with limited leadership and economic resources the power structure will be more likely to be dominated by political leaders, whereas in those with more fulsome internal resources it will probably be dominated by economic leaders."[5]

Chicago

Another political scientist, Edward Banfield, recently examined the exercise of political influence in Chicago.[6] Tracing the history of six controversies involving major community decisions, Banfield concluded that the notion of a power élite running the city is a myth. As in Dahl's New Haven, he found that the power structure is characterized by subunits of influence, each centering around a certain area or issue of public policy. In this structure the actions of many persons and groups, each having independent authority, must normally be in concert for a particular major proposal to be adopted. No one, Banfield insists, is in a position to survey the city of Chicago as a whole, much less the metropolitan area, and carry out any comprehensive policy of development. It is only after the pulling and hauling of various views and various forces that some kind of decision is finally reached.

Syracuse

A fifth and highly systematic study by a team of Syracuse University social scientists also probes into the mysteries of community

[5] *Ibid.*, pp. 410–411.
[6] *Political Influence* (New York: Free Press, 1961).

decision-making or leadership.[7] Selecting thirty-nine significant issues that had been resolved in the Syracuse SMSA over a recent five-year period, the investigators undertook to discover who had been instrumental in reaching the decisions. They began in each instance by identifying the individuals who were formally responsible; that is, those whose position—mayor, councilman, commissioner, board member, and the like—endowed them with legal authority for making the decision. Each person so identified was asked to name all others who were involved. The process was then repeated, first with those who had been mentioned by the formal authorities as "informal" participants, and then with the second level "influentials" nominated by the latter group. Utilizing the data made available in this leadership pool, patterns of participation were examined by statistical procedures and clusters of issues which shared a common core of decision-makers were identified.

The results of the study were closer to the findings of Dahl and Banfield than to those of Hunter. Nowhere did the Syracuse team find evidence of the existence of an old-fashioned monolithic or single élite. They discovered that twenty-nine of the thirty-nine issues grouped into nine clusters with common participants while the remaining ten showed no identifiable pattern. Not one leadership group, but many, were revealed, with approximately nineteen involved in the decisions selected for study. The fact that all but one of the clusters were predominantly content-oriented (dealing with issues in the same functional field, such as health or education) gave rise to an additional conclusion. As society increases in complexity, the trend in community decision-making is for specialized participation. In other words, when social organization is relatively simple, it may be possible for one group to make all kinds of decisions covering the whole range of community affairs. As society becomes more complex, the tendency is for each group to involve itself only

[7] Linton C. Freeman and others, *Local Community Leadership* (Syracuse: University College, 1960); and Linton C. Freeman and others, *Metropolitan Decision-Making* (Syracuse: University College, 1962). Also see Warner Bloomberg, Jr. and Morris Sunshine, *Suburban Power Structures and Public Education* (Syracuse: Syracuse University Press, 1963). Another major empirical study in the field of community power structures and decision-making is Robert E. Agger, Daniel Goldrich, and Bert E. Swanson, *The Rulers and the Ruled* (New York: Wiley, 1964).

in the combination of decisions that is of direct interest to it and in which it has special competence and skills.

These five studies and others of similar character give no definitive answer to the question of power configuration in urban communities. They offer no simple and universally applicable schema for describing and delineating influence. Hunter and his followers who use the "reputational" method of identifying leaders start with the assumption that society is stratified and social power structured. Those who adhere to the issue-oriented approach posit a society in which power is shared between the state and a multitude of private groups and individuals. The first, the "reputationists," have most often found a monolithic élite of upper class and economic dominants running the community; the second, the "pluralists," have generally found that power is widely dispersed among many competing groups with no significant overlap of leaders.[8] Critics of the "reputationist" position contend that its adherents have failed to demonstrate that persons who have a reputation for power successfully exercise this power. Those who question the "pluralist" theory charge that its supporters ignore the relationship between power and social structure by viewing the community simply as a collection of individuals who have different amounts of power depending on the issue. On one point, however, there is agreement: only an extremely small proportion of the community is normally involved in any single issue.

Despite the divergent views, the weight of evidence persuasively points to a pluralistic model of power in the large city and certainly in most metropolitan areas.[9] As the Syracuse study illustrates, the complexity of modern society leads inevitably to specialization of leadership. This very complexity militates against the possibility of any monolithic domination over all sectors of community affairs. In such a system no individual or group is likely to possess the resources, the technical know-how, the skill, or even the desire to play this

[8] For a thorough discussion of these two positions as seen by a "pluralist," see Nelson Polsby, *Community Power and Political Theory* (New Haven: Yale University Press, 1963).

[9] In this connection, also see Robert J. Mowitz and Deil S. Wright, *Profile of a Metropolis* (Detroit: Wayne State University Press, 1962). After examining in depth ten cases of metropolitan decision-making, the authors note (p. 630): "Our cases have not turned up a single master decision-maker for the Detroit metropolis in the form of a person, group, or organization."

role. Add to this the fragmented governmental character of metropolitan areas and the possibility of centralized or oligarchical control becomes even more remote. For here small power clusters can function with relative autonomy behind the legal walls of their political suzerainties. Moreover, it seems unlikely that this pattern will be significantly changed in the foreseeable future.

THE CIVIC ACTORS

If we cannot answer the broader question of who or what "crowd" runs the metropolis, it may well be because no one runs it. As one political scientist has observed, the overall organization of a metropolitan area is weak or nonexistent. "Much of what occurs seems to just happen with accidental trends becoming cumulative over time and producing results intended by nobody. A great deal of the communities' activities consist of undirected co-operation and of particular social structures, each seeking particular goals and, in doing so, meshing with others."[10] Certainly the formal structure of government provides no institutional machinery for centralized decision-making and control. Less evident, but probably of equal truth, the informal pattern of relationships that undergirds the community similarly furnishes no framework adequate for this purpose.

In the modern metropolis consensus is reached, progress achieved, and the system made operative by the continuous interaction that takes place among individuals and groups of various capabilities and with various power potentials. Each of them, while competing for the rewards of society, has an important stake in maintaining an ongoing and viable community. All but the most aberrant of them accept the fact that the system can function only if the participants voluntarily accept and play within the rules of the game. These constraints, as well as the balancing effect of the interplay among competing elements, serves to maintain equilibrium in the metropolis despite the unequal distribution of power among its heterogeneous parts.

The principal actors on the metropolitan scene now deserve consideration. Our attention will be concentrated mainly on groups,

[10] Norton E. Long, "The Local Community as an Ecology of Games," *American Journal of Sociology*, LXIV (November, 1958), 252.

not individuals, since the power of the latter must be structured into associational patterns to be effective in the civic and political arena. People of like interests join together and pool their resources for a wide variety of objectives: social, professional, religious, economic, and political. Such combinations of individuals form subsystems of power which cooperate and compete in the community. A number of these organizations are "politicized," that is, they seek regularly or occasionally to further their aims through the institutions of government. An examination of several major categories of organizational participants at the local and metropolitan level will serve to underscore this point.

Business

Businessmen and business-oriented organizations such as the chamber of commerce have long been active in civic affairs. Their resources and reputed influence are great and their economic stake in the community substantial. However, as we have already had occasion to observe, the picture is not one of a business élite scheming to direct the course of community action. As Banfield found in Chicago, big businessmen are to be criticized less for interfering in public affairs than for failing to assume their civic responsibilities. Their role in local public decisions is most frequently confined to rather passive membership on civic or governmental committees and to more active service in the private welfare sector of the community. The case may be different in a "company-dominated" town or in a small city where the Main Street merchants are in control; but today it is the exception rather than the rule for businessmen to play the role of civic overlords.

To deny the reputed power of the economic notables in the governance of the community is not to imply that they are without influence. As Peter B. Clark, a political scientist and newspaper executive, has observed: "If one looks at the outcomes of local government decisions over long periods of time, one finds that the interests and ends of businessmen taken as a group tend to be served more often than, to take the most contrasting case, the interests and ends of Negroes and Puerto Ricans."[11] Clark argues that the businessman's influence in local affairs is not so much directly ex-

[11] "Civic Leadership: The Symbols of Legitimacy." Paper presented at the 1960 annual conference of the American Political Science Association.

ercised as it is anticipated. Rather than being based upon conspiracies or control of wealth, this influence rests upon the usefulness of the economic notable to others, such as political leaders, who seek the prestige and legitimacy which he can lend to their undertaking. In the process of co-opting him to their cause, local governments and civic groups tend to anticipate and, at least to some extent, satisfy his wishes.

Changing Roles of Business. The role of the businessman in local governmental affairs was not always passive as it is today. In the not too distant past, the roles of businessman and political leader were interchangeable. Until well into the nineteenth century, in fact, the economic notable and the political notable were identical in most American cities. With the ruling élite sharing the same social and economic perspectives, community controversy was minimized and consensus on overall policy readily reached. By the end of the century, however, the situation had changed. As cities grew in size and heterogeneity as a result of industrialization and large-scale immigration, demands upon the public sector increased in scope and magnitude. Local governments found it necessary to assume new functions and undertake new services to meet the mounting needs of a rapidly expanding urban society. And as these developments occurred, the demands on local officials became more burdensome while at the same time the stakes of local public office grew more attractive. The stage was now set for a new breed of community leader, the professional politician.

Cooperating closely at first with the economic notables who were gradually withdrawing from active public roles, the new leaders soon established their own independent basis of support. Instead of social position and wealth, their principal resource was the strength of numbers. Appealing to the rising class of workers, the immigrants and low-income groups, they offered them access to opportunities and rewards that had been denied them under the passing system of oligarchical control. "Machine" politics, the "boss," and the "wardheeler" became the prevalent symbols of local government as the nineteenth century drew to a close. The response of the economic dominants—and ultimately of the middle class in general—to the new "working class" politics was withdrawal. One finds an analogue to this in the present-day flight from the central city to suburbia. The exodus in a sense dramatizes what has long been true in most large urban areas: the non-involvement of the upper and middle classes in the political and civic affairs of the core city.

After relinquishing the political reins, commercial and industrial leaders became content to influence the conduct of government indirectly through various citizen groups and reform leagues. More importantly, they began to play predominant roles in the private welfare sector of the community. Service on boards such as the Community Chest, Red Cross, and hospitals became a substitute for political involvement. Activity of this type served several purposes for the economic notable. It furnished him with a means of satisfying his traditional sense of civic obligation without becoming immersed in local politics. It provided him with a highly prestigeful and non-controversial role in civic affairs. And finally, it enabled him to retain certain responsibilities within control of the private sector of the community that otherwise would have to be assumed by government.

Changes in business organization and styles also contributed to the separation of economic and political power in community affairs. In place of the local proprietors, the family- and home-owned establishments, came the large and impersonal corporate enterprises, frequently branches of national firms or controlled largely by outside capital. Along with them came the modern business élite, the organization men described so graphically by William Whyte of Fortune magazine. The new managers and engineers of economic power were not imbued with the sense of personal commitment to the community that had characterized their predecessors. Mobile, subject to frequent transfer from city to city, engrossed with their careers, they were men of limited civic commitment. Their involvement in the affairs of the local community was minimal and generally restricted to the specialized economic interests of their organizations. Communication with governmental officials was rare, with both business and public sectors pursuing their own objectives under an implicit truce of "no intervention" in the other's bailiwick.

Today, the situation is somewhat different, although the basic chasm still remains. Corporations, increasingly sensitive to public relations, now advertise their responsibility to the communities in which their plants are located. Executives are encouraged to participate in local civic activities (preferably of a non-controversial nature); cooperative action is taken with city officials in urban redevelopment and similar programs; and closer relations and better rapport are established with the chief executives and administrative technicians of the public sector. Corporate involvement, however, remains peripheral to the main stream of local political activity.

Differing Business Attitudes. Up to this point, we have been speaking of business as though it were a unified force or monolithic influence in the community. Such is far from the case. Like most segments of society, the business sector is more pluralistic than hierarchic. Fundamental conflicts of interest and opinion exist among businessmen as they do among other groups. Some of the differences arise, of course, on purely business or economic grounds. Local plans or laws that are good for one segment of the business community may be harmful to another. Redevelopment plans may affect differently the interests of rival banking and financial institutions. Downtown real estate operators may have quite different ideas as to what should be done than those in the outlying areas. The differences extend even into civic issues where business interests are not at stake. Economic notables, for example, are often found arrayed on both sides of community issues, such as the consolidation of private welfare agencies or the location of a new music hall. A few hypothetical instances of the obstacles to a unified and determined exercise of business influence in questions of governmental reorganization of the metropolis will serve further to illustrate this point.

Industrialist Archer operates a factory in the central city and also resides there in one of the few remaining upper-income neighborhoods or in one of the new luxury apartments now arising on "renewed" land peripheral to the downtown area. Jones is a suburban dweller and president of a large manufacturing firm located in the core city. Smith, a business executive, resides in a fashionable suburban community and his plant is situated in an industrial satellite. Williams is a downtown merchant who also lives in suburbia. Each of these men is likely to look upon proposals for metropolitan governmental reorganization from different perspectives. Archer, committed to the central city both economically and residentially, sees no reason why the metropolitan area should be governed by a multiplicity of units. Accustomed to efficiency and centralized administrative control in business affairs, he perceives little rationality in a badly fragmented governmental structure. Jones has mixed feelings. He has a direct economic interest in the central city and,

like Archer, is intellectually appalled at the administrative "irrationality" of the local political system. At the same time, however,
he is well satisfied with his suburban enclave and regards it as a
bastion against invasion by "undesirable" elements from other sections of the metropolis.

Smith's commitment is primarily to suburbia even though he
may recognize the interdependence of the total community. With
both his plant and home in outlying municipalities, his ties to the
central city are less apparent to him than to the others. The location
of his factory outside the core city offers certain tax advantages; and
in addition, his company enjoys close working relations with the
village officials. Under these circumstances, Smith is not prepared
to jeopardize his amicable arrangements with the village authorities
by actively supporting reorganization plans that would destroy or
decimate their power. Williams, the downtown merchant, has a
large economic stake in the central business district. Although his
entry into suburban shopping centers with branch stores has lessened
his dependence on the downtown, he still regards with favor any
local reorganization movement that might enhance the importance
of the core and attract more people into the area. These hypothetical
instances of differences among businessmen touch only upon matters of metropolitan governmental reform, but they could be expanded to cover many other local issues.

Labor

A popular conception of "who gets what" in American society
centers around the triad of "Big Business, Big Labor, and Big Government." The contest in the public arena is pictured as a struggle
between the first two giants with the third acting as mediator and
controller and, in the eyes of some, as dispenser of lavish favors to
those on the "in." This view is not limited to the national and
state scenes; even at the local or metropolitan level murmurs are
heard about business or labor running the community or being the
recipients of political largess. The evidence, as noted previously,
offers little to substantiate the mythology of business dominance in
community affairs. The case with respect to labor is no different.

In discussing labor's role in community affairs, several observations may be made at the outset. First of all, if unions and business
are contesting for power over local civic matters, the struggle is

taking place behind the scenes. Seldom do clashes over issues of a noneconomic character stir the community waters. In civic causes, more often than not trade union leaders will be found in the same camp with the business notables, assisting a chest or hospital drive, endorsing a bond issue for public improvements, working to establish a cultural center, or supporting an urban redevelopment project. Second, like business, labor is not a monolithic aggregation of power. Differences among and even within unions militate against any effective system of centralized control. Third, union leadership is likely to be most effective in mobilizing support for those issues that the membership considers legitimate concerns of the organization.

The generalization that American unions do not display great interest in local governmental affairs has empirical support. When labor intervenes and uses its strength in the metropolitan arena it usually does so because matters of direct relevance to the economic interests of its members are involved. The construction trade unions, for example, will resist building code changes that threaten to reduce the job potential of their constituents. Or the joint AFL–CIO council will lend its support to public employee unions in disputes over wages and working conditions. Labor leaders will also speak out at times on various noneconomic matters of local concern, such as educational and recreational needs, but they will assiduously avoid more controversial questions such as racial discrimination in housing and job opportunities. Even though the national leadership of organized labor takes strong stands on issues of equality, the local leadership treads cautiously in this realm. The rank and file of union membership is by no means committed to the abolition of discrimination, particularly in its own house or at its own doorstep. For local union officials to act militantly in issues of this kind presents threats to their continuance as leaders.

Labor's principal access to influence in local affairs is through the elective officials who are concerned with the mass mobilization of numbers. In the large cities, labor is usually found closely allied to the Democratic party; and where partisan elections for local office are held, it normally supports candidates of this political faith. On occasions, the union will line up behind local political leaders to oppose charter reform measures that threaten to diminish the patronage or other perquisites of their allies in government. Their support of "friendly" candidates and their interests gives them access to the governmental structure and entitles them to certain rewards, such as the appointment of labor officials to various local boards and commissions.

Today, organized labor is also attaching increasing importance to participation in activities of private welfare agencies where its guarantee of financial support provides a means of penetration. Union officials are now found on the Community Chest and similar boards and on various civic commissions. Studies indicate, however, that despite its increased representation, labor has not materially altered the goals of these agencies or effectively challenged the controlling power of other groups.[12] Rarely, if ever, is a labor official selected to head the community welfare council or to serve as general chairman of the annual fund drive. These positions remain within control of the economic notables. Indicative also in this connection is the fact that lists of community influentials, whether compiled on the basis of reputation or participation, seldom include a high percentage of union members.

Beyond the acquisition of these trappings and symbols of civic legitimacy and the occasional intervention in matters of economic concern to its membership, labor still does not occupy a place in the community power structure commensurate with its numbers or economic strength. As a perceptive study of Lansing, Michigan concluded, "Organized labor's community power lags behind its economic power."[13] The reason for this lag is possibly as Dahl speculates: "If the local union group has had much less influence in political decisions than consideration of sheer numbers might suggest, this is partly because the leaders and members have had no clear-cut image of the functions unions should perform in local politics —or even whether unions should have any role in local government at all."[14]

[12] See, for example, Donald E. Wray, "The Community and Labor-Management Relations," in *Labor-Management Relations in Illini City* (Champaign: University of Illinois Institute of Labor and Industrial Relations, 1953), pp. 7–145.

[13] William H. Form, "Organized Labor's Place in the Community Power Structure," *Industrial and Labor Relations Review*, XII (July, 1959), 537.

[14] Dahl, *Who Governs?*, p. 254.

Political Parties

Generalization about the role of political parties in local governmental affairs is no easier than it is in the case of business and labor. Their influence and the degree of their participation vary from community to community. In Chicago and New York it is relatively high, in Cincinnati and Los Angeles, less evident. One important variable in determining the role and activity of parties at the metropolitan and local levels is their formal status in the governmental structure.

In some metropolitan communities, nonpartisan elections prevail throughout the area; in others the central city chooses its local officials on partisan tickets while suburban municipalities utilize nonpartisan ballots; and in still others different combinations are found. In Montgomery County, Ohio, for example, Dayton city officials are selected in nonpartisan elections, and county and township officers in partisan contests.

Form, of course, is not the all-determinative element in assessing the activity and influence of political parties in local elections. Some nonpartisan communities carefully observe the principle in practice and spirit as well as form; in others partisanship merely operates under a nonpartisan label. An extreme instance of the latter is found in Chicago where the highly partisan board of aldermen is selected on nonpartisan tickets. Generally, however, nonpartisan elections impose restraints on the extent of partisan activity and weaken party influence in the conduct of local government.

Where political parties are able to nominate and elect their candidates to municipal and county offices, their stake in local affairs will be greater than when they are excluded from these prizes. As Eugene Lee found in a study of nonpartisanship in California cities, ". . . removal of the party label tends to reduce the stake of the party organization and leaders in the outcome of the local races, and their interest and activity is correspondingly lessened."[15] Yet even in jurisdictions where partisanship prevails, the insignificant amount of patronage that generally remains at the local level diminishes the inducement for intensive involvement by the party leadership. When patronage jobs were available on a large scale,

[15] *The Politics of Nonpartisanship* (Berkeley and Los Angeles: University of California Press, 1960), p. 176.

the party could readily utilize these rewards to recruit loyal workers and strengthen its organization for pursuing the more important stakes at the state and national levels. Now, the widespread adoption of merit systems in municipal governments has lessened and in some cases virtually destroyed these opportunities.[16]

Party leaders themselves are far from unanimous in favoring the participation of political parties in local politics. Some feel that local issues have little connection with the policies of the two major parties. Others maintain that parties are too preoccupied on the state and national levels to expend their energies and resources on local affairs. Still others are of the opinion that extensive participation in community affairs offers little payoff while entailing considerable risk. They point out that such activity not only drains off organizational resources but also involves the party uselessly in highly controversial issues. It is one thing, they say, to support civil rights legislation in Washington; it is another matter to be responsible for passing open-occupancy ordinances and anti-discrimination measures in Middletown where the issues strike close to home.

Party Divisions and Decentralization. Two additional factors are relevant to a discussion of party influence in metropolitan affairs: the divisions within the parties themselves, and the many separate centers of political power arising from the fragmentation of the local governmental structure. The traditional image of a tight political hierarchy extending from the "boss" to the precinct captain is the exception rather than the rule today. Men like Hubert Humphrey, a political amateur when he was mayor of Minneapolis —Mayor Raymond R. Tucker of St. Louis is another example—were able to achieve local public office without party support and even against the opposition of their parties.[17] Mayor Robert Wagner of New York in a successful bid for re-election was able to defy important segments of the Democratic party and yet retain his office. Many examples could also be cited of differences over local issues between party officials in the white and Negro wards and between those in and outside the central city.

Governmental balkanization of the metropolis further diminishes

[16] See Frank J. Sorauf, "The Silent Revolution in Patronage," *Public Administration Review*, XX (Winter, 1960), 28–34.

[17] See, for example, Robert L. Morlan, "City Politics: Free Style," *National Municipal Review*, XXXVIII (November, 1949), 485–490.

the opportunities for political parties to exercise effective control or significant influence in area-wide public affairs. Even where only partisan elections are employed, each municipality has its own political cadre that vies for the rewards of local office. The "politicos" in each of these minor strongholds enjoy their own independent basis of operation, their own constituency, and their own interests. To be elected to office they must be attuned to the needs and desires of their individual local electorates; and these needs and desires, as conceived by the residents, do not always correspond to those of the metropolitan area as a whole. Programs that political leaders in the central city or at the county level might like to see adopted for the area may be anathema to inhabitants in the suburban municipalities. Public officials with stakes in the suburbs are unlikely to jeopardize their local interests by supporting the position of the area-wide party organization. It is unlikely also that the party leadership would demand such compliance. More probably the party would avoid taking a stand on such local or metropolitan issues.

The facts of political arithmetic in this fragmented system also discourage greater party participation in metropolitan affairs. Where the two-party system operates as it does in many urban communities with the core city Democratic and the suburbs Republican, the difficulties of area-wide policy formulation are compounded. The favorite strategy in such instances has been one of "live and let live." Political parties have thus exhibited little interest in reforming the governmental structure so as to make centralized decision-making institutionally possible. Amalgamation or even lesser schemes of functional consolidation and federation might either dilute the strength of the core city Democrats or submerge the influence of the suburban Republicans. If, as one observer has speculated, the city of Buffalo were consolidated with Erie County, control over the city would pass from the Democratic to the Republican party. Or if Chicago were combined with Cook County, the Democrats would have a chance of capturing the area-wide government; but why should they take the risk when control of Chicago is a sure thing.[18] The situation is different in some areas, as in Metropolitan Syracuse, where the central city, the suburban municipalities, and the county government are all controlled by the same party. In the

[18] Edward C. Banfield, "The Politics of Metropolitan Area Organization," *Midwest Journal of Political Science*, I (May, 1957), 77–91.

Syracuse area the concurrence of party membership has made it possible for a Republican mayor of the central city, who is also Republican county chairman, to bring about certain area-wide decisions such as integration of welfare functions on a county basis. This ability, however, is severely circumscribed, as the Syracuse studies show, and can be exercised only in limited spheres of a relatively non-controversial nature.[19]

The Formal Decision-Makers

No matter who may be the real wielders of power in a community, decisions on public policy ultimately rest with those who occupy positions of formal authority in the governmental system. Only the city council, for example, can appropriate public funds for a new park or rezone a parcel of land. Only the school board can approve the site for a new school or let the contracts for its construction. (Some decisions require voter ratification by referenda, but the vast bulk of local government business is carried on by the elected and appointed officials.) Individuals or organizations seeking to influence governmental action may be important in the community, but they will be badly handicapped in their efforts unless they have access to the appropriate legal authorities.

Individuals in governmental positions of power range from officials who follow relatively independent courses of conduct to those who are little more than puppets of various interests and from chief executives and councilmen to building inspectors and policemen. All of them are subject, in varying degrees, to various forces and pressures. A councilman dependent for election upon the support of his party committeeman or on campaign funds provided by tavern operators will not be unsympathetic to their interests. Nor is the mayor of an industrial community likely to slight the wishes of his working-class constituency. However, individuals and groups providing electoral support for public officials are normally concerned with only a limited number of issues that are of particular relevance to their own interests. They therefore will make no effort to influence the official policy-makers in most items on the local public agenda. In a heterogeneous community, moreover, many diverse groups will be competing in the governmental arena.

[19] See Roscoe C. Martin, Frank J. Munger, and others, *Decisions in Syracuse* (Bloomington: Indiana University Press, 1961).

Not all will have equal access to the ear of the formal decision-maker nor will everyone make equal demands for the attention of persons in authority. Nevertheless, the interests of no group of any significance (in terms of size, prestige, or economic resources) can be flagrantly ignored by policy officials no matter how politically indebted they may be to certain individuals or groups.

The possessors of formal authority frequently must mediate between the claims of contending groups, no one of which is dominant in the community. In such instances their role as decision-makers assumes greater importance. Holding the balance of power, they occupy a strategic position of influence which they can exploit to further their total program and objectives. The mayors of large cities, particularly, enjoy such opportunities. It would be grossly misleading, however, to assume that men who have reputations as strong mayors, such as Daley in Chicago, Lee in New Haven, or Tucker in St. Louis, rule by fiat or by arbitrary exercise of their official prerogatives. Requiring the support of many elements and influentials in the community, they cannot politically afford to limit access to any one group or small coterie of interests or to alienate any segment of the community by high-handed action. Their relationship with many divergent interest groups enhances their leadership potential at the same time that it imposes on them the necessity to compromise and steer a middle course in community affairs. Dahl's description of the role of the New Haven mayor sums up the situation well. There is no such animal in New Haven, he points out, as a neatly hierarchical system with the mayor at the top operating through subordinates in a chain of command. "The mayor was not at the peak of a pyramid but rather at the center of intersecting circles. He rarely commanded. He negotiated, cajoled, exhorted, beguiled, charmed, pressed, appealed, reasoned, promised, insisted, demanded, even threatened, but he most needed support from other leaders who simply could not be commanded. Because the mayor could not command, he had to bargain."[20]

The Governmental Bureaucracy. Political leaders in the government have received considerable attention in discussions of the community power structure of the metropolis, but the governmental bureaucracy usually has been overlooked. This neglect is unwarranted;

[20] Dahl, *Who Governs?*, p. 204.

the professional civil servant has come to play an important role in policy-making as well as execution. By virtue of numbers alone, the bureaucracy constitutes a force in metropolitan life that cannot justifiably be ignored. The pressures for new and expanded services generated by increasing urbanization have swelled the ranks of local governmental employees. At the time of 1962 *Census of Governments*, local units, including school districts, had 4.2 million employees (full-time equivalent) on their payrolls, an increase of almost 25 percent since the previous census in 1957. Approximately two-thirds of this total worked in SMSA's.

The importance of the local bureaucracy has been augmented not alone by numbers but more significantly by the growing need for expertise in government at the metropolitan level. As functional activities become more dependent on science and technology, political officials find themselves compelled to rely increasingly on the knowledge, specialized skills, and advice of professional administrators. Intuition, common sense, and native shrewdness, the stock-in-trade of the successful politician, are no longer enough. The central city mayor, the urban county executive, or the elected council of a large suburban government cannot afford, politically or otherwise, to formulate programs and determine policies without the assistance of administrative technicians and specialists. Political judgment in the attack on such complex problems as traffic, air and water pollution, juvenile delinquency, crime, and governmental financing must feed on bureaucratic appraisal and know-how. And as amateurs in the many technological aspects of community functioning, political officials find it more and more difficult to challenge policy advice based on specialized knowledge. The expert may be on tap and not on top but the demands of a technological society have increased his influence over political officials. Council-manager governments provide a readily observable illustration of this development. There the city manager, once looked upon as the employee and servant of the elected council, is now—by virtue of his expertise —frequently an influential policy-maker guiding the chosen representatives of the people.

The political and bureaucratic structure of government in urban areas, however, is not a monolithic giant that encompasses all public personnel within its administrative tentacles. Like other interested groups, and like government in the metropolis itself, local officialdom and its accompanying bureaucracy are highly pluralistic. Each unit, whether a school district, municipality, or countywide sewer district, has its own entrenched officials and employees and its own fenced-in area of jurisdiction. The central city mayor, the suburban manager, the school district superintendent, the county health commissioner, and the village police chief all constitute centers of power and influence, and all are contenders in the urban arena. Water departments in the city and county vie with each other to become the metropolitan supplier. A county health department seeks to expand its authority at the expense of municipal agencies. Autonomous sewer districts resist efforts of a metropolitan agency to bring them under its jurisdiction. County and municipal police departments argue over their respective jurisdictional spheres. A central city mayor and a county governing board member or chief executive compete for recognition as the major political figure of the area. In this interplay of forces, each segment or subunit of the structure cultivates clientele relationships and affords points of access to the private influentials of the community. The king has many ears.

THE METROPOLITAN WEB

A vast and intricate mosaic, the political system of the metropolis is at the same time both enigmatic and understandable. Enigmatic because it is difficult to comprehend how a system so diffused and fragmented can serve the needs of modern urban society. Understandable because it is equally difficult to see how an integrated and monolithic structure of public service and control can be imposed upon an urban area composed of so many divergent interests and lacking any real sense of community. But mysterious or comprehensible, rational or irrational, the metropolitan political system presents a fascinating study of the interaction of people and institutions in daily life. As spectators and participants we can observe the interrelationships among the actors, the maneuvering for advantage, the power plays and the bargaining, as each segment seeks to achieve its objectives; or, as the economist would say, maximize its utilities.

The metropolitan structure can best be viewed part by part, subunit by subunit. At the center of the stage is the core city dominating the political scene even though its sphere of governmental control stops at its legal boundaries. In less conspicuous places are the satellite municipalities, non-school special districts, and, in some states, townships or New England towns, each with its own retinue of court followers. Moving toward the front of the platform in some metropolitan areas is the county government, hoping to be tapped for the role of metropolitan major-domo. Scattered around the stage are the school districts, that of the central city occupying the most important spot. What distinguishes this drama from those of the past is the absence of a script and a director. The actors improvise their lines, establish working relations with each other, and jockey for more favorable positions. None of the participants is quite sure of the theme or objective of the play; they are certain only that the show must go on. Although rivals for attention, they are aware that no one of them is self-sufficient to keep the play moving. They are consequently willing to cooperate among themselves within limited spheres and to observe certain ground rules. Coalitions are formed, often aimed at the leading actor, bargaining is sporadic, understandings are reached. As crises arise, minimal accommodations in roles and positions are made to solve the immediate issue or problem and avert a more serious showdown.

This system of loose control and wide distribution of power is largely a function of the pluralism that characterizes American urban society. Every man may not be king in the metropolis but the numerous power clusters provide him with ample opportunity to further his personal aims and protect his vested interests. Unfortunately not all people have the means or capabilities to take advantage of this opportunity, nor are the results always conducive to the well-being of the total community. But such problems are inherent in any free society. Although inequities exist, some of them gross, all the diverse elements in the community partake in the rewards of the system. No group is powerless to defend itself or to make its demands felt on the decision centers that exist throughout the structure.

The risks in such a multicentered system are many. Possibly the most serious is not the proliferation of power but the lack of an institutional base for the exercise of area-wide leadership. Although formal and informal avenues exist to acquiring influence in the many sectors of the community, no path to metropolitan leadership is open. The central city mayor is the best known and most important political official on the local scene, but his influence is confined to a territorial segment of the total area. He can serve as initiator, bargainer, compromiser, prodder, and coordinator of matters pertaining to his own bailiwick, but when the issue transcends city boundaries his effectiveness is drastically curtailed if not obliterated. Similarly, no suburban statesman anywhere has emerged to play the role of tribune for a metropolitan populace; and with an institutional base even more spatially circumscribed than the core city mayor, none is likely to appear. Popularly elected county executives offer some possibility for the future, but few areas have established the office, and from all indications acceptance of a county governmental official as the metropolitan "father-image" is a long way off.

The web of the metropolis continues to be fashioned, for better or worse, in response to the forces of urbanization and industrialization. The political system embodied in it evolves organically rather than rationally. Governmental changes take place gradually and on an *ad hoc* basis while social, technological, and economic developments race out far ahead. But somehow the system, despite its seeming irrationality and lack of a sense of direction, shows no signs of succumbing. More favorable to defenders of the status quo than to innovators, the political system (including the governmental organization) of the metropolis faces the long haul ahead. Only the future will decide its fate.

CHAPTER 8

▷ **The Metropolitan Citizenry as Civic Participants**

ARISTOTLE IN HIS CLASSIC *Politics* described man as a social animal, one who by nature is an active participant in the public and political life of the community. Correlatively, he added that the polity, the governmentally organized community, comes into being to satisfy the minimum needs of man but continues in existence to promote the good life. Today, both propositions—at least as they apply to the metropolis—evoke considerable skepticism. Critics of the contemporary urban scene trenchantly comment on the lack of citizen interest and participation in local public affairs and on the failure of governmental institutions to provide a satisfactory community environment. If man is a political animal, they say, he scarcely demonstrates it in his civic involvement. And if the polity exists for the sake of the good life, they point out, the physical and social maladies of the metropolis and its unmet needs give little indication that this role is being performed.

The democratic dogma assumes an order based on control through the consent of the governed. As traditional community institutions have been modified or dissolved under the impact of new forces such as technology and urbanization, the nature of popular control has changed also. The Jacksonian ideology of rule by friends and neighbors may have been appropriate for the agrarian America of the early nineteenth century but it misses the mark altogether in twentieth century urban America. This is not to say that community participation today is less important than it was a century or so ago. It is merely to point out that the changing character of urban society has evoked new participation patterns, a new organizational topography, and new citizen attitudes toward the community and its institutions. These features in turn have given rise to the kind of criticism that we have just noted.

We have already described the metropolitan community as a vast social network of interacting individuals and groups—a complex of living patterns, as it were, on the local level. We saw, however, that the whole system is loosely interconnected despite the close relationship of its parts. Highly heterogeneous in character and comprised of many independent subgroups, power clusters, and governments, the metropolis provides both incentive and deterrent to citizen participation. It furnishes incentive, since the vast opportunities and rewards that it offers stimulate individual and group activity in its public life. But it also supplies deterrent, since its bigness, its complexity, and its impersonal facade tend to discourage a high degree of involvement by all except the most highly motivated.

"In a sense," as sociologist Roland Warren has observed, "the community is the meeting place of the individual and the larger society and culture."[1] It is here that he directly confronts his society's institutions, its manner of living, its ways of regulating human behavior, its processes of educating the young, and its forms of cultural and religious expression. It is here, also, through these locally based institutions and practices, that the individual encounters the forces and influences of the broader society or social system: the nation and even the world. This, then, is the milieu in which man functions as a citizen and member of a politically and socially organized community.

Against this background, what can be said about metropolitan dwellers as civic participants? To simplify matters, we will analyze

[1] *The Community in America* (Chicago: Rand McNally, 1963), p. 21.

the topic in terms of four aspects: the degree of citizen commitment or identification with the community, voting in local elections, membership in voluntary associations, and informal group activity. Until recent years our knowledge of political and social involvement at the local level depended largely on impressions and speculations. Starting, however, with the famous Middletown (Muncie, Indiana) study by Robert and Helen Lynd in 1929, a new era of systematic inquiry into this important and exciting field was opened. Although a majority of the studies of the Middletown genre such as Yankee City, Plainville, U.S.A., and Crestwood Heights, deal with the small community, they are now being supplemented by a growing number of investigations of larger urban areas.[2] These latter efforts make it possible to discuss metropolitan participation patterns and citizen attitudes with the help of empirical evidence, although it is still incomplete and tentative.

COMMUNITY IDENTIFICATION

People may be the community, as the familiar expression runs, but not all play an equal part in its life. For many, the city or the metropolis means little more than a place to reside, earn a livelihood, shop, and entertain and be entertained. People of this type are important as economic providers and consumers (and as taxpayers), but they contribute little to the civic life of the area. For others, identification with the community involves little beyond support for the local baseball or football team. Some of the more enthusiastic will even follow the team to distant cities to root for the "home-town" boys. For a minority, being a good citizen means taking part in community affairs by serving on school and hospital committees, voting and otherwise showing an active interest in government, assisting in welfare and chest drives, and supporting civic and institutional improvement projects.

Many reasons prompt individual or group involvement in community affairs. In one case the motive for participation may be

[2] W. Lloyd Warner and Paul S. Lunt, The Social Life of a Modern Community (New Haven: Yale University Press, 1941); James West, Plainville, U.S.A. (New York: Columbia University Press, 1945); John R. Seeley, R. Alexander Sim, and Elizabeth W. Loosley, Crestwood Heights (New York: Basic Books, 1956).

primarily selfish, as that of the businessman or property owner who is concerned only from fear that his economic interests would suffer should the area deteriorate or decline. In another, it may be a matter of social responsibility, as that of the civic notable or influential who feels a sense of obligation to contribute some portion of his time to the betterment of the community. For many, the motive centers around the needs of the family and its use of local facilities, particularly the ability of the community to serve the primary group requirements of childrearing, such as education and recreation. The motivational shades, in other words, are many, a fact reflected by the wide differences in the degree of individual and group participation.

Commitment to community is an illusory concept that is difficult to define or measure. It may be manifested in many ways: by actual civic participation; by household and business investments; by longtime residency; by support of local institutions; or simply by expressions of pride in the locality. It may consist of involvement with neighborhood affairs, joining in the organizational life of the larger community, or more directly participating as a voter, civic leader, or public official. Some indications of commitment, such as voting and length of residence, can readily be ascertained. Others of a less tangible nature, such as emotional attachment and attitude toward the community, are not easily measured. According to the findings of one survey—which are probably typical of the general situation—16 percent of urban dwellers have practically no commitment to their community while only 11 percent are heavily involved in local affairs.[3] The remainder are widely dispersed over the participation continuum.

Images

One clue to the degree of commitment or identification is the image which citizens hold of their community. Several years ago a representative sample of Metropolitan Dayton residents was asked this question: "If someone who didn't know the Dayton and Montgomery County area asked you what you were proudest of about it,

[3] Morris Janowitz, *The Community Press* (New York: Free Press, 1952), pp. 209 ff. Janowitz's study of three Chicago community areas deals primarily with the community press an an indicator of social cohesion but his findings have broad political implications.

what would you tell him?"[4] The responses were revealing. The most frequent answer, one given by more than one-half of the persons interviewed, pertained to the cleanliness and beauty of the area; some of these, for example, mentioned specific physical features such as wide streets and attractive homes and buildings. Other people referred to the generally high level of prosperity in the area, and a number cited the friendliness of the people. Significantly, only one in twenty mentioned local government or public services, and only one in fifty spoke of citizen interest and participation in community affairs as a matter of particular pride. The identification of Daytonians with their area was, as these replies indicate, predominantly in terms of a physical place to live or work. For residents of this particular metropolis (and there is no reason to believe them atypical), local government and its operations do not form an important part of the total image of their community.

When the subject is community commitment or involvement, the problem of identifying the unit that is being referred to again arises. The question presents no difficulty if we are dealing with the relatively small and territorially isolated town such as the Middletown of the Lynds or the Plainville of James West. When, however, the community is a metropolis composed of several or many cities and villages, the problem is no longer simple. Here we are confronted with the difficulty of discriminating between the attachment an individual may have for the municipality or local unit in which he resides and his identification with the larger metropolitan community of which he is also an integral part. Which has more meaning in his eyes, and which elicits greater response from him?

Some evidence dealing with this general question is also contained in the Metropolitan Dayton survey. Individuals who were interviewed were asked, "When you are away from this area, what do you say is your home town?" (The concept of home town suggests a feeling of "rootedness," thus furnishing a crude measure of identification with the community in which one lives.) Three of every four suburban residents named the central city while only one in ten mentioned their own municipality or township. The remainder gave a city outside the area. The import of the results

[4] *Metropolitan Challenge* (Dayton: Metropolitan Community Studies, 1959), pp. 22 ff.

from a question of this type, of course, can be exaggerated since individuals may when travelling list the central city as their place of residence merely because others would recognize the name. Yet, as in the case of Dayton, identification of many suburbanites with the central city and its institutions offers an indication of metropolitan consciousness and a realization of the linkages between parts of the same urban area.

Similar observations may be made of suburbanites in the Detroit area who identify themselves with the Tigers baseball team, or of those in the New York SMSA who regard the city's famed Metropolitan Opera and Metropolitan Museum as part of their cultural assets. Sports-minded readers also will recall the fracas over the team name when big league baseball went to the twin cities of Minneapolis and St. Paul a few years ago, a dispute that was finally settled by calling the Washington, D.C., expatriates the Minnesota Twins. These are small and rather superficial signs, yet they suggest the existence of deeper feelings of metropolitan identity that might possibly be exploited for more meaningful community purposes.

Man Versus the Metropolis

There is a tendency among many city dwellers to speak of their local government as if it were something separate and apart from them. It is a common experience to hear an individual refer to his municipal government as "it," "they," or "the city hall." When matters arise which bring him in direct contact with his local unit, he finds the whole process complicated and impersonal. He conceives of himself on one side and something called the city or the bureaucracy on the other. His disposition is that the less he has to do with this unknown quantity and with the "politicians" who run it, the better off he is. Those with this attitude are content to let local government go its way so long as it takes care of the community's normal housekeeping functions in fairly adequate fashion, avoids scandal, and keeps the tax rate within reasonable bounds. As a generalization of citizen attitude toward local government, this description has validity.

But local government means different things to different people. In the more extreme cases, those found most frequently among low-income ethnic and racial groups, the policeman and his nightstick symbolize city government. To the slum landlord trying to milk his property dry, the building and health inspectors are the bureaucracy. To the suburban mother and active P.T.A. member, the local school district constitutes the government. However local government is regarded, seldom is interest in it as a basic community institution high. In the Metropolitan Dayton survey, more than one-third of the respondents stated that they had little or no interest in local governmental affairs, and about half said that they had "some." Only a small minority, 15 percent, expressed "a great deal" of interest. Samplings of citizen attitudes elsewhere have resulted in similar findings.

This sort of live and let live philosophy in respect to local government is encouraged by the realities of modern urban existence, realities working against widespread citizen commitment and identification. Both bigness and specialization, two key attributes of metropolitan life, contribute to this result. The first makes direct participation in community affairs by individuals difficult. The simple fact of bigness engenders a feeling of personal helplessness in the presence of the leviathan. When a sample of Detroit citizens was asked, "Do you feel that there is anything you can do to improve the way the city is run?" one-half of the respondents said no. Only one in twelve believed that he could exert influence by means of personal criticism or by joining in group action. The authors of the study concluded that "great numbers of Detroit citizens feel helpless and indifferent about changing their city. They have few ideas how things can be made better and little understanding of how they personally can play a part."[5]

Equally important, the high degree of specialization of the metropolis focuses the attention and energies of the residents on their vocational responsibilities and interests to the almost total exclusion of the polity. Life in modern urban society becomes compartmentalized around one's business or work while an individual's leisure hours are devoted to the small world of his primary relationships: family, relatives, and friends. Little time or inclination remains for more than occasional and haphazard involvement in civic affairs. The unmistakable fact, moreover, is that the number of legitimate community concerns has now become so great as a result of urbanization and its accompanying features that individual citizens

[5] Arthur Kornhauser, *Detroit as the People See It* (Detroit: Wayne State University Press, 1952), p. 176.

cannot actively concern themselves with all of them even if they are so inclined.

THE REPUBLIC IN MINIATURE

This discussion prompts a question that merits examination before turning to the patterns of participation of urban residents. If the large-scale community discourages citizen participation in public affairs, as the evidence seems to indicate, is not the case of those who argue for the perpetuation of the small local government greatly strengthened? We hear much about the virtues of suburban communities and the desirability of maintaining their political autonomy in the face of metropolitan reorganization movements. In American political folklore, as Robert Wood notes, the justification for suburban legal independence "rests on the classic belief in grassroots democracy, our long standing conviction that small political units represent the purest expression of popular rule . . ." In such a milieu, "no voter is a faceless member in a political rally, but an individual citizen who knows his elected officials, can judge their performance personally and hold them accountable."[6]

A community newspaper in the Milwaukee metropolitan area put the case for small government less formally in an editorial that is worth quoting for its unrestrained expression of the suburban myth. Commenting on a decision of the Wisconsin Supreme Court that awarded a disputed portion of Brown Deer, a Milwaukee suburb, to the central city, the newspaper lamented:

A cold pall that is not of the people's doing hangs upon Brown Deer—the more the bitterness! Here is a young community, for the most part made up of young families dedicated to securing the best in local government for themselves and their children, denied the right of voice in its affairs.

The heartbreak is that all these young families, who so revivify the spirit of our founding fathers in securing a new way of life, seemingly are not to have any say about the kind of a community or government under which they are to live.

They would prefer a hamlet or town hall where they could talk over their common needs rather than become a segment of a city that in no way has ever helped with the development of raw lands until it proved

[6] *Suburbia* (Boston: Houghton Mifflin, 1959), p. 12.

worthwhile territory to gobble, a city that allowed its inner core to fester and then seek new but developed territory to annex.

It is a sad day in this twentieth century when people become mere pawns of state and have their grassroots government torn from under them. Sad, indeed it is, that the supreme court could so lightly toss aside a request for rehearing on the litigation question—to not let the people have voice.

If mourning were in fashion, the whole contested area would be in shrouds for the abruptness of the decision carries with it the seed of bitterness for those who served their country through their early years of manhood and came home with renewed determination they would own their own homes and dig deep into the grassroots of America.

After so much work by officials and citizenry to build a semi-rural area for children to play in, for neighbors to be real neighbors, helping each other and guarding the children, it is heartbreak and pain.

Our forebears found a way to self government via the Boston tea party, perhaps the outraged ex-Brown Deereans may also find a way. We wish them surcease of trials.[7]

The picture is a touching one, but how much of the myth conforms to reality? As we shall see later in this chapter when considering participation, little evidence exists to support the claim that suburbanites play a larger role or show greater interest in their local community and its government than do their central city counterparts. Suburban residents may be unwilling to surrender the legal independence of their local unit—witness their adverse vote in consolidation referenda—but seldom does this unwillingness grow out of any deep feeling of attachment and dedication to their miniature republic. In most instances it is the result of uncertainty or fear as to the consequences that change might bring: higher taxes, invasion by Negroes and other core city "undesirables," downgrading of the local public school system, or loss of certain privileges peculiar to the suburban enclave. Some, but hardly more than a minority, also feel that they have greater access to the small-town government than they would to the large city bureaucracy and that their wishes and complaints are better heeded.

Suburban living may have its advantages and attractions but would these be any different under a consolidated governmental system? Certainly the drawbacks of bigness alone do not support the argument of those who laud the virtues of the suburban village,

---

[7] *Fox Point-Bayside-River Hills Herald*, June 18, 1962.

for a suburb is as much a part of large-scale society as a neighbor-hood in the core city. It is probably true that small communities are more conducive to the formation of closely knit social systems. People are more likely to know each other and to interact among themselves to a greater degree because of their less specialized and more diversified roles. But here we are talking about something quite different, the small town or village territorially separated from other communities.

Contrary to the rhetoric of those who adamantly defend the integrity of the ring municipalities, suburban cities and towns are not isolated or autonomous units but little more than parts or neighborhoods of a larger urban complex. The individuals and groups who inhabit them are subject to the same forces and pressures that typically characterize metropolitan life and operate against citizen activity and involvement in the affairs of the local community. The suburban resident is no more immune from the effects of bigness and specialization than is the central city dweller. Both are caught up in the whirl of modern urban life and both tend to react to it in similar fashion. As a result, other factors being equal, their political behavior as local citizens shows no appreciable differences. There may be sound reasons for the politically autonomous suburb, but the grassroots argument is hardly one of them.

PARTICIPATION BY VOTING

Man is involved in many role relationships: as husband or parent, employer or employee, neighbor or stranger, producer or consumer. In this social matrix of seemingly endless interpersonal relations, the individual is also a political actor and as such a participant in the governance of his community. This participation may take many forms. It may be limited to the occasional act of voting, or it may also entail electioneering, standing for office, and exerting leader-ship in community affairs. It may involve membership in voluntary organizations, engaging in discussions about local issues, trying to influence public officials, or simply registering complaints about governmental services. For some, the degree of participation is ex-tremely small; for others, a minority to be sure, it is all-encompassing. Whatever the extent, man's involvement or political role in the community is a pivotal factor in determining the shape and character of government in the metropolis.

Voting provides the most objective if not the most relevant index of citizen interest in public affairs. The act of voting, as political scientist Robert Lane points out, involves an expenditure of time and energy, the making of a decision, a certain relatedness to society, and an affirmation that votes do make a difference.[8] That many citizens do not take the trouble to perform this function regularly is evident from election statistics. In fact, a conspicuously wide disparity exists between the potential size of the electorate and those who vote. Only 60 to 65 percent of those of voting age go to the polls in presidential elections while it has been estimated that 17 percent of the electorate has never voted in any national contest.[9] Studies dealing with national elections also show that non-voting is generally higher among women, the youngest eligible age group (21 to 30), and individuals with low socioeconomic status (education, occupation, and income).[10]

Although data on voting behavior at the local level are much less complete, the evidence reveals a pattern generally similar to that found in national and state elections. Turnout is low, actually far less than in presidential and congressional contests. Seldom do more than 50 percent of the registered voters go to the polls in municipal elections. The more likely figure is 30 percent, and it is not uncommon for the vote to drop to less than one-fourth of the registered electorate, with the usual turnout in school district and other non-municipal contests even lower. The percentage of those who never participate in local elections is also larger than that at the national level. The St. Louis and Dayton studies found that over one-fourth of those eligible to vote in local contests had never done so. Both studies further revealed that almost all who take part in local elections also vote in national contests but that the reverse does not hold true.[11]

The demographic characteristics of local voters and non-voters also follow the national pattern. Women tend to vote less than men

[8] *Political Life* (New York: Free Press, 1958), p. 47.

[9] Samuel J. Eldersveld, "The Independent Vote: Measurement, Characteristics, and Implications for Party Strategy," *American Political Science Review*, XLVI (September, 1952), 739.

[10] See, for example, Angus Campbell, Gerald Gurin, and Warren E. Miller, *The Voter Decides* (New York: Harper & Row, 1954).

[11] John C. Bollens (ed.), *Exploring the Metropolitan Community* (Berkeley and Los Angeles: University of California Press, 1961), p. 182; *Metropolitan Challenge*, p. 231.

although the difference is not great and is becoming progressively less so; young people and those individuals over 65 are less likely to go to the polls than the intervening age groups; and those with lower incomes and less formal education are more apt to refrain from electoral participation than individuals of higher social rank. Two additional variables—length of residence and home ownership—are also significant determinatives of community participation patterns. The longer a person lives in the same locality, the greater the likelihood that he will vote in local elections. Similarly, if he owns his home, he is more apt to vote than he is if he rents his dwelling quarters.

The male-female differential in voting participation is seemingly a result of less interest and less opportunity for involvement in public affairs on the part of women as well as less social pressure on them to vote. In recent years, however, women have so increased their electoral participation that when other factors are held constant, their rate of voting no longer differs greatly from that of men.

The lower rate of voting among young adults undoubtedly grows out of factors associated with their stage in the life cycle. Persons in their twenties and early thirties are often not yet involved in neighborhood and community networks of commitment and responsibility. Geographically and occupationally mobile, they are busily engaged in establishing new families, finding their way in new job situations, and meeting mortgage payments. These personal commitments consume their time and energies and channel their interests away from public affairs. Toward the other end of the age continuum, the rate of voting also tends to decline. Persons over 65 begin to find many of their community bonds falling away with the dissolution of their families and the relative isolation of old age. For them, voting and the round of civic participation tend to become more burdensome if not less meaningful.

Several factors help to explain the close relationship between socioeconomic level and voting rate. People with more education, better jobs, and higher incomes are likely to be knowledgeable about public issues, feel a high sense of personal efficacy in political matters, and have a large personal stake in the outcome of elections. Even if they do not have a sense of responsibility to their community —which they are more likely to have than those of lower socioeconomic rank—they nevertheless feel socially compelled to participate in the electoral process. Social norms in the lower status groups, on the other hand, place less emphasis on political and civic activity.

Both length of residence and home ownership are indicators of commitment to the community and both tend to stimulate participation in its public affairs. The individual who has lived in the same locality for a long time has struck deeper roots than the transient, knows more about the area, and is more likely to have acquired interests that he is anxious to protect. A similar statement may be made about the home owner as against the renter. Investment in a home gives a feeling of greater permanence as well as a vested stake in the neighborhood or community. Empirical findings support these propositions. The Metropolitan Dayton survey, for example, found that the non-voter in local elections is most likely to be an individual who has lived in his present location less than five years, does not own his home, and has a lower educational level. To the same effect, the St. Louis area study reported than 26 percent more owners than renters voted in local contests.

One further aspect of the voting pattern should be noted. The statement is frequently made that a smaller proportion of Negroes than whites vote. However, outside the South, with its barriers to Negro voting, racial background is not generally of great importance in determining electoral participation. Local surveys have found no significant differences between Negroes and whites in the extent of their activeness in local public affairs, including voting. The fact that a great proportion of Negroes are in the low educational, occupational, and income categories depresses the overall percentage of those who go to the polls and creates the impression of lower participation rates. When these factors are held constant, Negroes are found to be proportionately represented among community actives.

Voter Interest

The lower turnout rate in local as compared to national elections is at least partly a result of the degree of interest which each type generates. Recent surveys of citizen attitudes in several communities have probed into this question in different ways. One, a study of a group of small communities, inquired whether respondents were "most interested in what happens in the local elections, the state elections, or the national elections." Two-thirds of the sample expressed most interest in national, one-fourth in local, and less than one-tenth in state contests.[12] Another, the Metropolitan Dayton survey, asked the interviewees to rate their own interest in local governmental affairs. Only 15 percent said they had a great deal of interest; 50 percent "some"; 30 percent "little"; and 4 percent "none."[13] A third, the St. Louis area study, inquired as to whether respondents agreed or disagreed with the statement, "A good many local elections aren't important enough to bother with." One of every four individuals interviewed expressed agreement.[14]

Taken together, these findings from communities of different size and type point conclusively to the absence of a high level of interest in local elections. National contests involve such issues as war and peace, civil rights, and medicare; and these have considerable capacity to arouse the concern of the citizenry. Local elections, in a quite different vein, generally tend to center around such matters as inefficiency, poor administration, charter reform, service and house-keeping functions, and capital improvements. Issues of this kind are not likely to bring the voter screaming to his feet. Only on relatively few occasions are emotionally charged questions involved, and they usually fade into the background after the initial excitement passes. Yet individuals are by no means devoid of all interest in local affairs and elections. Actually, as the evidence demonstrates, they are more concerned with matters at the local than at the state government level. This concern, however, is generally not strong enough to stimulate a high degree of electoral activity.

Voting on metropolitan government proposals is a case in point. Many of the referenda have involved plans that would radically change the local governmental pattern and structure. Logically, this should be a matter of considerable concern to residents of the metropolis, but examination of the voter turnout in such elections leads to a different conclusion. Only 22 percent of the registered electorate, for example, cast ballots on the proposed merger of the city of Albuquerque and Bernalillo County in 1959. A special election on the creation of a multifunctional metropolitan district for the St. Louis area in the same year drew 40 percent of the qualified electorate in the suburbs and 20 percent in the central city. Also

[12] *The Fox Valley Survey.* Unpublished (Madison: University of Wisconsin Survey Research Center).

[13] *Metropolitan Challenge*, p. 234.

[14] Bollens (ed.), *Exploring the Metropolitan Community*, p. 184.

in 1959, Cleveland area voters rejected a comprehensive urban county charter, with 57 percent of the registered electorate in the city and 68 percent in the suburbs participating. An unusually active campaign in the Cleveland area preceded the higher than normal turnout for elections of this kind. More recently, the unsuccessful attempt to consolidate the governments of Memphis and Shelby County, Tennessee (November, 1962), drew 53 percent of the registered voters to the polls. Part of the turnout in this case is attributable to the fact that the issue was voted on at a general election.

Even the successful election on a comprehensive urban county charter in Dade County (Miami), Florida, in 1957 attracted only 26 percent of the voters. Commenting on citizen interest in this highly publicized experiment in metropolitan government, two University of Miami political scientists pointedly observed:

Any testing of levels of thought and feeling in the political sub-structure inevitably yields new evidence of abject apathy and gross ignorance in the citizen mass. This is particularly true in dealing with the subject of local government. To find, as we did . . . that only 15% of our registered citizens could think of anything good that the county commission had done in the preceding year, or that 24% could name something blameworthy that they had done (9% named a parks concession scandal) is routine.

However, somehow one expects a thing as big as Metro to make an impression. When only 32% say they have heard or read about a new county charter and had a sliver of a correct idea about it, while 13% have a quite wrong idea about it, that sinking sensation returns. It was not only in the telephone poll that 64½% said they did not know of any big change in the county government in the last couple of years. The same question had produced the identical 64½% shrugging response when asked in Survey #10 [an earlier sampling by personal interview].[15]

Political Alienation

Social scientists have written a great deal during the past decade about voter apathy and political alienation; in fact, a study of the Boston mayoralty contest in 1959 is entitled *The Alienated Voter*.[16] Emerging from this literature is a picture of a politically active

[15] Ross C. Beiler and Thomas J. Wood, "Metropolitan Politics of Miami," (Paper presented at the annual meeting of the Southern Political Science Association, Gatlinburg, Tenn., November 7, 1958), p. 13.

[16] Murray B. Levin, *The Alienated Voter* (New York: Holt, Rinehart and Winston, 1960).

minority directing the course of the polity while the larger segment of the citizen body plays a relatively small and essentially acquiescent part in community affairs. The low level of involvement by many urban residents is attributed to apathy or indifference, which in turn is linked to political alienation—a feeling on the part of the individual that his vote makes no difference and that his political or civic activity can have little influence in determining community policy. This feeling of futility tends to cause a withdrawal by the individual from political participation and a retreat into the little world of his own immediate and personal problems.[17]

Political alienation may involve not only apathy or indifference as a response to feelings of inefficacy but it may also lead to displeasure at being powerless and to a distrust of the persons in power. When such is the case, political alienation, given the opportunity for expression at the polls, is likely to be translated into a vote of resentment or protest against the "powers that be," or an ill-defined "them."[18] Local referenda particularly provide such opportunities. Such issues as fluoridation, charter amendments, and school bond elections tend to attract an exceptionally large number of individuals predisposed to cast a negative ballot. This phenomenon is also relevant to the cause of metropolitan governmental reorganization. Interviews with a sample of suburban residents in the Nashville, Tennessee, area showed that political alienation was significantly related to an unfavorable attitude and negative vote on the issue of consolidating the city and county governments of that metropolis.[19] Voting against issues of this kind, in other words, may be more than the rejection of the particular program; it may be, in

[17] David Riesman, *The Lonely Crowd* (New Haven: Yale University Press, 1950). Also see Morris Rosenberg, "Some Determinants of Political Apathy," *Public Opinion Quarterly*, 18 (Winter, 1954), 349–366; and Melvin Seeman, "On the Meaning of Alienation," *American Sociological Review*, 24 (December, 1959), 783–790.

[18] Wayne E. Thompson and John E. Horton, "Political Alienation as a Force in Political Action," *Social Forces*, 38 (March, 1960), 190–195; John E. Horton and Wayne E. Thompson, "Powerlessness and Political Negativism: A Study of Defeated Local Referendums," *American Journal of Sociology*, LXVII (March, 1962), 485–493.

[19] Edward L. McDill and Jeanne C. Ridley, "Status, Anomia, Political Alienation and Political Participation," *American Journal of Sociology*, LXVIII (September, 1962), 205–213.

addition, an expression of general discontent on the part of the politically alienated.

Political alienation is the response pattern most frequently found among the lower socioeconomic strata. It is a pattern that finds reflection in the high incidence of non-voting and in the expressions of civic unconcern typical of those at this end of the social continuum. But non-voting in local elections is characteristic of a far broader sector of the community than the low status groups or the socially estranged. One writer offers this explanation. "The principal reason for apathy in municipal elections, in fact, is likely to be a pervasive consensus, that is, there may be widespread agreement in the community as to the kinds of persons who are wanted in public office, as to expenditure levels, and as to public policies. Under such circumstances, there is little incentive for any but the most conscientious voter to go to the polls."[20] Another suggests that perhaps even many "well-adjusted citizens do not consider the trouble of registering, informing themselves of complex affairs, determining the position of candidates with respect to these affairs, and finally getting themselves to the polls, to be adequately compensated by the personal improvement which the act of voting promises to achieve for them."[21] The authors of a major voting study touch upon this latter point in an enlightening way:

An assumption underlying the theory of democracy is that the citizenry has a strong motivation for participation in political life. But it is a curious quality of voting behavior that for large numbers of people motivation is weak if not almost absent. It is assumed that this motivation would gain its strength from the citizen's perception of the difference that alternative decisions made to him. Now when a person buys something or makes other decisions of daily life, there are direct and immediate consequences for him. But for the bulk of the American people the voting decision is not followed by any direct, immediate, visible personal consequences. Most voters, organized or unorganized, are not in a position to foresee the distant and indirect consequences for themselves, let alone the society.[22]

[20] Charles R. Adrian, *Governing Urban America*, 2nd ed. (New York: McGraw-Hill, 1961), p. 93.

[21] William Buchanan, "An Inquiry into Purposive Voting," *Journal of Politics*, 18 (May, 1956), 296.

[22] Bernard R. Berelson, Paul F. Lazarsfeld, and William N. McPhee, *Voting* (Chicago: University of Chicago Press, 1954), p. 308.

Each of these views doubtlessly has a measure of validity. None of them offers or purports to offer a total explanation. Each recognizes that the causes of non-voting in local (as in national and state) elections are numerous and complex. We have touched upon several of the more general and pervasive of these causes. Others that might be mentioned include the general attitude of the citizen toward his community, the degree to which organized groups are active in local campaigns, and the type of election employed, that is, whether partisan or nonpartisan. We know, for example, that elections conducted on a party basis tend to engender more organized political activity and therefore usually turn out a higher vote than nonpartisan contests. Today, however, the majority of American municipalities employ the nonpartisan method of election. Approximately two of every three cities with 5000 or more population presently elect their local officials on nonpartisan tickets. So do almost 70 percent of the central cities and an even higher proportion of the suburban communities in the nation's metropolitan areas.

One may argue, as some people do, about the significance of low electoral participation for community government and its functioning. According to one school of thought, a low voting rate indicates the citizenry is generally satisfied with the way matters are going and is content to entrust the management of community affairs to those willing to undertake the task. High voting rates, in this view, may be signs of tension and social conflict that make community consensus and therefore community stability impossible. To the élitist-minded, low electoral participation is actually desirable since non-voting is most common among the uneducated, ignorant, and poorest social groups; and they would be most likely to employ their strength at the ballot box to society's disadvantage. Another view, expressed by some observers, shrugs off the fact that those who elect to vote constitute a small proportion of the population. By a process of self-selection, they say, the interested, informed, and those with community responsibilities will perform the civic acts which must be done.

We need not interject ourselves into this argument except to point out its existence. Low voting participation is undoubtedly a reflection of other factors affecting general community behavior. Whether it is caused by a sense of political impotence, by a lack of awareness about the public sphere, or simply by the fact that people have more interesting things to do with their time, the phenomenon itself is relevant to the functioning of the urban community. Low voting, for example, may mean that the socially and economically disadvantaged groups are underrepresented in local government. It may cause community goals to be "watered down" and encourage inactivity rather than action at the policy-making level. Finally, it may deter the modernization of local government in metropolitan areas by endowing the status quo with a protective mantle. Ideally speaking, and from the standpoint of a healthy community, it is desirable to involve the little as well as the big John Smiths in activities which give them a sense of participation in decisions that affect their daily lives. Voting is one such form of involvement.

PARTICIPATION IN GROUP LIFE

Voting is not the only, nor necessarily the most important, means of participation in local civic affairs. The role of the citizen in relation to his community goes considerably beyond the infrequent act of casting his ballot, basic as this function is to the selection of officials and the determination of ballot issues. Membership in voluntary associations that are concerned with local affairs is one form of non-electoral participation. By the simple act of joining an organization of this nature, the individual lends his support to its goals and operations. If he is an active participant in its life, he may help shape the group's stand on a community issue or problem; and this stand in turn may influence others including the official or governmental policy-makers. In short, organizational affiliation offers the citizen an opportunity to become a far more influential community participant than he could otherwise be, or than the mere act of voting implies.

Because of the importance of voluntary associations in the community fabric, we are interested in knowing the extent to which metropolitan dwellers take part in the life of such groups. We are also interested in determining whether the various socioeconomic segments of the community are characterized by different patterns of organizational activity. Last, we would like to know more about participation in informal groups, such as the family or neighborhood, and its relation to community behavior. These are more than academic topics. Like voting, they have direct relevance to the operation of the metropolis and the quality of its public life, as the degree of participation in formal and informal groupings is another indicator, perhaps an even more accurate one than voting, of citizen involvement in the polity.

Extent of Participation

More than a century ago, Alexis de Tocqueville, the noted French commentator on American mores and institutions, observed that "Americans of all ages, all conditions, and all dispositions constantly form associations."[23] Historians Charles and Mary Beard, writing in more recent times, commented that the tendency of which de Tocqueville spoke "has now become a general mania."[24] The habit of joining, of organizing human contacts around some cause or activity, is a well recognized feature of our cultural environment. Voluntary associations act as stimuli, arousing their participants to greater involvement in the political life of the larger society. They provide a far-flung although highly decentralized network for mobilizing citizen interest and activity on public issues and problems. Together with the formal structure of local government they constitute an integral part of the community's organizational system. Segmented in their membership and purposes, and frequently in competition with one another, such groupings enlist the allegiances of the citizenry in a variety of causes. In playing this role, they serve as important anchoring points for the political and associational life of the individual.

Although organizational membership is widespread and pervasive, a substantial number of individuals remain outside it. A study based on evidence from national sample surveys reveals that somewhat less than one-half of all adult Americans are members of voluntary associations (other than church-related groups); and of those who are joiners, only a small part have membership in two or more groups.[25] Other studies of individual communities have also

[23] *Democracy in America* (New York: Knopf, 1946), Vol. II, p. 106.

[24] *Rise of American Civilization* (New York: Macmillan, 1927), Vol. 2, p. 730.

[25] Charles R. Wright and Herbert H. Hyman, "Voluntary Association Memberships of American Adults: Evidence from National Sample Surveys," *American Sociological Review,* 23 (June, 1958), 284–294.

found considerable non-participation, with the rate varying from one-third to one-half.[26]

Membership in organizations that are primarily interested in or have some substantial concern with local public affairs and community action involves a much lower percentage of the population. Data gathered in national studies show that only 2 percent of the adult citizenry belong to a political club or organization and 31 percent to an association that sometimes takes a stand on such public issues as housing, better government, or school affairs.[27] (This latter figure includes membership in unions, chambers of commerce, and other groups that only occasionally become involved in local civic issues.) Less than one adult in ten belongs to an organization such as the League of Women Voters, neighborhood improvement associations, or good government clubs, that exist for the specific purpose of civic involvement.

Membership alone, of course, is not a reliable indicator of organizational participation. To belong to a formally organized group is one matter, but to play an active and meaningful role in its affairs is another. Many people are members in name only. They belong because it is occupationally necessary or socially desirable for them to do so but they have little inclination (some, in fact, have no capacity) to become involved in organizational activities. If we define the active member as one who attends meetings regularly and who holds office or serves on committees in the organization, the proportion of the citizen body in this category is probably as low as 15 or 20 percent. One study found that among those who belonged to voluntary associations, one-fourth had not attended any meeting during the three months preceding the interview while another one-third indicated that they rarely attended.[28] Thus like voting, active involvement in organizational life is confined to a minority of the population.

[26] Sampling of the Detroit area population in the mid-1950s disclosed that 37 percent of the respondents were not members of formal groups. See Morris Axelrod, "Urban Structure and Social Participation," *American Sociological Review*, 21 (February, 1956), 13–18. The Metropolitan Dayton survey similarly found that one-third of the adult residents belonged to no organization, one-fourth to only one, and the remainder to more than one (*Metropolitan Challenge*, p. 227).

[27] Lane, *Political Life*, p. 75.

[28] Axelrod, "Urban Structure and Social Participation," pp. 13–18.

Who Belongs?

To determine the extent and intensity of citizen participation in voluntary associations is not enough; it is equally, if not more important to know who belongs. Are those who join formal groupings randomly distributed throughout the population or disproportionately concentrated in certain socioeconomic categories? Because of the large role private associations play in the civic arena and in shaping public policy, the extent to which the community's organizational web is representative of the total populace is a matter of some concern. We would assume that those segments of the society which are highly organized are in a better position than the unorganized to make their influence felt in the public sphere. Studies show, moreover, that those who participate in voluntary associations are, as a group, different from other persons in the community in at least three respects: they are much more likely to be voters, they are more likely to remain voters, and they are more likely to become voters if they had been non-voters.[29]

When the demographic features of associational membership are examined, a pattern similar to that found in electoral participation emerges. Belonging to formal organizations is closely related to social rank (education, occupation, income), age, and length of residence in the community. Based on a nationwide sample, the Michigan Survey Research Center found that 47 percent of those with grade school education or less belonged to no organization while the comparable figure for those who had attended college was 19 percent. The study also revealed that 60 percent of those in the lower income brackets as against 20 percent in the higher categories were non-joiners.[30] The same situation prevails in the case of multiple memberships. Findings of the Metropolitan Dayton survey show that about one-fourth of metropolitan residents of lower educational status as against nearly three-fourths of those who had attended college belong to two or more organizations. They also demonstrate that socioeconomic variables bear a close relationship to organizational

[29] Herbert Maccoby, "The Differential Political Activity of Participants in a Voluntary Association," *American Sociological Review*, 23 (October, 1958), 524–532.

[30] Lane, *Political Life*, p. 78. Also see Mirra Komarovsky, "The Voluntary Associations of Urban Dwellers," *American Sociological Review*, 11 (December, 1946), 468–498.

activism. The college group in the Dayton area was four times as well represented as the lower educational categories among those who attend meetings regularly. And so were individuals in the higher occupational and income levels, thus again indicating the class-linked nature of membership in voluntary associations.

Age is a further determinative factor in organizational affiliation. Membership is highest among individuals between the ages of 35 and 65, with a significantly lower figure for those not yet 35 and a sharp drop among the oldsters. The heavy involvement of young adults in establishing careers, families, and homes detracts from their participation in the community's organizational life. Later, after they reach retirement, their roles in organizations and civic endeavors become less meaningful and less active. They find, moreover, that with increasing age useful participational roles become less available to them as society turns to more youthful leadership and new ideas.

Length of residence, the third variable found to be related to membership, reflects the degree of local identification and commitment held by the individual citizen. The relationship is a positive one: membership in voluntary associations tends to increase with length of time in the community. The highest rate of both membership and active participation occurs among natives and those residing in the neighborhood for more than twenty years. Less than one-half the newcomers to the Dayton area (those living there no more than five years) belonged to a formal organization of any kind, and less than one-fifth of those who did belong could be classified as active members.[31] Morris Janowitz also found in his Chicago study that almost one-third of his sample of leaders had resided in their present community since childhood.

The United States is a nation of families and individuals who often change their place of residence. So widespread is this trait that one of the first questions asked of a new acquaintance is, "Where are you from?" According to the 1960 census, almost one-half of the nation's 159 million people above the age of four were not living in the same dwelling where they had resided five years earlier. And of those who had changed their residence during this period, over 14

[31] Similar results are reported in a study of a medium-sized midwestern community by sociologist Basil Zimmer. "Participation of Migrants in Urban Structures," *American Sociological Review*, 20 (April, 1955), 218–224.

million had moved to a different state. This geographical mobility is a factor of importance to metropolitan living. Many urban residents do not remain in the same locality long enough to cultivate close ties or to become integrated into the associational web of the community. The constant moving back and forth across the country in search of better jobs or other opportunities, or as a result of corporate policies of transferring personnel, puts a premium, as one sociologist has said, "on the tree which can survive with shallow roots."[32]

Mobility within the borders of the metropolitan area itself is a further source of weak community ties. The ceaseless movement from central city to the ring, from suburb to suburb, from the fringe to exurbia (the area beyond the established suburbs), leaves little time for the family to sink its roots into the community soil. When one knows he is not going to remain long in a particular governmental jurisdiction or subsection of the metropolis, he is not likely to become deeply involved in its affairs. The number of people in this category is legion. A poll of residents in most metropolitan areas would probably reveal that 50 percent or more have at least tentative plans to move within the next four or five years. The desire for higher grade housing, better neighborhoods and schools, and more open space is a predominating stimulus in this game of musical chairs. Only a society with a steadily increasing standard of living could sustain the movement.

Informal Participation

Individuals participate in community life through informal and primary group relations as well as through voting and membership in voluntary associations. Relatives, friends, and neighbors serve as major anchors and points of interaction in the daily life of most people. As intimate and informal groupings, they provide an important source of the norms and attitudes which the members of a given society share. The family gatherings, the discussions with one's fellow workers at the plant or with friends at the poker or bridge table, the conversations over the back fence or round the barbecue pit, all leave their mark on the impressions and views of the participants and all are important channels of communication. The nature and extent of an individual's relation with others in these

32 Warren, *The Community in America*, p. 18.

informal, face-to-face situations inevitably affect his beliefs and his ways of thinking. If, to cite only one example, he enjoys close contact with relatives or friends who are active in civic affairs, this fact will probably be reflected in greater community involvement on his own part. If, on the other hand, those with whom he regularly associates are totally uninterested in local government and local public issues, the odds are that his own community participation will be low.

The implications here are clear. Although these primary or face-to-face groups do not appear on any organizational chart of the local polity or governmental system, they constitute key building blocks in its structure.[33] If nothing else, patterns of friendship and neighborhood contacts are indicators of community integration and cohesion. Earlier we spoke about political alienation and the "rootless" individual. The emphasis on this characteristic of political man can be overdone since, as we indicated, the majority of urban residents are neither alienated or rootless. They may be bored and uninterested in civic affairs, but many of them find gratification of their psychic needs in their informal group contacts. When these contacts or social ties extend beyond the local governmental boundaries, as many do, they also serve as unifying forces for the metropolitan community. When a suburbanite's close friends or kin live in the central city, each brings to the other a better understanding and appreciation of the linkages between the two sections of the larger community.

Some sociologists contend that urbanization leads to greater emphasis on voluntary associations at the expense of primary groups. Stressing the impersonality of relationships in the metropolis, they see the formal organization becoming a substitute for the kinship and neighborhood group. If this assumption is correct, individual involvement should be increasingly intense with respect to voluntary associations and correspondingly weak as to relatives, friends, and neighbors. Other sociologists deny that the role of informal groups is being taken over by organizations, contending that participation with kin and friendship circles is more widespread today than at any time in the recent past. Contemporary survey findings appear to support the latter position. The Metropolitan Dayton study showed

[33] See Sidney Verba, *Small Groups and Political Behavior* (Princeton: Princeton University Press, 1961).

that four of every five adults get together with relatives, neighbors, or friends at least once each week. In Janowitz's Chicago sample over 70 percent of the respondents reported regular visitations with neighbors. And in the Fox Valley survey over one-half the residents stated that they visited fairly often with their neighbors (10 percent "just about every day" and 25 percent "once a week or so") and almost two-thirds said they saw relatives at least once a week. These findings suggest that, in many ways, the informal associational web may be more important to the functioning of metropolitan communities than their formal organizational pattern.

PARTICIPATION IN SUBURBIA

What we have been saying about voting and other forms of civic involvement applies to suburbia as well as the central city. Little evidence exists to substantiate the common assumption that the small suburban community stimulates greater citizen activity. A study of electoral participation in forty-five cities in Los Angeles County, California, over a seventeen-year period found little relation between size of municipality and voting turnout. Los Angeles ranked twenty-sixth of the forty-five in the percentage of the qualified electorate who voted in municipal elections while one of the smallest cities had the poorest turnout.[34] A similar study of St. Louis area municipalities found no significant differences in rate of voter participation based on size. Voting turnout in the central city compared favorably and, in fact, exceeded that in over half the ring municipalities.[35] Given the relatively higher social rank of most suburban populations and the relationship between this variable and voting, the findings on electoral participation are even more telling than the figures indicate.

Is the picture any different when we turn to the organizational life of suburbia? If we can take the word of some commentators, the answer is "yes." William H. Whyte, in *The Organization Man*, says of suburban Park Forest and the amount of civic energy it swallows up, "Every minute from 7 A.M. to 10 P.M. some organi-

---

[34] Lawrence W. O'Rourke, *Voting Behavior in Forty-Five Cities of Los Angeles County* (Los Angeles: University of California Bureau of Governmental Research, 1953), p. 104.

[35] Bollens (ed.), *Exploring the Metropolitan Community*, pp. 87–88.

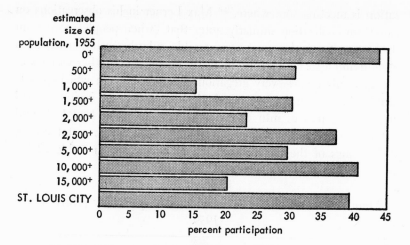

Figure 8.1 Average Percentage of Estimated Eligible Voters Participating in 1953 Municipal Elections, St. Louis City and 69 County Municipalities, by Size. From John C. Bollens, ed., *Exploring the Metropolitan Community*, University of California Press, 1961, p. 88.

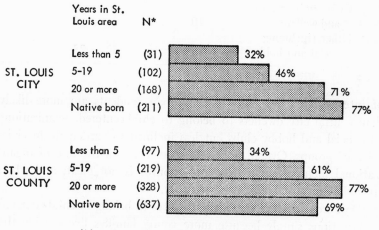

*N represents the number of cases or interviews.
Excluded: City 3 and County 4 "don't know."

Fig. 8.2 Length of Residence in the St. Louis Area and Voting in Any Area Election. From John C. Bollens, ed., *Exploring the Metropolitan Community*, University of California Press, 1961, p. 227.

zation is meeting somewhere."[36] Max Lerner in his observations on American civilization similarly notes that "when people move from the mass city to the more compassable suburb, their participation in club and associational life increases deeply."[37] Another writer sees the new suburbs as "very gregarious communities, in which people wander in and out of one another's houses without invitation and organize themselves into everything from car pools to PTA's and hobby clubs of numerous sorts."[38] In the light of these statements, the findings of the Dayton area survey as set out in Table 22 are

TABLE 22

Membership in Organizations, Montgomery County (Dayton),
1959

TYPE OF ORGANIZATION	CENTRAL CITY	SUBURBAN ZONE
Child-centered	18 percent	30 percent
Fraternal	19	21
Church-centered	21	15
Labor union	15	12
Other work centered	8	12
Community action	12	8
Community service and welfare	10	4
Other (including social and hobby)	14	23

SOURCE: *Metropolitan Challenge*, p. 228.

of interest. Here we find that suburban residents are more likely than central city dwellers to belong to child-centered organizations and social and hobby clubs but less inclined to participate in civic-oriented groups. Overall, the differences between the rate of organizational membership in city and suburbs is not great; and when controlled for social rank, it is negligible.

We would expect more suburbanites to belong to child-centered organizations simply because more young families live outside the core city. We would also expect them to belong to more social groupings because of the generally higher social ranking of suburban

[36] (New York: Doubleday, 1956), p. 317.
[37] *America as a Civilization* (New York: Simon and Schuster, 1957), p. 637.
[38] Frederick L. Allen, "The Big Change in Suburbia," *Harper's Magazine*, 208, (June, 1954), 26.

populations. On the other hand, we would anticipate that a greater proportion of central city residents would participate in civic-oriented associations because of the broader range of opportunities open to them and the higher significance of public affairs and issues in the metropolitan hub. Moving to suburbia does not transform one's participational and civic habits any more so than it does his political beliefs.[39] The non-joiner leaving a home in the central city for an outlying ranch house is likely to remain a non-joiner just as the migrating Democrat is unlikely to become a Republican.

Myth and Reality

Some observers argue that the low rate of electoral and other formal participation in suburban government is due less to lack of interest than to satisfaction. The average suburbanite, they say, is content with the way his community is being run. He feels, moreover, that access to the governmental structure is open to him at any time he may desire to reach into its official portals. Whether Jones or Smith is mayor makes little difference to him since neither is likely to act contrary to prevailing community norms or disturb the existing order in any substantial way.

Certainly suburbia provides a large body of elected officials—far more per citizen than the central city—who are accessible to the people and ready to listen to their grievances. How meaningful this accessibility may be is another question. The data on local power structures cast doubt on the proposition that the suburban community is an open and free political system. Control of the governmental machinery generally rests in the hands of a small minority. In some cases this may be the local merchants; in others the social notables or prominent citizens who seek assurances that the community will remain a preserve for the privileged; and in still others it may be simply a group that gets psychic enjoyment from the exercise of political power, small-scale as it may be. This concentration of formal power, however, by no means implies that it can be used as its holders desire. Whatever the controlling clique in the local political system, its members are conscious of the fact that they or their surrogates can best retain the trappings of power by offending no group and by disturbing the status quo as little as possible.

[39] Jerome G. Manis and Leo C. Stine, "Suburban Residence and Political Behavior," *Public Opinion Quarterly*, 22 (Winter, 1958), 483–489.

Thus, in a negative sense, it is probably true that the exercise of political power in the small suburban community is highly responsive to the citizenry. But this responsiveness is more attuned to the objector than the proposer. The suburban citizen may exercise a more effective veto over governmental action than the central city dweller; but by the same token he is less likely to be successful in pushing for changes or new programs that meet with objections from even a very small minority.

Studies of suburban council meetings emphasize the role of the citizen as objector. The sturdy villagers who appear at the town hall come, with few exceptions, as protestors. Shaken out of their lethargy by a proposed zoning change in the vicinity of their homes, a notice of assessment for costly street improvements, or the erection of an unsightly fence by one of their neighbors, they will descend on the miniature citadel of government with righteous indignation. Only the rare individual goes to learn more about the operations and goals of his local polity or to propose new policies and programs. As two sociologists concluded after an intensive investigation of a small community, the political managers are in a sense "actors who play to a passive audience and who, after all their histrionics, depend on their ability to please and entertain groups which frequently appear to be only observers. The players aim all their acting at the audience and the audience acts only to approve or reject. Only in extreme situations is the audience seen as the instigator in the interchange between player and audience."[40]

It is hardly surprising that reality contradicts the image of the suburban community as a modern Athens where the citizen body is actively engaged in the vital process of self-government. What, after all, is there to stimulate a high level of political participation in such a setting? The majority of suburban municipalities are essentially homogeneous in social composition and have few divisive issues to arouse their residents. Governmental policy-making is confined largely to routine matters of administration and the provision of non-controversial services. Even competition for public office is usually low, probably because the stakes and potential rewards are not high. (The St. Louis area study found that the smaller the suburb, the less the competition for office.) Suburban man may be well satis-

[40] Arthur J. Vidich and Joseph Bensman, *Small Town in Mass Society* (New York: Doubleday, 1960), p. 289.

fied with his government and believe it closer to him, but he shows no greater civic activity than his core city counterpart. The irony is that few rule in suburbia but many believe they could.

Suburbia evokes different reactions among individuals. To some it represents the fulfillment of the middle-class dream, but to others it constitutes a dreary blight on the American landscape. It is easy to make suburbia the butt of our barbs and jokes, and the temptation to do so is great. Our purpose here is not to ridicule, but only to point out the fallacies of the suburban myth. It is important to recognize that suburban life styles would exist whether metropolitan areas were under a single government or not. We would still have our ranch houses, spacious lots, barbecue pits, and socially segregated neighborhoods. These are values which the people hold, and whether we agree or not, we accept them as social facts. What we should get straight is that suburban living takes place in mass society and within a metropolitan context. Its government and the extent of its citizen involvement are not necessarily better or worse than that of the central city. Once metropolitan dwellers discard the notion of the central city as the stronghold of evil and corruption and the suburbs as the haven of goodness and virtue, they may perhaps begin to see some of their problems in clearer perspective.

THE SIGNIFICANCE OF PARTICIPATION

Metropolitan residents are caught in the maelstrom of modern society with all its advantages and liabilities. Their reaction to this environment takes many forms: from social conformity to deviance, from aggressive behavior to submissiveness, from community involvement to withdrawal, from commitment to the system to estrangement. It is against this backdrop that the participation patterns of metropolitan communities are shaped. If we recognize the forces implicit in such a setting, we can begin to understand why "get-out-the-vote" campaigns and other exhortations to civic activity are so pathetically inadequate.

Within the borders of the metropolis, amorphous as they may be, individuals vie for the rewards that society has to offer. As businessmen, professionals, skilled craftsmen, or just common laborers, they daily pursue their economic objectives in a milieu too complex to understand and too large to conquer. In their role as community citizens these same individuals participate in a political system whose function is to maintain order, provide services, and adjust conflicts among the members and social categories of the area. The role would seem to be a vital one, yet society is structured in such a way that many of the crucial decisions relating to the local community are made miles away from it: in the halls of Congress, in the offices of national agencies, in the state highway commission, or in the plush corporate board rooms in the skyscrapers of New York. True as this is, the residual functions of the metropolitan polity involve stakes of substantial significance to the local citizenry. Where a park is located, how land is zoned, what portion of community resources is allocated for educational purposes are but a few such matters. How these issues are determined is greatly influenced by who participates in the civic arena and in what manner.

Voting and organizational activity are measures of citizen involvement in the community. They, particularly the latter, are also indicators of communications channels and of the interconnectedness between the members of the society and its power centers. In the course of this chapter, we observed how the division of the metropolitan population helps to explain community participation. We also saw how voluntary associations and informal groups are important reference points for the formation of attitudes and decisions about local and metropolitan issues. It is these groupings which frequently give political meaning to community affairs in terms relevant to the individual and his interests. Finally, we called attention to the relatively low rate of participation in civic affairs and some of the probable causes for this phenomenon. This last aspect of contemporary metropolitan life should occasion no surprise. Commentators on the national scene—at least until the racial crisis of mid-1963—consistently complained of the immense public apathy toward the issues before Congress. They concluded that the nation felt too well off to embrace reforms, such as those that had been proposed by the Kennedy administration. And there is not much point, as one political scientist put it, "in exhorting a self-satisfied public to a state of mind it doesn't care to embrace. . . . Changes will come only when our complacency is jolted, and this will be achieved not by hortatory words but by new conditions that affect our lives."[41]

[41] Andrew Hacker, "America Follows the Middle of the Road," *The New York Times Magazine*, May 5, 1963, p. 112.

CHAPTER 9

▷ *Social and Economic Maladies*

A MAJOR WEAKNESS of American domestic affairs that is gravely damaging to the nation's reputation and prestige is "the unhinged and disorderly quality of our urban society and the consequent squalor, delinquency and crime."[1] So writes John K. Galbraith, widely-known economist and former ambassador to India. Galbraith is not alone among contemporary writers in expressing concern about the conditions and fate of the modern urban community. Starting in 1958 with *The Exploding Metropolis*, a steady stream of popular as well as scholarly books about the ills of cities have poured off the presses. One of the more recent literary efforts in this genre is significantly entitled *Sick Cities: Psychology and Pathology of American Urban Life*. Its author, newspaperman Mitchell Gordon, has this to say:

An observer of the sprawling urban scene today might be compelled to concede that the superficial monotony of physical similarity must be the least important of all the ailments of the squatting modern metro-

[1] *The Liberal Hour* (Boston: Houghton Mifflin, 1960), p. 18.

politan region whose air grows fouler and more dangerous by the day, whose water is threatened increasingly by pollution, whose mobility is undermined by accumulations of vehicles and withering transit, whose educational system reels under a growing variety of economic, social, and national emergencies, and whose entire pattern is assuming an ominous shape and sociological form, with well-to-do whites in their suburban cities ringing poverty-ridden minority groups widening at the core.[2]

These olympian forebodings strike a responsive chord in few urban residents. Most citizens pass over them with scarcely a second thought or a flash of anxiety. Only the more observant express concern over present developments and the course of the future. The situation is far from satisfactory, but is it actually as alarming as Gordon and other commentators would have us believe? Certainly the sophisticated way to talk about metropolitan areas these days is to speak ominously and fearfully about their problems and plight. To pass as an urban expert, one must warn that the metropolis is on the verge of catastrophe and is doomed, as Thomas Hobbes' man in the state of nature, to a "poor, nasty, brutish, and short life" unless immediate and massive action is taken to redeem it. Whatever the element of truth in these prophecies, the simple fact remains that the metropolis is surviving and continuing to grow. Its most optimistic defenders, however, would have to admit that it is surviving despite its great problems and not because man is making any significant strides in finding solutions or in achieving a more satisfying environment in which to live.

THE WEB OF PROBLEMS

Americans have discovered, however belatedly, that they are a metropolitan nation and that most of their troublesome domestic problems are related to urban growth and change. Some congressmen and state legislators, together with a small number of local officials, still refuse to acknowledge this simple truth even though the trumpets are sounding at the walls. But for most of us who live in metropolitan areas, the presence of urbanization is patently evident although its nature and meaning may be blurred and confusing. The individual who wants to behave like a metropolitan ostrich will find little sand in which to bury his head. Even the most unobservant

[2] (New York: Macmillan, 1963), pp. 339–340.

city dweller cannot fail to sense the changes that are sweeping over and around him, impinging upon numerous aspects of his life, affecting his activities and goals, and conditioning his behavior.

Living together amicably in contemporary urban society is not easy. No matter how imbued we may be with the American credo of rugged individualism and self-reliance, we are compelled to recognize our dependence on other people. We have to attend school with our fellow citizens, work and do business with them, shop with them, drive on the same streets with them, and compete with them in a variety of fields. In the process, we are compelled to submit to restraints, accept controls over our behavior, and compromise our demands on other individuals and on the community and its institutions. For complex as the metropolitan system is, it cannot function without a high level of disciplined organization based on the recognition of mutual social responsibility.

Problems are an integral part of this environment, the common lot of men everywhere and at all times and the inevitable concomitants of living together. These problems, moreover, are continually changing just as the community itself is constantly, if slowly, evolving into new forms. What constitutes a minor source of difficulty today may be a major issue tomorrow. Nothing is more certain than that if we solve one troublesome problem, another will soon appear in its stead. Thus we may drain a swamp to get rid of the mosquitos only to find that the water table drops because rain is no longer being absorbed into the earth. Or we may speed up production by automating the factories only to discover that we have an unemployment problem on our hands. Or we may build massive expressways or freeways to move people swiftly in and out of the central business district only to learn that we have created a gigantic parking problem. To paraphrase the old adage, "one man's solution is another man's problem." We cannot expect to find the total answer for our rapidly urbanizing communities, for the future is never finished. Nor can we ever expect to have enough resources and enough agreement on goals to make everybody happy.

Non-Service Problems

Political scientists and civic reformers have tended to limit the discussion of metropolitan problems to those of a service or "housekeeping" nature. Looming large in their catalogue are such items as water supply, sewage disposal, fire and police protection, and traffic control. This emphasis on the service role of the metropolis finds expression in the notion that local government is a business institution to be structured and administered on a businesslike basis. Such being the case, the most important metropolitan task to many people is to organize the bureaucratic machinery so that it can furnish the necessary services in an efficient, economical, and apolitical manner.

Accompanying this preoccupation with service problems is a heavy emphasis on the city as a physical plant. Paul Ylvisaker, director of the Ford Foundation's public affairs division, called attention to this fact when he said:

> Examine the literature on the city and the substance of action programs and you will find them dominated by a concern with physical plant. The going criteria of urban success are the beauty and solvency of the city's real properties, not the condition of the people who flow through them. As a result, the civilizing and ennobling function of the city, mainly its job of turning second-class newcomers into first-class citizens, is downgraded into pious pronouncements and last-place priorities. We despair of our wasting city property, and count the costs of urban renewal in building values. These are nothing compared to the wasting resources of the human beings who get trapped in these aging buildings, and the value of their lost contribution to their own and the world's society.[3]

No one would deny that the problems of service, governmental organization, and physical development are of vital importance to the metropolis and its people. Nor would anyone deny that efficient and economical operation of the governmental machinery is a desirable goal. The caveat offered here is that such matters by no means exhaust the list of politically relevant issues. We can put water in the taps, dispose of the waste, develop an outstanding fire and police force, build countless miles of expressway to accommodate the automobile, and bulldoze the slums, yet leave unresolved some of the most critical issues facing the urban complex. How can racial strife be mitigated and minority groups, particularly the Negro, assimilated into the life of the community? What can be done to provide adequate housing and equal opportunities for all members of the society? How can crime and juvenile delinquency be curbed?

[3] Address to the World Traffic Engineering Conference, Washington, D.C., August 21, 1961.

What steps can be taken to alleviate the effects of unemployment resulting from automation?

One might argue that the major social and economic problems of modern urban society lie outside the sphere of local government and cannot be solved by action at the local or metropolitan level. Some would even maintain that their resolution lies in private hands, by business, labor unions, social agencies, property owners, and people acting individually and together. Arguments of this kind are valid up to a point. Obviously, a problem such as technological unemployment is national in scope and cannot be met by local means. Its solution lies in the combined efforts of industry, labor, and all levels of government. Even the control of crime and juvenile delinquency, while primarily a community function, is affected by national conditions such as poverty and unemployment.

But whether these problems are "national" or not, they exist principally in the metropolis. Local government cannot escape involvement with them, for they are part and parcel of the local environment. Urban renewal is a case in point. Even though the national government furnishes the lion's share of the money, it is local authorities who must design and initiate the project, resolve the differences among competing interests, and administer the program. The same is true of race relations. The national constitution may bar racial segregation in public schools and state laws may forbid discrimination in employment on account of color, but the full enforcement of these rights will depend upon the active cooperation of local governments and private groups.

Whose Responsibility?

Some myopic defenders of suburbia go so far as to say that the major socioeconomic problems of urban society are problems of the central city, not those of the total metropolitan community. Where but within the boundaries of the core city, they ask, does one find an abundance of racial strife, crime, blighted housing, and welfare recipients? Superficially, their logic may seem sound since they are in general correct about the prevalent spatial location of these maladies. Although crime and other social problems exist in suburbia, their magnitude and extent are substantially less than in the central city. But why in an interdependent metropolitan community should the responsibility of suburbanites be any less than that of the central city dwellers? Certainly no one would think of contending that

residents of higher income neighborhoods within the corporate
limits of the city should be exempt from responsibility for its less
fortunate districts. What logic then is there in believing that neighborhoods on the other side of a legal line can wash their hands of
social disorders in these sections?

Low-income areas are unfortunately a part of every large urban
complex. Without the workers that these neighborhoods house, industrial production would be curtailed and the service trades seriously
crippled. It was not too long ago, for example, that factories in the
northern cities were conducting active recruiting campaigns for low-
income southern workers. Automation may be reducing this demand,
but it has not stopped the migration of dispossessed rural dwellers,
also victims of the new technology, into our urban centers. In fact,
it would be difficult to find any industrial community that did not
have its concentrations of the poor and underprivileged. These concentrations most often happen to be in the central city simply because it is here that cheap and available housing is located. Were
the reverse true, as it is in some smaller metropolitan areas, these
groups would be found in the suburban ring. No large community
can hope to reap the benefits of industrialization and urbanization
and yet escape their less desirable by-products. The suburbanite
and the central city resident share responsibility for the total community and its problems. Neither can run fast enough to escape
involvement sooner or later.

Effects of Urbanization

At a 1963 conference on urbanism hosted by the internationally
famous city planner, Constantinos Doxiades, and attended by emi-
nent representatives of a wide variety of professions and academic
disciplines, strong feeling was expressed that the modern metropolis
is failing to satisfy many crucial social needs. In a formal statement
called the "Declaration of Delos," the group noted that the modern
city is "profoundly involved in the deepest and widest revolution
ever to overtake mankind." It concluded that failure to adapt human
settlements to change "may soon outstrip even disease and starva-
tion as the gravest risk short of war, facing the human species."[4]

[4] A description of the conference is contained in Lyle C. Fitch, "The
Delos Symposium," Address before the Columbia University Seminar on the
City, New York, February 5, 1964.

The effects of the revolution referred to by the conference participants are evident on all sides of us. From Maine to Singapore, in
the emerging and underdeveloped nations as well as the highly industrialized countries, urban communities are undergoing vast transformations. And as always, changes bring with them new problems
and new demands on the social, economic, and governmental structure.

We need not concur fully in the broadly stated conclusions of
the Doxiades conference to accept the elementary fact that most
metropolitan problems are correlates or consequences of urbanization. If we run through the list of domestic maladies that are
causing national concern, we will notice that the majority of them
are connected with the urban community. The Negro problem is
illustrative of this phenomenon. All the current manifestations of
race conflict have appeared in the cities, not in the rural hinterlands.
Urban opportunities, triggered by advancing technology and industrialization, have attracted many Negroes from their back-country
sharecroppers' cabins to the gaudy neon lights and shabby tenements
of the metropolis. Uneducated, unversed in middle-class mores, and
flagrantly discriminated against, they have often become social casu-
alties in their new and seemingly hostile environment. Or take the
problem of housing and the appearance of slums and blighted areas.
These disorders can also be directly tied to the great population
shifts that have occurred in the course of urbanization. Like the
early frontiersmen, the urban pioneers exhausted the land—in this
case the neighborhoods and housing of the central city—and then
moved on to the virgin soils and ranch-style homes of the new
suburban frontier.

In other chapters we deal with various service and organizational difficulties that are peculiar to metropolitan areas. Here we
direct our attention to several of the more important socioeconomic
problems that plague these communities. Our purpose is not to deal
definitively with these questions—for each would require a large
volume—but to describe the dimensions of a selected few and to
show their relevance to the functioning of the metropolis. For this
purpose we have chosen three sets of problems which figure prominently in the news and in the concerns of urban dwellers: blight
and slums, racial strife, and crime and juvenile delinquency. These
by no means encompass the whole range of dysfunctions in metro-

politan society, but they include some of the most pressing and aggravating problems.

THE "DETERIORATING" CITY

In 1953, economist Miles Colean wrote a book for the Twentieth Century Fund which he titled *Renewing Our Cities*. The term "urban renewal" caught on and became the symbolic designation for the efforts of public agencies and private groups to eliminate slums and curb the spread of blight in American cities. Urban renewal is not a modern invention; only its technical aspects are. Man has been engaged in the construction and reconstruction of cities since antiquity. Athens, for example, was rebuilt under Pericles, Rome under Augustus, and Paris under Napoleon III, and one might even say with tongue in cheek, New York City under Moses—that is, Robert Moses. Renewal, however, is not always so spectacular or dramatic, yet it is constantly taking place in one fashion or another regardless of whether we are aware of the fact. The city we live in today, if not destroyed or abandoned in the interim, will be completely rebuilt—renewed if you please—for better or worse within the next 100 years.

A city or a metropolitan area is not like frozen sculpture. It is forever undergoing change, being added to and subtracted from, shaped and reshaped like pliable clay, sometimes with deliberate intent, more often without conscious design. The visitor to any major American city today—and many of lesser size, such as New Haven, Connecticut—is invariably amazed at the physical transformations that are taking place. In New York, Chicago, Philadelphia, St. Louis, Detroit—and the list could go on—huge sections of the community have been stripped naked to the ground. This planned destruction is being followed by rebuilding, in some cases at a feverish pace, in others more slowly and even hesitantly.

It is an eerie experience to walk through a redevelopment area after the occupants have been cleared out but before the bulldozers and demolition squads have begun their task of devastation. The streets are empty and silent, the houses which once teemed with laughter and cries starkly devoid of human life, the area a giant neighborhood or abandoned island in an urban sea. But what we observe is only a strange interlude, a passing moment in the city's travail of renewal. We know that soon the dilapidated houses and run-down shops will be replaced by impressive new apartments and office buildings. But there is much we do not know. What happened to the families who were evicted? How have their lives been affected? What impact will these physical changes and their consequences have on the community as a social and political organism? These are among the questions troubling some of the more sensitive observers of the urban scene.

Housing

According to the 1960 *Census of Housing*, a total of 34 million of the nation's 53 million dwelling units is located within metropolitan areas. Of this number approximately 3.5 million are classified as deteriorating and 1 million dilapidated. These figures point to the dismal fact that almost one of every seven metropolitan families lives in substandard housing. Universally condemned as slums, the areas where most of this housing is located serve as the home of the poor and the outcast, classes that have not been integrated into the life of the community presumably because of lack of formal training and the existence of color barriers. These pockets of poverty and blight exist in the midst of wealth and affluence. They represent a huge waste of human resources and one of the most serious domestic problems of American society.

Slums are nothing new; they have been with us ever since the middle-class families abandoned the task of rebuilding the original areas of settlement and moved outward in search of better neighborhoods and better homes. Boston, New York, Chicago, Los Angeles, San Francisco, and other large communities had their slums long before the wave of southern migrants began to enter the large industrial cities of the North and West. It was not, however, until the 1930s and the New Deal programs that Americans began to become conscious of blighted areas and substandard housing. During the great depression period there was, as Coleman Woodbury, a pioneer in the urban field, describes it, "the general mood of self-criticism . . . and the recognized need for new enterprise and outlets for labor and materials."[5] Housing surveys made

[5] "Human Relations in Urban Redevelopment," in H. Warren Dunham (ed.), *The City in Mid-Century* (Detroit: Wayne State University Press, 1957), p. 115.

by various public agencies at that time revealed large areas of blight in central cities. Why, concerned officials and community leaders asked, was deteriorating real estate not being replaced?

The first efforts at the national level to attack the problem embodied the curious combination of goals—economic pump-priming and social amelioration—that characterized many of the New Deal programs. To stimulate the home building industry and at the same time clear away some of the worst slums, the national government offered loans and subsidies to local agencies for construction of public housing. One condition of the grant, as set out in the Federal Housing Act of 1937, specified that the city must eliminate dilapidated dwelling units equal in number to the new units to be constructed. Yet even at the time the act was passed, it was already clear that broader machinery for dealing with slums would ultimately have to be fashioned. The war temporarily delayed steps in this direction, but in 1949 Congress enlarged on the original act by authorizing generous grants to local units to acquire and clear blighted areas, which could then be used for public housing or sold to private developers. In the new program, the rehousing of slum dwellers became subordinate to the goal of clearance and redevelopment. Subsequent enactments by Congress have emphasized this latter aspect while placing less and less stress on public housing.

Urban Renewal

The Housing Act of 1949 and subsequent authorizations by individual states for the creation of local redevelopment authorities met with little opposition, largely because the various interests regarded the objectives of the program differently. As Catherine Bauer Wurster—a veteran participant in the field of urban planning—observed, various groups of people like the blind men feeling the elephant made entirely different assumptions about the purpose of the legislation.[6] Welfare groups viewed it as an enlargement of the power to get rid of bad living conditions. Others saw it as a means of bolstering waning property values in central areas and facilitating slum clearance without extending public housing. It was this latter

[6] "Redevelopment: A Misfit in the Fifties," in Coleman Woodbury (ed.), *The Future of Cities and Urban Redevelopment* (Chicago: University of Chicago Press, 1953), p. 9 ff.

aspect that captured the interest and support of the business leaders. Typically the worst slums were adjacent to the downtown district. The economic attractions of rebuilding these areas were appealing to the civic influentials as well as central city officials. By demolishing the slums, space would be made available for industrial and commercial expansion and, more importantly, for middle- and high-income housing that might lure back some of the city's former residents, the consumers and taxpayers of substance who had fled to the greener pastures of suburbia. Many businessmen supported the program primarily because they would profit economically by a revitalization of the core of the community, but some among them saw in urban renewal an opportunity to restore the lost civic glory of the central city and revive its prestige.

Whatever the motives of the individuals who have promoted urban renewal, it has been the economic rather than the social appeal that has sustained the program. The characteristic American trait of reducing most things to dollars and cents has forced political leaders and social reformers to couch their arguments in economic terms and to picture slum clearance projects as self-liquidating business ventures. Consequently we hear that decent housing means less crime, less juvenile delinquency, lower costs for police and fire protection, and fewer welfare cases. From these assertions we get the impression that all the community has to do is remove the slums and by this act it will wipe out social ills and their human and material costs. A documentary film of some years ago describes the metamorphosis in idyllic terms. First we see a shocking slum area with filthy and dilapidated buildings, rats running along the gutters, dirty and poorly clothed children playing amidst refuse and debris, traffic moving slowly and impatiently in a bumper-to-bumper procession on the congested streets. Then the change takes place. Bulldozers and giant cranes move in to tear down the old buildings while construction crews follow closely behind to put up the new. Out of the ashes rises the new Phoenix: bright and shiny apartments insulated from the traffic of the city streets, happy children romping about in orderly and supervised play areas, neatly dressed mothers sitting on decorative benches sewing or chatting gaily with their neighbors.

Several things are wrong with this picture. Certainly there is much evidence to substantiate the argument that the incidence of poverty, disease, vice, and crime is far greater in slum districts than in other parts of the metropolis. What the picture overlooks, however, is that the housing problems of slum occupants are generally inseparable from family and community disorganization, poverty, and disease. Human lives as well as houses are blighted in these areas. Merely moving occupants into better dwelling units will not cure other physical and social ills. Empirical evidence, in fact, is accumulating to show that improved housing does not have many of the social benefits initially attributed to it. An investigation of housing as a factor in juvenile delinquency, to cite one inquiry, ends with this statement: "The one unmistakable conclusion that emerges from the study is that there is no relationship between bad housing in its physical aspects and juvenile delinquency as revealed by court records."[7] Another careful look, a study of families who moved from slum areas to new housing, found that although the incidence of illness and disability was markedly reduced, the social effects were less than had been expected.[8] Yet the belief that delinquency, prostitution, alcoholism, crime, and other forms of social pathology magically inhere in the slums and will die with their demolition continues to persist.

Although the arguments for urban renewal are not necessarily compatible, they reflect the different assumptions on which the program was originally inaugurated. If the principal objective is to bolster the tax base of the community, efforts should be directed at developing the cleared land at its highest income-producing use. The fate of the people who are to be relocated becomes secondary in this case. If, on the other hand, the primary and overriding purpose is to provide better housing for the low-income and underprivileged classes, the economic argument must give way to the social. In most communities, the former goal has prevailed. Private investors are seldom interested in building low-income housing on renewal sites since the land is too expensive, even with the federal and local write-down (the difference between the cost of buying, clearing, and preparing the land for redevelopment and its selling

[7] John Dean, "The Myths of Housing Reform," *American Sociological Review*, 14 (April, 1949), 281–288.

[8] Daniel M. Wilner and Rosabelle P. Wakely, "The Effects of Housing on Health and Performance," in Leonard J. Duhl (ed.), *The Urban Condition* (New York: Basic Books, 1963), pp. 215–228.

price). An alternative to private development is to erect public housing on the cleared land for the existing population of the area, but in this case the return from the property will do little to bolster the tax base of the community.

In those instances where renewal areas have been used for public housing, land costs have generally led to the construction of high rise projects of uniform design and forbidding appearance. By isolating the tenants from the rest of the community and exhibiting them as the recipients of public subsidy, the program places a stigma on the disadvantaged families who inhabit them. In some localities the prejudice against public housing is so great that the only families willing to live in such units are predominantly non-whites who cannot find other dwellings and whites in the very lowest income category. As a result, public housing projects often tend to become social and economic ghettos with large concentrations of problem families. The condition tends to perpetuate itself since those families who achieve a measure of success in the commercial and industrial world are forced to move out when their income exceeds the limits for eligibility.

Given the emphasis on the economic argument—understandable in view of the central city's struggle to maintain fiscal solvency and bring back some of its expatriated middle-class citizens—it is hardly surprising that slum areas have generally been rebuilt for new occupants and not for the slum dwellers themselves. Public housing, moreover, symbolizing governmental encroachment in the private sector, has become a nasty term in many cities while urban renewal, standing for private enterprise, has retained its respectability. Public housing has been erected to be sure—some 700,000 units when the current authorization is completed—but this is only 1.3 percent of the nation's total housing and a small fraction of the substandard dwelling units in urban areas.

Relocation

What happens to the families who are displaced and who do not move into public housing? Surprisingly little information is available about them. What data are available indicate that most move to neighborhoods similar to those from which they were cleared, usually on the fringe of renewal projects. As one sociologist has commented, "The dispossessed enjoy as their reward a distant view of luxury apartments rising over their old homes."[9] A study of families displaced by land clearance in San Francisco, for example, showed that most of them clustered around the project areas. Since some of these adjacent neighborhoods were marked for clearance in subsequent projects, many households faced further displacement at a later date. The study also revealed that although a majority of the persons evicted moved to somewhat better housing, the proportion of their income spent on rent increased from 17 percent to 25 percent.[10] Other observers have estimated that between 15 and 50 percent of the families displaced by redevelopment move to slum property in other sections of the city and a large portion of the remainder into deteriorating areas.

These findings demonstrate that new slums will inevitably be created as the old ones are demolished if uprooted Negroes and low-income whites are forced to move into other overcrowded and deteriorating areas. They also suggest that a large portion of the relocated families have achieved only marginal improvements in housing at the cost of substantially higher rent. The Housing Act of 1949 states as the nation's goal "a decent house in a suitable living environment for every American family." This objective, as we well know, is far from realized for a sizable proportion of our population. The simple fact is that there is not enough good low-rent housing in decent neighborhoods to accommodate the less affluent members of the urban community. As a conference on housing attended by nationally recognized civic, business, and professional leaders concluded, efforts to achieve the goal of the 1949 act "have been inadequate and disillusioning. We are making little or no progress in getting rid of our slums. The residences left behind in the older centers of our cities as well-to-do families move to the suburbs are becoming blighted and turning into slums almost as rapidly as older slum dwellings are eliminated."[11]

Urban redevelopment has remained popular with the business interests, but the wholesale clearing of land has met with increasing

[9] Peter Marris, "The Social Implications of Urban Redevelopment," *Journal of the American Institute of Planners*, XXVIII (August, 1962), 182.

[10] Nathaniel Lichfield, "Relocation: The Impact on Housing Welfare," *Journal of the American Institute of Planners*, XXVII (August, 1961), 199–203.

[11] *Interim Report on Housing the Economically and Socially Disadvantaged Groups in the Population* (Chicago: Metropolitan Housing and Planning Council of Chicago, 1960), p. 2.

resistance from the general public, and particularly from residents in the areas to be razed. It has also been subjected to a barrage of criticism from economists who question the economic arguments advanced in its behalf and from articulate observers of the urban scene, such as Jane Jacobs, the author of the controversial *The Death and Life of Great American Cities*, who stress the preservation of neighborhood life and the possibilities of upgrading blighted areas through encouraging and aiding local owners to improve their property. Joined to these voices of protest are those of socially conscious individuals and groups who have become alarmed at the "human impact" of renewal projects and the emphasis on physical rehabilitation to the seeming exclusion of social consequences.

Faced with these countervailing forces, the pace of redevelopment or land clearance is slowing down. The days of unilateral action by the city fathers in league with the business leaders appear over. It is less and less possible to view plans for the clearing of blighted areas as matters which can be decided by technicians and experts in collaboration with the community's business interests. Almost everywhere urban redevelopment programs which ignore the needs and desires of the affected residents and which fail to enlist the counsel and support of representative citizen groups are running into serious difficulties.

In the renewal programs, more emphasis is also being placed on neighborhood rehabilitation and property conservation. Through amendments to the Housing Act in 1954 and more recent acts, the program has been broadened by extending assistance to projects that involve less drastic steps than public acquisition and clearance. The underlying philosophy of the new approach is to help the residents of affected areas help themselves. It contemplates a combination of governmental action and private effort. Local governments are to use their powers in upgrading and stabilizing the neighborhood environment through public improvements, creating additional new open space, reducing heavy traffic on residential streets, providing new playgrounds and other recreation facilities, and stepping up enforcement of minimum housing standards and zoning. At the same time individual owners are to be encouraged to improve their property by making liberal government-insured financing available to them. Rehabilitation and conservation are obviously applicable only in neighborhoods that are still sound but beginning to show signs of blight and deterioration. They cannot be effective in slum areas that have decayed to the point where large-scale clearance is the only possible remedy. Nor can they be effective in areas where poverty and social disorganization are

| ♔ | 500 families |

Figure 9.1   Estimated Relocation Families—Next Decade —Newark, N.J. From *Renew Newark,* Central Planning Board, 1961, p. 41.

rampant or where the residents are contemplating flight because of threatened invasion by racial minorities or evicted slum dwellers.

Progress in urban renewal, whether by way of slum clearance or conservation, will continue to be agonizingly slow so long as the basic social causes of blight and deterioration remain. Yet any criticism of the housing reformers for their failure to combine rehousing with extensive programs of social welfare measures must be tempered by the realization, as Housing and Home Finance Administrator Robert C. Weaver points out, that the social right of every American family to a decent house is still disputed by a substantial number of people in our society.[12] The tradition of individualism which has seriously circumscribed even the limited objective of the public housing program continues, in other words, to impede the development of improved programs based upon social reconstruction. Progress in overcoming the pragmatic consequences of this ethos is being made but the pace is slow and hesitant.

THE PROBLEM OF RACE

Some of the most acute social problems in metropolitan areas revolve around the racial question. It is difficult to discuss any of the major issues of local concern such as housing, unemployment, or crime and delinquency without involving the matter of race. It is estimated, for example, that non-whites constitute more than 70 percent of the families displaced from their homes by renewal projects and expressway construction; that the unemployment rate among them is about double the national average; and that they account for 20 percent of the incidence of juvenile delinquency although they make up only about 10 percent of the nation's population. Racial undertones also underlie and impede efforts at reconstructing the metropolitan governmental system. The white suburbs fear that closer administrative alignment with the central city will open the door to Negro "encroachment" on their residential preserves, while the Negro himself is wary of any governmental rearrangement that might possibly dilute his growing political power in the core municipality.

Negroes constitute the largest portion of the newest migrants to the major urban settlements in the United States.[13] In 1910, eight of every ten Negroes lived in the southern states, mostly in the rural areas where they worked as sharecroppers and farm hands. Since World War I, and particularly since 1940, they have been

[12] "Major Factors in Urban Planning," in Leonard J. Duhl (ed.), *The Urban Condition* (New York: Basic Books, 1963), p. 108.

[13] Some metropolitan areas have also experienced the arrival of Appalachian Mountain whites, Puerto Ricans, and Mexican-Americans. Although these groups face many of the same problems as Negroes, they do not suffer from the disability of race.

pouring into the cities of the North and West in large numbers. Today over 70 percent of the approximately 21 million Negroes are urban dwellers.

Earlier in-migrant groups have been able to rise out of their lower strata and enter the mainstream of American life. They achieved the goals of better housing, improved neighborhoods, and better schools once they had demonstrated adherence to the dominant culture and had secured the economic rewards which the system offered. The Negro has not been as fortunate. Although his economic status has improved considerably in recent decades and although a significant Negro middle class is emerging, racial prejudice continues to bar him from the place of residence, the type of employment, and the social recognition to which his income and behavior qualify him. As a result, a troubling pattern of racial segregation and socioeconomic differentiation has developed beneath the patchwork of local governments that comprise the metropolitan political system. From 1950 to 1960 the percentage of the nation's white population residing in suburbia increased from 15 percent to 23 percent while the proportion of the non-white population living in central cities leaped from 39 percent to 54 percent.[14] (The relatively small proportion of Negroes who do live in suburbia is largely in segregated communities or in the less desirable neighborhoods of industrial fringe cities.) These figures provide further evidence of the increasing racial division between central city and suburb.

The New Migration

The migration we are now witnessing is not a new phenomenon. Throughout history the advantaged have fled from the disadvantaged. The core areas of our major municipalities have long served as ports of entry for ethnic migrants at the lower end of the economic ladder. So also the earlier in-migrants, as they acquired middle-class stature, moved outward to the periphery to find better housing and to escape from residential proximity to the newcomers. If this pattern had continued, we would expect to find a substantial number of the later migrants, the Negroes, now residing in the outer reaches of the metropolis. Instead, we find the overwhelming majority still confined to restricted areas of the core city and denied access to

[14] Weaver, "Major Factors in Urban Planning," pp. 101–103.

the broader opportunities of the larger community. Today these same areas can no longer be considered way stations on the road upward.

Two factors distinguish the current situation from that of the past: the governmentally fragmented character of the metropolitan community and the skin color of many of the new migrants. The flight of the middle class in the past usually did not involve an avoidance of the social welfare and other municipal costs which the underprivileged in-migrants generated. Most of those who fled remained within the expanding boundaries of the central city and therefore continued to bear their share of financial and social responsibility for the core areas. However, with the governmental balkanization of the metropolis that began early in this century, the new and legally autonomous suburban retreats offered an opportunity not only to flee the ugly specter of the city but also to escape obligation for its problems.

Of even greater importance in distinguishing the earlier circumstances from those of recent decades is the matter of race. The migration in mid-twentieth century America is bringing large numbers of southern rural Negroes into the metropolitan orbit. Most of them come poorly equipped for the highly competitive system into which they are thrust. Handicapped by restrictive education, lacking in the skills necessary for an industrial society, and standing at the bottom of the socioeconomic hierarchy, they are the most vulnerable to economic fluctuations ("the last to be hired and the first to be laid off") and the most dependent upon public welfare services. Denied the social, residential, and employment mobility enjoyed by earlier migrant groups because of the color of their skin, and arriving in the middle of a technological upheaval when unskilled jobs are in ever shorter supply, the majority of them remain marginal members of the dominant society and its culture. This low rate of mobility, moreover, has limited the growth in numbers of Negro intellectuals and the professional and business élite who provided much of the leadership for various other ethnic groups.

Race and Housing

The metropolitan character of the racial problem is vividly demonstrated in the field of housing. The prevailing practice of containing Negro families in certain areas of the central city is a matter of common knowledge. Some Negroes have been able to break through this barrier and find homes in white neighborhoods, but accommodation of the rapidly increasing non-white population in metropolitan areas has taken place almost wholly by expanding the limits of the ghetto or black belt. The phenomenon of racial segregation, moreover, is not confined to the South. On more than one occasion, as in the suburban town of Folcroft in Metropolitan Philadelphia, the nation has witnessed the spectacle of screaming, rock-throwing crowds of northern whites seeking to prevent Negro families from moving into their neighborhoods or communities.

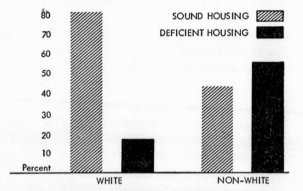

Fig. 9.2 Allegheny County Condition of Housing, by Race, 1960. From *Summary, Urban Renewal Impact Study*, Action-Housing, Inc., Pittsburgh, 1963, p. 50.

The hostility of whites to residential integration stems in part from the belief that entrance of Negroes into a neighborhood lowers property values. Although this myth has been demolished by studies which show that non-white occupancy in most cases does not adversely affect such values, the fear continues to exist.[15] Unscrupulous real estate operators commonly play upon this fear to generate panic selling in neighborhoods "threatened" by Negro invasion. Frequently in such cases they purchase the property themselves at depressed values and sell to Negro families at premium prices. Both the white seller and the non-white buyer are penalized by these tactics.

Several undesirable consequences flow from the practice of restricting the non-white market to certain sections of the central

[15] See Luigi Laurenti, *Property Values and Race* (Berkeley and Los Angeles: University of California Press, 1960).

city. First, there is the matter of injustice involved in denying the Negro equal opportunity in a supposedly free market and barring him from choosing the kind of house and neighborhood that his economic means warrant. This denial is repugnant to the basic tenets of our democratic system. Second, failure to recognize the achievements of non-whites by granting them access to such rewards as good housing and better living conditions tends to lessen or destroy their initiative and motivation. When this occurs among a group that comprises a significant segment of our urban population, it redounds to the economic, political, and cultural detriment of the metropolis.

Third, from the standpoint of sound economics and the most efficient operation of the market, private industry is ignoring a potential and growing source of demand for new housing. The following colloquy between Congressman Barrat O'Hara of Chicago and William Levitt, developer of the massive eastern residential communities, is revealing in this regard:

MR. O'HARA: Now in the homes that you are building, are they open to all Americans regardless of race or religion?

MR. LEVITT: You really pick a ticklish subject now, don't you, Mr. Congressman?

MR. O'HARA: I would regard it as a pertinent question to a congressional study of our over-all housing problem. In Philadelphia, 1 out of 4 of the people who live in Philadelphia belong to a minority group. They are as much entitled to good housing as anybody else. Is private industry furnishing them these houses?

MR. LEVITT: No, private industry is not. Someday I hope they will, and I hope we will be the leaders in it.

MR. O'HARA: Now the houses you are building, are they open to all Americans?

MR. LEVITT: Unfortunately, no.

MR. O'HARA: They are entirely for the white people?

MR. LEVITT: Yes, and I repeat, I hope someday that will not be so, and I hope we will be the ones who make it not so.[16]

---

[16] Testimony before the Subcommittee on Housing of the Committee on Banking and Currency. *U.S. Congress, House, Hearings, Investigation of Housing,* 1955. 84th Congress, 1st Session, 1955, p. 415.

Most suburban builders and developers defend their racial policies on the assumed basis that the presence of non-whites in a residential area will destroy the demands of whites for housing there. They also complain of the difficulty of obtaining financing and of the obstructing tactics of local public officials when Negro or racially integrated housing is involved. In instances where suburban builders have turned to the non-white market, they have developed projects intended specifically for sale or rent to minority families. This practice has been most prevalent in the South where communities have hoped to counter pressure for housing desegregation by providing a supply of good segregated buildings. Although such action augments the supply of dwelling units for non-whites, it serves to intensify racial segregation.

Fourth, if Negroes were able to enter freely the total housing market of the metropolitan area, their demand for better housing would be spread over the entire community. The volume in any single neighborhood of the central city would thereby be reduced and the incentive for the whites to vacate would be correspondingly lessened. There is a "tipping point" in any neighborhood—even those trying to effect integration—at which whites will move out when the proportion of non-whites reaches a certain size. Russel Woods, a middle-class Detroit neighborhood in the path of non-white expansion, provides a typical example of this tendency.[17] With a heavy sprinkling of persons of liberal outlook among the residents, the neighborhood did not respond to the Negro advance with either all-out resistance or panicky flight, the two most common reactions. Yet by the time the proportion of Negro residents reached 50 percent, all hope that Russel Woods would remain a stable mixed neighborhood had vanished. Several factors contributed to this result, but perhaps the most important was the fear of white residents that educational standards in the local schools would be downgraded. Persons who are most liberal on the subject of living in mixed neighborhoods are also the most sensitive to the quality of their schools.

[17] The Russel Woods experience is described by Albert J. Mayer, "Russel Woods: Change Without Conflict," in Nathan Glazer and Davis McEntire (eds.), *Studies in Housing and Minority Groups* (Berkeley and Los Angeles: University of California Press, 1960), pp. 198–220. For a discussion of other factors determining the rate and extent of racial change in neighborhoods, see Eleanor P. Wolf, "The Tipping-Point in Racially Changing Neighborhoods," *Journal of the American Institute of Planners*, XXIX (August, 1963), 217–222.

Fifth, metropolitan well-being is best promoted when satisfactory working relations exist between the central city and suburbs. The social and racial bifurcation characteristic of many urban areas makes it more difficult to achieve these relationships. Intergovernmental cooperation, for example, is more easily obtained among communities of similar socioeconomic rank than among those which are highly differentiated.[18] Thus if the core municipality becomes increasingly the home of the non-white and low-income families and the suburbs the exclusive residence of the white middle class, the social and racial distance between the two geographical sectors will aggravate the problem of area-wide consensus and reduce the possibilities of joint action in metropolitan affairs.

To say that housing is a metropolitan problem is not to imply that its solution rests in a restructuring of the local governmental system. The fundamental causes of blight and poor housing are unrelated to the way urban areas are governmentally organized. As one study emphasizes, changes in the local governmental structure will not eliminate slums or neighborhood obsolescence nor alter the racial distribution in the metropolis.

To take one striking example, there is ominous significance in the population movements that threaten to make many central cities into lower-class ethnic islands. These islands exist because the people who live in them have low incomes and because they are excluded, frequently by illegal means, from other sections of the cities and from the suburbs. The consequences of this *de facto* segregation for the cultural, political, and business life of the nation are deleterious. Clearly no solution to this problem would come from the structural reform of integrating the governments of central cities and suburbs; nor is it possible to imagine any local government or combination of local governments taking effective action with their own resources to achieve a reversal of the present population distributions. What is needed is a whole range of measures to make central cities more attractive to upper- and middle-class whites and to allow nonwhites to live where they can afford to live and want to live. Such measures can be achieved only through a major effort of all levels of government and must include large-scale financing, public education, nondiscrimination laws, and experimentation with new programs of urban renewal and relocation housing.[19]

[18] See Thomas R. Dye, Charles S. Liebman, Oliver P. Williams, and Harold Herman, "Differentiation and Cooperation in a Metropolitan Area," *Midwest Journal of Political Science*, VII (May, 1963), 145–155.

[19] Edward C. Banfield and Morton Grodzins, *Government and Housing in Metropolitan Areas* (New York: McGraw-Hill, 1958), pp. 154–155.

Governmental reorganization at the local level might possibly provide better mechanisms and a more suitable political arena for considering the issues of race and population distribution, but no such restructuring can give any assurance of bettering the situation. Even within a single governmental unit serious difficulties arise in connection with such matters as the selection of sites for low-income housing projects. In Chicago and other metropolitan centers across the nation, residents of outlying sections within the central city itself have successfully opposed public housing projects that threatened to bring residents of the core area into or near their neighborhoods. The mere creation of an area-wide authority would by no means lessen these pressures or change the nature of political realities. In fact a metropolitan general-purpose government heavily weighted with suburban representatives would probably make the passage of open-occupancy and other anti-discrimination ordinances even more difficult than is now the case.

CRIME AND DELINQUENCY

Crime and juvenile delinquency are not maladies unique to the metropolis; they are widespread social disorders affecting rural as well as urban areas. Their heaviest incidence, however, is in the large population centers where the sheer number of people congregated in close proximity to each other magnifies the problem and compounds the difficulty of handling antisocial behavior. Crime statistics reveal that the criminal elements of the society are more active and more concentrated in cities and metropolitan areas. During 1960 law enforcement authorities in the United States reported a rate of 39 arrests per 1000 inhabitants for all criminal offenses. The city rates were almost three times as high as the rural. In metropolitan areas the crime index for serious offenses showed a rate of 1327.9 per 100,000 people; in rural areas the rate was 423.2.[20]

Crime in the United States, according to the Federal Bureau of Investigation, is increasing at more than five times the rate of population growth. Between 1950 and 1960, while the population was rising approximately 18 percent, the number of serious crimes almost doubled. No single causal factor or well-established set of them can

[20] Caution must be observed in using crime statistics for comparative purposes because of the inadequate reporting by some local law enforcement agencies.

explain this increase. Some people attribute it to a breakdown in family life, others to the emphasis that modern society places on material goods, and still others to a general weakening of the moral and religious fiber of the nation. Most sociologists subscribe to some form of multiple causation theory, holding that crime is the product of the integration of many associated variables that defy simple analysis, citing the fact that maladjustment and disorder are characteristic of rapid social change. They point out that the process of transforming a nation from an agricultural and rural society to an industrial and urban civilization—a development we are now witnessing on a worldwide scale—cannot be accomplished without social costs. One such cost appears to be the increased rate of adult crime and juvenile delinquency.

Law enforcement, which is concerned with protecting the lives and property of the citizenry, is primarily the responsibility of the local government, while punishment and rehabilitation of the offenders rest with state and, in some cases, with federal agencies. Obviously, no local unit or combination of local units can cope with or treat all of the causes of social disorganization. Citizen inertia and poor law enforcement by municipal and county authorities may contribute to increased crime rates but in the final analysis the problem transcends the local and metropolitan community. Like poverty and racial discrimination, crime and delinquency have their roots in national as well as local conditions.

Some Ecological Characteristics of Crime

Within the metropolitan area the heaviest incidence of antisocial conduct is found in the central segment of the core city. As demonstrated by studies in large urban communities, the tendency is for crime and delinquency to decrease with distance from the center of the city. In Baltimore, for example, it was found that 88 percent of both white and Negro delinquents lived within a radius of three miles from the center of the city. (This pattern, it should be emphasized, merely indicates spatial dimension; it does not imply a causal relationship between the core area and the incidence of crime.) The residential neighborhoods that spread out around the central business district in the so-called "gray" and slum areas of the larger urban concentrations are generally characterized by all or most of the following factors: low social cohesion, weak family life, low socioeconomic status, physical deterioration, high population mobility, and high rates of school dropouts and unemployment.[21] One sociologist, examining the phenomenon on a worldwide scale, describes the neighborhoods of deviant behavior in the following way:

. . . they are often areas of great diversity in social norms and values, and they lack stability. People migrate there from rural and urban areas and from other cities. Social contacts in the entire area are often less numerous or intimate and, although there is more tolerance, there is less concern for the welfare of one's neighbor. Shared activities of the entire neighborhood are less frequent and seldom involve common problems. One may find enclaves based on regional, tribal or caste ties, but they are often small. Even where they are larger, they often become disorganized and are unable to compete successfully with the different norms and ways of life of the surrounding area.[22]

Neighborhoods of this type also frequently have different norms of conduct than the rest of the community. Fighting, gambling, prostitution, alcoholism, bootlegging, and narcotic addiction may have tacit approval or be tolerated by the residents. High delinquency rates can be expected among the children exposed to such norms.

Poor housing and physical deterioration are conspicuous earmarks of high crime areas but, as previously indicated, it is doubtful that these are controlling factors. Families which are forced to settle and to continue to live in such neighborhoods are for the most part already affected by the causal forces that produce social disorders. However, life in such an environment serves to intensify the latent capacities of these families and individuals for antisocial conduct. It also affords them more opportunity to pursue criminal careers and become demoralized.

Although public attention has been focused mainly on social disorganization in the core areas of the metropolis, the rate of juvenile delinquency has increased among children in the better sections of the central city and in the suburbs. Acts of vandalism, rowdyism, automobile theft, and shoplifting by young people in these neighborhoods have been growing since World War II. The spread of juvenile delinquency among children of middle-class families again sug-

[21] Calvin F. Schmid, "Urban Crime Areas," *American Sociological Review*, 25 (August, 1962), 527–542; and 25 (December, 1962), 655–678.

[22] Marshall B. Clinard, "The Organization of Urban Community Development Services in the Prevention of Crime and Juvenile Delinquency," *International Review of Criminal Policy*, No. 19 (1962), 5.

gests that the causes of antisocial conduct are more than poverty and slum living. That these conditions breed deviant behavior is evident from the degree of slum-centered crime and delinquency. But what is relevant to note is that although economic conditions have improved for all segments of the population, the rates of delinquency are rising and becoming more widely dispersed among the general population. As some analysts point out, a new form of juvenile delinquency has developed, one not produced by material deprivation but having its roots in the very abundance of our society.

Government alone cannot eradicate the basic causes of crime and delinquency. It cannot eliminate prejudice or the cultural factors that build up vast reservoirs of resentment and frustration by depriving certain groups of the opportunity to participate fully in the society. Nor can it strengthen or assume the role of the family, church, and other institutions that are influential determinants and molders of behavior. Whatever steps it takes in the field of crime and delinquency beyond apprehending and punishing the offenders are closely circumscribed by the cultural environment in which it functions and the underlying consensus of its citizenry.

From the standpoint of government in the metropolis, law enforcement is seemingly a functional area in which closer coordination among local units could be generally achieved. Prevention of crime and juvenile delinquency is an objective desired by residents throughout the metropolitan area. Unlike some problems, such as public housing and racial discrimination, where general consensus is lacking, strong public support might well be mustered for greater cooperative work in the fields of crime and delinquency prevention and control.[23] This would seem to be one function where determined and imaginative leadership might overcome the provincialism of local officials and local bureaucracies.

THE GOOD LIFE

The growth of the metropolitan economic and social system has brought expanded opportunities for millions of Americans in the form of better jobs, improved educational and cultural facilities, and greater

[23] This point is made by Daniel J. Elazar in *Some Social Problems in the Northeastern Illinois Metropolitan Area* (Urbana: University of Illinois Institute of Government and Public Affairs, 1961).

social mobility. At the same time it has also brought problems of far greater magnitude than those experienced by less complex societies. We have discussed some of these difficulties in this chapter and others. We have also observed that burgeoning urbanization and its accompanying features have decreased the self-sufficiency of individual metropolitan areas and made their economy and well-being more dependent than ever before on national and even international events and trends. Whether a particular metropolis thrives can be affected only partially by what its local governments do or fail to do. Greater forces are at work than the zeal and resources of local leaders and officials. Nevertheless, within these circumscribed limits, achievement of the good life for the city or the metropolis can be fostered or deterred by the spirit and acts of the local citizenry and its governments.

For some urban dwellers the "good life" or its approximation has become a reality. The goal seems within the grasp of many others. For the economically and culturally deprived whites and a majority of non-whites, the American dream appears a hollow mockery. Throughout a century in which the Negro enjoyed freedom from legal servitude, equality remained for him little more than an abstraction and an unattainable ideal. All this has been changed with the events of the 1960s. The series of protest demonstrations that are taking place in cities all over the United States, north and west as well as south, is a manifestation of the growing impatience among Negroes with the progress being made to assure them social, economic, and political equality. "Gradualism" has become a thoroughly discredited term. The mounting clamor is for equality here and now —today—not in a distant tomorrow. No longer is the Negro willing to adjust his hopes and behavior to a system in which he is relegated to second class citizenship. Passage of the historic Civil Rights Act by Congress in 1964 represents one response by the nation to the demands of its racial minority.

Non-whites who were formerly apathetic and resigned have now been drawn into a massive campaign of social action. Sparked by the new national and international status achieved by the peoples of Africa and by the infamous events in such communities as Selma, Birmingham, and St. Augustine, the American Negro has turned from the regular channels of democratic decision-making to the strategy of peaceful mass protest. The movement is of crucial relevance to metropolitan life, for the battleground is the city. Equality has ceased to be an abstraction for the Negro and has now become directly related to the house in which he lives, to the job opportunities available to him, to the schools where he sends his children, and to the public and private accommodations and facilities open to him. These are matters in which local governments cannot escape involvement.

In our discussion of non-service problems, we have concentrated attention on only several of a much larger number of social and economic maladies plaguing metropolitan areas. We have omitted such relevant items as the high rate of school dropouts among children in the lower socioeconomic strata, the necessity for upgrading the school system and broadening educational opportunities for all segments of the society, the social needs of the rapidly increasing number of older persons, the impact of automation on the worker, and the technological and industrial changes that are accelerating economic growth in some urban areas and deterring it in others. Some of these matters are touched upon in other chapters, but a comprehensive treatment of them is not within the scope of this book. Most of our attention in this chapter has been focused on urban renewal and the racial question not only for purposes of demonstrating the relevance of social and economic issues to the functioning of the metropolis, but also because these are the two key factors in the internal life of the contemporary American city and metropolis. Progress in achieving the goal of a satisfactory urban environment and realizing the potentialities of metropolitan living will depend largely on the advances made in solving these problems.

CHAPTER 10

The Planning Challenge

No ONE CONCERNED with metropolitan planning, writes a perceptive scholar, "can observe the city from the air without a sense of both wonder and dismay—a wonder at the richness and variety, a dismay from a vague sense of discontent, the nagging thought that the problems of the metropolis have somehow gotten ahead of us, that we are in the grip of forces greater than our comprehension and beyond our powers of control. As one views the urban region from this vantage point, the reflection automatically arises as to whether one mind or any organized group of minds can ever really grasp this restless entity as a whole, or being grasped, whether human efforts can control it."[1]

Incomprehensible as the modern community may appear, it is a reality, a human artifact, that urban man must live with here and now. Moreover, it is a dynamic and constantly evolving entity that he must shape and guide to the best of his ability, imperfect as the

[1] William A. Doebele, Jr., "Key Issues in Land Use Control," *Planning, 1963* (Chicago: American Society of Planning Officials, 1963), p. 5.

current state of knowledge and understanding of metropolitan phenomena may be. To leave the future of this complex organism to
chance would be to tempt fate. For without control and direction
intelligently and humanely exercised, the course of urban development can only be disappointing and in the long run self-defeating.
/ The implication of these observations should therefore be clear: there
is a critical need for planning in the process of growth and expansion./
Planning is not a nostrum for urban ills nor does it promise the
millennium. It gives no assurance that metropolitan change will be
rational and orderly and in the common interest, but it does increase
the chances of achieving a more satisfactory community environment.

Planning is now a familiar and respectable term, but not very
many years ago the mere mention of the word conjured up visions of
governmental regimentation, creeping socialism, and infringement
of private rights. These fears have largely faded into the background
with the course of contemporary events. Although resistance to community planning still exists among those with strong emotional and
financial investments in the status quo, the process is generally recognized as a legitimate function of local government. Businessmen,
as well as civic reformers and newspapers, have become its strong
advocates. Even those people who were originally most hostile to the
concept, such as real estate operators and builders, have reluctantly
come to accept the fact that land use expansion and development
cannot be left entirely to the decisions of the market and the ingenuity of its participants but must be subjected to responsible public
control.

The rapid pace of urbanization and its resultant problems have
encouraged this more favorable attitude toward planning. Local
officials and citizens alike have become increasingly aware of the
imprudence of letting their communities grow like Topsy. To put it
simply, the tidal wave of metropolitan growth has set off the alarm,
bringing urban dwellers face to face with the realities of twentieth
century metropolitan life. On the one hand, they see their hopes of
semi-rustic life in suburbia vanishing with absorption of land on the
fringe of the metropolis at an incredible rate. On the other hand,
they can no longer avoid recognizing the social and economic
threats implicit in the spreading blight and deterioration within
the core city. The awakening, it is true, has been only partial,
but the voices crying in the wilderness are beginning to be heard.

Today, the need to regulate metropolitan change is no longer seriously debated; the question is the extent of the controls and whether they shall be based on *ad hoc* decisions or comprehensive planning.

Planning is not a new or novel public responsibility. The cities and towns of the world have always made some kind of blueprints for their physical development. Community building based on clearly determined plans can be found in the cities of ancient Greece and Rome, in the villages of medieval Europe, and in many New England towns. Major l'Enfant's design for the physical pattern and development of our national capital is one of the more outstanding instances of American city planning, but other examples can be found in colonial Philadelphia and in Salt Lake City. Although planning in these earlier communities was elementary in the light of modern needs and conditions, its continued use and development would undoubtedly have given us cities of greater beauty and livability today. The tragedy is that urban planning was largely ignored during the past century in the wake of the industrial revolution and the craze for land speculation, and in what one writer refers to as the "intellectual blight of laissez-faire."[2]

Despite its long, if disregarded, tradition, city planning has only in recent decades become established as a distinct process within the framework of local government. Land decisions in the past were made by private businessmen, realtors, and developers with no governmental guidance or control. Only occasionally did public agencies intervene to prevent flagrant abuses. The first municipal plannning commission was established in 1907 in Hartford, Connecticut, but several more decades were to pass before land planning with controls could be said to exist. The Detroit experience is typical in this respect. A city charter adopted in 1918 provided for the appointment of a commission charged with preparing a comprehensive plan for the physical development and improvement of the community. For years the agency operated on a shoestring budget and with virtually no staff. Not until 1940 did the city enact a zoning ordinance and not until eight years later did it adopt a master plan. Thus by the time the commission had become established as the recognized agency for guiding Detroit's development, most of the vacant land within the city had disappeared and much of the physical layout set. The new suburban communities which came into existence after World War

[2] Coleman Woodbury (ed.), *The Future of Cities and Urban Redevelopment*, (Chicago: University of Chicago Press, 1953), p. 637.

II were in a far better position: they could plan before intensive development occurred. Unfortunately, only a few took full advantage of this opportunity.

The Detroit example is not unique. Until very recently, planning agencies in most large cities enjoyed low status in the local bureaucracy. Even after achieving acceptance, they were able to do little long-range planning but were mainly, and in some cases exclusively, occupied with zoning and subdivision regulation. The situation is changing for the better, but improvement is painfully slow. All but a handful of American cities of over 10,000 population now have official planning commissions; this is encouraging, but it would be a mistake to conclude from this fact that planning (as distinct from zoning) is widely practiced in the United States.

In this chapter, we first discuss the planning function itself and the various tools used in its implementation. We next observe how the process operates in the central city and in suburbia. Only then do we turn to its use at the metropolitan level. The reason for this approach is that although the metropolis is not a wholly undesigned artifact, whatever planning goes into it is carried out individually by its legally autonomous parts: the municipalities, special districts, and counties which constitute its governments. It has been only in recent years that planning agencies of area-wide scope have been established, but even in virtually all such cases, the basic responsibility for carrying out developmental decisions still remains with the local units.

WHAT PLANNING MEANS

Up to this point we have been speaking about planning as though it were a commonly understood concept. The contrary, however, would be more accurate. Not only the general citizenry but many local officials as well hold erroneous notions about its nature and scope. Some confuse it with zoning or official mapping; others assume that it is a legally binding blueprint of land use development; and still others regard it as some esoteric process of curing urban ills. The confusion is not surprising since the professional planners themselves have not been very successful in making their roles clear. Here is a sample of the types of definitions that appear in the literature:

Planning is a generic term that refers to any activity which contributes to the establishment of objectives for the future and their attainment over time.

Planning is the coordination in space and over time of those activities which affect the physical characteristics of the city.

Planning is concerned with the orderly relation of all functions which government performs directly or through regulation.

Planning is essentially a process of understanding human needs and of influencing and shaping future public policy to serve those needs most effectively.

Planning is the process whereby a community attempts to anticipate future developments, prepare for them, and guide them into desirable patterns of growth.

Planning is a means for systematically anticipating and achieving adjustment in the physical environment of a community consistent with social and economic trends and sound principles of civic design.

The common element in all these definitions is the anticipation of and preparation for the future. A booklet prepared by the Community Planning Division of Sears, Roebuck and Company answers the question "Why do we plan?" in these simple terms: (1) to meet events we expect to happen; (2) to accomplish things we want to happen; and (3) to avoid or prevent things we do not want to happen.[3] Three broad groups of functions are implicit in this listing: research (Where are we now?); goal formation (Where do we want to go?); and plan-making (Specifically, how do we get there?) A report prepared by the Planning and Zoning Commission of High Point, North Carolina, sums up the meaning and objective of planning in this way :

The goal of planning is the efficient utilization of the physical resources of the community and the provision of a healthy and satisfying environment in which to live and work. In order to insure the maintenance of already developed portions of the community, and in order to insure that the best use will be made of land which will be developed in the future, High Point must look ahead. Before we can know how much land ought to be provided for industry and for homes, before we can know how much water and how many roads we are likely to need, we must have some idea about the growth potential of our community. How many of these new people will be living in High Point City? How many will be working in the city's factories and mills? How many children will be attending High Point's schools and playing in High Point's parks? How many automobiles will be traveling to and

[3] *ABC's of Community Planning* (Chicago: Sears, Roebuck and Company, 1962), pp. 4–5.

from and through the city every day? How many people will be shopping on Main Street?[4]

Planning results in blueprints for future development; it recommends courses of action for the achievement of desired goals. But as is true of any design, whether for the construction of a house or the building of an expressway, community plans are not self-executing. The political and administrative officials responsible for policy determination must provide the necessary ways and means and the tools, such as zoning, subdivision regulations, and capital improvement programming, for carrying them out. These implementing techniques are frequently employed in communities where no comprehensive plan exists, but this situation is an invitation to costly mistakes and undesirable growth patterns.

THE MASTER PLAN

The overall blueprint for community development is known variously as the master plan, comprehensive plan, or general plan. It is not a rigid and static physical design attractively presented on a large and colorful chart but a composite of maps, programs, and policy statements that are intended to serve as guides for both public and private action. Its basic components include plans for land use, transportation, and community facilities.[5] The Connecticut statute authorizing municipalities to formulate and adopt a master plan provides a typical legislative definition of the scope of such instruments. Under the terms of the statute, the plan may include recommendations:

for the most desirable use of land within the municipality for residential, recreational, commercial, industrial, and other purposes; for the most desirable density of population in the several parts of the municipality; for a system of principal thoroughfares, parkways, bridges, streets, and other public ways; for airports, parks, playgrounds, and other public grounds; for general location, relocation and extent of public utilities and terminals, whether publicly or privately owned, for water, sewerage, light, power, transit, and other purposes; and for the extent and location of public housing projects.[6]

[4] *High Point: The City and the Region* (High Point, North Carolina: City of High Point, August 1, 1958), p. 1.
[5] For an incisive treatment of the elements of land use planning see F. Stuart Chapin, Jr., *Urban Land Use Planning*, 2nd ed. (Urbana: University of Illinois Press, 1964).
[6] General Statutes of Connecticut (1949 Revision), title 8, chap. 45.

The emphasis in this broad mandate, as in virtually all such laws, is on physical development. City planning traditionally has tended to concentrate on the formulation of blueprints for the physical community without serious inquiry into the overall social, economic, and political objectives that local government should seek to obtain. Today, however, planners are giving increasing attention to these goals and to the forces that motivate people's actions and aspirations. They are also coming to recognize that physical planning cannot be separated from the planning of services and programs. In the words of one authority, "The physical plan represents social planning practice only to the extent that it serves to further sound public policies as represented by all the major functions that government performs."[7]

The master plan as such is not legally binding on anyone. Only those elements of it which the governmental policy-makers see fit to adopt and incorporate into law through zoning and other implementary means have this effect. The execution or enforcement of the plan, in other words, is strictly a political act. Planners are powerless to effectuate their work except as their proposals are appealing to the policy-makers. They may carefully and arduously prepare a comprehensive plan for community development but unless the mayor and council are willing to employ it as the basis for decisions on circulation patterns and public improvement projects, it will stand merely as a collection of attractive maps and noble statements. For no matter how imaginative and well conceived a plan may be, "it is unlikely to achieve success as an organizing force unless planning is well established and an astutely directed function of local government situated in the mainstream of the decision-making process."[8]

This last statement points to a major difficulty planning has faced in this country. In most communities, responsibility for the preparation and adoption of the master plan rests with a semiautonomous agency or commission appointed by the mayor or council. The location of this function in a body outside the regular administrative channels of government was largely the result of reformist zeal. Pressure for planning (or more accurately for zoning) originated with

[7] Donald H. Webster, *Urban Planning and Municipal Public Policy* (New York: Harper & Row, 1958), pp. 558–559.

[8] F. Stuart Chapin, Jr., "Taking Stock of Techniques for Shaping Urban Growth," *Journal of the American Institute of Planners*, XXIX (May, 1963), 80.

civic improvement groups during the municipal reform era early in the present century. By assigning the responsibility to an independent commission, the reformers hoped to make the program secure from politics and politicians. This insulation, desirable as it may have been at that time, has had the effect of separating the planning process from the mainstream of public decision-making. Planners, as a result, have been able to play a less effective role in urban development than might otherwise have been the case.

The pendulum has swung in the opposite direction in recent years until today many scholars and general practitioners of public administration urge the abandonment of the idea of autonomy and the integration of planning into the administrative structure. Some even propose the elimination of the lay plan commission and the transfer of its functions to a department directly responsible to the chief executive.[9] Chicago, for example, moved in this direction in 1957 when it reconstituted its planning agency as a full-fledged executive department and retained the commission only as an advisory board to the department. Those advocating this approach maintain that the planners have been most successful when they have managed to establish close working relations with the mayor (or the manager) and other agencies of government concerned with policy-making and administration. This view is becoming more prevalent, although many planners continue to insist on the value of the semi-autonomous agency. It seems clear, however, that whether or not formal structural changes are made, the future is almost certain to bring a closer alignment between the planner and the political official.

TOOLS OF IMPLEMENTATION

We have referred several times to the tools necessary to transform planning proposals from intellectual and artistic exercises into public policies. Three of these processes are of particular importance to the control of urban growth and development: zoning, subdivision controls, and the capital improvement program.

[9] For a cogent expression of this viewpoint see Robert A. Walker, *The Planning Function in Urban Government*, 2nd ed. (Chicago: University of Chicago Press, 1950).

Zoning

Zoning is often regarded as planning; in fact, it serves as a substitute for it in many communities. Some planning obviously is involved in the zoning process, since local policy-makers are designing a pattern for future development when they draw up districts for the various types of land use. However, unless this design is based on a knowledge and evaluation of the many interrelated elements influencing community growth and change, it is likely to be unrealistic as well as dysfunctional. How, for example, could local officials intelligently estimate the amount of land that should be reserved for residential use, or for industrial and commercial purposes, without reference to a host of other factors? Zoning, if it is to be employed rationally, must be related to future needs and trends, community resources and potentialities, the road and utility systems, and demographic characteristics. It must, in short, be grounded on a comprehensive plan that reveals these interconnections and provides perspective for coordinating and harmonizing the numerous pieces of the urban puzzle.

Zoning is commonly defined as the division of a community into districts for the purpose of regulating the use and development of the land and buildings. It is an exercise of the police power directed primarily at the use of private property. It originated in efforts to segregate noxious activities from residential areas and to protect property values by the similarity of uses in each zone. Frequently zoning was brought into operation as the result of a local emergency. Stuart Chase, the well-known author, relates how zoning came to his town when a small drug-preparation shop opened in a residential area and began emitting an unpleasant smell. He also tells of a similar awakening in a neighboring town when it was suddenly confronted with a project for a large trailer park. In this case, Chase notes, zoning "heretofore held to be un-American by the good people of Hartland was rushed through in an emergency town meeting."[10]

Comprehensive or community-wide zoning is accomplished by means of an ordinance specifying the types of districts and the permissible uses within each type. The boundaries of the various districts are then indicated on an official map which is adopted as part

[10] "Confessions of a Town Planner," *The Reader's Digest*, 83 (July, 1963), 133–137.

of the zoning ordinance. Three broad categories of zones are customarily established—residential, commercial, and industrial—with each divided into several classifications or grades. In addition to governing

EXISTING LAND USE

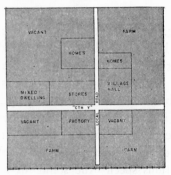

LAND USE PLAN

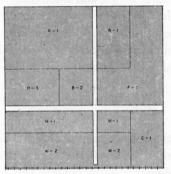

EXISTING ZONING MAP

FUTURE ZONING MAP

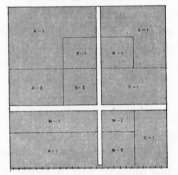

A-1 Agricultural   M-1 Light Industrial   R-1 Single Family Residential
B-2 Commercial   M-2 Heavy Industrial   R-3 Multi-Family Residential
C-1 Conservancy

Figure 10.1   Relation of Zoning Map to Land Use Plan.
From Southeastern Wisconsin Regional-Planning Commission, Planning Guide No. 3, April 1964, p. 13.

the kind of development permitted in each type of district, the zoning ordinance also contains regulations pertaining to the height of buildings, the proportion of the lot that the structure may cover, the setback and side lines, and, in the case of multi-family and business uses, the amount of off-street parking facilities. Once adopted, the ordinance is enforced by the building commissioner who has authority to deny building and occupancy permits for structures not complying with provisions of the zoning law.

Subdivision Regulation

Subdivision regulation, like zoning, is of relatively recent vintage. It grew out of the many problems and abuses, such as disconnected street patterns and lack of essential utilities, that flow from the uncontrolled division of land holdings for developmental purposes. Whereas zoning concerns the type of building and use that may take place on the land, subdivision control is concerned with the manner in which the land is divided and made ready for improvements. Enacted under the police powers of the municipality or other local governmental unit, subdivision regulations specify the standards to be followed by developers in laying out new streets and building lots and the site improvements that they must provide, such as sewers, water mains, and sidewalks. With relatively little raw land remaining in the central city, such regulations are of greater applicability in the expanding suburban communities. However, many states permit their municipalities to exercise subdivision control in the fringe areas outside their boundaries, usually for a distance of three to five miles.[11]

Capital Improvement Program

Zoning and subdivision regulation are primarily protective functions. They prevent land use development that the community deems undesirable, but of themselves they have no power to effectuate desirable development. This task depends more on private initiative and private resources than on public action. Zoning an area for an industrial park is no assurance that industry will locate there; or redesigning the central business district is no guarantee that the merchants and property owners will make the investments in building construction and alterations necessary to carry out the plan.

One implementary device, which is positive in character and both directly and indirectly contributes to plan execution, is the capital improvement program. This program is simply a planned schedule of public projects designed to meet present and future

[11] For a detailed treatment of subdivision regulation, see Webster, *Urban Planning and Municipal Public Policy*, chap. 9.

public needs. As such, it is a key element in carrying out the community master plan and serves two purposes in this connection. First, it provides for the execution of that portion of the plan which calls for public investment, such as the acquisition of park sites or the redesigning of the road network. Second, it influences private investment decisions by the timing and allocation of public expenditures for various programs. Thus a governmental decision to give priority to an urban renewal project in the older section of the city over a program to extend sewer and water mains into an undeveloped area would probably have much to do with the direction of private developmental activity.

A long-range capital improvement program has certain other practical advantages. By revealing the total picture of immediate and future needs, it enables public officials to evaluate these requirements better in relation to other facets of the master plan and to available resources. This procedure reduces the possibility of costly mistakes and permits the establishment of realistic priorities for public facilities. The existence of such a program also affords local officials a degree of protection from political pressures in resolving capital allocations. Few of us are so naive as to believe that public expenditures, or zoning for that matter, can be insulated from politics and the demands of special interest groups. Yet a carefully worked out program and schedule of priorities give public officials a sound basis on which to stand in resisting ill-conceived or untimely action. Without such a program, there is danger that the policy-makers will spread the capital budget over a wide range of projects in efforts to satisfy all interests. When this occurs, needs which should be given priority inevitably suffer.

PLANNING THE CENTRAL CITY

Planning in the central city has a distinctly different emphasis and orientation than its counterpart in new suburbia. The former involves the task of redesigning an already built-up community, which is obsolescent in some respects. The latter is concerned with guiding expansion into the virgin soil of yesteryear's pastures and cornfields. The same principles may be applicable in both cases, but the conditions and circumstances in which they are utilized are thoroughly different. Few planners in the United States are presented with the opportunity of designing a Brasilia or a British New Town from its inception. Our postwar suburban towns and villages come closest to offering this chance, but in most cases their governments are the least planning-conscious. When they do plan, it is usually with their eyes shut to the possible consequences of their acts for the metropolitan community as a whole.

Lack of planning or poor planning has saddled our older cities with many of their current problems; and the mistakes are being repeated in suburbia today. A physical plant, once constructed, endures for years and years. The downtown business district may have outlived its usefulness and the grid pattern of streets may have become obsolete, but these early developments continue to circumscribe the city's planning efforts. The huge investment of capital which such developments represent cannot easily be ignored in the programs and policies of local officials. To change the deeply entrenched pattern would require radical action and massive rebuilding. This is the typical physical plant with which the planner in the core city must work. In such a context, he must plan for renewal, for gradual change. It is as though he must patiently await obsolescence before corrective measures can be taken.

Events during the past decade have altered this picture in certain respects. The federal housing program has done for American core cities what the last war did for many European communities: it has given them the opportunity to plan anew by destroying the old. In Europe, however, the destruction was by bombing; in the United States it is being accomplished by the bulldozer and the iron ball. Judicious use of this opportunity offers a means of speeding up the redevelopment and modernization of our older cities by several decades. It has permitted Philadelphia to revitalize a portion of the gray area around its central business district in an imaginative and attractive manner. In St. Louis, it has enabled municipal authorities to clear out several hundred acres of abysmal slums in the heart of the city. The story is the same elsewhere: New York, Detroit, Chicago, Pittsburgh, New Haven. In all, approximately 1530 projects have been undertaken in 762 cities and have involved more than $4.2 billion in federal capital grants. The consequences have not all been salutary, as we have discussed in Chapter 9, but the program has given central cities "new" land with which to work and a new implementing tool with which to carry out the community master plan.

"Renewing" the City

Urban renewal is closely related and supplementary to the capital improvement program. Under it, the city makes an investment in the acquisition and clearing of blighted land (with the national government bearing at least two-thirds of the costs). In embarking on such a program, local policy-makers face many difficult decisions. What are the boundaries of the areas to be cleared? Which sections of the community should be given priority? To what uses should the cleared land be put? Where will the displaced families and businesses be located? Decisions on these and similar questions can best be made when the community has a comprehensive plan for its development. Congress has given recognition to this need in the requirement that municipalities must have a "workable program," including a comprehensive development plan, in order to qualify for federal assistance. More recently, the Housing Act of 1959 took further steps in this direction by authorizing grants to cities for the preparation of Community Renewal Programs (CRP).[12]

The success of urban renewal as a device for renovating the physical plant of the city depends heavily upon private action and capital, just as execution of most aspects of the master plan does. When the land is cleared, that portion which is not utilized for public housing and civic improvements is placed on the open market. It is at this point that the density, open space, housing specifications, and other concerns of the city planner may run counter to the ideas of the private developer who is interested in maximizing his economic return. The pressure on municipal officials to get the land back on the tax rolls once it is cleared may lead to serious compromising of the city's original plans. This demand can be mitigated, certainly not altogether avoided, if the planning of the project is realistic in light of the community's needs and potentials and based on a "total approach" to the renewal of the city.

Let us take a typical renewal project and discuss some issues that commonly arise in planning the reuse of the land. The project is in the "gray" zone adjacent to the downtown business district. Prior to

[12] A community renewal program is designed to provide a coordinated approach to urban renewal by identifying and measuring the total renewal needs in the community, relating these needs to available resources, and developing a long-range program for carrying out the necessary projects.

clearance, a large portion of the area was residential, but intermingled with the houses were a number of small shops and businesses, several warehouses, and a trucking terminal. Studies showed a strong need for low- and moderate-priced housing in the community and the city planners originally intended that the land be used for this purpose. Inquiries among private developers, however, indicated an interest only in high rent apartments and in office building construction. After weighing various alternatives, the local agency in charge of redevelopment tried to work out a plan it thought would attract private investment and at the same time help to meet community needs. Its tentative proposals allocated one portion of the land, that immediately adjoining the central business district, to office buildings; another to luxury apartments, and a third, in the most remote section of the project, to low-income or public housing.

When the plans of the redevelopment agency were announced, many interests became activated. Downtown property owners objected strenuously to the inclusion of office buildings in the project and contended that such action would further undermine the economy of the central business district and lead to its demise. Private developers, who were not happy about the provision for public housing, maintained that the proximity of such units would destroy the market for the high rent apartments. NAACP (National Association for the Advancement of Colored People) and CORE (Congress of Racial Equality) spokesmen argued that the plan was designed to keep out Negroes and that it did little to meet the housing needs of low-income families who had been evicted to make way for clearing the land. The warehouse and truck terminal operators informed the mayor and councilmen that they would have to relocate their businesses outside the city unless reasonably priced land was made available to them in the project area. Chamber of Commerce officials not only supported this position but went further in urging that part of the land be devoted to an industrial park.

Can issues of this type be resolved in a manner that will preserve the integrity of the city's overall plan of development? Or will the pressures for solution lead to decisions made without reference to the project's effects on other parts of the community? Each case, of course, has to be judged by its own results. The tendency, however, has been for supporters to justify a project on the dubious assumption that what is good for one section of the city must be good for

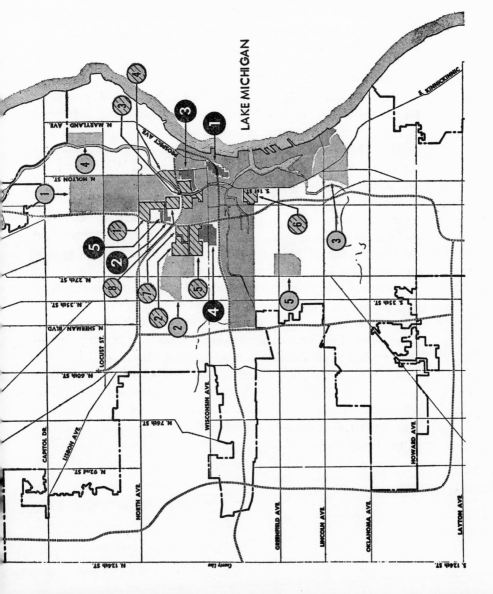

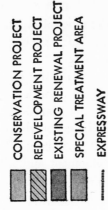

CONSERVATION PROJECT

REDEVELOPMENT PROJECT

EXISTING RENEWAL PROJECT

SPECIAL TREATMENT AREA

EXPRESSWAY

Figure 10.2 Urban Renewal Projects and Special Treatment Areas, City of Milwaukee, 1960. From *Milwaukee's Community Renewal Program*, Department of City Development, City of Milwaukee, May 1964, p. 20.

the whole city. Ideally, the renewal programs should be closely tied into the community's long-range goals and its planning for other projects, but this intermeshing is not always easy to achieve. The redevelopment agency, particularly if it is headed by a strong director, usually has its own ideas about priorities and plans. If these coincide with the views of the planning commission, no problem is involved; if they do not, action may be taken which is not in accord with the city's comprehensive plan. Where basic differences of this kind arise, the position of the redevelopment authority to proceed with a particular project will likely prevail over the planning commission's objections since the mayor and other political officials are naturally anxious to show concrete accomplishments. Renewal offers them this opportunity and makes them more amenable to the modification or deferment of other plans when such action is necessary to get a project under way.

The Case of the Detroit Expressway

The street network presents another serious planning problem for the central city. Today, almost every major metropolis is engaged in the frantic development of expressway systems. Some observers question this trend, asking whether it will not lead to the demise of the core city by making access to suburbia easier. Whether or not this fear is justified, we are unlikely to see the impetus for urban expressway construction slacken in the near future. No central city policy-maker can afford to let traffic jams take their course. Public pressure for quick automobile transportation is too great for political officials to disregard; and a metropolis which cannot boast of at least one expressway is looked upon as "backwards."

The city is by no means the master of its own house in designing its road system. The cost of expressways and major arterials is now beyond the fiscal capacity of most urban communities; and even if they possessed the means, highway building on their periphery would greatly affect their individual street plans. Cities today have little choice in the matter. They must depend heavily on federal and state funds to meet their expressway and road construction needs. This reliance necessarily subjects them to certain controls by the granting agencies and gives the latter an influential voice in the determination of the local transportation system. A case study by two political scientists of the expressway network in the Detroit area graphically underscores this point.[13]

In 1957, the Michigan state highway commissioner announced a ten-year expressway plan for the Detroit metropolitan area that called for $632 million of federal and state funds to construct eighty-one miles of new roads. The first step in carrying out the program required formal agreements among the city of Detroit, the Wayne County road commission, and the state highway commissioner covering the specific projects to be built, allocation of costs, and other details. At the time the negotiations began, the Lodge Expressway which stopped three and one-half miles short of the city limits was the only existing north-south expressway in Detroit. Extension of the expressway would take it through a neighborhood that ranked among the highest in the city in terms of home values and average income. When this extension had earlier been discussed by city officials, it had received a cool reception. One councilman expressed what doubtlessly was in the minds of many others when he declared that he was not for tearing out a large number of homes and businesses and taking much needed assessed valuation from the tax rolls so that suburbanites could save time getting to and from work.

Aware of the city's reluctance to tamper with the Lodge Expressway but convinced that no integrated metropolitan expressway system could be created without such action, the state highway commissioner included the Lodge extension as part of a package which contained other projects Detroit officials were eager to obtain. City negotiators balked at this inclusion but agreed to it after the state held out additional bait on another project. When the contract came up for formal approval before the Detroit common council, a flood of complaints poured in from residents along the proposed route. The protests led to further negotiations between the city and the state and a change in the contract to provide that each of the three parties— city, state, and county—must approve the exact route before work could begin.

Soon after the amended contract was formally ratified by the council, a plan calling for the extension of Lodge by a double deck expressway running along the center mall of James Couzens, an

[13] Robert J. Mowitz and Deil S. Wright, *Profile of a Metropolis* (Detroit: Wayne State University Press, 1962), pp. 403–463.

existing arterial street, was presented to the council. Organized opposition was quickly formed among neighborhood and civic associations in the area. In the face of this opposition, the council again refused to act and asked that an alternative plan be prepared. This time the negotiators proposed a depressed expressway along the Couzens right-of-way. During the long series of public hearings and neighborhood meetings that followed, the issue became not whether to have an expressway but what type. Although some of the groups continued to oppose any form of expressway, the majority had become convinced that the no-expressway position was a lost cause. Finally in March, 1959, eighteen months after the original negotiations had begun, the council approved the depressed roadway plan. The state highway commissioner's strategy of insisting on a package deal had placed city officials in a position where they had to act on the Lodge extension or risk further delay on other projects they badly wanted.

We cite this case for two reasons. First, it shows the role that higher governmental agencies, in this instance, the state highway department, play in certain crucial aspects of city planning. Second, it illustrates how neighborhood resistance can alter the shape of a plan. These are not atypical variables but factors that commonly enter into the planning process. Whether the state's influence led to a better expressway system for Detroit or whether the neighborhood resistance resulted in a solution that was in the best interest of the city are questions on which reasonable minds might well differ. Whatever the answer, the controversy demonstrates that planning does not take place in a social and political vacuum. The products of the drawing board must be subjected to the tempering and at times devastating fires of reality. The process may be a game, as some describe it, but the play is for keeps and deadly serious.

PLANNING IN SUBURBIA

Generalizations about suburban planning are subject to the same weakness as those about other aspects of metropolitan life. Unless they are so broad as to be almost vacuous, significant exceptions can be made to each statement. The heterogeneity of the subject makes this inevitable. Some of the older suburbs face developmental problems similar to those of the central city: lack of room for expansion, blight, obsolescent structures, a deteriorating central business district, and traffic congestion. Other suburban settlements are products of the last two decades and have a quite different set of problems. A few in the total complex are industrial communities, a large number contain mixed land uses, and many are predominantly residential. Some have engaged in careful planning; most have made growth and developmental decisions on an *ad hoc* basis. Still, our stereotype of suburbia—a land of relatively new and rapidly expanding communities with single-family homes and young occupants in the childrearing stage of the life cycle—contains enough accuracy to permit a measure of analytical license.

Pleasant Meadows, an imaginary but "typical" suburb situated fifteen miles from the heart of Big City, serves as a good case in point. When incorporated in 1945, an event precipitated by fear of annexation by the central city, the community consisted of about 200 families and many acres of vacant land. At first the village government did little except provide for a part-time police force and a voluntary fire department. Soon, however, residents began to complain about some of the land use developments that were taking place. The area previously had been subject to the county zoning ordinance which, although inadequate, had provided some measure of protection. With incorporation, however, county jurisdiction over zoning and subdividing had been terminated and the land released to the free play of the economic market place and the whims of the developers.

Awakened from its lethargy by the complaints, the village governing board on the advice of its attorney zoned the whole community as single-family residential. This step was taken to give the board immediate control over land use. Now a developer who wanted to build anything other than single-family dwellings would first have to seek a zoning change. Some time later, subdivision regulations and a building code modelled after those of an adjacent municipality were also adopted. Requests for zoning changes to permit commercial uses were generally granted in cases where there was no significant opposition from the residents. Most of this development occurred along the state highway which ran through the village.

During the course of the next few years, subdivisions blossomed indiscriminately over the area and population mounted rapidly. The village board found itself increasingly pressed to provide necessary services. Both municipal and school district tax rates spiralled upward as public expenditures increased. Alarmed at the trend, village officials reacted by raising the minimum lot size in the zoning ordinance from one-quarter of an acre to one acre. This change forced developers to construct higher-priced homes in order to justify the increased land costs. With larger lots, fewer families could be accommodated in the community, and with fewer families the burden on the school system would be less. The change also meant that families of low or modest income would be kept out of the village due to the housing costs.

By this time Pleasant Meadows authorities had become convinced of the need for broadening the tax base of the community. They realized that the most effective way of doing this was to attract industry. To do this the village board zoned for light industry certain tracts along the highway and along the rail line which cut across one corner of the community. It also appointed an industrial development committee of local citizens to search out prospective users. These efforts met with a measure of success as they brought into the municipality several firms formerly located in Big City.

The influx of people, commerce, and industry continued to create new problems for the village fathers. The old system of private wells and septic tanks had to go. Industry demanded water and sewers as a condition of location; even in the residential sections, the increase in the number of septic tanks was causing health and sanitation problems. New roads were also required to accommodate the increased traffic; additional fire stations would have to be built and hydrants installed if residents were to receive the financial benefit of lower fire insurance rates. Businessmen were insisting that more street lights be installed in the commercial areas; school authorities were calling for sidewalks in the vicinity of the school buildings. Parents were urging the provision of recreational areas for their children— and so the list of needs multiplied.

Up to this time, the village board had occasionally retained a planning consultant on certain zoning matters, but it had made no effort to develop a master plan for the community. The city manager whom it had recently hired after a revamping of the governmental structure now suggested the desirability of such a plan, pointing out that federal matching funds were available for this purpose. The board welcomed the proposal and authorized the filing of an application for assistance with the Housing and Home Finance Agency (HHFA). Upon approval of the request, the village board entered into a contract with a consulting firm to prepare the plan. By this time in the community's history, commercial and industrial uses were strung out along the highway; sections that might have been ideal for industrial development were covered with houses; few sites large enough for parks or other public facilities remained; residential building had been permitted along creeks and watercourses that were now subject to periodic flooding because of the increased runoff from new building construction; and the road system could not be modernized without tearing down property erected less than ten years earlier. Attractive residential subdivisions were scattered throughout the municipality but the total pattern appeared incongruous and unrelated. Thus, two decades after its incorporation, the village found itself in a position not unlike that of its much older neighbor, Big City. Instead of fields of raw land, the master planners of Pleasant Meadows had to work with a physical layout that was already fixed in major respects by the haphazard development of recent years. The old story of the central city was repeating itself in suburbia; all that remained to complete the cycle was the next phase: blight and renewal. For some suburban communities this stage has already arrived.

PLANNING THE METROPOLIS

The High Point report, mentioned earlier in this chapter, emphasizes that in order to plan intelligently a community must take into consideration its position as an integral part of a larger geographical and economic region. As the authors note, "High Point has outgrown its political boundaries. While there is much which can be done to improve the city as a place to live and work, the future of High Point and the solution of its development problems lie beyond the city limits."[14] The same statement can be made of most American cities. The task of guiding urban growth has simply outstripped the ability of municipal planning agencies to cope with the economic, social, and physical developments that have made many local political boundaries obsolete and have led to the creation of special districts. Although these events have magnified the need for area-wide

[14] *High Point: The City and the Region,* p. 2.

planning, public recognition of its importance has been slow to evolve.

The bulk of planning that has taken place up to now has been primarily for individual municipalities rather than for entire metropolitan areas. As a recent study prepared for a United States Senate committee by the Joint Center for Urban Studies of the Massachusetts Institute of Technology and Harvard University points out:

> In the absence of well-developed metropolitan plans, the urban patterns that are emerging today are a random collection of local plans and policies designed to meet local objectives. Yet each community, in seeking an optimum solution to its own problems, does not necessarily work in the interests of the people in the larger metropolitan area. Many suburban towns, for example, have chosen to promote the development of single-family houses on large lots as a means of forestalling costly investments in new utility systems. From their own point of view, these strategies have often been effective. But when large numbers of communities in an area limit their development in this way, the net result has often been to force a vast outward movement of people to the fringes of metropolitan areas, creating a need for new and expensive utility systems in the peripheral communities, and forcing long commuting trips to the central cities. A pattern of development that is economical for many suburbs can be very costly for the metropolitan area and the Nation at large.[15]

Number of Metropolitan Planning Agencies

A list prepared by the National Municipal League staff in 1962 showed sixty-three planning commissions created on a multi-jurisdictional basis within standard metropolitan statistical areas.[16] Three-fourths of these commissions had been established since 1950. A survey conducted the following year by the Housing and Home Finance Agency showed 126 "metropolitan" planning commissions in 142 SMSA's where some form of area-wide planning activity was under way.[17] (The HHFA total is larger than that of the National Muni-

---

[15] U. S. Senate Committee on Government Operations, Subcommittee on Intergovernmental Relations, *The Effectiveness of Metropolitan Planning* (Washington: 1964), p. 3.

[16] For an annotated list of these agencies see *National Civic Review*, LI (July, 1962), 384–390.

[17] Housing and Home Finance Agency, *National Survey of Metropolitan Planning* (Washington: 1963). Several of the agencies have territorial jurisdiction in more than one SMSA, thus explaining the discrepancy between the number of commissions and the number of SMSA's.

cipal League since it includes county planning agencies.) Although both inventories must be regarded with caution since many of the commissions listed by them are metropolitan planning bodies in name or pretense only, the tabulations reflect a growing trend toward broadening the territorial scope of planning.

Geographical Area

The term metropolitan or regional planning commission is generally applied to planning agencies which are set up on a multi-jurisdictional basis. It includes those serving two or more counties, several municipalities, a combination of counties and municipalities, or a city and county jointly. About one-fourth the total number serve areas larger than the SMSA as defined by the national government: well over one-half are coterminous with it; and the remainder cover areas smaller than the SMSA. The Detroit Metropolitan Area Regional Planning Commission and the Southeastern Connecticut Regional Planning Agency are examples of the first. The former covers an area of 5 counties, only 3 of which are part of the SMSA; the latter has jurisdiction over the New Haven SMSA and 6 additional towns. In the second category are such bodies as the Atlanta Metropolitan Regional Planning Commission serving the 5 counties in the Atlanta, Georgia, SMSA, and the Tri-County Regional Planning Commission covering the 3 counties of the Lansing, Michigan, SMSA. The third group includes the Pueblo Regional Planning Commission which serves only a part of Pueblo County, Colorado, and the Portland Metropolitan Planning Commission which excludes that portion of the Portland SMSA in the state of Washington.

Membership

The majority of metropolitan planning agencies are established by joint action of local units under state enabling acts. With no single policy-making body, no metropolitan government to which they can relate or of which they are a part, they must look to the group of local units they serve as their constituency. In most cases, the participating local governments appoint the members of such commissions (in some instances a portion of the membership is named by the governor). The provisions regarding appointment and size are so varied that generalization is not possible. The Capitol Regional Planning Agency in Hartford, for example, consists of 56

members, two appointed by each town in the region. The Northeastern Illinois Metropolitan Area Planning Commission is composed of 19 members, one named by each of the 6 county boards,
5 by the mayor of Chicago, and 8 by the governor; the Detroit agency
has 72 members, half selected by the local governing bodies and half
by the governor; and the Cleveland Regional Planning Commission
contains 54 members, 5 of whom are county officials (ex officio), 5
citizens appointed by the county board, and the remainder named
by municipal planning commissions.

Structural Relation to Local Units

The formal relationship of metropolitan planning bodies to the
local units varies widely. At one end of the continuum are the agencies which are established and financed by private organizations and
groups. Those in this category have no official standing but seek to
interest the citizenry and local governments in metropolitan-wide
planning through research, preparation of land use plans, economic
analyses, and publicity concerning the problems of the area. The
New York Regional Plan Association and the Pittsburgh Regional
Planning Association are two of the better known private organizations in this field. At the other end are those agencies which are
constituent parts of a general metropolitan or area-wide government
in much the same way that city plan commissions are component
units of their municipal governments. The Metropolitan Toronto
Planning Board and the planning department of Metropolitan Dade
County, Florida, fall into this classification. Between these two extremes are the majority of metropolitan or regional planning bodies
with varied degrees of relationship to their local units.[18]

Private planning associations have played a useful role in stimulating interest in area-wide planning and in performing a function
that government has been slow in assuming. However, they cannot,
nor do they claim to, serve as substitutes for officially constituted
metropolitan planning bodies. As private groups with only advice and

---

[18] The financing of these agencies differs. Only a few of the multi-jurisdictional commissions, such as the Southeastern Wisconsin Regional Planning
Commission, have the power to levy taxes or assessments on the member units.
Most must rely on voluntary contributions or appropriations by other governmental agencies. The burden of support is borne largely by the national government and the counties, with the states and other local units contributing
only a relatively small proportion of the total amount.

TABLE 23

Areal Characteristics of Metropolitan Planning Agencies, by Jurisdiction

AREAL CHARACTERISTICS	ALL TYPES	MULTI-JURISDIC-TIONAL	CITY-COUNTY	COUNTY
	TYPE OF AGENCY JURISDICTION (NUMBER OF AGENCIES REPLYING TO QUESTIONS SHOWN IN PARENTHESES)			
Areal jurisdiction determined by	(112)	(34)	(36)	(42)
State legislature	45	6	14	25
State code department	15	13	2	0
Participating jurisdictions	53	15	21	17
Other	8	3	3	2
Boundary may be revised by	(97)	(31)	(34)	(32)
State legislative action	24	5	8	11
Agreement of participating units	57	18	24	15
Annexation or incorporation	9	0	3	6
State planning agency	11	9	2	0
Other	4	0	1	3
Action to secede subject to	(53)	(25)	(16)	(12)
Approval of participating units	13	5	2	6
State approval	3	3	0	0
Unilateral act of secession by any government	32	18	11	3
Other	7	1	3	3

SOURCE: *The Effectiveness of Metropolitan Planning*, p. 125.

expertise to offer, they are severely handicapped in seeking to influence public policy. Lacking official status and divorced completely from the governmental structure, they are unable to relate their planning closely to the operations of the public agencies involved or participate in the decision-making process of these units except as outsiders.

The most desirable arrangements for metropolitan planning exist in those few instances where the responsible agency is an integral part of an area-wide government. In such cases the planning function can more easily be tied into the programs and decision-making processes of an ongoing public body that has operational powers. Such a situation exists in Toronto where the Metropolitan Toronto Planning Board is a component unit of a government possessing jurisdiction over an impressive range of area-wide functions. It also exists in the Miami, Florida, SMSA (Dade County) where the county government serves as the metropolitan instrumentality. In the case of

TABLE 24

Organizational Characteristics of Metropolitan Planning Agencies, by Jurisdiction

| ORGANIZATIONAL CHARACTERISTICS | TYPE OF AGENCY JURISDICTION (NUMBER OF AGENCIES REPLYING TO QUESTIONS SHOWN IN PARENTHESES) | | | |
	ALL TYPES	MULTI-JURISDIC-TIONAL	CITY-COUNTY	COUNTY
Commission members selected by	(114)	(34)	(39)	(41)
County board or chairman	33	0	0	33
City government and county board	26	0	26	0
Each government represented on commission	37	25	8	4
Plan boards of governments on commission	3	3	0	0
State	4	3	1	0
Other	11	4	4	3
City and county officials can serve on commission	90 (121)	34 (37)	22 (37)	34 (47)

TABLE 24 (*Continued*)

ORGANIZATIONAL CHARACTERISTICS	TYPE OF AGENCY JURISDICTION (NUMBER OF AGENCIES REPLYING TO QUESTIONS SHOWN IN PARENTHESES)			
	ALL TYPES	MULTI-JURISDIC-TIONAL	CITY-COUNTY	COUNTY
Commission members are	(47)	(14)	(20)	(13)
Elected officials only	6	3	1	2
Elected officials and citizens	20	8	8	4
Elected and appointed officials and citizens	18	2	9	7
Citizen members only	3	1	2	0
Number of different government types on commission	(123)	(38)	(40)	(45)
1	26	6	0	20
2	54	18	28	8
3	29	9	10	10
4 or more	14	5	2	7
Number of times government-type represented on commission	(126)	(38)	(41)	(47)
State	11	9	1	1
County	108	27	40	41
Incorporated city	92	31	40	21
Township	36	10	7	19
Special district	12	7	4	1

SOURCE: *The Effectiveness of Metropolitan Planning*, p. 129.

Toronto, municipal planning commissions remain in existence, but authority to veto local plans that conflict with the area-wide master plan is vested in the metropolitan government. In the Miami area, efforts to implement the provisions of the Metro charter vesting broad formulation and enforcement powers over planning and zoning in the county government have thus far failed so that each city still retains control of its municipal zoning. Marion County, Indiana (which constituted the Indianapolis SMSA until it was redefined in 1963 and two adjacent counties were added) has on the other hand succeeded in making planning a metropolitan responsibility. By act of the state legislature in 1955, all powers of planning and zoning were removed from the municipalities and townships and transferred to the county government. In this instance, not only authority for area-wide planning but also one of the important implementing powers for executing it, namely zoning, are vested in a single government of general jurisdiction. The Marion County case, as well as the two others, are exceptions to the rule, however, and efforts to import similar practices in other areas have met solid walls of resistance.

A somewhat more common arrangement in use is the joint city-county planning body. One of the strongest agencies of this type is the Tulsa Metropolitan Area Planning Commission formed in 1953 to take over the planning functions of the city of Tulsa and Tulsa County. The commission's area of jurisdiction includes the central city, a five-mile perimeter around it, and the unincorporated sections of the county. Because of its structural relationship to the two major operating governments of the area, the commission is in a strategic position to function effectively as a metropolitan planning agency. In other communities where joint city-county planning is in operation, this relationship is generally not as close. The more usual arrangement is for both governments to retain their separate commissions but employ a single professional staff. Although not as effective as consolidation of the commissions themselves, this system does offer the opportunity for coordinating the respective planning programs through use of the same staff.

The type of area-wide planning agency that is currently becoming more popular is the metropolitan or regional commission serving a multiplicity of governments throughout an urban complex. These agencies have no organic relationship to the local units although their board membership may be appointed by the participating governments. The Northeastern Illinois Metropolitan Area Planning Commission is a prominent example of this type. Within its planning area of 3700 square miles in the Chicago SMSA are 250 municipalities and over 700 other governments. To relate to this number of public bodies and attempt to coordinate their planning activities in matters of regional concern is a herculean task. As Paul Oppermann, the former executive director of the commission, has observed: "A critical difference becomes visible here between the conditions of city planning and metropolitan planning. In the city or village, the whole governs while the parts advise, petition, and seek to amend. At the metropolitan scale, the situation is reversed, and the parts govern while the viewpoint of the whole is . . . recommended to units of government."[19]

In a number of metropolitan areas, voluntary associations or councils of governments have been formed to provide a continuing forum for discussion of area-wide problems and to promote coordinated action in solving them.[20] These councils offer a possible means of relating metropolitan planning more closely to the operating agencies. This result has been partially achieved in the Detroit area where the regional planning commission enjoys an informal working relationship with the Supervisors Inter-County Committee. Some tendency has also been evidenced by several other metropolitan councils to engage in their own planning activities. The Mid-Willamette Council in the Salem, Oregon, area, for example, is conducting a large-scale regional transportation study, and the Association of Bay Area Governments (ABAG) in the San Francisco area is conducting an inventory of existing land use and general plans of the cities and counties in the region.

Metropolitan or regional planning is at the stage today that city planning was about fifty years ago. It is winning recognition but it still remains outside the mainstream of local governmental life. The growing number of area-wide planning agencies furnishes tangible evidence of the current fermentation in this field. So also does the movement toward the establishment of metropolitan councils of public officials, a movement that gives promise of providing an institutional mechanism, imperfect as it may be, for relating planning to the executing agencies. This latter development may well offer the most advanced solution that can be expected in improving the governmental processes of the metropolis.

THE ROLE OF METROPOLITAN PLANNING

In 1962, a committee of the American Institute of Planners issued a statement on the role of metropolitan planning that is of considerable

---

[19] "Five Years of Metropolitan Planning: A Special Report," *Inland Architect* (April, 1963).

[20] These councils are discussed more fully in Chapter 13.

significance since it expressed the consensus of professionals on a relatively new activity in the local government field. The committee outlined the nature and objectives of metropolitan planning in the following terms:

Metropolitan planning is comprehensive planning applied to areas containing a large urban concentration where dominant economic, social and physical factors may over-arch local and even state boundaries. The function of metropolitan planning is to contribute to the formulation and implementation of optimal public policy for the metropolitan area.

Metropolitan planning functions at a new level in the governmental hierarchy, one which, however, includes fundamental roles for governments at all levels. On the one hand, metropolitan planning serves as a framework and a vehicle for the municipal, county and other local units of government and for relating these plans to the desirable development of the metropolitan area as a whole. On the other hand, planning at the metropolitan level seeks to integrate local and metropolitan plans with the plans of the state and of the nation.

The metropolitan planning agency should seek the development of a unified plan for land use, density and design, the provision and correlation of public facilities, services and utilities, and the preservation of open space and wise use of natural resources. It should strive to coordinate local planning, both public and private, with planning at the metropolitan level; similarly, the metropolitan plan should be coordinated with state and national plans—particularly those affecting transportation, public facilities and natural resource programs and functions that are metropolitan in scope. To this purpose, there should be a legal requirement that the agency review the content, conformity or compatibility of all proposals affecting the metropolitan area.

. . . The metropolitan planning agency should seek establishment and acceptance of goals, both long-range and immediate, for the metropolitan area's physical development (with due regard to economic and social factors). These goals should be the basis for the formulation of the comprehensive metropolitan area plan—and that plan, in turn, should serve as a framework within which may be coordinated the comprehensive plans of municipalities, counties and other units of government in the metropolitan area.

The metropolitan planning agency should seek to establish especially close relationships with other institutions concerned with metropolitan-wide development such as water supply and development authorities, mass transportation agencies, special districts, highway departments, park and recreation agencies and air pollution control bodies. Efforts should be made to participate in the decision-making processes of such agencies as a major means of accomplishing area-wide development goals.[21]

[21] American Institute of Planners, *The Role of Metropolitan Planning* (Chicago: 1962), pp. 1, 4, 5.

Several facets of the AIP memorandum are worth noting. First, metropolitan planning is regarded as supplementary to local planning, not as a substitute for it. The comprehensive area-wide plan should provide a broad framework within which local units can plan for their own growth and development. For this purpose, it should deal primarily with functional elements of metropolitan significance, such as the transportation network, conservation of natural resources, open space, economic potential, water pollution, drainage and flood control, and general patterns of land use. To take a simple example, if local officials are provided with a plan for developing the major arterial system of the region, they can more intelligently plan their own road network and land use to fit into the overall pattern.

Second, a metropolitan planning agency is basically a coordinating mechanism. Since it must depend on other governments for the execution of its proposals and recommendations, it must operate in working partnership with planning units at all levels. In this capacity, it serves as a sort of catalyst or broker seeking to relate the activities of all the affected agencies of government in integrated efforts to achieve area-wide planning objectives. Again using the road system as an example, we know that many governmental units are involved in the process of locating a major metropolitan throughway: the federal Bureau of Public Roads, the state highway commission, the county, and various municipalities. A metropolitan agency with a carefully prepared plan for regional development is in a position to effect a consensus among the parties that will be in the best interests of the entire area.

Third, metropolitan planning is advisory in nature and depends for its acceptance on the voluntary acquiescence of the local units. Provision is made in a few states for mandatory review by the area-wide agency of all local plans affecting the metropolitan region. This power, however, is only the power to be heard, not to approve or reject. Ultimate authority to heed or ignore the recommendation rests in the hands of the locality. The success of a metropolitan agency, in other words, resides largely in its ability to persuade and convince its numerous and autonomous constituents. This is not an easy task even under the best of circumstances. As C. David Loeks, the director of the Twin Cities Metropolitan Planning Commission (Minneapolis-St. Paul), describes it: "Metropolitan planners in this country are laboring under formidable odds. They have been given a dictaphone, a calculator and fist full of prisma color pencils and have been directed to sally forth and slay the giant of urban disorder. Unlike the original David—who had something quite tangible with which he rendered his Goliath *hors de combat*—the contemporary metropolitan planner must be content to throw ideas, suggestions and proposals."[22]

PLANNING IN PERSPECTIVE

Planning, whether at the local or metropolitan level, involves proposals and commitments that pertain to an indefinite future. People find it much easier to act when they are confronted with a self-evident problem or when a decision is forced on them by the pressure of circumstances. At the same time, they are less ready to commit themselves to community plans that may involve present self-sacrifices on their part in return for some projected future benefit. Planning, for this reason, requires the strong support of political leaders who are in a position to articulate community needs and goals and rally public support. It is precisely in this respect that metropolitan planning is seriously handicapped. Since the governmental or institutional pattern in most urban complexes is not conducive to the emergence of political leaders who consider the general good of the whole area as their primary responsibility, the task of guiding metropolitan growth is relegated to numerous locally-based officials with locally-oriented allegiances.

Coupled with the general lack of public appreciation for long-range goals and the absence of metropolitan political leadership, the possibility of meaningful area-wide planning is further impaired by the near-feudal isolationism and internecine rivalry that exists among the various governmental units which make up the metropolis. The picture would indeed be bleak were it not that the pressures of contemporary events are forcing even the most provincial officials to be less intransigent in their opposition to certain forms of action at the metropolitan level. Steps thus far taken in this direction have been reluctant rather than enthusiastic, timid rather than bold. What is important, however, is that progress is being made. Metropolitan areas are creating planning commissions, preparing comprehensive

[22] "Taming Urban Giant," *National Civic Review*, LI (July, 1962), 354.

land use and transportation plans, and setting up area-wide councils of governments. These developments may fall far short of the demands of the modern urban era, but in typical American fashion adjustment will be made as the people and their elected representatives are brought face-to-face with immediate and concrete needs. By that time, the less sanguine would say, it will be too late.[23]

No subject on the metropolitan agenda has received more attention in recent years than planning. Conference after conference has been devoted to its discussion, and expert after expert has emphasized its central role in controlling and shaping urban growth. Well-known authorities in the planning profession, such as F. Stuart Chapin, Jr. and Henry Fagin, have been calling for local units to adopt some kind of developmental policies instrument to provide a unified framework for steering public programs in metropolitan areas. The national government, moreover, is beginning to use its financial incentives to encourage area-wide planning. New sections of the Federal Highway Act, for example, required every area of a population of 50,000 or more to develop a continuing transportation plan by July 1, 1965, in order to retain its eligibility for federal highway funds. Similarly, bills introduced in Congress in 1963 and 1964 called for review by a metropolitan planning agency of applications for certain federal grants within the area. All this activity is a good omen. It indicates wide acknowledgment of the concept that urban growth should be consciously shaped and not left to the whims of chance. What is not yet revealed, as the results demonstrate, is public acceptance of the substantive proposals for carrying out this shaping process. And unless acceptance comes fairly soon, metropolitan areas will be confronted with future problems that will be staggering by today's standards.

[23] The previously mentioned study by the Joint Center for Urban Studies takes a more optimistic view about the future prospects of metropolitan planning. In its words: "The problems in making metropolitan planning effective do not sound as signals of impending failure, nor do they appear to be insurmountable. It would seem, therefore, that now is the time to move ahead in encouraging the growth of the existing embryonic system into a more permanent and responsible structure for metropolitan planning." (*The Effectiveness of Metropolitan Planning*, p. 38.)

CHAPTER 11

⇨ *The Service Challenge*

RIDING ABOUT New York City, the visitor is inevitably struck with awe and wonder. He is amazed at the bigness, the congestion, the noise, the bustle of activity, the polyglot population. He sees subway and railroad stations packed with commuters, streets jammed with taxi-cabs, buses, trucks, and passenger cars, sidewalks crowded with shoppers and tourists, and huge office buildings filled with workers. How, he may ask, is government able to manage the mammoth task of servicing this vast complex? How is it able to maintain order, keep traffic moving, dispose of the waste, supply water, and perform the numerous other functions necessary to keep the city operating? As Wallace Sayre and Herbert Kaufman have pointed out in their study of the New York city government:

It takes two billion gallons of pure water a day, removal of four million tons of refuse, thousands of miles of sewers and huge sewage disposal plants, regulation and inspection of food and food handlers and processes, disease control to prevent epidemics, air pollution control to prevent the poisoning of the atmosphere, and a fire-fighting organization

capable of handling every kind of blaze from small house fires to immense conflagrations in tenements, skyscrapers, industrial structures, and
the waterfront. The basic physical and biological requirements of urban
life are either provided or guaranteed by government.[1]

The New York case is, of course, exceptional. No other American metropolis approaches it in population size, density, or economic
importance. Yet the same general problem of providing basic public
services is faced by local government in each of the nation's many
SMSA's; only the scale is smaller and the degree of intensity less.
Growth and change are no respectors of size; they confer their benefits and inflict their penalties on the small metropolises as well as on
the giants. But whether in Sacramento, California, or Chicago, Illinois, the service problems which expansion engenders are not so
much indicators of weakness in the governmental system as they are
evidence of the dynamic forces that are reshaping the urban world.

LOCAL VERSUS AREA–WIDE FUNCTIONS

Before turning to several of the major service problems that plague
metropolitan areas, it would be well to note a distinction that is commonly made when discussing governmental reorganization, that between local and area-wide functions. The first are assumed to be those
which can be provided separately by the individual municipalities or
other units with less than area-wide jurisdiction; the latter those
which require administration on a metropolitan basis.[2] The area-wide
approach is said to be necessary when the function is of such nature
that it transcends individual municipal, and in some cases county,
boundaries (such as the control of air and water pollution); or when
it would be economically unfeasible for the local units to perform
individually (such as the operation of a sewage treatment plant).

[1] *Governing New York City* (New York: Russell Sage Foundation, 1960),
p. 34.
[2] A report of the Advisory Commission on Intergovernmental Relations
employs a threefold classification of urban functions: local, intermediate, and
area-wide. The first includes those performed by units whose jurisdiction extends only to a portion of the metropolitan area, such as municipalities, townships, school districts, and small special districts. The second are those administered by a single unit, or a number of local units acting jointly, and having
jurisdiction over a substantial portion of the area. The third are those performed
throughout a metropolitan area by a single unit or a number of local units
acting cooperatively. (*Performance of Urban Functions: Local and Area-wide*,
Washington: 1963, p. 34.)

It is impossible to draw a clear line of distinction between the two categories, "local" and "area-wide." Most attempts to make the differentiation are based more on impression than objective criteria. Virtually all functions performed by the various governments of a metropolis have some impact on the larger area. Poor police protection in one municipality may be detrimental to the neighboring units. Or an inadequate building code in one city or village may adversely affect property values in surrounding areas. Even if we assume that these traditional local functions are performed reasonably well by the individual units, the classification still presents difficulties. Police protection, for example, can normally be handled locally if the municipality is large enough to support a professional department. Yet certain aspects of this function, such as communications, training, central records, and laboratory facilities can often be provided more efficiently and economically on an area-wide basis.

In the case of urban functions of this latter character, how is one to determine the level to which they should be allocated? Should the function itself be divided and appropriate portions assigned to both the local and area-wide units? Or should responsibility for the total function be vested in one or the other level, depending on which aspects—local or area-wide—are predominant? No systematic attempt has been made to resolve these questions either theoretically or empirically. Local government proponents have generally resisted any division of individual functions, fearing that such action would open the door to eventual absorption of the total service by the higher echelon. Supporters of metropolitan reorganization, on the other hand, have preferred the transfer of whole functions, maintaining that confusion and inefficiency would result if portions of the same service were allocated to two different levels. However, in recent years their attitude has tended to shift to the point where many of them have come to accept the notion as feasible.

One of the few attempts to develop a set of standards for judging whether a function should be performed at the local or area-wide level was made by the Advisory Commission on Intergovernmental Relations in one of its many reports.[3] The Commission suggested seven criteria for making this determination:

[3] A more theoretically oriented attempt to develop criteria for the areal division of governmental powers is contained in Arthur Maass (ed.), *Area and Power: A Theory of Local Government* (New York: Free Press, 1959).

1. the unit of government responsible for providing a particular service should have territorial jurisdiction large enough to minimize
   the spillover of benefits or social costs into other jurisdictions;
2. it should be large enough to permit realization of the economies
   of scale;
3. it should have a geographic area of jurisdiction adequate for effective performance;
4. it should have the legal and administrative ability to perform the
   service;
5. it should be responsible for a sufficient number of functions so that
   it provides a forum for resolution of conflicting interests and is
   able to balance governmental needs and resources;
6. it should be so organized that the performance of its functions
   remains controllable by and accessible to its residents; and
7. it should be able to maximize the conditions and opportunities for
   active citizen participation while still permitting adequate performance.[4]

We cite these criteria because they illustrate the difficulty of
devising operational standards for making an areal distribution of
functions. As is evident, the list is a mixture of economic, administrative, and political tests that are not altogether in harmony with
each other. The political criteria in the sixth and seventh categories,
for example, may run counter to the economic standards in the second
and third specifications. The latter may call for a governmental unit
of such large size that citizen control and accessibility would be limited and participation discouraged. To arrive at allocational decisions,
moreover, each of the factors would have to be weighted since all are
not of equal value. But on what basis is the relative importance of
each to be determined? It is easy to say that an accommodation must
be made between the traditional values commonly associated with
local government and the realities of modern urban society; but again,
how is such a balance to be struck? A list of criteria, such as that
developed by the Advisory Commission, serves a useful purpose in
focusing attention on the most patent factors involved in the areal
division of powers. It does not, however, provide a pat formula or a
quantitative measuring device for making allocational determinations
in concrete cases.

[4] *Performance of Urban Functions: Local and Areawide* (Washington:
September, 1963), pp. 41–60.

The Local-Areawide Continuum

The Advisory Commission, in the same report, used its set of criteria to rank fifteen urban functions on a scale from "most local" to "least local." (See Table 25.) The ranking is based more on impression than on measurable data and is, as the Commission admits, only a rough approximation of the possible order.

TABLE 25

Rank Order of Urban Functions According to Local-Areawide Criteria

	RANK	FUNCTION
	1	Fire protection
	2	Public education
Most	3	Refuse collection and disposal
Local	4	Libraries
↑	5	Police
	6	Health
	7	Urban renewal
	8	Housing
	9	Parks and recreation
	10	Public welfare
	11	Hospitals and medical care facilities
↓	12	Transportation
Least	13	Planning
Local	14	Water supply and sewage disposal
	15	Air pollution control

SOURCE: *Performance of Urban Functions: Local and Areawide*, pp. 9–23.

Many analysts of the metropolitan scene would undoubtedly disagree with the ranking of particular functions. To some, public education and libraries would be less local than, say, police or urban renewal, or health more area-wide than parks and recreation. Others would point out that the listing fails to take account of the various aspects of individual functions and their differing degrees of "localism." Refuse collection, for example, is more local than its complementary element of disposal, and the operation of a sewage treatment plant is less local than the maintenance of the lateral sewer lines. What is of interest, here, however, is not the validity of the ranking but the approach which was employed. Instead of starting with the assumption that administrative reorganization is needed and then documenting the problems to justify this conclusion, the Commission focused its attention on the optimum scale of operation for each of the major urban services without reference to governmental structure. By divorcing these two aspects for analytical purposes, such an approach is capable of providing greater insight into the kinds of governmental accommodations that are necessary to keep a metropolitan system functional.

These preliminary observations furnish the general framework and background for our examination of seven major urban services: transportation, water supply, sewage disposal, air pollution, fire protection, police, and parks and recreation. The first four rank high on the area-wide or "less local" end of the scale, the fifth is one of the "most local," and the last two are in the intermediate category. Although this list is by no means exhaustive, it is representative of the range and kind of governmental services that are provided in metropolitan areas. (Other functions including planning, housing, urban renewal, and several organizational aspects of public education are discussed in other chapters.)

TRANSPORTATION

April 1, 1898, marks a memorable occasion in the annals of urban life, for it was on that day that the first recorded sale of an automobile took place: a one-cylinder Winton. Fifteen years later, the age of the rubber-tired motor vehicle began in earnest with the advent of Henry Ford's mass-produced car. By 1920 there were nine million motor vehicles registered in the United States; in 1964 there were over eighty-two million. Approximately 80 percent of all American families now own at least one car and 10 percent more than one. When the automobile was first introduced, the hard-surfaced roads in this country, if laid end to end, would not have stretched from New York to Boston. Today, there are 2.6 million miles of such facilities, enough to circle the earth at the equator more than 100 times.

It is sometimes said that the automobile is the cause of most metropolitan problems. Critics charge that it has precipitated urban sprawl, rendered the central city obsolete, destroyed the beauty of the community by generating unsightly expressways, polluted the air with gas fumes, and led to mass congestion. Few would deny the element of truth in these charges. Relying upon the automobile to satisfy most of the travel needs in the metropolis has led to serious consequences. Yet consider the other side of the coin. The transportation of people and goods is basic to the life of the modern urban community, and the motor vehicle has provided a dynamic instrument for fulfilling this need. It has also given man greater freedom of choice in his place of residence and greater mobility to pursue his cultural and recreational goals. If we did not have the automobile, we would have to invent it.

Consider also the role of the motor vehicle in the American economy. In 1963, automotive retail sales, including vehicles, accessories, parts, repairs, and gasoline totaled $67 billion. During the same year nearly $12 billion in motor vehicle taxes were collected, and one of every seven wage earners was employed in some phase of the automotive and transportation industries.[5] The enemy is not the automobile; it is the long prevalent policy of putting our transportation eggs in one basket by developing facilities for the private motor car to the virtual exclusion of every other form of transit.

Trends in Urban Transportation

The increasing popularity of the automobile has been accompanied by a steady decrease in mass transportation. Although the population of the nation's SMSA's gained 26 percent between 1950 and 1960, the transit industry provided 45 percent fewer passenger rides during 1959 than it did ten years earlier. Profits of the industry have fallen substantially in recent years despite upward adjustments of fares, financial institutions have shown little inclination to invest new capital in a declining enterprise, and many private lines have either ceased operations or been taken over by public agencies. The cycle has been a vicious one since lower patronage has led to fare increases and service curtailments, and these developments in turn have contributed to further rider losses.

Practically all metropolitan areas in the United States, large as well as small, depend wholly on their street systems to accommodate the movement of people. (Only New York, Boston, Chicago, Cleveland, and Philadelphia have rapid transit systems utilizing rails. The San Francisco–Oakland area is now building such a system.) Since

[5] These statistics are from *Automobile Facts and Figures* (Detroit: Automobile Manufacturers Association, 1964).

the street patterns in the older cities were laid out before the automobile age, they are wholly inadequate to meet the demands of modern traffic. Even the "post-auto" communities such as Los Angeles designed their circulation systems seemingly oblivious to the flood of automobiles that was soon to inundate them.

Since World War II most metropolitan areas have made frantic efforts to enlarge their street and road capacity. In the mad scramble, freeway building became the popular response to congestion. The Los Angeles area alone had 310 miles of such facilities by the end of 1960, and the story, in lesser degree, has been repeated all over the nation. The freeway boom received a boost from the Federal Aid Highway Act of 1956 which provides for the financing of a 41,000-mile interstate network. This total includes 5500 miles of urban expressways that will skirt or penetrate virtually all cities over 50,000 population. With the national government bearing 90 percent of the cost of such roads, there has been little incentive for urban areas to seek alternative solutions to their transportation ills.

A Balanced System

Traffic experts have long pleaded for the development of a balanced transportation system in which mass transit takes its place alongside the private automobile. They point out that it is wholly unrealistic to build costly new expressways but neglect the needs of public transportation. Every additional motor vehicle which appears on the streets during the peak hour traffic periods in the morning and evening requires an increase in the load-carrying capacity of the network as well as additional road maintenance, parking space, and policing. Experience has also demonstrated that new expressways fill to the point of saturation almost from the day they are opened. This outcome is ironic since in creating easier and more rapid driving conditions, the new roads encourage greater use of private vehicles in the work-home trip and thereby further aggravate the congestion problem.

At the present time, the automobile reigns supreme as the predominant mode of commuter conveyance, with no possible competitor in sight. Only 12 percent of the nation's labor force travel to their place of employment by public transportation and the proportion is decreasing yearly. The battle against the ensuing congestion has been fought primarily by building more and larger roads and converting more of the community's land area to off-street parking facilities. This strategy, however, has been self-defeating since it has ignored the plight of mass transit. Congestion simply will not be conquered by the cement mixer and the paving roller; it will be eased only by diverting a substantial number of commuters from private automobiles to public conveyances.

Motorists will not be lured away from their self-powered vehicles by advertising campaigns or other gimmicks. Unless public transit is upgraded to the point where it can compete with the private automobile in terms of speed and convenience, present trends will not be reversed. This revitalization, as traffic analysts emphasize, cannot take place without decisive public action. All indications point to the fact that congestion will grow progressively worse until urban communities and higher levels of government see fit to devote a far greater share of their energy and resources to the development of mass transportation facilities than they do at the present time. The resistance of the citizen body to any "subsidization" of public transit has severely handicapped efforts in this direction. Voters have been willing to support huge expenditures for road and freeway construction but at the same time they have insisted that public transit be self-supporting. In doing so they have disregarded the fact that urban transportation—both public and private—is conceptually a single function that, like education, includes large indirect social benefits as well as direct individual benefits.

Current Developments

The demonstrated inability of local government to deal with the transportation problem is causing the initiative to shift to higher echelons of public authority, particularly to the national level. State governments, with few exceptions, have thus far done little to assist their metropolitan areas in achieving a balanced system for moving goods and people. When they do take cognizance of the need to bolster mass transportation, they are usually unwilling to discard the shibboleth of self-support. The action in 1963 of the Pennsylvania legislature in creating a metropolitan transportation authority to operate an integrated mass transit system for Philadelphia and four surrounding counties provides a typical illustration of this reluctance. No taxing power was given to the authority and its revenues were restricted to fares and to funds contributed by the participating cities and counties. A similar situation faces the Bi-State Development Agency which in 1963 took over the more than twenty private transit lines serving the St. Louis SMSA. It too must depend upon its fare revenues to finance operations and expansion. The policy of barring such agencies from tax sources prevents them from making the large-scale capital investment in facilities and equipment that is called for if public transportation is to be placed on a competitive basis with the private automobile.

Once again, as in the case of planning, housing, and urban renewal, the national government is stepping into the breach. In 1961 Congress provided funds for demonstration projects to determine the effects of fare reductions and service improvements on public transportation. This action was followed in 1964 by passage of the Urban Mass Transportation Act authorizing $375 million in matching funds over a three-year period to aid urban areas in financing mass transit improvements. These are timid steps, to be sure, yet they give official recognition to the crucial role of public transit and the need for governmental assistance in this field.

Two instances in which federal demonstration grants have contributed to encouraging developments—one in Skokie, Illinois, and the other in Boston—are worthy of note. Early in 1964, a rapid transit system was organized jointly by the village of Skokie and the Chicago Transit Authority with federal financial assistance. Utilizing a five-mile stretch of abandoned right of way of a discontinued commuter line, the new agency inaugurated a nonstop shuttle operation between Skokie and Chicago. The response surprised even the most optimistic. The "Skokie Swift," as the new line is called, carried more than 4000 passengers on its first day of operation. Because of the heavy patronage, schedules were quickly revised to reduce the time interval between trains from ten minutes to five during the peak hours and from thirty to fifteen at other times.

In the Boston case, a $5.4 million demonstration project financed by federal and state funds was undertaken in late 1962. The purpose was to study the effects of various service and fare changes on transit ridership. Many interesting findings emerged from the study, leading to the general conclusion that the declining trend in the number of riders of public transportation can be reversed.[6] More

[6] See Mass Transportation Commission, *Mass Transportation in Massachusetts* (Boston: 1964).

important than the findings themselves, however, the project sparked the passage of comprehensive state legislation to attack the problem of urban mass transit. In June, 1964, Governor Endicott Peabody signed into law a bill establishing the Massachusetts Bay Transportation Authority with responsibility for mass transit in the city of Boston and seventy-seven other municipalities in the area. Significantly, the measure recognizes the need for the state to participate financially by earmarking proceeds from an increase in the cigarette tax for mass transit purposes.

Transportation Administration

Urban transportation by any meaningful criterion is an area-wide function. The network of roads and mass transit facilities in an urban complex cannot be divided up by local governmental jurisdictions. As origin and destination surveys show, a large portion of the trips that begin in one section of the metropolis terminate in another of its sections, passing through the boundaries of two or more localities in the process. To facilitate this movement, the entire urbanized area must be considered as the geographic base for coordinating the planning and operation of the transportation system.

Several approaches may be taken to the question of governmental jurisdiction in relation to the urban transportation function. The most extreme, and the one preferred by many experts, is an overall regional agency to plan and administer the total system. The Metropolitan St. Louis Survey in recommending an integrated system for that area in 1957 put the case in this way:

> The traffic and transportation problem in St. Louis City-St. Louis County must be attacked on an area-wide basis by correlating expressways, major arteries, feeders, bridges, and parking facilities with an efficient and rapid mass transportation system. This objective can be attained only if a single governmental authority is endowed with power over the planning, construction and maintenance of expressways, principal arteries and major off-street parking facilities, and with control over mass transit facilities.[7]

No such agency presently exists in the United States. A number of area-wide transit authorities have been created but their jurisdiction does not extend to other segments of the transportation network.

[7] *Path of Progress for Metropolitan St. Louis* (University City: 1957), p. 59.

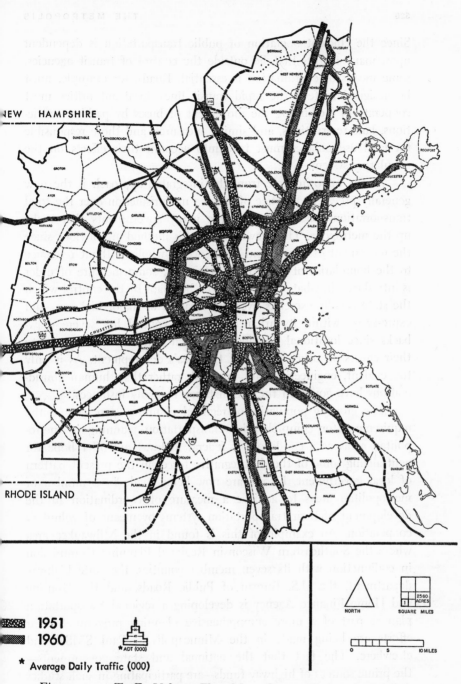

1951
1960
* Average Daily Traffic (000)

Figure 11.1   Traffic Volume Flow Map, Greater Boston Area, 1951 and 1960. From *Mass Transportation in Massachusetts*, Massachusetts Department of Public Works, Massachusetts Transportation Commission, 1964, p. 5.

Since the efficient operation of public transportation is dependent upon many factors that lie outside the control of transit agencies, some means of coordination is essential. Roads, for example, must be designed to feed the rapid transit lines, local authorities must cooperate in facilitating the movement of buses by parking restrictions, lane reservations, and similar measures, and those responsible for land use policies must take into account their effects on the circulatory system.

At the opposite pole from the integrated approach is the now generally prevalent practice of carving up jurisdiction over the total transportation function among the many governments that make up the metropolis. The drawbacks to this method are obvious since the movement of people and goods occurs wholly without reference to the boundaries of these units. However, some measure of order is introduced in what would otherwise be chaos by the control which the state usually exercises over the location of major highways and expressways within its urban areas. This control has severe drawbacks since locational decisions are often made without regard to their effects on other aspects of the area's development. As is only too evident, engineering and financial, rather than human considerations have governed the action taken in many instances.

The growing popularity of regional planning agencies and the requirement for comprehensive transportation planning in metropolitan areas as a condition of federal highway aid offer hope for neutralizing some of the disintegrative forces in the present pattern of local government. Efforts are now being made in a number of metropolitan areas to achieve a measure of coordination in the development of their transportation systems by means of voluntary cooperation. An example of this is found in the Milwaukee area where the Southeastern Wisconsin Regional Planning Commission in conjunction with its seven member counties, the state highway department, the U.S. Bureau of Public Roads, and the Housing and Home Finance Agency is developing a regional transportation plan as part of a more comprehensive planning program. Similar efforts are being made in the Minneapolis-St. Paul SMSA and elsewhere. The fact that the national and state governments—the prime sources of highway funds—are participating in such studies gives some assurance that future road and expressway construction in these areas will be based on coordinated planning. This development appears to offer the most promising approach to the transportation problem under existing circumstances.

A middle course between integrated control of transportation and voluntary cooperation is based on the idea that individual functions can be divided and allocated to different levels of public authority. The most prominent example of this practice is found in the Toronto area where the metropolitan government has jurisdiction over the main highways and major arteries while the municipalities retain responsibility for local streets and roads. Recommendations embodying this concept have occasionally been advocated by metropolitan survey commissions in the United States but they have met with little favorable response. To a limited degree, however, this arrangement exists in the present system. Generally, the states administer the main trunk highways in their urban areas, the counties in some instances operate the expressways and secondary roads, and the municipalities control the remainder of the streets within their boundaries. The division is wholly inadequate and lacking in coordination, yet the practice furnishes precedent and a possible basis for strengthening the transportation network.

WATER SUPPLY

Urban areas require water for a variety of purposes including human consumption, waste disposal, manufacturing, and recreation. As in the case of our other natural resources, the amount of water consumed has risen steadily. Part of the increase is due to population growth but a substantial portion is attributable to the rise in per capita use, the result of improved living standards that have made such appliances as automatic dishwashers, washing machines, and air conditioners common household items. The concentration of industry in metropolitan areas has also caused urban water needs to soar. Industrial requirements are enormous; the manufacture of a ton of paper, for example, takes 25,000 gallons of water, and that of a ton of rayon fiber 200,000 gallons. In all, the nation's average daily consumption exceeds 300 billion gallons.

The problem is less one of overall shortage than lack of facilities for transporting usable water from where it is to where it is needed. According to reliable estimates, the United States as a whole has ample water to meet its foreseeable needs, but this supply is not

uniformly distributed and in some cases it is of poor quality. This
latter characteristic is a cause of major concern in the eastern cities
where water is fairly abundant. There, intense urban and industrial
concentration has caused severe pollution of the rivers and lakes and
magnified the task of providing pure water. In the western states
where rainfall is substantially below the national average, the problem is one of quantity. Many communities must rely on distant
sources for their needed supply. San Francisco's reservoirs are located
as far as 150 miles away from the city, and Los Angeles will be
drawing its water from as far away as 550 miles when the Feather
River Project is completed in the early 1970s.

Water Administration

The pattern of providing water in metropolitan areas is extremely
diversified. In the Sacramento SMSA, for example, there are 44
public and 55 private agencies engaged in this task; in the Minneapolis-St. Paul complex, 64 municipalities, including the twin cities,
have water systems of some kind. In Chicago the central city plant
supplies water on contract to approximately 60 suburban communities, a practice followed in other large cities such as Detroit, Cleveland, New York, and San Francisco. Special districts provide another
type of water supplier. The 1962 Census of Governments lists 764 such
agencies operating within standard metropolitan statistical areas. The
largest is the Metropolitan Water District of Southern California
which serves communities, including Los Angeles and San Diego, in
three metropolitan areas.

Most central cities in the metropolis are served by their munici-
pally-owned and operated water systems. Outside the West, supply
has seldom been a problem for them since the majority are located
on rivers or lakes that provide ready quantities of surface water. The
metropolitan suburbs, on the other hand, have been in a less fortunate
position. For many of them supply has been a real problem, aggravated by rapid expansion and lack of access to surface water. Individual household wells, the initial source of supply, have long since
proved inadequate in all but the yet undeveloped peripheral sections.
As experience has shown, to the dismay of many a suburbanite,
water tables usually drop and artesian wells become subject to contamination by septic tank seepage as the area is built up. When this
happens, the outlying communities are left with two choices: secure

their water from the central city plant or establish their own facilities by sinking deep wells to tap underground sources.

Some core cities have offered their suburbs the more drastic alternative of annexation. Both Milwaukee and Los Angeles at one time used water as a weapon to press annexation on fringe areas that did not have the resources to develop their own systems. The more common practice, however, is for the central city to furnish water to its suburbs on a contractual basis. Arrangements for accomplishing this vary widely. In a majority of cases the city sells water wholesale to the neighboring municipalities or water districts and these in turn handle the distribution to the consumers. In other instances, the city provides direct extensions of service to the individual users. Often both methods are employed, as in Seattle where 14 percent of the city's suburban customers are served directly and the remainder through the distribution systems of thirty water districts and municipalities.

None of these methods has been considered satisfactory by those seeking metropolitan reorganization. As a Select Committee on National Water Resources of the United States Senate noted in 1960, a serious problem affecting the provision of water in urban areas "stems from difficulties in the field of political structure or organization."[8] Because of these difficulties, most survey commissions have tended to favor a unified system for the entire area. The advantages claimed for such a solution include (1) economies of scale, (2) elimination of disputes over water among local units, (3) comprehensive planning for the total system, (4) orderly extension of facilities, and (5) more effective conservation of water resources.

Logically, there is no more compulsion for consolidating water administration than for integrating control over other functions such as transportation. The major question is not whether there should be a single supplier; it is whether some institutional means should be established to assure the coordinated planning and development of the overall system and to see that the water needs of all sections of the metropolis receive proper consideration. As one authority has commented:

A plan for a regional system does not necessarily mean that a region has to have a single integrated regional facility. It merely means that

[8] *Water Resource Activities in the United States: Future Water Requirements For Municipal Use* (Washington: 1960), p. 19.

all of the alternatives for supplying water or disposing of it have been studied, and that combination adopted which is best suited to the topography and geography of the region, and will most efficiently and economically provide the required service with the least interruption or damage to people, property and resources. The selected combination might very well include several sources of water, several points of waste disposal and several separate systems and operating agencies.[9]

The function of water supply in the metropolis readily lends itself to a division of responsibility. Even if a single regional agency were established, local units could still retain the task of distributing the water to the consumers. The same arrangements could be employed if the central city were the sole supplier. When this latter practice is followed, many objections would be eliminated if the city were compelled to operate as a utility subject to the regulatory powers of the state public service commission. In this way suburban customers would be protected against arbitrary rates or practices by the city, while the latter would have the monopoly rights of a utility and be assured of a reasonable return on its investment.

As a final observation, it should be noted that the problem of water supply often extends beyond the boundaries of individual metropolitan areas. Southern California's struggle with Arizona interests over the use of Colorado River water is one example of the territorial extent of the problem. Chicago's attempt to utilize additional water from Lake Michigan for sewage disposal purposes, an attempt opposed by five Great Lakes states and Canada, is another. Water supply, in other words, is a national—and in a few instances an international—problem. It involves all levels of government and its proper administration requires that local units relate and integrate their water policies and programs with state and national agencies as well as among themselves.

SEWAGE DISPOSAL

The publisher of the *St. Louis Globe Democrat* is reported to have remarked, "Every time you take a glass of water from a faucet in St. Louis, you are drinking from every flush toilet from here to

[9] Melvin E. Scheidt, "Water Management Problems in Urban Areas," Paper presented at Residence Course on Urban Planning for Environmental Health, U.S. Public Health Service, Cincinnati (April 3, 1962), pp. 7–8.

Minnesota."[10] And in portions of Long Island where suds have been known to flow from faucets, residents facetiously refer to a glass of water as a "detergent cocktail." These vivid remarks point up the close relationship between the supply of water and the disposal of sewage. No matter how large a quantity of water may be available to a community, inadequate waste disposal can seriously limit its use and affect its quality.

In the past urban areas devoted considerable effort to supplying their residents and industries with water but paid much less attention to the task of getting rid of the waste. Until well into the present century, it was common practice for cities to dump their sewage untreated into the watercourses that conveniently flowed by their doorsteps and from which they drew their needed water. In fact, as late as 1950 every major city on the Missouri, including Kansas City and St. Louis, was discharging raw sewage into the river. The U.S. Senate's Select Committee on National Water Resources reported in 1960 that almost 2900 new sewage systems were required for communities that have never provided treatment for their wastes and another 1100 plants to serve residents in areas with overloaded facilities. Two years later, the Department of Health, Education, and Welfare estimated that $6 billion would be required over the next ten years to eliminate the backlog of sewer needs, replace obsolete units, and serve population increases.

The growing pollution of the nation's watercourses prompted the national government to intervene actively in the field after World War II. In 1948, Congress passed the first comprehensive federal legislation on the subject. The measure was designed principally to stimulate state action in establishing effective enforcement programs. When the state follow-up proved disappointing, Congress enacted the Water Pollution Control Act of 1956. As amended in 1961, this measure gives the national government pollution control powers over all navigable waters situated in the United States. It authorizes the Secretary of Health, Education, and Welfare to call conferences of affected parties in areas where serious pollution problems exist and to initiate court action when satisfactory solutions cannot be worked out. The cooperative approach, although time-consuming, has been successful in eliminating some of the worst

[10] Mitchell Gordon, *Sick Cities* (New York: Macmillan, 1963), p. 84.

sources of pollution. So far court action has been taken in only one instance, that of St. Joseph, Missouri, where the voters had stubbornly refused to approve funds to construct a treatment plant for the raw sewage the city was dumping into the Missouri River.

Sewage Disposal Administration

The administrative pattern for the function of waste disposal varies widely. At least five different types of arrangements are in effect in metropolitan areas:

1. municipal operation of both collection and treatment facilities;
2. administration of the total sewerage system in all or most of an urban area by a special district government;
3. operation by a series of special districts, often in combination with municipal systems;
4. various contractual combinations;
5. municipal operation of the local collection systems and special district management of the disposal facilities.

A majority of central cities fall into the first category, operating all aspects of the sewerage function. Some of the older and larger suburbs likewise maintain their own systems, but most of the smaller suburban communities do not possess adequate resources to warrant construction of treatment plants. Moreover, those that are not located on watercourses have no economical way of discharging their effluent even if they have the financial means to build disposal facilities. The second method, integrated administration for the total metropolis, has not been fully achieved in any major SMSA. In the St. Louis area, for example, a metropolitan sewer district operates all sewerage facilities in the central city and in most of the urbanized portion of St. Louis County, but the remainder of the area is served by a variety of systems. The third approach, a profusion of special sanitary districts, is becoming less popular as costs mount and the disadvantages of maintaining many separate systems become more apparent. The fourth approach, contractual arrangements, is employed with reasonable success in some metropolitan areas such as Detroit where the central city handles sewage from approximately forty suburban communities.

The last arrangement, that of splitting responsibility between local units and a regional agency, has received increasing attention in recent years. Some metropolises, such as Milwaukee with its Metropolitan Sewerage Commission and Chicago with its Metropolitan Sanitary District of Greater Chicago, have long employed this device. Others, such as Seattle which entered the field in 1958 with creation of a special district (misleadingly called the Municipality of Metropolitan Seattle) to operate the area's treatment plants

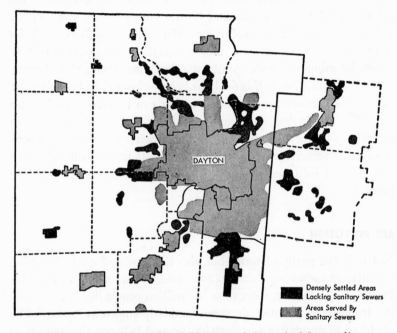

Densely Settled Areas
Lacking Sanitary Sewers
Areas Served By
Sanitary Sewers

Figure 11.2   Sewered and Unsewered Areas in Metropolitan Dayton, 1959. From *Metro Reporter*, Metropolitan Community Studies, March, 1959, no. 5, p. 2.

and trunkline sewers are relative newcomers to this device. With increasing emphasis by federal and state authorities on pollution control, many suburban communities and even some central cities find themselves faced with the need for large investments in treatment facilities. Where this is the case, local units are generally more receptive to proposals involving the transfer of responsibility to an overall agency.

The ideal solution to the problem, as many reform advocates suggest, might well be a metropolitan district with jurisdiction over both water supply and waste disposal. Such an agency would be in a position to plan for the coordinated development and expansion of these two highly interrelated functions. However, there is little indication of any serious movement in this direction at the present time. What appears to be evolving in sewage disposal administration is more in the nature of a threefold allocation of responsibilities with (1) the municipal level handling the construction and operation of local sewage collection facilities, (2) the metropolitan level furnishing the major interceptor sewers and the treatment plants, and (3) the state and national governments providing the policy framework for water resource management and stimulating the lower levels to action by minimum water purity standards and financial assistance. Federal intervention in this field has been welcomed by lower governments since national enforcement action can remove incentives for industries to penalize states and local areas that adopt strong water pollution control programs by moving their operations elsewhere. It can also remove some of the political costs to local officials when they support increased expenditures for facilities to correct pollution problems.

AIR POLLUTION

Not only the purity of water but also the purity of air is becoming a matter of increasing metropolitan concern. According to the U.S. Public Health Service, more than 104 million people live in communities troubled by polluted air, more familiarly known as "smog." The plight of Metropolitan Los Angeles, penned between the mountains and the sea, is a well-publicized fact, but other large population centers are just as severely affected. Tests by the Public Health Service during the first six months of 1964 showed that three metropolitan areas—Washington, D.C., Philadelphia, and St. Louis—had smog concentrations as high as Los Angeles. Mayor Robert Wagner of New York has described the local metropolitan area as the terminus of a 3000-mile-long sewer of atmospheric filth starting as far away as California and growing en route like a dirty snowball.

Contamination of the air is one of the prices of an industrialized and motorized civilization. It is estimated that motor vehicles alone daily emit into the air more than one-half million pounds of carbon monoxide, sixty-six million pounds of hydrocarbon, and eight million pounds of nitrogen oxide. There would be little problem if the pollutants were dispersed evenly throughout the atmosphere, but they are concentrated primarily in the metropolises that produce them. The physical damages from such contamination—to horticulture, paint on homes, clothing, fabrics, and other commodities—are as high as $11 billion annually according to some sources. More important is the possible damage to health. Medical scientists feel that polluted air can aggravate heart conditions and respiratory diseases such as asthma, chronic bronchitis, and lung cancer.

The remark has been made that there is nothing small about the air pollution problem in the United States except efforts to solve it. Considering the nature of the problem, the statement contains more truth than exaggeration. Although a majority of states have adopted legislation directed at air contamination and many local units have established control programs, the total effort has been surprisingly small. As late as 1961, only seventeen states and eighty-five municipalities had programs involving expenditures of $5000 or more each year. Only six states were engaged in "enforcement" activities, the remainder confining their role to technical assistance and encouragement of local programs.

The national government first entered the field in 1955 when Congress authorized the Public Health Service to conduct research and provide technical aid to state and local agencies. In 1964, Congress approved the Clean Air Act which greatly enlarges the role of federal authorities in pollution control. The measure directs the Department of Health, Education, and Welfare to (1) initiate an expanded national program of research and training on the causes, effects, and prevention of air pollution, (2) award grants-in-aid (up to two-thirds of the cost) to local and state agencies for initiating or expanding their programs, and (3) engage directly in abatement and enforcement activities when the health or welfare of citizens in one state is found to be endangered by air pollution emanating from another state. One research area designated to receive special attention is the control of exhaust contamination from motor vehicles.

Air Pollution Control Administration

More so than in the case of other functions, local units are helpless to protect themselves against the failure of their neighbors to control air pollution. It is surprising therefore that so few area-wide agencies have been created or designated to administer abatement programs. In a small number of metropolitan communities, such as Milwaukee, the function has been transferred to the county government. In a relatively few instances, special districts have been created to handle the problem. These include the Bay Area Pollution Control District with jurisdiction over the nine-county area centering on San Francisco, and the Metropolitan Air Pollution Control District of the Boston area. One agency has been set up by interstate compact, the Interstate Sanitation Commission of New York, New Jersey, and Connecticut. However, it has no enforcement power and is limited to making studies of air pollution within its territory. The task of controlling the purity of the air rests, in short, largely on the municipal governments.

TABLE 26

Number of Places and People Exposed to Urban Air Pollution Problems, 1950 and 1960

YEAR	MAJOR PROBLEM		MODERATE PROBLEM		MINOR PROBLEM		TOTAL	
	NUMBER OF PLACES	NUMBER OF PEOPLE[a]	NUMBER OF PLACES	NUMBER OF PEOPLE[a]	NUMBER OF PLACES	NUMBER OF PEOPLE[a]	NUMBER OF PLACES	NUMBER OF PEOPLE[a]
1950	224	36,710	636	22,450	1,407	21,920	2,267	81,080
1960	308	42,940	847	30,160	1,818	31,200	2,973	104,300
Increase	84	6,230	211	7,710	411	9,280	706	23,220

[a] In thousands.
SOURCE: U.S. Department of Health, Education, and Welfare, *Health, Education, and Welfare Indicators* (Washington: 1964).

The nature of the problem obviously calls for "air basin" control. In few cases will this be the area covered by a single municipality and in some instances its territorial scope will be larger than the metropolitan community. A 1960 report of the Air Hygiene Committee of the American Public Health Association outlined what the group considered the proper role for the various levels of government in this field. The following allocation of responsibilities was suggested:

1. The national government should limit its activities to research, training of personnel, and technical assistance to state and local agencies;

2. State governments should undertake all aspects of the air pollution programs except those relating directly to the enforcement of regulations;
3. A local agency, which may be a municipality, county, or special district, depending on the extent of the air basin, should administer the controls.[11]

The Clean Air Act passed by Congress in 1964 gives the national government a stronger role than had been suggested by the APHA since it authorizes the Department of Health, Education, and Welfare to abate interstate air pollution along the general lines of previously enacted water pollution measures. A similar strengthening of controls and enforcement agencies at the state and metropolitan levels is necessary if the problem is to be met successfully.

FIRE PROTECTION

Fire protection is an essential function of urban government. An adequately manned and equipped department not only minimizes the loss of life and property from fire hazards but it also substantially reduces insurance costs to the owners of homes, commercial establishments, and factories. The task of protecting a large city against fire is both quantitatively and qualitatively different from that in the small and predominantly residential suburb. Fighting conflagration in a densely settled community of tall office buildings, apartments, factories, and department stores is a highly complex responsibility. Specialized equipment and expertly trained personnel are absolute requirements. These needs are far less in the small suburban village where the houses are farther apart and the tall buildings few or nonexistent. Here, only a pumper or two and less skilled personnel, even volunteers, may be all that is needed to provide an acceptable level of protection.

Each year over 10,000 people perish in fires in the United States, and each year the nation suffers a loss of more than $1.5 billion worth of property from this source. Any substantial reduction in these figures depends less on increasing the efficiency of fire-fighting agencies than on more effective fire prevention activities. It is in

[11] "Role of Public Health Agencies in Air Pollution Control," *American Journal of Public Health*, 50 (October, 1960), 1591–1603.

the latter that most communities have been deficient. Smaller departments seldom have the qualified personnel to carry out the necessary inspections and to see that the fire code is properly enforced. Larger agencies are often precluded by budgetary limitations from hiring enough inspectors to do the kind of job they feel essential in prevention.

Fire Protection Administration

Of the major functions administered by local government, fire protection is one of the "most local." Spillover effects from the performance of this service are not geographically extensive. Residents in one community receive no direct benefits from the fire protection activities of neighboring municipalities other than those derived from mutual aid pacts or informal understandings of assistance in emergencies. Nor do they suffer any serious disabilities from the failure of adjacent jurisdictions to maintain an adequate level of protection as they do, for instance, in the case of water and air pollution. Although it is true that a fire in one city or village could spread into the surrounding area, the likelihood of this occurring is seldom strong enough to cause any significant expenditures for additional fire-fighting equipment or personnel on the part of other communities.

The pattern of fire protection administration is relatively simple —although varied. Most municipalities maintain their own departments, some with full-time professionals, others solely with volunteers, and still others with a combination of the two. A number of the smaller incorporated communities, and even some of medium size as in California, purchase their fire protection from other cities or the county government. The unincorporated areas are served in a variety of ways: by volunteer departments, special districts, the county government, and private companies on a subscription basis. Numerous mutual aid pacts are in existence among communities providing for each party to render assistance to the others upon call. For example, in Erie County, New York, which contains Buffalo, all the towns, cities, and villages participate in a countywide mutual aid fire protection system that is linked by a radio network.

Fire protection is not a critical organizational problem in metropolitan areas. Economies of scale could undoubtedly be realized by consolidation of the smaller departments, and more efficient services could be provided if the training of personnel was standardized and central communications systems created. But these and other deficiencies which now exist hardly call for a radical reorganization of the system. It is likely that the future will bring greater emphasis on the establishment of minimum area-wide standards and their enforcement by county or state fire marshals. Cooperative efforts by local units to develop a coordinated system of protection will also continue. These measures should upgrade the present system sufficiently to serve at least the basic fire protection needs of the metropolitan community.

POLICE

Police administration, like that of fire protection, is a function related to the safety of the public and is therefore one of the key services provided by local government. The protection of lives and property against law violations is a complex and highly specialized task in a metropolitanized and industrialized society. Crime has become a social problem of front rank with the growth of urban concentrations, the multiplication of wealth, and the development of speedier automobiles and better roads that allow criminals to escape more easily across the boundaries of local jurisdictions. No one actually knows how much crime costs the nation each year, but estimates range as high as $15 billion, not to mention the loss in lives.

According to one police chief, "The attack on crime, accidents and traffic congestion, juvenile delinquency, and other important phases of police operation is the same in cities of two million as in towns of 50,000. There is simply a difference in the extent and sometimes the degree of application of fundamentals generally accepted."[12] Implicit in this statement is the principle that the police forces of the small communities in the metropolis should be as well versed and as well trained in the fundamentals of law enforcement as their larger neighbors. There is sound basis for such an assumption since adequate protection against major crimes requires coordination of police activities over a wide geographical area. If weak links exist in certain portions of the network, the effectiveness of the total system is correspondingly reduced.

[12] John M. Gleason, "Policing the Smaller Cities," *The Annals of the American Academy of Political and Social Science*, 291 (January, 1954), 14.

The wide diversity among police departments in the typical metropolitan area militates against efficient and uniform law enforcement. This diversity is not simply one of size; it relates to training, equipment, record keeping, and even attitude as well. Some smaller communities operate with only part-time departments; many employ untrained or partly trained personnel; a majority do not have adequate facilities for crime prevention and detection. Yet each individual department constitutes, in effect, a part of a single system that has as its objective the maintenance of law and order in the metropolis.

Police Administration

The police function has a long tradition of local autonomy in the United States. Regardless of size or financial resources, virtually every city, town, or village regards itself capable of providing adequate law enforcement within its boundaries. Over 40,000 separate police departments exist throughout the country, ranging in size from those with no full-time personnel to the New York City force of approximately 25,000. In many of the larger metropolitan areas, the number of individual departments runs well over one hundred. Within a fifty-mile radius of Chicago, for example, there are approximately 350 locally maintained police forces, Cook County alone having ninety; and in the five counties surrounding Philadelphia the number exceeds 160.

County governments, through the sheriff's office, usually provide police protection to the rural sections and the urbanized unincorporated areas. A limited number, such as Los Angeles and St. Louis counties, offer police services to the municipalities on a contractual basis. Similar arrangements also exist among cities, but the contractual device is employed nationally far less extensively than it is in fire protection. The same is true with respect to special districts. In contrast to the more than 3200 such agencies utilized for fire protection purposes, special police districts are virtually nonexistent.

Although the police and fire functions are closely related, the spillover effects of the former are substantially greater. Inadequate law enforcement in one community can have important social costs for the remainder of the area. Fires cross corporate boundaries only occasionally but law violators are highly mobile. Police departments throughout an urban area must therefore be trained and equipped to detect and apprehend criminals within their territorial limits no matter where the crimes are committed. This mission requires the close coordination of police activities, an effective communications network, and modernized facilities for record-keeping and identi- fication. The more fragmented police administration is in a metrop- olis, the more problematic is the task of achieving a coordinated system of law enforcement.

Some authorities maintain that a consolidated department is the only satisfactory answer to the problem of police administration in metropolitan areas. Suggestions of this nature, however, have fallen on deaf ears. No American metropolis has seen fit to follow the example of the Toronto area where the police function was assumed by the metropolitan government in 1957. In recent years there has been some movement toward centralization of certain functions such as communications, record-keeping, laboratory facili- ties, and training. There also has been some feeling that either the state or an area-wide agency such as the county should be given authority to establish and enforce minimum standards for local departments. New York was the first state to take steps in this direction when it enacted legislation in 1961 to require all local police officers to have formal training before assuming the respon- sibilities of law enforcement.

The middle approach is illustrated by the recommendation of the Metropolitan St. Louis Survey which called for the county police department in that area to become the agency for correlating the municipal forces and for providing centralized services of the type mentioned above.[13] Proposals of this kind are typical. They rest on the assumption that area-wide needs can be balanced against the claims of local autonomy by dividing the police function in such a way as to satisfy both. Reasonable as this solution may seem, it has met with little favor among suburban departments. As a result, progress in achieving metropolitan coordination in the police field has been far from spectacular.

PARKS AND RECREATION

The rise of recreation as a governmental responsibility in the United States is largely a product of the present century. The opening of

[13] *Path of Progress for Metropolitan St. Louis*, pp. 87–88.

the nation's first playground, a large sandpile in front of a children's home in Boston, did not occur until 1885. Some of the larger cities began to develop park systems earlier, more for their aesthetic qualities than their recreational potentialities. New York City acquired Central Park in 1853 but the purchase was condemned by many as an extravagant waste of public funds. Most of the smaller municipalities did not begin to acquire park acreage until after 1900, and a majority of the suburban communities created since World War II have ignored this responsibility altogether. St. Louis City, to cite one example, has over 2800 acres of parkland; this exceeds the area maintained by local governments throughout the remainder of the seven-county SMSA where the population is almost double that of the city.

The need for parks and outdoor recreational areas has become more imperative as urban populations have multiplied and as leisure time has increased because of the shorter workweek and earlier retirement. In 1964 attendance at state parks exceeded 300 million and at national parks and forests 200 million. No figures are available for the countless millions who utilized the 25,000 parks and the more than 150,000 playgrounds under the jurisdiction of local governments. Local public expenditures for this function are now approximately $1 billion a year, but the gap between need and availability of facilities continues to widen.

Land for park and recreational purposes, once plentiful in and around urban areas, is now in scarce supply. The title of a Department of Interior booklet, "The Race for Inner Space," reflects the urgency of this situation. The nation still has lots of open space but little of it is available where it is needed most. Several states, such as New York, New Jersey, Massachusetts, and Wisconsin, have become active in financially assisting their local units to acquire land while the opportunity still exists. The national government's concern in this field was similarly expressed in the Housing Act of 1961 which authorizes federal grants to state and local governments for acquisition of open space land.

Park and Recreation Administration

All levels of government—local, state, and national—are engaged to one extent or another in providing public recreational facilities. The greatest burden, however, falls on municipalities in urban areas where the day-to-day needs of burgeoning populations must be met. County participation in this function has increased in recent years but is still relatively minor in comparison to that of the incorporated communities. The special district device is also employed for park and recreational purposes to a very limited extent; the 1962 *Census of Governments* reports 488 such agencies in existence, over one-third of them in the state of Illinois. State agencies maintain and operate approximately 2700 parks and the national government 201 parks and monuments (exclusive of the national forests) with a combined acreage of over 25 million.

The spillover benefits from parks and recreational facilities rank relatively high among urban functions. A large park, zoo, or public beach invariably attracts many users from outside the immediate governmental jurisdiction in which it is located. Furthermore, open space areas, wherever they are located, enhance the attractiveness of the entire metropolitan complex, give psychic benefits to the residents, and serve an important conservation function by helping to maintain the ecological balance of nature. On the other side of the ledger, the social costs of failing to provide adequate facilities in one densely settled community may be substantial for the surrounding area in terms of lowered health standards and juvenile delinquency.

The administration of the park and recreation function lends itself to a division of responsibilities, largely on the basis of the benefits it confers. One such division, that into local and metropolitan, has been suggested by George D. Butler, research director of the National Recreation Association. Under his proposed breakdown, facilities and services that primarily benefit the local residents, such as playgrounds, neighborhood parks, and supervised recreational programs, would be handled by the municipalities. The larger parks, golf courses, zoos, beaches, and similar facilities serving the entire area would be administered by the county or, where the SMSA is comprised of more than one county, by a special park district.[14] This division might be extended to one additional level, that of the state. A large urbanized population should have available within reasonable distance large tracts of land that are kept in their natural condition for hiking, camping, picnicking, boating, and fishing. These

[14] "Recreation Administration in Metropolitan Areas," *Recreation*, LV (September, 1962), 349–351.

regional parks or reservations, which may serve several metropolitan areas, can most appropriately be administered by the state government.

Little agreement has as yet evolved among the various governments as to their proper roles with respect to parks and recreation. Each local unit in a metropolis has its own ideas as to what it should or should not do, and each proceeds on its own way without reference to any overall plan for the area. With the shortage of open space in and around the nation's large urban areas becoming increasingly critical, the fragmented and uncoordinated approach characteristic of existing policy in this field is extremely shortsighted and unrealistic.

The park and recreational problem, along with the other service difficulties that have been considered in this chapter, differ from each other in their functional characteristics, territorial scope, and administrative requirements. Our purpose here has been to call attention to the various dimensions of these problems and to possible avenues of solution. In doing so, we have considered each function as an individual activity separate and apart from the others. In reality, of course, many of the problems are interrelated in such a way that a satisfactory solution of one cannot be achieved without action on the others. But whether citizens interested in improving the urban governmental system should concentrate their resources on a single function or strive for a larger or "total" package can only be answered in the light of many considerations. Subsequent chapters will deal with the various overall approaches to metropolitan reorganization and the factors they involve.

C H A P T E R   1 2

Financing
Government in
the Metropolis

THE METROPOLITAN "problem," like the proverbial elephant, has many aspects. One of the most critical, as every taxpayer and public official knows, is that of finance. What can be done to meet the rising costs of local government? Where can new revenues be obtained? How can expanding public services be financed on a basis equitable to all residents of the community? What kind of taxes will be least harmful to urban economic activity? Answers to questions of this nature do not come easily. The era of population explosion and the emerging metropolis is not without its social costs in the form of new problems and aggravations of already existing ones. It is an era that places mammoth burdens on governmental agencies and public facilities and calls for ever expanding services to meet the needs which it generates. All of this costs money—lots of it. But if the pipers are to play, they must be paid even though the fee is high and there are many pipers. For not only has the audience increased many times in size, but its demands have also become intensified because of higher standards of living and greater service expectancies. The result has been inevitable—a frantic scramble for funds to operate the governments of the metropolis.

THE FISCAL DILEMMA

Some observers contend that public finance, not governmental structure, is the nub of the metropolitan problem. They argue that given sufficient funds and equitable distribution, most of the difficulties, whether traffic, blight, or pollution, can be overcome without major changes in the existing governmental pattern. Others agree on the importance of the fiscal problem but maintain that it is precisely the lack of adequate administrative machinery which gives rise to much of the trouble. They point to the numerous local units competing for the tax dollar, the wide range of fiscal capacity among local jurisdictions, and the difficulty of relating benefits and taxes when public activities extend across corporate boundaries as they do in the metropolis. Both positions have a measure of validity. Certainly the most thoroughgoing reorganization of the governmental structure will not in itself assure better schools, more parks, improved transportation facilities, or the elimination of blight. The new structure, as that of the old, would still be confronted with the problem of securing sufficient revenue to finance the rapidly growing needs of an urban populace. On the other hand, a rational reordering of the machinery would make possible the mobilizing of an area's resources more effectively and the elimination or reduction of the inequities which now exist in the system.

Many observers have also commented on a paradox in the metropolitan fiscal problem. Although the bulk of the nation's wealth is concentrated in SMSA's, they note, a great part of the difficulties of governmental units in these areas is attributed to their financial condition. This seeming contradiction is accepted with an air of resignation by most local officials who are well aware of the political perils attached to tax increases. Their attitude is realistic, if not politically courageous, since basically the contradiction is related to the more fundamental question of public versus private spending. At one extreme are those individuals and groups who paint a dark picture of the growing governmental bureaucracy and the perils inherent in transferring activities from the private to the public sector. At the other end are those who argue that the American economy is suffering from underspending in the sphere of social investment and public services. In the opinion of the latter, too much attention is being paid to private wants and not enough to public needs. By way of illustration they point to the individual who spends several thousand dollars for an automobile, yet resists the allocation of sufficient funds to the governmental sector for an adequate road system. Economist John Kenneth Galbraith describes this "unbalanced" emphasis in pungent terms:

> The family which takes its mauve and cerise, air-conditioned, power-steered, and power-braked automobile out for a tour passes through cities that are badly paved, made hideous by litter, blighted buildings, billboards, and posts for wires that should long since have been put underground. They pass on into a countryside that has been rendered largely invisible by commercial art. . . . They picnic on exquisitely packaged food from a portable icebox by a polluted stream and go on to spend the night at a park which is a menace to public health and morals.[1]

Increase in Public Spending

Regardless of the direction in which our own sentiments may run, we cannot disregard the hard reality of financing present-day urban needs. Reshaping the governmental pattern of the metropolis, a remedy some suggest, may provide more efficient machinery for tapping a community's resources but it will not overcome public resistance to increased spending by local units nor produce adequate revenue in poorer areas. Since World War II, the local political climate has reflected an intense preoccupation with governmental spending and a growing tax consciousness. The reason for this resistive mood is not difficult to ascertain. Governmental expenditures at all levels have increased astronomically during the last two decades. In 1942, federal, state, and local agencies spent a total of $45.5 billion. Twenty years later, the amount exceeded $165 billion or approximately $900 for every man, woman, and child in the nation. During this period, the annual outlays of local governments alone jumped from under $10 billion to well over $40 billion, an average yearly increase of 8.5 percent. In metropolitan areas, the rate of increase of local expenditures has been over one-third more than that for federal domestic expenditures.[2]

[1] *The Affluent Society* (Boston: Houghton Mifflin, 1958), p. 253.
[2] See Alan K. Campbell, "Most Dynamic Sector," *National Civic Review*, LIII (February, 1964), 74–82.

No one, of course, likes to pay taxes, Justice Oliver Wendell Holmes' dictum that "with taxes we buy civilization" to the contrary. Faced with ever mounting levies, many a citizen has come to regard his tax load as oppressive and unreasonable. This reaction may seem logical but it ignores the fact that increasing governmental expenditures have also been accompanied by rising standards of living, higher productivity, and greater capacity to foot the bill. When local spending is considered in relation to these other changes in the economy, the picture takes on a different hue. For one thing, it costs more dollars today than it did in 1930 to obtain the same service. Even if the amount or level of public activity had been held constant during the last three decades, costs of local government in dollar terms would have increased appreciably. As in every sector of the economy, wages of governmental employees have risen and the prices of materials consumed by public agencies have gone up. When adjustments are made for these inflationary factors, we find that the real cost of local government on a per capita basis has not increased greatly despite expansion of services, and in some cases has actually declined. For example, Los Angeles City tax revenues, measured in constant dollars (dollars of the same purchasing power) were $54.41 per capita in 1928 and $51.90 in 1958.[3] Similarly, in the Cleveland metropolitan area, when price increases were taken into account little change was found in per capita spending by local governments from 1940 to 1956.[4]

The rising economic status of the citizen consumer must also be kept in mind when discussing the subject of increased governmental expenditures. As the Committee for Economic Development reported some years ago, disposable income per person—income left for the individual to spend or save after payment of taxes—has tripled since 1880.[5] Thus as governmental costs have increased, personal income has soared to new heights. In similar vein, a recent analysis disclosed that the total national tax burden—federal, state, and local—expressed as a percentage of total income did not increase during the period from 1952 to 1962. The increase

[3] John A. Vieg and others, *California Local Finance* (Stanford: Stanford University Press, 1960), p. 90.

[4] Seymour Sacks and William F. Hellmuth, *Financing Government in a Metropolitan Area* (New York: Free Press, 1961), pp. 45–65.

[5] *Economic Growth in the United States* (New York: Committee for Economic Development, 1958), p. 28.

in taxes, in other words, corresponded almost exactly with the rise in the nation's income. Total taxes per $100 of income in 1952 were $24.48 and in 1962, $24.42. Computed on this basis, federal taxes declined by $2.23, while the state burden increased by $1.02, non-municipal 93 cents, and municipal by only 22 cents.[6]

As a percentage of national income, local government outlays have gone up slightly in recent years, a not unexpected consequence in view of the tremendous expansion of population and the resulting demands on local public facilities. In 1929, local expenditures for all purposes claimed slightly over 7 percent of the national income, a figure that increased to 15 percent at the height of the depression. By 1946, it had dropped to 5 percent, and since that time has risen to approximately 9 percent.[7] These figures, although they show some increase, demonstrate that no massive diversion of income or capital to local public purposes has taken place.[8]

Although these facts run counter to the folklore of urban fiscal plight, they do not eliminate the financial headaches of local governments or ease their hard-pressed budgets. The ability to pay for needed services may exist but the task of finding equitable and persuasive ways of drawing upon this capability still remains. Moreover, what is true of the whole is not necessarily true of each of the parts, as wide differences in fiscal ability and need exist among the various public jurisdictions within the governmentally divided metropolis. To some of the poorer units, the old adage that you cannot get blood out of a turnip is peculiarly applicable; to the wealthier enclaves, the demand that their tax resources be shared with their less affluent neighbors has little appeal.[9] Additional factors also

---

[6] Reuben A. Zubrow, "Recent Trends and Developments in Municipal Finance," *Public Management*, XLV (November, 1963), 247–254.

[7] *Guiding Metropolitan Growth* (New York: Committee for Economic Development, 1960), p. 25.

[8] Robert Wood made a similar observation in his study of the New York region. See his *1400 Governments* (Cambridge: Harvard University Press, 1961), p. 184.

[9] As several writers have pointed out, lack of uniformity in resources among local units has important implications for metropolitan governmental reform. When there are notable differences in local revenue sources, strong motivation exists for the wealthier communities to resist political or functional unification. See Donald J. Curran, "The Metropolitan Problem: Solution from Within," *National Tax Journal*, XVI (September, 1963), 213–233; and Jesse Burkhead, "Uniformity in Governmental Expenditures and Resources in a Metropolitan Area: Cuyahoga County," *National Tax Journal*, XIV (December, 1961), 337–348.

enter the picture: the allocation of tax resources among the different levels of government, the economically competitive position of one metropolitan community vis-a-vis others, popular attitudes and myths, and the patchwork nature of the whole fiscal structure of government. When all these are taken into consideration, an already intricate problem assumes even greater complexity.

REVENUE PATTERNS

According to the 1962 *Census of Governments*, there are 91,236 units of local government—municipalities, counties, towns and townships, school districts, and special districts—in the United States. Of this total, 18,442 are located within standard metropolitan statistical areas. The fiscal importance of these latter units far outranks their numbers. Even though they represent only about one-fifth of the total, they have approximately twice as much revenue and expenditures and three times as much indebtedness as all the other local governments in the nation. Vast differences exist in their size and affluence, but all of them are participants in the vital task of providing for the day-to-day public needs of their urban dwellers. How they raise their money is our next topic of discussion.

General Property Tax

National, state, and local governments are in a very real sense competitors for the tax dollar. Each level has found it necessary to draw more heavily on existing revenue sources and to seek out new sources to meet enlarged responsibilities. In this competitive system, a rough division of revenue sources has developed between the three jurisdictional levels. The bulk of federal funds is derived from income taxes on individuals and corporations; states rely heavily on sales and gross receipt taxes; and, since the turn of the present century, the general property tax has been acknowledged as the almost exclusive domain of local government. Competition for tax resources, moreover, is not confined to the interplay between the three levels of government; it occurs with even greater intensity among overlapping local units within urban areas. The county government, municipality, school district, and other autonomous special districts draw on the same taxpayer, and all rely on the property levy in varying degrees for a portion of their revenue. This competition is not conducive to a rational tax system, but it is a fact of life that cannot be ignored.

The general property levy has provided the historical base of support for local governments since colonial times. Next to federal income and excise taxes it has been the most productive source of public revenue in the American system. In fact, as late as 1932 it was contributing more than all other federal, state, and local taxes combined. Today it yields well over $18 billion, or almost $100 per capita, for local government use.

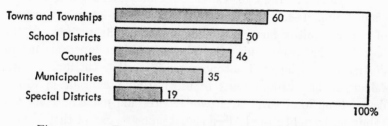

Figure 12.1   Property Tax as Percent of Total General Revenue, by Type of Local Unit, 1962. Source: U.S. Bureau of the Census, *Census of Governments: 1962*, Vol. IV, Nos. 1, 2, 3.

Not all types of local units, as Figure 12.1 shows, rely equally on the property tax. Towns and townships are the most dependent, and special districts the least; the latter obtain the bulk of their income from utility and service charges. School districts receive virtually all their locally-derived funds from the property tax and practically all of the remainder from state aid. Municipalities, as a result of their success in tapping other sources, now draw only about 35 percent of their operating revenue from property taxation. County governments, like school districts, depend on the property levy for almost one-half their total funds and on state aid for a substantial portion of the remainder. Since the property tax is commonly utilized by all types of local units, those which overlap each other in territorial jurisdiction must look to the same property owner for much of their support. The urban dweller therefore must customarily pay the traditional municipal, county, and school district levies and, in addition, property taxes assessed by such other local agencies as fire protection and sewer districts. The unexpected elasticity of the tax has permitted this extended use.

The general property tax is primarily a levy on real estate (land, buildings, and other permanent improvements) and on tangible personal property such as household goods and business inventories.[10] In 1961, property values that were officially set or assessed for local general property taxation in the United States totalled $355.7 billion, more than 70 percent of which was located in metropolitan areas.[11] Approximately four-fifths of this amount consisted of assessments on real estate and the remainder on personalty. These values represent the base for local property tax collections.

Property Tax Base. Because of the heavy local reliance on the general property levy, the property tax base is an important measure of a community's financial ability to support its services. In this regard the balance or mix between residential, commercial, and industrial uses is equally if not more significant than the total assessed valuation. The various types of urban land use result in diverse demands on local governments for services and make differing contributions to public funds. Residential property, except that of more than average value, pays only a portion of the costs of local public services it generates while commercial and industrial uses contribute as much as two to three times the cost of services rendered them.[12]

From the standpoint of tax base, the well-balanced municipality is one which has a mix of residential and nonresidential properties. So also the well-balanced metropolis is one which contains a similar blend of land uses. In the latter case, however, it would be no more possible or even desirable for each autonomous unit in the area to embody this mix than it would be for each neighborhood of the central city to do so. Yet an effort to achieve this very end takes place within the metropolitan community as each local government

[10] Intangible personal property—stocks, bonds, bank shares, and the like—was also assessed under the general property tax at one time, but this practice has now been terminated in all but a small number of the states.

[11] The relationship between assessed value and market or sales price varies considerably among governments. For the nation as a whole the level of assessments stands at about 30 percent of market value.

[12] See in this connection W. N. Leonard and W. F. Clarke, *Does Industry Pay its Way?* (Hempstead, New York: Hofstra College Bureau of Business and Community Research, 1956). For an analysis of the net fiscal effect of an industry on school districts when indirect costs such as those related to the education of the workers' children are taken into account, see Werner Z. Hirsch, "Fiscal Impact of Industrialization on Local Schools," *The Review of Economics and Statistics*, XLVI (May, 1964), 191–199.

seeks to attract the kind of development that will produce more in tax revenues than it costs in public services. The economics of the market place frustrates these efforts to some extent but the results are still deleterious in terms of rational physical development, fiscal capabilities, and fairness to taxpayers. Some industry does get located where it should not be; some local governments do enjoy overly lucrative tax bases while their neighbors are revenue-starved; and residents of some localities do receive a low level of services despite a proportionately high tax effort on their part.

Land Use Patterns. Because of the different cost-benefit ratios associated with servicing the various land uses, the spatial distribution of property types in the metropolis is a matter of considerable importance to the taxpayer. It is not uncommon to find large industrial concentrations in one local unit, low or medium priced homes in another, and luxury housing in a third. When this pattern prevails, as it does in most metropolitan areas, fiscal resources and public needs are poorly correlated. The lower income unit with little or no industrial property finds itself hard pressed to pay for its municipal services and educate its children. Its two neighboring communities, on the other hand, are able to enjoy higher levels of service with less tax effort. Robert Wood cites the case of a Bergen County municipality with an assessed valuation of $5.5 million per student.[13] This well-heeled industrial enclave draws its manpower from the surrounding municipalities which house the workers and educate their children but which derive no direct tax benefits from the concentration of the high yield property. The Bergen County case is an extreme example but the story, although less dramatic, is the same elsewhere.

Wide variances in the property tax base lead not only to inequities among taxpayers but also to broad diversity among local units in the quantity and quality of governmental services. The differences are particularly significant to the financing of public education, a service which relies heavily on the property levy. An industrial area with great financial resources and few school-age children may be situated next to a district with modestly-priced suburban homes and hordes of children. The result is unevenness in the quality of the area's school system and in educational oppor-

[13] Wood, *1400 Governments*, p. 55.

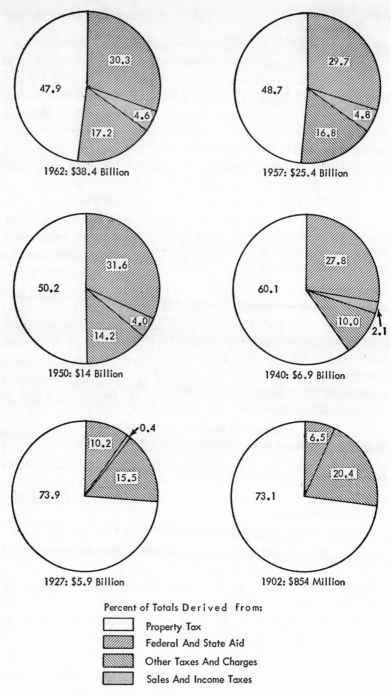

Figure 12.2 General Revenue Sources of Local Government, 1902–1962. From *Guiding Metropolitan Growth*, Committee for Economic Development, 1960; U.S. Bureau of the Census, 1957 *Census of Governments*, Vol. III, No. 5, and 1962 *Census of Governments*, Vol. IV, No. 4.

tunities for its children. In suburban St. Louis, for example, the school district with the highest assessed valuation per capita was found to spend five times more per pupil than the district with the least fiscal capacity. Yet residents of the latter were paying a substantially higher tax rate for school purposes than those of the former.[14] This situation makes little sense in a metropolitan community that is dependent on the same economy and the same labor pool for its material well-being.

The general property tax has long been the subject of criticism by experts on public finance. It has been condemned as regressive (not based on ability to pay), inflexible, and difficult to administer fairly. These are well-known frailties which we will not discuss here. Valid as they may be, it is unlikely that we will see the property levy disappear or be severely reduced in the foreseeable future. The mere lack of satisfactory and politically acceptable alternatives will undoubtedly be sufficient to assure the maintenance of this tax as a prime source of local government revenue for some time to come. The problem is to find better ways of administering the tax and distributing its benefits more equitably.

Non-Property Taxes

The relative importance of the property tax to local public financing has declined in recent decades although its dollar yield has continued to increase. Rising costs and mounting needs have made total reliance on this source unfeasible and politically unacceptable. Fear of repercussions on the local economy together with the anguished cries of property owners has set public officials scurrying about for new revenue lodes. Part of the answer has been found in a broad array of non-property levies such as those on municipal income, utility and business gross receipts, retail sales, gasoline and motor fuel, motor vehicles, cigarettes, and alcoholic beverages.[15] The assortment of these taxes differs widely from community to community. In each instance it generally represents the results of *ad hoc* and unrelated responses to local revenue needs as they arise.

[14] *Background for Action* (University City: Metropolitan St. Louis Survey, 1957), pp. 61–63.

[15] For a discussion of these various types, see Robert L. Funk, "Trends in Municipal Nonproperty Taxes," *Public Management*, XXXVII (June, 1955), 126–128.

Municipal Income Tax. One of the more lucrative of the non-property levies is the municipal income tax, sometimes referred to as an earnings or payroll tax. It is used most extensively in Pennsylvania and Ohio and to a lesser extent in several other states. As of 1962, nine of the fifty largest cities in the country had turned to this revenue source.[16] The levy is relatively low, in no case more than 2 percent on the gross earnings of individuals and on net profits of businesses and professions. As commonly employed, it taxes residents for all income earned regardless of source and non-residents for that portion of their income earned within the municipality. Central cities are attracted to this device because it provides them with a means of reaching suburbanites or urban fringe dwellers who derive their income within the core boundaries. They defend this "extra-territorial" aspect of the tax on the grounds of equity, contending that it enables them to recoup some of the added costs of the services and facilities which they must provide to the nonresident working population.

On the surface, this position seems reasonable enough. The suburban commuter clearly adds to the operational and capital costs of the central city. His presence during the workday requires the city to provide more road and parking space, public utilities, police protection, and similar services than would otherwise be necessary to accommodate its resident population. But the costs and benefits are not one-way streets. The commuter-worker spends money in the shops, restaurants, and entertainment spots of the central city, and these expenditures are reflected in increased tax returns for the municipality. More importantly, he helps man the business and industrial enterprises that enrich the core municipality's tax base while at the same time relieving the city of the costly burden of educating his children.

To what extent these costs and benefits balance out has not been conclusively demonstrated.[17] There are studies which indicate that the per capita expenditures of the central city are associated with the population size of the satellite area. Expressed in another

[16] For a résumé of local income taxes, see Milton C. Taylor, "Local Income Taxes after Twenty-One Years," *National Tax Journal*, XV (June, 1962), 113–124.

[17] Julius Margolis, "Municipal Fiscal Structure in a Metropolitan Region," *Journal of Political Economy*, 65 (June, 1957), 225–236.

way, the expenditures of the core municipality tend to rise as the proportion of people living outside its boundaries increases.[18] However, this finding in itself does not establish the case that residents of suburban areas impose a net burden on the central city since it tells us nothing about the reciprocal benefits which such increase may bring to the city.

A municipal earnings tax, moreover, may work an undue hardship on lower income commuter-workers by increasing the proportion of their income that is taken for local taxes. They are obliged not only to support the full panoply of services at their place of residence but also to contribute tax payments to the community in which they work. To the affluent commuter, the American stereotype of the suburbanite, the earnings levy presents no problem; to the lower-income worker living outside the central city, it may be a real burden.

Local Sales Tax. Another innovation of the post-World War II years, the local sales tax, has received a somewhat wider acceptance than the municipal income tax. In fact, total nationwide receipts from this source are greater than those for any of the other non-property levies. The tax is frequently collected by the state as additions to the state sales tax and returned to the local governments. Over 300 local units in California and 1300 in Illinois are among those tapping this revenue source. However, like most non-property levies, the local sales tax is not without its drawbacks when employed in metropolitan areas. The most obvious is that merchants in a municipality having a sales tax may be penalized if residents can avoid the levy by shopping in an adjacent city or town where no such tax is imposed.

Some of the deficiencies of a local sales tax and other non-property levies would be eliminated if they were imposed by a metropolitan-wide unit, since in this way all individuals and businesses in the area would be uniformly reached. Other defects, however, would remain, such as the general regressiveness of these taxes, the difficulties of administering them, their general nuisance, and the increase of compliance costs on the part of taxpayers. Un-

---

[18] See, for example, Amos H. Hawley, "Metropolitan Population and Municipal Governmental Expenditures in Central Cities," *Journal of Social Issues,* VII (Nos. 1 & 2, 1951); and Harvey E. Brazer, *City Expenditures in the United States* (New York: National Bureau of Economic Research, 1959).

restrained emphasis on their use is creating an entrenched crazy-quilt pattern of local taxation that is raising more problems than it solves. The "hand-to-mouth" operations characterizing metropolitan area financing in recent years give little consideration to long-range effects and objectives, or even to the relations among the various types of levies and their impact on different segments of the population. In this setting, the rush to non-property taxes has proved more of an uncertain palliative than a constructive approach to a sound fiscal system.

Service Charges

In addition to taxes, local governments derive a portion of their income from fees, permits, and user charges of various kinds. The most important of these non-tax revenues in terms of total dollars are utility or service charges which are collected in return for specified services supplied to the consumers. These charges are based on the measurable benefits received. The citizen consumer who is furnished with a specific service by his local government pays for it just as he would if the supplier were a private agency. The provision of water by a municipality or special district is a case in point. The consumer is billed for the amount of water he uses, that is, for the benefit he receives. In this way, a householder will pay less than the florist or the factory owner whose water needs are greater. The same principle has been applied in many jurisdictions to sewage disposal, garbage collection, and other services.

If viewed as taxes, such charges would be classified as regressive, but so also would electricity, telephone service, and other commodities purchased in the private market place. As economists point out, each local government competes for available resources with every other public activity as well as with the private sector of the economy. Where services and goods are bought by individuals, each consumer takes part in the decision-making process of allocating his resources by determining what service or product and how much of it he will buy. In brief, he is able to choose that combination of goods and services which, within the constraints of his income, will give him maximum satisfaction. On the other hand, where purchases are made by groups—as in the case of most local public services—decisions as to how much to spend and for what purposes are political judgments that are reflected in the budgets of the various governmental units.

The market mechanism obviously cannot be applied to all local public services since some of them, such as education and welfare, are designed to meet social rather than private needs; and for others, such as water pollution control and police protection, the connection between individual benefits and costs is less evident. The resort to user charges instead of general taxation is therefore limited. Such charges provide a means of helping to distribute the burden of local expenditures only when the benefits to the individual citizen or business are direct and measurable. Yet even though this device offers no complete solution to the fiscal difficulties of the metropolis, attention might profitably be paid to extending its use both as a means of enlarging local governmental revenues and as a mechanism for reaching those in one jurisdiction who benefit from but escape payment for services furnished by another.[19]

State Aid

Since World War II, local governments have come to rely increasingly on state assistance to meet their budgetary requirements. In 1942, they received a total of $1.8 billion from their parental benefactors; by 1962 this figure had risen to $10.9 billion.[20] This latter amount in per capita terms was over four times as big as the payments in 1942 and 40 percent more than in 1952. Currently, state aid provides more than one-fourth of the total general revenue of local governments.[21] For school districts and counties the proportion is substantially higher (approximately 37 and 36 percent, respectively) while for special districts the amount is negligible

[19] The case for greater use of service charges is competently made in Garth L. Mangum, "The Benefit Principle," *Municipal Finance*, XXIV (February, 1962), 125–136.

[20] Federal grants-in-aid also play a role in the financing of local units but most of these are channeled through state governments and hence are included in the state aid figures. Grants by the national government directly to local units constitute only a slight proportion of local revenue. In 1962, they totalled $749 million or about 2 percent of local governmental income.

[21] The term "general revenue" as used here and in reports of the U.S. Bureau of the Census includes revenue from all sources except from the operation of publicly-owned utilities, such as water supply and mass transit systems, and from employee–retirement deposits.

(see Figure 12.3). The pattern differs considerably from state to state with the heaviest reliance on this source in the South and the least in New England. Interstate comparisons must of course be used with caution because of the great variations which exist throughout the country in the allocation of state-local responsibilities for particular functions. One state government may directly provide public assistance and maintain the county highway system while another will make grants to the local units for the performance of these functions. The amount of state aid in each instance may be similar but it will not appear in the fiscal records as such.

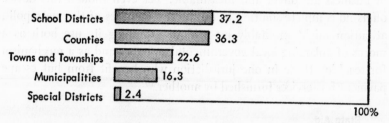

School Districts	37.2
Counties	36.3
Towns and Townships	22.6
Municipalities	16.3
Special Districts	2.4

100%

Figure 12.3 State Aid as Percent of Total General Revenue of Local Governments, by Type of Unit, 1962. Source: U.S. Bureau of the Census, *Census of Governments: 1962*, Vol. IV, Nos. 1, 2, 3, and Vol. VI, No. 2.

State aid takes the form of either grants for the support of particular services such as education and welfare, or of specified shares of state-collected taxes on such items as motor fuel, liquor, cigarettes, and income. The first, which provides by far the larger portion of state financial assistance, is usually distributed with reference to some measure of local need: for education, school age population or enrollment; for welfare, number of cases or estimated expenditures; for highways, miles of road or number of vehicles. In education particularly, the grant formulas commonly aim at some degree of equalization between the relatively poor and more prosperous local districts or units.

Under the second type of monetary aid, the state imposes and collects the tax and then returns a portion of it to the local unit. Since these levies are actually local taxes with the state acting as collecting agency, the recipients are generally allowed to use the revenues for whatever legal purposes they see fit. This shared tax device has the effect of substituting the greater taxing capacity of the state for the inferior capacity of the smaller units. It also helps local officials meet their growing revenue needs without incurring the political risks involved in raising or levying additional local taxes.

Both grants-in-aid and shared taxes have been the subject of criticism, some of it merited but much without foundation. One of the most frequently heard objections is that such devices constitute a threat to local self-government and responsibility. This danger, however, is more mythical than real. As one student of public finance has remarked, "There seems to exist, all too commonly, a kind of implicit assumption among those who talk about inter-governmental relations, that the purposes of policy-makers at different levels of government are diametrically opposed to each other, that they have goals which are incompatible, that the larger unit invariably plots the destruction of the smaller. It seems that, on the other hand, a decent respect for the dangers of centralization might well exist along with a willingness to use central authority where the nature of the problem to be solved is moving beyond the unaided capacity of the smaller units."[22] Critics also say that state aid stimulates extravagant expenditures by local officials and leads to disproportionate emphasis on those functions receiving grants. Again, these charges are based more on impression than empirical study.

There are two other criticisms of state aid which have more basis in fact. The first is the patchwork system of grants-in-aid. Developed through the years as the result of many *ad hoc* political decisions and governed by no coherent or consistent philosophy, the pattern of state fiscal assistance to local subdivisions is unduly complicated and in many cases inequitable. The second criticism, applicable mainly to shared taxes, is that such assistance often bears little relation to need. Since shared taxes are generally returned to the local jurisdiction where they originate, wealthy communities receive an added boost to their already sufficient resources while the poorer units derive proportionately less than their greater needs call for. Neither of these objections indicates defects that are irremediable, although their correction may be politically difficult. The patchwork nature of state grants could be cured by overhauling the

[22] Carey C. Thompson, "Financing Government in Metropolitan Areas," *Proceedings of the Texas Conference on Metropolitan Problems* (Austin: University of Texas Institute of Public Affairs, 1958), pp. 33–34.

system and setting it up on a more rational basis. Similarly, the imbalance occasioned by shared taxes could be overcome by returning the local portion to an area-wide government, such as the county, rather than to the individual units. In this way the money would be pooled for use throughout the metropolis on the basis of need.

EXPENDITURE PATTERNS

Local units within a metropolis serve up different packages of public programs. At one extreme is the government of the small dormitory suburb which operates with part-time personnel, relies on volunteers instead of professional firefighters, avoids installing curbs and sidewalks, and provides no parks or recreation facilities. At the other end of the spectrum is the central city government with its broad range of services encompassing everything from tiny-tot play areas to hospitals and museums. The same differences, perhaps not as extreme, prevail among school districts. Beyond meeting the minimum requirements of the state department of education, local districts vary widely in their educational offerings and facilities. One may provide courses in music, art, and specialized types of vocational training, employ school psychologists and nurses, conduct extensive recreational programs, and furnish bus transportation to the pupils. Another may offer none of these services but limit itself to a "skin and bones" or 3 R's educational program.

Current Expenditures

In examining the output side of the local public budget, it is helpful to distinguish between two broad categories of expenditures: current operations and capital outlays. The first refers to the cost of running the various departments and agencies and providing services to the citizen consumers; the second includes appropriations for the acquisition or construction of public buildings, roads, parks, sewers, and other facilities and for the purchase of major items of equipment. Of the $39 billion spent by local units for general governmental purposes in 1962, approximately $31 billion was for current operations and the remainder for capital improvements. In addition to these totals, local units also expended some $5 billion for the operation and development of publicly-owned utilities, such

as water, electric, and transit systems. These latter items cover revenue-producing facilities that are generally self-sustaining.

In no two metropolitan areas is the expenditure pattern identical. Available resources as well as public demands and expectations
differ from community to community. Good roads, an attractive
park system, and well-groomed public buildings greet our eyes in
one governmental unit while potholed streets, lack of open space,
and a poorly maintained city hall or court house appear in another.
The pattern among local units is further distinguished by the total
amount expended per resident for public purposes and by the way
in which this total is distributed among the various functions. One
community may allocate a higher proportion of its revenue to
education than its neighbor. Or one may spend substantial funds
on the development and maintenance of park and recreational facilities while another allots little or nothing for this purpose. Close
examination of a community's public spending pattern can tell us
a great deal about the characteristics and aspirations of the people
who reside there.

The percentages in Figure 12.4 show the average distribution
of current expenditures by all local units in the United States. Education, as we might anticipate, dominates the fiscal picture. Almost
one-half the total operational outlay (exclusive of utility costs) of
all local governments combined is devoted to this function. Health
and welfare is a poor second with 14.5 percent and police and fire
protection third with 9.4 percent. When these proportions are
broken down on the basis of population, as in Table 27, we see
how the size of an area affects its spending pattern. Local governments in the smaller counties tend to allocate most of their resources
to a limited number of services while the budgets of the larger
areas are spread over a broader range of items. For example, approximately 67 percent of total current outlays in counties under
25,000 population is preempted by two items: education and roads.
The corresponding figures for areas of 1 million and over is less
than 43 percent. Although expenditures for these two items are
inversely related to size, those for other services show a positive association. Thus the larger the area, the greater is the proportion
of the budget spent on such functions as health and welfare, police
and fire protection, waste disposal, and parks. Similar results are

obtained when the areas are ranked by density instead of population size.[23]

The main reason for these differences can easily be determined. Local governments in rural counties and small urban areas may discharge their principal responsibilities and meet the demands of

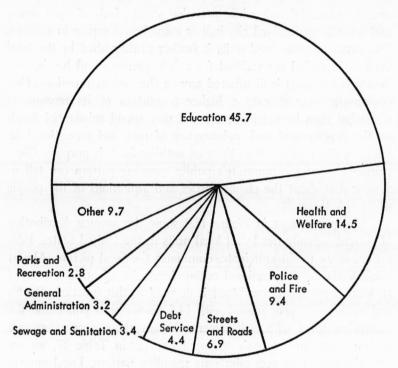

Education 45.7

Other 9.7

Parks and Recreation 2.8

General Administration 3.2

Sewage and Sanitation 3.4

Debt Service 4.4

Streets and Roads 6.9

Health and Welfare 14.5

Police and Fire 9.4

Figure 12.4   Percentage Distribution, by Function, of Current Expenditures of Local Governments, 1962. Utility Expenditures have been excluded. Source: U.S. Bureau of the Census, *Governmental Finances in 1962*.

their clientele when they provide educational facilities for the children and maintain adequate roads. The householder or industrialist in this rural or semirustic setting takes care of his other service needs with a modicum of governmental participation. Increasing urbanization interrupts this practice of self-help by generating a

[23] See Henry J. Schmandt and G. Ross Stephens, "Local Government Expenditure Patterns in the United States," *Land Economics*, XXXIX (November, 1963), 397–406.

need for common sewage and waste disposal systems, public health and sanitation measures, professional police and fire protection, and similar services, all of which compete with educational and road requirements for the budget dollar. Narrow public service ranges are not, of course, confined to rural areas; witness some of the

TABLE 27

*Percent of Mean Per Capita Operating Expenditures
of 3096 County Area Aggregates for Selected
Functions, by Population Size, 1957ᵃ*

POPULATION SIZE CLASS	EDUCA-TION	ROADS	HEALTH AND WEL-FARE	POLICE	FIRE	SEWAGE AND SANITA-TION	PARKS
Under 5000	47.1	19.7	10.9	2.4	0.4	0.4	0.4
5000–15,000	52.9	15.3	10.6	2.6	0.5	0.6	0.5
15,000–25,000	52.7	14.6	11.9	2.4	0.8	0.9	0.5
25,000–50,000	51.5	14.0	11.3	3.2	3.1	1.3	0.8
50,000–100,000	48.0	10.5	12.1	3.9	2.5	1.9	1.2
100,000–250,000	47.5	8.3	11.7	4.8	3.6	2.4	2.0
250,000–500,000	45.1	6.4	13.5	5.7	4.8	3.4	2.7
500,000–1,000,000	39.1	5.3	15.2	7.2	5.3	3.7	3.6
1,000,000 and over	37.2	5.5	14.8	8.1	4.3	5.0	4.0

ᵃ Figures are for all local units within the county.
SOURCE: Henry J. Schmandt and G. Ross Stephens, "Local Government Expenditure Patterns in the United States," *Land Economics*, XXXIX (November, 1963), 401.

smaller suburban villages in the metropolitan maze. These latter units, however, are able to operate at a minimum level only because of the spillover benefit which they receive from the services and facilities of their larger neighbors.

Capital Outlays

Urban growth affects not only operating expenditures but it also compels local governments to invest heavily in the enlargement of their physical plants. Along with the demand for more teachers, policemen, firemen, sanitarians, engineers, and other workers, expansion is accompanied by the need for additional classrooms, police and fire stations, hospitals, roads, sewers, and parks. In 1962 local expenditures for these latter (capital) items, including publicly-owned utilities, totaled over $9.5 billion. The largest share, almost one-third, went into educational facilities, with streets and roads next and locally operated utilities third (see Table 28).

Both central city and suburban units in the metropolis have large-scale capital requirements, but they have different emphases. For the former, the major physical needs are those of renewal: redevelopment of blighted and deteriorating neighborhoods, replacement of obsolescent and worn-out public structures and utilities, and modernization of road and transportation systems to facilitate

TABLE 28

Local Governmental Expenditures for Capital Outlay, 1962
(in millions of dollars)

FUNCTION	AMOUNT	PERCENT OF TOTAL
Education	$3,021	31.5
Streets and roads	1,575	16.4
Local utilities	1,481	15.5
Health and hospitals	207	2.2
Sewerage	886	9.2
Housing and urban renewal	779	8.1
Parks and recreation	269	2.9
Airports	227	2.4
All other	1,132	11.8
Total	$9,577	100.0

SOURCE: U.S. Bureau of Census, *1962 Census of Governments*, Vol. IV, No. 4 (Washington: 1964).

the movement of people and goods. For the latter, the basic needs center around the building of schools and libraries where none existed before, construction of new streets and roads, installation of water and sewer mains, and the acquisition and development of park lands. In short, the suburban problem, as contrasted to that of the central city, is the rapid expansion of new public facilities, not the renovation or enlargement of an already existing physical plant.

Both expansion and renewal are costly processes, but the burden of capital investment in the suburbs has exceeded that of the central city since World War II. In the St. Louis metropolitan area, for example, almost two-thirds of the total capital outlay in 1962 was made by local units outside the central city. The proportion was even greater in Boston (83 percent) and San Francisco (76 percent).

The item principally responsible for the variance between city and suburban capital expenditures is education. Of the total outlay for public school expansion in Metropolitan St. Louis in 1962, only 9 percent was spent by the central school district. The comparable figure in both Boston and San Francisco was 10 percent. The experience of Metropolitan Cleveland typifies this reversal of city-suburban positions in the capital expenditure pattern. In 1940, 70 percent of the area's capital outlays for schools was made by the city of Cleveland. By 1962, the reverse was true, with school districts outside the city accounting for almost three-fourths of total capital expenditures for educational facilities.[24]

Capital outlays may be financed in one of two ways: on a pay-as-you-go basis or by borrowing. Most Americans in their capacity as individual consumers are well acquainted with the distinction. Relatively few could buy a new home or automobile if compelled to pay the full purchase price in cash. Public agencies are in a similar position. If they were required to finance new expressways, school buildings, and sewage treatment plants from current revenues, construction of many badly needed facilities would be deferred simply because taxpayers could not or would not bear the load. Through borrowing, governments, like householders, are able to buy items of a durable nature and spread the cost over a period of years. For public agencies, the acquisition of capital funds is normally accomplished by issuing bonds of two types: general obligation, which are backed by the full credit and tax resources of the local unit; or revenue, which are paid out of the proceeds of some self-liquidating project. Publicly-owned water supply systems, toll bridges, and parking garages

[24] There are indications that the growth in educational expenditures is slowing up slightly in the older suburban areas—those which experienced their population boom in the late 1940s and early 1950s—but rising in the central city because of the special educational problems associated with the increasing number of culturally disadvantaged pupils. At the same time, the newer communities on the fringes of the built-up areas are currently faced with the rapidly rising educational costs experienced earlier by the now well-established suburban units. See Campbell, "Most Dynamic Sector," pp. 74–82.

are commonly financed in the latter way; school construction, park acquisition, and urban redevelopment by the former.

The capital indebtedness of local governments has been growing at a rapid pace. During the five-year period from 1957 to 1962, the total outstanding debt of the nation's local units rose from $37.3 billion to $55.9 billion, an increase of 50 percent (see Table 29). The sharpest gain in dollar amounts occurred in outlays for public education (almost $7 billion) while hospital facilities recorded the largest

TABLE 29

Total Long-Term Indebtedness of Local Governments, 1957 and 1962
(in millions of dollars)

PURPOSE	1957	1962	PERCENT INCREASE
Education	$11,461	$18,119	58.1
Streets and roads	3,459	4,366	26.2
Local utilities	9,231	12,280	33.0
Sewerage	3,459	5,592	61.6
Housing and urban renewal	2,977	4,801	61.3
Hospitals	615	996	61.9
Airports, ports, and terminal facilities	1,464	2,042	39.5
Other	4,657	7,736	66.3
Total	$37,323	$55,932	49.8

SOURCE: U.S. Bureau of the Census, *1957 Census of Governments*, Vol III, No. 5 and *1962 Census of Governments*, Vol. IV, No. 4.

percentage (61.9 percent). Road and street outlays showed a gain of 26.2 percent, but this figure does not reflect the huge federal and state expenditures for highway and expressway construction within urban areas. About 70 percent of the total indebtedness is represented by general obligation issues, the remainder by revenue or non-guaranteed bonds. The relative reliance on each of these methods of financing varies by type of unit. School districts depend wholly on general obligation debentures, while special districts finance the bulk of their capital needs by means of revenue bonds. Slightly over one-third of the long-term debt of municipalities and substantially smaller proportions of county and town and township indebtedness are represented by the latter.

DETERMINANTS OF EXPENDITURE PATTERNS

Most of us, including the experts, are baffled at the complexity of the local fiscal pattern and find it difficult to generalize satisfactorily about the wide variances that exist throughout the nation. As Figure 12.5 shows, the differences in per capita expenditures among the nine regions is substantial, with local governments in the Pacific Coast

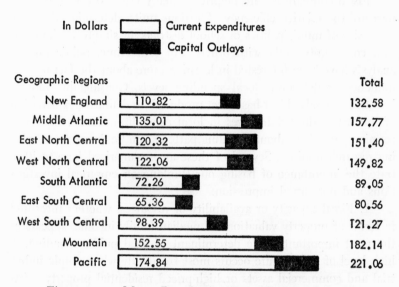

Figure 12.5   Mean Per Capita Expenditures of Local Governments by County Area Aggregates, by Geographical Regions, 1957. From Henry J. Schmandt and G. Ross Stephens, "Local Government Expenditure Patterns in the United States," *Land Economics*, 39:401, 1963.

states spending almost three times as much as those in the South. Even within the same metropolitan area, wide variances exist among local units, as current research well documents. Per capita operating expenditures among municipal governments in Metropolitan Cleveland in 1956, to cite one example, ranged from $527 in Cuyahoga Heights to less than $14 in the village of Oakwood.

The common impression is that size is the most important determinant of local public expenditures and that the larger a unit is

the more it will spend.[25] Clearly total outlays will mount as a community grows since there are more people to service. But the cake
cuts both ways. With more people, there are also more taxpayers to
share the total load. Researchers usually adjust for this fact by measuring expenditures on a per capita basis. When this is done comparisons can be made between communities of different size as well as
those with the same number of residents.

Fiscal comparisons are helpful in many ways. We may wish to
measure the relative efficiency of various units, determine the optimum size of municipalities or school districts, or simply see how our
own community ranks with others. For some time, public finance
analysts have been interested in learning more about the factors that
influence or determine local spending levels. Considerable inquiry
into this general subject has as yet produced no definitive explanation
of the tremendous differences in local expenditure levels. However,
certain conclusions about spending patterns can be drawn from existing research findings. Several of these are summarized here to illustrate the importance of basing our thinking on empirical investigations and not casual impression.

1. Fiscal capacity or availability of resources, whether measured
in terms of property valuations or median family income, appears as
the most important single determinant of local public spending. A
high level of expenditure occurs most frequently when ample industrial and commercial assets or high-priced residential property exists
within the taxing unit.

2. Per capita expenditures tend to go up in all functional categories with increase in median family income but the rise is particularly marked in respect to police and fire protection. Wealthy communities have more property per resident to guard against hazards
and hence generate more demand for police and fire services.

3. State grants-in-aid show a significant positive relationship to
local spending levels, particularly in the case of welfare, streets and
roads, and public education, the three functions that depend most
heavily on outside financing. By increasing the funds available to

[25] Central city and suburban partisans frequently engage in verbal controversy over this question. The former contend that suburban units are generally uneconomical and inefficient because of their small size while the latter
maintain that there are diseconomies of scale in the larger governments. The
argument obscures many factors of a more relevant nature but it has received
wide publicity.

local governments, these aids constitute a further measure of a community's ability to provide services.

4. Earlier studies indicated that a statistically significant and positive relationship existed between local per capita expenditures and population size.[26] *Compendium of City Government Finances,* published annually by the Bureau of the Census, furnished support for this conclusion by revealing that cities in the higher-class intervals spend on the average more per capita than those in the lower categories. More recent research, while acknowledging the generally higher spending levels of the larger governments, casts considerable doubt on the assumption that population size is the major determinant of this phenomenon. The findings of these investigations point to other factors, wealth and resources in particular, as far more important in explaining the variance.[27] As economist Harvey Brazer concluded after a systematic and statistically rigorous study of city expenditures in the United States: "There is little, if any, demonstrable positive relationship between the population size of cities and their levels of expenditure per capita when other independent variables are taken into account and the sample studied is a large one. Assertions to the contrary have typically been based upon simple correlation analysis or observations of data for broad groups of cities. Careful study of such groups discloses the fact, however, that variations in the mean level of per capita expenditures between groups is not significantly greater than that within groups."[28]

5. Density appears to be a more important factor than population size in affecting local governmental spending. Tightly packed settlements make the provision of municipal services more complicated and usually require a greater range of public activities than do communities with the same population but lesser density. The relationship is not, however, particularly significant except in the case of several individual functions. For example, as density increases, per

[26] See, for example, Mabel L. Walker, *Municipal Expenditures* (Baltimore: The Johns Hopkins University Press, 1930) where the conclusion is reached (p. 117) that "per capita costs of government increase rapidly as the population increases."

[27] Stanley Scott and Edward L. Feder, *Factors Associated with Variations in Municipal Expenditure Levels* (Berkeley: University of California Bureau of Public Administration, 1957); Harvey E. Brazer, *City Expenditures in the United States* (New York: National Bureau of Economic Research, 1959).

[28] Brazer, *City Expenditures in the United States,* p. 66.

capita costs for police and fire protection tend to go up; but conversely, those for streets and roads decline. These results are not surprising since the need for police and fire protection in the same spatial area increases with the concentration of people while the per capita street mileage to be maintained decreases.

These various findings suggest that local government expenditure levels are in large part reflections of the resources available to a community. High spending patterns are associated with superior fiscal capacity and low with correspondingly smaller assets. On this basis we would expect lower per capita spending in the southern states where industrial development has been slow and where median family income is proportionately less than it is in the remainder of the nation. Similarly, we would expect higher spending levels in the larger metropolitan areas since it is there that the greatest wealth is concentrated and personal and corporate income highest.

Granting that wealth is the most important determinant of local spending patterns, as the studies indicate, it nevertheless explains only a part of the variation among and within metropolitan areas. Many other factors contribute to the wide differences. Some are not readily identifiable and others cannot be reduced to quantitative terms. Among those which are thought to have some effect are type of community, political and ethnic backgrounds of the residents, rate of growth, quality of services, popular attitude toward government, ratio of central city to metropolitan area population, and the property mix. But as local public finance experts readily admit, there is no facile means of explaining the tremendous range of per capita expenditures.

THE QUEST FOR SOLUTIONS

To a considerable extent, as economist Lyle Fitch has observed, the American system of local finance still operates as though the various activities of the urban polity were concentrated in one governmental jurisdiction.[29] It blatantly ignores the fact that political splintering has arbitrarily divided up the tax resources of metropolitan areas and has left some units with insufficient capacity to provide needed services. Under a single government, the spatial differentiation of eco-

[29] "Metropolitan Financial Problems," *Annals of the American Academy of Political and Social Science*, 314 (November, 1957), 67.

nomic activities and wealth does not affect an area's financial structure; in a governmentally divided metropolis, this differentiation normally results in an uneven distribution of tax capabilities among the individual jurisdictions. The problem is not one, as commonly posed, of central city versus the remainder of the area. It involves all units and their fiscal position in the metropolitan matrix. Actually, greater discrepancies between financial ability and need exist more often among the suburbs than between the core city and the suburban aggregate.

The present system also disregards the spillover effects which result from the extension of activities across jurisdictional lines and which make it virtually impossible to relate benefits and taxes. A high quality of police protection in one unit will be reflected in a lower incidence of crime in an adjacent community; efficient sewage treatment by one jurisdiction will benefit its downstream neighbors; a first-rate school system in one district will enhance the economic potentialities of the total urban complex. Obviously each unit will be both the source and beneficiary (or victim) of such spillovers, but it is highly unlikely that the scales will be balanced for each.

How can the inequities and weaknesses in the metropolitan fiscal system be resolved or mitigated, given the likelihood that a fragmented governmental structure will be with us for quite some time? Three broad approaches to this problem are worthy of mention, all of them based on the principle of expanding the taxing jurisdiction: (1) superimposing new operating agencies on the existing governmental structure; (2) shifting responsibilities or functions to units of broader territorial scope; and (3) redistributing tax resources.

The first approach is represented by the familiar device of the special district, both school and non-school. We have already noted that a single government in urban areas would eliminate the inequities resulting from spillovers and uneven distribution of taxable capacity. Similar results may be achieved on a lesser scale when individual services are administered by special districts. By permitting the pooling of area resources for carrying out certain functions, these units help mitigate the effects of territorial differentiation in wealth. The special school district for handicapped children in St. Louis County illustrates this point. Invested with power to levy a countywide property tax to support its activities, the district is able to draw on the wealth of the area to serve handicapped children regardless of their place of residence in the county. In this way, those who live in the poorer districts where lack of funds would prevent such services are able to benefit from the tax resources of the larger community.

The second method, transfer of functions to a larger unit of government, has the same effect. If responsibility for such items as public health and hospitals is assumed by the county, or if welfare programs are administered directly by the state, the problem of logistics—getting the service distributed where it is most needed—is solved. In other words, there is a close positive association between the equitable fulfillment of needs and the proportion of the local service package that is handled by area-wide units. The more services of a local nature are administered by the county, special districts, or the state government, the less territorial variance will exist in the system between need and fiscal ability.

The third approach, redistribution of tax funds, offers another means of partially overcoming the uneven spatial distribution of metropolitan resources. State grants-in-aid that are based on need serve this purpose to a limited extent. A more direct method is for the county or a metropolitan taxing agency to collect and distribute funds to the local units according to some equalization formula. The Toronto area follows this practice in the case of education. The metropolitan government, through a metropolitan school board, subsidizes the local school districts of the area by direct grants designed to provide a reasonable standard of education for each child. The Toronto arrangement permits the retention of local school districts but, by tapping the resources of the total area, assures each of sufficient funds to maintain a basic level of education. Individual school districts that wish to go beyond this level are free to do so by financing the additional costs through local levies.

These various approaches are not mutually exclusive. All three may be, and occasionally are, utilized in efforts to resolve the fiscal difficulties that plague metropolitan areas. They provide no total solution but only partial remedies. Nor are they without their serious disadvantages and dangers. One might argue, for example, that the creation of special districts only compounds the difficulties of administering metropolitan public affairs, or that the redistribution of tax funds permits the continued existence of local units which should not survive as autonomous entities. Valid as these arguments may be, the governmental system of the metropolis operates in a political world where change, short of revolution, occurs by gradual accretion rather than rational design. A shrewd observer of political life, Niccolo Machiavelli, gave classical expression to this fact many years back: ". . . there is nothing more difficult to take in hand, more perilous to conduct, or more uncertain in its success, than to take the lead in the introduction of a new order of things. Because the innovator has for enemies all those who have done well under the old conditions, and lukewarm defenders in those who may do well under the new."[30]

THE CHOICE AHEAD

Financing local government is a major facet of the metropolitan problem. By means of taxes and other revenue-producing devices, local units are able to maintain an environment in which people can live and business and industry function. Insufficient funds or uneven distribution of resources may seriously impede the governmental structure in performing this task. So also may the organization of the political system and its capacity to operate effectively. To say that present arrangements are grossly defective would be inaccurate; if this were true the metropolis would have perished before now. To say that they are adequate or satisfactory would be equally misleading; if this were true the fiscal problem of the urban community would be less pressing and of small magnitude.

The question of whether present mechanisms for allocating resources pay too much attention to private wants and not enough to public needs cannot in the end be resolved wholly by recourse to fact or logic. One's conception of the good community is, after all, subjective and a matter of values. Residents of a community have considerable freedom to select the kind of environment they want. But specification of the choices is a responsibility of political and civic leadership. We do not have to be practicing psychologists to know that people's preferences are based on their perception of alternatives. Therefore, unless a community's leaders articulate the communal stake in such public goods as education, urban renewal, and cultural development, the taste for private goods—which are not lacking in such articulation—is likely to dominate. Thus far such leadership in metropolitan affairs has been a scarce commodity.

[30] *The Prince*, Everyman's Edition (London: J. M. Dent and Sons, 1958), p. 29.

Aside from the question of public versus private allocation of resources, metropolitan areas are faced with the problem of moderating the gross inequalities that arise from the widely different fiscal abilities of their local units. Given the governmentally divided nature of the metropolis, it is extremely doubtful that this problem can be handled locally. For to attempt to resolve it at this level, as a report of the Advisory Commission on Intergovernmental Relations points out, merely adds to its ramifications, since local governments resort to protective devices that tend to generate more, rather than less, inequity. They carry on interlocal economic warfare through competitive underassessment; they help to create tax havens for concentrations of industry; and small suburban communities engage in protective planning and zoning that may be a deterrent to sound land use planning for the well-balanced economic development of the metropolitan areas in which they are located.[31] That the state governments must ultimately assume more responsibility for this problem is inevitable. The question is how long we must wait before they take action.

[31] *The Role of the States in Strengthening the Property Tax* (Washington: June, 1963), p. 12.

CHAPTER 13

The Cooperative Approach: Agreements and Metropolitan Councils

WITH THE continued growth of intercommunity needs and problems in the metropolitan age, cooperation among local governments has greatly increased in efforts to meet the challenges of adequate services and facilities. As we shall see, particularly in the two succeeding chapters, interlocal cooperation is not the only approach that has been devised in metropolitan areas to confront such difficulties. Nor is it a recent innovation or one used exclusively in the metropolis. However, the marked upsurge in interlocal cooperation since World War II has occurred mainly in the major population complexes. Indeed, the cooperative method is now primarily and most importantly a metropolitan trend.

Interlocal cooperation is a broad term and takes many implementing forms. At one extreme are informal, verbal understandings, often called "gentlemen's agreements" and involving such elementary matters as the exchange of information by administrators of two local governments operating in the same substantive field, such as public health. At the other end of the range are formal, written agreements among a sizable number of local units that decide jointly to build and operate a major facility, such as a sewage treatment plant. Without in any sense downgrading the importance of informal arrangements, which often reduce the abrasions of metropolitan living and help the system function without major disaster, we will focus our attention here on two types of formal interlocal cooperation: one relating to specific functions or services, the other to a more general mechanism for reaching consensus on area-wide issues and policies.

The first type is composed of three kinds of formal agreements, in which: (1) a single government performs a service or provides a facility for one or more other local units, (2) two or more local governments perform a function jointly or operate a facility on a joint basis, and (3) two or more local governments assist or supply mutual aid to one another in emergency situations, such as a large fire or a serious riot. The second type of cooperation consists of the formation and operation of metropolitan councils, permanent associations of governments that are convened regularly to discuss and try to agree on solutions to common difficulties and needs.

An increasing number of individuals and organizations, especially those made up of local public officials, are strong adherents of the cooperative device. Its greatest attraction to them is that it provides a process for dealing with needs and problems on a voluntary basis and a means of retaining local determination and control. Moreover, its advocates view the cooperative approach as an effective countermove to demands for the creation of powerful metropolitan governments that would substantially reduce the authority of existing local units and possibly eliminate many of them. Supporters also look upon it as contributing to increased efficiency and lower cost since this process makes it unnecessary for each local government to hire its own personnel and construct its own facilities for each service for which it has a legal responsibility. Far from everyone, however, agrees to the wisdom of the cooperative approach. Its most vigorous detractors consider it to be a weak palliative that is incapable of handling the total major area-wide difficulties of the metropolis.

THE GROWTH OF COOPERATION

Many factors have prompted the recent rapid spread of interlocal governmental cooperation to the point where many thousands of agreements on services and facilities are now in operation in

American metropolitan areas. As we stressed earlier, the number and intensity of certain functional problems have been mounting in the metropolis. The resultant effects have made it increasingly apparent that these shortcomings cannot be adequately dealt with on an individual community basis. One response for dealing with them has been the cooperative approach. In some instances, as just noted, it has been employed deliberately as an alternative to other means; thus, in a number of areas the threat of establishing a metropolitan government has served as a whiplash in speeding the growth of interlocal cooperation. In other instances, the cooperative method has been utilized as a last resort—one employed, at least extensively, only after other types of reform have been suggested and turned down by the local voters.

An important common difference between the cooperative method and alternative approaches has also facilitated the expansion of the voluntary principle. In general, cooperative agreements are negotiated by administrators of the respective local governments and go into effect after their governing bodies pass the necessary ordinances or resolutions. In contrast, alternative approaches generally become operative only after they have surmounted the often difficult hurdle of obtaining the sanction of the local voters. Unquestionably, cooperative arrangements, often accomplished without general public awareness that they exist, are subject to a much easier adoption procedure.

The Role of Counties

Changes in county governments have also been a big contributor to the increased popularity of interlocal cooperation. Many counties in metropolitan areas have widened their span of functions and have become providers of important urban services. In addition, a number of them have improved their organizational structures and their operational procedures and have thereby generated increased confidence in their ability to carry out contractual agreements efficiently and effectively. As a result of these two developments, county governments have become increasingly active participants in cooperative arrangements.

More Authorizations and Advocacy

More and more states have enacted laws making cooperation legally possible. A wide variety of such enabling legislation has been adopted since World War II—an amount far exceeding the prewar quantity. The constitutions of the two newest states, Hawaii and Alaska, illustrate this strong trend. At the time they were written, the device of interlocal cooperation had become of sufficient importance to warrant permissive provisions in these documents which are noted for their brevity and concentration on the essentials of state and local government.

A final contributor to the growth of the cooperative approach has been the support it has recently received from national, state, and local organizations composed entirely or partly of state or local officials. Both the national Advisory Commission on Intergovernmental Relations, a permanent bipartisan body created by Congress in 1959, and the Council of State Governments, the official spokesman for all fifty states, have advocated use of interlocal cooperation and have prepared draft legislation on the subject for the consideration of state legislatures. And the National League of Cities (formerly the American Municipal Association) and the National Association of Counties have been vigorous supporters of the metropolitan council idea and in 1962 established a joint program of service to these councils. Various state leagues of cities have also been active in promoting the cooperative approach.[1]

INTERLOCAL AGREEMENTS: SCOPE AND CHARACTERISTICS

In terms of its total use in metropolitan areas, the cooperative method embraces an exceedingly broad sweep of local services and facilities and involves every type of local government. Some of the important functions included are airports, building inspection, civil defense, construction and operation of public buildings (including not only the headquarters of governments but also auditoriums, hospitals, libraries, memorials, and stadiums), correctional and detention facilities, election services, fire protection, flood control, public health activities, and hospital services. Others include law enforcement (particularly communications and identification), library services, parks

[1] See, for example, *State Legislative Program of the Advisory Commission on Intergovernmental Relations* (Washington: October, 1963), pp. 145–154; Council of State Governments, *Program of Suggested State Legislation: 1957* (Chicago: 1956), pp. 95–97; and American Municipal Association and National Association of Counties, *Voluntary City-County Regional Cooperation: A Collection of Exhibits* (Washington: July, 1963).

and recreation, personnel services, planning, purchasing, refuse disposal, road construction and maintenance, sewage disposal and treatment, tax assessment and collection, public welfare activities, and water supply. Especially numerous are arrangements relating to libraries, personnel services, public health, public welfare, purchasing, and tax assessment and collection. Many of the functions furnished under cooperative agreements are direct services to the public. Others, such as personnel examinations, purchasing, and tax collection and assessment, are services provided to government to enable it to operate more efficiently or economically.

Municipalities are by far the most numerous participants in interlocal agreements. They have many such arrangements with one another as well as a substantial number with other types of local units, especially counties. The latter, in fact, are becoming increasing users of the cooperative method, largely on a county-municipal rather than an intercounty basis. School districts, too, are more frequently entering into various arrangements with one another and with municipalities. School-municipal agreements on recreational and library services, for instance, are growing markedly. In New England, many towns are active in intertown and town-city endeavors. Townships and non-school special districts are the least frequent participants in cooperative enterprises, largely because their narrow range of functions makes them less likely prospects for such activity.

One Function, Two Governments

Some common characteristics of interlocal cooperative agreements on services and facilities can be delineated despite the great diversity of such arrangements. First, most consist of agreements between two governments concerning a single activity. For instance, a city and a county may sign a contract specifying that the latter will collect the city's taxes on a fee basis. Or a number of municipalities in the metropolis may want the county government to perform this function for them; again, a separate contract for only one activity is negotiated between each interested city and the county. Thus where interlocal cooperation is used extensively there will be a plethora of contractual arrangements, encompassing in total many local governments and many services and facilities, with the vast majority of agreements, however, relating to only two governments and one specific function. The limited nature of most individual interlocal arrangements should be remembered before one is overawed by the number of cooperative efforts. The significance of the device can be properly gauged only if the quantity is related to its piecemeal or fragmented character.

Service Orientation and Time Factors

Second, most interlocal agreements pertain to services rather than facilities. Cooperative arrangements have been completed for the building of civic centers, hospitals, and other public buildings, and for the construction of water and sewage disposal plants, roads, and bridges; but they are the exception rather than the rule. Agreements concerned with services (such as public health, libraries, and protective activities) are much more numerous. Interlocal cooperation, in other words, has a predominately service orientation.

Third, these agreements are not necessarily permanent. In fact, they contain one or more time factors, thus emphasizing their possible temporary nature. For example, either party can terminate such a contract. A common provision is that an agreement may be abrogated at the beginning of a new fiscal year by a party making its intent known in writing at least two months before the proposed date of termination. (The situation is similar in those fewer cases where an agreement involves a number of governments; the withdrawal of any one unit may make the contract unworkable for the remaining governments.) Also, many contracts provide that they are effective for only a specified period of years after which there must be mutual consent for their renewal. At this time the financial terms of the agreement may be renegotiated and, unless the terms are satisfactory to the participants, the contract will terminate. However, many agreements in practice have had a long life and have not been rescinded. In particular, those relating to facilities have tended to be long lasting, in part because a withdrawing government would immediately have to invest in the construction of a replacement facility.

Many interlocal cooperative agreements represent a type of functional consolidation characterized by two features: their voluntary nature and their possible temporariness. This kind of functional consolidation contrasts with two other types: the first is based on state laws that require the transfer of functions from one kind of local government to another (say the transfer of public health services from all municipalities in a county to the county government);

the second involves the abdication of a function by one government to another (for example, the relinquishment of the health functions of a big city to the county government for economy or other reasons). The former kind of consolidation is mandatory and both types are permanent. Thus they differ basically from the agreements dealt with in this chapter.

Frequent Standby Arrangements

A fourth characteristic of interlocal agreements is that many of them are standby arrangements. They are operative only when certain conditions come into existence and they remain in operation only so long as these conditions are present. Known as mutual aid pacts, such commitments are activated only when fire, disturbance, or other local emergency cannot be adequately handled by the personnel and equipment of the affected contracting party. The extent of the aid furnished is determined by the supplying government, which may at any time, and solely at its own discretion, withdraw the aid.

One factor prompting the execution of many mutual aid pacts is the question of legal liability when a government participates in activities beyond its boundaries in the absence of appropriate agreements. Such contracts providing for the operation of a government outside its normal jurisdictional limits protect it while rendering emergency aid from damage suits, loss of personnel rights to its employees, and loss of workmen's compensation rights. As a report of the Cleveland Metropolitan Services Commission notes:

The principal purpose of the "mutual aid" agreement would appear to be *legal* rather than *operational* [operational in the sense of providing systematic coordination of an activity]. It is believed to reduce possible legal problems *in the event* that a department should respond to external calls. (One has reason to believe that law officers have been influential in persuading municipalities to adopt such agreements, with this end in view.)[2]

Although mutual aid pacts commonly specify that they do not relieve the parties from the obligation of providing adequate protective services within their respective boundaries, some of the participants do not comply with these requirements. The key element of

[2] Matthew Holden, Jr., *Inter-Governmental Agreements in the Cleveland Metropolitan Area* (Cleveland: Cleveland Metropolitan Services Commission, 1958), pp. 19–20.

mutual aid pacts is reciprocity, and some small cities having mutual aid agreements with an adjacent large city know the latter will immediately come to their aid if a major fire or other serious emergency occurs within their borders. As a consequence, numerous small cities that do not or cannot finance adequate protective services improperly rely on mutual aid to compensate for the deficiency. This unjustifiable use of the device contributes to the continuance of inadequate fire and police departments in various metropolitan areas.[3]

Specific and General State Laws

A fifth and final characteristic of interlocal agreements is that a majority of them are based on specific state legislative authorizations, each allowing cooperation in simply one particular field. The tendency has been for lawmaking bodies to respond in a highly restricted or unifunctional way to individual needs as they arise. The amount of enabling legislation has thus proliferated as the demands for cooperative authorizations for an increasing number of services and facilities have been heeded.

In recent years, two types of deviations from this highly restricted approach have been gaining increased acceptance, both involving the concept of a general interlocal cooperation act. In the one, the legislature lists a number of services and facilities that can be subject to cooperative arrangements. In the other, the legislature authorizes a general permission of either narrow or broad scope without making any specific enumeration. The narrow form provides that any power within the authority of each of the contracting governments can be exercised jointly by them or by one government for the other. The broad form specifies that any power possessed by one of the contracting governments can be employed jointly by them or by one of them on behalf of the other. Although in a legal sense the broad form of general legislation seemingly endows contracting governments with a wider range of action, in practice there has been no significant difference in the purposes for which the two forms have been used.

[3] For evidence of this effect on fire service in Metropolitan Los Angeles, see Frank P. Sherwood, "Legislative and Administrative Powers for Intergovernmental Cooperation for Metropolitan Affairs in California," in Governor's Commission on Metropolitan Area Problems, *Metropolitan California* (Sacramento: 1961), p. 95.

THE COOPERATIVE MOVEMENT IN PRACTICE

The nature and the direction of the movement involving interlocal cooperative agreements can be more fully perceived by considering the use made of this approach in various sections of the United States. The Philadelphia, Cleveland, St. Louis, and Los Angeles areas and the state of California provide good illustrations for this purpose. Although they are all leaders in the development, each of them has employed the technique somewhat differently—some more intensively than the others and some along lines not utilized much, if at all, by the others.

The Philadelphia Area

The most prominent features of the interlocal cooperative development in the Philadelphia area are the very widespread use of agreements, the large number of participating governments, and the frequency of cooperation among suburbs (rather than central city-suburban contracts). A survey of an eight-county area, completed in 1953, discovered that 427 local governments were involved in 756 agreements; more than three-fifths of the cities, boroughs, and townships and about three-fifths of the school districts were participants.[4] A similar study, made seven years later but limited to five counties, found a continuation of the high level of cooperative activity, the greatest amount of participation by densely populated suburbs which most commonly entered into agreements with one another, and a high concentration of cooperative relations in law enforcement, fire protection, education, and sewage disposal.[5]

The Cleveland Area

The Cleveland area, although making proportionately less use of agreements than the Philadelphia region, has a more even distribution of them among the central city, the county government, and

[4] Jephtha J. Carrell, "Inter-Jurisdictional Agreements as an Integrating Device in Metropolitan Philadelphia." Unpublished doctoral dissertation (Philadelphia: University of Pennsylvania, 1953); a summary of this work is contained in "Learning to Work Together," National Municipal Review, XLIV (November, 1954), 526–533.

[5] George S. Blair, Interjurisdictional Agreements in Southeastern Pennsylvania (Philadelphia: University of Pennsylvania Institute of Local and State Government, 1960).

the suburban municipalities. Cleveland occupies the pivotal position of contract supplier of sewerage, water, and civil defense services to many suburbs. The county government is most prominent as the provider under contract of street maintenance, public health, public welfare, and sewer management services and jail detention facilities to a number of municipalities. And agreements between suburbs are fairly numerous, most notably in fire protection.[6]

Metropolitan St. Louis

Still another pattern of development in interlocal cooperation has emerged in Metropolitan St. Louis. The government of St. Louis County was reorganized and strengthened in 1950 by the adoption of a charter which, among other powers, permits the county to enter into contracts with municipalities. This invigorated government has become the hub of many service agreements. More than four-fifths of the municipalities in the county, including all those of at least 1000 population, have signed a total of 241 contracts with the county government under which the latter provides one or more services to them. The most common contracts are for electrical inspection, but there are a number of other fields in which agreements are quite prevalent; included are law enforcement, health and sanitation, libraries, tax collection, and fire protection.

The extensive number of interlocal agreements existing between St. Louis County and its suburban municipalities, however, has not been duplicated elsewhere in the metropolis. Very few agreements, for example, have been completed between the city of St. Louis and either the municipalities or county government of St. Louis County.[7]

THE COOPERATIVE MOVEMENT IN CALIFORNIA

Local governments in California in general and those in Los Angeles County in particular are very prominent in the interlocal cooperative

---

[6] Holden, *Inter-Governmental Agreements in the Cleveland Metropolitan Area*, pp. 24–32. Municipal-school agreements were not included in this study.

[7] Governmental Research Institute, *Municipal Services Made Available to Cities, Towns, and Villages by St. Louis County* (St. Louis: December, 1959); Metropolitan St. Louis Survey, *Background for Action* (University City: February, 1957), pp. 41–47; John C. Bollens (ed.), *Exploring the Metropolitan Community* (Berkeley and Los Angeles: University of California Press, 1961), pp. 74–77.

movement. Their prominence extends to several features: the total number of agreements, the range of functions included in the cooperative arrangements, and the number of participating governments, which includes all the types of local units operating in the state—municipalities, counties, school districts, and other special districts. Statewide, there are approximately 3000 city-county agreements, most of them involving county services to municipalities. These agreements involve practically every county government and a very large share of the municipalities in the state. They are especially widespread in jail detention, law enforcement communications, tax assessment and collection, and public health services. Substantially more than half of them are in operation in counties located in metropolitan areas.

There are also approximately 2000 intermunicipal agreements in California. A majority of the cities are participants and the most extensive use of these arrangements occurs in metropolitan areas. The agreements embrace a wide range of activities. Included among the most frequent are sewage collection and disposal, jail facilities, engineering services, animal control, library services, recreation facilities, and refuse disposal.

An examination of a few instances of cooperative agreements in California metropolitan areas is helpful to a fuller understanding of this approach to problems. Such an analysis demonstrates the diversity of cooperative arrangements, the reasons for them, the procedures through which they evolved, and the controversies that arose. Three illustrations, each involving a number of governments, have been chosen for consideration: an equipment and manpower exchange, a cooperative library system, and the financing of a railroad grade separation.[8]

Equipment and Manpower Exchange

The equipment and manpower exchange agreement developed among twelve cities in the southwestern section of Los Angeles County. It emanated from discussions among city managers and

[8] League of California Cities, *Inter-Municipal Cooperation Through Contractual Agreements* (Berkeley and Los Angeles: July, 1963), pp. 26–33, 37–40. For examples from another state, see New York State Office of Local Government, *Local Government Cooperation: Uses-Procedures-Case Studies* (Albany: April, 1963), pp. 24–33.

administrative officers of most of these communities at their regular meetings. (Administrative officers are similar to city managers but have fewer formal powers.) These officials found that many of the municipalities were not fully utilizing the specialized equipment they owned and the specialized personnel on their payrolls. They also discovered that some cities could not justify large capital investment for such equipment or full-time salaries for specially trained personnel because they had only occasional need for them.

As a consequence of these findings, a joint powers agreement was drawn up, prescribing the terms and methods under which equipment and manpower could be exchanged between the contracting governments. Each city also prepared a list of available equipment and its rental rate, together with qualified equipment operators and their rates. Rental rates were derived from a guide issued by a contractors' association, while operators' rates were based on actual salaries, plus the overhead costs of items such as fringe benefits, retirement, and workmen's compensation insurance. In addition, each city specified what pieces of equipment had to be manned by its own operators. The names and telephone numbers of persons authorized to acquire or release equipment were noted and the storage point of each piece of equipment was designated.

The joint powers agreement provided that each participating government could permit every other contracting government to use its available equipment upon payment of the fair rental value and operational cost of the equipment. The agreement also stipulated that any contracting government could withdraw from the arrangement upon giving written notice thirty days in advance of terminating its participation. The agreement and each city's list of equipment, operators, and charges were approved by the city councils of all the municipalities.

The lone controversy that emerged during the negotiations concerned insurance coverage of equipment and coverage of personnel with respect to such matters as injuries, workmen's compensation, and retirement. City attorneys and insurance companies gave assurances that municipal employees performing work outside the limits of their cities in accordance with a formally adopted agreement authorizing such services are entitled to the same rights and benefits as when they work in their own city. It was also determined that insurance coverage of equipment would apply to the same risks outside the owning city as inside.

The equipment and manpower exchange has been in operation for several years and has been successful. The participating governments are highly satisfied with its results and no government has withdrawn from the arrangement.

Cooperative Library System

The cooperative library system materialized because of the desire of a number of small libraries to pool their resources in a more efficient manner. The system, created in 1960, consists of sixteen small public libraries operated by eleven municipalities, four counties, and one school district in a six-county area north of San Francisco Bay. None of the public libraries in the North Bay area is very large, which precludes the establishment of a centralized system in which, for instance, a central city with a large staff and holdings could provide and make charges for library services to nearby smaller communities.

These libraries were confronted with a variety of problems that prompted them to cooperate. One, the separate processing of new books by each library, including evaluation, ordering, cataloguing, and preparing books for the shelves, produced very costly duplication of effort. Two, no individual library had the resources to buy an adequate collection of specialized books and documents. Three, each library was giving valuable space in its cramped quarters to little-used materials, such as files of old newspapers and periodicals. Four, no library could afford an adequate collection of educational films for use by local organizations. Five, there was a lack of sufficient consultant services to children.

Stimulated to cooperative action by the availability of a federal grant and the leadership of the state librarian, representatives of these North Bay libraries completed a joint powers agreement that covered each problem and various other related subjects. Among the items included were cooperative book evaluation, cooperative in-service training, subject specialization of book collections, and sharing of specialized and periodical resources. Other items were joint film collection, centralized processing, establishment of a regional deposit center, interchangeable borrowing privileges, employment of a consultant in children's work, and teletype or telephone communication among member libraries. Where an item called for a centralized operation, as in establishing a depository for seldom used materials or a film pool, a particular member library undertook the responsibility and was compensated for it. As long as a majority of the member libraries remain in the system, the agreement continues in force. Any member, however, may withdraw at any time by resolution of its governing body and new members may join by majority vote of the existing participants.

A controversy developed while discussions about organizing the cooperative system were in progress. The board of one small library system in the North Bay area refused to become a partner to the agreement, although its librarian had taken part in the earlier stages of the development. The board concluded that federal or state aid would result in federal or state control of libraries. This view, however, was not widely shared among administrators in the cooperative system. Most of them favored some sort of state aid to encourage cooperative library arrangements throughout the state. In addition, they were convinced that even without such financial assistance substantial improvements in library services could be achieved through interlocal cooperation.

Grade Separation Agreement

In Metropolitan San Jose the traffic congestion and accident hazard caused by a railroad crossing located in a sliver of unincorporated land between two cities and close by a third brought forth a pressing need to work out a means of financing a grade separation. The consent of the state public utilities commission to closing the grade crossing and constructing the grade separation, the authorization of the state department of public works to pay half the cost, and the agreement of the three cities, the county government, and the railroad company, all had to be gained. The central problem was for one of the local parties to convince the others that each would benefit to the point of justifying its financial participation.

One of the cities took the lead and pointed out the benefits to be received by the other local governments: access to an industrial area in the second municipality would be improved, commuter traffic originating in the third would flow more rapidly, and the overpass would be a major step to developing a thoroughfare into a multilane expressway as recommended in a recently completed county traffic-ways report. Although these arguments were presented persistently but tactfully, they might not have been persuasive by themselves. In any event, the turning point in the negotiations came after the state public utilities commission denied the motions entered by two of the municipalities to have themselves dismissed from the proceedings before the regulatory body. The proceedings included an application by the city most interested in the overpass which stated that the commission should determine the allocation of costs if the parties failed to agree.

A formal agreement was completed among the three cities and the county. It provided for the allocation of local governmental costs among them and gave the most interested city responsibility for preparing the plans and specifications and supervising the construction. By the terms of the contract this city also agreed to annex the land containing the overpass and to maintain the grade separation. This is a significant example of how cooperative agreements are sometimes reached under pressure from outside agencies.

COOPERATION IN LOS ANGELES COUNTY

The most extensive use of cooperative agreements in California has taken place in Los Angeles County. Although a number of inter-municipal arrangements exist there (the equipment and manpower exchange is an outstanding illustration), most of the agreements involve the county government as the provider of services to municipalities. This role is a major reason why Los Angeles County offers one of the most prominent illustrations in the nation of the urban county development.

Five Forms of the Urban County Development

The designation, "urban county development," is so widely used and embraces so many kinds of actions that it requires further explanation. The term is applied to five types of practices.[9] First, it is used to refer to an increase in the number and levels of services which a county provides to unincorporated urban areas within its boundaries. Thus it can mean, for instance, that the manpower and equipment of the sheriff's department have been augmented to the point where

[9] Approximately 250 counties in the United States are involved in one or more of the five forms of the urban county development.

the county furnishes extensive law enforcement in unincorporated urban areas. In fact, the level of law enforcement supplied by some counties in heavily populated unincorporated sections approximates, and sometimes exceeds, the level of such protective work offered by small municipal governments within city limits. This urban type of law enforcement stands in decided contrast to the county's traditional role as supplier of a modest level of police protection in rural areas only.

A second use of the designation pertains to the transfer of a function, usually under mandatory state law, from cities to counties so that the latter may carry out the urban-type activity on a countywide basis. An example is state legislation that requires transferring to counties the responsibility for checking the accuracy of meters on taxicabs, rented cars and trucks, and private ambulances.

A third use of the term, "urban county development," relates to the intensification of a long-established function or the assumption of a new function by the county government throughout the entire county. Recreational programs, regional parks, and libraries are frequent examples. A fourth refers to the completion of cooperative agreements under which a county provides services to municipalities. And a fifth and final use pertains to the conversion of a county government into a metropolitan unit through the installation of a comprehensive plan of governmental reorganization that simultaneously reallocates many urban functions from all cities in a county to the county government.[10]

Los Angeles County as an Urban County

The government of Los Angeles County is a leading representative of the urban county development in terms of the first four types of practices. As for the first of them—the provision of urban-type services to residents of densely settled unincorporated areas—the Los Angeles County government supplies high levels of such services as

[10] The fifth use of the term is in operation only in Dade County (Miami), Florida. A discussion of this use of the term and its utilization in Dade County is presented in Chapter 15. For a consideration of various forms of the urban county development, see Victor Jones, "Urban and Metropolitan Counties," *Municipal Year Book: 1962* (Chicago: International City Managers' Association, 1962) pp. 57–66, and his earlier, similar article in the *Municipal Year Book: 1954*, pp 133–147.

law enforcement, streets, and traffic signals to its many residents who live in such sections. For instance, the county sheriff's department is the fifth largest police operation in the nation and is widely recognized as a first-class law enforcement agency. Indeed, the urban services rendered by the county (and to a lesser extent by some other county governments in the state as well) were at such a high level in the early 1950s that a bitter controversy developed. The cities claimed that since their inhabitants were paying both city and county taxes they were being forced to subsidize services extended by the county to residents of built-up unincorporated sections.[11] The controversy has subsided in recent years, in part because many areas incorporated and contracted for urban-type services from the county government, and in part because the county government cut back on some services to unincorporated urban areas. However, occasionally some city officials still get agitated about the matter, which they continue to regard as inequitable. And it is a fact that some communities remain unincorporated largely because of the urban services they can obtain from the county government out of general county tax funds.

The second practice—transferring functions from cities to the county government by action of the state legislature—is illustrated by a state law of 1962 that forced the county government to take custody of city prisoners booked on drunk charges. This law has compelled the county to lease the drunk farm of the city of Los Angeles, add 125 officers to the sheriff's department, and spend an additional $2.5 million annually. Noteworthy illustrations of the third practice—a county government intensifying an old function or taking on a new one on a countywide basis—are the ownership and operation by Los Angeles County of a considerable number of parks and the administration of extensive, diversified recreational programs.[12]

[11] California Legislature, *Final Report of the Assembly Interim Committee on Municipal and County Government Covering Fringe Area Problems in the State of California* (Sacramento: 1953).

[12] The urban county development in Los Angeles County is also discussed in Winston W. Crouch and Beatrice Dinerman, *Southern California Metropolis* (Berkeley and Los Angeles: University of California Press, 1963), chap. 7, and pp. 222–225. In addition, see Winston W. Crouch, "Expanding Role of the Urban County: The Los Angeles Experiment," in Stephen B. Sweeney and George S. Blair (eds.), *Metropolitan Analysis: Important Elements of Study and Action* (Philadelphia: University of Pennsylvania Press, 1958), pp. 99–122.

Los Angeles County as a Contractor

The wide use of any one of these three practices would qualify Los Angeles County for recognition as an urban county, but its most notable urban county attribute is the provision of services to municipalities under cooperative agreements. It has approximately 1500 such agreements, involving all seventy-six municipalities in the county, with the number of services ranging in each case from four to forty-five.

The provision of some types of services to municipalities is universal, or virtually so. The county supplies election services for all cities, tax assessment and collection for all but two, and the housing of prisoners and the enforcement of state health laws and city business licenses for all except three. In addition, the county provides a variety of other services to at least one-half of the cities: emergency ambulance service, prosecution of violations of city ordinances, subdivision final map check, enforcement of city health ordinances, inspection of mobile homes and trailer parks, and library service. And many other services are rendered to at least one-third of the cities, including hospitalization of city prisoners, building inspection, engineering services, industrial waste regulation, rodent control, animal pound, law enforcement, and fire protection.

Establishment of the Lakewood Plan

The catalyst to the rapid growth in recent years of county-city service agreements was the establishment in 1954 of the Lakewood Plan (or as cities other than Lakewood operating under the same arrangement prefer to call it, the contract cities plan). Under this system a municipality receives a sizable package of municipal services—virtually all municipal services in some instances—from the county government under contracts and through county-administered districts (special county taxing areas for fire protection and library services, for example). The Lakewood Plan was the product of a combination of factors. Some were the passage by the state legislature of a uniform local retail sales and use tax that made it financially attractive for areas to incorporate as municipalities, the controversy over whether city residents were subsidizing urban services that certain unincorporated areas were receiving from the county government, and the continued rapid growth of the county's population, particularly in some of its unincorporated sections. Other important factors were the existence of highly respected county departments already staffed and equipped to furnish municipal services and the willingness of county officials to think through the idea of a package of services (at least partly because of the fear of some county department heads that the size of their operations would be reduced as burgeoning unincorporated sections found it necessary to incorporate or annex to a municipality). A final significant influence was the desire of built-up unincorporated sectors to escape annexation by incorporating (and thus being vested with local control, especially of land use)—but at the same time avoiding the necessity for large capital investments for facilities like police and fire stations and for recruiting a corps of city employees.

The Lakewood Plan: Differences and Characteristics

The Lakewood Plan differs in several important respects from the earlier city-county service agreements. It entails the purchase of a package of services instead of individual services on a piecemeal basis. It includes for the first time county law enforcement and fire protection services to cities. (Previously the sheriff's department did not enter into contracts with cities, and newly incorporated areas withdrew from county-administered fire districts.) Use of the Lakewood Plan has been confined entirely to communities incorporated since Lakewood became a city in 1954—that is, to municipalities not already having long-established departments of their own.

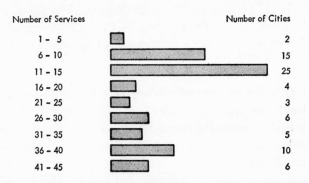

Figure 13.1   Number of Municipal Services Provided to Cities by the Los Angeles County Government. Data as of July 1, 1964. From the County–City Coordinator's Office, County of Los Angeles.

The Lakewood Plan system has been accepted by practically all of the thirty-one municipalities, both medium-sized and small, established since 1954. At the time of incorporating, Lakewood had a population of approximately 60,000 and immediately became the fifteenth most populous city in the state. Its population has since grown by another 20,000 and there are various other Lakewood Plan cities that currently have between 30,000 and 100,000 people.

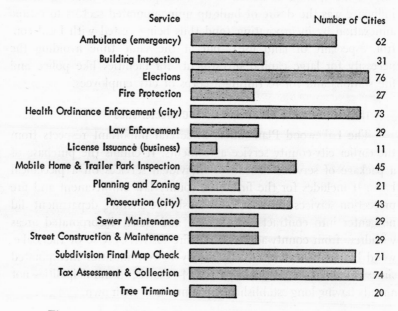

Service	Number of Cities
Ambulance (emergency)	62
Building Inspection	31
Elections	76
Fire Protection	27
Health Ordinance Enforcement (city)	73
Law Enforcement	29
License Issuance (business)	11
Mobile Home & Trailer Park Inspection	45
Planning and Zoning	21
Prosecution (city)	43
Sewer Maintenance	29
Street Construction & Maintenance	29
Subdivision Final Map Check	71
Tax Assessment & Collection	74
Tree Trimming	20

Figure 13.2 Selected Types of Municipal Services Provided to Cities by the Los Angeles County Government. Data as of July 1, 1964. From County-City Coordinator's Office, County of Los Angeles.

Although the package of services idea is central to the Lakewood Plan, cities operating under the system do not all purchase the same package from the county. The common practice has been for the newly incorporated cities to purchase at the outset virtually all the municipal services they need. Over a period of time, however, a number of them have terminated some contracts and withdrawn from particular county-administered districts. Such action was usually taken after they had determined on the basis of studies that they could perform certain services more economically than the county government, or when they decided to undertake some functions on their own for such non-financial reasons as preference by community residents. (The county's contract rates must be set at full cost—the direct costs for the number of units of each service rendered and a share of the county's general administrative or overhead expenses; the rates are subject to revision annually to reflect changes in the factors making up the costs, such as pay scales.) The contents of the service package thus vary according to a community's decisions as to what it initially needs from the county and what subsequent changes should be made in the original arrangements.

While the Lakewood Plan has flourished, the number of service agreements between the county and older, pre-Lakewood cities (often called "old-line" or "traditional" cities) has also grown. These older municipalities have become increasingly interested in obtaining specialized services such as sewer maintenance, storm drain design, traffic signal maintenance, and traffic striping and marking.

The Future

Arthur G. Will, the former county-city coordinator (a position established in the county government soon after the inception of the Lakewood Plan to handle the expanding volume of details about contracts) has commented optimistically about the possible significance of the cooperative agreement device as an evolutionary means of determining a logical allocation of functions between city the county governments. In speaking at a national conference of county officials, Will stressed:

We [in Los Angeles County] are now well into *the process of natural selection* [italics added] between the county and the various cities for allocation of the local services between the two agencies. . . . cities very probably will amend our contract operations over the years to provide for themselves the primary services involving identity and direct and frequent contact with their citizens. These services will generally be the bread-and-butter . . . services such as responding to complaints for repair of streets and other public works facilities, the handling of routine day-to-day planning and zoning matters, the handling of certain engineering design functions, and many others. The county will more and more step back and assume those supporting functions requiring highly specialized personnel and equipment and less direct contact with the public.

We think that through the splitting of these services and the allocation of a portion to the city and a portion to the county, it will strengthen the position of both and provide a more permanent service operation. . . .

We think that much of what is going on in our county right now is an accomplishment of what has been stated academically in studies of metropolitan area problems in the matter of allocation of functions. Rather than talking about them, we have been in the process of actually making these allocations by experience and settling these service areas into the proper location in our governmental structure. The County of Los Angeles has a great deal of work to do and we hope that other counties can very materially benefit from our experience.[13]

THE METROPOLITAN COUNCIL

The metropolitan (or regional) council is the newest form of co-operation in the metropolis. Employed so far in only a few areas, the council idea is viewed by its advocates as a highly significant development and by most of its opponents as a toothless tiger or—even worse—a protector of the inadequate status quo. In brief, a metropolitan council is a voluntary association of governments designed to provide an area-wide mechanism for key officials to study, discuss, and determine the means—cooperative means, if possible —of solving common problems.[14] This mechanism is not a government; it has no power to implement its decisions by compelling compliance with them. Instead, it is a continuing forum for deliberation and discussion and an advisory, recommendatory, and coordinating organization.

Limited Number, Recent Origin

There are seven active metropolitan councils. The pioneer was the Supervisors Inter-County Committee established in the Detroit area in 1954. It was followed by the creation of the Metropolitan Regional Council in the New York area in 1956 and the Metro-

[13] Arthur G. Will, "Another Look at Lakewood," (Paper delivered at the annual conference of the National Association of Counties, New York, July 11, 1962), pp. 14, 15. For other observations about the Lakewood Plan, see Samuel K. Gove, *The Lakewood Plan* (Urbana: University of Illinois Institute of Government and Public Affairs, 1961), and Crouch and Dinerman, *Southern California Metropolis*, pp. 201–205, 222–225.

[14] The refusal of a number of important local governments in the New York area to become formal members of the Metropolitan Regional Council caused its reorganization in 1964 into an association of local elected officials.

politan Washington (D.C.) Council of Governments and the Puget Sound Regional Governmental Conference in the following year. The more recent additions were the Mid-Willamette Valley Council of Governments (Salem, Oregon, area) in 1959, and the Association of Bay Area Governments (San Francisco) and the Regional Conference of Elected Officials (Philadelphia), both in 1961.[15]

Other Features

In addition to their general purposes and recent origin, metropolitan councils have many other features in common:

(1) All of them emanate from agreements which are based on state legislative authorizations, governmental compacts, or simply by-laws accepted by the participants.

(2) The members of the organization (with the exception of the New York council which is an association of elected officials) are exclusively or largely local governments, most often municipalities and counties. In the case of the Salem organization, the state government and a school district are also participants; in that of the Washington, D.C., agency, state governments, the national government, and the government of the District of Columbia are members; and in that of the Detroit area committee, the membership consists solely of representatives of county governments.

(3) The overwhelming number of representatives on such councils are elected officials, not appointed administrators.

(4) The councils are financed by contributions of the member governments, usually determined on the basis of each government's share of the total population of all the participating units.

(5) A member has the right to withdraw from the association at any time. The tendency, however, has been for additional governments to join the organizations rather than for original members to drop out. (The latter does happen occasionally, as in the case of the withdrawal of Montgomery County, Maryland, from the Washington organization in 1963.)

(6) The councils are multipurpose in nature; they are able to consider any area-wide problems to which they decide to give their attention.

[15] Formation of the Southern California Association of Governments is under way; another organization, the Metropolitan Area Council in the Baltimore area, established in 1961 through the efforts of one man, is now defunct.

(7) Although multipurpose in scope, the councils tend to look at problems separately on a function-by-function basis.

(8) Each council strives for unanimity of agreement on recommendations for action, even though some provide that decisions can be reached by majority vote of the representatives in attendance (or in the case of the San Francisco Bay council separate majorities of the city and county members).

(9) All the councils have professional staffs which manage the organizational activities and undertake research.

(10) The councils originated for one of two reasons or a combination of the two: a realization that collaborative governmental decisions and actions were necessary to deal with area-wide problems and a fear that local units were about to lose powers to proposed metropolitan governments.[16]

Three Councils in Action

A review of some of the principal work of three metropolitan councils in 1963 is revealing.[17] The Supervisors Inter-County Committee of the six-county area centering on Detroit continued to work for implementation of recommendations contained in regional aviation and water studies and published a new edition of its metro-

[16] The two following statements illustrate each type of rationale:
"Your metropolitan area is confronted by problems that cannot be solved by any one local government acting individually." (Metropolitan Washington Council of Governments, *Report for Sixty-Four*, p. 1).
"The threat of new state-imposed metropolitan governments brought home forcefully . . . the possibility of a revolutionary approach to the solution of metropolitan problems. [It] made clear to California cities the need for an affirmative program to cope with metropolitan problems." (Paper delivered by Lewis Keller of the League of California Cities at American Municipal Association Workshop, Seattle, August 24, 1961, p. 1).
[17] For other summaries of council activities, see John C. Bollens, "Metropolitan and Fringe Area Developments," *Municipal Year Book: 1964* (Chicago: International City Managers' Association, 1964), pp. 57–59, and Roscoe C. Martin, *Metropolis in Transition: Local Government Adaptation to Changing Urban Needs* (Washington: Housing and Home Finance Agency, September, 1963), chaps. III and IV. Additional discussions of councils are contained in Henry J. Schmandt, "The Area Council—Approach to Metropolitan Government," *Public Management*, XLII (February, 1960), 30–32; Samuel Humes, "Organization for Metropolitan Cooperation," *Public Management*, XLIV (May, 1962), 105–107; and John K. Parker, "Cooperation in Metropolitan Areas through Councils of Governments," *Public Management*, XLV (October, 1963), 223–225.

politan area planned public works program. The latter was offered in testimony before congressional committees as evidence of the need for continuation of the federal accelerated public works program. The Committee also sponsored a conference that led to the establishment of the Forum for the Detroit Metropolitan Area Goals, which was assigned the task of defining the area's governmental and non-governmental objectives, and endorsed a considerable number of bills for presentation to the state legislature (half of the measures passed), including a proposal to implement the county home-rule provisions of the recently adopted state constitution.

The Metropolitan Regional Council of the New York area held a national conference on the jet-noise problem, backed legislation for the creation of a strong tri-state regional transportation agency, and supplied technical assistance to an intermunicipal refuse disposal project. It also set up a tri-state organization of all police chiefs and sheriffs in the area, prepared a manual of emergency procedures to be followed in the event of airplane crashes in crowded sections, and requested Congress to reinsert in the federal budget $12 million for a comprehensive water quality and supply program for the area.

In the San Francisco Bay area, the Association of Bay Area Governments (a designation that was quickly shortened to the unromantic-sounding abbreviation of ABAG) concentrated its attention on other matters. It actively proceeded to establish itself as the agency responsible for regional planning in the area. In this connection, it obtained the agreement of eight counties to provide matching funds or services to finance a regional planning program and applied for federal planning assistance money. In addition, it distributed an agreement relating to the preservation of open space, which was signed by a number of local governments.

As this summary indicates, councils are engaged in a broad sweep of activities involving much more than merely research. Some of them, moreover, have assumed the role of unified spokesman for their member local governments in certain relations with the state and national governments. And in the case of ABAG, one such agency has moved forward vigorously to add the metropolitan or regional planning function to the customary council activities of research, discussion, and advice.

THE COOPERATIVE APPROACH: THE FUTURE

The cooperative approach, as exemplified by both service agreements and metropolitan councils, is in a period of rapid growth and an era of good feeling toward the device.[18] Expanding as a defense against more thorough approaches, which are discussed in the next two chapters, and as a result of the necessity of employing some integrative device in view of the general resistance of metropolitan areas to comprehensive approaches, cooperation is being promoted by a variety of individuals and organizations. Among them are local public officials, their state and national associations, and groups that include state and national officials, such as the Council of State Governments and the national Advisory Commission on Intergovernmental Relations. Furthermore, a favorable image of cooperation has been fostered by making it a leading topic at local, state, and national conferences of governmental representatives and private citizens.

What is surprising about the cooperative approach is not that it has been receiving greatly increased use recently, but that its expansion did not come much earlier. Certainly it would be logical to expect that the most moderate method of attacking problems— one based on voluntary agreement and no major disturbance of existing governments in the metropolis—would have received widespread use when interlocal problems were first developing. But such was not the case. Equally astonishing is the fact that service agreements are still not in common use in most metropolitan areas and the existence of metropolitan councils in only seven of a total of more than 200 metropolises surely must be regarded as a modest attainment. Similarly, it would be expected that the mildest form of cooperation—mutual aid in emergencies—would be in effect among all governments in an area. However, a recent tragedy in a southern

[18] An exception is the New York area where the Metropolitan Regional Council has been subjected to vociferous opposition by what the mayor of New York has called "an organized campaign to attack all attempts at interlocal cooperation. In the past year, M.R.C. has been the target of irrational and scurrilous attacks by extremist groups. . . ." *The New York Times*, June 8, 1963. For further details, see U.S. Senate and House Committees on Government Operations, Subcommittees on Intergovernmental Relations, *Joint Hearings: Government in Metropolitan Areas* (*New York Metropolitan Region*), 88th Congress, 1st Session (Washington: 1963).

California community, where a call about a drowning was rejected by a city rescue squad two minutes away from the scene because the home was a few feet outside the city limits, brought to light the complete absence of intermunicipal emergency aid agreements covering such situations.

The piecemeal nature of service agreements—each normally concerned with only two governments and one service or facility—means that the device would have to be used very extensively in order to produce an area-wide approach to needs and problems. Although a growing amount of interlocal contracting is taking place, it is only in rare instances that the total use of the method in relation to any function constitutes an area-wide solution to a difficulty. (Two significant exceptions are the multigovernmental sewage disposal agreements in effect in the Phoenix and San Diego metropolitan areas under which the central cities serve most or all the communities.) Even in Los Angeles County, where the greatest number of agreements involving a single government (the county) are in operation, the cooperative method has emerged in only a very few non-controversial functions as an area-wide approach. The nationwide metropolitan pattern, therefore, is one of a limited number of governments reaching agreement about a single function and a limited number (but not necessarily most of the same governments) making arrangements about another matter. The common result is a patchwork of agreements, usually relating to long-standing non-controversial matters, and a lack of an overall design and system.

The severest limitation on interlocal agreements is found in their financial nature. In the overwhelming number of instances, they involve the provision of services for an exchange of money. But a number of local units in most metropolitan areas do not have the financial resources to contract and pay for certain services even when they are available on this basis. As the Cleveland Metropolitan Services Commission well stated the case in its final report:

. . . Since, for example, a contract assumes an exchange of values between the parties involved, this presumes that the receiver of the services has the financial means to make the required payment. A major part of the metropolitan service problem, however, arises as a result of service inadequacies in communities where there are insufficient resources for the task. An inter-governmental contract cannot very easily meet this type of difficulty.[19]

[19] Cleveland Metropolitan Services Commission, *Prologue to Progress* (Cleveland: 1959), pp. 40–41.

The prospect is that at least in the years immediately ahead interlocal service agreements will continue to grow in number, mainly because of the rising pressure to deal with certain needs and problems and the lack of appeal of more comprehensive methods. But it also appears likely that such agreements will remain ineffective for dealing with area-wide needs. Moreover, there seems to be little probability that most county governments soon will take on the role of major contract supplier as performed most prominently by the Los Angeles County government and to a lesser extent by certain other counties. Not very many counties in metropolitan areas are ready in terms of personnel, equipment, or facilities to undertake this assignment.

Service contracts also generally will continue to be of restricted value because of the common requirement of an exchange of money for service rendered. It is true that the use of such agreements would grow if more state laws (California, for example, has one in the health field) were passed which required counties to perform certain services for cities at the request of the latter and without additional charge to them. The political controversy that would be generated by such legislative proposals and the probable confinement of such state-imposed service request arrangements to activities which counties already perform in unincorporated areas or as agents of the state (and thus have existing departments and personnel to handle) make it unlikely that service agreements will increase significantly by this route.

The future for metropolitan councils, the other type of cooperation considered in this chapter, may be more promising. Two developments in particular make this possible. First, the number and significance of contacts between the local governments in the metropolitan area and the state and national governments are increasing and with them is growing the realization by local officials of the need for a unified spokesman. The metropolitan council, which is multigovernmental in membership and outlook, can fill this area-wide role. Second, the state and national governments are becoming increasingly metropolis-conscious in preferring to deal with one organization and in attempting to foster a greater amount of interlocal coordination. As an example, recent federal highway legislation calls for the preparation of area-wide plans for metropolitan areas to be eligible for grants. This requirement is compelling local units to cooperate in developing such plans. Federal and state legislation containing grants to stimulate metropolitan-wide coordination will undoubtedly grow in volume. The time therefore seems ripe for area-wide councils and planning agencies to increase in number by serving as the focal points for increased coordination.

A word of caution should be interjected at this point, however. Metropolitan councils are voluntary and advisory; thus governments can join and abandon them at will and council decisions are simply wishful thinking unless at least the major local governments in an area want to follow the recommendations. It therefore takes a great deal of continuing cooperation by many local governments, which may have quite divergent aspirations, to make the council idea a success.

Norman Beckman, an assistant director of the national Advisory Commission on Intergovernmental Relations, has incisively summarized both the positive and negative roles metropolitan councils can play:

How effective the council approach actually will be depends in large part on whether it brings out the full expression of conflicting views, creates an awareness of varying problems and interests among jurisdictions, uses existing local government machinery to implement council decisions, develops that crucial but currently missing ingredient of the metropolitan mix—regional leadership, and presents a united front in negotiations with federal and state agencies. Alternatively, the voluntary councils could serve to neutralize or obscure the real conflicts and to protect the status quo. The returns are not in yet on this new approach.[20]

[20] Norman Beckman, "Alternative Approaches for Metropolitan Reorganization," *Public Management*, XLVI (June, 1964), 130.

CHAPTER 14

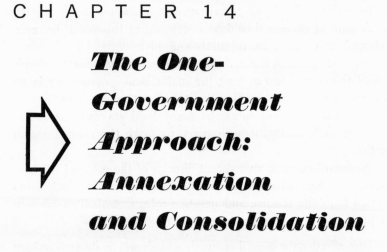

The One-Government Approach: Annexation and Consolidation

THE IDEA of a single local government functioning throughout an entire metropolitan area has long had many advocates. Support for the idea is rooted in various convictions. Some proponents maintain that an integrated governmental operation produces greater efficiency and economy. Others point to the ability of such a government to allocate public financial resources on the basis of needs of the different parts of the common area, thus eliminating the great disparities between resources and needs that prevail when there are many local units. Still others emphasize the ability of a single, territorially large government to handle functions of an area-wide nature in a unified and coordinated manner. In contrast to these claims, opponents of the one-government concept most frequently argue in terms of loss of local control, decreased citizen access to public officials, and reduced attention to local services.

Activities to implement the one-government concept have taken several principal forms and have met with varying degrees of success. Almost always, one or more of three types of local governments have been involved: municipalities, counties, and school districts. The efforts, however, have seldom been concerned with merging these three types into a single unit. In fact, the most prevalent attempts have consisted of two distinct movements: one relating to municipalities alone or in combination with counties and the other pertaining to school districts.

Interest in other kinds of unification has existed, but activity on behalf of such proposals has been highly sporadic and very unproductive. For example, discussion has occurred from time to time, mostly by scholars and consultants, about combining school districts with municipalities or counties, but despite this talk school districts remain strongholds of governmental separatism. Similarly, the merging of counties and the combining of townships have also been urged, especially during times of economic depression, but no major results along either line have followed. Also, with the rapid increase of non-school special districts in the last few decades, isolated proposals have been advanced to consolidate them with one another and with general local governments, such as municipalities and counties. The trend, however, continues in the opposite direction, as the proliferation of these districts moves on.

The single-government approach centering on municipalities has involved three techniques: absorption of nearby unincorporated land (a process commonly known as annexation); merger of two municipalities (municipal consolidation); and merger of some or all of the municipal governments in a county with the county government (city-county consolidation). On the other hand, the single-government approach involving school districts has concentrated on their consolidation with each other. We will consider and analyze each of these approaches in this chapter.

MUNICIPAL EXPANSION: THE HALCYON AND DORMANT YEARS

Municipal annexation—a municipality's acquisition of adjacent unincorporated territory—has consistently been the most common means of changing governmental boundaries in urban areas. As we shall see, however, annexation has generally changed over the years in both extent and nature.[1]

[1] Some state laws speak of the annexation of one municipality by another. In this book, for purposes of clarity, the term "municipal annexation" is used to refer only to the absorption of unincorporated territory and the term "municipal consolidation" refers to the absorption of one municipality by another or the combining of two or more municipalities to create a new unit.

The Original Plan

From the early years of our national history, each state government acknowledged the basic necessity of setting up several processes for the creation and expansion of municipalities. In addition to annexation, these procedures were incorporation, the marking out of certain land to be within the boundaries of a newly established municipality, and municipal consolidation, the merging of two or more municipalities into a single government. In acknowledging the importance of these three processes, the states recognized that what became urban should also become municipal—that is, possessing the type of local government to satisfy the service and regulatory needs of population centers.

This rationale for accommodating urban growth was generally accepted until the turn of the present century. Its acceptability, however, was based primarily on the fact that urban settlements had tended to be scattered and geographically apart. Consequently, as an area became urban in the sense of becoming a concentration of people, it was incorporated as a municipality; and as urbanization spread beyond the muncipality's original boundaries into the surrounding countryside, the newly populated land was annexed to the existing municipal government. There seldom was any thought of doing otherwise. Here was a municipal government, a going concern, that could promptly provide the adjacent land with the necessary urban services and controls. It therefore was judged to be a logical action, a natural extension of the original city, to have the adjoining area become part of this municipality. And on a number of occasions when two municipalities, through the annexation activity of one or both of them, eventually became territorially contiguous, they were consolidated into one unit.

Up to about the beginning of the twentieth century, the three processes were generally used successfully and operated to the advantage of the one-government concept. Annexation was usually accomplished by a special act of the state legislature, action of the governing body of the municipality seeking to annex the territory, or a combined vote of the electorate of the municipality (which practically always was much more populous) and that of the outlying area. Consolidation was most often completed by either an act of the state legislature or the combined vote of the electors of the municipalities involved. And incorporation, utilized principally in widely separated locations, was realized by a state legislative act or favorable successive actions by the property owners of and the voters residing on the affected land.

The Boom Period

In the pre-1900 era the expansion of municipal boundaries, principally through annexation, largely kept pace with population expansion. Thus in many urban areas boundary extensions enabled an initially small municipality, which for some time was often the only incorporated place for miles around, to become large in population and territory. Today, these units are the central cities of many metropolises. Without annexation (and, to a much lesser degree, municipal consolidation and city-county consolidation), few large central cities would have developed. Instead, clusters of numerous small cities, none being the governmental, economic, and social hub, would exist in most metropolitan areas. Furthermore, the governmental pattern of many metropolises would now be far more complicated if annexation in particular had not been frequent during this early period.

The pre-1900 annexation movement had three highly prominent characteristics. One, many municipalities absorbed much territory, often through very few annexation actions. Two, the land annexed was usually not intensively urbanized at the time of absorption. Three, in a number of instances, annexation was used simultaneously with another area reorganization approach, such as municipal consolidation or the separation of a city from the remainder of a county.

A comparison of the areas of various major cities at the time of incorporation and in 1900 demonstrates the great magnitude of municipal territorial expansion, solely or chiefly through annexation, in this early period. Chicago, for example, increased from 10.5 to 190 square miles, Boston from 4.5 to 38.5, and Baltimore from about a half square mile to 31.5. Similarly, Pittsburgh grew from a half square mile to 28, St. Louis from a similar size to 61 square miles, and Minneapolis from 8 to 53 square miles.

Although annexation was the principal spur to expansion, two related activities were also influential: municipal consolidation and other methods of boundary adjustment used in combination with annexation. As municipalities stretched outward, some existing smaller cities and towns eventually came to stand in the path of the further, "natural" territorial growth of the expanding units. Consequently, smaller municipalities frequently were consolidated with their larger neighbors, usually by state legislative act or a combined vote in the two affected areas. Municipal consolidation was important, for instance, to the continued expansion of both Chicago and St. Louis. In this early period, however, the employment of this merger device was generally slight in comparison to annexation, the difference being largely due to the infrequent existence of adjoining municipalities and the prevalence of nearby unincorporated territory. Also, on occasion, annexation was utilized concurrently with some other method of adjusting local governmental boundaries. A conspicuous example is St. Louis, which in 1876 more than tripled its area through annexation at the same time that it territorially separated from St. Louis County.[2]

The Time of Decline

The nature of municipal annexation changed quickly and decidedly around the turn of the century, and from about 1900 until the end of World War II its usage was generally infrequent and of minor significance. During this time, annexations decreased in number, in total territory absorbed, and in the average size of the annexed areas. The total amount of territory absorbed, for example, in the decade of the 1920s was substantially smaller than in the 1890s. By the 1930s, only a handful of municipalities were completing annexations, most of them of minuscule size. A few cities—most prominently Detroit and Los Angeles—made sizable annexations between 1900 and 1945, but these were notable exceptions.

Municipal consolidation was even less active and less consequential than annexation during this time. Again, as in annexation, there were occasional exceptions, almost always fostered by extraordinary circumstances. Los Angeles, for example, using its control of the area's major water supply as a club, was able to persuade a number of municipalities to consolidate with it. In general, however, the device became almost completely disused.

[2] R. D. McKenzie, *The Metropolitan Community* (New York: McGraw-Hill, 1933), pp. 191–198, 336–337, and Richard Bigger and James D. Kitchen, *How the Cities Grew* (Los Angeles: University of California Bureau of Governmental Research, 1952), pp. 143–151, describe the early annexation activities of a number of cities.

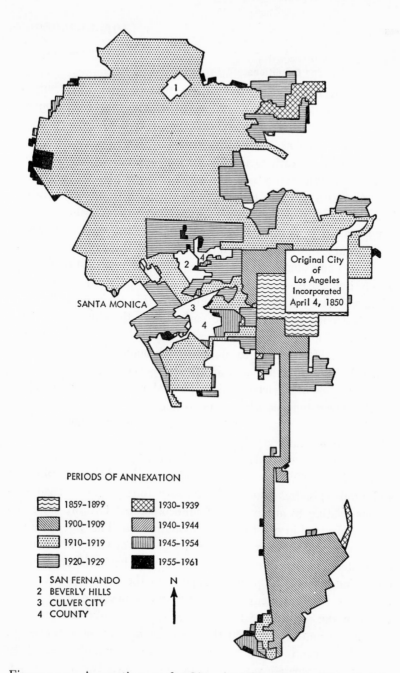

PERIODS OF ANNEXATION

1859–1899	1930–1939
1900–1909	1940–1944
1910–1919	1945–1954
1920–1929	1955–1961

1 SAN FERNANDO
2 BEVERLY HILLS
3 CULVER CITY
4 COUNTY

N

Figure 14.1   Annexations to the City of Los Angeles, by Time Periods.
From Winston W. Crouch and Beatrice Dinerman, *Southern California Metropolis*, University of California Press, 1963, p. 161.

The Changing Conditions

The precipitous decrease in annexation and the near demise of municipal consolidation were directly related to the pronounced urban and metropolitan growth of this period. Technological improvements, such as the increasing availability and acceptance of the automobile, greatly facilitated the expansion of urbanization over greater and greater areas and converted many people into commuters traveling many miles to their work locations. As these newly urbanized sectors outside the old established large municipalities gained in population, their residents established their own municipal governments or at least avoided becoming parts of those already in existence. Formerly many small but old municipalities had been fairly or completely isolated from the big city, but now they often found themselves to be its neighbors as a result of the big city's annexations of the nineteenth century. In the early 1900s, therefore, many new urban developments and most small neighboring municipalities developed stiff resistance to absorption through annexation or consolidation. In sum, the halcyon years of governmental assimilation by large cities of adjacent unincorporated urban areas and nearby small incorporated places had come to an end.

In order for opposition to the one-government concept to be effective, it was necessary to get state legislatures to make municipal annexation and consolidation difficult to use successfully. In many states this objective was accomplished, with a coalition of suburban and rural legislators usually the decisive force. General legal provisions relating to annexation of unincorporated territory were frequently changed in one to three important ways. The procedure was made extremely complex. The property owners or voters in the unincorporated territory were given the sole right to begin the annexation. Obtaining a favorable popular majority in the unincorporated area was made a requirement to complete the annexation, thus giving voters in the outlying section a conclusive veto over the proposal, even if the municipality had the power to initiate the proceedings. Similarly, general consolidation laws were commonly altered to stipulate that separate voter majorities (sometimes two-thirds majorities) had to be obtained in both municipalities. And in states that still used special legislation to effect specific annexations and consolidations, the suburban representatives alone or in combination with rural legislators were ordinarily able to defeat such bills. The number of such states had decreased by this time in the face of the upsurge of municipal home rule and the greater use of general state laws.

The Continued Ease of Incorporating

In contrast to annexation and consolidation procedures, municipal incorporation provisions remained extremely lax. Moreover, when urban development began to spread over a wide area in the present century, the process of incorporation became interrelated and interacting with the processes of annexation and consolidation. Thus, the ease of incorporation affected the successful utilization of the other two devices and contributed importantly to the marked decline in their use.

Incorporation laws continued to specify that an area with a very small number of residents—a figure seemingly satisfactory in earlier years but ridiculous in an age of growing urbanization—could incorporate and thus establish a municipal government. The incorporation laws, which have largely remained unchanged to the present, commonly required an area to have only 100 to 500 inhabitants and in at least one state called for merely an assemblage of houses or places of business. Then as now, most states did not have a set of legal standards to be applied in determining when areas should be permitted to incorporate and whether they should annex or be consolidated with existing municipalities. In the case of incorporation, the only requirement usually was and still is a small resident population.

Greatly stiffening the terms of annexation and consolidation but retaining excessively liberal incorporation provisions naturally resulted in extensive use of incorporation as a technique for avoiding the other two processes. Annexation related only to the acquiring of unincorporated territory; consequently, if a small amount of land was incorporated as a municipal government, the annexation process, regardless of its liberal or highly restrictive nature, could no longer be applied to this area. In like manner, use of incorporation in an area generally meant that two incorporated places could not be consolidated unless a majority of the voters in both approved the proposition separately. Such consent was difficult to obtain and seldom forthcoming.

THE REBIRTH OF ANNEXATION

Municipal annexation arose from its long dormancy in the closing year of World War II, despite the obituaries written by many analysts only a few years before. Their conclusion seemed sound, for by the 1930s annexation was in its fourth consecutive decade of general inactivity. The error of that conclusion became evident in 1945, however, when 152 cities containing at least 5000 people completed annexations, a total greatly exceeding the prewar level of the 1930s. And in the following year the number of comparable municipalities annexing land passed 250 and in 1947 neared 300.

During this early stage of the annexation revival, various researchers reached another conclusion: the resurgence would be short-lived. The postwar spurt, they reasoned, was simply being produced by unjamming the backlog of actions that had been postponed because of economic depression and recession, international crises, and the United States' involvement in war, a series of events stretching over a considerable period of years. But this conjecture also proved erroneous. The renewed vigor displayed by annexation in the immediate postwar period did not flag but increased later, and the movement has continued to exhibit considerable strength. Basically, this resurgence is attributable to two interrelated factors: the continuance of metropolitan growth and the general lack of public acceptance of comprehensive plans of governmental reorganization in the metropolis.

Much Annexation Activity

In most years since the termination of World War II, the number of annexing municipalities has increased. In 1962, for example, 754 such units of at least 5000 residents completed annexations; this was practically five times as many as in 1945. There were, of course, substantially more municipalities of this population size at the end of this eighteen-year period (an addition of approximately 1000, to be more precise), as a result of many small cities becoming larger and many newly urbanized areas taking advantage of liberal incorporation laws. This increase in number of cities partly accounts for the virtually continuous rise in annexation activity. But the fivefold gain in municipalities annexing land can be traced chiefly to the much greater proportionate use of the annexation device. To illustrate, only about one of each twelve municipal governments of at least 5000 population annexed territory in 1945, but about one of every five did so in 1962. In addition, the total amount of land annexed by cities of this population size has become considerable. Although upward and downward spirals have occurred in various years, the total in 1962—968.5 square miles—was almost seven times as much as that of 1948.[3]

A large portion of this revitalized annexation activity has taken place in metropolitan areas, with many central cities and suburbs employing the device to increase their territorial size. Notwithstanding the impact annexation has had in such areas, not all of it beneficial, it seldom has been a successful mechanism for dealing with area-wide policy matters and difficulties.

An extensive number of municipalities have participated in postwar annexation activities, but the most important general characteristic of the movement has been the smallness of the areas annexed. In year after year the overwhelming majority, usually about four-fifths, of the municipalities completing annexations have acquired less than one-half square mile of land. And very frequently the continued difficult nature of many annexation laws has made it necessary for these governments to proceed successfully many times through an intricate legal procedure in order to obtain a tiny total amount of land.

While the annexation trend has generally continued to feature the absorption of small areas, many new incorporations but few municipal consolidations have taken place. In the 1950s, for example, only about twenty such mergers occurred in the entire nation, many of them involving small incorporated places lying outside metropolitan areas. The restricted size of most annexations, the consider-

---

[3] In 1963 the number of annexing cities (679) decreased somewhat and the total amount of land annexed (488.8 square miles) declined considerably in relation to the 1962 levels. Nevertheless, the total amount annexed in 1963 was more than triple the comparable figure of 1948. The data on the number of municipalities of 5000 or more people annexing territory and the total amount of land absorbed in the postwar years through 1962 are derived from John C. Bollens, "Metropolitan and Fringe Area Developments in 1962," *Municipal Year Book: 1963* (Chicago: International City Managers' Association, 1963), p. 53. Details about annexation activities in specific years will be found in similar articles by the same author in previous editions of this publication, beginning with the one issued in 1949.

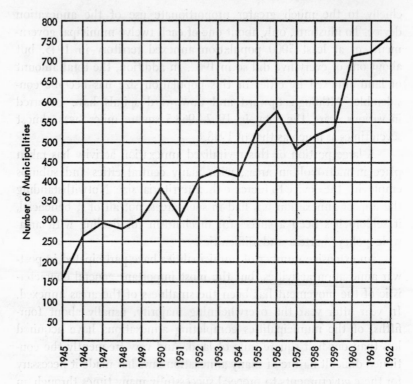

Figure 14.2   Number of Annexing Municipalities of 5000
or More Population, 1945–1962. From *Municipal Year
Book: 1963*, International City Managers' Association,
1963, p. 53.

able number of incorporations, and the dearth of municipal consolidations have together produced an increased, at times complete,
hemming in of the major cities of many metropolises. Milwaukee
and Minneapolis, for instance, have become entirely encircled by
other incorporated places that are legally immune from merger unless
their separate approval is obtained. In the meantime, too, the land
of various metropolises has become largely covered by incorporated
communities.

The limited general utility of annexation in recent years is
further demonstrated by the degree to which it has been employed
by the nation's most populous cities—those possessing populations of
at least 100,000. In the 1950s, one-third of these municipalities (44
of 130) did not annex any land and about another one-fourth (36)

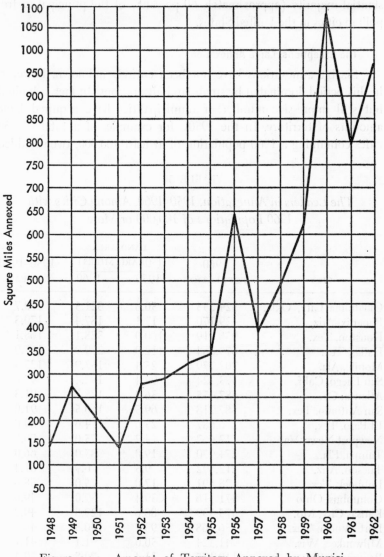

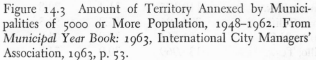

Figure 14.3   Amount of Territory Annexed by Munici-
palities of 5000 or More Population, 1948–1962. From
Municipal Year Book: 1963, International City Managers'
Association, 1963, p. 53.

absorbed a small total ranging from a fraction of a square mile to
less than ten square miles. Thus, in this ten-year period of rapid
metropolitanization, annexation was of limited or no value to a sub-

stantial majority (approximately 60 percent) of the principal metropolitan cities in the United States.

The Exceptions: Large Annexations

Sizable annexations have not been entirely unknown, however,
in this period dominated by small land absorptions. In fact, a limited
but still impressive number of municipalities have acquired large
amounts of territory. In the 1950s, for example, of a total of 130
cities containing a 1960 population of at least 100,000, twelve added

TABLE 30

*The Leaders in Annexation, 1950–1960, Among Cities with
1960 Populations of 100,000 or More*

		LAND AREA (SQUARE MILES)		
CITY	1960 POPULATION	1950	1960	1950–1960 INCREASE
Oklahoma City, Okla.	324,253	50.8	321.5	270.7
Phoenix, Ariz.	439,170	17.1	187.4	170.3
Houston, Tex.	938,219	160.0	328.1	168.1
Dallas, Tex.	679,684	112.0	279.9	167.9
Mobile, Ala.	202,779	25.4	152.9	127.5
San Diego, Calif.	573,224	99.4	192.4	93.0
Atlanta, Ga.	487,455	36.9	128.2	91.3
San Antonio, Tex.	587,718	69.5	160.5	91.0
El Paso, Tex.	276,687	25.6	114.6	89.0
Newport News, Va.	113,662	4.2	75.0	70.8[a]
Tampa, Fla.	274,970	19.0	85.0	66.0
Tucson, Ariz.	212,892	9.5	70.9	61.4
Lubbock, Tex.	128,691	17.0	75.0	58.0
Columbus, Ohio	471,316	39.4	89.0	49.6
Kansas City, Mo.	475,539	80.6	129.8	49.2
Fort Worth, Tex.	356,268	93.7	140.5	46.8
Milwaukee, Wis.	741,324	50.0	91.1	41.1
Beaumont, Tex.	119,175	31.4	70.8	39.4
San Jose, Calif.	204,196	17.0	54.5	37.5
Charlotte, N.C.	201,564	30.0	64.8	34.8
Amarillo, Tex.	137,969	20.9	54.8	33.9
Greensboro, N.C.	119,574	18.2	48.6	30.4

[a] This increase in area resulted from the consolidation of the cities of Newport
News and Warwick.
SOURCE: Reports by cities as of April of 1950 and 1960 to the Bureau of the
Census for the *1960 Census of Population.*

between 60 and 270 square miles, while another ten gained between
30 and 60 square miles (see Table 30). Annexation of unincorporated
land accounted for practically all the territorial expansion by these
twenty-two units. Newport News, the only major exception, grew by
means of municipal consolidation; it merged with the city of Warwick in 1958.

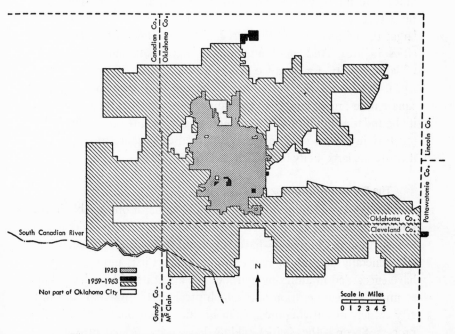

Figure 14.4   The Growth of Oklahoma City, 1958–1963.
Data compiled by Thomas M. Ballentine, Unpublished
Thesis, University of Oklahoma, 1964.

Some of these cities of at least 100,000 made highly spectacular
use of annexation in the decade of the 1950s. Oklahoma City had
the most dramatic annexation activity, one of almost incredible scope
and undertaken, according to its officials, as the only feasible method
by which proper and orderly development of the area could be provided. Fairly large in territory (about 50 square miles) but only
moderate in population (about a quarter of a million) at the start of
the decade, in the following ten years Oklahoma City annexed 270
square miles, a total area larger than that within the boundaries of
Chicago, the nation's second most populous city. Phoenix, with an

area of 17 square miles in 1950, annexed 170 square miles, thus increasing its land size by more than ten times. Both Houston and Dallas similarly annexed approximately 170 square miles.

By 1960, as a result of large-scale annexation, Oklahoma City and Houston, in terms of territorial size, had both surpassed New York City, still by far the largest population center in the United States and the second largest in area in 1950, and stood second and third to Los Angeles. Also by 1960, Dallas had become territorially larger than Chicago, and Phoenix had become one of the ten largest cities in area. And giant annexations have not come to an end. Oklahoma City, for instance, has continued its torrid pace; between April, 1960, and the end of 1963, it annexed approximately 320 square miles, more land than the fantastic total it had brought within its boundaries in all of the previous decade. By this time, it included territory in several counties and contained 641 square miles, making it easily the largest city in area in the United States.

The Favorable Factors

Recent large land acquisitions through annexation—sizable in the sense of adding at least thirty square miles or more in a decade or ten square miles in a year—have largely taken place under conditions not generally present in metropolitan areas. First, most cities that have succeeded in annexing considerable amounts of land have done so under state annexation laws which preclude the residents or property owners in outlying areas from having a controlling voice in the process. Second, these cities seldom have been located near a large number of other incorporated places.

As to the first factor, most large annexations have been completed under a procedure that does not provide the outlying area with a veto power. There are four such procedures: (1) an annexation ordinance enacted by the council of the annexing city; (2) a favorable vote by the electorate of the city undertaking the annexation effort; (3) a special act passed by the state legislature; and (4) an order by a court that has reviewed the annexation proposal.

The relation of these four procedures to the acquisition of large amounts of land is readily apparent from considering a few representative examples. Oklahoma City's unrivaled annexation accomplishments were realized by means of ordinances passed by its city council. The huge annexations by the Texas cities of Dallas, El Paso,

Fort Worth, Houston, and San Antonio also were made through council ordinance action. Kansas City, Missouri, has grown in area through the affirmative responses of its voters who have the legal right to pass on annexation proposals. Most of the land added to Atlanta in recent years was obtained by an act of the Georgia legislature in 1951. And Norfolk, Virginia, was able to annex a total of almost twenty-two square miles in the 1950s because of favorable determinations by a specially constituted annexation court composed of circuit court judges. A number of these actions were of such large size because it was legally possible to annex across county lines, a permission not available in some states.

The existence of considerable unincorporated territory adjacent to the annexing city, the second factor important to large annexations, has been basic to the successful use of these laws. The presence of liberal or equitable processes would have been meaningless to the leading users of annexation in the postwar period if these municipalities had been surrounded by other incorporated places. Under such circumstances these cities in order to expand would have had to follow the stipulations of municipal consolidation laws, which virtually always require the separate consent of the neighboring municipality. Thus, to cite several examples, Oklahoma City, Phoenix, Houston, and Dallas were bordered by ample unincorporated land when they launched their major postwar annexation drives. This condition had long before vanished in many other metropolises where the major cities are in a veritable sea of many municipalities.

Since the highly fortuitous combination of these two circumstances—liberal or equitable annexation laws and sizable adjoining unincorporated land—has generally been necessary in the postwar years to accomplish large annexations, such expansions have been mostly confined to certain types of metropolitan areas, particularly those of small or medium size, such as Oklahoma City, Phoenix, Mobile, San Antonio, Charlotte, and Amarillo. Not one of the principal cities of any metropolitan area of 1,000,000 people or more in 1950 was a leader in the use of annexation in the 1950–1960 period (see Table 30). In contrast, ten of the twelve most populous cities as of 1950 annexed little or no land during this same decade. (Milwaukee and Chicago were the exceptions, absorbing 41.1 and 16.7 square miles, respectively.) In fact, half of them had acquired all or virtually all of their present land by 1900.

Some large annexations have materialized in metropolitan areas that have been undergoing rapid population growth in the postwar years, however. As a consequence, a significant number of the recent annexation leaders—Houston, Dallas, San Diego, Atlanta, Kansas City (Missouri), and Milwaukee—are now located in highly populated metropolitan centers which currently have more than 1,000,000 inhabitants. (Due largely to annexation, the city of Houston had become the seventh most populous city in the United States by 1960, rising from the fourteenth position it had occupied only ten years before.)

But there has been a more important consequence of large annexations in booming metropolises. In some of these SMSA's annexation has been used early and comprehensively enough so that the areas contain far fewer municipalities than most of their older counterparts. The latter generally completed annexations earlier and at a much slower pace, in part because urbanization of land then materialized much less rapidly. Thus some metropolises of medium size at present, such as Phoenix, are likely to become heavily populated but still remain relatively uncluttered in terms of number of municipalities as a result of their sizable land absorptions. A few examples demonstrate the possible long-range importance of some of the recent large annexations. In 1962, the Houston metropolitan area had 25 municipalities; the San Diego area, 11; and Metropolitan Phoenix, 17. The situation in various older large metropolises was distinctly different; for instance, the Cleveland area had 75 municipalities; the St. Louis area, 163; and the Chicago SMSA, 246. The variations are pronounced even when the comparisons are confined to metropolises of approximately the same population size. The Cleveland area has three times as many municipalities as Metropolitan Houston and almost seven times as many as Metropolitan San Diego, even though all three SMSA's are in the one million to two million population range.

Annexation as a Metropolitan Device

Although dramatic, large-scale annexation in recent years has not by itself produced an adequate governmental instrument for dealing with metropolitan-wide services and problems. Such annexation developments have brought an appreciable portion of land within the jurisdiction of a single municipal unit in the metropolis, thus

guaranteeing a unified governmental operation in the entire territory occupied by that city. They also have greatly simplified the
existing governmental system in at least parts of the metropolis by
eradicating numerous non-school special districts that had operated
in the formerly unincorporated territory. At times, however, large
absorptions have produced defensive incorporations, thereby contributing to the proliferation of municipalities.

Large annexations offer no panacea as a metropolitan-wide
device, falling short in two important ways. First, they have taken
place in metropolises already containing a considerable number of
municipalities (and frequently many special districts and one or
more county governments as well). Second, cities that have utilized
this device in a large-scale way still embrace merely a portion, most
often a relatively small part, of the total metropolitan area. These
shortcomings, moreover, are likely to persist in view of the continued
geographical expansion of metropolitanization.

Some metropolises where large annexations have recently occurred are less complicated governmentally than some longer established ones, but generally the difference is one of degree of complexity rather than the absence or presence of complexity. The
Houston, San Diego, and Phoenix areas have fewer municipalities
than many of their older counterparts, but nonetheless they range
between eleven and twenty-five, which are sizable numbers. Before
1900, annexation was repeatedly used to keep all of the urban area
within the boundaries of one municipal government; since 1945 not
a single use of annexation has produced a similar result.

The latter has inevitably been the situation, even under the most
favorable conditions, largely because (1) metropolitanization has
spread rapidly over a widening area, thereby bringing a number of
formerly isolated municipalities within the metropolis, (2) various
unincorporated communities located in the path of metropolitan expansion have incorporated to avert absorption, (3) many of the recent sizable annexations have been completed in metropolitan areas
that already have a high degree of governmental complexity, and (4)
regardless of the total amount of territory annexed by any city in
recent years, the current boundaries of that city are far short of
being the same as the territorial limits of the metropolis.

Since large-scale annexation does not in itself provide a comprehensive metropolitan approach, the establishment of widespread

cooperation among the principal governments of the metropolis (extensive contracting, for instance) or the formation or reconstitution of some area-wide instrumentality such as a new metropolitan government or a renovated county government is still required. This need is evident from the number of metropolitan areas that have completed large annexations but in which studies or actions involving area-wide approaches have later been undertaken—Houston, San Antonio, and Milwaukee are illustrations. At best, therefore, annexation can be viewed as no more than a supplementary or stand-by device.[4]

Despite its inability, even when employed on a large scale, to provide an area-wide approach to services and problems, annexation continues to be a significant device for dealing with certain difficulties in the metropolis. And in all likelihood this will remain true so long as there are unincorporated urban areas in SMSA's, a probable situation in most of them for some time to come. Even the installation of various area-wide approaches to problems—such as extensive cooperation among existing units, the conversion of the county into an urban unit, and the establishment of metropolitan districts and certain other types of metropolitan-level governments— does not eliminate the existence of unincorporated urban territory. Only consolidation of all existing municipalities, a county, and unincorporated sections into a single government wipes out all unincorporated territory and furnishes a unified means of attacking the service and regulatory deficiencies of the unincorporated fringes. Such a plan has seldom gained acceptance.

ANNEXATION AND THE URBAN FRINGE

Annexation now is significant principally as a method of resolving problems concerning a municipality, whether the central city or a

[4] Annexation has been used on a large-scale basis in a variety of situations. For example, it has been utilized (1) after the rejection of a more comprehensive plan (the Knoxville annexation of 1962), (2) as a conscious or unintentional stimulant to prompt acceptance of a comprehensive proposal (Nashville, 1960), and (3) as a corollary to implementation of another approach, as in the annexation of 23.5 square miles to the city of Baton Rouge in 1949 when a modified city-county consolidation plan was adopted in Baton Rouge city and parish (county), and as in the annexation of 82 square miles to Atlanta in 1951 when a redistribution of functions between the city and the county also was made.

suburb, and an adjacent unincorporated urban area. (The latter is often called the urban fringe because it has undergone urban development, has urban needs, and borders but is not part of a municipality.) By annexing the urban fringe, a city assumes jurisdiction over territory that usually has numerous shortcomings in services and controls —shortcomings detrimental to the inhabitants of both the land being absorbed and the city. The existence and the spread of such areas and their problems are major reasons prompting the spurt of annexation activity by municipalities in the postwar years.

Fringe Characteristics and Defects

The magnitude of urban fringe areas and their difficulties is frequently underestimated or largely ignored; yet they contribute some of the most troublesome conditions in the metropolis. A survey of a representative sample of these areas, undertaken in 1960 under the auspices of the International City Managers' Association, conclusively demonstrates their significance and deficiencies.[5] First of all, many such areas are large in population and territory; in fact, although generally less densely settled, a considerable number of them contain more land than the cities they border. Second, virtually all unincorporated urban areas are wholly or predominantly residential, usually medium- or low-income developments, rather than commercial or industrial, and consequently tend to have limited financial resources. Third, their residents frequently resist annexation or incorporation, preferring to choose services cafeteria-style—that is, to select a few public services that meet, sometimes only in part, their most pressing needs from whatever sources are willing to provide them, whether a private company, one or more special districts, the county, or even the adjoining city. Fourth, many urban fringes are seriously deficient in some or even all basic urban-type services and regulatory activities: water supply, garbage collection, streets, sewerage, fire protection, police protection, parks and recreational facilities, zoning controls, and subdivision regulations.

[5] John C. Bollens, *Urban Fringe Areas: Zoning, Subdivision Regulations, and Municipal Services* (Chicago: International City Managers' Association, Management Information Service, September, 1960). A summary of this report is contained in "Urban Fringe Areas—A Persistent Problem," *Public Management*, XLII (October, 1960), 218–221. For an earlier, somewhat similar study, see John C. Bollens, *Municipal Policy on Fringe Areas* (Chicago: International City Managers' Association, Management Information Service, June, 1953).

As a consequence, many unincorporated urban areas are poorly constructed developments with inadequate sanitation, fire hazards, low-level law enforcement, mud-rut streets in incompleted subdivisions, illogical mixtures of land uses, and other basic inadequacies. Many effects of these various deficiencies spill over into the neighboring city and plague its residents. Furthermore, the defects in zoning and subdividing are deleterious to a pleasant living environment. Corrective measures in such instances are exceedingly costly if they are undertaken after unincorporated land is fully developed. And most municipalities are unable to prevent these developments since they either have no extraterritorial power (the authority to exercise their zoning and subdivision controls for a specified distance beyond their limits) in the fringe or can exercise such power in only a limited portion of it. Obviously, then, the existence of urban fringes produces serious problems in many metropolitan areas, even though these defects are not necessarily metropolitan-wide.

Resistance to Annexation

On the surface, annexation seems a relatively simple method of solving the difficulties of many unincorporated urban fringe areas. By absorbing such land, a city can usually supply services and regulations of such a level as to eliminate the inadequacies; but this is easier said than done. The key to understanding the situation lies in the fact that in most cases annexation proposals are matters of local determination in which the fringe often has the advantage. As we saw earlier in this chapter, the authority to initiate an annexation proposal or to vote separately on the proposition, or both, frequently rests with the outlying unincorporated area where residents are often likely to resist the move.

The urban fringe may oppose annexation for a variety of reasons. It may not want to pay city taxes, although in some instances, apparently not realized by its inhabitants, the city tax rate is lower than the total rate of various special districts operating in the unincorporated sections. It may not want to have comprehensive city subdivision and zoning regulations, some residents and property owners claiming such rules would unduly interfere with their freedom and others fearful these regulations would mean personal costs to them. It may take a short-range view by concluding that it gets a sufficient number of services at adequate levels from a

variety of suppliers (a generally erroneous belief). It may fear that
it will not have a potent voice in local affairs, but instead will be
dominated by people who currently control the city government.
Or, finally, it may want to remain "countryfied," to escape being a city or part of one by remaining rural or semirural, even
though it already is, or is fast becoming, urban in appearance and
needs.

In most instances fringe residents or property owners are responsible for the continued unincorporated status of such areas,
but the situation does not always result from the fringe playing the
role of the devil and the city the innocent but powerless angel.
On a number of occasions when the city has occupied the controlling position in a locally-determined annexation question, it has
absorbed only the financially attractive portions of adjacent territory. By completing leap-frog annexations, it has bypassed those
sections that would cost far more to serve than they would return
to the city in revenue. Yet, these are often the sections most in
need of city services, regulations, and corrective actions and the
principal sources of the major problems affecting both the city and
the fringe. Similarly, other municipalities with the power to effectuate annexations have been very reluctant to do so because of the
feeling that territorial expansion will increase their financial obligations. Some of them have begrudgingly resorted to annexation
in the belief that an increased financial burden is a lesser evil than
the continuance of irritating problems at their borders. The effectiveness of annexation as a means of attacking problems in unincorporated urban areas thus is substantially diluted by the frequently
parochial attitude of either the fringe or the city.

The use of annexation in fringe situations is further lessened,
in fact often eliminated, by the availability of easy incorporation
processes. In most states a fringe area containing relatively few
residents can block annexation (as well as consolidation) by incorporating as a separate municipality. When fringe areas possessing
low financial resources and numerous deficiencies become separate
municipalities, their problems remain and even increase in time. At
the other extreme, when wealthy but unincorporated areas bordering a municipality incorporate, they are able to capitalize on all
the benefits of the adjacent city but escape their equitable share
of its burdens.

MUNICIPAL EXPANSION: DIFFERENT APPROACHES

At the midpoint of the twentieth century it seemed as if the urban fringe problem would generally continue to be approached illogically and emotionally, often on the basis of counteracting maneuvers by cities and their adjacent unincorporated areas. During the first half of this century, Virginia was the only state to adopt and use a distinctly improved process for adjusting municipal boundaries. In 1904, its legislature provided for judicial determination of proposals calling for the annexation of unincorporated territory or the consolidation of a city (or a town) and another town. (In Virginia, towns usually have fewer than 5000 people.) Moreover, the legislature prescribed standards, although in the very general terms of "the necessity for and the expediency of" the proposal, that had to be followed by the annexation court, composed of three circuit court judges and specially organized to consider a particular boundary adjustment proposition.[6]

The Virginia Model

The Virginia procedure of determination by an impartial body rather than by either a city or a fringe has received wide acclaim both inside and outside the state. Some observers have complained about one element of the procedure—the use of circuit court judges instead of persons possessing special technical competence—or have bemoaned the absence of proposed incorporations from the purview of the review body. However, virtually all observers have vigorously supported the basic idea of the plan, namely, the vesting of power to decide annexation and municipal consolidation issues in an impartial body with authority to sift the evidence and make its judgments to approve, modify, or deny the proposals on the basis of

[6] For detailed considerations of the judicial determination process in Virginia, see John C. Bollens, *The States and the Metropolitan Problem* (Chicago: Council of State Governments, 1956), pp. 40–49, and Chester W. Bain, "Recent Developments in the Virginia Annexation System," *Virginia Law Review*, 46 (June, 1960), 1023–1035. In 1962, a general moratorium was declared on annexations and consolidations in Virginia, pending a study by the Virginia Advisory Legislative Council. The temporarily suspended procedures were reactivated in 1964 when the state legislature rejected the Council's recommendations.

prescribed standards and relevant facts.[7] Despite the long-time praise of the Virginia procedure, not even its basic concept was transplanted to and placed in general use in any other state for many years.

Anti-Incorporation Laws

Breakthroughs in methods of dealing with urban fringe areas (and to a lesser extent, with those various small municipalities that are uneconomic and functionally inept) came on two fronts around 1960: one involving restrictions on incorporation, the other review of incorporation and annexation proposals and the establishment of standards for evaluating them. These changes, which are substantial and encouraging departures from the long-established haphazard practices, are still exceptions; up to now they have been adopted by only a limited number of states, but the prospect that one or both of them will spread is promising.[8]

The first change relates to the prohibition or imposition of strong controls on the creation of incorporated places in the vicinity of existing municipal governments. In 1961, Arizona, Idaho, North Carolina, Nebraska, and New Mexico all passed state legislation of this type, appropriately termed "anti-incorporation" laws. Several others, including Georgia, Ohio, and Wyoming followed suit in 1963.[9] The acts differ in particulars, but they all contain the significant idea of creating around a municipality a buffer zone in which additional incorporations cannot take place under any circumstances or only if the existing municipality consents to the proposed in-

[7] A factor complicating the use of the procedure in Virginia, but non-existent in other states, is the practice of automatically separating a city, when it attains a population of 5000, from the county (city-county separation). Consequently, territory awarded to a city by an annexation court ceases to be part of the adjoining county; in time, through a number of such actions, only a "rump" county without financial resources to be a viable government may remain, although an annexation court may decide it is too large to be annexed.

[8] Annexation laws, for example, continue to show great diversity. For a recent review, see Frank S. Sengstock, *Annexation: A Solution to the Metropolitan Area Problem* (Ann Arbor: University of Michigan Law School Legislative Research Center, 1960), pp. 9–41. This publication was prepared while the breakthroughs in annexation procedures were being made and thus includes only some of them.

[9] These laws somewhat parallel the legislation enacted in Indiana in 1953, but which applies only to the Indianapolis area; in contrast, all of the more recent laws are of statewide application.

corporation or refuses to annex the territory when the latter makes such a request. (Frequently the zone is larger for the more populous municipalities.)

The Arizona anti-incorporation law is typical. No territory within three miles of the boundary of a city or town of less than 5000 population or within six miles of the official limits of a more populous municipal government may incorporate as a separate municipality, unless one of two conditions develops. One, the governing body of the nearby municipal government adopts a resolution approving the proposed incorporation. Two, the municipality does not respond affirmatively to a petition for annexation from an unincorporated fringe area.

Texas adopted a similar, but stronger law in 1963. The legislation is comparable to some of the anti-incorporation laws recently passed elsewhere; it established a zone around each city, with the width of the band varying with the population of the city (a five-mile zone for cities of at least 100,000 population is the largest) and prohibited any further incorporations without the city's approval or unless it declines to annex part or all of the territory in the zone that so desires. But the Texas law goes beyond any of the recent anti-incorporation laws in other states by stipulating that a city may regulate the subdivision of land in the zone. This provision endows the city with extraterritorial power to prevent undesirable physical developments in the unincorporated area.

Several aspects of this anti-incorporation trend deserve explanation. First, its value is limited to the present and the future; none of the laws has a retroactive effect. Any municipalities already located in such a zone continue to function as separate governments unless the regular legal channels of municipal consolidation are successfully employed. These laws, therefore, are preventive rather than remedial; their objective is to stop the further proliferation of municipal governments, not to reduce the existing total through consolidations. Second, only some of the anti-incorporation laws place any requirement on municipalities to annex part or all of the "frozen" unincorporated territory, and those that do require annexation only when the fringe is the initiator. At that time, the municipality must annex or allow incorporation to proceed. (In practice, in some of the states, particularly those with liberal annexation procedures, the municipalities are annexing the reserved land.) A third aspect is that the anti-incorporation development so far has not generally taken hold in states having the heaviest concentrations of population in metropolitan or urban areas. Fourth and finally, the anti-incorporation plan, if supported by adequate annexation procedures, will do much in particular states to eliminate unincorporated fringe areas and their problems.[10] However, the process established by the plan favors the municipalities and therefore it does not work impartially or necessarily equitably.

Review and Standards

The second recent breakthrough, one which is a more comprehensive and more impartial process than the anti-incorporation approach, has two basic elements: review of proposed incorporations and annexations (and in two states, proposed municipal consolidations as well) by an administrative agency or official endowed with quasi-judicial powers; and use of standards for evaluating and making determinations about the proposal. Alaska, California, Minnesota, Washington, and Wisconsin enacted laws of this type between 1959 and 1963. This change is similar in some important respects to the Virginia practice inaugurated in 1904. Both feature a disinterested party making a determination about a boundary question in the light of specified criteria. However, while in Virginia a few members of the regular judiciary are specially convened to consider one matter, in the other states the review and determination are made by administrative agencies or officials possessing quasi-judicial powers and, except in Washington, having regular and continuing responsibilities along these lines.

Although differing in certain major ways, the process of review and determination recently established in various states has common characteristics. A commission is the usual form of organization; it may be entirely or largely a state agency, a mixed state-local body, or a strictly local group. Both municipal incorporations and annexations with one exception (annexation only in Washington) are within the purview of the agency or individual. The Alaska and Minnesota commissions also can consider municipal consolidations,

---

[10] The Texas law, for one, recognizes that fringes tend to re-emerge beyond municipal boundaries despite the extension of the city limits through municipal annexation. The legislation specifies that the no-incorporation zone expands outward as the city increases territorially.

the latter only in metropolitan areas. The California commissions —one exists in each county—cannot consider such consolidations, but they can review the proposed formation of non-school special districts and proposed annexations by districts. The process of review normally involves approval or disapproval of proposals made to the commission. Disapproval is final and terminates the progress of the proposal. Commission approval, on the other hand, is generally a screening action, one permitting the matter to proceed to a popular vote. (In some states the commission may modify or attach conditions to a proposal before approving it.)

The review procedure includes standards that must be applied to each proposition before a decision is reached. They tend to be of a general nature, broad guidelines allowing the commission wide discretion. For example, the commissions in California must consider three sets of factors and may include others they deem relevant. The first consists of total population and density, land area and uses, per capita assessed valuation, topographical features, proximity to other populated areas, and the likelihood of significant growth in the area and in adjacent incorporated and unincorporated land during the next ten years. The second relates to the need for organized community services and the present cost and adequacy of, and probable future needs for, governmental services and controls in the area. And the third is concerned with the probable effects of the proposed action and alternative actions on the area and on adjacent areas, on mutual social and economic interests, and on the local governmental structure of the county.[11]

Review of proposed new local governments and boundary changes by a disinterested party can be an important step away from the irrationality of the older practices. The late acceptance of the idea in the metropolitan age and the severe limitations usually placed on the review agency—inability to initiate proposals, exclusion of municipal consolidations from its jurisdiction, and lack of

[11] Analyses of the procedures, including the standards utilized, in states and several foreign nations employing such a process are made in Stanley Scott, Lewis Keller, and John C. Bollens, *Local Governmental Boundaries and Areas: New Policies for California* (Berkeley: University of California Bureau of Public Administration, 1961). The California and Washington laws were passed later and the California legislation used the standards recommended in this study. North Carolina also recently enacted standards for annexation, but it has no review commission; its municipalities have unilateral annexing power.

authority to put its affirmative decisions into effect—may be decried. Even so, if properly implemented, the device can still have profound effects in view of the expected continued population growth in metropolitan and urban areas.[12]

CITY–COUNTY CONSOLIDATION

City-county consolidation, which is generally a broader one-government approach than either municipal annexation or municipal consolidation, has been a subject of discussion for many years. The process usually consists of the complete or substantial merger of a county government with the principal city or all municipalities in the county. (The retention of the county government as a separate legal entity for limited purposes, a situation that persisted in the Philadelphia area for more than a century, constitutes substantial rather than complete city-county consolidation.) There are variations of this common pattern; on some occasions more than one county government is involved or school districts or other special districts are also parts of the consolidation proposal.[13]

Notwithstanding widespread consideration and advocacy, city-

[12] The Local Boundary Commission in Alaska has broader jurisdiction than any of the other agencies and its decisions are not referred to the local voters. It can initiate actions, consider all types of local boundary changes—annexations, incorporations, and consolidations, including the merger of a district with a city—and its recommendations in support of change automatically go into effect unless disapproved by a resolution adopted by both houses of the state legislature.

[13] Distinct from, but often confused with, city-county consolidation is another process of area adjustment, city-county separation. Separation features the detachment of a municipality, sometimes after its territorial enlargement, from the remainder of the county. The separated government then performs both municipal and county functions, although not necessarily all of the latter. A contributor to public confusion over the two processes is the legal identification of some separated cities, Denver and San Francisco for example, as city-counties. City-county separation is an act of withdrawal, and therefore cannot be currently viewed as a metropolitan approach. Except in Virginia, where separation automatically occurs in every city when it reaches a population of 5000, all other city-county separations are of ancient vintage: Baltimore (1851), San Francisco (1856), St. Louis (1876), and Denver (1902). Many examples of various types of governmental reorganization in metropolitan areas are analyzed in Paul Studenski, *The Government of Metropolitan Areas in the United States* (New York: National Municipal League, 1930), in Victor Jones, *Metropolitan Government* (Chicago: University of Chicago Press, 1942), and in Jones' essay, which is Part IV in Coleman Woodbury (ed.), *The Future of Cities and Urban Redevelopment* (Chicago: University of Chicago Press, 1953).

county consolidation has seldom been put into effect. Indeed, only six areas, plus several localities in Virginia, function under this type of governmental reorganization.[14] Four of them—New Orleans (1813), Boston (1821), Philadelphia (1854), and New York (1898) —antedate the twentieth century; consequently, for many years of the present century this type of reorganization was generally regarded as a matter of historical record. "Often proposed, never adopted" might well have been the consolidation theme in the early decades of this century. The installation of the system in more recent years in the Baton Rouge and Nashville areas, however, has given renewed encouragement to supporters of consolidation elsewhere.

The Pre-1900 Consolidations

A significant common thread runs through the four city-county consolidations of the pre-1900 era: all were accomplished by state legislative acts, not by affirmative verdicts of the local voters. Moreover, all of them originally were not complete consolidations since a remnant county government or at least a skeletal county official-dom continued to operate apart from the consolidated government. The New Orleans and Boston consolidations each involved only one county (called parish in Louisiana) and one city; the Philadelphia and New York consolidations, on the other hand, merged many local governments and also brought public education into the new system. The New York plan was the only one of an inter-county nature, the city's boundaries being extended to embrace four counties, one of which (New York County) was later divided into two counties. The New York consolidation also was unique in retaining and reconstituting local areas, which were renamed boroughs, and granting them several administrative functions (minor public works, for instance) and membership on a major policy agency of the consolidated government (the Board of Estimate, which exercises a large share of the city's legislative authority).[15]

[14] A number of city-county consolidations have taken place in Virginia—for instance, in the Lower Peninsula in 1952 and in the Virginia Beach and South Norfolk areas in 1962. Such actions usually have grown out of a unique practice in that state which removes land annexed by a city from the jurisdiction of a county.

[15] The boroughs have no legislative powers, however, and New York is not therefore an example of a two-level or federal governmental system.

These four early city-county consolidations stand as impressive governmental changes, particularly since each of the principal affected cities is the hub of a highly important metropolis. (This is true despite the fact that the territorial limits of the metropolis now extend far beyond the consolidation's original boundaries, which have been altered little or not at all since their inception.) The New York reorganization is especially impressive because even in 1898 the city was preeminent among American urban centers in population and financial importance.

The Unproductive Years

The period from 1900 to the end of World War II was characterized by considerable interest in city-county consolidation and by its supporters' inability to put it into operation in any metropolis in the United States. These were years of growth of metropolitan areas and their number of incorporated suburbs. These developments, moreover, fostered stronger resistance by suburbanites to the absorption of their communities into a unified government. Arguments that consolidation would result in greater efficiency, economy, and equity and would establish a government capable of dealing with area-wide problems left these people unpersuaded. Instead they continued to insist on local autonomy, which enabled them to control local zoning and local financial resources. Many also expressed fear that they would not have sufficient access to officials in a larger government, which might be remote and indifferent to important local needs and viewpoints.

In this setting of strong resistance, the advocates of city-county consolidation waged uphill and totally unsuccessful battles in many metropolises up to 1945. In brief, formidable legal barriers were constructed and proved insurmountable. Many states added municipal home rule provisions to their constitutions, thus prohibiting their legislative bodies from passing laws that would produce city-county consolidation. In other states, where the state legislatures still had this authority, they were disinclined to use it, often because of the opposition of rural and suburban forces. Thus, the avenue used in the four consolidations completed in the nineteenth century —state legislative action—was effectively sealed off.

To achieve consolidation, two legal hurdles had to be overcome: (1) passage of a state constitutional amendment or legislative enabling act authorizing metropolitan areas to adopt city-county consolidation, and (2) approval of the proposal by the local voters, which usually involved obtaining at least two and occasionally more local majorities: the central city and the remainder of the county. Most consolidation efforts in the 1900–1945 period fell before the first hurdle. This was true in King County (Seattle) in 1923, Cuyahoga County (Cleveland) in 1925, Multnomah County (Portland, Oregon) in 1927, the Boston area in 1931, Jackson County (Kansas City, Missouri) in 1933, Jefferson County (Birmingham) in 1936, and Jefferson County (Louisville), Wyandotte County (Kansas City, Kansas), and Milwaukee County (Milwaukee) in 1937. Only three city-county proposals reached the stage of local voter consideration and all were defeated: St. Louis-St. Louis County, 1926; Macon-Bibb County, Georgia, 1933; and Jacksonville-Duval County, 1935.

Success in Baton Rouge

In the face of the long list of unproductive efforts which seemingly had brought permanent oblivion to city-county consolidation, adoption of this form of reorganization by Baton Rouge and East Baton Rouge Parish (County) in 1947 came as a surprise. A combination of highly fortuitous factors, however, greatly aided its adoption in this relatively lightly populated area, which was not then, but is now, of metropolitan status. First, it was easy to get proposed constitutional amendments of strictly local application on the ballot in Louisiana, unless the local legislative delegation opposed them. In this case, legislators from the Baton Rouge area had little knowledge of the proposed constitutional amendment to permit a county home rule charter to be written for that area. Not realizing the effect the proposal could have on the local political organization and desiring to please the local industries which favored the amendment, they recommended its submission to the state electorate.[16]

Second, unlike the people in many other states, Louisiana voters are accustomed to repeatedly amending their state constitution. Accordingly, it was not surprising when the amendment was ap-

---

[16] Thomas H. Reed, "Progress in Metropolitan Integration," *Public Administration Review*, IX (Winter, 1949), 8. An analysis of the reorganization a number of years after its effectuation is contained in William C. Havard and Floyd C. Corty, *Rural-Urban Consolidation: The Merger of Governments in the Baton Rouge Area* (Baton Rouge: Louisiana State University Press, 1964).

proved by a margin of almost four to one in 1946. Third, the charter board specified in the amendment was made up of representatives of a number of organizations, including the president of the state university, who could not be controlled by the local political machine. Six of the nine votes on the board were therefore consistently cast in favor of city-county consolidation and improved governmental structure and processes. Four, the plan of government written into the charter needed to obtain only a single parish-wide majority to be adopted. It acquired that majority in 1947 by the narrow margin of 307 votes of approximately 14,000 cast, with only about one-third of the electorate participating.

The Baton Rouge-East Baton Rouge Parish plan involved only partial consolidation; it provided for retention of both the city and parish governments and preservation of two small municipalities, which were prohibited, however, from further expansion of their boundaries. A prominent innovation of the plan was the interlocking of the city and parish governments. The seven members of the city council and two other persons elected from the rural area constitute the parish council. The mayor-president, who serves as the chief administrator of both governments, presides over both councils, but has no vote, and is elected on a parish-wide basis. He appoints the finance director, personnel administrator, public works director, and purchasing agent, all of whom serve both the city and the parish. He also selects the police and fire chiefs, who function only in the city. The parish council appoints the attorney, clerk, and treasurer, who are both city and parish officials. The city and the parish share equally in the cost of operating the finance department. Thus, the two governments are integrated at many key points, although there continue to be separate governing bodies and separate budgets and accounting for city and parish funds; moreover, a number of officials and boards continue to have independent status.

A second innovation of the Baton Rouge plan was the establishment of taxing and service zones throughout the consolidated area. The parish was divided into three types of zones or areas: urban, industrial, and rural. Under the charter, the boundaries of Baton Rouge were extended to the limits of the urban area, thus increasing the territory of the city from about six square miles to thirty square miles and its population from about 35,000 to more than 100,000. The city government provides police and fire protection, garbage and refuse collection and disposal, street lighting, traffic regulation, sewerage, and inspectional services in the urban area, which is subject to both city and parish taxes. (Uniform parish taxes are also levied in the rural zone and the two industrial zones.)

Bridges, highways, streets, sidewalks, and airports are provided on a parish-wide basis by the public works department, which serves both the city and the parish, and are financed by parish taxes. City-type services needed in the industrial areas are provided by the industries at their own expense. The rural zone cannot receive city-type services (except the services of the sheriff's department) unless special taxing districts are established there by the parish council to pay for them. Built-up, adjacent portions of the rural zone can be annexed to the urban area with the consent of a majority of the owners of the affected property and the city council. No further incorporations can take place in the parish. The idea of creating tax and service differentials on the basis of differing needs and land use development instilled an important degree of flexibility into the city-county approach that had previously been lacking. The idea did not go unnoticed elsewhere.

Interest in city-county consolidation showed marked acceleration in the 1950s and early 1960s, but the movement failed to register another success until 1962. During this time, consolidation proposals were submitted to a local vote in a considerable number of metropolises and were rejected (see Table 31). With the exception of the St. Louis area, all such attempts were concerned with medium- and small-sized metropolises, predominantly in the South. Practically all of them required dual majorities—one in the principal city, the other in the remainder of the county. In most of them, the proposition obtained the necessary majority in the former, but failed to do so in the outlying area. However, the plan did not acquire either majority in the Memphis or Columbus, Georgia, areas. This may indicate a growing resistance to consolidation by central cities, long the main sources of support for the idea.[17] In addition, most consolidation plans provided for the creation of taxing and service

---

[17] Unlike a similar reorganization proposition of 1926 which required dual local approval, the St. Louis area consolidation effort of 1962 was attempted by means of a state constitutional amendment. The proposal lost by three-to-one in the state, by six-to-five in St. Louis, and by almost four-to-one in St. Louis County. The election results represent another example of recent opposition by a central city to the idea of complete city-county merger.

zones (usually a county-wide general services zone and an urban zone) in the consolidated city-county.

TABLE 31

Voter Defeats of City-County Consolidation,
Since 1950[a]

YEAR	AREA
1950	Newport News–Warwick County–Elizabeth City County, Virginia
1953	Miami–Dade County, Florida
1958	Nashville–Davidson County, Tennessee
1959	Albuquerque–Bernalillo County, New Mexico
	Knoxville–Knox County, Tennessee
1960	Macon–Bibb County, Georgia
1961	Durham–Durham County, North Carolina
	Richmond–Henrico County, Virginia
1962	Columbus–Muscogee County, Georgia
	Memphis–Shelby County, Tennessee
	St. Louis–St. Louis County, Missouri
1964	Chattanooga–Hamilton County, Tennessee

[a] Similar proposals were defeated earlier in two of these areas: in St. Louis–St. Louis County and Macon–Bibb County in 1926 and 1933, respectively.

Victory in Nashville

The fifteen-year drought for adoption of city-county consolidation ended in 1962 in the Nashville–Davidson County area. It thus terminated in a locality where only four years before a similar plan had been rejected by the suburban voters. The new plan needed and obtained dual majorities. The proposal received almost as large a proportion of affirmative votes in the outlying areas as in the core city; four years earlier, the comparable proposition had passed decisively in Nashville, but had garnered only 42 percent of the tallies in the remainder of the county.[18]

The most prominent feature of the Nashville–Davidson County consolidation is the two district (or zone) arrangement. One part

[18] Nashville's annexation of approximately fifty square miles between the two consolidation efforts was a decisive factor in the success of the second attempt. A discussion of the various reasons for the change of attitude by many suburbanites (as well as by the mayor of the central city) is contained in Chapter 16.

is an expandable urban services district, consisting initially of only the city of Nashville. The entire county, including Nashville, is in the general services district in which all residents receive and pay for area-wide services. Six suburban municipalities, which in total contained only 16,000 people at the time of the consolidation, are in the general services district and are therefore subject to the jurisdiction of the metropolitan countywide government for area-wide services and controls. These municipalities remain outside the urban services district, which may be expanded by the metropolitan government, however, whenever areas need urban services.

Functions performed by the metropolitan government and financed only in the urban services district include fire protection, intensified police protection, sewage disposal, water supply, and street lighting and street cleaning. Functions performed by the metropolitan government and financed on an area-wide basis, that is, in the general services district, include schools, public health, police, courts, public welfare, public housing, urban renewal, streets and roads, traffic, transit, library, refuse disposal, and electrical, building, plumbing, and housing codes. An elective metropolitan county mayor and an elected forty-member metropolitan county council, five at large and thirty-five from districts, are central organizational features. At the time of the consolidation, the area contained 533 square miles and approximately 415,000 inhabitants.[19]

SCHOOL DISTRICT CONSOLIDATION

The large amount of school district consolidation (or reorganization or redistricting, as many professional educators prefer to call it) in the last several decades stands in pronounced contrast to the handful of city-county and municipal consolidations accomplished in the same period. School districts continued their long-time trend

[19] When passed in 1957, the Tennessee enabling legislation permitting the drafting of city-county consolidation charters applied only to the more populous counties. In 1963, the law was revised to extend the authorization to all counties. Also in 1963, the privately-financed Research and Planning Council of San Antonio recommended city-county consolidation for San Antonio and Bexar County; one of its most prominent features was its use of the interlocking governments idea of the Baton Rouge consolidation of 1947: the members of the council of the central city also serving on the governing body of the county. San Antonio Planning and Research Council, *Bold Plan for Bexar County* (San Antonio: 1963).

of rapid proliferation until the early 1930s; by 1932, they had reached the staggering total of approximately 127,000, making up almost three-fourths of the governmental units in the nation. Since then, the nationwide total has steadily decreased, with the rate of consolidation accelerating noticeably in the years since World War II. By 1962, the number had dropped to 34,678, less than one-third of the total of thirty years before, and represented less than two-fifths of all governments.

School district consolidations have been taking place in many metropolitan areas, but generally at a slower pace than in rural America. In 1962 the number of school districts in metropolitan areas was 6004. Granting the existence of a great overabundance of school districts at the time the movement got under way and the continuance of still far too many of them according to most observers, this development constitutes the first sizable use of consolidation in the governmental history of the United States. And it has been occurring at a time when various other types of governments are continuing to grow in number.

Concern by the States

Why has the consolidation of school districts so often materialized? What elements have been present that have been lacking in city-county or municipal consolidation and even in other forms of reorganization of general local governments? Two factors stand out as contributing most to the success of the school district consolidation movement. One has been recognition by many state legislatures of the need to foster such reorganization, a recognition prompted by the spiraling proportion of school support obtained from the states since the 1930s. The other has been the increased advocacy of the device by many professional educators and lay educational leaders who are convinced of the relationship between this kind of reform and higher quality education.

Many state legislatures have used two means to prompt school district consolidations. One, they have made major changes in the school reorganization laws, which had required local initiation of a proposal and usually majority consent of the voters in each affected district. Two, they have made financial grants available to districts that merge, thus supplying an adequate incentive, an enticing carrot on the end of a stick, as numerous educators have termed it.

The consolidation legislation has taken various forms, some quite drastic. In a number of instances, existing county boards of education or specially constituted county school reorganization committees have been empowered to order a merger without a local popular vote. In others the law has specified that on a certain date all school districts (or all except those in particular large municipalities or those not operating schools or not containing a specific number of students) would be combined into one school district. In still other states, the legislation has called for study and recommendations in each county by the county board of education or a special countywide committee, approval or disapproval of the plans by the state board of education, the state school superintendent, or a special state commission, and submission of the proposals to the voters in the affected districts. However, many laws of this type, called the comprehensive-planned-permissive approach, do not require majority consent of the voters of each affected district for the proposal to pass. For example, a number of them simply require a single, overall majority in the area of the proposed district, a far easier requirement to meet. (Many consolidations, it should be pointed out, have involved the simultaneous merger of more than two school districts.)[20]

Professional and Lay Leadership

Professional and lay leadership in school district reorganization has been exhibited in several ways. Strong support has been given to the passage of new state consolidation laws, including often the providing of financial incentives. Professional educators, working through their state associations, have been particularly effective in this regard. Both the professionals and private leaders have taken on major roles in implementing the legislation through activities in regular and special state and county education agencies. In brief, the certainty of public officials (state legislators and educators in this instance), of private leaders, and of seemingly a fairly large segment of the general public that school district consolidations produce better service and more economic use of public funds accounts in large part for the widespread acceptance of this type of merger.

[20] For a more detailed analysis of the techniques of school district consolidation, see John C. Bollens, *Special District Governments in the United States* (Berkeley and Los Angeles: University of California Press, 1957), pp. 197–227.

The lack of a comparable conviction by similar elements, on the other hand, helps substantially to explain the long-time slow rate of municipal and city-county consolidations.

THE ONE–GOVERNMENT APPROACH: THE FUTURE

The expected continuance of urban and metropolitan growth seemingly assures the continued annexation of unincorporated land by many municipalities. In general, the device will be used in metropolitan areas, particularly to eliminate the problems of urban fringes, but it will not be used as a means of creating a metropolitan government. The prevalence of incorporated places in most metropolises precludes annexation on a scale that would be necessary to produce such a government. The recent establishment in a few states of annexation-incorporation review commissions furnishes hope that these boundary questions will be decided more rationally than in the past and with proper attention to their probable effects on the entire metropolis. If these commissions carry out their responsibilities impartially, their powers will probably be increased to include the authority at least to initiate proposals and conceivably to effectuate annexations and incorporations without a local popular vote. And if the commission idea is successful, it will spread to other states. It is even possible that in time some commissions may be granted the authority to order the consolidation of very small, financially poor municipalities.

In the immediate decades ahead, it is very unlikely that local boundary commissions will be permitted to order city-county consolidations, although some school reorganization agencies already have comparable power. There is a growing feeling that a number of functions in the metropolis are of an area-wide nature (and therefore in some instances should be handled by an area-wide government), but there is also a strong belief, often valid, that various functions are not of such a nature and therefore can best be performed by local governments smaller in territory than the total metropolitan area. There may be too many local governments in the metropolis, but this does not mean they should all be replaced by a single government performing both metropolitan and local services. As a consequence, city-county consolidations almost certainly will continue to be slow in coming and confined largely to small and medium-sized metropolises that are not governmentally complex. Most, if not all, of those that materialize will encompass both urban and rural land and will feature tax and service zones. Furthermore, city-county consolidation is almost always a one-county concept, both in legal authorizations and proposals, but more and more metropolises are becoming intercounty, even interstate. Many proponents of this form of reorganization do not believe it should be applied in situations involving two or more large counties, admitting that a consolidated local government should not cover so much territory. And apparently no one has ever proposed the application of the consolidation idea to an interstate metropolitan area, a proposition that would be fraught with many legal problems.

Conversely, school district consolidation will persist. Public officials and private leaders are caught in the swirl of growing school enrollments and costs and of dealing with a government performing a single but crucial function, thus excluding the possibility, as in the case of municipalities, of establishing an area-wide government to assume some of their activities, but not all of them. They therefore will probably move ahead with the merger of more school districts. There is, however, mounting support in various states for some type of area-wide financial equalization as a countermove to school district merger.

In general, the one-government approach to area-wide problems has passed its heyday, although it will retain its vigor in many situations concerning only part of the metropolis; the latter is apparent in both municipal annexation and school district consolidation. But in terms of the entire metropolitan area, the one-government approach is almost certain to be bypassed increasingly in favor of other techniques.

CHAPTER 15

The Two-Level Approach: Districts, Comprehensive Urban County Plan, and Federation

THERE IS widespread admission of the seriousness of area-wide service problems and of the need to solve them. At the same time, many people are convinced that neither the one-government approach (large-scale annexation and city-county consolidation) nor the piecemeal, cooperative method is the most satisfactory way to deal with the difficulties. Opposition to the one-government concept is particularly formidable, based largely on the prevalent notion that local governmental functions in the metropolis, in contrast to area-wide needs, should be handled by various local units rather than a single, territorially larger government. Similarly, although piecemeal transfers of functions and voluntary cooperative efforts are undergoing expanded use, many observers regard them as incapable of producing sufficiently comprehensive and prompt results. As a consequence of the negative attitude toward these two opposite approaches, another type of governmental reorganization has received increased advocacy and use: the two-level or federal concept. Under this plan, area-wide functions—one or many—are allotted to area-wide governments while local functions remain with local units, thus creating a metropolitan-local system.

As we have seen in the case of both other types, the two-level arrangement also takes various forms. The first is the metropolitan district, a governmental unit usually encompassing a substantial part or all of the metropolis but generally authorized to perform only one function or a few closely related activities of a metropolitan nature. The second is the comprehensive urban county plan, which calls for the simultaneous transfer of selected functions from municipalities (and at times from other local units) to the county government. The third is federation, which features the establishment of a new area-wide government (customarily replacing the existing county government if the metropolis covers only one county) that is assigned numerous responsibilities. In brief, the two-level arrangement in its varied forms represents a halfway house between the extremes of very drastic and very moderate techniques of attacking metropolitan problems. It seeks to preserve much of the existing governmental system of the metropolis while making only those modifications deemed necessary to combat serious area-wide difficulties.

METROPOLITAN DISTRICTS

Metropolitan district governments represent the mildest variation of the two-level approach with respect to their functional nature, but not their territorial scope. In terms of the latter, each of them generally includes the entire metropolis or a major part of it, such as the central city and the heavily populated suburbs.[1] Some even extend far beyond the confines of the metropolis and are in fact regional governments. In terms of functions, however, such districts are usually limited to a single service or a very small number of

[1] A few metropolitan districts (some bridge districts, for instance) do not have defined areas or they have within their official boundaries only the small amount of land on which their facilities have been built. Comprehensive analyses of metropolitan districts will be found in John C. Bollens, *Special District Governments in the United States* (Berkeley and Los Angeles: University of California Press, 1957) and Max A. Pock, *Independent Special Districts: A Solution to the Metropolitan Area Problem* (Ann Arbor: University of Michigan Law School Legislative Research Center, 1962). Also see Robert W. Tobin, "The Metropolitan Special District: Inter-county Metropolitan Government of Tomorrow," *University of Miami Law Review*, XIV (Spring, 1960), 333–354.

activities. Therefore, although such entities are area-wide in territorial scope (and the only metropolitan governments in existence in many localities), they are units of strictly limited purpose.

Metropolitan districts have become common in urban areas. Although a few were established before the present century (one in the Philadelphia area as early as 1790), they are chiefly a post-World War I development that has accelerated in the years since World War II. Approximately 100 districts of this type are now in operation; they are active in about one-fourth of the SMSA's and particularly prevalent in the larger metropolises of 500,000 or more. Found in all sections of the nation, they are most numerous in California, Illinois, Ohio, and Texas.[2]

Many Functions and Accomplishments

Taken altogether, metropolitan districts perform a wide range of service activities. Providing port facilities and sewage disposal are easily the most frequent functions, followed by airports, mass transit, parks, public housing, and water supply. Others less common are air and water pollution control, bridge construction and maintenance, electricity, flood control, hospital facilities and care, and libraries. Still others include insect pest control, public health, transport terminal facilities, and tunnel construction and maintenance. Strangely enough, however, certain functions considered by many people to be definitely metropolitan in character—law enforcement in particular—are not provided by any metropolitan districts.

The record of accomplishment of metropolitan district governments is impressive, despite their functional restrictiveness. In total, they have done much to satisfy or alleviate some of the most pressing area-wide needs of the metropolises they serve. A sampling of their significant activities, often unrecognized as district operations by most of the citizenry where they function, is illuminating. The

[2] There are many district governments other than metropolitan districts in the metropolis. School districts and urban fringe districts (special units confined to providing services to unincorporated urban areas) are the most prominent examples; they make up a large portion of the district governments in metropolitan areas. A relatively few of the former are of metropolitan territorial size, but they are not included in this chapter. Also, metropolitan districts are governmental units and should not be confused with state and municipal authorities and dependent districts that are adjuncts of state and local governments.

Port of New York Authority runs airports, port facilities, bridges, tunnels, and bus, motor truck, and railroad freight terminals. The Chicago Transit Authority and the Bi-State Development Agency (St. Louis area) operate mass transit systems and the latter also owns port facilities; the Cleveland Metropolitan Park District, the Huron-Clinton Metropolitan Authority (Detroit area) and the East

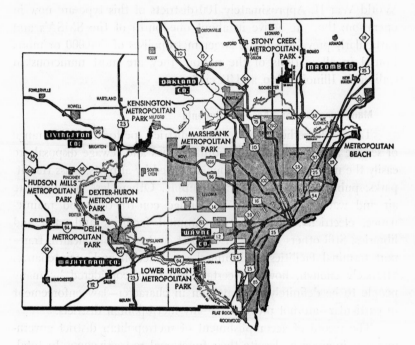

Figure 15.1   The Huron-Clinton Metropolitan Authority, 1960. From the *Eleventh Biennial Report,* Huron-Clinton Metropolitan Authority, Detroit, Mich., 1963, p. 29.

Bay Regional Park District (San Francisco Bay area) provide regional parks; and the Metropolitan Sanitary District of Greater Chicago, the Metropolitan St. Louis Sewer District, and the Municipality of Metropolitan Seattle (a district government) handle sewage disposal. The Metropolitan Water District of Southern California is the wholesale supplier of water (after transporting it hundreds of miles from the Colorado River) to a large number of cities and other water agencies in six southern California counties.

And soon the Bay Area Rapid Transit District (San Francisco Bay area) will be operating an extensive rapid transit system, the first completely new dual-rail system established in the nation in nearly fifty years.

The magnitude of their personnel and finances gives even greater significance to metropolitan districts and offers a strong reason why these big governments should receive close and continuing public attention. The Port of New York Authority, for instance, has more long-term outstanding debt than most state governments, and the Chicago Transit Authority has both more employees and more annual revenue than a number of state governments.

Facilitating Factors

The mildness of the metropolitan district device, as exemplified by the usual single-function restriction, has certainly been a factor facilitating its widespread use for reform. Another prompting factor is that most such districts are not given the power to tax or are severely limited as to the amount of tax they can levy. A large number must rely wholly or mainly on service charges, tolls, and rents and on revenue bonds whose principal and interest must be paid from operating funds. Although such limited financial authority makes these districts more palatable to taxpayers, it restricts the kinds of activities in which they can successfully engage. Certain area-wide problems such as air pollution control cannot be handled on a profit-making basis; consequently, such difficulties will remain outside the orbit of metropolitan districts that lack the taxing power or have only minor access to it.

Another factor facilitating the spread of metropolitan districts is the liberal nature of most legal provisions authorizing their formation. Many of these units have been established under state laws requiring only a single area-wide popular majority, a process uncommon to most other reorganization methods. Many others have been created without any popular vote at all, a procedure totally unknown in the current century in connection with federation, comprehensive urban county, and city-county consolidation proposals. Districts in this latter group have been formed by special acts of state legislatures (the air pollution control and rapid transit districts in the San Francisco Bay area are examples), state legislation providing a non-voter means of activation (the metropolitan park district in the Cleveland area), and interstate compacts (the Port of New York Authority and the Delaware River Basin Commission).

Frequent Remoteness from Public

Metropolitan districts have registered important attainments, but they have also drawn increasing condemnation. One of the strongest criticisms is the remoteness of many of them from the influence and control of the residents of the areas they serve. This remoteness takes various forms: the authority of the directors in some districts to issue bonds on their own judgment without submitting the proposals to voter approval; annexations of territory to districts through state legislative action, thus bypassing the consent of residents within either the existing district or the area to be attached; and the indirect method of selecting the district governing boards. All three elements are present in a number of metropolitan districts established under interstate compacts. The governing body can float bonds after its own unilateral decision. The district boundaries can be enlarged by amending the interstate compact. The governing body consists of appointed or ex officio members.

Complexity of Governing Board Composition

The composition of many district governing bodies also makes adequate accountability to their constituencies extremely difficult, if not impossible. Two illustrations will point up the difficulty. The governor appoints three of the seven members of the Chicago Transit Authority with the consent of the state senate and the mayor of Chicago; one of these three must reside outside Chicago. The mayor of Chicago appoints the other four members with the approval of the city council and the governor. In the St. Louis area, the mayor of St. Louis with the sanction of the judges of the circuit court in the city appoints three members of the governing body of the Metropolitan St. Louis Sewer District and the county supervisor, the elected county executive of St. Louis County, selects the other three members with the approval of the local district judges. In both of these cases, the district board is at least one step removed from the public and the divided method of appointment leaves the members without direct responsibility to any one public official or elected body.

Constituent-Unit Principle of Representation

The constituent-unit principle of representation for metropolitan districts—meaning that members of the governing body are
appointed by, and often from, the governing boards of the cities
and counties located within the district—has received growing support and use in recent years.[3] There are three major reasons why
interest in this method of representation has been expanding. One
is the irrationality of the system of board representation used in
many instances and the desire to avoid a similar practice as additional districts are established. (The constituent-unit principle has
been confined to new district legislation; it has not been used
to change the method of composition of any existing districts.)
Another is the opposition to making the governing bodies of new
districts popularly elected, thereby adding to the load of an already
overburdened electorate. And the third is the desire to link metropolitan districts more closely to the cities and counties they overlie.
Such interlocking assures greater intergovernmental cooperation and
coordinated planning, and places the cities and counties in a position to control these agencies.

This factor of control has been very important in fostering
acceptance of the constituent-unit idea. Cities and counties, realizing the probability of new metropolitan districts being created, have
often made effective use of the old political maxim, "If you can't
beat them, join them." By successfully advocating the installation
of the constituent-unit system of representation, they not only assure themselves of a direct association with these governments but
also acquire means of controlling them.

The constituent-unit principle has taken various forms. In the
Municipality of Metropolitan Seattle, extensive use is made of city
and county officials with the amount of representation divided
almost equally between the central city and the rest of the county.
The sixteen-member governing body is composed of the mayor and
seven councilmen of Seattle, the three county commissioners, the

[3] For additional discussions of the constituent-unit idea, see Arthur W.
Bromage, *Political Representation in Metropolitan Agencies* (Ann Arbor: Uni-
versity of Michigan Institute of Public Administration, 1962), and Stanley
Scott, *Metropolitan District Legislation: Some Problems and Issues* (Berkeley:
University of California Bureau of Public Administration, December 15, 1958).

mayors or councilmen of the three largest municipalities other than the central city, a mayor or a councilman from one of the remaining eight municipalities (selected by ballot by their mayors), and a chairman, who cannot be a public official, chosen by the other fifteen members.

The Bay Area Air Pollution Control District (Metropolitan San Francisco), which currently is active in six counties, has a governing body of twelve members, two from each county, all public officials. One member of each pair is a county supervisor, chosen by the county board of supervisors, which is the county governing body in California. The other member is a mayor or a councilman of a city chosen by a selection committee, which is composed of the mayors of all the cities within the county. The San Francisco Bay Area Rapid Transit District, which also employs the constituent-unit principle, follows a similar formula except that the more populous county areas are entitled to a larger number of representatives.[4]

Although the constituent-unit principle represents a more logical system of selecting district governing boards than do other methods of appointment, it is doubtful that it affords sufficient accountability to the metropolitan electorate. At most, such a system offers indirect, remote, and cumbersome public control. It is particularly indirect when private citizens, instead of public officials, are chosen as board members. Moreover, when local officials constitute such boards the process of public control can be strange indeed. These members ran successfully for city or county offices in campaigns that rarely if ever were concerned with the affairs of the district. Nevertheless, if the voters become dissatisfied with the performance of these officials as district board members, they can recall them from the city and county offices (in the relatively few states where recall is permitted) or they can defeat them if they make bids for

[4] Individuals appointed to the district's governing body may not serve concurrently as county supervisors, mayors, or city councilmen, according to an opinion of 1957 of the state's Attorney General. Concurrent service as both a supervisor, mayor, or councilman and a transit district board member, the opinion held, on seemingly doubtful grounds, involves the exercise of duties of two offices that may require contradictory or inconsistent action to the detriment of the public interest, and may result in a conflict of interests. Stanley Scott, a veteran researcher on California government, effectively demolished the bases of the Attorney General's opinion in A "Golden Gate Authority" for the San Francisco Bay Area—The Problem of Representation (Berkeley: University of California Bureau of Public Administration, June, 1960), pp. 9–11.

re-election. Doing so, however, means disregarding or playing down the records of these officials in the positions to which they were elected—records that may be satisfactory or superior—and focusing on their subsequently obtained, tangential responsibilities relating to the district. Another peculiarity of concurrent office holding is that in some instances officials spend less time on the activities of the positions to which they have been elected than on those of the district governing boards to which they have been appointed.[5]

So long as each metropolitan district performs only a single function or at most a few (and those recently created continue to fall within this general pattern), the element of representation will be beyond rational solution. Election of district governing board members furnishes a direct means of popular control, but as these agencies proliferate in number such control becomes increasingly ineffective. Conversely, the constituent-unit method of representation avoids increasing the number of elected officials but provides circuitous channels of accountability.[6]

Advocacy of Multipurpose Districts

In addition to criticism of their frequent remoteness from public control, metropolitan districts have been widely condemned because of their generally restricted functional nature. This limited-purpose approach has resulted in a fragmentary and usually un-coordinated attack on area-wide problems. It has also produced an even more complicated and confusing pattern of government, and by dealing with a few acute problems, it has on occasion lulled metropolitan residents into the false belief that no major area-wide service difficulties exist. As a consequence of their functional restrictiveness, interest and efforts to make these agencies multipurpose governments—authorized to undertake a considerable range of dif-

[5] Stanley Scott and Willis Culver, *Metropolitan Agencies and Concurrent Office-Holding: A Survey of Selected Districts and Authorities* (Berkeley: University of California Bureau of Public Administration, April, 1961), Legislative Problems No. 7, pp. 12–13.

[6] Some supporters of the constituent-unit system recognize the problem of adequate public accountability. They admit that, as a district becomes multipurpose in the functions it performs, direct election of some or all members of the governing body may be preferable. Racial and ethnic minorities have expressed concern about the constituent-unit system in terms of both adequate public control and sufficient representation of the cross section of groups in the metropolis.

ferent types of area-wide functions—have been growing in recent years.

Scattered advocacy of the metropolitan multipurpose district idea, and even isolated adoptions of legal provisions permitting its implementation, are not recent developments. The California legislature passed the Municipal Utility District Act in 1921, providing that any district organized under the legislation could furnish light, water, power, heat, transportation, telephone service, sewerage, and refuse and garbage disposal; and an analyst of district governments urged nationwide utilization of the multipurpose district idea as long ago as 1936.[7] Major impetus for the concept, however, has come in recent years, particularly through three officially sponsored efforts: a study prepared for the nationwide Governors' Conference in 1956, the Metropolitan Municipal Corporations law passed in Washington State in the following year, and a report released by the national Advisory Commission on Intergovernmental Relations in 1961.[8]

Implementing the Multipurpose District Idea

The metropolitan multipurpose district idea can materialize in three ways: through endowing existing metropolitan special districts with more functions, through consolidating those in existence, and through enacting new legal provisions of broad functional scope to be used by districts formed in the future. There is no substantial evidence that the first is likely to take place in the years immediately ahead. Districts of limited purpose have shown little or no desire to take on additional functions. The vast majority have been content to perform their one service or few closely related activities. When local residents have urged them to seek a broader functional authorization, they customarily have turned aside the request by

[7] California Statutes, 1925, p. 245 ff.; Ralph F. Fuchs, "Regional Agencies for Metropolitan Areas," *Washington University Law Quarterly*, 22 (December, 1936), 64–78. Coleman Woodbury also later supported the proposal in a book of which he served as editor, *The Future of Cities and Urban Redevelopment* (Chicago: University of Chicago Press, 1953), p. 521.

[8] John C. Bollens, *The States and the Metropolitan Problem* (Chicago: Council of State Governments, 1956), pp. 133–135; Washington Laws, 1957, Chapter 213; Advisory Commission on Intergovernmental Relations, *Governmental Structure, Organization, and Planning in Metropolitan Areas* (Washington: 1961), pp. 26–30, 67–74.

suggesting that another district be set up. The interested persons, wanting a service and not feeling strongly about which particular agency provides it, even though it might seem logical to them that the activity be assigned to an existing district government, organize still another special district. This is accomplished under an available law or under a new law submitted by a state legislator on their behalf. State legislatures are usually very willing to accommodate requests for new laws of this type. By complying with such proposals, they please individuals and groups wanting a specific service and at the same time they escape making enemies of those who are opposed to any significant enlargement of the powers of existing metropolitan districts.

The built-in positions of influence of persons in control of existing special districts makes merger of these agencies into multipurpose governments unlikely.[9] Advocates of the constituent-unit system of representation are hopeful that in time the interlocking type of governing board membership will promote the consolidation of such districts. They cannot point to any evidence of such a trend, however. For example, in the San Francisco Bay area, where the constituent-unit principle is used most extensively, metropolitan special districts have shown no serious inclination toward consolidation.

Slow Progress

The most current interest in implementing the multipurpose idea centers on the passage and the effective use of state laws, state constitutional provisions, and interstate compacts authorizing new districts to perform numerous diversified functions. Although this method of gaining implementation of the idea strikes many people as untidy, if not unsound, since it does not build on and seek to improve existing metropolitan districts, it has become the most discussed approach. Supporters point out that if this method receives

[9] Other ways exist to reduce the number of metropolitan special districts, such as converting them into dependent entities of the state or county government. There are numerous metropolitan districts which are not independent governments but adjuncts of county governments; however, they have been dependent agencies since their inauguration and have not been changed from independent to dependent status. Strong resistance, based on the extensive desire for metropolitan operations to be controlled by the metropolitan public, exists to transforming independent metropolitan district governments into agencies dependent on the state government.

thorough use, its potential is great in many metropolises that still have few or no metropolitan special districts. But so far effective use has not been made of the few legal provisions of this type that have been enacted nor has widespread acceptance by state legislatures and metropolitan voters of such proposals been realized. Regarding the former, no metropolitan district operating under a broad multipurpose grant has utilized most of its powers. For example, the East Bay Municipal Utility District (in the San Francisco Bay area), which was organized in 1923, performed only the function of water supply until the late 1940s when it added sewage disposal. Interest by its governing body in undertaking any of the numerous other functions included in its broad grant of powers has never developed, despite periodic public advocacy. The District's record is typical of the relatively few metropolitan districts that are legally permitted to undertake a broad, diversified series of activities: potentially multipurpose, they continue in practice to provide simply one function or very few.[10]

State legislatures have generally been reluctant to enact metropolitan multipurpose district laws; and when passed the legislation has usually been substantially circumscribed. In 1959, an interim committee of the California legislature presented a persuasive case on behalf of metropolitan multipurpose district legislation, but the bill did not survive the legislative session of the same year. Again, in 1960, the Governor's Commission on Metropolitan Area Problems recommended similar legislation, but it failed to be adopted the following year.[11] Also in 1960 the executive secretary of the Minnesota state commission on municipal laws unsuccessfully advocated

[10] The Port of New York Authority carries out many activities, but they are all within the single functional field of transportation.

[11] California Assembly Interim Committee on Conservation, Planning, and Public Works, A Metropolitan Multipurpose District for California (Sacramento: March, 1959); California Governor's Commission on Metropolitan Area Problems, Meeting Metropolitan Problems (Sacramento: December, 1960); California Assembly Bill No. 1896, 1959; California Assembly Bill No. 267, 1961. The functions allotted to these districts in the 1959 bill were planning, air pollution control, water supply, public transportation, regional parks, civil defense, and metropolitan administrative planning and coordination in local affairs. Civil defense was omitted from the 1961 bill, but this significant omnibus coverage was added: "any other metropolitan areawide function when delegated as provided in this chapter," meaning when a proposal to add a function is approved by overall majority popular vote.

the establishment of a multipurpose district in the Minneapolis–St. Paul area.

The much publicized Metropolitan Municipal Corporations bill enacted by the Washington state legislature in 1957 (creating metropolitan multipurpose districts to handle a maximum of six area-wide functions: sewage disposal, water supply, public transportation, garbage disposal, parks and parkways, and comprehensive planning) was circumscribed in two important particulars. First, the functions to be undertaken by the district were required to be named in the ballot proposal (instead of allowing such decisions to rest with the agency's governing board) and the proposal had to receive dual majorities in the central city and in the rest of the metropolitan area. Second, any functions not specified in the initial proposal could be carried out by the district only by gaining the consent of the voters, in this instance on a single overall majority basis.

The experience of Metropolitan Seattle with this law is revealing. In March, 1958, a proposal to create a district to perform three of the six functions—sewage disposal, public transportation, and comprehensive planning—received an overwhelming overall majority vote but failed to obtain the required majority outside Seattle. In September of the same year, a proposition to establish a district limited to sewage disposal was approved, receiving the more decisive majority outside Seattle where the sewage problem was worse. In 1962, the district, legally named the Municipality of Metropolitan Seattle (nomenclature that surely will not aid the public to distinguish different types of governmental units), tried to add public transportation as its second function; but the proposal failed to acquire an overall popular majority. Thus, the widely heralded Seattle district remains as most metropolitan special districts: multipurpose in potential but single-purpose in operation.

Another method of implementing the multipurpose district idea—placing the authorization in the state constitution and permitting a locally-appointed charter commission to determine what functions should be assigned to such an agency—has also proved ineffective. Such a procedure, applicable to St. Louis and St. Louis County, was written into the new Missouri constitution of 1945. The first use of the constitutional section in 1954 resulted in the acceptance by dual majorities of a single-purpose district for sewage

disposal. Although the district charter provided for assumption of
other functions with the consent of the voters, no effort has ever
been made to broaden the agency's activities. In 1955, a second
use of the constitutional authorization produced a proposal to organize another single-purpose district, to operate a transit system,
but the measure was soundly defeated in both the city and the
county. In 1959, a third utilization of the authorization resulted in
a proposed multipurpose district to handle such area-wide functions
as the metropolitan road system, master development planning,
sewage disposal (by absorbing the previously established metropolitan sewer district), and civil defense. The plan went down to
a smashing defeat, by a two-to-one count in the city and a three-
to-one margin in the county. As in the case of Metropolitan Seattle,
the St. Louis area continues to employ multipurpose enabling provisions in a single-purpose manner.

COMPREHENSIVE URBAN COUNTY PLAN

The comprehensive urban county plan, a second major variation
of the two-level approach, involves the simultaneous reallocation
of various functions from all municipalities, and sometimes other
local units, to a county, thus transforming the latter into a metropolitan government. The functional shifts are comprehensive in
scope and they all occur at the same time, usually through local
adoption of a charter.[12] A county thus assumes functions deemed to
be of an area-wide nature while municipalities and other local governments remain in existence to perform local services.

Much of the appeal of this plan emanates from the basic geographical fact that most metropolitan areas lie within the boundaries
of a single county. However, the concept is even attractive in many
intercounty metropolises where the greatest number of the residents
and the most serious aspects of their problems are found in the central county. The plan is also appealing in that, unlike the metropolitan district and federation methods of reform, it does not require

[12] The combination of two characteristics of this plan—comprehensiveness
and simultaneity—differentiates this method of reorganization from other forms
of the urban county development, which are discussed in Chapter 13. It should
also be noted that although the original reallocation of functions under the
comprehensive plan is extensive and simultaneous, later grants of authority may
be made in smaller quantity, even singly.

the creation of still another unit of government in an already badly fragmented system. These factors have made the comprehensive urban county plan the decided choice of many people who favor some type of two-level arrangement. Stimulated by the possibility of making an existing, long-established government of sufficient territorial size a vehicle to deal with significant metropolitan problems and by the opportunity to avoid city-county consolidation, the number of proponents of this approach has increased. They have succeeded in advancing their objective to various stages—a package of recommendations, an official proposal submitted to the voters, and public acceptance of the idea. However, they have also encountered numerous difficulties along the way so that in only one locality (Metropolitan Miami) has the concept become a reality.

The Cuyahoga County Efforts

Recent efforts on behalf of the comprehensive urban county idea in four areas—Cleveland, Pittsburgh, Houston, and Dayton —are typical and, in combination, they reveal many of the major hurdles encountered in attempts to put the concept into operation.[13] The most persistent activity has taken place in the Cleveland area (Cuyahoga County), where comprehensive urban county charters were submitted to the voters in both 1950 and 1959. The first called for the transfer to the county of airports, health and welfare services, public institutions, sewers, water supply, and mass transit (the last named, however, only if the voters approved a separate referendum on that question). It further proposed enlargement of the county governing board, substantial reduction in the number of elected county officials, and the establishment of a strong elected county

---

[13] The principal recommendations of the three-year study that influenced the Cuyahoga County charter of 1959 are contained in Cleveland Metropolitan Services Commission, *Prologue to Progress* (Cleveland: 1959). For the interesting reflections of the person who directed that study, see James A. Norton, *The Metro Experience* (Cleveland: The Press of Western Reserve University, 1963). The recommendations relative to the Pittsburgh area appear in Metropolitan Study Commission of Allegheny County, *An Urban Home Rule Charter for Allegheny County* (Pittsburgh: 1955) and those for Metropolitan Houston are in Harris County Home Rule Commission, *Metropolitan Harris County* (Houston: 1957). Supporting evidence for the Dayton area proposals are found in Metropolitan Community Studies, *Metropolitan Challenge* (Dayton: 1959); the proposals were published as a special supplement to the January 16, 1960, edition of the *Dayton Journal Herald*.

executive. The state constitutional requirements for authorization to adopt such a plan were severe, requiring four separate electoral majorities: countywide; Cleveland; the county exclusive of Cleveland; and a majority of the cities, villages, and townships. The charter attained none of these majorities, although it came within a few percentage points of gaining the first three.

The 1959 charter similarly provided for reallocation to the county government of many important functions and facilities and for structural reorganization. By this time the constitutional provisions for adoption had been eased for the heavily populated counties, although they still required separate popular majorities inside and outside the central city. The charter failed to obtain a majority in either area; in fact, it fared better in the suburbs where it lost by merely 8000 votes than it did in Cleveland where it garnered only about two-fifths of the ballots.

The Allegheny County Attempt

The comprehensive urban county plan experienced less progress in the other three metropolises. In the Pittsburgh area, the official Metropolitan Study Commission of Allegheny County recommended in 1955 a constitutional amendment authorizing the local adoption of such a plan. The Commission urged that the county government be endowed with broad regulatory powers over many local activities and take over certain functions (property tax collection, for example) and that the elective status of some county officials be eliminated. The movement for large-scale change collapsed when the necessary constitutional permission to draft a county charter was not obtained.

The Harris County Study

The experience was quite similar in Metropolitan Houston. The official Harris County Home Rule Commission, in 1957, called for the addition of a new, workable county home rule amendment to the state constitution, which would allow the county government to undergo major structural reorganization and to expand its functions substantially. The proposed new constitutional amendment did not materialize; finally, in 1961, an attempt to revise the existing county home rule amendment was turned down in the state legislature.

The Montgomery County Movement

In the Dayton area (Montgomery County), Metropolitan Community Studies, a privately financed organization, prepared a report containing recommendations for adoption of the comprehensive urban county arrangement. The staff recommendations, issued in 1959, focused on thoroughly reorganizing the county governmental structure and endowing the reconstituted county with authority to prepare and adopt a countywide general plan, which would control the location of all major roads and highways, regional parks, recreational sites, industrial parks, and major sewer and water facilities. Such changes could be effectuated only through the adoption of a home rule charter by the voters. Although the area had accomplished major reforms in the early years of the present century (Dayton was the first sizable city in the nation to adopt the council-manager form of government and a much acclaimed conservancy district was established after a disastrous flood), the movement succumbed at the first action step. In late 1961, the county voters defeated a proposal to elect a county charter commission by a margin of almost 34,000 votes.[14]

Legal Authorizations and County Reorganization

Based on the attempts in these four metropolises and others, it is clear that at least five formidable obstacles stand in the way of utilizing the comprehensive urban county concept. First, legal authorization to use the concept does not exist in many states and the authorization must take the form of state constitutional permission.

[14] Promotion of the antithesis of the comprehensive urban county plan is not unknown. The most prominent example is the Plan of Improvement for Atlanta and Fulton County, enacted by the Georgia legislature in 1951 and fully operative since the following year. In addition to annexing eighty-two square miles to Atlanta and establishing a procedure involving judicial determination for future annexations, the plan provided for the reallocation of functions between the city and the county and largely excluded the county from performing municipal functions. For instance, fire protection, garbage collection, law enforcement, parks and recreation, sewerage, and water were made the exclusive responsibility of Atlanta. For additional details, see Fulton County Local Government Commission, *Plan of Improvement for Atlanta and Fulton County* (Atlanta: 1950) and M. Clyde Hughes, "Annexation and Reallocation of Functions," *Public Management*, XXXIV (February, 1952), 26–30.

Second, there is widespread agreement that a structurally integrated county government, one capable of efficiently performing its functional assignments, must be an essential part of any such plan. Although some improvements in the organization and processes of county governments have developed in recent decades, few counties in the metropolis have undergone the thorough reorganization advocated by most proponents of the comprehensive urban county idea. Without doubt, the sweeping nature of the structural reorganization called for as a basic condition of converting the county into a metropolitan government is a strong deterrent to securing the necessary legal authorization. Numerous incumbent county officials see such authorization as an opening threat to their continuance in office and naturally work quietly or openly against it.

Composition of County Governing Body

Determining the most appropriate method of constituting the governing body of the comprehensive urban county is a third frequent source of difficulty. Although many counties have gradually taken on more urban functions over the years, little attention has been paid to changes needed in the composition of their governing boards. In numerous counties the board has a small membership, as few as three in some instances, and in others it has an excessive number of members, as many as forty or more. Moreover, in many cases where the county board members are elected from districts (wards), no realigning of their boundaries has occurred in many years or they have been periodically reshuffled to retain the overrepresentation of the less populated areas. This situation has prevailed despite major changes in the relative number of people or voters residing within the respective districts. For instance, before 1963, when a state supreme court decision started a number of corrective actions, in four-fifths of the counties of California a voter in the least populous district had at least twice the voice in county government as did a voter in the most populous district; indeed, in one county, one district contained about half the county electorate while another had only about 1 percent.[15]

---

[15] For further details, see Winston W. Crouch, Dean E. McHenry, John C. Bollens, and Stanley Scott, *California Government and Politics*, 3rd ed. (Englewood Cliffs, N.J.: Prentice-Hall, 1964), pp. 236–238, and Stuart C. Hall, *County Supervisorial Redistricting in California* (Berkeley: University of Cali-

The basis of county board representation becomes a central consideration when a comprehensive urban county plan is being prepared since important new responsibilities are to be assumed by the county government. Answers are therefore necessary to many questions about representation. Should all governing board members be nominated and elected at large or by districts (wards), or should a combination of the at-large and district methods be used? If the district method of representation is employed, should the districts be constructed solely on a population (or voter) factor so that they will contain reasonably equal numbers of people or voters? Or should existing municipalities, separately or in some combinations, be an additional basis for determining such representation, thereby utilizing the constituent-unit principle? In addition, judgments have to be made about the size of the governing board, the length of the terms of office and, in cases where the legal authorization permits local determination, whether the elections should be officially partisan or nonpartisan.

The system of representation decided upon may importantly affect what sections of the county (and in some instances what political party) will have control of the greatly strengthened county government. Very often, therefore, the proposed scheme of representation differs greatly from the existing one. The Cuyahoga County charter of 1959, for example, would have supplanted the governing board of three members, elected at large, with a council of 19 members, 9 elected at large and 10 by districts. Not unexpectedly the representation formula frequently becomes a point of major controversy and may be decisive to acceptance or disapproval of the plan.

Assignment of Functions

A fourth major difficulty in achieving a comprehensive urban county plan concerns the functions to be assigned to the county government. In developing such a plan, judgments must be made

---

fornia Bureau of Public Administration, 1961). As a result of the apparent nationwide impact of the United States Supreme Court decision in *Baker* v. *Carr* in 1962 and subsequent related federal and state court decisions ordering more equitable congressional and state legislative reapportionment, county governing board representation seems destined to be in greater imbalance than either congressional or state legislative representation—unless the reapportionment principle is generally applied to it. A recent Wisconsin Supreme Court decision made such an application.

as to what functions should be reassigned and how many of them should be reallocated at the inception of the plan. In other words, what compelling problems need to be handled on an area-wide basis and what degree of change will be acceptable to the electorate? If the transfer of merely a few functions to the county is proposed in the belief that a conservative approach will be welcomed by the voters, the electorate may decide the plan is inconsequential and turn it down. If on the other hand, the transfer of a considerable number of functions is offered, the voters, often led by disgruntled city officials, may decide the plan is too revolutionary. Furthermore, the decision to include a particular activity may be decisive to approval or rejection. The formulators of a comprehensive urban county plan therefore have to strike a balance between the too moderate and the too drastic redistribution of responsibilities; and an accurate judgment on this matter is not easy. For instance, the commission that wrote the unsuccessful Cuyahoga County charter of 1959 decided to propose a far-reaching reallocation of functions. This decision generated the opposition of the influential mayor of Cleveland, who had no desire to see certain important activities and assets of his city taken away.

Financial Powers

A final difficulty, which is more than an occasional point of harassment to implementation of the comprehensive urban county plan, is the inadequacy of the financial powers of many county governments. Heavily dependent on the property tax and often faced with constitutional tax limitations, many counties lack the financial means to assume the functional responsibilities called for in this approach. The seriousness of these restrictions to the successful working of such a plan has been frequently acknowledged. Here, for example, are the strong conclusions about a basic phase of the problem reached by the staff of Metropolitan Community Studies in its recommendations report on the Dayton area:

The 10-mill limitation was adopted by state constitutional amendment in 1933 during a period of depression and low prices. Under its terms, the total or combined property tax rate that can be levied by all local units and the state government without a special vote of the electorate cannot exceed 10 mills or $10 per $1,000 of assessed valuation.

Home rule municipalities, such as Dayton, may provide for higher millage rates in their charters.

The absurdity of this limitation is apparent. Operating costs in every local school district alone require more than the 10-mill rate. In fact, the total tax levy in virtually all of the urbanized portion of Montgomery County is at least three times this limit. The restriction imposes a severe handicap on the local units, particularly the school districts and the county government, since it compels them to appeal constantly to the electorate for even basic operating funds. If the powers of the county government are enlarged, the millage limitation would constitute a serious impediment to the execution of its new responsibilities.

Unfortunately, removal or modification of the 10-mill limitation can be accomplished only by constitutional amendment. . . .[16]

METROPOLITAN MIAMI: COMPREHENSIVE URBAN COUNTY GOVERNMENT ON TRIAL

When its charter went into effect in July, 1957, exactly two months after being adopted, Dade County (Miami) became the first metropolis in the United States to put the comprehensive urban county idea into operation. The institution of this major reform was preceded by overcoming two barriers that have thus far proved insurmountable elsewhere: state constitutional authorization to draft a county charter and local voter approval of the proposed document.

By the mid-1950s, the Miami area, fast growing in population (up almost 400,000 in ten years) and fast growing in problems, had undergone considerable functional consolidation and had experienced much agitation for city-county merger.[17] A countywide system of schools and consolidation of the functions of public health, welfare, hospitals, airports, and harbors had all been accomplished in the 1940s. In addition, three unsuccessful efforts had been made to merge various municipalities with the county government, in 1945, 1948, and 1953. The last, which would have abolished the city of Miami and transferred its functions to the county, lost by a hairline margin of less than 1000 votes in a city referendum. The closeness of the defeat served as a catalyst for establishing comprehensive urban county government.

---

[16] *Dayton Journal Herald,* special supplement, January 16, 1960.

[17] Various other characteristics of the area, particularly as related to its residents and interest groups, are considered in Chapter 16.

Constitutional Authorization and Popular Approval

In securing state constitutional permission to prepare a plan of governmental reorganization for the Miami area, the state legislative delegation from Dade County, under the leadership of its astute senator, R. "Bunn" Gautier, succeeded where the proponents of reform in a number of other metropolitan areas have failed.[18] In 1955 the Florida legislature placed a proposed constitutional home rule amendment for Dade County before the voters of the state. The response in the following year was decisive, with a 70 percent favorable vote. Unlike most such enabling grants, the amendment required only a countywide popular majority to adopt a charter. On May 21, 1957, the charter, prepared by a board appointed by the governor, barely gained the necessary single majority (44,404 to 42,620); with only about one-fourth of the county's registered voters taking part in the special election, a heavy affirmative majority in the city of Miami brought victory for the plan.

The County's Functions

The new charter for Metropolitan Miami provided for a powerful and structurally integrated county government and for the continuance of the existing twenty-six (later twenty-seven) municipalities, nineteen of which had fewer than 10,000 people. The county government, encompassing 2054 square miles, was empowered to construct expressways, regulate traffic, and own and operate mass transit systems and transportation terminals; maintain central records, training, and communication for fire and police protection; provide hospitals and uniform health and welfare programs; furnish parks and recreational areas; establish and administer housing, urban re-

[18] Following the vote on consolidation in 1953, the city of Miami created a study group, the Metropolitan Miami Municipal Board, which employed Public Administration Service, a consulting firm, to prepare a report on local government in Metropolitan Miami. Some important conclusions of that report (*The Government of Metropolitan Miami*) are discussed later in this chapter under federation. The county's legislative delegation objected to the study board's recommendation to eliminate the existing county government. The constitutional amendment introduced by the county's delegation and passed by the legislature stipulated that the board of county commissioners would be the governing body of the new metropolitan government, thus transforming this reorganization proposal from the federation approach to that of the comprehensive urban county.

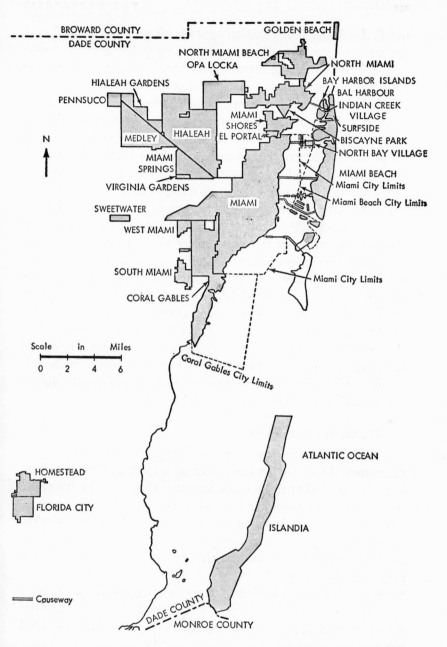

Figure 15.2 The Municipalities of Metropolitan Dade County, Florida.
Courtesy Metropolitan Dade County Planning Department (© Atlantic
Research Corporation, 1962).

newal, flood and beach erosion control, air pollution control, and drainage programs; regulate or own various public utilities (under certain limitations); and engage in industrial promotion. It was also authorized both to prepare and to enforce comprehensive plans for the development of the county, thus gaining a grant of authority of potentially great significance that is seldom even proposed for a metropolitan government. On related fronts, it was permitted to adopt and enforce zoning and business regulations and uniform building and related technical codes throughout its territory.

The county government was also empowered to set reasonable minimum standards for all governmental units in the county to meet in the performance of any of their services or functions and to take over an activity if there was failure to comply with the standards. Additional municipalities can be created in the county only upon the authorization of the county governing body and after affirmative majority approval by the voters in the proposed incorporation. However, no municipality existing at the time of the charter's adoption can be abolished except by majority consent of its electors. The sanction of the county governing board must be gained before annexation of land to municipalities is completed. Finally, this board may establish and govern special districts and finance district services and facilities by charges made within such areas.

The County's Organization

The charter also brought on a thorough revamping of county governmental organization and processes. It specified that the county commissioners, elected on a nonpartisan ballot, were to constitute the legislative and governing body with power to appoint and remove a county manager. Administrative operations were brought under the manager's jurisdiction, a far cry from the supplanted rambling structure. The charter abolished the elective status of the assessor, tax collector, surveyor, purchasing agent, and supervisor of voter registration, and made the holders of these offices appointees of the manager. It also conferred authority on the county board to eliminate the election of the sheriff and constables, a power that the board subsequently exercised.

The five county commissioners in office at the time the charter went into effect in July, 1957, were continued in those positions under a provision of the charter. Their four-year terms had just begun in the previous year and until 1958 they constituted the entire member-ship of the board. In that year, other original provisions of the charter relating to the governing board became operative; they called for one commissioner to be elected at large from each of five districts, one to be elected from each of these districts by the district voters only, and one to be elected from each city containing an official population of at least 60,000. When these charter sections first became appli-cable, the governing board consisted of eleven members, as Miami was then the only municipality to qualify under the 60,000 population rule. After the federal census of 1960, the board's size increased to thirteen since both Hialeah and Miami Beach then exceeded 60,000 people.

The Early Turbulent Days

The new governmental arrangement in Dade County has had a rocky road to travel, but seemingly it has survived its own initial mistakes and the continuing harassment by various municipal officials and former county office holders. Perhaps the initial period of travail and uncertainty, which covered seven years, should not have been unexpected in a metropolis characterized by a dearth of strong political leaders and a somewhat complacent attitude among business groups—and in a state without previous experience with county home rule.[19] Some observers of metropolitan developments have concluded (perhaps somewhat harshly) that metropolitan government could scarcely have materialized in a more unlikely place or in one less equipped at the outset to make a success of thorough governmental reorganization.

Initially it seemed as if the newborn metropolitan government would be killed before it learned to walk. Upon approval of the charter by the voters, the members of the county commission, who were all new to their jobs, authorized the new county attorney to

[19] These characteristics of the area are by Edward Sofen, a University of Miami political scientist, who has written the most thorough study of Dade County's experience with metropolitan government. See his *The Miami Metro-politan Experiment* (Bloomington: Indiana University Press, 1963); the com-ments about the area are on page 60. Also see Edward Sofen, "The Politics of Metropolitan Leadership: The Miami Experience," *Midwest Journal of Political Science*, V (February, 1961), 18–38, and Reinhold P. Wolff, *Miami Metro: The Road to Urban Unity* (Coral Gables: University of Miami Bureau of Business and Economic Research, 1960).

draft proposed ordinances spelling out the basic relations between the county government and the municipalities as well as the details of county administration. The attorney, an individual who had a reputation for attacking any task with vigor, argued that adoption of these implementing ordinances was necessary by July 21, 1957, the day when the charter officially took effect. Some analysts who had closely studied the new plan of government questioned the necessity for this deadline and unsuccessfully urged the postponement of ordinance drafting until the appointment and arrival of the first county manager. O. W. Campbell, then city manager of San Diego, was offered the chief executive position by a three-to-two vote of the commission, an ominously narrow margin, and accepted the post the day after the charter became operative.

The proposed ordinances, generally drastic in nature and pertaining to a number of highly sensitive subjects, including zoning, certification of contractors, public works, traffic enforcement, and automobile inspection (some of which would seriously affect municipal revenues, were promptly attacked by municipal officials. Whether the county commissioners who were at best unenthusiastic about the new government deliberately set out to wreck it or whether their inexperience prompted them to rely too heavily on an overly zealous county attorney may never be known conclusively.[20] Whichever is the case, the commissioners barged ahead in the fashion of "a runaway freight train," to use the words of John Wilmott, former head of a local research foundation, and started public hearings on eighteen proposed ordinances.

The Local Autonomy Amendment

Their confidence buoyed by the close vote on adoption of the charter as well as by the acrimony generated from the nature of the implementing ordinances and the ramrod speed employed in preparing them, the opponents of the metropolitan reorganization made their move. They proposed a local autonomy amendment which, if passed, would have virtually reinstated the precharter governmental

[20] Edward Sofen tends to support the latter view (*The Miami Metropolitan Experiment*, p. 91). As possible counter evidence, however, it should be pointed out that one of the commissioners later spearheaded an effort to dismantle the metropolitan government through a series of emasculating charter amendments.

system. Tax assessment and collection and permission to set reasonable minimum standards for service performance would have been the only charter powers not stripped from the county government. In October, 1957, less than three months after the charter took effect, initiative petitions in support of the amendment were filed to force an election on the issue. When the local autonomy amendment finally came before the voters in September, 1958, after a delay caused by a lower court ruling, it met resounding defeat by a vote of 74,420 to 48,893. The vote of confidence for the charter was substantial as compared to its marginal adoption in the previous year. The new governmental arrangement thus had survived its first major test, but it continued to be badgered by hundreds of law suits, many brought by municipal officials and a number not reaching final settlement for years.[21]

A Barrage of Amendments

Harassment of the new government persisted after the defeat of the local autonomy proposal through repeated use of the same technique—the submission of amendments to weaken the area-wide government. Not all of the amendments submitted to the voters have been proposed by anti-metro people. For example, some, such as the proposition to change the county's name from Dade to Miami (rejected in both 1958 and 1963), involved minor matters and certainly did not constitute attacks on the comprehensive urban county plan. Another, which called for abolishing the mandatory reassessment of property required by the charter, was supported by the county manager. Others, which have been concerned with the size and method of selection of the county commission, although sometimes promoted by metropolitan government opponents, were not in themselves weakening modifications. Still others, such as the adopted proposal of 1963 to stiffen the requirements for qualifying amendments by initiative petitions, have definitely strengthened the metropolitan governmental system.

The anti-metro amendments, however, have been numerous and have been presented in both small and large packages. The contents of the small packages have been of three main types. The first is to return the positions of assessor and sheriff to elective status. These

[21] Joseph Metzger, "Metro and Its Judicial History," *University of Miami Law Review*, XV (Spring, 1961), 283–293, considers a number of these cases.

propositions were both defeated in 1959 and again in 1961 (in the latter case as part of a large package); in 1963 the elective assessor proposal again lost, but the one relating to the sheriff won by approximately 1000 votes. The passage of this amendment weakens the county manager plan, but is far from fatal to it. The second type is to return functions to the municipalities or to make activities independent of the county government, as illustrated by the unsuccessful efforts in 1962 to restore the traffic courts to the cities and to establish an independent port authority. The third type is to place restrictions on the county manager, as exemplified by the victorious amendments of 1962 to require commission approval of the manager's appointments of department heads and of his administrative orders to create, merge, or combine departments. As in the case of making the sheriff elective, these amendments also make inroads into council-manager operations but can be successfully overcome by a manager who knows the basic importance of personal relationships to his accomplishments in office.

The big anti-metro package was presented to the voters in October, 1961. More comprehensive even than the local autonomy proposal of three years before, this proposition (known as the McLeod amendment due to its promotion by a former county commissioner of that name) called for thirty-seven charter changes and was in effect a new charter. In brief, the amendment provided for stripping the county government of its area-wide functions, replacing the council-manager form with the commission form of government, restoring the elective status of the sheriff and the assessor (the latter to be supplanted later by a five-member board appointed by the county commission), and reducing the county commission to five members elected at large and more than doubling their salaries. The amendment was defeated by the close tally of 97,170, for, to 105,097, against, which was a margin of support for the urban county charter only slightly larger than that given to it at the time of its adoption in 1957.

The Manager's Tenure

The other major crisis point for the Miami plan has been the tenure of the county manager. Hired as the first occupant of the position by a closely divided vote of the carryover Commission in July, 1957, O. W. Campbell never knew when the pivot man on the board might shift sides and bring on his dismissal. But even after the Commission was increased in size, the stability of the manager's tenure did not improve. Accusations about the members' interference with administration and their obstructionist tactics and counter contentions by the Commission and the manager that the other party had failed to assume leadership were made. Finally, in February, 1961, the Commission, with only one dissenting vote, dismissed Campbell.

Campbell's successor was Irving G. McNayr, then city manager of Columbia, South Carolina, and formerly manager of Montgomery County, Maryland. He took over the position on May 1, 1961, and immediately sought to reassure municipal officials of the county's intention to cooperate fully with them. Prompted by the unfavorable public reaction to the reassessment program required by the charter (all property in the county was to be reassessed by 1961), McNayr recommended an amendment to postpone this requirement. The change, approved by the voters in August, 1961, was considered to be a deciding factor in the defeat of the McLeod anti-Metro amendment later that year. But the basic problem still remained since Florida law required assessment at cash value and that in Dade County was only at about 50 percent of such value. When the court in July, 1964, ordered the doubling of all assessments to comply with the law, the resulting public uproar precipitated the firing of McNayr. Although there had been increasing signs of tension between him and the Commission newly elected in 1964, the immediate cause of his dismissal stemmed from the assessment fiasco.

County Governmental Activities

What has the county government accomplished since the plan of metropolitan government went into effect? Here are a number of examples. It has integrated a haphazard administrative organization and installed modern governmental practices by consolidating departments, standardizing procedures, and developing a full battery of staff services such as data processing, records management, and internal auditing. It has completed a countywide land use plan. It has purchased and unified bus lines. It has set up a uniform traffic code and has undertaken countywide traffic engineering. It has made progress on an extensive expressway system. It has begun construction of a seaport, designed to make the metropolis a highly modern cruise and freight center. It has adopted stringent regulations to prevent pollution of air and water. It has improved the professional standards of a public hospital. It has taken steps to establish service standards and regulate the rates of private water and sewage disposal companies.[22] (One sign of the rapid urbanization of Dade County is that most of its residents still rely on septic tanks for sewage disposal.) The county government has made progress in terms of both its organization and processes and its functional activities, but it should be remembered that in Metropolitan Miami almost any change from the precharter system could only be an improvement.

Problems and Challenges

Finance and leadership are two vexing and persistent problems in Dade County. The constitutional county home rule amendment furnished the means of creating a metropolitan government but it did not confer additional taxing powers on that government. In essence, the county government has had to utilize its pre-reorganization tax structure to finance new and improved area-wide services as well as municipal-type services to the hundreds of thousands of residents in the unincorporated areas, which contain about two-fifths of the total population. Moreover, although the charter authorizes the county commissioners to establish special districts to finance added services in urbanized fringe areas, employment of the procedure has encountered legal complications and remains under a legal cloud.

Lack of sufficient community leadership, including an absence of strong political leaders and aggressive civic organizations, has handicapped the metropolitan government. In November, 1963, a charter amendment was approved which provides for a county commission of nine members, one elected as mayor and serving as permanent board chairman. In the light of this development, the key question is, will the office of mayor become the focal point of the needed political leadership?

The Dade County experience raises serious doubts about the appropriateness of the council-manager form of government for a

[22] For an early listing of activities, see Miami-Dade County Chamber of Commerce Government Research Council, *Metropolitan Dade County—Its First Four Years* (Miami: 1961).

metropolitan complex. The dismissal of two managers within a period of seven years, one of whom (Campbell) tried to exercise forceful leadership, the other of whom (McNayr) followed a more conciliatory and less aggressive path, lends support to those who argue for an elected county executive. In fact, just before McNayr's ouster, a group headed by two university professors and a former county commissioner began to circulate petitions for a charter amendment to substitute a strong mayor plan for the existing arrangement. The group charged that the council-manager plan made impossible the allocation of responsibility for the failures of the reassessment program and other shortcomings and that it did not provide the dynamic political leadership necessary for the proper functioning of a metropolitan government.[23]

Another challenge immediately confronting the Dade County governmental system is adoption of a sound general land use master plan. In 1964, a series of public hearings got under way on a preliminary draft of such a plan, which had been more than four years in preparation. Even before public discussion, however, the county governing board officially rejected one of the proposal's major road features, a possible indication of the obstacles that lie ahead. The broad planning power, both to adopt and enforce comprehensive plans, vested in the metropolitan government provides an unexcelled opportunity to guide the area's development. Whether this rarely provided authority will be intelligently exercised or whether it will be squandered is a critical question facing Metropolitan Miami.

In appraising the comprehensive urban county plan in operation in Dade County, both successes and failures can be noted. The successes have been registered by the metropolitan government in terms of improvements in many area-wide services and facilities. Although additional powers were granted to the county government, the improvements are chiefly the product of the replacement of archaic county organization and practices by a modern structure and professional top-level administrators. On the negative side, the metropolitan government has not been able to develop an equitable method of furnishing municipal services to unincorporated urban areas (due partly to legal difficulties). Nor has it used its authority to develop and enforce reasonable minimum standards for services

[23] Thomas J. Wood, "Dade Commission Dismisses Manager," *National Civic Review*, LIII (October, 1964), 498–499.

provided by municipalities. This failure has been due largely to the heavy backlog of countywide work it has faced and to its desire to appease the municipal units which have generally been unfriendly at best.

The greatest uncertainty about the long-range value of the two-level system in Metropolitan Miami centers on the municipalities. The municipal level includes a number of incorporated places that may never be viable units capable of adequately performing a variety of local services. But an even more important factor causing uncertainty about the future of the system is, to use the words of former County Manager Irving McNayr, "the political opposition that municipal officials have placed in the path of almost every area-wide endeavor attempted." According to Mr. McNayr:

> The concept of Metro Court was fought all the way to the United States Supreme Court in a two-year court battle. When that failed, the recently proposed charter amendment attempted to do at the polls what the courts refused to do. County-wide traffic engineering was attacked in the courts. Work on the Dodge Island Seaport was delayed for years by the opposition of officials of Miami Beach. The City of Miami attempted to stop the transit take-over by court action and by every other means. The cities have refused a county-wide automobile inspection system and the City of Miami Beach even refuses to use a uniform inspection sticker. City councils have openly favored charter amendments restricting Metro even though their residents have consistently voted pro-Metro. They have fought uniform hours for the sale of liquor, a uniform building code, a uniform traffic code, and virtually every effort made to implement the Charter. These are the public and open areas of opposition. We daily encounter others in every area of contact.

> · · ·

> In every transfer of a function to the county, we have had to pay taxpayers' money for equipment and facilities already paid for by taxpayers who would still get the same benefit from it. As we increase our taxes, in assuming these new functions, the cities do not lower their taxes.

> · · ·

> Municipal cooperation to date in developing area-wide services has occurred only rarely, and every bit of progress by Metro has been made despite, rather than in concert with, municipal officials. If we are ever to move ahead, it must be with unity of purpose. City officials have openly and defiantly demonstrated they do not intend to cooperate in the development of metropolitan area government.[24]

[24] Irving G. McNayr, "Recommendation for Unified Government in Dade County," (A Report of the County Manager to the Board of County Commissioners, Miami, September 25, 1962), pp. 5, 6, 7.

The worth of the two-level arrangement in the Miami area has yet to prove itself. Certainly such a "federal" system cannot operate properly so long as one of its vital elements, the municipalities, is uncooperative. Any governmental structure involving a division but interlocking of powers depends upon a high degree of cooperation for success. If the attitude of many municipal officials in the Miami area stays unchanged, a two-level system may be unworkable in Dade County.

FEDERATION

Federation, the third variation of the two-level approach, involves the creation of a new area-wide government of intercounty or one-county territorial scope. The new unit, usually designated as the metropolitan government, carries out area-wide responsibilities. The municipal governments continue to exist, perform local functions for which the metropolitan government is not responsible, and retain their governing boards. Under some federation plans the municipalities are territorially enlarged by adding adjoining unincorporated land and are renamed "boroughs." Another feature of all federation plans proposed in the United States is local representation, generally from the municipal or borough areas, on the metropolitan governing board.

Similarity Between Federation and Other Two-Level Variations

Federation has considerable similarity to the comprehensive urban county and metropolitan multipurpose district arrangements. In fact, virtually indistinguishable federation and comprehensive urban county plans can be developed for a one-county metropolis. For example, when a metropolis occupies a single county, the principal difference is that the federation plan calls for replacing the existing county government and its incumbent officeholders by the new metropolitan agency, whereas the comprehensive urban county plan retains the county government as the area-wide unit. At first glance, this seems a broad distinction, but it need not be so.

Utilization of the county government under the latter plan is generally predicated upon substantial reorganization of its structure. Such renovation means the conversion of many elective positions to the appointment method of selection. It also often includes the immediate or eventual reconstitution of the county governing body

and in some cases the nomination or election of the board members
from local areas. When reorganization encompasses all these changes,
the difference between one-county federation and the comprehensive
urban county arrangement is minor at most. (The enlargement of
municipalities as called for in some federation proposals might be
the only important point of variation.) Of course, these two types
of reform do differ importantly in terms of an intercounty metropolitan area; there only federation is usable.

Federation and the metropolitan multipurpose district can likewise be very similar. Since both can be used in both intercounty and
one-county situations, their major distinction at times is that some
federation proposals have included the boundary enlargement of
municipalities. This stipulation is unknown to the metropolitan
multipurpose district concept.

Considerable advocacy of federation developed in the late nineteenth century and the early twentieth century. To many people
who supported governmental reform in the metropolis, this method
seemed a logical and suitable solution since it fulfilled the desire for
a metropolitan government while retaining more localized units for
local public purposes. But support for federation has practically disappeared in the United States in recent years, due to the rising
interest in the other two variations of the two-level approach and
the failure to secure adoption of plans based on this concept. In
fact, federation is the only widely discussed approach to area-wide
problems that has not been adopted by a single metropolis in the
United States. Oddly enough, in the early 1950s, at the very time
interest in this approach virtually vanished in the United States, it
grew in neighboring Canada to the point of adoption in the major
metropolitan area of Toronto.

The Major Federation Attempts

For many years federation was discussed in generalized terms,
much in the manner of fashionable conversation, but few serious
attempts were made to formulate specific plans and to obtain their
adoption. The first proposal emanated from a three-member commission appointed by the governor of Massachusetts to study forms
of governmental organization for the Boston metropolitan area. In
1896 the commission recommended the enactment of a bill by the
state legislature that would require a popular vote in the area on the

question of federation. The bill failed to pass, and little activity was generated on behalf of the idea in any metropolis for twenty years. A major effort got under way in Alameda County (Oakland) in 1916, culminating in the drafting and presentation to the electorate of a federation charter, the first to be submitted to a popular referendum in the United States. The county voters defeated the charter in 1921.

Another federation plan—the second and last to come before the voters of a metropolis—was rejected by the electorate of Allegheny County (Pittsburgh) in 1929. In the following year, a proposed constitutional amendment to permit St. Louis and St. Louis County to prepare a federation charter failed to gain the necessary statewide electoral support. During the 1920s a detailed plan of this type was drawn up under private auspices for San Francisco and San Mateo County, its neighbor to the south; although the plan was partially included in the new San Francisco charter of 1931, it was never officially presented to the area-wide voters.[25] In 1931, the Massachusetts legislature had two federation bills for the Boston area before it, but did not enact either of them, thus repeating its decision of thirty-five years before.

Then came a lengthy period of only limited activity. Intermittent or short-lived efforts to revive the federation movements in the San Francisco–San Mateo County area, Alameda County, and Allegheny County developed in the 1930s, but none met with success. It was not until 1955 that a major attempt was again made in any metropolis in this nation. In that year, Public Administration Service, a professional consulting organization, prepared a plan of federation for Dade County (Miami), which was approved by a countywide study board created by the city of Miami. A constitutional amendment to permit the adoption of federation and other types of governmental reorganization was transmitted to the state legislature. The legislature, however, changed the amendment to require the existing board of county commissioners to be the governing body of the metropolitan government, thereby converting the reform measure from federation to a comprehensive urban county plan (as discussed

[25] The Alameda County and the San Francisco–San Mateo County federation activities are reviewed in detail in John C. Bollens, *The Problem of Government in the San Francisco Bay Region* (Ann Arbor: University Microfilms, 1964), chap. IV.

earlier in this chapter). No significant support has been organized elsewhere in the United States in later years.

General Characteristics

A number of common characteristics of federation attempts in the United States stand out prominently; some of them also demonstrate major difficulties in adopting this type of reform. First, federation efforts in specific areas, with the exception of those pertaining to Metropolitan Boston, had to obtain state constitutional authorization before they could proceed to the stage of official formulation. This step has proved to be a formidable hurdle, as demonstrated in the St. Louis and Miami areas. Second, all federation plans (other than the Boston area proposals which were presented as legislative bills) took the form of charters, practically all of which were to be drafted by locally elected charter boards. (The exception was the Pittsburgh area charter which was prepared by a commission appointed by the governor.) In both these characteristics, therefore, most federation proposals have been similar to comprehensive urban county plans but unlike metropolitan special districts which have usually been authorized (and even created in some instances) through the enactment of state legislative bills.

A third characteristic of federation efforts has been the requirement of local popular approval for adoption of this kind of arrangement (again the Boston area proposals have been the sole exceptions). And frequently the obtaining of multiple majorities has been required—majorities so numerous as to make such consent a virtual impossibility for any type of proposal, even consent for motherhood, as one wag has suggested, let alone a complex and politically sensitive matter such as federation. Three illustrations show the difficulty of the approval requirement: a majority in each of the ten cities in Alameda County; a countywide majority and a two-thirds majority in each of a majority of the municipalities in Allegheny County; a majority in San Francisco, in San Mateo County, and in each of the municipalities in San Mateo County. Federation plans have usually had to acquire more majorities than the comprehensive urban county proposals, a surprising circumstance in view of the comparable nature of the two approaches. (In the case of the comprehensive urban county plan in Dade County only a single area-wide majority was necessary, a stipulation identical to that required to form many metropolitan special districts.) In fact, the voting requirements to put some city-county consolidation plans into effect—the Nashville area, for example, where dual majorities were the rule—are far simpler than those applied to most federation propositions, surely an illogical situation since city-county consolidation is far more drastic in its effects.

A further common characteristic of proposed federations has been the method of constituting the governing board of the metropolitan unit. Exclusive of most of the Boston area proposals, all other federations called for direct election of all governing body members and for the nomination or election (or both) of some or all the members from areas smaller than the entire territory of the metropolitan government. This matter of board composition has proved to be as sensitive an issue in federation attempts as in comprehensive urban county endeavors.

Differing Characteristics

Proposed federations have also exhibited mixed rather than common characteristics. In terms of area, for instance, the Alameda, Allegheny, and Dade proposals were cast in a one-county context, while the Boston, San Francisco, and St. Louis plans extended beyond a single county. Those for the Boston area concerned one entire county and parts of three others; the San Francisco proposition involved a city-county and a county; and the St. Louis effort related to a city (which does not lie within the boundaries of a county) and a county.

In terms of allocation of functions, pronounced differences are also apparent. Should the metropolitan government or the municipalities have enumerated powers, or should the powers of both levels be specified? All three possibilities have been proposed. In the Alameda and San Francisco–San Mateo County plans, the powers to be exercised by the municipal governments or boroughs were enumerated. In contrast, the Allegheny County charter and the Boston area bills listed the functions of the metropolitan government. In the Dade County federation plan approved by the countywide study group, the powers of both levels of government were specified. One of the most imaginative elements of the Dade County plan was the division of many functions between the metropolitan and municipal levels rather than the assignment of all phases of a function to one or the other level. Thus, for example, refuse collection in municipalities was to be a municipal responsibility while refuse disposal throughout the county was to be handled by the metropolitan government.[26]

Another functional difference in federation proposals involves the magnitude of the responsibilities assigned to the metropolitan government. Since area-wide problems are not identical in all metropolises and since certain advocates of federation take a conservative approach and others a drastic one, some difference would be expected. But the diversity has been extremely broad. In both the Alameda County and the San Francisco–San Mateo County plans, the powers enumerated for the municipal governments or boroughs were relatively few in number, thus endowing the metropolitan government in both instances with sweeping authority. Under the Alameda County charter, the boroughs were limited to (1) passing local ordinances to protect the welfare of persons within their corporate limits, (2) appropriating funds for street repair and maintenance, sewer construction exclusive of main sewers, and police and fire maintenance, (3) assuming bonded indebtedness after local voter approval, (4) making borough improvements through special assessments, and (5) investigating the expenditure of borough funds. The boroughs were expressly forbidden to deal with planning, traffic, building regulation, harbor development, and licenses other than liquor licenses. The powers vested in the municipal governments or boroughs in the San Francisco–San Mateo County plan were also few but somewhat different. The boroughs were restricted to (1) creating zoning and planning areas, (2) constructing, improving, and maintaining streets, bridges, and sidewalks, (3) constructing and maintaining public libraries, parks, local sewers, and public buildings, (4) passing local police ordinances, and (5) incurring debt for public improvements.

On the other hand, in Allegheny County and Metropolitan Boston, where the proposed federations gave the metropolitan governments enumerated powers and the municipalities residual duties, the functional distribution would have made the former less power-

[26] For further details about the proposed division of many services into metropolitan and local phases in the Dade County federation, see Public Administration Service, *The Government of Metropolitan Miami* (Chicago: 1954), pp. 89–90.

ful than its counterparts in the Alameda County and San Francisco area plans. In Allegheny County, the powers of the metropolitan government involved such matters as street construction and maintenance, traffic regulation, mass transit service, smoke control, law enforcement, and health regulations, but the latter two only to supplement the work of municipalities. In the proposal of 1896 for the Boston area, which was typical of plans recommended for that metropolis, the responsibilities of the metropolitan government were severely limited, being confined to the provision of sewage disposal, water supply and distribution, and metropolitan parks, activities which at that time were carried out by three state agencies.

The proposed federation for Dade County established still another pattern of distributing functions and a somewhat different role for the metropolitan government. The metropolitan unit was assigned very few functions in their entirety, chiefly sewage disposal and water service. In addition, it was allotted some but not all aspects of many other functions, including planning, streets and highways, traffic, and public housing.

METROPOLITAN TORONTO: FEDERATION IN ACTION

Metropolitan Toronto, Canada's second most populous urban area, has succeeded where various metropolises in the United States have failed. Federation has been in effect in this area for a number of years; it came into being in April, 1953, when the metropolitan governing body was organized, and became fully operative on January 1, 1954. The combination of three forces was largely responsible for realization of the idea: the criticalness of certain service and financial problems, the recommendations of an impartial board, and the receptivity of the Ontario provincial legislature (the equivalent of a state legislature in the United States).[27]

The Prompting Events

The series of events leading to federation in the Toronto area began in 1912, when the city of Toronto halted its long-time policy

[27] Federation acts for two other Canadian metropolitan areas, Montreal and Winnipeg, were subsequently passed by the Quebec and Manitoba provincial legislatures in 1959 and 1960, respectively. However, the metropolitan governments created under these laws have far fewer powers than the metropolitan government in the Toronto area.

of annexing nearby areas as they became fairly populous. Bringing
their municipal services up to the city's standards was proving very
costly, as the large amount of territory absorbed between 1909 and
1912 clearly demonstrated. Toronto officials, fearing that further
large expenditures might endanger the community's financial status,
decided to reverse the city's traditional policy. After World War I
there was heavy population growth, much of it in sections beyond
Toronto's city limits. With annexation halted, a number of separate
local governments were organized to accommodate this growth, and
by 1930 thirteen municipalities were operating in the area.

After World War II population increased greatly outside
Toronto, particularly in the outer ring of municipalities, while it
declined slightly in the central city. Each of the municipal governments continued to be concerned with a strictly local pattern of
land use and to be largely disinterested in area-wide needs and
progress. Some communities possessed extensive financial resources
as a result of having attracted industries, important commercial establishments, and families who could pay for high-value homes. Others
had low financial resources as a consequence of becoming bedroom
communities for people of very moderate means; but they often had
large-scale needs, as in education.

During the 1940s a number of problems became critical. Various
suburban municipalities, developed as modest residential areas and
lacking substantial industries, found their locally-derived revenues
insufficient at reasonable tax rates to finance their many service
needs. And some of these localities, burdened by an increasingly pre-
carious financial condition, found it impossible to borrow money
at reasonable interest rates. These fiscal shortcomings, coupled
with the inability of localities to work out adequate solutions through
interlocal agreements, caused serious service deficiencies.

Of the numerous problems of area-wide importance, three grew
particularly acute: education, water supply, and sewage disposal.[28]
All municipalities were experiencing drastic percentage increases in
school taxation, ranging in an eight-year period (1944–1951) from
about 100 percent to almost 1000 percent in most suburbs, with the

[28] Frank Smallwood, Metro Toronto: A Decade Later (Toronto: Bureau
of Municipal Research, 1963), p. 10; Frederick G. Gardiner, "Metropolitan
Toronto: A New Answer to Metropolitan Area Problems," Planning: 1953
(Chicago: American Society of Planning Officials, 1953), pp. 38–47.

gain being particularly large in the three outer ring municipalities where rapid growth was continuing. Many communities were having great difficulty in paying for a minimum level of education and needed school construction was lagging seriously. Water supplies became deficient and several suburban communities, separated from Lake Ontario by the city of Toronto, resorted to wells, which soon proved inadequate. Sewage disposal also became increasingly deficient, producing health hazards. Various sewage treatment plants were loaded beyond capacity and the rivers in the area were rapidly becoming open sewers.[29]

There were other serious deficiencies, too. No system of arterial highways existed to aid the development and serve the needs of the entire area; decisions about these lifelines of the metropolis were stalemated because of the disagreement of municipal officials over location and financing. Streets that had long been inadequate proved less and less capable of handling the constantly growing volume of traffic. Mass transit continued to deteriorate, thereby failing to contribute positively to the vital function of circulation. Housing, especially low-cost housing, was in very short supply; Toronto was largely built up and its land was high-priced, but many suburbs that had available land were unsuitable because they could not finance necessary public services. Many official metropolitan planning studies had been made but they were largely ineffective because each municipality controlled its own land use policies and practically always took a parochial view on such matters.

Applications to the Ontario Municipal Board

The swelling fiscal and service aggravations made the time propitious for governmental reorganization of the metropolis, but there was broad disagreement locally over what course should be followed. The crucial factor in resolving these differences was the existence of the Ontario Municipal Board, a province-appointed quasi-judicial and administrative agency. This board exercises control over aspects of

[29] Toronto's water and sewage facilities were adequate for the needs of its residents and for a number of years this central city supplied water to the suburbs and allowed connections to its sewer system up to the limit of the capacity of its plants. Having reached a stable population size, Toronto did not want to make costly expenditures from its own funds to expand the capacity of its plants and intermunicipal agreements providing the necessary means of financing could not be successfully negotiated.

local governmental finance and, upon application by one or more municipalities, can order boundary adjustments permitted under existing provincial legislation, including the consolidation of any number of communities, annexation of one municipality to another, or the creation of certain new governmental authorities.

The movement for reform started in 1946 when the small suburban municipality of Mimico applied to the Ontario Municipal Board for an order to create an area for the joint administration of education, fire and police protection, administration of justice, health and welfare, planning, sewage disposal, and public utilities, including transportation and main highways. The proposal to create such an area involved the formation of a new government headed by an elected governing body; its territory would include ten of the municipalities in their entirety and the three others in part. The Board took no action at that time.[30]

Applications to the Ontario Municipal Board resumed in January, 1950, when Long Branch, another small suburban community, filed two petitions, one requesting the consolidation of four municipalities and the other asking for the merger of eleven in their entirety and substantial parts of the other two. In the following month, Toronto filed an application, which in its final form called for the consolidation of all thirteen units into a single government.

The Board determined that the Toronto and Mimico applications were related matters and gave priority to the former, with the understanding that the evidence and material submitted at the hearing would be applicable to the Mimico proposal. The Long Branch petition was postponed indefinitely. The hearing, which started in June, 1950, was very long and detailed; it covered a year and involved considerable participation by local public officials and private leaders and the submission of hundreds of reports and other exhibits. Only Toronto and Mimico favored the application; the eleven other municipalities and York County vigorously and bitterly opposed it. The Board took the matter under advisement in June, 1951, but

[30] Ontario Municipal Board, *Decisions and Recommendations of the Board* (Toronto: January 20, 1953), p. 3. This publication, also known as the Cumming Report (after the board chairman, Lorne Cumming), is a very thoughtful analysis and certainly one of the most interesting and significant commentaries on government in a metropolis in the twentieth century.

did not release its decisions and recommendations until January, 1953.

The Board's Decisions and Proposal

The Board denied both the Toronto and Mimico applications, but stated that it felt obliged to "assume the responsibility of presenting its own proposals for the organization of a suitable form of metropolitan government in the Toronto area . . . [largely because the present applicants] have clearly established the urgent need for some major reform of the existing system. . . ."[31] It accordingly submitted to the provincial premier a plan of federation for the thirteen municipalities. The premier responded favorably and had a bill introduced in the provincial legislature. The proposal, which largely followed the recommendations of the Ontario Municipal Board, was promptly enacted by the legislature in April, 1953; the metropolitan governing body was established in the same month, and the act went into full effect on the first day of the following year.

Functions of the Metropolitan and Municipal Governments

The main features of the Metropolitan Toronto federation are (1) the establishment of an area-wide government, the Municipality of Metropolitan Toronto, encompassing the areas of all thirteen municipalities (a total of 241 square miles, containing at the plan's inception about 1,200,000 residents), to perform functions deemed essential to the entire metropolis; (2) the continued existence of the city of Toronto and of the twelve suburbs (the latter now separated from York County), to carry out functions not assigned to the metropolitan government; and (3) representation from each municipality on the metropolitan governing body.

The plan set up a strong metropolitan government, one endowed with many powers relating to many functions—assessment of property, water supply, sewage disposal, arterial roads, transit, health and welfare services, administration of justice, metropolitan parks, public housing and redevelopment, and planning. In a number of functional areas certain responsibilities were assigned to the new government and others remained with the municipalities. In some

[31] Ontario Municipal Board, *Decisions and Recommendations of the Board*, p. 42. The reasons for denial of the Toronto and Mimico applications appear on pages 28–32 and 33–39 of this publication.

instances of shared functions—water and sewerage are prominent examples—the metropolitan government took on the role of wholesaler. It was given responsibility for construction and maintenance of pumping stations, treatment plants, trunk mains, and reservoirs in supplying water. It sells water at a wholesale rate to the municipalities, which own the local distribution systems and supply water to consumers at locally-determined retail prices. Similarly, it constructs and maintains trunk sewer mains and treatment plants

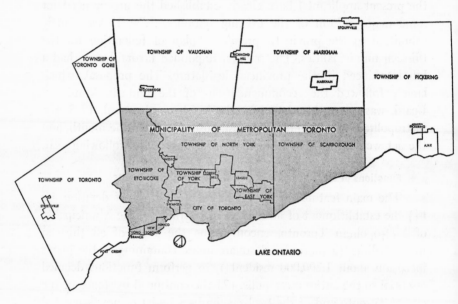

Figure 15.3 The Municipality of Metropolitan Toronto and Its Thirteen Member Municipalities. Source: Metropolitan Toronto Planning Board.

and disposes of sewage from municipalities at wholesale rates. The latter in turn operate the local sewage collection systems.

In other instances, the sharing of a function was devised on a different basis, that of making the metropolitan unit a financial overseer. For example, in the field of education the metropolitan government, on the advice of an independent metropolitan school board, determines the amounts of funds to be approved for the purchase of school sites and the construction of buildings, and issues bonds for such purposes against its own credit. (In addition, to

bring about a greater degree of equalization of educational opportunities, the metropolitan school board pays some of the debt
charges for schools and makes uniform per pupil payments to
local school boards.) On the other hand, eleven locally-elected
school boards operate the public elementary and secondary schools
in the municipalities. The metropolitan government also reviews the
bond proposals of municipalities and floats bonds in its name for
those propositions it approves.

In still other instances of shared functions, the Municipality
of Metropolitan Toronto was assigned various aspects of a service
on the basis of a clear area-wide need. It was, for example, made
responsible for building and maintaining a system of arterial highways (but not local streets) and developing and operating large
metropolitan parks (but not local parks).

The metropolitan government also was given the power to appoint the members of the Toronto Transit Commission, which
consolidated all existing systems and became the area's exclusive
supplier of public transportation. And the metropolitan unit was
authorized to undertake public housing and redevelopment projects;
provide a courthouse, jail, and juvenile and family court; and assess
property at a uniform rate throughout the area for use in both
metropolitan and local tax levies. Finally and very importantly, the
new government was empowered to adopt an area-wide general
plan, which would be controlling in the municipalities after the
approval of the provincial minister of planning development.

This constituted the metropolitan government's package of
service responsibilities until 1957, when provincial legislation added
several others: law enforcement, air pollution control, most aspects
of licensing, and civil defense. Although this action represented a
further diminution of local powers, the local governments still retain a number of functions; some of them, such as the provision
of public elementary and secondary education, libraries, fire protection, and most phases of public health, are of great importance.

The Metropolitan Governing Board

The Metropolitan Council, the official name of the governing
body, consists of twenty-five members (twenty-four if it decides to
select a chairman—who serves as the government's chief executive

officer—from among its own membership instead of from outside). So far there have been only two chairmen, both former municipal officials and chosen from outside.

The federation act provides for equal representation between the central city and suburbs (both have twelve members) and for equal representation among the suburbs (each of the twelve has one member). It also stipulates that officials of the municipalities would serve as the governing board members of the metropolitan unit. Thus, Toronto's representatives are the mayor, the two controllers who received the highest number of votes in the last city-wide election, and the nine aldermen (councilmen) who acquired the largest number of ballots in their respective districts at the last municipal election.[32] The heads (mayors and reeves) of the other municipalities are the suburban representatives. The federation law further specifies two-year terms for Metropolitan Council members, but most of them must face annual elections to retain their positions in their own municipalities, a fact making possible a considerable annual turnover in the Council membership.

The representation formula spelled out in the law has been a constant point of controversy. From the beginning, most dissatisfaction has centered on the equality of representation for the suburban units. Some suburbs had ten times the population of others at the inception of the federation plan and these differences have subsequently become even greater. In addition, discontent has been expressed recently with the equality of representation between the central city and the suburbs. At the time of the plan's inauguration, the city of Toronto had 57 percent of the area's population, but with the continued suburban growth it now has only about 40 percent.

Progress Under Federation

In a short time, the Municipality of Metropolitan Toronto has registered a variety of major accomplishments, many of them realized because of the vigorous leadership of the Council's first chairman, Frederick G. Gardiner, and his emphasis upon improving the phys-

[32] Four Toronto controllers, along with the mayor, make up a board of control, which has important financial and personnel authority in the Toronto city government.

ical facilities and public finances of the metropolis. Gardiner, a former suburban reeve (mayor), a well-to-do corporation lawyer, and a dynamic, hard working, and practical man, served as council chairman from 1953 through 1961.[33] And the progress made since his retirement has largely been in the mold he shaped.

In the first ten years of the new government's existence (1953–1963), major advances were particularly evident in water supply, sewage disposal, and education—needs which had been critical before the federation arrangement. During this period, the water supply capacity was increased by almost one-half and the number of miles of trunk distribution mains was more than doubled. A comparable achievement was recorded in sewage disposal through an increase of 70 percent in sewage treatment capacity. A gigantic school construction program was completed, involving 175 new schools and about 300 additions to schools.

There were other noticeable gains, too, during this decade. A metropolitan park system of several thousand acres was established. An extensive program of expressway construction was launched and many road improvements were made. Construction of a second subway for mass transit got under way. Air pollution was brought under effective control. Unified law enforcement helped to produce a reduced crime rate and an increased level of clearance of crimes. In addition, the metropolitan government had acquired a triple "A" credit rating in Canada and a double "A" rating in New York City, the highest classification a foreign corporation can receive in the United States. One of the consequences of this excellent financial standing was the savings on interest charges of more than $50 million in the decade. "Without fear of contradiction," Mr. Gardiner emphasized in a speech delivered shortly before his retirement, "I can say that we never could have made the progress we have under our old system of thirteen locally autonomous municipalities."[34]

[33] William R. Allen, Mr. Gardiner's successor, was a former controller in the city of Toronto.

[34] Frederick G. Gardiner, "Getting Things Started," National Civic Review, LI (January, 1962), 10–11. Various accomplishments are recounted in Municipality of Metropolitan Toronto, Metropolitan Toronto, 1953–1963: A Decade of Progress (Toronto: 1963). Also see Smallwood, Metro Toronto: A Decade Later, pp. 12–13, and G. Arthur Lascelles, "Financing Metropolitan Improvements," Municipal Finance, XXXII (August, 1959), 46–51.

Criticisms of the Toronto Area Federation

Although the federation system in Metropolitan Toronto has had much success, it has not been free of criticism. A study made in 1959 by John Grumm, a political scientist, well illustrates the general nature of the censure. While praising the various types of progress that had been made, Grumm noted that the emphasis had been upon tangible public works, where concrete results could be rapidly achieved, whereas the metropolitan government had moved slowly on those problems requiring the use of powers that might disturb local interests and local loyalties.[35]

Frank Smallwood, also a political scientist, completed another analysis of the federation experience in 1962. His praise and criticism partly paralleled those of Professor Grumm. Smallwood called the metropolitan government's success in eliminating crisis situations involving physical plant needs "a highly notable accomplishment," but he also observed that "Ten years' cumulative experience indicates that the Metropolitan Council has been consistently aggressive in tackling the so-called 'hard-core' problems where results are concrete and obvious, and considerably less assertive in meeting some of the 'softer,' more socially-oriented issue areas where results are usually less tangible and more controversial."[36]

Professor Smallwood was particularly critical of the metropolitan government's lack of assertiveness in public housing, planning, and publicity and information. On the first count, he pointed out that only 5000 units of public housing were completed in Metropolitan Toronto in the first ten years of the government's existence, despite the proliferation of housing authorities in the metropolis. On the second count, he complained that although the metropolitan planning board had prepared a master plan for the area, it had not yet been approved by the Metropolitan Council and put into effect. On the third count, he observed that the Metropolitan Council had viewed its public information effort as an added chore and relegated it to the metropolitan planning board, an operational unit

---

[35] For fuller details, see John G. Grumm, *Metropolitan Area Government: The Toronto Experience* (Lawrence: University of Kansas Publications, Governmental Research Series No. 19).

[36] Smallwood, *Metro Toronto: A Decade Later*, pp. 11–12, 35.

that already had a full-time responsibility. Professor Smallwood then concluded:

> In addition to its responsibility to respond to existing crisis situations, any strong leadership agency must be prepared to anticipate future developments and to educate the public with regard to their implications. . . . Metro's forte to date, however, has most decidedly been an emphasis upon response to already apparent crisis situations to an extent where the other components of the leadership process, most especially public information and education, have been largely ignored.
>
> .   .   .
>
> During the formative years, one of the reasons Metro has been able to achieve a considerable degree of consensus among its member municipalities has been due to the fact that the basic problems that have represented its primary fields of interest have been relatively obvious in their priorities and relatively non-controversial in their implications. . . . As Metro now places increasing emphasis on welfare, housing, recreation, and the like, the considerably more contentious nature of these new priorities (complete with all their implications of 'unnecessary frills') promises to place increasing strains upon the original federation framework. In short, Metro has been suffering from a growing lack of resolution during its first decade in precisely those fields that will demand an increasing amount of its attention during the next decade. It is highly debatable whether the existing Metro municipalities will be able to achieve a degree of consensus on these newly emerging issues of social reform that will be comparable to the degree of consensus they have been able to achieve in the past when considering the more tangible, 'hard core' problems that have monopolized Metro's first decade.[37]

Acceptance of Metropolitan Government

On balance, the metropolitan government concept is clearly well established in Metropolitan Toronto, where it has received a far different reception from that given to it in Dade County. There is no interest in returning to the totally fragmented arrangement that existed before federation in 1953; this is true even among the many suburbs that so strongly opposed consolidation at that time. Instead, the changes that have been completed or advocated have been in the direction of more comprehensive reform, witness the functions added by provincial legislation to the metropolitan government's original assignment of functions in 1957 and the proposals of an official study group in 1961 (the Gathercole Report)

[37] Smallwood, *Metro Toronto: A Decade Later*, pp. 37, 38–39.

which called for the consolidation of the thirteen municipalities into four or five cities or boroughs of more equal population and financial resources. Similarly, various political leaders and newspapers, mostly based in the central city, have long urged consolidation of the whole area as a replacement for federation.[38]

The matter of governmental reorganization will doubtlessly remain on the civic agenda of Metropolitan Toronto for some time to come. Debate will continue to revolve around such questions as the basis of representation on the Metropolitan Council, the division of powers between the metropolitan and local levels of government, and the respective merits of federation and consolidation. The situation could not be otherwise, as no governmental arrangement can be considered final in a dynamic and rapidly growing urban community.

THE TWO-LEVEL APPROACH: THE FUTURE

The various comprehensive forms of the two-level approach—the metropolitan multipurpose district, the comprehensive urban county plan, and federation—will continue to be appealing to reformers, at least on a theoretical basis, because these devices grant only certain functions to a metropolitan unit and generally have the members of its governing body chosen from local areas. But these very elements which make this approach appealing will remain major obstacles to gaining acceptance for any of its variations. Once the decision has been reached to construct a two-level arrangement, it is very difficult to reach consensus on what functions should be vested in the upper or metropolitan level and how its governing board should be constituted. Whatever determination is made on these two matters, there is almost inevitably considerable dissatisfaction.

Neither of these troublesome issues haunts metropolitan special

[38] Some consolidation adherents argue their case in part on the premise that the Ontario Municipal Board, in drawing up its proposals in 1953, regarded federation as a short and immediate step to consolidation. Actually the Board said, "The board is convinced that the local governments will always have a vital role in the general scheme of metropolitan government." Ontario Municipal Board, *Decisions and Recommendations of the Board* (January 20, 1953), p. 45. The governmental organization of Metropolitan Toronto is now under study by a royal commission established in 1963.

districts; each is assigned only one function or a very few and generally little thought is given and little concern is expressed about the composition of their governing boards, even when the districts are of an interstate nature. Moreover, each such district has usually been created to deal with a particular problem, one on which a considerable portion of the citizenry wants action; it thus has built-in public support, a favorable factor that has customarily been lacking in efforts on behalf of the more comprehensive forms of the two-level approach. In addition, the metropolitan special district has great territorial flexibility (some districts are the only interstate metropolitan governments in existence) and its establishment does not cause a major upheaval in the governmental system. For all of these reasons, this type of district seems likely to grow in use.

On the other hand, there is at present no substantial evidence foretelling the probability that metropolitan special districts will evolve into or will be replaced by multipurpose districts. In fact, as the metropolitan multipurpose district concept has become more widely advocated and understood, opposition to it has increased, even to the point of successfully blocking the passage of enabling legislation to permit its use. Such a unit poses a threat to the powers of established governments, including previously created metropolitan special districts, all of which have proprietary interests in avoiding extensive changes.

Next to the metropolitan special district, the comprehensive urban county plan seems the most likely prospect among the two-level arrangements for expanded use in the future. It has a distinct advantage over other multipurpose two-level forms: it utilizes an existing governmental unit instead of creating a new one. The advantage can be deceptive, however, since employment of the plan generally calls for substantial structural and functional (and often financial) renovation of the county government. In the past the strength of the county bureaucracy in opposing major structural change, a strength enhanced by the fact that county organization is often imbedded in the state constitution, has been such as to block the drive for adoption of the comprehensive urban county plan in practically all cases. There are no important signs of change on this matter; consequently there is little prospect of widespread adoption of this idea in the near future. The much more likely prospect is that many county governments in metropolitan areas, most of which still embrace only a single county, will gradually become more important through piecemeal transfers of functions and contractual relationships involving municipalities.

Federation conceivably may be proposed and actually adopted in a limited number of urban areas. Like the metropolitan multipurpose district, however, it is confronted by a lack of public knowledge and enthusiasm, the latter emanating in part from the fact that use of this device produces still another government. Furthermore, in some instances creation of a federation system would result in elimination of the county government, an action that would encounter strong opposition, particularly from county officials and their supporters. Finally, as in the case of the other comprehensive types of the two-level approach, federation faces strong competition from two already widely used alternatives: the metropolitan special district and the gradually evolving county government.

CHAPTER 16

The Politics of Reform

CIVIC LEADERS of recent decades have tended to view metropolitan governmental reform as comparable to the reorganization of a private business corporation. The issue to them has been less a political question than one of proper management methods and administrative tidiness. Unlike the city reformers of the early 1900s, who effectively utilized the battle cry of "throw the rascals out," the modern advocates of metropolitan restructuring have invoked the culturally respected symbols of efficiency and economy. In place of the charges of corruption and machine politics, they have aimed their fire at overlapping jurisdictions, governmental fragmentation, confusion of responsibility, and outmoded administrative structures. Disdaining the rhetoric of emotion and fear, they have appealed to the good sense and rationality of the citizenry. At times they have been shocked by their opponents' tactics, but mostly they have been disillusioned and disheartened by the apathetic public response to their proposals.

The drive for metropolitan reform has rested on what appear to be sound premises. Supporters of the movement have consistently emphasized the theme that problems which are metropolitan in scope and impact demand treatment by an agency with area-wide authority, not by a fragmented local polity or governmental system. This position may be difficult to refute rationally; but reason, as we well know, does not always prevail in the world of reality. In basing their case on logic, the reformers have generally ignored, or at least minimized, the fact that governmental reorganization is a highly charged political question as well as an exercise in management efficiency. Although not unaware of the political obstacles, they have assumed that once the public was informed of the "convincing" facts, the resistance of "petty" interests and "small minds" would be swept aside in an inexorable march toward civic redemption.

The optimistic appraisal of the reformers has missed the mark by a wide margin. General public response to the "logic" of the situation has been lukewarm and disappointing, while political resistance to change has been strong and largely insurmountable. Why has this been so? When alterations are made in an existing system of government, the stakes of various individuals and groups are affected in one fashion or another. To some, the prospect of change may hold out inducements and promises of rewards; to others, it will appear as a threat to their interests. Metropolitan reform is no exception to the rule. Unfortunately for its success, however, the potential rewards of a reconstituted polity have seemed too remote in the eyes of most social and economic interests to call for deep involvement on their part. Hence, while many of them have been sympathetic to the objectives of metropolitan reorganization, few have been willing to commit more than token resources to the cause. The same cannot be said of the opposition. Reshaping the governmental structure of the metropolis directly impinges upon a variety of change-resistant interests and clusters of power, particularly on the established local public bureaucracy. These interests, as case after case has demonstrated, can be quickly mobilized into an effective opposition through the existing network of relationships among public officials and their allied cliques, such as political party organizations and leagues of municipalities.

No amount of wishful thinking can make metropolitan reform an apolitical issue. It is a question that must be resolved in the civic arena with the aid of political weapons and political techniques. It is not, as some would have us believe, a battle between the enlightened and unselfish on the one hand, and the ignorant and self-seeking on the other. The tendency to view urban governmental reorganization in these simple and moralistic terms has handicapped the movement by divorcing it from reality. Neither side has a monopoly on virtue. Just as the most active opponents of reform are those who profit from retention of the status quo, so the most highly motivated supporters of reorganization are frequently those who stand to gain by the proposed alterations in the existing system. Actually, the weakness of the reform cause is that too few in its cadre have seen any real personal benefit in change.

In this chapter, after first noting several commonly cited barriers to metropolitan governmental change, we identify the major groups and interests that are usually involved in reform efforts and the values that each seeks to advance or protect. We next examine in some detail four reorganization campaigns: two of the very few cases, Miami and Nashville, where significant change has been accomplished, and two of the numerous instances, St. Louis and Cleveland, where it has failed. Last, we present some propositions and generalizations about the politics of metropolitan reform that have emerged from current research efforts.

BARRIERS TO CHANGE

Scott Greer, in his brief but incisive analysis of metropolitan civic life, lists three groups of interrelated impediments to governmental restructuring: (1) the underlying cultural norms of Americans concerning local government; (2) the resulting legal-constitutional arrangements; and (3) the political-governmental system built upon them.[1] To these we would add (4) the indifference of the citizenry to structural change; and (5) the increasing scale of urban society. All of these relate, in one way or another, either to the ideology and theory that underlie the American urban polity or to the forces that are questioning the traditional concept of the metropolis and its governance.

The norms that have helped shape our system of local government are derivatives of Jeffersonian and Jacksonian ideologies. From

[1] *Governing the Metropolis* (New York: Wiley, 1962), pp. 124–125.

Jefferson we inherited the "grass-roots" concept of government and the distrust of those who exercise the powers of office. His ideas on local government were always couched in terms of the small community of educated yeomen rather than the large city with its teeming populace. To him, the New England town with its meetings of all the citizenry was "the wisest invention ever devised by the wit of man for the perfect exercise of self-government and for its preservation." Jacksonians, too, stressed the "sacred right" of local self-rule, but unlike their aristocratic predecessors, they welcomed the urban masses to share in the function of government. Public office was opened to all on the premise that any citizen of normal intelligence could satisfactorily manage the affairs of his city or county. Rotation in office, popular election of numerous officials, and the spoils system became standard features of local government during the second half of the nineteenth century.

The municipal reform movement, at the turn of the present century, was a repudiation of Jacksonian practices but not of its grass-roots ideology. To combat the corruption of city politics, the reformers offered the short ballot, professional management, nonpartisan elections, and the initiative, referendum, and recall, which exposed the governmental system to the direct action or veto of the voter. The inherent right of the community to govern itself free from undue interference by the state legislature, a right implicit in both Jeffersonian and Jacksonian theory, was also institutionalized during this period by state constitutional and statutory provisions relating to municipal "home rule." These enactments supplemented the earlier guarantees of local self-determination, which included generous incorporation laws for the indiscriminate creation of municipalities. They were also accompanied by difficult annexation requirements permitting intransigent groups of fringe area dwellers to remain outside the corporate citadel and by legal conditions making it virtually impossible to consolidate or eliminate existing governmental units. So deeply entrenched in American folklore are the norms which these measures purport to safeguard that those who attempt to alter the system must be prepared to face charges of removing government from the people, infringing on basic human rights, and destroying local self-rule.

The political-governmental pattern that has evolved at the local level, grounded as it is on these norms and beliefs, stands as a formidable obstacle to change. Cloaked in the protective mantle of statutory and constitutional legitimacy and defended by the entrenched bureaucracy, the system has managed to maintain itself without submitting to major surgery. Any alteration of significance is viewed as a threat to the "establishment" and its retinue of followers. Few incumbent officeholders or others who benefit from existing arrangements are willing to gamble on possible gains that a reordered structure might bring them. Similarly, those who aspire to the rewards of local public office are willing to play the game within the existing system and according to its rules. The local "establishment," moreover, holds a strategic weapon for defending its stronghold against attack. Unlike the reformers who have no ready-made machine for mobilizing support but must carry their message through the mass media and from the lecture podium, it has access to political cadres and mass-based organizations that serve as important reference points for voters. Add to this advantage the experience of local officeholders in the art of political in-fighting and the odds against major change become impressive.

The defense of the status quo is further favored by the apathetic attitude of the citizenry toward metropolitan reorganization. We commented on this phenomenon earlier in Chapter 8, in citing the relatively low rate of participation and interest that characterizes local political affairs generally. An important reason for this indifference rests in the fact that urban dwellers are fairly well satisfied with their local governments and see no impelling reason for change. Both the St. Louis and Dayton surveys, for example, showed that residents in those areas had no strong criticism of any of their governments and few complaints about services.[2] In St. Louis, only one unit among the 149 was considered to be performing poorly by as many as 10 percent of the residents—and ironically, this was the sewer district, an area-wide agency. In Dayton, only about one of each ten persons felt that his local government was performing inefficiently or was unresponsive to the people. Less than one-half the residents had even registered a complaint or even felt like complaining about a local governmental service. Almost 60 percent could

---

[2] See John C. Bollens (ed.), *Exploring the Metropolitan Community* (Berkeley and Los Angeles: University of California Press, 1961), pp. 188–190; and *Metropolitan Challenge* (Dayton: Metropolitan Community Studies, 1959), pp. 241–251.

name no more than one service with which they were dissatisfied. Similar results were obtained in a group of Wisconsin communities. Only a relatively small number (less than 20 percent) of the citizens said that their local governments were inefficient or the performance of their public officials poor.[3] The story was the same in Cleveland, as Table 32 clearly demonstrates. To convince a relatively satisfied electorate of the need for major change is a substantial undertaking.

TABLE 32

Citizen Evaluation of Local Governmental Services,
Cleveland Metropolitan Area, 1958

SERVICE	PERCENT COMPLETELY SATISFIED	PERCENT PARTLY SATISFIED	PERCENT NOT AT ALL SATISFIED	PERCENT NO OPINION
Water service	90	6	2	2
Fire protection	89	7	1	3
Public health	72	13	4	11
Police protection	70	22	7	1
School	67	22	6	5
Sewer services	64	17	13	6
Public welfare	61	15	5	19
Main thoroughfares	55	27	14	4
Bus and transit	40	24	28	8

SOURCE: James A. Norton, The Metro Experience (Cleveland: The Press of Western Reserve University, 1963), p. 61.

Urban life is characterized by increasing size: the concentration of large aggregations of people, growth in the size of business corporations and private associations, widespread expansion of the communications and transportation network. Made possible by technological progress and the resulting organizational transformation of society, the twentieth century metropolis finds itself in an ever-expanding web of activity and an ever-widening radius of interdependence. To work out a satisfactory and acceptable system of government for this complex entity is a challenging task. External as well as internal forces and factors impinge upon the local political

[3] Henry J. Schmandt and William Standing, Citizen Images of the Fox River Valley (Madison: University of Wisconsin Survey Research Laboratory, 1962), p. 13.

process. Decisions made at the distant headquarters of a locally-based industrial plant or department store, in the Washington offices of a federal agency, or in the administrative bureaus at the state capital can often shape local policy. So also the cumulative effect of numerous land use decisions by private developers and financial institutions can do much to alter the face and even character of the metropolitan community.

It seems anomalous that the governmental organization of the metropolis should move in a direction opposite to that of other major segments of the society. While the local polity has become more fragmented, business, labor, and other associations have been able, by means of increasing organizational scale, to achieve a measure of control over their environment that is denied the metropolitan community. Some observers have speculated that the local governmental system represents for many the last stronghold against the growing societal scale, against "bigness."[4] They reason that this feeling accounts for much of the lack of popular enthusiasm in reorganization matters and makes voters more receptive to the "grass-roots" argument.

Whether this speculation is sound or not, the reformers are at a disadvantage in answering the rhetoric of the opposition. The intricate nature of the problems which the metropolis faces is not easily comprehensible. Because of this complexity, neither the problems nor the possible remedies can be articulated and expressed in clear-cut and readily understandable terms. The opponents of change may have little logic on their side, but they have the effective myths and symbols; the reformers may possess the logic but they lack myths and symbols with popular appeal. To the cry of "keep government close to the people," the reformers can only speak of the brighter future and better environment that reorganization will presumably assure. To the challenge, "show the people why the system which has served them for so long should be discarded," the proponents can only reply with generalized and vague statements about efficiency, orderly growth, and future dangers, or with arguments so complex that their importance escapes the average citizen. As one Cleveland official remarked in telling of the advantage he had in fighting the proposed comprehensive urban county charter,

[4] See, for example, Robert Wood, *Suburbia* (Boston: Houghton Mifflin, 1959).

"I'd say to them, 'Say, what's wrong with the present situation? You've got a good government. What's wrong? Show me.' "[5]

WHO GETS INVOLVED

In a large-scale society, individuals acting alone are handicapped in affecting collective behavior. It is primarily through organizational membership that they enlarge their opportunities and resources to influence social action. Hence, the question of who gets involved in metropolitan reform efforts pertains less to the individual actors than to the groups or associations of which they are a part. To answer the question, it is necessary to ascertain what organizations initiate change. Who provides the resources for carrying on the campaign? Where does the opposition arise? What stakes do the various participants have in the outcome? We need not throw our net wide in this undertaking, since the active participants in metropolitan reform campaigns constitute a relatively minor segment of the organized populace. The issue has not generated deep community conflict or seriously involved a broad range of urban interest groups.

Civic Organizations

Much of the impetus for metropolitan governmental restructuring comes from two sources: civic organizations (sometimes referred to as the "good government" groups) and the central city daily newspapers. At times, a maverick politician or underemployed young lawyer seeking publicity may spark the revolt, but the flame will be short lived unless the fuel to keep it burning is supplied by the established groups. Most often, the initial push will come from organizations that are heirs of the municipal reform spirit and philosophy of the early 1900s: citizens' leagues, bureaus of municipal research, good government councils, and leagues of women voters. These groups began to turn their attention to the larger community as central cities became better governed and the critical urban problems outgrew individual corporate boundaries. Gradually, over the years, metropolitan reorganization came to occupy the place on the civic agenda that municipal reform held earlier.

The interests of the social and economic influentials were channeled into the metropolitan reform field largely by the profes-

[5] Greer, *Governing the Metropolis*, p. 16.

sionals who staff the key civic organizations, by concerned political scientists, and by the promptings of the National Municipal League, the patriarch of the good government groups. Few of the notables who support such movements are motivated by prospects of personal gain. Some feel that reorganization will result in a better business and industrial climate, but most act out of a sense of *noblesse oblige*. As persons of civic reputation and stature, they have a feeling of responsibility for the well-being and governance of the area. Metropolitan reform provides them with a respected outlet for meeting this obligation. However, the role, as they see it, does not necessarily imply personal involvement; more often, it means legitimizing the issue as worthy of community support. The actual task of carrying the campaign forward is left to the professional staffs and younger aspirants in the group, to public relations hirelings, and to the workhorse civic organizations such as the League of Women Voters.

One element of the business community, the downtown interests, has a more personal stake in metropolitan reorganization. Concerned with the economic position of the central business district, many merchants and property owners feel that area-wide governmental change may in some way aid the center by giving it greater prominence in a reconstituted polity. In the Miami area, the downtown groups pushed vigorously for metropolitan government, seeing in it a means of relieving the tax pressure on property in the core city by spreading the base over a larger area. Central city or metropolitan chambers of commerce serve as the organizational mechanism for articulating and executing the support of these interests.

Aside from the nebulous prospect of direct economic gain for their members, chambers of commerce are ideologically disposed to regard such movements with favor. The "booster" spirit which permeates their operations finds expression in the gospel of "a bigger and better community." Most of the groups see metropolitan restructuring as a symbolic aid in promoting the image of a progressive community, one distinguished by civic vitality and modernized government. Typical was the plea in the Dade County charter campaign: "Give Miami a chance to be a big city." This view of metropolitan aggrandizement through governmental integration is not shared by the suburban chambers of commerce and the local merchants they represent. To them, reorganization means a loss or diminution of their influence over the public affairs of the suburbs in which they operate. As a consequence, they are usually found in the ranks of those actively opposing change.

The Press

The daily newspapers in the central city are usually staunch advocates of metropolitan reform. In some areas, such as Miami, they have been prime instigators of reorganization movements. In others, such as St. Louis, they have editorially tried to prod the civic élite into action. As organs with an area-wide audience and outlook, they are attracted to metropolitan reorganization as an appropriate cause for their crusading zeal. And by championing the vision of the larger community, they can fulfill their role expectations as "integrative" symbols of the metropolis.

In contrast to the large dailies, the suburban community press is almost always opposed to major change in the existing system. Long characterized by bias against the central city and an equally strong anti-metropolitan press attitude, the suburban papers find area-wide reorganization measures useful targets. By picturing such proposals as the products of central city politicians or of "undesirable" elements seeking to invade suburbia, they can pose as protectors of small-community virtues. Metropolitan reorganization gives them an opportunity to launch a "safe" crusade of the type they can rarely afford on local issues for fear of alienating some of their readership. As locally based and locally oriented instrumentalities dependent on the business advertising of the village merchants and the subscriptions of residents in their limited area, they feel a personal stake in keeping the existing governmental system intact. The fiction of small community autonomy is a strong legitimizer for their existence. Any movement which threatens to undermine this fiction or lessen the importance of the suburban governments is a cause for battle.

The Local Bureaucracy

Wherever a "going system" of local government exists, we can expect it to react against radical transformation. If it did not, it could hardly be called a system. We can thus generalize that incumbent officeholders will usually be found in the camp of the opposition. There are, of course, many exceptions, some of them significant. The city manager of Miami, the county engineer of Cuyahoga

County, the president of the St. Louis Board of Aldermen, the mayor of Nashville (in the 1959 campaign), all supported metropolitan reorganization efforts in their areas. In each instance, however, the incumbent could see in the proposed reform an opportunity to extend his sphere of control or obtain other rewards. Only on rare occasions will an individual support change that will abolish or reduce the powers of his office.

In the past, many central city officials strongly espoused plans for total merger. They viewed consolidation as an enlargement of the city's boundaries and hence an enhancement of its political power. On the other hand, they reacted negatively when lesser remedies were proposed—a federated system, for example—which would reduce the powers of the core city. Now the tendency is for central city officials to oppose even merger. This solution involves the risk that control may shift to the periphery where the suburban population in many metropolitan communities is rapidly approaching or exceeding that of the core. The risk is particularly great in areas where the politics of the central city is predominantly Democratic and that of the suburbs Republican. Central city officials have also become apprehensive that assuming responsibility for the suburbs might increase rather than diminish the city's fiscal difficulties. Mayor Raymond R. Tucker of St. Louis, for example, opposed a consolidation of the governments of that area in 1962, fearing the impact of such action on the redevelopment and other ongoing programs of the city and on its tax structure.

Suburban officialdom stands solidly against any major restructuring of the existing system. Only an occasional mayor of an upper socioeconomic community will support a metropolitan multipurpose district or other reform measure short of consolidation. Not uncommonly suburban officials express their willingness to have "true" metropolitan functions handled on a unified basis. Such a function, as they conceive it, is one which they badly need but cannot perform for themselves because of cost. Water supply and sewage disposal are two common examples. In such cases, officials of the affected communities will usually acquiesce in the assumption of the service by the county government or the creation of a metropolitan single-purpose district to handle it. This kind of area-wide administration finds acceptance because it involves little or no loss of power for the local units and wards off the possible danger of more thorough changes by taking care of the most immediate and trouble-some deficiencies.

Other Participants

In addition to the principal protagonists already mentioned, other groups such as political parties and labor unions are often found among the participants in the reform drama. The extent of their activity varies considerably, depending on the circumstances and the issues at stake. Occasionally, one or more of them may play a major role, but usually their participation is not great. The political parties provide the best illustration of this low degree of involvement. In few of the recent campaigns have they taken an official stand. Party regulars at the ward, township, and state legislative district levels in some instances have utilized the organizational machinery in their bailiwicks to mobilize support or opposition, usually the latter, but the extensiveness of these activities has varied from area to area. Individual political leaders have also taken public positions on the issue, but few have used their political "muscle" to influence the outcome. Neither the reorganization issue nor the potential rewards of an altered system seem to provide sufficient motivation for this kind of commitment. Moreover, the insignificant amount of patronage at the municipal level and the widespread use of nonpartisan elections contribute to this result by dampening party interest in local governmental affairs. Ironically, these two major accomplishments of municipal reformers now seriously impede the efforts of the metropolitan reformers.

Organized labor is another group frequently found among the participants in reorganization campaigns, but the degree of its involvement ranges only from token endorsement or opposition to moderate activity. Like the political parties, labor does not consider its stake in the outcome sufficiently great to warrant substantial expenditures of its resources. Its position and the extent of its activity in each case will be dictated largely by the possible effects of the proposed restructuring on existing political arrangements and coalitions. If the influence of those officials or political groups with which it has established working relationships will be expanded by the change, labor is likely to favor the movement; if the interests of these groups is threatened, it will probably join the opposition. In neither case, however, is it likely to make large-scale commitments of energy and resources.

The Negroes are another group that has become of increasing importance in reorganization issues. For the most part, Negro political leaders look with disfavor on efforts to reorder the system. Their base of operation and strength lies in the central city. An area-wide government poses a threat to their hard-won and long-incoming major political influence by joining the predominantly white electorate of suburbia to that of the core municipality. It is not surprising, therefore, that both the comprehensive urban county proposal in Cleveland and the multipurpose district plan in St. Louis drew heavy opposition from the non-white wards. As a study of the vote on metropolitan reform issues in Cleveland over a period of years showed, the attitude of Negro voters toward area-wide reorganization became more negative as the political strength of the non-whites increased in the central city.[6] By 1957, their opposition had firmly crystallized, for by then they had acquired a considerable stake in the political status quo with seven Negroes on Cleveland's thirty-three member city council. There have been similar cases in other places like Miami, where Negro leaders opposed the metropolitan county charter. There, they had been able to establish a *modus vivendi* and an understanding with central city authorities in such matters as the allocation of city jobs; naturally, they have no desire to see these arrangements disturbed.

METROPOLITAN MIAMI

Ratification of a comprehensive urban county charter by the voters of the Miami, Florida, area in May, 1957, was widely heralded as a major breakthrough for the cause of metropolitan reform. The victory bolstered the hopes of reorganization proponents throughout the United States, leading many to believe that American urban areas were standing on the threshold of significant governmental change. These hopes, however, proved to be short-lived. Out of the numerous reform efforts that developed after the Miami success,

[6] Richard A. Watson and John H. Romani, "Metropolitan Government for Metropolitan Cleveland: An Analysis of the Voting Record," *Midwest Journal of Political Science*, V (November, 1961), 365–390.

none bore fruit until the Nashville-Davidson County consolidation five years later. If anything, the reorganization fires have subsided in recent years, until now little serious talk is heard of radically altering the existing pattern of local government. The Miami and Nashville successes continue to stand out as rare exceptions, not as probable harbingers of events to come.

Metropolitan Miami differs in a number of ways from other areas.[7] Its suburban population is constantly shifting and growing, not with the overspill from the central city but with in-migration from other sections of the nation. Its tourist atmosphere and the high mobility of its population are not conducive to the development of deep roots and emotional ties to individual municipal units. It is almost wholly devoid of strongly organized political factions and strong labor unions. Its business leadership is sporadic, although effective when motivated. Its "social élite" is made up largely of wintertime residents. Metropolitan Miami, in short, is under-organized when compared to most other metropolises.[8] Because of this organizational and leadership vacuum, the mass media, particularly the two metropolitan daily newspapers, have been able to assume a role of decisive importance in metropolitan affairs. As Edward Sofen points out, the large number of voters who are relatively new to the area have no place to turn for their political education other than to the press and television.

Formal reorganization movements began in Dade County about the time of World War II. As we have seen in the preceding chapter, certain services were placed on a countywide basis during the decade of the 1940s and an effort was made in 1953 to abolish the city of Miami and transfer its functions to the county. In each of these endeavors, the *Miami Herald* and central city businessmen were the prime movers. The recurring theme in their arguments was the inequity of saddling the city with the costs of maintaining facilities

[7] The Miami reorganization movement is carefully documented in Edward Sofen, *The Miami Metropolitan Experiment* (Bloomington: Indiana University Press, 1963). Also see his article, "Problems of Metropolitan Leadership: The Miami Experience," *Midwest Journal of Political Science*, V (February, 1961), 18–38; and Ross C. Beiler and Thomas J. Wood, "Metropolitan Politics of Miami," (Paper delivered at annual meeting of Southern Political Science Association, Gatlinburg, Tennessee, November 7, 1958).

[8] On this point, see Thomas J. Wood, "Dade County: Unbossed, Erratically Led," *Annals of the American Academy of Political and Social Science*, 353 (May, 1964), 64–71.

used by all residents of Dade County. The reformers regarded functional consolidation as only partial remedy for this situation; their ultimate goal was city-county consolidation, a solution which they were convinced would result in more efficient and economical administration.

Supporters and Opponents

The closeness of the 1953 vote alarmed municipal officials in both the central city and the suburbs and led to adoption of the state constitutional amendment granting home rule to Dade County and subsequently, in May, 1957, to the presentation of a metropolitan charter to the electorate (see Chapter 15). The lineup of the protagonists in the charter campaign was not unlike that in other metropolitan reform battles. The supporters included civic groups, the Chamber of Commerce, and the metropolitan press; the hard core of opposition was supplied by municipal officials and employees. There were, however, at least two important exceptions to the common pattern. First, central city businessmen did more than pay lip service to the reorganization cause. Motivated by what they considered a direct economic stake in the outcome, they committed energy as well as financial resources to the campaign. Second, the newspapers of the central city also did more than serve as publicists. The associate editor of the *Miami Herald*, for example, was a key strategist in the movement. Largely through his efforts the support of the major newspapers throughout the state was secured for the home rule amendment. His influence was also evident in the actions of Dade County's delegation to the state legislature, which steered the amendment through that body and later supported the charter. Miami newspapers enjoy greater influence in area-wide public affairs than most of their counterparts elsewhere. In a metropolitan community where party organization is weak and where politics is played on an "each man for himself" basis, support of the large dailies is an important factor in election campaigns. This fact makes candidates more sensitive to newspaper blandishments and pressures. As Edward Sofen describes the role of one of the newspapers:

Aspirants for political office eagerly seek the *Herald*'s endorsement which is extremely important in this no-party area. Some of Miami's most important businessmen, elected officials, and administrative officers meet and consult with Mr. Pennekamp [the *Herald*'s associate editor] on important community problems . . . Mr. Pennekamp has successfully used the power of the *Herald* to crusade for many civic reforms. He has an almost artistic touch in the manner in which he gradually builds a case for or against an issue. His sense of righteousness makes him a devoted ally—and an extremely dangerous foe.[9]

Circumstances also helped to dull the edge of the opposition. The Dade County League of Municipalities campaigned against the charter but in a relatively mild and restrained manner. Its members had no liking for the proposal, but convinced that some form of metropolitan integration was inevitable, they were torn between accepting the present scheme or risking total consolidation later. This ambivalent attitude diluted the strength of their opposition. There were municipal officials, moreover, who deserted the ranks of the localists to campaign actively for the reorganization plan. The Miami city manager was the most prominent officeholder to take this step. The office of county manager to be created under the charter appealed to him, and he saw himself as the logical choice for the post. Later, he became a bitter opponent of the new government when the position went to another candidate.

The proponents also were able to invoke a time-tested reform symbol to their advantage. Miami city politics had been marked by considerable in-fighting among council members and by recurring charges of corruption. In particular, the police department had long been under fire for its alleged failure to enforce the laws against gambling and other forms of vice. In contrast, the county government was generally well regarded and free from any taint of corruption. These circumstances enabled proponents to juxtapose the "good" county against the "evil" city government. Reform, spelled out in these terms, had popular appeal.

Post-Charter Difficulties

Passage of the charter proved to be only the beginning of a long struggle to establish Metro, as the new government is known, on a firm basis. Since its inception, it has been under constant attack both in the courts and at the polls. No less than 600 lawsuits have been brought to curtail its powers, and crippling amendments to the charter have been placed on the ballot almost yearly. Part of the difficulty arises from the fact that the charter was essentially a com-

[9] *The Miami Metropolitan Experiment*, p. 78.

promise between the consolidationists and localists. Both purportedly accepted the principle of federalism but in different ways. The consolidationists looked upon it simply as the doorway to complete merger; the localists interpreted it as a narrow and static division of power that was more favorable to the maintenance of the status quo than to significant change. The language of the charter was left ambiguous enough to accommodate both interpretations.

The conflict between these two forces has kept the new government in constant turmoil. The mergerites, led by the *Miami Herald*, have pushed for the more rapid assumption of municipal functions by Metro while local officials have vigorously resisted any change in the distribution of power. Those committed to a workable two-level or federal system find themselves in the middle of the fray. The same tendency has been evident in Toronto where the metropolitan government was the product of compromise between the central city and its demand for amalgamation and the suburbs with their insistence on the retention of local autonomy. There, also, the consolidationists have not accepted the federated scheme as the final form of metropolitan government for the area.[10] This ambivalence keeps the system in an uneasy equilibrium.

METROPOLITAN NASHVILLE

A second departure from the pattern of defeat in metropolitan reform campaigns occurred in June, 1962, when consolidation of the governments of Nashville and Davidson County, Tennessee, was approved by popular referendum. Just four years earlier, a similar plan had been rejected by the voters. The two instances provide a rare opportunity to examine the factors that contributed to defeat in one case and victory in another.[11]

[10] See Frank Smallwood, *Metro Toronto: A Decade Later* (Toronto: Bureau of Municipal Research, 1963).
[11] The Nashville experience is analyzed in David A. Booth, *Metropolitics: The Nashville Consolidation* (East Lansing: Michigan State University Institute for Community Development and Service, 1963). See also Daniel J. Elazar, *A Case Study of Failure in Attempted Metropolitan Integration: Nashville and Davidson County, Tennessee* (Chicago: National Opinion Research and Social Science Division, University of Chicago, August, 1961); Daniel R. Grant, "Urban and Suburban Nashville: A Case Study in Metropolitanism," *Journal of Politics*, XVII (February, 1955), 82–99, and "Metropolitics and Professional Political Leadership: The Case of Nashville," *The Annals of the American Academy of Political and Social Science*, 353 (May, 1964), 72–83.

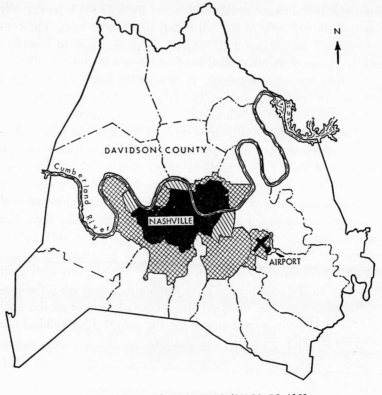

N
↑

■ CITY OF NASHVILLE (PRIOR TO 1958
    AND 1960 ANNEXATIONS)
▨ 1958 ANNEXATION (INDUSTRIAL)
▩ 1960 ANNEXATION (RESIDENTIAL)

Figure 16.1   Former City Limits of Nashville, and An-
nexations of 1958 and 1960. Adapted from David A. Booth,
Metropolitics: The Nashville Consolidation, Institute for
Community Development and Service, Michigan State
University, 1963, p. 74.

The First Campaign

At the time of the first referendum, in 1958, the population of
Davidson County was approximately 368,000. More than one-half
resided outside Nashville in unincorporated territory. The governmental structure was relatively simple: central city, county, six
small suburban municipalities, and six special districts. Nashville's
failure to annex for thirty years had resulted in the growth of a
large fringe area that had few urban services. It was this development

that finally touched off the movement for reorganization in the early
1950s. Before the end of the decade, in 1958, a charter calling for
consolidation of the city of Nashville and the county government
had been drafted and presented to the voters.

The lineup of adversaries in the battle for "Metro" was a
familiar one. The two daily newspapers, the *Nashville Tennessean*
and the *Nashville Banner*, which normally take opposite stands, en-
thusiastically endorsed the charter and devoted considerable space to
its promotion. All the civic groups joined in support, with the
Chamber of Commerce playing an important but unobtrusive role.
The Chamber, which initially had worked to gain the enabling legislation to permit the drafting of the charter, was instrumental in
setting up and manning the citizens' committee which formally
guided the campaign. The civic amateurs were joined by the two
leading politicians of the area, the Nashville mayor and the presiding
officer (called the county judge) of the county governing board. The
mayor, generally regarded as the certain choice for the new office of
metropolitan chief executive, worked hard to get the plan adopted.
The county judge also campaigned for the charter, even though it
would abolish the office to which he had just been elected.

Arrayed against the plan were suburban private fire and police
companies, many county board members (called magistrates) and
city of Nashville councilmen, and the operators of small business
establishments in the fringe area. The opposition was relatively
quiescent until the final week of the campaign when it launched a
vigorous attack on the charter, employing the usual time-tested symbols to defend the status quo: higher taxes, bigger government, loss
of individual rights. From neither side, however, did the campaign
elicit a large-scale commitment of energy and resources. The great
majority of community influentials interviewed by political scientist
David Booth readily admitted that they expended little personal
effort on the cause, while those in opposition seemed to feel that a
high level of activity on their part was unneeded.

In February, 1958, in a very light turnout, the charter carried in
the central city, but lost by a substantial margin in the remainder
of the county. (Separate majorities were required in each area for
adoption.) The Negro districts in Nashville voted against the plan,
although the active support of two Negro leaders who had served on
the charter commission kept down the margin of loss. Heaviest oppo-

sition came from the low-income suburban areas, where the argument of higher taxes was particularly effective, and from the rural areas, which voted more than eight-to-one against the proposal.

Revival of the Consolidation Movement

Following the defeat of the charter, the city of Nashville took two steps that were deeply resented by suburban residents. First, it adopted a ten dollar "green sticker" tax on automobiles to be paid by all city residents and all other persons whose automobiles used city streets during more than thirty days a year. Second, taking advantage of the strong annexation powers granted by the Tennessee legislature in 1955, the city moved quickly to more than triple its territorial size. Without a vote in the affected sections, it annexed seven square miles of largely industrial land in 1958, soon after the consolidation referendum, and forty-two square miles of residential area with over 82,000 residents in 1960. Among other effects, the two annexations drastically reduced the road tax revenue of the county government and created serious financial difficulties for the schools which remained outside the city.

These actions of the city administration led to the revival of the consolidation crusade. Sensing that merger or Metro was now becoming an attractive issue, a number of political leaders began to support it actively. Elections to the county board (known in Tennessee as the county court) in 1960 indicated the direction of popular sentiment when the leading champion of reorganization led a field of thirty-four candidates from Nashville, while the main consolidation opponent outside the core city was defeated by a huge majority. The election also marked the turning point in the political fortunes of Ben West, the mayor of the central city. The incumbent whom he had endorsed for sheriff was swamped by a political newcomer favorable to Metro, and only eight of eighteen candidates whom West's organization had backed for the county board were elected. The political defeat for the mayor was closely related to the consolidation movement. Although he had actively supported the first charter, he and other Nashville officials subsequently opposed any further efforts to revive the issue, preferring to solve the metropolitan problem by expanding the central city boundaries. In following this policy, Mayor West became the prime target of the resentment caused by the automobile tax and the 1960 annexation.

511 THE POLITICS OF REFORM

The Second Campaign

Despite the objections of Nashville city officials, the charter commission was reactivated and a new document drafted. The plan submitted to residents of Davidson County early in 1962 was virtually the same as the 1958 proposal. However, the campaign that followed its presentation differed markedly from the first contest. This time, the participants on both sides were well organized and willing to make a heavy commitment of resources. David Booth observes that "it was as if the professionals and the politicians had taken over from the amateurs and do-gooders."[12] Mayor West, knowing that a victory for the charter forces would be a serious blow to his political career, worked extensively to defeat the proposal. The full weight of his political organization was brought into the fray and city employees were mobilized for the fight. Police and firemen, as well as schoolteachers, were used to distribute anti-Metro literature. West was joined in the battle by the pro-administration *Banner* which had vigorously supported consolidation in the first campaign but which now portrayed it as an attempt to wreck the city's "planned program of annexation."

Charter advocates were likewise better organized. Spearheaded by a citizens' committee for better government, the pro-Metro forces set up cadres in virtually every city and county precinct and held more than 250 well-publicized neighborhood meetings. Support also came from sources not usually friendly to metropolitan reorganization. Schoolteachers and principals outside Nashville, for example, turned to consolidation as a remedy for the fiscal ills of the outlying schools that had been precipitated by the city's annexation. Even the private police and fire companies that had figured prominently in the defeat of the 1958 effort endorsed the charter, viewing it as a lesser evil than annexation which had already put some of them out of business. The forces favoring consolidation were effectively augmented by the *Tennessean* which hit hard at the "city machine" theme, carrying front-page stories of anti-Metro activities by city police and firemen.

In the election in June, 1962, Metro proponents were triumphant. The charter passed by a vote of 21,064 to 15,999 in the city of Nashville and by 15,914 to 12,514 in the remainder of the county. Annex-

[12] *Metropolitics: The Nashville Consolidation*, p. 85.

ation stood out as the critical issue that reversed the earlier defeat. Vengeance-minded residents of the area that had been involuntarily annexed to the central city voted six-to-one in favor of consolidation. In the suburbs, fear of annexation led many voters to turn to Metro in preference to their uncertain status. By his vigorous action in enlarging Nashville's boundaries, Mayor West had unwittingly provided the reformers with an issue that could readily be articulated. Instead of the usual abstract arguments of administrative efficiency and economy, charter proponents could point to the "high-handed" actions of the "city machine" and the threat it posed to suburbanites. Instead of alluding to vague dangers and future difficulties, they could play on the dissatisfaction and sense of outrage felt by residents in the newly annexed areas. West, in effect, became the symbol around which the battle raged. He provided a target not only for the reformers but also for his political opponents who seized upon the charter issue as a means of discrediting him.

METROPOLITAN ST. LOUIS

Like the Nashville area, Metropolitan St. Louis was the scene of two major reorganization efforts within a short period of time—in 1959 and 1962—but unlike the Nashville experience, both movements failed. The first involved the creation of a multipurpose metropolitan district; the second, city-county consolidation.[13] In both cases, the margin of defeat was overwhelming. Experience with metropolitan reform campaigns was not new to St. Louis. The long-standing legal separation of the city from the county (an event that had taken place in 1876) had led to many previous efforts to reshape the governmental pattern. The first major move came in 1926 when a plan of consolidation was turned down by the voters; the second followed four years later when a constitutional amendment to permit the establishment of a federation of local governments in the area was rejected by the state electorate. Two attempts involving less comprehensive plans were made in the early 1950s: creation of a metropolitan sewer district; and establishment of an area-wide transit authority. The former was adopted, the latter failed.

[13] See Scott Greer, *Metropolitics* (New York: Wiley, 1963); and Henry J. Schmandt, Paul G. Steinbicker, and George D. Wendel, *Metropolitan Reform in St. Louis* (New York: Holt, Rinehart and Winston, 1961).

The Metropolitan District Campaign

At the time of the 1959 reorganization campaign, the population of the city of St. Louis was approximately 750,000, while the suburbs were rapidly approaching this figure. The governmental structure of the county was badly fragmented, with responsibility divided among 98 municipalities, 20 fire protection districts, 27 individual school systems, the metropolitan sewer district, and the county government. The original impetus for the 1959 effort came from a young and politically ambitious St. Louis alderman, A. J. Cervantes, who was looking for a "live" issue to promote his candidacy for president of the city council. In Cervantes' words:

It had all started when I tried to get three councilmen each from the City and County together to do something about traffic problems. A reporter told me about this constitutional possibility, and I started the move for a new City-County charter. I called a meeting at Medart's Restaurant in April of 1955. I got the labor guys, the politicians, the Teamsters, and others out, and we formed the Citizens Committee for City-County Consolidation. The Teamsters helped out, and we got out our petitions.[14]

The constitutional provision to which Cervantes referred provides for establishment of a metropolitan charter board by popular initiative. This board must then draft and present to the voters a reorganization plan based on one of four alternative approaches: city-county consolidation, re-entry of the city of St. Louis into the county, enlargement of the St. Louis city boundaries, and creation of a metropolitan district for the administration of services common to the area.

Mayor Raymond R. Tucker, obviously irked at Cervantes' bid to preempt the role of metropolitan statesman, condemned the movement as premature and simultaneously announced his support of a pending proposal by the two local universities to undertake a broad-scaled examination of the area's governmental problems. Cervantes at first demurred at delaying his signature-gathering campaign but soon acquiesced when top business and civic leaders joined the mayor in urging that official charter drafting await the university survey. Sometime later the study got under way, financed by a Ford Foundation grant and local funds. In August, 1957, the university

[14] Greer, *Metropolitics*, p. 38.

researchers issued a report recommending creation of a metropolitan multipurpose district for the city and county.[15] Appointment of a metropolitan charter commission followed; and in April, 1959, this body, by a ten-to-nine vote, adopted a plan which closely resembled the recommendations of the university group. The dissenting members had insisted on complete merger of the local units (other than school districts) as against the less extensive district proposal, once again illustrating the basic difference over remedies that has plagued the reform cause.

In the ensuing campaign, the major business interests, civic groups, and the two metropolitan daily newspapers supported the plan, while the St. Louis County League of Municipalities, labor, the suburban press, and the top political leaders, including the central city mayor and the county supervisor (the county's elected executive) opposed it. Ironically, the district proposal drew the opposition of both the consolidationists who charged that it was too timid and the defenders of the status quo who attacked it as too far-reaching.

The campaign proved to be desultory. It was as though the proponents were not seriously committed to winning, while the opposition was convinced that the plan did not stand a chance of adoption. Most of the influentials who endorsed the proposal lent their names and financial support and then took no further part in the campaign. Their peripheral commitment to the cause was described by one of the active participants in this fashion:

> When I came in, the present campaign leaders were asked to serve by a small group of men who derived their precedent, their jurisdiction, just from their own desires and interest. (Who were they?) Shepley, Chancellor of Washington University, Ed Clark of the telephone company, Kurth of the Chamber of Commerce—and that, by the way, was the last we heard from them except money.[16]

The closely divided vote in the charter commission and the opposition of Mayor Tucker, who stated that the district proposal would not solve the city's problems, raised doubts about the wisdom of the plan even among its proponents. Tucker's position was particularly damaging since his political judgment was highly respected by the civic notables. When they discovered that he was not in

---

[15] See *Path of Progress* (University City: Metropolitan St. Louis Survey, August, 1957), pp. 53–82.

[16] Greer, *Metropolitics*, p. 64.

favor of the proposal, they lost whatever enthusiasm they may have had for it. Their abdication as active participants left the task of organizing and directing the campaign to a relatively small number of individuals of lesser stature and to groups such as the League of Women Voters and the Junior Chamber of Commerce.

The political parties remained officially neutral, although individual ward and township organizations worked quietly against the plan. In one township, where the Democratic committeeman had long been hostile to any form of metropolitan reorganization, the proposal lost by a margin of eleven to one. Similarly, in one of the Negro wards where the committeeman let his disapproval be known, the vote was seven to one against adoption. Cervantes tried to rally the Democratic politicians in the city behind the plan but succeeded in getting endorsements from only three of the twenty-eight committeemen. Ward politicians in the city felt they would gain little by the creation of the new government, while county Democrats wanted no part of any arrangement that would align them closer to their city counterparts in local governmental affairs. County Republicans also wanted no change that might open the door to further Democratic gains in county offices. The outcome was a foregone conclusion. City residents rejected the plan by a vote of two to one, suburbanites by three to one.

The Consolidation Campaign

Most local observers felt that the overwhelming defeat of the metropolitan district proposal would bring an end to further efforts at large-scale reorganization. Much to their surprise, announcement of another attempt to change the system was made in less than a year. This time, the movement was spearheaded by the chairman and several other members of the first charter board who had supported consolidation in preference to the district plan. During the first campaign they had publicly pledged that they would seek to have a merger plan presented to the voters if the district proposal was rejected, a gesture that few observers then took seriously. However, the chairman of the charter board, a well-to-do suburban land developer turned "statesman," had become morally convinced that consolidation was in the best interests of the metropolitan community. He personally took charge of the new campaign and provided most of the financing. Convinced that no merger plan would emerge from a locally appointed charter commission, he and his supporters resorted to the initiative to place such a proposal before the voters in the form of a constitutional amendment. (The amendment was self-executing so that on its adoption consolidation would have gone into effect.) This procedure required them first to collect signatures throughout the state and then to rely on a statewide referendum.

Support for the movement came principally from labor, which traditionally has favored consolidation in the St. Louis area, from a few political leaders in the central city, and from a number of prominent citizens. The opposition, as in the earlier election, was made up of two divergent elements: those who favored change but not of the kind proposed, and those who espoused the status quo. The first element of the opposition was composed chiefly of suburbanites who had been strong supporters of the district plan; the second consisted of a coalition of suburban officeholders, ward and township political organizations, and neighborhood or community newspapers. St. Louis city politicians at the ward level reacted as strongly against the proposal as their suburban counterparts, looking upon such a sweeping change as a threat to their established positions of power. The Democratic city committee went on record against the amendment by a vote of fifty-three to one and the board of aldermen (city council) by twenty-one to three. Negro political leaders openly condemned the proposal, telling their constituents that "consolidation would take us back twenty-five years and force us to begin fighting again just to get back what we have already won."

Mayor Tucker, although personally sympathetic to consolidation, also announced his opposition because of his fear of the plan's effect on city programs and taxes. Many civic groups that had endorsed the earlier district plan, such as the League of Women Voters, took no stand on the issue. Newspaper support was also lacking, the *Post Dispatch* opposing consolidation as too radical a remedy (the *Post* was apparently unwilling to back what it regarded as a hopeless cause), and the *Globe Democrat* belatedly endorsing the movement "as a matter of conscience, principle, and responsibility, though we never felt it had any real chance of success."

The battle was waged largely in the St. Louis area. Neither side made any real effort to conduct a statewide campaign: the proponents because they lacked the resources, the opponents because they saw no need to do so. Sponsors of the movement had become discouraged long before election day when they realized that they had greatly overestimated the sentiment for consolidation. They had counted heavily on the mayor of St. Louis, the prestigious groups, and the metropolitan newspapers, but all of these backed away from the issue. The proponents were certain that central city politicians would welcome the opportunity to work for consolidation, but the opposite proved to be true. They had hoped that organizations in the other urban areas of the state, such as Kansas City, Springfield, and St. Joseph, would lend their support, but as one of the proponents commented, "The outstate people were polite and expressed sympathy for our cause, but they just weren't interested." They had expected labor leaders to be active in mobilizing the vote, but union interests were too peripheral to involve a major commitment.

The results of the referendum held in November, 1962, confirmed the gloomiest expectations of the consolidationists. Statewide, the plan received slightly more than 200,000 votes of a total of well over 600,000. In St. Louis city, the vote was six to five against and in the suburbs four to one in opposition. The margin in the city was surprisingly close in view of the organized opposition. In fact, the plan fared far better there than the metropolitan district proposal had in the earlier election when the city vote was two to one. Suburban residents reacted in opposite fashion, voting more heavily against consolidation than they had against the district charter. The radical nature of the proposal had obviously alienated many suburbanites who were favorably disposed toward moderate change. One relatively well-to-do township, for example, which had rejected the metropolitan district by only a small margin, voted four to one against merger. The dilemma which these results pose for the reformer in the St. Louis area is seemingly insoluble. Many central city residents apparently will accept consolidation but not a lesser remedy; many suburbanites will support moderate change but not merger. For neither solution, however, does a majority appear to exist in either city or county.

METROPOLITAN CLEVELAND

Metropolitan reorganization was placed on the civic agenda in the Cleveland area as early as 1920 when the Citizens League began its campaign to modernize the county government of Cuyahoga County. Since then the reformers have not deviated from the goal of making this unit the metropolitan instrumentality for the area. On five occasions since 1920, the question of establishing a charter-drafting commission was placed before the voters of the county. Three times they answered the question affirmatively, but in each instance they later rejected the resulting charter. The latest attempt, in 1959, involved the most elaborate preparation, the most money, and the largest outpouring of civic activity in the history of metropolitan reform. Despite the herculean effort, the charter failed to pass, losing decisively in the central city and by a small margin in the suburbs.[17]

The Metropolitan Charter

Cuyahoga County was the subject of an intensive metropolitan survey that began in 1956 and continued for three years. Impetus for the study came from the usual sources: good government groups, civic leaders, and the newspapers of the central city. With the active backing of top business leaders and supported by nearly one hundred community organizations, a research agency known as the Cleveland Metropolitan Services Commission was created to examine the problem of government in the area. Before it finished its work in July, 1959, the commission had spent $500,000 (about one-third of this amount came from the Ford Foundation) and had involved several hundred influential citizens, public officials, and political leaders. Also during this time, it kept up a continual flow of publicity aimed at the citizen through its wide coverage by the three daily newspapers.

The members of the official charter-drafting commission, who were elected during the last year of the study, met throughout the spring of 1959 and placed their proposal on the November ballot. The document provided for a reorganized county government to be headed by an elected chief executive and for the assumption of certain area-wide functions by the county. There was little disagreement among the members as to the general course to be followed; the question was the extent of functional power to be given the county

[17] For a more detailed account of the Metropolitan Cleveland experience, see James A. Norton, *The Metro Experience*; Greer, *Metropolitics*; and Matthew Holden, Jr., *Decision Making on a Metropolitan Government Proposition: The Case of Cuyahoga County, Ohio, 1958–59*. Unpublished doctoral dissertation, Northwestern University, June, 1961.

government. Some argued for a "hard charter" which would transfer a large number of functions from the existing local units to the county; others supported a "soft charter" which would conciliate existing power blocs by making minimal changes but which would leave the door open to later enlargements of county jurisdiction. The Democratic party "regulars" who dominated the charter board tended to support the former position, seeing in it an opportunity to extend their sphere of influence; the civic representatives favored the latter, convinced that the local units would balk at any major change in the existing division of powers.[18] To the politicians, the gains to be derived from the "soft" approach were not worth the effort. As a result, the hard line generally prevailed, with certain powers being included that aroused strong opposition from the adversely affected governments and officeholders.

The Charter Campaign

The charter was endorsed by an impressive list of organizations and individuals, including labor, both political parties, the three daily newspapers, and the Cleveland Chamber of Commerce. The Mayors' Association was the only organized area-wide group to declare its opposition. Particularly damaging, however, was the stand of Mayor Anthony Celebrezze of Cleveland, who opposed the charter purportedly because it would take away several important functions and assets from the city, including its water works, airport, and harbors. Although Celebrezze had little control over the regular Democratic party organization—he belonged to the wing headed by Frank Lausche—his opposition did much to weaken support from this source. As one Democratic leader described it:

When we saw Celebrezze was against it, we said, "Well then, we'll go to the wards." And I said to the Chamber guys, I said, "If the men are going to work in the wards, we're going to need some money for them to work with." And they said, "Okay." No question about it.

But they waited so late in order to get the money to me that I couldn't use it to get people committed. Therefore, I didn't know who to back and who not to, and since the Democratic organization had endorsed it unanimously, we decided to give the money to the organization. Miller (boss of the regular party organization), however, felt he could not use party discipline on the matter. So instead, he took it and instead of giving it to the people who cared about the charter and were

[18] Greer, Metropolitics, pp. 51–52.

going to fight for it, he divides it up evenly among the Democratic candidates in all 33 wards. Those who were for it, against it, and neutral—all of them got a share![19]

Put to them in this way, the local ward leaders and candidates simply accepted the largess and generally took whatever position seemed most popular in their district. Thus, in Scott Greer's words, "The campaign in Cuyahoga County, although it probably neutralized the political party organization, did not harness it."[20]

The coalition in favor of the charter followed the same route and employed the same tactics that had been used in the St. Louis area in both of the most recent efforts. Speeches were given, debates were held, newspapers were filled with news stories and favorable editorial comment, the League of Women Voters and others conducted telephone campaigns, and some precinct activity took place. The opposition criticized the technical aspects of the charter, invoked the grass-root symbols, and charged that the proposal went too far in depriving the local units of their powers and assets. The most effective campaigners among the opposition were the heads of the two city departments who had the most to lose in the way of functions and powers. Their colorful attacks made news which even the pro-charter press could not ignore. As the director of the local citizens' league commented: "They made headlines over and over again because they said and did the things that make headlines, while charter proponents were taking the 'educational' approach that left the reporters empty handed when they wrote their stories."[21]

In the end, the charter received 42 percent of the vote in the central city but lost by only 8000 of approximately 226,000 votes cast in the remainder of the county. (Separate majorities in both areas were required for passage.) The heavy opposition in the Negro wards of Cleveland, where 70 percent of the vote was negative, contributed importantly to the margin of defeat. The suburban showing was better, but the efforts of the supporters, extensive as they were, could not overcome the mobilized status quo. Unlike Metropolitan Nashville, where reorganization became an issue between opposing political factions as well as a crusade by the reformers, the

[19] *Ibid.*, p. 93.
[20] *Ibid.*, p. 95.
[21] Estal E. Sparlin, "Cleveland Seeks New Metro Solution," *National Civic Review*, XLIX (March, 1960), 143.

campaign in the Cleveland area was left largely to the "good govern-ment" forces despite formal political endorsement. Except in Metro-politan Miami, with its atypical characteristics, these forces have not proved sufficient to effect significant change in the governmental structure of the metropolis.

METROPOLITAN REFORM FACTORS

Until recent years, the work of researchers in the metropolitan field was focused on substantive problems and reorganization plans and little or no attention was given to examining reform campaigns systematically. The long persisting tendency was to consider the process of translating proposed structural changes into reality as a righteous crusade that somehow transcended politics. Only gradually has it become clear that reconstituting the governmental system is a political question to be treated as any other public policy issue. This realization has led to more realistic appraisals of reorganization movements and to a better understanding of the forces and factors that control the outcome.

Although the reform campaigns just discussed took place in four metropolitan areas of widely varying characteristics, the pattern is strikingly similar. For the most part, the same classes of protag-onists, the same evolutionary steps (from study commission through official charter-drafting board to public vote), the same demographic and political factors, and the same type of public response were present in each instance. The experiences in these four areas provide a basis for certain conclusions about metropolitan reform efforts.

1. The crusade for metropolitan governmental reorganization has not been the product of grass-roots dissatisfaction nor has it been initiated by public officials. It has been largely the creature of good government groups and civic notables who have been disturbed by the "irrationality" of the system.

2. The general public is indifferent to the reorganization issue. A sampling of residents in Cuyahoga County several weeks before the charter election in 1959 revealed that one of every three persons did not remember reading or hearing anything about the proposed new document despite the extensive publicity that had been given to it. More than three-fourths of the people could not name a single reason advanced for or against it. A survey in the St. Louis area

after the district election also showed convincingly that the voters knew little about the issue and those who were involved in it. In 40 percent of the cases, leaders mentioned as supporters of the plan by the persons who had been interviewed were publicly on record as opposed to it.

Transmitting to the electorate the complex issues inherent in governmental reorganization of the metropolis is an extremely difficult, if not impossible, task. Change of this type does not ordinarily give rise to the use of effective and attention-capturing symbols. Thus, as Greer describes the recent campaigns, they proceeded behind a massive facade of logical argument:

> Seldom have so many thorny problems, involving theoretical and empirical unknowns, been aired on the front page of the daily papers. Seldom have so many businessmen, lawyers, elected officials, politicians, administrators, and League ladies taken public stands on abstract and difficult issues. Seldom have so few worked so hard and succeeded in confusing so many.[22]

Caught in a crossfire of conflicting and abstract arguments, and with the groups to which he normally looks for guidance on public issues silent or only slightly involved, the average voter is frequently confused and uncertain in reorganization elections.

3. Metropolitan reform movements involve only a small segment of the community's many organizations and of its "power structure." Seldom are the mass-based interest groups, such as the political parties and labor unions, seriously committed as either supporters or opponents. By concentrating on organizational efficiency, reformist activity has avoided the deeper and more controversial issues that can motivate such groups and enlist their active participation.

4. Except in loosely structured communities such as Metropolitan Miami, no major reorganization plan is likely to succeed without organized political support. Without such backing, civic groups cannot mount an effective campaign at the grass roots, an essential factor particularly when popular approval of proposed changes is required. The second Nashville consolidation attempt illustrates the importance of actively involving professional politicians in metropolitan reform movements. What in the earlier campaign had been simply a question of administrative reorganization fostered by the good government groups became a political issue in the later

[22] *Metropolitics*, p. 193.

effort when two opposing factions, vying for the stakes of public office, seized upon it as a major point of disagreement. Voters who identified themselves with one or the other political faction had an "authoritative" referent to which to look for guidance in reaching a decision on the charter, even though they may have been completely ignorant of the plan it embodied or its effect on their own interests.

5. Voters who support metropolitan reform tend to be drawn from the better educated and high socioeconomic categories. In the Miami area, the precincts highest on the social scale favored the charter most sharply while those at the bottom voted against it most strongly. In Metropolitan Nashville, the findings were the same: the higher the level of an individual's income or education, the more likely he was to hold a pro-Metro attitude. These results are not surprising. We would expect the better educated voter to be more familiar with the issue and more likely to be persuaded by the logic and rationality of reformist arguments. Such an individual is also more likely to identify himself with the socially respected civic groups that customarily champion reorganization plans.

As an analysis of one of the Cleveland charter elections indicates, however, socioeconomic status is by no means the only variable in determining the direction of the vote. Using multiple correlation techniques, it was found that the combined effect of income, education, and occupation—the typical components of social rank—accounted statistically for only 48 percent of the variation in the voting.[23] This finding means that less than half the variations in the vote can be attributed to differences in socioeconomic status.

One factor or intervening variable that may help to explain the deviation in voting behavior within social categories was suggested by Booth in the Nashville study. He found that individuals who were members of formal organizations exposed to campaign propaganda tended to favor the side of the issue to which their group had been exposed at significantly greater rates than others of the same social rank.[24] The St. Louis area study suggested another variable, that of home ownership, thus indicating that property owners are more susceptible than renters to the usual opposition arguments.

[23] Watson and Romani, "Metropolitan Government for Metropolitan Cleveland," pp. 382–385.

[24] Metropolitics: The Nashville Consolidation, pp. 45–54.

Some observers have speculated that a small turnout is advantageous to reorganization elections since persons of higher social rank are more likely to participate and since they tend to favor change. This, however, is a dubious assumption. The Miami survey, for example, found no important difference between the high- and low-status precincts in voter turnout on the charter issue. A similar finding was made in St. Louis where the proportion of those who voted on the district plan did not differ significantly among the various social ranks. One explanation for this deviation from the general pattern of voting behavior is found in the more intensive organizational activity displayed by opponents at the grassroots level. This activity, coupled with lack of concern by many people in the higher socioeconomic categories, leads to a disproportionate turnout of lower-status voters in reorganization elections.

6. Because the strategies of support for change in metropolitan reform campaigns are usually determined by the good government groups and civic notables, effective communication is seldom established with the mass audience. Proponents have relied on the newspapers to perform this function, but the ability of the press to influence the public is limited by the interests and predispositions of its readers, their readiness to listen, and their capacity to understand the question. Thus far the strategists have been unable to translate comprehensive plans of reorganization into terms which are meaningful in the political vocabulary of local or neighborhood affairs. Change which must rely on the results of the ballot cannot move far beyond the understanding and interest of the voters. Political leadership, not civic exhortation, is required to foster this understanding and kindle this interest.

Regardless of the fate of major reform efforts, the governmental structure of the metropolis is certain to undergo modification with the passage of time. Only by so doing can it survive the great changes in the urban environment that the future will bring. This adjustment may be only a minimal accommodation to the emerging forces or it may involve a thorough alteration of the system. Whatever the change, it will probably take place through political channels, under the initiative of political actors, and through the process of political bargaining. Civic groups and civic leaders will remain important, but more as legitimizing symbols for the cause than as carriers of the movement.

CHAPTER 17

The States and the Nation

THE DESTINY of each metropolis is determined by a multitude of public and private decisions, actions, and interrelationships only some of which originate within its boundaries. The activities of its local governments and the developmental decisions of locally-controlled private companies have far-reaching effects, but these elements are merely some of the important influences that help to mold the metropolis. Large private corporations operating sizable branch facilities that follow policies made at some distant headquarters likewise have a major impact. So also do the state and national governments, the subjects of this chapter.

Each metropolitan area is therefore the hub of a large number of intergovernmental relations. Its local governments do not function as a set of tightly sealed compartments, each insulated from the other local units and from the operations of the state and national governments. Instead, they stand at the crossroads of an extensive series of interactions with one another (as was noted in Chapter 13) and with the state and the nation.

The states occupy the fundamental legal position in relation to local units. The powers of the latter—their functional and financial authority, organizational structure, areal jurisdiction, and even their creation and continued existence—depend upon provisions in state laws and state constitutions. Thus as the ultimate repositories of all local public powers, the states, and particularly their legislatures, have always had a very substantial impact on the form and substance of the local governmental pattern in metropolitan areas. In addition, the states exert great influence on these areas by directly providing a number of services and facilities and by helping to finance others handled by local units. The national government likewise has a substantial impact on metropolitan areas by its many programs of grants—some routed through the states and others made directly—for the performance of specific activities by local governments such as urban renewal and public housing. It also has important effects on some urban communities by its decisions on the location and alteration in size of military installations and by its defense contracts with private firms.

EXPANDING ROLES

In the first half of the current century the roles of state and national agencies in the metropolis grew greatly in importance, but they expanded on a helter-skelter basis. Although the states increased their direct services and financial assistance to local units, they were often slow to respond to local demands. The national government's program of grants meanwhile mounted in volume from a mere trickle to a forceful stream. Neither level of government, however, gave any attention to the total effect of its programs on metropolitan areas. In fact, at times the projects of one agency of either the state or national government directly conflicted with or deviated materially from related projects of another department of the same government.

Lack of Coordination

In these years of increased state and national activity in the metropolis, lack of program coordination was a frequent occurrence: various programs of agencies of the same government and of different governments were not synchronized. A typical pattern of financial assistance, for example, was for administrators of different governments to reach agreement and grants to be made without sufficient, if any, concern for their effects on associated programs in other parts of the two governments. As a result of the isolated state and national activities, local governments many times found themselves caught in the crossfire of contradictory programs and on some occasions their chief executives and governing boards were forced into the embarrassing position of trying to explain the inexplicable conflicts to the local public. There were many state and nationally sponsored programs but their value was sharply dissipated by the disorderly manner in which they were utilized.

The states affected metropolitan areas in other important ways during the first half of the present century. Most of these effects were negative in nature, growing out of the continuance or adoption of restrictions on local governments and the failure to provide new authority to local units to deal with problems of the metropolitan age. Among the major deficiencies were those which pertained to local financing, powers, and organization, and the legal means of solving interlocal problems.

The States and Finance

One highly serious drawback involved state constitutional or legislative limitations on the local property tax, a major revenue source for local governments. These restrictions took three forms: a maximum limit on the allowable tax rate related to the assessed value (not the market value) of taxable property; limits on the maximum dollar amount of the local property tax levy; and limits on the amount by which the local property tax levy could be increased from one year to the next. A second defect was the failure of many states to authorize local units to levy non-property taxes for revenue purposes instead of confining the use of such taxes to licensing and regulation. The third part of the financial strait jacket consisted of restrictions on the borrowing power of local units. These were of two types, ceilings on the total debt, expressed as a percentage of the assessed valuation of the local government's tax base, and requirements of voter approval, often by extraordinary majority vote, of bond proposals.

The States and Services

Many states further handicapped their local governments by failing to broaden the grant of functional authority enough to enable them to meet demands for new services. Both long existing and recently revised grants of power were often circumscribed by requirements and conditions that greatly reduced their effectiveness. This inadequacy of functional authority was noticeable among various municipalities, but was particularly evident and crucial among many counties that were subjected to local pressures to take on urban responsibilities.

The States and Organization

The practice in a number of states of saddling local governments with antiquated and inflexible organizations constituted another important shortcoming. Requiring the election of various administrative officials of department head status (especially prevalent in counties, but noticeable in many cities as well), failing to endow local units with discretion in structural matters where local preference should be dominant (such as election of governing board members at large or from wards), and placing limitations on the forms of government that could be employed are all illustrations of state-imposed confinements within which many local units had to operate during this period.[1]

The States and Problems

A still further type of deficiency—one that had profound effects on the metropolis—was the unresponsiveness of many states to furnishing appropriate legal means by which local governments could deal effectively with interlocal and area-wide problems. This deficiency was not always due to state inaction; it was also the result of measures adopted by the states. In the case of municipal annexation, for example, many changed their laws in the first half of the current century to make it more difficult for municipalities to absorb

[1] Some cities and a more limited number of counties in certain states gained a measure of relief from extensive restrictions on their activities and organization by making use of recently won constitutional local home rule powers. In some instances, however, court interpretations of these powers have greatly narrowed their scope.

nearby unincorporated urban land (a development treated in detail in Chapter 14). At the time they took such action, they generally left unchanged their overly liberal incorporation laws and thus unconsciously or deliberately failed to recognize the intimate relationship between the annexation and incorporation processes.

A great deal of the difficulty, however, was rooted in the failure of states to act positively. Many failed to provide legal authorization to permit even an extremely modest approach to problems—interlocal cooperative agreements for the provision of a service or facility or for the joint handling of a function or service. Similarly, many did not make it legally possible for local units to complete interlocal transfers of functions. There was even less general state response to permitting the use of the more thoroughgoing forms of governmental reorganization in the metropolis—city-county consolidation, federation, comprehensive urban county plan, and metropolitan multipurpose district. Finally, state technical or expert assistance to local units, particularly to the smaller governments, in such increasingly complex fields as finance and planning lagged substantially behind the needs.[2]

THE BEGINNING OF INCREASED CONCERN

Not until the mid-1950s and early 1960s was systematic attention given to a long overdue item of public business—determining the roles for state and national governments that were designed to produce positive, coordinated results in metropolitan areas. As will be seen, efforts in this direction were sometimes made separately for the two levels of government and at other times jointly. So far, however, only moderate success has been realized in implementing the various elements of the two roles.

The Kestnbaum Commission

The stage was set for working out specific state and national roles by the establishment and work of the Commission on Inter-

---

[2] In considering the effects of state action or inaction on the metropolis, it should be remembered that while responsibility usually belonged to the state legislatures, in some instances it rested on the voters who did not amend state constitutional provisions—a difficult procedure in some states. It should also be stressed that these various deficiencies, although frequent, did not exist in all states.

governmental Relations (the Kestnbaum Commission). Created by act of Congress in 1953 and composed of appointees of the President, the President of the Senate, and the Speaker of the House of Representatives, the Commission was charged with intensively studying national-state-local relationships—"the first official undertaking of its kind since the Constitutional Convention of 1787," as the group's final statement noted. The Commission reported to the President in 1955 by presenting him with sixteen documents, a general report and fifteen special publications. Most of the latter were concerned with federal aid in particular fields such as highways, public health, welfare, education, airports, and natural resources. Three of the special documents, however, pertained to local government in general and to the overall impact of federal grants on state and local units.[3]

The Kestnbaum Commission made no attempt to delineate the specific details of the state and national roles in the metropolis, but it strongly emphasized that both governmental levels had important and unmet responsibilities to fulfill in this regard. As to the states, the Commission declared that it was clearly their responsibility to assume leadership in seeking solutions to metropolitan areas problems. These solutions, the Commission observed, would require state constitutional changes as well as legislative and administrative actions. Moreover, new forms of action and cooperation by the states would probably be needed to deal effectively with interstate SMSA's. As to the national government, the Commission warned that this level of public authority had an obligation to facilitate state action concerned with area-wide problems. It suggested that the national government begin by analyzing the impact of its activities on metropolitan communities and by working with the states for better coordination of national and state policies in such areas.[4]

[3] The general report of the Commission is A Report to the President for Transmittal to the Congress (Washington: 1955). The publications on local government and the overall impact of federal grants are An Advisory Committee Report on Local Government, Summaries of Survey Reports on the Administrative and Fiscal Impact of Federal Grants-in-Aid, and A Survey Report on the Impact of Federal Grants-in-Aid on the Structure and Functions of State and Local Government, all published in 1955.

[4] Commission on Intergovernmental Relations, A Report to the President, pp. 52, 53. The Advisory Committee on Local Government of the Kestnbaum Commission discovered that the growing number of federal grants received by local governments lacked coordination, cohesion, and consistency. An Advisory Committee Report on Local Government, p. 38.

Assumption of Responsibilities by the States

The first breakthrough in deciding upon exact metropolitan roles for either the states or the national government was made by the former in 1956 when a study was published that focused on their responsibilities. This work was certain to have an impact for several reasons. First, the Council of State Governments, under whose sponsorship the analysis was made, is the only nationwide organization representing all the states and is a respected and persuasive force in the state capitals. Second, it had been directed to undertake the work by the Governors' Conference, its most potent constituent unit. Third, the organization's common practice is not only to have studies made but also to seek adoption of their recommendations. It does such follow-up work through direct contacts with state executives and legislators and by presenting its recommendations as draft laws and policy statements in a widely circulated program of suggested legislation. Fourth, the study was designed to document the states' central position in a number of metropolitan affairs and to present a specific program of action.

The study pointed out that although the national and local governments have indispensable roles in the metropolis the states are the key units for solving many complex urban difficulties. "To achieve adequate results," it urged, "the state governments—the legislative and executive branches and the people [through constitutional amendments and direct legislation]—need to exert positive, comprehensive and sustained leadership in solving the [general metropolitan] problem and keeping it solved."[5]

To place the states in a position of metropolitan leadership, a five-point program was advocated. First, the states should provide authorizations—laws and where necessary constitutional provisions and interstate compacts—to permit the creation of general metropolitan units that are adequate in functions, financing ability, and structure. These units may be of one or more of three types: metropolitan multipurpose district, federation, and urban county. To be adequate in functions, they must be permitted to perform a range of activities wide enough to eliminate or substantially reduce area-

[5] John C. Bollens, *The States and the Metropolitan Problem* (Chicago: Council of State Governments, 1956), p. 132. Part Three contains the suggested program for the states.

wide service and regulatory deficiencies. As for financing, they must be given a broad and equitable fiscal base, including the powers to tax and issue bonds. As for structure, they should be responsible to and controlled by the metropolitan public.

Second, the states should determine the method—legislation, local voter decision, or administrative or judicial determination—for putting the selected type or types of general metropolitan units into effect.

Third, the states should provide suitable legal provisions for annexation and interlocal agreements, which would generally be supplementary devices, and for incorporation.

Fourth, the states should appraise the adequacy of local governments in terms of area, financial ability, administrative organization and methods, and amount of discretion in the exercise of powers; and they should make necessary changes on the basis of these appraisals.

Fifth, each state should establish a single agency to serve two major purposes: it should aid in determining the present and changing needs of metropolitan and non-metropolitan areas, and it should analyze the effects of current and proposed programs, both of the several levels of government and of major private organizations. Such a state-level research and service agency would thus be the focal point for information and evaluation about metropolitan and local conditions and relations and would propose both remedial and preventive programs. Moreover, such agencies would cooperate when parts of their states were in interstate metropolitan areas.

The Council of State Governments moved immediately for implementation of the recommendations. A few months after public release of the study, the Council issued draft legislation concerning establishment of a state office for local affairs and authority for local units to enter into cooperative agreements. At the same time it distributed policy statements about legal authorizations for creating the three recommended types of metropolitan government and about changes in incorporation and annexation laws.[6] Within a short time these matters were receiving increased attention and a limited number of states adopted some of the proposals, most often

[6] Council of State Governments, *Program of Suggested State Legislation: 1957* (Chicago: 1956).

those pertaining to annexation, incorporation, and interlocal agreements.

Establishment of the National Advisory Commission

A major impetus to promoting both state and national leadership in metropolitan areas occurred in 1959 with the establishment by Congress of the Advisory Commission on Intergovernmental Relations (ACIR). This agency differs in a number of important respects from the earlier Commission on Intergovernmental Relations chaired by Meyer Kestnbaum. First and most important, it is to be a permanent body. Second, it is intimately tied into all levels of government since many of its members are chosen by the President from panels of names submitted by the Governors' Conference and by nationwide associations of municipalities, municipal officials, and county governments. Third, it devotes a considerable portion of its resources to the promotion of legislative and administrative action in support of its recommendations. Fourth, metropolitan areas, along with taxation and finance and governmental structure and functions (which are also relevant to urban complexes), constitute the principal fields of its work.

There is a significant interlacing of governmental levels, units, and branches in the ACIR—a fact that gives its reports and recommendations considerable authority and political strength. The previously noted use of nationwide organizations of state and local governments and officials as nominators of a substantial part of the membership assured representation of state and local viewpoints and a greater likelihood that these governments would be receptive to the Commission's recommendations. The selection for membership of the chairmen of the intergovernmental relations subcommittees of the two houses of Congress provided an effective transmission belt to the national legislature. The initial choice for membership of the Secretary of Health, Education, and Welfare (three secretaries served in sequence) and then of the administrator of the Housing and Home Finance Agency furnished liaison with federal agencies that have become increasingly involved in metropolitan affairs. The appointment of Frank Bane, the veteran and recently retired executive director of the Council of State Governments, as the Commission's first chairman—a position he has occupied under Presidents Eisenhower, Kennedy, and Johnson—supplied an important bridge to all three levels of government. (Bane has a large number of close acquaintances in Washington and the state capitals and among local officials, accumulated during a lifetime of public service.)

In July, 1961, less than two years after holding its organizational meeting, the Advisory Commission on Intergovernmental Relations presented broad-ranging, vigorous programs of action and leadership in metropolitan affairs for both the states and the national government. The report was given a significant title, *Governmental Structure, Organization, and Planning in Metropolitan Areas: Suggested Action by Local, State, and National Governments*. Also, it was published not by the Commission but by the House of Representatives' Committee on Government Operations, which has an intergovernmental relations subcommittee—thus demonstrating how the Commission from its inception has sought to establish close relationships with public authorities possessing the power to carry out its recommendations.[7]

The ACIR and the States

The Commission laid out a twofold program for the states: enactment of a package of permissive powers for use by metropolitan residents (which it called "an arsenal of remedial weapons"), and a series of direct state actions involving assistance and control. Three items in the permissive package built directly upon the Council of State Governments' recommendations and policy statements of a few years before. They were simplification of the legal requirements for municipal annexation of unincorporated territory, authorization for interlocal contracting and joint performance of services, and permission to establish metropolitan multipurpose districts. Three other permissive items consisted of authorizations for voluntary transfers of functions between cities and counties, creation of metropolitan study commissions to develop proposals to improve local governmental structure and services, and formation of metropolitan area planning agencies. A final item called for the states,

[7] For reactions by fifteen scholars to the study's recommendations, see *Government in Metropolitan Areas: Commentaries on a Report by the Advisory Commission on Intergovernmental Relations*, issued by the same congressional committee in December, 1961.

when granting local home rule, to reserve sufficient authority so that their legislative bodies could act on intercounty metropolitan problems not solvable through interlocal cooperation.

The Commission's suggestions on direct state action were also highly important. Two recommendations in this field were carry-overs from the recent work of the Council of State Governments. The first called for the passage of state legislation to establish a state office of local affairs to give continuous attention to metropolitan areas and the problems of local governmental structure, organization, finance, and planning. The second, a follow-up of the Council's proposal for review of the adequacy of state incorporation laws, urged the passage of legislation to provide rigorous standards for the creation of new municipalities in metropolitan areas. Other elements of the proposed program of direct action by the states specified the establishment or expansion of programs of financial and technical assistance to urban areas in such activities as planning, urban renewal, and building code modernization, financial and regulatory action to secure and preserve open land in and around metropolitan areas, and state assumption of an active role in resolving disputes among local units when they cannot reach mutual agreement.

The ACIR and the Nation

A dual approach was likewise formulated for the national government, one phase concerned with expanded and improved financial and technical assistance and the other with improved coordination of federal programs affecting the metropolis. In advocating this enlarged role, the Commission spoke out even more forcefully than the Kestnbaum group had six years earlier: "The National Government . . . must be prepared to accept, as a permanent and continuous responsibility, the stimulation and support of State and local efforts to achieve an effective and orderly pattern of metropolitan area development."[8] The Commission then proceeded to put forward four methods of increasing or improving federal assistance: (1) financial support on a continuing basis to metropolitan planning

[8] U.S. House of Representatives, Committee on Government Operations, *Governmental Structure, Organization, and Planning in Metropolitan Areas: Suggested Action by Local, State, and National Governments* (Washington: July, 1961), p. 44.

bodies, (2) technical assistance to state and local agencies concerned with metropolitan planning, (3) advance congressional approval to interstate compacts creating planning agencies in metropolitan areas that cross state lines, and (4) review (but not necessarily formal approval) by a metropolitan planning commission of applications made by local units within the area for certain federal grants.

The Commission's recommendations for improved coordination of federal programs having major impact on metropolitan development were less specific. The group, however, was blunt in stating the need for such action:

> The Federal response to metropolitan problems has not only tended to bypass the States; it has also operated on a single-purpose functional basis, with insufficient attention paid to the need for planning or coordination of the various functions on a comprehensive basis at the Federal level. While large sums of Federal money have been spent on such programs as urban renewal, public housing, highways, airports, hospitals, sewage treatment facilities, river and harbor improvements, etc., little attention has been given to developing a coordinated plan of action at the national level to overcome the conflicts and gaps in their impact upon particular metropolitan areas. Such Federal coordination includes the need for Federal institutional arrangements for properly relating those aspects of the activities of the various Federal departments which are concerned with urban affairs.[9]

The Commission urged improvement along two lines. One recommendation was to formulate national goals and policies for urban and metropolitan development—a matter to which this body gave more attention in later years. The need here, the group pointed out, was to break down each federal program into its component parts as they affect metropolitan areas and then reconstruct these parts into a new metropolitan policy which is reconcilable with national goals. The other recommendation was to coordinate operating programs of the national government. This would eradicate a debilitating situation: too much unilateral functional programming and too little interagency synchronization. The Commission took no stand, however, on whether a federal Department of Urban Affairs of cabinet rank, which was then a subject of growing controversy, should be established. In fact, in a letter written to the Senate

[9] *Governmental Structure, Organization, and Planning in Metropolitan Areas*, p. 52.

Government Operations Committee at about the time of the report's release, the group stated its belief that the matter should be determined by the President and Congress, since it dealt primarily with the organization of the national government's executive branch.[10]

THE PERSISTENCE OF CONCERN

Almost simultaneously with the publication of the ACIR's metropolitan areas report, the states through their national organization, the Council of State Governments, made it evident that their recently expressed interest in assuming metropolitan leadership had not been fleeting. For one thing, the Council incorporated into its annual program of suggested state legislation draft laws and policy statements on all the items the national commission had just recommended for assumption by the states.[11]

In addition, the Governors' Conference of the Council in 1961 passed resolutions directing the organization to prepare a report on the appropriate roles of the different levels of government in urban and regional development, together with a policy statement on comprehensive statewide physical planning and on a more thorough and coordinated approach to joint federal-state planning. One of the resolutions stressed the central position of the states in metropolitan affairs as against the secondary role of the national government. It asserted that the responsiveness of the latter to local needs is necessarily limited by its broad responsibility for international affairs and the national security, its relative remoteness from local problems, and its need to treat varied and disparate problems

[10] U.S. Senate Committee on Government Operations, Subcommittee on Intergovernmental Relations, *Intergovernmental Relations* (Washington: 1963), p. 31.

[11] Council of State Governments, *Program of Suggested State Legislation: 1962* (Chicago: 1961). In a reinforcing action two years later, the national commission published *State Legislative Program of the Advisory Commission on Intergovernmental Relations* (Washington: 1963), which showed the wide support given to its proposals for the states. Such support had come not only from the Council's committee on suggested state legislation but also from two other Council units, the Governors' Conference and the National Legislative Conference, and three influential local organizations, the U.S. Conference of Mayors, the American Municipal Association (since renamed the National League of Cities), and the National Association of Counties.

uniformly. On the other hand, the resolution declared, the states are close to the people and have the ability to deal intimately with urban and regional problems.[12]

The States and Urban Development

The two publications resulting from the resolutions were issued in 1962. The report on responsibilities of the states in urban and regional development contained numerous conclusions, mostly implying rather than explicitly stating recommendations.[13] Here are some of the principal findings:

1. Solutions to many problems require joint governmental effort, but it is chiefly the states that possess the implements to provide the proper setting for intelligent urban development.

2. The states' major task may be to equip local units with a wide array of permissive powers.

3. Local units in many states need additional legislative authorization to organize for planning and to use planning techniques and controls effectively.

4. Many states do not fully meet the need for comprehensive statewide planning that relates local and regional requirements to state policies.

5. The traditional home rule concept can be modified to satisfy current needs by allowing local home rule for strictly local problems and metropolitan home rule for area-wide problems, with the state free to act on intercounty problems and those not solvable through interlocal cooperation.

6. State technical and financial assistance can both stimulate local planning and increase the competence of local governments.

7. A state office of local affairs can furnish systematic, interrelated, and continuing consideration of local needs and problems.

8. Improving annexation and incorporation laws, strengthening counties, and permitting functional transfers, interlocal cooperation, and the establishment of metropolitan multipurpose districts and metropolitan councils are all helpful devices for dealing with problems in the metropolis.

[12] The complete text of the resolution is in *State Government*, XXXIV (Summer, 1961), 191–192.
[13] Council of State Governments, *State Responsibility in Urban Regional Development* (Chicago: 1962).

The States and Planning

The report on state planning, in contrast to that on urban development, contained many specific recommendations.[14] One of the most important was for each state to create a central planning unit, located close to the governor, which would take account of all state development efforts and help integrate them into an over-all plan. Close cooperation should be fostered between this unit and persons responsible for planning in the state operating departments. A second recommendation urged the states to encourage state-wide networks of self-sustaining local planning agencies and to establish close ties with them. In addition to these proposals for state action, the report directed several suggestions to the President. One requested that he consider issuing directives to all federal departments and agencies on the importance of working directly with the governors for improved coordination of planning programs at all governmental levels. Another recommended that he encourage preparation of a comprehensive, long-range national program for effective use of all physical and human resources. Still another stressed the need for establishing a formal relationship between the national and state governments, possibly through a newly created section in the Executive Office of the President, for continuous cooperation and communication between the national and state chief executives.

Advocacy of Greater Coordination

The national Advisory Commission on Intergovernmental Relations soon made recommendations about one of the most serious gaps in a program of state and national metropolitan leadership. In 1964 a report was published under the auspices of the Senate Committee on Government Operations (note again the close relationship between the Commission and an important governmental agency) that emphasized the need for better coordination of federal programs influencing urban and metropolitan areas.

Concerning the national government's forty-three aid programs for urban development, the Commission reached these candid conclusions:

. . . No evidence was found to indicate the existence of a unified Federal policy or organizational machinery for coordinating aid programs

[14] Council of State Governments, Governors' Conference Subcommittee on State Planning, *State Planning: A Policy Statement* (Chicago: 1962).

in the field of urban development. Although general purpose local governments [such as municipalities and counties] are, or may choose to
become, involved as participants in a number of programs, the tendency
to accept, encourage, or even require special purpose units [special district
governments] is more general. There is only a limited tendency to accept
joint project sponsors [those involving the collaboration of two or more
local governments] as an alternative to requiring a single legal entity.
Federal requirements for an adequate geographic area of jurisdiction promote areawide planning and administration in some cases but not
in a majority.

Although planning requirements are almost universally imposed in
one form or another by the [federal] programs surveyed, the largest
number of programs that do so actively promote functional planning
only, and do not relate the aided function with the other functions in a
comprehensive plan designed to achieve orderly development of the
entire urban area. A majority of the [federal] programs that do recognize
comprehensive planning, do so only passively. They do not require that
such planning be done, but only that if it is done, it should not be
disregarded.[15]

The key element in the Commission's report was concerned
with vastly improved coordination among national agencies. It
called for congressional legislation to establish the principle of federal interagency coordination in all programs affecting urban development. To facilitate the achievement of this objective, a draft
of suggested language for a unified federal urban development policy
was presented in the report.[16]

The Commission had further counsel for the national government: federal aid programs in urban development should favor
general local governments over non-school special districts as recipients, they should require and promote effective local planning,
they should encourage joint participation by local units in area-wide
projects,[17] and they should be channeled through the states when
the latter also provide significant financial contributions.

On the matter of favoring general local units for federal aid,
the ACIR noted that the blame for the growth of special districts
was shared by all three levels of government. The national govern-

---

[15] U.S. Senate Committee on Government Operations, Subcommittee on
Intergovernmental Relations, *Impact of Federal Urban Development Programs
on Local Government Organization and Planning* (Washington: 1964), p. 22.

[16] *Ibid.*, pp. 41–44.

[17] The Commission also advised the states to enact legislation to permit
interlocal cooperation.

ment has encouraged the creation of districts and made grants to them. The states have placed severe financial restrictions on general local units, thus causing people to turn to the district device. Too many municipal and county officials have avoided controversial decisions by shunting to special districts responsibility for vital urban development functions. Strengthening general local units, it was pointed out, would simplify intergovernmental relations, make urban development processes more understandable to the local public, and reduce the need for local officials to try to coordinate the activities of additional governments. While speaking out strongly against special districts, the Commission excluded from censure metropolitan multipurpose districts, especially those governed by elected municipal and county officials. (Although this condemnation of special districts is generally well taken, it should be remembered that the local representatives on the ACIR are all from general units, a fact also related to the stated preference for multipurpose districts to be governed by city and county officials.)

The Commission's recommendations had two general objectives in mind. The first was to strengthen existing general local governments and to encourage them to cooperate in dealing with area-wide needs and problems. The second was to bolster the states and to stimulate them to take on fuller responsibilities in urban and metropolitan development. This dual approach represents efforts to improve the workings of the American federal system.

The proposal to channel federal urban grants through the states when they provide supplementary financial assistance was designed to strengthen the position of the states by compelling their local units to deal with them in development matters. At the same time, the proposal sought to awaken the states from their lethargy in responding to urban challenges and induce them to assume greater financial responsibility for the needs of their local metropolitan governments. However, this recommendation, unlike any of the others, precipitated dissents from a formidable minority of the Commission.[18]

Two Commission members—Don Hummel, its vice-chairman and a former mayor of Tucson, and Robert C. Weaver, the administrator of the Housing and Home Finance Agency—argued that

[18] U.S. Senate Committee on Government Operations, *Impact of Federal Urban Development Programs*, pp. 30–31.

the decision about channeling federal urban development grants through the states should continue to be left to the discretion of the individual states. Such decisions, they reasoned, should not be imposed by the national government unless an overriding national interest requires uniformity.[19] The three mayor members of the Commission—Raymond R. Tucker of St. Louis, Arthur Naftalin of Minneapolis, and Neal S. Blaisdell of Honolulu—concurred in their dissent. They contended that no meaningful principle existed which required the involvement of all levels of government in all governmental activities and that this recommendation unwisely sacrificed substance for form. Urban renewal and public housing programs, they added, were uniquely adaptable to local administration and this proposal would therefore disrupt a relationship which had worked well and had been attacked up to this time only by enemies of these programs. Moreover, Edmund S. Muskie, a Commission member and chairman of the Senate's Subcommittee on Intergovernmental Relations, maintained that channeling all federal urban grants through the states would undermine the flexibility that had contributed greatly to the success of various programs. In addition, he warned, the failure of many states to develop an understanding of and sympathy for these cooperative efforts should not be overlooked.

RECENT STATE ACTIONS

What has been the response of the states in recent years to the urging by important organizations to assume increased leadership in urban and metropolitan areas? Among the most obvious developments have been the increased attention to metropolitan matters in many governors' inaugural addresses and messages to legislatures, the expanded number of governors' commissions and legislative committees conducting urban and metropolitan studies, the in-

[19] Earlier in late 1962 Mr. Hummel had spoken out vigorously along another line in opposition to the channeling of all federal urban grants through the states. In testifying in late 1962 before the Senate Subcommittee on Intergovernmental Relations, he emphasized that the states had made direct federal-local relations necessary by turning a deaf ear to metropolitan needs. The states could not expect any change in the situation, he admonished, until they had proven their willingness and ability to cope with modern urban challenges. U.S. Senate Committee on Government Operations, Subcommittee on Intergovernmental Relations, *Intergovernmental Relations*, p. 34.

crease in statewide conferences, and the mounting volume of legislative bills relating to metropolitan affairs.[20] But much more than
accelerated interest has been evident. Various states have taken
concrete action along different lines involving procedures and organization. Laws have been passed to permit local governments
to enter into cooperative agreements, transfer functions among
themselves, form metropolitan planning commissions, and choose
among more forms of government. (This last has sometimes involved
constitutional amendments.) Some states have tightened their incorporation procedures and have revised their annexation legislation
so that unincorporated areas no longer have a controlling voice in
land absorption efforts. A few states have taken another type of
action on annexations and incorporations by establishing state or
local commissions to pass upon such proposals. The gains represented
in these various efforts have been modest thus far and the adoption
of the changes has been sporadic.

State Offices of Local Affairs

Action to create a state office of local affairs—a move that could
have long-range effects on promoting and evaluating the kinds of
changes just mentioned—has occurred only rarely. The first major
development in this field in recent years took place in New York
in 1959, when legislation was enacted to establish the Office for
Local Government in the executive department. The new office
was vested with substantial powers: to assist the governor in coordinating the activities of departments and agencies having relationships with local governments, to provide advice and assistance to
requesting local units and make studies of local problems, to serve
as a clearinghouse for information about local governmental affairs,
and to encourage and assist cooperative local efforts to solve common problems.[21] Somewhat similar agencies were formed in Washington State and Tennessee in 1961 and 1963, respectively.

Proposals to establish state offices of local affairs have often

[20] For specific examples of such governors' addresses and messages and
gubernatorial and legislative study groups in a recent year, see the March–April,
1963, and November–December, 1963, issues of *Metropolitan Area Problems:
News and Digest*, published by the State University of New York Graduate School
of Public Affairs, Albany.

[21] The office was subsequently expanded when several agencies, including
the state board of equalization and assessment, were relocated in it.

encountered stiff and decisive opposition. Opponents have argued that such an agency will increase the dependence of local governments on the state. What is needed, they contend, is not a new state agency but more legislation making it possible for local governments to solve their own problems. They also maintain that the services to be provided by such an agency are already generally available through leagues of cities and university bureaus and institutes of governmental research. State activities affecting urban areas are so vast, they further hold, that reshuffling all of them into this new agency would collapse many existing relationships between the two levels and place a substantial part of all state services in a single unit. Although these three arguments can be answered (and at least the third one is specious since no proposals have specified the assignment of all or even most urban functions to a state office of local affairs), the opposition, composed mainly of local officials and their organizations, has proved a formidable barrier to widespread acceptance of the idea.[22]

Growing Services

A number of states—still simply a minority—have also acted in functional fields of significance to the metropolis. Legislation has been enacted to acquire open space in and near metropolitan areas, to aid mass transit, and to assure the availability of adequate supplies of water. Some states have also assumed greater responsibilities —in both facilitating local action and directly providing service and regulation—in such fields as air and water pollution control and urban highway planning and construction. A substantial number, moreover, have been increasing the amounts of their direct expenditures and grants in metropolitan areas.

Interstate Areas

Many states have found it increasingly important to act on metropolitan affairs for another reason: growing proportions of their populations live in urban complexes that transcend state lines. The twenty-six interstate metropolitan areas now existing contain more than one-fifth of the nation's people and more than one-third of

[22] For a further consideration of such state agencies, see John G. Grumm, A State Agency for Local Affairs? (Berkeley: University of California Bureau of Public Administration, 1961).

its metropolitan population. Furthermore, many of them—New York–Northeastern New Jersey, Chicago–Northwestern Indiana, Philadelphia, St. Louis, Washington, Cincinnati, and Kansas City, for example—are among the principal population and economic centers of the United States.

Adjacent states having parts of their territory in the same SMSA have been confronted with the growing necessity of establishing an instrumentality to deal with mutual difficulties. Consequently, in an increasing number of instances interstate agreements or compacts have been worked out to take care of certain common problems or needs. Such compacts normally create a board, composed of appointees of the governors, and assign it responsibility in one or more functional fields—building and maintaining bridges and tunnels, operating parks and ports, and managing mass transit facilities are all existing examples. Although use of the compact is increasing, this device has often proved to be a cumbersome procedure. The respective state legislatures must pass identical forms of the agreement and negotiations frequently take years to complete successfully.[23] In addition, any subsequently needed revisions of the arrangement must obtain common consent.

The outstanding recent use of the compact device materialized in 1961 when the Delaware River Basin Commission was formed for the four-state area centering on Philadelphia. The Commission has broad powers in terms of river basin planning and developing and operating water resource projects. Moreover, it is authorized to review (and thereafter disapprove or require modification of) proposals by other agencies that affect the region's water resources —proposals such as those relating to flood protection, recreation, hydroelectric power, and water withdrawals or diversions. This agency is of further importance because it is based on a compact signed by four states (Delaware, New Jersey, New York, and Pennsylvania) and by the national government. This marks the first time the latter has become a partner with states in a compact. And the national-state association is a continuing working relationship, as the President

[23] On the question of congressional approval of interstate compacts and other legal points, see John M. Winters, *Interstate Metropolitan Areas* (Ann Arbor: University of Michigan Law School Legislative Research Center, 1962), pp. 12–45. A listing of interstate compacts will be found in Council of State Governments, *Interstate Compacts, 1783–1956* (Chicago: 1956).

of the United States and each of the four governors have a representative on the governing board. The possible significance of this interstate-federal arrangement was recognized at its inception. As political scientist Roscoe Martin has observed, "The Delaware River Basin Compact represents a new departure in intergovernmental relations in the United States. It constitutes an experiment that will be watched with interest by all concerned either with regional [including metropolitan] administration or with the Federal System."[24]

In sum, the states have recently exhibited increased interest and activity in metropolitan affairs, although generally the effort has been far from equal to the challenge. Many people have long held that a major reason for the states' inadequate response to urban and metropolitan needs has been the rural domination of many of their legislative bodies. This dominance is giving way, largely as a result of extensive litigation over legislative apportionment produced by the Supreme Court's decisions in *Baker* v. *Carr* in 1962 and *Reynolds* v. *Sims* in 1964. The first held that the apportionment question was "within reach of judicial protection under the Fourteenth Amendment;" the second held that members of both houses must represent substantially equal populations. In the past, urban areas have often been unable to get the ear of the lawmakers because representatives from central cities and suburbs have failed to agree on a united program. It will be interesting to see if they work in greater harmony when their legislative strength is increased.

RECENT NATIONAL ACTIONS

The national government has been increasingly active in metropolitan affairs along a number of fronts in recent years. A substantial proportion of its grant programs, including those concerned with mass transit and outdoor recreation, has been inaugurated during this period. Requirements or incentives have been placed in such programs—the highway and open space acts, for instance—to stimulate area-wide planning. Congress has increased the enforcement authority of federal agencies dealing with certain metropolitan

[24] Roscoe C. Martin, *Metropolis in Transition* (Washington: U.S. Housing and Home Finance Agency, September, 1963), p. 25. Professor Martin presents an interesting case report on the development of this compact in Chapter X of this study.

problems. For example, the national government, at the governor's request, can now take court action against a city or an industry which violates federal water pollution abatement measures even though the body of water being polluted lies wholly within one state. Congress has given advance consent to interstate compacts concerned with the establishment of interstate metropolitan planning agencies. The Housing and Home Finance Agency has created an office of metropolitan development and made it responsible for coordinating the agency's varied urban programs and for promoting increased program coordination with other federal departments and agencies active in urban and metropolitan affairs.[25]

A Federal Department of Urban Affairs

Various people have pinned their hopes for effective federal interagency coordination of programs affecting metropolitan areas on the creation of a federal Department of Urban Affairs. Others have felt a preferable coordinating device would be a staff assistant, agency, or council (the last named patterned along the lines of the Council of Economic Advisers) in the Executive Office of the President.[26] Although bills in support of an urban affairs department had been regularly introduced in Congress since 1954, the idea did not come to a peak until the administration of John F. Kennedy. In his special message on housing in 1961, President Kennedy recommended the establishment of such a department of cabinet rank because an "awareness of these [urban] problems and programs should be constantly brought to the Cabinet table, and coordinated leadership provided for functions related to urban affairs but appropriately performed by a variety of departments and agencies." Soon after the House Rules Committee in January, 1962, pigeonholed a bill to establish a Department of Urban Affairs and Housing, the President, acting under his congressionally-granted reorganization powers, submitted a plan that closely resembled the tabled

[25] For a penetrating review of increased national and state efforts in metropolitan areas, see Norman Beckman, "Our Federal System and Urban Development: The Adaptation of Form to Function," *Journal of the American Institute of Planners*, XXIX (August, 1963), 152–167.

[26] A discussion of an urban affairs department and a metropolitan area council at the national level is contained in Robert H. Connery and Richard H. Leach, *The Federal Government and Metropolitan Areas* (Cambridge: Harvard University Press, 1960), chaps. 4 and 5.

bill. Basically, the plan would have upgraded the Housing and Home Finance Agency to cabinet status, although a number of officials and observers viewed the action as simply an opening wedge to reallocating various urban programs from other agencies to the new department. Such a reorganization plan would have gone into effect provided neither house of Congress disapproved it within sixty days after submission. In late February, 1962, the House of Representatives by a roll-call vote of 264 to 150 adopted a resolution vetoing the plan. President Lyndon Johnson, like his predecessor, has demonstrated a deep concern for the problems of urban and metropolitan areas and has renewed the call for an urban department of cabinet rank.

Unquestionably state and national governments will assume even larger roles in metropolitan affairs in the future. The growing number of votes in urban communities will doubtlessly make both state and national officials increasingly sensitive to the demands of these areas. So also the Supreme Court's decision in *Wesberry* v. *Sanders* in 1964, which held that congressional districts should be roughly equal in population, will probably lead to greater responsiveness by the House of Representatives to the desires of the metropolitan public. And as the national Advisory Commission on Intergovernmental Relations has stated:

. . . While the primary responsibility for solving metropolitan problems lies with State and local governments, many considerations, including the number and size of the interstate metropolitan areas, make these problems a national issue. Economic considerations alone, and the predominant position of the metropolitan areas in the national economy, are enough in themselves to make the fullest development of those areas a vital concern of the Federal Government.[27]

The question is no longer whether the states and the nation are to be highly active in the metropolis. The question now is whether local governments will cooperatively work out metropolitan problems, with the national and state governments playing facilitating and supplementary roles, or whether direct intervention by the latter levels will be forthcoming.

[27] *Governmental Structure, Organization, and Planning in Metropolitan Areas*, p. 43.

CHAPTER 18

The Metropolitan World

ALONG WITH the cold war and the end of colonialism, the most striking aspect of the modern era is the steady increase in the proportion of the world's population residing in urban areas. At the present time, approximately one-third of the population lives in communities of more than 2000 inhabitants; by the end of the present century it is estimated that this figure will be over 50 percent. The degree of urbanization varies widely, ranging from about 80 percent in England to less than 15 percent in some of the African and Asian nations. However, as industry and trade develop in these latter areas, the relative position of the Western world with respect to the other continents will gradually change. In fact, urban growth rates in parts of Asia are now running 400 percent higher than those in the West.

The population of the globe stood at the three billion mark in 1960, and if growth continues at the current rate the total will exceed six billion by the year 2000. Most of this increase, moreover, will take place in urban areas. A century ago, only five cities in the world had a population as large as one million; today there are well over

100. In 1960, 285 million persons lived in metropolitan areas of this size; by the end of the century it is estimated that this figure will be 1285 million. The number residing in smaller metropolitan areas, those from 300,000 to one million inhabitants, will likewise multiply during this period from 154 million to 820 million.[1]

The story is the same everywhere—in southeast Asia, in India, in South America, in Africa—as population increases and as people crowd into the cities in search of economic opportunities and a new way of life. Ninety percent of the four million increase in Japan's population from 1955 to 1960 was concentrated in two metropolitan regions, Tokyo and Osaka. In Latin America, Colombia's five largest metropolitan areas are now averaging an annual growth rate of 6 percent while the country's population as a whole is gaining only 3 percent. The consequences of this seemingly irresistible trend are only too familiar to American city dwellers: increasing congestion, the trek from the farms and hinterlands to urban centers, the battle against slums, the assimilation of newcomers, the demands on the local governmental system. Americans who are staggered by the problems of urbanization in the United States are really amazed when they see such cities as Tokyo or Calcutta. The Japanese capital, one of the world's most populous metropolitan cities, has no sewerage facilities for 80 percent of the area, while in Calcutta, where the population doubled during a recent twelve-year period, almost two-thirds of a million people have no homes but the sidewalks and alleys.

A glance at some of the titles now beginning to appear in social science literature illustrates the universal nature of the urban-metropolitan problem:

Migrant Adjustment to City Life: The Egyptian Case
Urban Planning in Pakistan
Congestion and Overcrowding: An African Urban Problem
Some Aspects of Urbanization in the Belgian Congo
Political Implications of Rapid Urbanization in Caribbean Countries
Local Migration and Urbanization in Sweden
Metropolitan Area Problems and Solutions in Australia
The Impact of Urbanization in Israel

[1] See Homer Hoyt, World Urbanization (Washington: Urban Land Institute, 1962).

Present State of Air Pollution in Cities Caused by Automobile
    Exhaust Gases and Problems Related with Its Control,
    U.S.S.R.
New South African Town Designed to Prevent Traffic Problems

Observations like the following also have a familiar ring for
Americans interested in metropolitan affairs:

While some 400,000 live and pay taxes to the municipality of Tel
Aviv, about the same number of non-residents use the city's services
each day but pay taxes in the surrounding townships. . . . Lack of coordination among the different local administrations in the area has led
to confusion and inefficiency. Separate tax systems, health systems,
municipal codes, and separate governments in the neighboring towns
result in needless duplication of effort.[2]

Lack of coordination [among the 28 separate bus companies in
Bangkok, Thailand] results in one of the most inconvenient mass transit
systems in any capital city of the world. The plan to consolidate these
companies into a single mass transit system serving the entire metropolitan area was purposely chosen as being of high impact value. It is hoped
that public support for putting other services on an area-wide basis would
be engendered by the successful operation of such a system.[3]

Tokyo has a population of more than nine million people, swelling to ten million by day as workers flow into the city from beyond the
metropolitan limits. Unplanned sprawl of built-up areas, worsening of
residential surroundings, lack of open space, increasing traffic congestion,
poor provision for public facilities, and severe housing shortages have
resulted from this excessive concentration of population.[4]

If one shows this study of Bombay's urban politics to a specialist
on the political behavior of American cities, as I have done, his reaction
will be: "Every major feature is familiar." Ethnic groups challenged by
functional roles and associations; the absorption of urban newcomers in
little urgent personal problems, the parties' inability to find vote-getting
issues and resorting to individual or group patronage—the American
political scientist recognizes them all.[5]

The approaches to most East African towns are through fringe
areas of sub-standard housing. Africans who have been evicted from

[2] *Metropolitan Area Problems: News and Digest,* VI (May–June, 1963), 3.
[3] *Ibid.,* V (January–February, 1962), 2.
[4] *Ibid.,* VI (January–February, 1963), 3.
[5] Henry C. Hart, "Bombay Politics: Pluralism or Polarization," *Journal of
Asian Studies,* XX (May, 1961), 267.

the center, as building standards are enforced because the land is needed for development, had little choice but to settle on the fringes of the towns. To those evicted have been added an ever-increasing number of Africans from rural areas seeking employment in the towns.[6]

THE METROPOLITAN TREND

Metropolitan society is a nonagricultural society. The greater the degree of industrialization in a nation, the higher will be the proportion of its people residing in urban areas.[7] The world, of course, had known cities long before the development of large-scale industry, but the achievement of high levels of urbanization (the ratio of people living in cities to the total population) had to await the Industrial Revolution. Before the invention of the steam engine and other forms of energy-producing devices, the economy of most nations could not support a large urban populace. The Industrial Revolution, however, led to a rising demand for workers in the cities and towns while technological advances in agriculture simultaneously created surplus labor on the farms. These developments in turn opened the doors to a metropolitan civilization.

In 1959 the International Urban Research Center at the University of California published a study entitled *The World's Metropolitan Areas.*[8] Departing from the usual practice of gathering and presenting demographic data by "cities" when urban communities are considered on a worldwide basis, the study attempted to delimit metropolitan areas in each country by criteria similar to that employed by the U.S. Bureau of the Budget in defining American SMSA's. Some 1064 such areas were identified as in existence at the middle of this century. The largest number outside the United States was found in the Soviet Union (129) with Communist China (103) and India (70) following next in order.[9]

[6] Peter C. W. Gutkind, "Congestion and Overcrowding: An African Urban Problem," *Human Organization,* 19 (Fall, 1960), 129–134.

[7] See, for example, Jack P. Gibbs and Leo Schnore, "Metropolitan Growth: An International Study," *American Journal of Sociology,* LXVI (September, 1960), 160–170.

[8] (Berkeley and Los Angeles: University of California Press, 1959).

[9] Other substantiating evidence of the worldwide urban and metropolitan trends was presented earlier, in Chapter 1 in the section "A Worldwide Development." See particularly Tables 3 and 4.

The pattern of settlement varies from nation to nation. The constant in each case is the rural-metropolitan migration that is contributing far more to urban numbers than the natural increase in city population. In some countries, the tendency is to concentrate in one or two large centers. Egypt is one example, with migration from the rural sections favoring the largest city, Cairo, while bypassing those of moderate and small size. Saigon in South Vietnam, Bangkok in Thailand, Manila in the Philippines, Accra in Ghana, Nairobi in Kenya, and Leopoldville in the Congo are other illustrations of the same phenomenon. Where this trend is evident, the largest city in most instances is also the national capital.

Metropolitan growth, apart from its spatial and geographical dimensions, is not confined to any particular type of nation or civilization. The rate of increase may be radically different but the trend is the same whether in the old and highly industrialized states of Western Europe or in the new and predominantly rural nations of Africa. It is taking place not only in countries like India and Egypt that have old and complex civilizations and a long heritage of great cities, but also in areas such as those in central and west Africa where primitive tribal life has been dominant until recent decades. It is occurring in countries like Great Britain, with a strong tradition of local rule, as well as in nations such as France, where the central government exercises considerable control over local units. In such widely diversified settings, substantial variance is likely to be found in the responses of local political and social institutions to emerging urban developments.

International comparative studies of urban problems and metropolitan political systems are still in their infancy. The endless variety of local customs and institutions—both among nations and even within the same country—presents formidable obstacles to such inquiries and makes generalization exceedingly hazardous if not impossible. What we shall do here is to give a sample or broad overview of local government and its responses to urban growth in various regions of the world. For this purpose we have chosen four widely scattered urban centers: the venerable metropolis of London, the indigenous African town of Ibadan, the oriental city of Tokyo, and the Brazilian metropolis of São Paulo. Although representing different cultures, each of them faces the same relentless pressures of urbanization.

LONDON

Known as a nation of townspeople, England has been highly urbanized for many decades. Its present density of 790 persons per square
mile is exceeded by only one other major European country, the
Netherlands. The urban population first surpassed that in the rural
areas around 1850. By the end of the nineteenth century, three-fourths
of the people lived in cities and towns. Since 1939, when the number
of urbanites reached 80 percent of the total population, there has
been little change in the proportion. However, the long prevalent
pattern of migration from farm to town has given way to the movement from one urban area to another, particularly from the older
industrial centers of the north to London and other cities in the
southeast. Today, over 40 percent of the population is concentrated
in London and five other smaller metropolitan areas.

Physical and Demographic Characteristics

The metropolis of London dominates British life. As the political
and cultural capital of the nation, the center of its commerce, and
the headquarters of its major financial institutions, London exercises
an enormous gravitational pull on the rest of the country. Someone
once remarked that to create an approximate American equivalent
we would have to merge New York, Washington, and Chicago into
one overwhelmingly dominant metropolis, compared with which all
other urban centers in the United States would appear provincial.

In speaking of London, it is necessary to recognize that there are
several Londons. There is the ancient city at the center, "a small
island of obstinate medieval structure," which contains but one
square mile of territory and a population of less than 7000. There is
the former county of London with 117 square miles and slightly
over three million people. There is the Greater London conurbation,
which is composed of the former county and the adjacent ring of
suburbs and encompasses a total area of 723 square miles and a
population of 8.2 million, over 60 percent of whom live in the suburban belt. Finally, there is the London region which, in addition to
the conurbation, includes an outer ring extending to about a fifty-
mile radius from the center. (As its boundaries are defined by the
Ministry of Housing and Local Government, the London region
contained a total of approximately 12.5 million people in 1961.)

Separating this outer regional ring from the Greater London conurbation is a metropolitan greenbelt varying in width from five to fifteen miles.

The London Region is growing substantially in population but the accretion is taking place in the outer ring beyond the greenbelt. During the intercensal period, 1952–1961, the number of inhabitants in this area increased by 891,000 in contrast to a decrease of 183,000 in the county of London and 29,000 in the remainder of the conurbation. This pattern is a continuation of the trend which started late in the last century as the British government began a planned program to reduce density and congestion in the center. The city of London, for example, had a population of 130,000 in 1850; today it has less than 7000. Since 1921, the county of London has lost steadily in the number of residents while the suburban ring has recorded substantial gains.

Planning for urban growth began early in Great Britain. Before the concept was discussed in other than a few American municipalities, Parliament passed a town planning act in 1909, the same year that the University of Liverpool inaugurated the first formal program in city planning offered by an academic institution. British planning has been strongly influenced by the "garden-city" movement as it found expression in the work of Ebenezer Howard and his followers. They proposed that the large urban centers, such as London, be decentralized by establishing and developing small satellite towns in the outlying reaches of the region. London planners have followed this general concept. Even before World War I, the London County Council had taken steps to effect a redistribution of the population by a program of slum clearance and the construction of new housing outside the central area. The program was accelerated in the 1940s as a result of the war damage which necessitated reconstruction of large sections of the core. It was also aided by the wartime evacuation which reduced the population of the county of London from four million in 1939 to 2.5 million at the end of 1944.

Starting in the 1900s, various "advisory" plans were drafted for the London area, some commissioned by the national government, others by local authorities and private organizations. Probably the most influential has been the Greater London Plan of 1944, which was prepared under an appointment from the Minister of Works and Planning. The plan called for a continuation of decentralization by moving out large numbers of people and their related employment from central London to new towns in the outer ring. It also proposed a metropolitan greenbelt encircling the built-up urbanized area of the conurbation. Drafters of the plan regarded the greenbelt as a strategic device for halting the continued spread of suburban growth. As they conceived it, such a belt, aided by the creation of self-sufficient new towns in the outer region and the barring of new industrial development in the interior, would serve as a barrier to the further enlargement of the London commuting zone.[10]

Many of the provisions of the Greater London Plan have been followed in principle, including redistribution of population, creation of the greenbelt, and the channeling of new industry into the outer zone. But the forces of growth and change have proved too strong to permit the degree of decentralization envisaged by the planners. Like the borough of Manhattan in New York City, the heart of postwar London has served as a powerful attraction for the location of new office sites, an attraction too great to be overcome by the public planners. As a result, the central area gained approximately 260,000 jobs, mostly of white-collar or clerical nature, during the 1952–1961 census period. Thus while a drastic reduction in the area's resident population was accomplished by the redistribution plans, the problem of traffic and congestion in central London has increased as more than 1.3 million persons commute to the core each week day. As one scholar has observed, the Greater London planning experience provides an object lesson in the relentless forces of growth. It demonstrates that containment is extremely difficult even when implemented by controls far more powerful than those available to public authorities in the United States.[11]

A measure of coordinated planning has been achieved in Greater London despite the usual fragmentation of local units. Until the reorganization of the governmental structure in 1963, as explained later, the planning function was shared by the six counties and three county boroughs in the metropolis. Each was charged by law with the responsibility of preparing a redevelopment plan and administering planning controls for the area within its jurisdiction. In formu-

[10] See Daniel R. Mandelker, *Green Belts and Urban Growth* (Madison: University of Wisconsin Press, 1962).

[11] Donald L. Foley, *Controlling London's Growth, Planning the Great Wen* (Berkeley and Los Angeles: University of California Press, 1963), p. 157.

lating their plans, local authorities were required to follow the broad policies laid down by the national Ministry of Housing and Local Government. This latter agency also reviewed and approved the local development plans and oversaw the administration of planning controls. These centralized checks tended to promote a higher degree of coordinated planning among the local units than would otherwise have been possible. They also enabled area-wide advisory plans, such as the Greater London Plan, to have more impact than similar documents prepared by regional planning agencies in the United States.

Governmental Pattern

Prior to 1964, the governmental structure of the London conurbation consisted of 117 local units including six counties and three county boroughs (larger cities detached from counties). Within the county of London were 28 metropolitan boroughs and the city of London; in the surrounding counties were 42 municipal boroughs, 28 urban districts, three rural districts, and six parishes. In addition, the area was overlayed with 16 special-purpose authorities such as the Metropolitan Police Commission (responsible to the Home Secretary in the national cabinet), the Metropolitan Water Board, and the London Transport Executive. The picture, in other words, was not unlike that in any large metropolis in the United States. The most notable difference was the far greater degree of control exercised over urban growth in the British system.

During the 1950s there was increasing feeling on the part of many analysts and observers of the London scene that either the existing system of local government had to be revitalized and modernized or the national government had to impose greater centralized controls. Although not as diffused as in the typical American metropolitan area where planning and zoning powers are exercised by dozens of independent units without supervision by a higher authority, the local governmental setup in the London area was by no means satisfactory. William A. Robson, the distinguished British political scientist, called it "obsolete." A royal commission charged that it was not only failing to achieve many essential aims but was "not conducive to the health of representative government."[12]

[12] *Report of the Royal Commission on Local Government in Greater London* (London: 1960), para. 189.

In December, 1957, a Royal Commission was appointed to "examine the present system and working of local government in the Greater London area; and to recommend whether any, and if so what, changes in the local government structure and the distribution of local authority functions in the area, or in any part of it, would better secure effective and convenient local government." After three years of study, the Commission presented its report recommending a radical reorganization of the area's local governmental structure. It proposed a two-tier structure or what is often referred to in the United States as a "borough system." Area-wide functions were to be administered by a directly elected Greater London Council which would have jurisdiction over the area roughly to the limits of the greenbelt. All other functions were to be assigned to fifty-two boroughs that would replace all existing units of government except the city of London.[13] The recommendations met a cool reception from local officials and also aroused the opposition of the Labour Party which feared that it could not control the proposed new and larger metropolitan council as it did the London County Council.

The government, at this time under Conservative party leadership, regarded the proposals favorably. In 1961 it introduced a bill in Parliament to effect a reorganization of London local government along lines closely following the Commission's recommendations. However, several modifications in the original proposals were made, including a reduction in the size of the area to be covered by the new metropolitan council from 760 square miles to 630 square miles, and also a reduction in the number of boroughs from 52 to 32. The new boroughs or cities would be created by consolidating existing units and would have populations ranging from 170,000 to 340,000. The smaller number of boroughs was favored by the Government since it wanted assurance that each would be sufficiently large to be a viable and efficient unit. The effect of the reorganization is to

[13] For a discussion of the report, see William A. Robson, "The Reform of London Government," *Public Administration*, 39 (Spring, 1961), 59–71; and L. J. Sharpe, "The Report of the Royal Commission on Local Government," *Ibid.*, 73–92. Also see Robson, *The World's Greatest Metropolis: Planning and Government in Greater London* (Pittsburgh: Institute of Local Government, Graduate School of Public and International Affairs, University of Pittsburgh, 1963) and Frank Smallwood, *Greater London: The Politics of Metropolitan Reform* (Indianapolis: Bobbs-Merrill, 1965).

abolish the counties of London and Middlesex and eighty-five other local governments. The city of London remains unchanged in territorial size, but it now has the same status in the new governmental pattern as that of the boroughs.

The bill, enacted by Parliament in late 1963, specifically charges the new metropolitan council with carrying out a survey of Greater London and the preparation of a general development plan, including policy with respect to land use. Each borough is required to formulate a redevelopment plan for its own area embodying the relevant features of the metropolitan plan. The metropolitan council is also vested with responsibility for traffic management throughout the area, main roads, trunk line sewers and sewage disposal facilities, major cultural and recreational facilities, refuse disposal, fire protection, and civil defense. All remaining local governmental functions including education (except in central London where the school system is to be administered by a special committee of the metropolitan council) are borough responsibilities.

The London experience poses the dilemma that the architects of metropolitan reorganization face. Although the plan is far-reaching and its territorial coverage large, it still falls short of constituting an answer to the problem of governmental structure *vis-à-vis* urban growth. That the adopted arrangements will bring more efficient and effective local government and greater control over land use and physical development within the territorial boundaries of the new council can scarcely be denied. That they will provide a solution to the more crucial problem of guiding and controlling the continued outward expansion of the metropolis is another matter. For even though the areal jurisdiction of the Greater London Council will be very extensive, it will still lack control over the outer ring where much of the new development is taking place.

There is obviously a limit in territorial size to which a unit can expand and yet retain its essential characteristics as a local government. On the other hand, planning for the limited area may be impaired or nullified by independent action on the periphery. The plan for lowering population density in central London, for example, can be effective only if provision is made for accommodating the displaced families in the outer zone. Here the London reorganization plan is deficient since it gives the new government control only over the already built-up area; it provides no assurance that the independent local units outside the territorial jurisdiction of the Greater London council will be willing to accommodate the overspill, particularly if lower-income families are involved. Superimposing national controls on the outer zone authorities can at least partially substitute for centralized local direction. Such action, as we have seen, is possible in Great Britain; it would not be at the present time in the United States.

IBADAN

The tendency toward urbanization, as an UNESCO study shows, is one of the outstanding characteristics of present-day life in Africa.[14] Virtually the entire continent is in a state of rapid transition. Colonialism has been brought to a speedy and often abrupt termination, new nations are coming into being, industrial expansion is taking place at an accelerated pace, and migration from the rural areas to the cities and towns is a common phenomenon. As in the more advanced countries, the urbanizing trends in Africa have brought with them overcrowding and slum conditions in the population centers, the emergence of a labor class, important social and cultural changes, the formation of new types of associations connected with occupations, cults, and recreational activities, and the progressive disintegration of wider kinship groups and family stability.

The problems of governmental reconstruction facing the new and underdeveloped nations are monumental. Sweeping away the foundations of a colonial structure and adapting traditional political institutions to the changing needs of an emerging urban society have everywhere produced difficulties. At the local level, it has required the transfer of authority from tribal councils to new elective assemblies and the creation of native administrative systems to replace the body of professional civil servants utilized by colonial powers. The shortage of educated and skilled personnel among the native population contributes to the difficulty of building up an efficient local bureaucracy. In addition, the influx of migrants into the towns often overstrains the labor market and the local economy, not to

[14] *Social Implications of Industrialization and Urbanization in Africa South of the Sahara* (Paris: United Nations Educational, Scientific, and Cultural Organization, 1956).

mention public facilities, and thus helps to create restlessness and insecurity.

Although no individual city can be said to be typical of African municipalities, we have chosen Ibadan, Nigeria, the famous center of the Yoruba tribe, as an example of a major community and its travails of urban growth and adjustment. We might have selected the far larger city of Johannesburg in the Union of South Africa, where a metropolitan complex resembling those in the United States and Great Britain has developed. Or we might have gone north of the Sahara to Cairo, where population is soaring and migration from the rural hinterlands heavy. We wanted, however, to examine an African city that is in an earlier stage of urban development, and neither Johannesburg nor Cairo comes within this category. The first is a highly industrialized metropolis with well established social and political institutions and with control firmly in the hands of its white minority. The second is an Arab community that is in a more advanced stage industrially and administratively than the vast majority of African towns. Ibadan, on the other hand, is a "Negro" city, the largest, in fact, on the African continent. As a unit of a country which only recently achieved statehood (1960), it is in the throes of adapting its governmental structure and institutions to the needs of independence. Its industry, although expanding, is still predominantly oriented toward the processing of agricultural crops from the surrounding countryside. These are characteristics common to many African towns.

Physical and Demographic Features

Nigeria, a federal parliamentary state and an independent member of the British Commonwealth, is divided into four regions: North, East, West, and Mid-West, the last being carved out of the western section in 1962. Ibadan, the capital of the western region, is located inland, seventy miles northeast of Lagos, the national capital, and had an estimated population in 1960 of 600,000, an increase of almost 100,000 in less than five years. The urban populace in Nigeria is increasing more rapidly than the rural. As in most of Africa, the percentage of its people now living in towns of 5000 or more varies from region to region. In the East it is approximately 14 percent; in the North around 10 percent; and in the West, one of the most highly concentrated areas on the continent, it is nearly 50 percent.

Although the majority of African towns owe their origin in large measure to foreign initiative, Ibadan is an outstanding example of a town founded by the indigenous peoples. It originated as a small forest settlement or war encampment of the Yoruba tribe around 1821, and by the time formal British control was established over western Nigeria in the late nineteenth century, the population of the town was well over 100,000. Under colonial administration the influx of newcomers was accelerated as wider trade relations and better communications (including the construction of a railroad from the coastal city of Lagos) were developed. The successful cultivation of cocoa, which began early in the present century, converted the Ibadan area into a rich agricultural district and increased the city's importance as a service and trading center. In 1948 the University of Ibadan was established by the national government and more recently large-scale industries of a European type have been introduced into the city.[15]

The core or oldest part of the city extends out for about a half mile on all sides of the town hall. Density is remarkably high (as many as thirty houses to the acre in some sections), open space is negligible, roads are few, and access to many of the houses is by means of footpaths. More than a third of Ibadan's inhabitants, generally the poorer families, are concentrated in these congested districts, many of them living in what were once compounds surrounded by mud walls. The walls have since disappeared but a few to several hundred inhabitants are still found congregated together in the same small space. Ibadan has a town planning authority that could effect a population redistribution as was done in the Greater London area, but the problems that would result from displacing so many people have caused officials to shy away from such efforts including slum clearance.[16]

The inner core with its large market and town hall was at one time the economic heart of the city. However, with the arrival of the railway at the turn of the present century, the town began to attract numerous European economic institutions such as department stores, banks, trading firms, specialized shops, and motor garages, as well as

[15] For a description of Ibadan, see N. C. Mitchel, "Yoruba Towns," in K. M. Barbour and R. M. Prothero (eds.), Essays on African Population (London: Routledge and Kegan Paul, 1961), pp. 279–301.

[16] Akin Mabogunje, "The Growth of Residential Districts in Ibadan," Geographical Review, LII (January, 1962), 56–77.

the colonial administrative agencies. Since land for these various activities could not be found in the congested core of the city, they located at the periphery, thus creating a large commercial section, the equivalent of the American downtown or central business district. This development caused the economic center of gravity to shift from the core to the suburban ring. It also made further expansion of the old town impractical and lessened economic incentive to redevelop the now obsolescent areas in the inner city.[17] One might speculate what the fate of American CBD's and their surrounding areas would have been had the commercial center of the metropolis been shifted to an outer location early in the twentieth century.

The suburban areas surrounding the inner city house the more affluent members of the community, including the Europeans and other "wealthy" immigrants who began to enter Ibadan after the British assumed control. Here the housing is better, the lots more spacious, and the density far lower. Today, the newcomers who are flocking into the city settle where their means permit. The poor and uneducated Africans must seek homes in the crowded districts of the core, while the educated Africans, or those with some means, settle in the suburbs. (The growing number of non-Africans also turn to the lower-density residential neighborhoods of suburbia.) A surprisingly large proportion of recent African migrants are young men and women who have had some education or training and are therefore better equipped than many of the indigenous population to compete in the rapidly changing society. Spatial patterns, not unexpectedly of course, have become almost a measure of social and economic status as migrants from different cultures and with different skills and competencies tend to congregate together in different sections of the community.

Governmental Pattern

Great Britain, particularly in the years following World War II, sought to develop in its African territories a system of local government that was patterned after the English model. This approach called for the establishment of popularly elected councils which were both legislative and executive in character. The council is the formal center of British local government, whether at the municipal

[17] See A. L. Mabogunje, *Yoruba Towns* (Ibadan, Nigeria: Ibadan University Press, 1962), p. 13.

or county level; it not only formulates policy but directly manages the work of the administrative staff—the permanent career employees—through its committees. It also chooses the mayor who serves as the presiding officer and as the ceremonial head of the municipality but not as an administrative officer. These features embody the traditional British policy of spreading responsibility widely among elected representatives.

With the advent of independence and the conclusion of colonial rule, Britain's former African territories continued the efforts to reproduce the English system of local government. But the adoption by one country of the political institutions of another is no simple task. The difficulties are compounded when the two countries are as different in tradition, culture, and stage of political development as Great Britain and Nigeria. The English system of local government, for example, makes demands of a kind that cannot always be met in the new African nations. It presupposes, among other factors, the existence of a cadre of politically and administratively knowledgeable individuals who can serve as councillors, a complement of trained civil servants, and a reasonably educated body of voters. It also presupposes willingness on the part of the council to recruit qualified personnel for its staff, to protect them from dismissal for political reasons, and to entrust them with administrative discretion. Such a system will not function well in a situation where a high proportion of local council members are in local government for material gain, where nepotism is widely practiced, and where little respect is accorded the staff—a situation not uncommon in West Africa.

The British, in governing their African colonies, early instituted a policy of "indirect administration" by which native leaders or chiefs acted as local officials. Later they set up local councils which included both elected representatives and traditional leaders. Since independence, the tendency has been to further modernize the system by making the councils wholly elective. Following the English pattern, there is no elected mayor or chief executive. The administrative function is carried out by civil servants who are appointed by and responsible to the council.

As in federal states generally, local government in Nigeria is a responsibility of the regional or provincial governments. In the western region, the organization and authority of the local units are spelled out in the Local Government Law of 1953. This act gives municipal councils a wide field of jurisdiction but provides for controls by the regional government. The main link between the two levels is the Regional Ministry of Local Government and its field staff of inspectors. Ministerial approval, for example, is required for development plans and for senior administrative appointments. To the extent that this supervisory power is exercised, some of the difficulties arising from the diffusion of local units can be overcome.

The problems of local governmental organization in Ibadan and other African urban areas are not greatly different from those in Western nations. If anything, the difference is a matter of degree rather than kind. The observations of Ronald Wraith, formerly of the University of Ibadan, are pertinent in this regard. He notes that the difficulty in developing countries like Nigeria is that the mass of people are not sufficiently informed to be able to think of local government in terms of areas suitable for efficient administration. (For that matter, neither are they in developed nations such as the United States, although the difficulty may not stand out as sharply.) The ordinary citizen in these countries tends to see local government in terms of traditional rivalries and distrust of neighboring towns or townspeople with whom he is unwilling to share his own resources and whom he suspects of getting more than their fair share of benefits. The solution, as Wraith sees it, and the one toward which Western Nigeria has been slowly working is to "leave the 'neutral areas,' in which peoples' local loyalties reside, untouched; to give them as much to do as possible; but not to give them powers and duties in connection with the major services on which the progress of Nigeria as a nation depends."[18] The philosophy underlying much of the current thinking on metropolitan reorganization in the United States is closely akin to this approach.

TOKYO

Asia, the largest of the five continents, has almost three-fifths of the world's population and more than a third of its land surface. The sharp reduction in mortality in recent decades (due largely to antibiotics and other products of the laboratory) has combined with

[18] *Local Government in West Africa* (New York: Praeger, 1964), pp. 87–88.

continuing high fertility to produce rates of population growth unparalleled in human history.[19] The people of Asia are predominantly village-dwelling agrarians, but the degree of urbanization is showing gains as both old and new nations seek to step up their industrial output. The number of cities with populations of one million or over, for example, increased from thirteen in 1935 to thirty-four in the mid-1950s. Not unexpectedly, the problems resulting from this massive growth have been intense for the local as well as national governments.

Of the Asian countries, Japan is the first to reach western levels of urbanization and the first to approach western standards of living. The world's fourth ranking industrial power, Japan is already in an advanced stage of urbanization. More than three-fifths of its 95 million people live in cities, and the proportion is steadily increasing. In 1950, the farming population accounted for 45 percent of the total; by 1960 this figure had dropped to 37 percent. Density is also high, 660 persons to the square mile, with concentrations as large as 50,000 in some of the Tokyo wards.

Administratively, Japan consists of two tiers below the central government: provinces (called prefectures) and municipalities. Each of the forty-six provinces into which the country is divided is governed by a popularly elected council and an elected chief executive. Before World War II, local government was rigidly controlled by national authorities; in 1947, the governmental system was decentralized and local units given a large measure of autonomy. Since the end of the United States military occupation in 1952, the trend has again been toward greater centralization, especially at the provincial level. During the 1950s a program of urban amalgamation was undertaken to increase municipal efficiency, with the national government offering financial inducements to communities that would agree to merge. Under the program, the number of cities and towns was reduced from 9622 to 3475.

Physical and Demographic Characteristics

Tokyo, the capital of Japan, is the largest urban concentration in Asia and one of the most intensely crowded cities of the world.

[19] See Irene B. Taeuber, "Asia's Increasing Population," *Annals of the American Academy of Political and Social Science*, 318 (July, 1958), 1–8.

Like Egypt's legendary bird, the Phoenix, Tokyo has risen from its ashes twice in the space of two generations. It was destroyed by an earthquake followed by a tidal wave and fires in 1923; and in World War II large portions of it were leveled by Allied fire bombs. Today it is a teeming, congested, and expanding metropolis, the political, cultural, financial, and industrial center of Japanese life. In 1950 the population of the ward area (the equivalent of a central city) was 5.4 million and that of the metropolitan area 8.0 million; in 1963 these populations were estimated to be 8.6 million and 10.2 million, respectively.

As is the case with the typical large American metropolis, Tokyo is experiencing severe growing pains. Schools are overcrowded, the street system is wholly inadequate, housing shortages exist, public facilities and services are badly overburdened, and the suburban development continues to move further out. Each year approximately a quarter of a million people are added to the area's population, 70 to 80 percent of whom are migrants from rural areas seeking better employment and other opportunities. Since most of the newcomers are unskilled laborers of little means, this influx places a heavy burden on the city's welfare and service resources.

In 1962 the Tokyo Metropolitan Government, to be discussed later, announced a ten-year program to attack such problems as over-concentration of population, urban sprawl, and inadequacy of public facilities. The program is designed primarily to carry out the Metropolitan Government's responsibility of enforcing plans made by the National Capital Regional Development Commission, a body appointed by the central government. According to national law, local authorities are required to cooperate in the development of the capital region, an area within a radius of approximately 65 miles from the center of Tokyo.

Plans prepared by the Commission provide for a greenbelt six miles wide around the presently built-up area. Hospitals, universities, and other institutions, and airports and cemeteries will be located in this setting of forests and farmlands. Beyond the greenbelt, a necklace of satellite towns is to be developed. These are not to be bedroom suburbs but communities with industry and other sources of employment. To facilitate this development, the central government assures local authorities of necessary funds to build home sites and public facilities. It also makes funds available to private entrepreneurs for constructing railways and factories in these areas.[20] The major objective of these plans is to restrict further industrial growth in the highly built-up sections of Metropolitan Tokyo and to redistribute or channel a portion of the population to the new towns on the periphery. The similarities to the Greater London plan can be seen in these developments. So also can the contrast between the Japanese and American approaches to urban growth be observed. Not only are greater governmental controls exercised over expansion in Japan, but public funds are also used far more extensively there to encourage and direct development in accordance with comprehensive plans.

Governmental Pattern

Metropolitan Tokyo, an area of approximately 1600 square miles, includes 23 wards (the equivalent of a central city), 11 cities, 3 counties, and several small offshore islands. The principal governing body is the Tokyo Metropolitan Government which has general jurisdiction over the entire area and which serves both as a local unit of self-government and as an administrative arm (a province) of the national government. It consists of a popularly elected governor or chief administrator and a metropolitan assembly of 120 members elected from 36 districts on the basis of population. Each of the cities also has an elected council and administrator.

The Tokyo wards are not electoral districts as city wards are in the United States but local governing units with an elected council and a head or chief administrator selected by the council with the consent of the governor. There is no separate overall government for the wards other than the Tokyo Metropolitan Government whose jurisdiction extends over a far larger territorial area. Following World War II, the wards were vested with strong self-governing powers equal to those of the ordinary city, but since then a considerable diminution of home rule has taken place.

The wards, as the cities and towns, are authorized to deal with local matters prescribed in the Local Autonomy Law or delegated to them by the governor. These include such functions as the operation of small parks and playgrounds, libraries, community centers, and

[20] For a more extended description of these developments, see *An Administrative Perspective of Tokyo* (Tokyo: The Tokyo Metropolitan Government, 1963).

street lighting. The wards also enjoy a limited power of taxation as prescribed by metropolitan ordinances. Generally their administrative powers are less than the other local units in the Tokyo area since the Metropolitan Government is responsible for certain services in the wards—refuse collection for one—that the other authorities provide for themselves. All powers and activities of the wards and towns are subject to the governor's supervision and his authority to coordinate relations among the various local units.

The Tokyo Metropolitan Government has jurisdiction over a wide range of functions, including health and sanitation, major parks, roads, parking facilities, water supply, sewage disposal, fire protection, and public housing. Police protection is also an area-wide function under the general supervision of the Tokyo government. However, the superintendent general of the metropolitan police department is appointed by national authorities, and he and other top officials of the department are treated as national public service personnel. Education is a dual responsibility of the two levels of government. Primary and junior high schools are operated by locally-appointed boards of education in each of the municipalities and wards, with senior high and special schools provided by the metropolitan unit.

As can be seen from this summary, local government in the Tokyo area is basically a two-level system with some services handled exclusively by the upper tier or Metropolitan Government, some relegated to the lower or municipalities and wards, and others jointly administered. What distinguishes this system from the American practice of local federalism is the high degree of control exercised by the upper tier over the local units and their activities. The Tokyo structure, in other words, unlike the typical American pattern, provides a means of minimizing the debilitating effects of governmental fragmentation on metropolitan development and functioning.

The Tokyo experience, however, indicates that even where these controls exist, the problem of government in rapidly expanding metropolitan areas is far from solved. A consultative body to the governor of Tokyo pointed this out in a report submitted in 1962. It noted, among other things, that (1) the task of providing public facilities and other services for a city growing as rapidly as the Japanese capital is so voluminous as to overtax the administrative structure badly; (2) no effective system of coordinating the activities of the many local units has yet been devised; and (3) with population spillover into adjacent provinces, it has become difficult for the Tokyo Metropolitan Government to deal with its administrative affairs effectively without some institutionalized system of cooperation with neighboring prefectures.

These difficulties have led some Japanese scholars and statesmen to propose a larger role for the national government in metropolitan affairs. It has been suggested, for example, that a new agency under national control be established to take over responsibility for certain metropolitan functions, particularly the construction of public facilities and the formulation of development plans. As the following quotation shows, the Tokyo government reacted strongly to this suggestion:

> Even if it is an admitted fact that the administration of the metropolitan area now carried on by the Tokyo Metropolitan Government is still far from perfect, its cause may be attributed to a lack of a centrally and locally coordinated plan and to the central government's various financial restrictions upon metropolitan administration. It is no wonder that the central government should make studies in the metropolitan system, but such ideas from some authoritative sources as tramping upon home rule are reckless and unconstitutional.[21]

SÃO PAULO

Contrary to popular impression, the fastest growing population in the world today is found not in India or Communist China but in tropical South America, a 5.3 million square mile area encompassing nine nations: Bolivia, Brazil, Colombia, Ecuador, Peru, Venezuela, and the three Guianas. This area, with a population in 1963 of approximately 121 million, is growing at an average rate of 3.2 percent annually compared to about 2 percent for India and China. As elsewhere around the globe, most of this increase is occurring in urban areas.

Brazil, by far the largest of the South American nations in both population (estimated at 78 million in 1963) and territorial size (3.2 million square miles, an area almost equal to that of the United States), is a federal republic composed of twenty-one states, five federal territories, and the federal district containing the new capital, Brasilia. The country is still basically agricultural with approximately 60 percent of its labor force engaged in farming and related em-

---

[21] *An Administrative Perspective of Tokyo*, p. 8.

ployments. However, the increased emphasis on industrial development during the last several decades is rapidly altering this picture. Production of crude steel, to cite one indication of the trend, increased almost eighteen times between 1940 and 1960. During this same span of time, the percentage of the population classified as urban also increased significantly: from less than one-third in 1940 to almost one-half by 1960.

Physical and Demographic Characteristics

São Paulo, 200 miles southwest of Rio de Janeiro, is Brazil's largest urban area and the most industrialized center south of the Rio Grande River. Referred to by some as the "Chicago" of South America, it is one of the fastest growing metropolises in the world. It celebrated the 400th anniversary of its founding in 1954, but until the latter part of the nineteenth century it was a quiet town of 25,000. Today, it is a center of great industrial and commercial activity, shining skyscrapers, and congestion. Its population, approximately 4 million in 1963, is growing at the rate of 150,000 a year, largely the result of internal migration from the rural areas.

The city is laid out in the shape of an irregular polygon. At the core is the historic "triangle," the community's economic and bureaucratic center, where the department stores, banks, private and governmental office buildings, and hotels are located. The residential neighborhoods near the core, formerly the quarters of the aristocrats, have become favorite points for middle-class penetration. Only the construction of centrally located luxury apartments has prevented the total flight of the élite to the gardened sites of suburbia. Growth outward from the core has been concentric and has occurred at immense speed without zoning regulations or comprehensive land use plans. This development has been under way for some time. For example, in the period from 1934 to 1940 the population increase within a two-mile radius of the city center was less than 10 percent; between 2 and 4.5 miles, it was 50 per cent; and beyond this circumference it was over 85 percent.[22]

Outside the city proper but within the metropolitan area are a host of suburban nuclei of various types that range from modern industrial aggregations to rural settlements lacking electricity and

[22] Richard M. Morse, *From Community to Metropolis* (Gainesville: University of Florida Press, 1958), p. 272.

piped water. In one section are industrial suburbs that include the plants of such well-known American companies as General Motors and Firestone. In another are residential sub-communities of middle- or lower-class families. And in still another are the attractively laid out residential enclaves of the well-to-do that stand in stark contrast to the crowded slums of the industrial areas. Beyond the urbanized portions of the municipality's 700 square miles of territory are the rural villages and agricultural areas.

People and goods in São Paulo are moved over a road network dominated by a loop-and-spoke system of broad radial and circumferential avenues. As in the typical metropolis in the United States, people converge on the core or central business district from all directions. The city has a good public transit system but the demands placed on it are too great to handle this volume of traffic with facility. Moreover, the street and parking system is wholly inadequate to accommodate the area's growing automobile population. The result is intense congestion in and around the core.

Despite gestures by local authorities to encourage decentralization of central business district activities, the core of the metropolis retains a strong pull on commercial and civic functions and on office building use. Some large department stores are invading the suburbs and a few radial streets offer retail shops and service establishments at a distance from the "triangle," but these developments have in no way detracted from the prominence of the city center. Tall skyscrapers continue to rise within its confines and large luxury apartments continue to be constructed on its periphery. Fortunately, the industrial suburbs provide a degree of decentralization for the area that helps to spread peak-hour traffic loads and affords some relief, however small, to the problem of congestion.

Governmental Pattern

The basic, in fact the only, unit of local government in Brazil is the municipality (*municipio*). Since each of the twenty-one states is completely subdivided into municipalities and no other units such as counties, townships, or special districts exist, Brazilian local government has an apparent simplicity that contrasts strongly to the pattern in the United States. The municipality is more comparable to the American county than to a city or town since it includes suburban settlements and rural villages in addition to the urban center or city. Unlike the American county, however, the Brazilian municipality does not share governmental responsibility with any other local entity. Instead, it enjoys jurisdiction over the entire area with no separately incorporated towns and villages or other autonomous units to challenge its authority.

The municipalities are territorially divided into districts (*distrito*), which are primarily administrative units or branch offices of the municipal government. Suburbs have no administrative or political significance although they constitute very definite social areas in large communities such as São Paulo and Rio de Janeiro. They are also functionally specialized subnuclei, as we have seen in São Paulo, with industrial and residential settlements scattered over the landscape. All they lack to make them analogous to the ring communities of metropolises in the United States are separate governments.

Brazilian municipalities have the strong mayor-council form of government. The council, which numbers from five members in the smaller communities to fifty in the larger metropolises, is elected by a system of proportional representation. It exercises no administrative functions but has power to legislate on all matters of purely local interest. The mayor (*prefeito*) is popularly elected except in municipalities which are state, federal, or territorial capitals. In the case of the state capitals such as São Paulo, he is appointed by the governor and in the other instances by the president of the republic. The chief executive plays the role of both administrative head and political leader. His strength in the latter connection is often important in determining the extent to which a municipality receives state and federal subsidies in such matters as public works.[23]

Despite the fact that the municipalities are granted substantial powers by the national and state constitutions, local self-government has developed far less in Brazil than in the Anglo-Saxon world. A major reason for this difference is the heavy financial dependence of the local units on higher levels of government. With the exception of São Paulo and possibly a few other major communities, municipalities seldom collect over 10 percent of their total revenue from local levies. For the remainder they must rely on state and federal grants and shared revenues and on the direct financing and

[23] For a summary description of Brazilian local government see Samuel Humes and Eileen M. Martin, *The Structure of Local Governments Throughout the World* (The Hague: Martinus Nijhoff, 1961), pp. 342–346.

administration of certain local services by these higher levels. State-operated primary schools, for example, outnumber those administered locally by more than a two-to-one margin. This reliance has encouraged the political subservience of municipalities to the upper-governmental echelons. Evidence of this subserviency is found in the considerable importance that municipal officials place on maintaining favorable political relations with state and national authorities.[24]

A second, although lesser, reason for the inability of local units to exercise their full panoply of powers is territorial instability. In many municipalities there has been a tendency to elevate the subunits or districts to municipal status, thus introducing an element of governmental fragmentation into what is otherwise a simplistic pattern of organization. The tendency has been particularly strong in the outlying suburban and rural sections where residents feel their needs are given short shrift by the city-dominated administration. This development is interesting to American observers of metropolitan political institutions because of its implications for governmental consolidation. Most importantly, it suggests that there are limits to the territorial size of a local unit for responsible and equitable policy-making and administration. Making the units larger still leaves the problem of how to provide government which is both effective and convenient for those who live in the villages and peripheral communities.

São Paulo occupies a more favored position that most municipalities in the Brazilian local governmental system, due largely to its economic status. Because of its degree of industrialization, its resources are substantial and its standard of living high compared to other communities in the country. The median per capita income of its residents is about three times that of the entire nation. These factors make the city less dependent financially on the state and national governments and enable it to exercise a greater degree of control over its local affairs.

Public services and facilities in São Paulo are among the best in Latin America. Utilities, recreation areas, transportation arteries, hospital and social welfare services, sanitation, and the primary and secondary school system are well developed despite persistent material and administrative deficiencies. There are, of course, chronic

[24] See L. Donald Carr, "Brazilian Local Self-Government: Myth or Reality?" *Western Political Quarterly*, 13 (December, 1960), 1043–1055.

problems, a common feature of metropolitan areas everywhere. Water distribution, for example, has not kept pace with population growth; inadequate land use planning and control have permitted the indiscriminate intermingling of commercial, industrial, and residential zones; and park and playground facilities are inadequate. Many of São Paulo's difficulties are, of course, attributable to its rapid growth, and no amount of governmental resources or foresight could have coped fully with this development.

METROPOLITAN COMMUNITIES IN A WORLD SETTING

No thorough consideration of the metropolis in time and space can overlook either its social and economic facets or its governmental institutions. The informal means of social control which once regulated the communal affairs of primitive settlements have given way to the more formal methods of modern society. As the populations of cities and metropolitan areas have grown in size and heterogeneity, larger and more complex governmental organizations have evolved as instruments of control and direction. Historically, it has been the emergence of local government that has weakened the bonds of familial or tribal social organization and marked the transference of local loyalties to the broader community.

The patterns of local government that have emerged and are still evolving show great diversity, not only between countries but within individual nations as well. To a large extent these patterns and the manner in which their formal and informal structures function are conditioned by the culture of the country and its subparts. We have had occasion to note this relationship in the case of Nigeria where British institutions and practices have been modified under the pressures of local tradition. The same phenomenon is observable elsewhere where the governmental forms imposed by colonial powers have been reshaped or modified in the crucible of local culture.

The basic tasks of urban government are everywhere the same, whether in the cities of Nigeria and Brazil or those in Great Britain and the United States. Throughout the world, metropolitan communities and their governmental systems are being subjected to heavy strains and incessant demands. The responses to these forces have varied from nation to nation. At one extreme, local units have tended to abdicate their responsibilities and become mere administrative arms of the state or national governments. At the other extreme, too great an emphasis on local autonomy has hindered the development of effective public mechanisms for meeting the problems and needs of an increasingly technological society.

Despite the great variations, however, the overall trend has been toward greater centralization, and this has been so even in cases where the fragmentation of local units continues unabated. Key functions are assumed by or transferred to area-wide agencies, provincial and national governments exercise greater control over local operations either by direct fiat or by means of financial inducements, and the power to make and execute many decisions affecting the small units is increasingly passing upward to higher echelons of public and private authorities. The phenomenon is universal; it differs only in degree and particulars. Metropolises in all sections of the world have a common kinship and a common set of problems. All of them are striving to work out their destiny in a world that is daily becoming more urbanized and more complex.

CHAPTER 19

The Shape of the Future

As THE second half of the twentieth century moves on, the metropolis becomes an ever more predominant feature of contemporary society. The urbanizing trend which has produced vast settlements of human beings and reduced the agricultural population to a shadow of its former self shows no signs of abating. Cities continue to break out of their old bounds and invade the "open country" in their quest for *lebensraum*. Ring upon ring of suburbs continue to be added to what were once single and relatively compact communities. Census figures on population, density, and territorial area—we need not repeat them here—present a picture of massive change and astonishing growth. The "exploding metropolis" is more than a figure of speech.

Demographic and spatial statistics, however, do not tell the whole story. They document the increase in volume and scale of urban society but they do not reveal how this growth has altered the traditional concept of the city or how it has required twentieth century man to think of his metropolitan habitat in new terms.

They indicate changes in crime rates, welfare assistance, and school enrollment, but they give us little feel for the wide range of problems and issues—social, economic, physical, governmental, political—that confront the community. They enumerate the increase in water usage, waste disposal, recreation, and automobile ownership, but they fail to disclose how these developments have drastically modified the nature of urban problems and the kinds of approaches necessary to cope with them. They show the increasing variety of economic activities and the growing degree of specialization, but they tell us little about the social and political consequences of such changes or their effects on community values and goals. These facets of the metropolis can be understood only by going beyond the impersonal figures of the statistician, important as they are for objective analysis, to the insights of the scientist, the social critic, the artist, and the philosopher.

Living in an urbanized society, modern man experiences mixed emotions as he contemplates the metropolitan scene and ponders its meaning and import. On the one hand, he is struck with the vigor and force of the system and with the impressive achievements in metropolitan community-building. He observes a broadbacked and boisterious land of "tense, turbulent cities, with fingers of power reaching out into space." Everywhere in urban areas he sees evidence of technological miracles, industrial might, and intense human activity. Impressive office buildings, factories, and apartments are being constructed, slums are being cleared, expressways are carving huge paths through dense settlements, and civic monuments are rising in tribute to the new metropolitan age. The picture is one of bold strokes and bright paint, perhaps gaudy and in poor taste, but exuding strength and vitality.

Strong as man's pride and wonder at this scene may be, gnawing doubts nevertheless keep disturbing his peace of mind. He cannot avoid a feeling of deep concern at the apparent looseness of control over present developments, the uncertain directions they are taking, and their long-range effects on human living. If he is in an inquiring and philosophical mood, he will ponder over many questions. What future is in store for the metropolis? What changes are likely to take place in its form and structure? Will its governmental machinery undergo radical transformation? Will the central city, as we now know it, survive? Can viable democratic institutions be retained at the local level in a large-scale society? Can man fulfill himself in such a milieu? What should be our response and attitude toward the unfolding metropolitan panorama?

The answers to these and related questions do not come easily, if at all; the world of the metropolis is too complex for the pat replies that masquerade as truth. Only diligent and imaginative research, careful analysis, and well-formulated theory can provide reasonably sound propositions that give some understanding of urban phenomena. True, without Cassandra's gift of prophecy, we can only speculate about the shape of events to come. Yet our efforts to look into the metropolitan future, if based on the experience of the past and on the emerging trends of the present, can be productive of more than sheer fantasy. To those who are concerned with the quality and livability of metropolitan living, recognition of the forces that are shaping our urban environment is critically essential. For unless we are prepared and willing to capitalize on our knowledge of these forces to guide change in the direction most likely to further human goals and aspirations, we can only rely on fate, luck, and drift to fashion the metropolis of tomorrow.

THE EXISTING SYSTEM

Many processes are at work indicating that modifications in the future character and role of the metropolis will inevitably take place, whether by rational design or not. The forces for change are relentless; they will not by stayed by indifference or inactivity. Technological miracles, new life styles, increasing citizen expectations, and the general pressures of growth are but a few of the factors that must be accommodated. Most aspects of the metropolitan system, including its social organization, land use patterns, and functional distribution of economic activities, have undergone substantial modification during the past half century. Of the key elements, only the governmental pattern has been able to avoid major alteration. Adjustments have been made in the traditional arrangements, new expedients such as special districts have been employed, and considerable school district consolidation has taken place, but basically the system remains as it was before large-scale urbanization. Lack

of serious crisis in the existing governmental structure and the strong
forces for continuing the present pattern of balkanization are important factors contributing to this result.

It would be difficult today to find an American metropolis in
which the governmental system is in danger of breakdown. Despite
dire predictions, disaster has neither struck nor even appeared im-
minent. The basic public needs of metropolitan residents, whether
in an area of 100,000 or 10 million, are being provided for in one
fashion or another. Lives and property are being protected, goods
and people transported, sewage and garbage disposed of, water
supplied, and general order maintained. Somehow, in spite of the
political and administrative fragmentation, governmental activities
manage to be coordinated and policies harmonized at least well
enough to keep the system functioning. Deep-seated differences may
exist between the central city and outlying governments, and dis-
agreements may occasionally arise among the suburban units, but
the degree of conflict has at no time been sufficiently great to im-
peril the existing structure.

The fact that catastrophe has been avoided does not by any
means imply that all is well. It is not enough for local metropolitan
government merely to prevent service crises or meet minimal expectations. It should help us realize the potentialities of urban
existence which large-scale society promises. If it is to fulfill this
latter role, it must assure orderly growth, formulate area-wide goals,
mitigate social conflict, and aid in fashioning a pleasant, stimulating,
and vigorous living environment. It must be ready for the future
and prepared to meet the challenges and dangers that metropolitan
communities will inevitably face. The likelihood is slim, however,
that urban man will give more than a passing thought to these prospects so long as the existing system functions tolerably well. Instead
he will continue to tinker with the machinery to get rid of the worst
annoyances, preferring to put up with the devils he knows rather
than take chances with those he does not know.

As political scientist Norton Long reminds us, metropolitan
areas are going concerns and hence can be expected to react vigorously to attempts at major alteration. For if the existing system of
local government could be easily changed, "it would be intolerably
unstable." And if no powerful interests were vested in the status
quo, "the existing order would have so little allegiance, it could

scarcely run, much less endure."[1] Earlier we saw an illustration of this in the case of Miami, where area-wide restructuring was aided by the lack of any strong organizational interest in keeping the old governmental pattern. In virtually all other metropolitan areas the forces with large stakes in the status quo were too powerful to overcome.

Previous chapters have called attention to some of the elements hostile to governmental reorganization: the established bureaucracy, the favored tax position of various units, central city-suburban antagonisms, political differences among sections of the area, and the general lack of community bonds. Another strong factor favoring the retention of the present system, according to Robert Wood, is the opportunity a governmentally fragmented structure affords for social segregation. Modern suburbs may use their political boundaries "to differentiate the character of their residents from their neighbors," and their governmental powers—zoning, residential covenants, taxation, selective industrial development—"to promote conscious segregation." From the variety of classes, occupations, income levels, races, and creeds in the metropolis, "a municipality may isolate the particular variant it prefers and concentrate on one type of the metropolitan man."[2] In this way socially homogeneous subcommunities with protective armor can be maintained within the larger complex. And as in the case of other vested interests, any attempt to reconstitute the governmental system so as to destroy or minimize this power of segregation can expect to meet bitter resistance from the affected suburban enclaves.

EMERGING TRENDS

Each metropolitan community faces important policy decisions in seeking to determine its future. It cannot avoid questions of how it shall organize governmentally, how it shall develop economically and physically, and how it shall deal with social issues. Nor can it disregard the processes by which it evolves over a period of time or the day-to-day interaction that takes place within its territorial confines. It must, in short, be conditioned to accept change and to

[1] *The Polity* (Chicago: Rand McNally, 1962), p. 161.
[2] "Metropolitan Government, 1975: An Extrapolation of Trends," *American Political Science Review*, LII (March, 1958), 117.

make the decisions that will guide this change in the direction most conducive to the furthering of community values and goals.

In making an assessment of the future, individuals concerned with the governmental organization of the metropolis must keep in mind certain emerging trends. Three of the more significant are: (1) the rise of the megalopolis; (2) the movement of community decision-making powers to higher echelons of public authority; and (3) the increasing emphasis on cooperative devices as an alternative to formal restructuring of the governmental pattern.

The Megalopolis

More than 2000 years ago, a group of Greek settlers founded a new community in the Peloponnesus which they called *Megalopolis*, to express their hope that it would become the largest of the Hellenic city-states. In subsequent centuries, the word's dictionary definition as a "very large city" was largely forgotten. Recently, however, it has reappeared in the vocabulary as a result of the writings of geographer Jean Gottman, who used the term to designate the cluster of metropolitan areas in the northeastern part of the United States. Gottman's description of this section of the nation portrays its amazing character:

> An almost continuous system of deeply interwoven urban and suburban areas, with a total population of about 37 million people in 1960, has been erected along the Northeastern Atlantic seaboard. It straddles state boundaries, stretches across wide estuaries and bays, and encompasses many regional differences. . . . Crowded within its limits is an extremely distinguished population. It is, *on the average*, the richest, best educated, best housed, and best serviced group of similar size (i.e., in the 25-to-40-million-people range) in the world. . . . It is true that many of its sections have seen pretty rural landscapes replaced by ugly industrial agglomerations or drab and monstrous residential developments; it is true that in many parts of Megalopolis the air is not clean any more, the noise is disturbing day and night, the water is not as pure as one would wish, and transportation at times becomes a nightmare.[3]

Along similar lines, political scientist Charlton Chute had earlier employed the term "urban region" to designate an area in which two or more SMSA's adjoin each other. Identifying nineteen such regions in 1955, Chute argued that the historic concept of a metropolitan area as a core city surrounded by suburbs is no longer ade-

[3] *Megalopolis* (New York: Twentieth Century Fund, 1961), pp. 7, 15.

quate for analytical purposes. It is now necessary, he stated, to take into account the interrelationships between neighboring SMSA's and to study clusters of such areas as closely as we do clusters of cities and other urban groups.[4]

The trend toward megalopolis or urban regions has several clear implications for local government. First, as urbanized agglomerations expand in population and territorial size, integration of local units as an answer to the problem of government in such areas loses all meaning. It would be ridiculous, for example, to talk in terms of forming one municipality or other type of local government out of the congeries of units extending almost continuously from Boston to the District of Columbia, or out of the group bordering the southern end of the Great Lakes. Such a solution may still be desirable in the case of the smaller and spatially separated SMSA's. But even if a consolidated government were feasible for those in this category on the basis of their present size, what happens as urban growth continues? Is the territorial jurisdiction of the government also expanded repeatedly to keep pace with this growth? If so, at what point does the area become too large for governance by a single unit? Or at what point do the qualities that are customarily associated with local government disappear?

Second, the emergence of megalopolitan areas also casts doubts on the adequacy of the two-tier arrangement as the ultimate solution to metropolitan problems. This approach, as commonly understood, is based on the purported distinction between local and area-wide functions. But how is area-wide to be defined when a cluster of metropolises is involved? One function like flood control or air pollution may be of common concern to the entire group of metropolitan areas; another, such as sewage disposal or water supply, may lie within the competency of the various parts of the megalopolis; and still others, such as refuse disposal and public health services, may be adequately handled by individual metropolises within the complex. The phenomenon here is not unlike that within a single SMSA where certain problems of the central city and suburbs spill over into adjacent units; the difference is that in this case, the spillover occurs between one metropolis and another, thus necessitating even broader areal treatment than is normally contemplated.

[4] "Today's Urban Regions," *National Municipal Review*, XLV (June, 1956), 274–280.

Third, the persistent expansion of urban settlements raises an interesting question as to the future of local government. If we consider the comprehensive urban county and other types of metropolitan agencies as essentially local in character, what is the case when an area becomes so large as to require either some form of regional government or the assumption of critical urban functions by the state? In the first instance, does the possible need for a unit of larger areal scope than the individual SMSA imply the need for a tripartite division of powers: local, metropolitan-wide, and regional-wide, with the last administered by a third tier of government that would transcend state as well as municipal and county lines? In any event, when area- or region-wide agencies are created in the large metropolis, can they retain any of the classical characteristics of local government, such as closeness to the people and accessibility to the citizenry? If the answer to this query is negative —and a strong case can be made that it is—would it not be better to turn over to the state those functions which cannot be handled adequately by the traditional local units—the municipalities and counties—rather than to complicate the system by creating new metropolitan or regional governments? In whichever direction we move, the need for integrated control of certain vital functions, such as air and water pollution, over a large territorial area will eventually have to be met.

The Upward Shift of Power

Metropolitan areas develop and take their particular form as the result of countless decisions by both public and private agencies. These decisions are controlled by various criteria including market facts, professional standards, and community attitudes and values.[5] Governmental policies at the metropolitan level can influence these developments, but the extent of such influence is limited. A decision by local public officials to encourage industrial growth can have real meaning only if economic factors are favorable to such expansion. Or a decision to undertake a major program of public works can be realistic only if the existing or potential resources of the com-

[5] See William L. C. Wheaton, "Public and Private Agencies of Change in Urban Expansion," in Melvin M. Webber and others (eds.), *Explorations into Urban Structure* (Philadelphia: University of Pennsylvania Press, 1964), pp. 154–196.

munity are sufficient to warrant such expenditures and the voters are willing to support them.

When government acts, moreover, it must do so within an environmental framework shaped by the cumulative past policies and actions of public agencies and private organizations. Local authorities, for example, may consider it desirable to relegate the central business district to a lesser role, but earlier investment decisions relative to buildings, transportation arteries, and public utilities may compel them to take the opposite tack and promote additional investment in the area to protect what already exists. Or past policies of the planning commission and city council may have resulted in the establishment of land use patterns that severely circumscribe the extent to which future changes in the physical design and ecology of the city can be accomplished.

In addition to these limitations, the ability of individual metropolitan communities to control their own destiny has been steadily diminished by the increase in scale of the urban world. Policies which at one time were determined largely at the local level are now dependent upon the decisions of agencies outside the community. As one observer has appropriately noted, "The discrepancy in organizational scale between local government and the nature of large-scale society results in a movement of power upward, to organizational centers outside the control of the local polity. Such organizations wield power that is area-wide in scope and consequences. But the use of such power does not require either concern for the interdependence of different aspects of the metropolitan community, or the concern for the ultimate nature of the city that a local polity might implement. In consequence, existing trends are simply accelerated."[6]

Urban renewal decisions provide an illustration of this trend. Although local authorities must take the initiative in rehabilitating the physical plant of the community, their actions are affected in important respects by congressional policies and the decisions of the Housing and Home Finance Agency. If Congress, for example, should curtail urban renewal appropriations or restrict their use to conservation rather than slum clearance projects, local communities would be compelled to reshape their redevelopment policies ac-

[6] Scott Greer, *The Emerging City* (New York: Free Press, 1962), p. 162.

cordingly. Or if the HHFA should decide to approve the construction of only high-rise apartments in cleared areas, the discretionary range of local officials over community renewal would be correspondingly reduced. Decisions by the federal Bureau of Public Roads and state highway commissions relative to the location of major freeways in metropolitan areas furnish further examples of extra-community influence on local development activities. So also do the mortgage guarantee policies of the Federal Housing Authority (FHA) which have greatly influenced the urban residential patterns of the present generation by favoring suburban or fringe area development over that in the older sections of the central city. The examples could be multiplied many times: the cost of aid to the poor and handicapped are largely borne by the national and state governments; the old age pension aspects of the social security program are administered by federal authorities, and the expenditures for hospital and school construction are shared by outside agencies.

While state control is often more direct, national agencies through grants-in-aid have been able not only to support particular local functions but also to cause communities to undertake completely new programs in such fields as vocational training and public health. The growing extent of federal participation in urban affairs is graphically documented: at the close of 1962, the national government was administering more than forty separate programs of financial aid for local communities, more than half of which had been authorized after 1950.[7] When one considers that such grants usually impose certain requirements and restrictions as a condition of assistance, the actual and potential impact of high-level policy determinations on local and metropolitan operations becomes patently evident.

The upward shift of power is by no means confined to government; the same phenomenon is occurring in the private sector with similar effects on the metropolis. The rapid disappearance of the family-owned enterprise (which traditionally has had a strong personal commitment to the local community) and its displacement by the national corporation with headquarters in one city and

[7] See U.S. Senate Committee on Government Operations, Subcommittee on Intergovernmental Relations, *Impact of Federal Urban Development Programs on Local Government Organization and Planning* (Washington: January, 1964).

branches in many others has caused drastic shifts in the spatial location of power. Many investment decisions which at one time were made locally are now determined at the main offices of the absentee owners who have no emotional attachment to the affected communities. These decisions may have important implications for the development or functioning of individual metropolitan areas, but the latter have no voice in their formulation.

As the channels of power increasingly bypass locally based institutions and agencies, those concerned with effecting change at the metropolitan level must devise new strategies to cope with the evolving trend. Most importantly, they must seek ways of relating these external forces, both public and private, to the strengthening of local structures. Little will be gained by decrying a trend that is well-nigh inevitable in large-scale urban society. The task is to harness the emerging forces and guide them into paths that will enhance the metropolitan polity as an influential unit in the American democratic system.

The "Cooperative" Fad

Early efforts at reform of the governmental pattern of the metropolis sought to achieve its complete integration by extending the boundaries of the central city through annexation or consolidation. The underlying rationale for this approach was expressed by such veteran political scientists as Chester C. Maxey and William Bennet Munro who stoutly maintained that as an organic and economic unit the metropolitan community demanded a unified government. Although recognizing the case for local rule, they saw little reason for granting political autonomy to what they regarded as neighborhoods or sections of a single community. In their view, the necessary concessions to local sentiment could be made in other ways, such as by the creation of administrative subdistricts within the larger complex.

By 1930, governmental integration had been largely abandoned as the proposed general solution. In its place, various remedies based on the principle of "local federalism" began to make their appearance. In the first comprehensive work on the governance of metropolitan areas published in this country, Paul Studenski gave expression to the new approach when he wrote that "a form of government must be found that will foster the development of a vigorous

metropolitan consciousness in the entire area, promote proper standards of service throughout, preserve and cultivate a healthy consciousness of locality in the constituent parts, and secure the proper
treatment of purely local as distinguished from metropolitan affairs."[8]
This view was repeatedly echoed in the survey-type studies of individual metropolitan areas which appeared during the decade of
the 1950s. In fact, much of the history of the reorganization movement since World War II could be written around attempts to
modernize the governmental structure of the metropolis without
disturbing local autonomy.

In more recent years, the emphasis has shifted to cooperation
as reorganization plans involving the federal or two-tier device have
continued to meet with no greater success than their predecessors.
A Rockefeller Foundation study of 1958 advanced the currently
popular theme when it said of urban problems: "Cooperation among
existing governmental units, under existing authority, can often go
far to meet these problems, and this, rather than the creation of
new layers of government, may be the most effective means of
coping with metropolitan growth."[9] Since the Rockefeller report,
considerable talk has been heard of interlocal cooperation through
voluntary action while little has been said of methods involving
coercion or control.

The cooperative approach in practice has represented more a
defense of the status quo than a serious effort to meet major service
needs. In the vast majority of instances, its use has involved little
more than joint action of limited scope by two or more local units
in minor and non-controversial matters. There are important exceptions to be sure, as noted in Chapter 13, but the total effort in
this direction constitutes a disappointingly small contribution to the
task at hand. Despite this fact, however, many urban analysts have
reluctantly come to the conclusion that the cooperative principle
offers the most realistic, if not the most desirable, answer to the
problem.

On its face, this acceptance of the cooperative approach would
appear to be a major victory for the status quo. Yet the retreat

[8] *The Government of Metropolitan Areas in the United States* (New York:
National Municipal League, 1930), p. 41.
[9] *Prospect for America: The Rockefeller Panel Reports* (Garden City:
Doubleday, 1961), p. 304.

from more comprehensive remedies is prompted by several promising factors. First, both the national and state governments are likely to bring increasing pressure on local governments in metropolitan areas to effect greater administrative coordination and more orderly development. Second, responsible local officials are beginning to realize that in view of the upward movement of power, they must mobilize in self-defense if they are to retain a voice in critical developmental decisions affecting their communities. Devices of a potentially integrative nature such as regional planning agencies and voluntary metropolitan councils are some of the by-products of this concern.

Third, the concept of cooperation has been broadened to include working relationships with state and federal agencies as well as arrangements among local units. Efforts in the past have concentrated on revamping the local governmental structure or on interlocal cooperation, with little attention given to the actual or potential roles of higher units. Luther Gulick reflected the new orientation in a series of lectures at the University of Michigan in 1961, in which he called upon the local, state, and national governments to coordinate these programs and responsibilities in the metropolitan field. Substituting the term "extension" for the more formal stipulation of "levels" of government, Gulick proposed that "aspects" of functions rather than whole functions be assigned to the appropriate agencies of each. In his words, "We will get nowhere trying to assign whole functions, like education, health, crime, highways, or even pollution control to any one type of government. There are aspects of most functions which belong to the federal government, some to the state government, and some to the local government."[10]

This type of "partnership" requires some mechanism for reaching agreement among the participants as to what aspects of what functions shall be assigned to each. Supporters of the cooperative approach who are sympathetic to Gulick's proposal suggest that representatives from each governmental level be formed into task forces to work out such arrangements in specific problem areas such as highways, urban renewal, and water pollution. They also urge that the persuasive powers of the higher governmental echelons be employed to stimulate agreement and action on the part of the local

[10] *The Metropolitan Problem and American Ideas* (New York: Knopf, 1962), p. 164.

units. This latter plea grows out of the general belief that inter-governmental cooperation can be a meaningful device only when pressure is exerted from above.

THE FUTURE METROPOLIS

A Boston public official a few years back gave this capsule descrip-tion of his city's core area: "The average building in downtown Boston is 75 to 100 years old. Our downtown streets are winding cow pastures. Traffic is so chaotic that an expressway we just built which was to have been adequate for nearly a decade was filled to capacity on the rush hour almost as soon as it was opened. It would cost us $2 billion to get the city core back into shape again and then we couldn't begin to show results for a good ten years."[11] The Boston picture is not atypical; it might be applied, with changes in details, to most of our large metropolitan areas and to an increas-ing number of smaller urban communities. The spread of blight, particularly in the older metropolises, continues to outrun the clear-ing of slums and the upgrading of neighborhoods despite extensive redevelopment efforts. Competent observers estimate that the na-tion could continue its present rate of spending for urban renewal for the next twenty years and still not be within sight of completing the job.

But blight is only one aspect of the problem. Some critics main-tain that the failure of local governments within the metropolis to plan in unison and their insistence on public austerity to the neglect of such vital amenities as parks and open spaces is creating a disorderly asphalt jungle of appalling ugliness. Walter Gropius, the well-known architect, charges that the development of our cities is guided by zoning laws that merely "forbid the worst." Lewis Mumford sees the metropolis as an accumulation of people accom-modating themselves "to an environment without adequate natural or cultural resources: People who do without pure air, who do with-out sound sleep, who do without a cheerful garden or playing space, who do without the very sight of the sky and the sunlight, who do without free motion, spontaneous play, or a robust sexual life."[12]

[11] Quoted in Mitchell Gordon, Sick Cities (New York: Macmillan, 1963), p. 318.
[12] The Culture of Cities (New York: Harcourt, Brace & World, 1938), p. 249.

And Yale University planners Christopher Tunnard and Boris Push-
karev and their associates complain that "The expertly engineered
automobiles are seen against a background of ramshackle slums,
the winding rivers are dark with pollution, the waterfronts are
crowded with ancient factories, and the spreading suburbs seem to
have no centers of life or evidence of individual distinction."[13]

Physical Design

The physical design and appearance of the metropolis stand in
close relation to man and his activities. Given this basic premise,
the ultimate objective of all land use planning should be the creation of the most favorable spatial arrangements for man's social
and economic life and his development as an individual. A carefully
planned community of pleasing aesthetic qualities is not only functionally efficient but also stimulating to the human spirit. The everyday routine of life takes on new meaning and value in such an
environment. Conversely, a community characterized by ugly and
shoddy commercial ventures, drab housing developments, lack of
open spaces, intense congestion, and a poorly conceived pattern of
land use has little capacity to evoke feelings of identity and commitment on the part of the residents or to intensify civic energy
and cohesion.

Is the physical shape of the metropolis likely to undergo major
transformation in the foreseeable future? Will the present pattern
of development continue or will growth be directed into satellite
cities separated from the main metropolitan centers by open space
and greenbelts? Will most Americans soon be living, as some writers
predict, in a dozen or so vast "super" or "strip" cities, which are
really not cities but great sprawling complexes covering hundreds
and even thousands of square miles? No one, of course, can answer
these questions with assurance. Events such as a nuclear war or
new technological breakthroughs in transportation and communication could result in drastic alterations in the present urban pattern.
So also might a change in the life styles or values of the average
American family. But discounting the unexpected, we see no indications on the immediate horizon of a major shift from current
trends. Changes, some of substantial significance, will undoubtedly

[13] *Man-Made America: Chaos or Control* (New Haven: Yale University
Press, 1963), p. 3.

occur, but most of them will likely be adjustments in existing arrangements rather than a radical departure from them.

We can certainly expect more coordinated land use planning and a higher degree of control over development in the coming years. The pressures which are building up are too great to be disregarded. Metropolitan dwellers, for example, are showing signs of greater awareness of the need for rational physical planning. State governments are beginning to take a closer look at the development of their urban regions. The national government is steadily adding to its requirements for long-range and coordinated planning on an area-wide basis as a condition of aid. Regional planning agencies are becoming more popular and growing in influence. Finally, hundreds of local communities (with the assistance of federal "701" grants) have prepared or are in the process of formulating comprehensive land use plans. The outcome of this fermentation is yet to be seen but it is encouraging that far more planning is going on in our metropolitan and urban areas today than at any time in the past. The task ahead is to see that this planning is properly coordinated and translated into concrete results. If we cannot achieve the "city beautiful" we can at least improve considerably upon the present situation.

Social Pattern

Observers of the contemporary metropolitan scene have often expressed fear that the central city will become increasingly the home of low-income workers and non-whites while the suburbs will continue to attract the middle- and upper-income whites. Some, however, are quick to point out that a simple social dichotomy between the core city and its periphery does not now exist and is unlikely to do so in the future. The suburban portion of the metropolis, contrary to the common stereotype, does not constitute a socially homogeneous settlement but a mosaic of sub-communities segregated by income and classes. There are working-class suburbs as well as fenced-off islands of the well-to-do; industrial as well as residential satellites; blighted as well as carefully maintained and manicured fringe-area villages. This pattern could mean, as Coleman Woodbury suggests, that "socially and psychologically, both the metropolitan and suburban bodies politic will remain split up into groups and classes unable to communicate effectively, mutually suspicious, incapable of defining their common interests or of cooperating to realize them."[14]

As in the case of its physical design, there is little reason to believe that the social structure of the metropolis will undergo major modification in the near future. The pattern will likely continue to evolve along present lines with the central city shouldering a disproportionate share of responsibility for the economically and culturally deprived segments of the populace, and the suburbs continuing to attract a large proportion of white families in the lower-middle to upper-income range. However, the revolution in race relations now taking place will inevitably lead to a substantial increase in non-white penetration across the core city border. Construction of expressways and circumferential highways will further accelerate suburban dispersion by reducing the time-space ratio and making new and farther-out sections of the metropolis accessible to settlement. Decentralization of activities throughout the area will continue, with cultural facilities, such as little theatres and music halls, making their appearance at various points in the suburban complex along with the commercial and industrial enterprises.

In looking ahead, a number of emerging developments pertinent to the social structure of metropolitan communities deserve notice. Although their potentiality for change is still to be determined, they cannot be ignored in speculations about the future. First, the continuous upward movement of urban dwellers in socioeconomic rank will give a higher proportion of the metropolitan population greater freedom of choice in housing, life style, and place of residence. This in turn may serve to dilute the homogeneity of suburban communities by reducing the extent of economic segregation of the present system. The increasing freedom from racial barriers will further enhance the possibility of greater social diversity in suburbia.

Second, the steady rise in income levels for all segments of the urban community will add to the number of citizens with a stake in the social order. This fact, once the racial issue is settled, should lead to a greater degree of internal order and less social tension. It could also lessen central city-suburban hostility and pave the way for a more effective organization of the governmental system to meet the problems of metropolitan living.

[14] "Suburbanization and Suburbia," *American Journal of Public Health*, 45 (January, 1955), 9.

Third, extensive urban renewal programs will provide quality housing in the metropolitan core and make this section a safer and more attractive place to live. As a result, the central city will be in a better position to stem the exodus of leadership talent to suburbia and to achieve a more balanced social pattern. This latter development seems a remote possibility at present with the wave of migrants from the rural hinterlands inundating the central community. However, the number of these migrants will diminish in the future as the surplus population of the rural areas is drained off. This fact, coupled with economic betterment of the urban populace in general, makes the prognosis somewhat more hopeful than present events appear to warrant.

The social structure of the metropolis, in brief, exhibits both encouraging and disturbing trends. The growing affluence of the total society, the rising level of education, and the upward mobility of an increasing proportion of urban residents constitute elements of strength in the system. At the same time, the slow progress in eliminating racial discrimination, the relatively feeble efforts to upgrade the disadvantaged and culturally deprived members of the community, and the spectre of technological unemployment serve warning on the future.

Economic Structure

The economic structure of the metropolis has undergone substantial modification in the present century. Continued growth in size has been accompanied by increasing specialization and industrial diversification. It has also been accompanied by major changes in the location of commercial and industrial enterprises. At one time, not too many decades ago, economic activities were overwhelmingly concentrated in the core city. Today, the situation is strikingly different. Decentralization which began early in this century has created an entirely new pattern. Retail trade has followed the population movement outward. Suburban industrial parks have developed along the new circumferential highways and at other strategic points on the periphery. Office buildings have appeared in large suburban communities, and warehouse and distribution centers have become common sights along the outlying arteries.

The forces which are generating the spatial diffusion of homes, factories, and shopping centers are not likely to diminish in the future. Manufacturing and wholesaling enterprises will continue to respond to obsolescence and changing technological requirements by looking for new quarters. The outward movement of people will continue to be accompanied by the outward movement of jobs, stores, and service establishments. These developments have caused some analysts to regard the future of the core city, and more particularly its downtown area, with a high degree of pessimism. Certainly many central cities will decline in importance as manufacturing centers in relation to the suburban hinterlands. So also will they experience a diminishing share of the total retail market as the proportion of suburbanites in the metropolitan population increases. In many cases these will be absolute losses, a result already observed in some of the large SMSA's where the number of jobs and total retail sales in the core municipalities declined significantly during the 1950s.

Despite these trends, the central city is likely to remain a viable economic unit. The tremendous amount of fixed capital, public and private, invested in existing facilities makes it highly improbable that this section of the metropolis will be abandoned to the vagaries of fate. Although it may not capture as high a proportion of the area's economic activity as it has in the past, redevelopment of its physical plant and changes in its functional role should reverse the downward trend. The central business district will become more reliant for its economic existence upon office activity; cleared areas will provide room for certain types of commercial and light industrial enterprises; new housing construction, much of it in the form of middle- and upper-income apartments, will provide a ready clientele for the shops, restaurants, and theatres; and the assumption of a greater portion of the city's welfare costs by higher echelons of government will lessen the tax strain on the local economy.

Governmental System

Mark Twain once said: "Thunder is good, thunder is impressive, but it is lightning that does the work." The mid-twentieth-century movement to redesign the metropolitan governmental system has been characterized by much thunder but little lightning, and in recent years even the thunder has died down. To the extent that any action at all is taking place in the matter of governmental reorganization, the devices receiving most attention are the transfer of area-wide functions to the county, creation of special districts, and voluntary cooperation. It appears likely that the SMSA's which lie within single counties will make greater use of the county government as the area-wide instrumentality. Special districts will remain popular for functions, such as water supply, sewage disposal, and air pollution, that require administrative areas larger than the county. Intergovernmental agreements of significant scope will be increasingly employed in efforts to ward off more drastic solutions. Finally, state and federal agencies will play expanding roles in the governance of metropolitan areas.

If the governmental system of the metropolis is to serve its full purpose, it must be capable of striking a balance between the particularizing and centralizing forces in the urban community. It must, in other words, possess institutional mechanisms for satisfying localistic needs and aspirations on the one hand, and meeting the overall demands of the total metropolitan complex on the other. Frequently, these two tendencies are in direct conflict. Residents of a suburban community, for example, may desire to maintain a "country-like" atmosphere in their environs, but metropolitan needs may require the construction of a major highway through the village. Or residents in one section of the area may want to retain control over their own school system but find consolidation with neighboring districts necessary in order to upgrade the quality of education for the larger community.

The two-tier or federal plan of local government in its various forms is designed to accommodate both of these tendencies. This approach acknowledges the pressures of localism by seeking to preserve a meaningful sphere of activity at the sub-metropolitan level and to provide a symbolic anchoring post for community identification and civic participation. At the same time, it recognizes the centripetal forces in the metropolitan aggregate by endeavoring to fashion an institutional framework for the exercise of leadership and policy-formulation in matters of area-wide concern. The principle of local federalism is logically sound and acceptable to most Americans; the difficulty—aside from that mentioned previously when clusters of metropolitan areas are involved—lies in a lack of consensus as to how it should be implemented and what the functional division should be. These are issues, moreover, that will not be settled by any grand design or total plan. Given our long-demonstrated penchant for making marginal rather than major adjustments in the local governmental system, problems of this nature will be resolved only by the gradual accumulation of lesser changes made in response to immediate and concrete problems.

In final analysis, it really matters little to the shaping of the urban environment whether a metropolitan area has a unified police force or a host of smaller departments, or whether water is supplied by one special district, refuse disposal by another, and mass transit by a third. Such a fragmented service pattern does raise problems of coordination and efficiency, but these difficulties need not render the system dysfunctional. Telephone, gas, and electric utilities, for example, have been able to respond to metropolitan needs effectively even though they operate as separate entities. What is important is that there be some established means of formulating community goals and policies, of coordinating and guiding overall development, and of giving the metropolitan electorate a voice in the critical issues that affect the total complex. Instead of concentrating efforts on restructuring the local governmental pattern as it relates to service problems, future emphasis might be more profitably placed on the creation of institutional mechanisms designed to bring all affected public agencies—local, state, and federal—to bear on the achievement of broad metropolitan goals.

THE GOOD METROPOLIS

Urban man is so immersed in his personal pursuits and day-to-day problems that, like the Muckraker in *The Pilgrim's Progress,* he does not raise his head to see the broader vision of the good community. The full potential of the modern metropolis escapes his thought as the difficulties and maladies which plague urban living capture his attention. Traffic congestion and overcrowded schools have meaning for him, as do crime and physical blight. He is unhappy about the racial problem and he grumbles occasionally at the rising costs of local government. But none of these developments seems to impair seriously the attainment of his own goals or to disturb him to the point where he is ready to take action to reconstruct the system. Perhaps, as political scientist York Willbern has expressed it:

. . . the great sprawling urban areas of this country fall short not so much in their achievement of the goals and ambitions of their residents, as in the degree to which they achieve or fail to achieve the speculative constructs of the intellectuals who concern themselves with the matter. The disparity is not between the metropolis as it is and the metropolis as its residents wish it; the disparity is between the existing metropolis and the City of God of the planners and the dreamers.[15]

But as Bloody Mary in *South Pacific* exclaimed, "You can't make a dream come true without first having a dream." It is the function of those who have caught the vision of a better city and metropolis—planners, philosophers, poets, novelists, social critics— to provide the dream. It is the function of political and civic leaders to seize upon those aspects of the vision which are in the realm of possibility, to define them in concrete terms, and to present them to the people for debate and consideration. It is the function of the citizenry to make the choice and to determine the goals that the community should seek. If general consensus could be reached as to the kind of community that is wanted, refashioning the governmental machinery for the purpose of achieving this objective might then be more readily accomplished.

The system of local government in a metropolitan area exists to assure order and supply public services. Beyond these basic tasks, it exists to nurture civic life and to foster the values of a free and democratic society. It serves this higher role to the extent that it is able to fashion an environment suitable for the expression and development of human potentialities and for the personal growth of its individual members. Government is by no means the sole or possibly even the most important instrumentality for promoting men's goals. This is a task for which all community institutions share responsibility. The special role of the governmental system is to provide an appropriate framework within which the energy and resources of the community can be mobilized and directed at improving the quality of urban life. Pessimistic as the outlook may seem to some, the good metropolis is more than a figment of utopian fancy. Its achievement is within the capabilities and resources of modern man. The choice of the future is his to make.

[15] *The Withering Away of the City* (University, Ala.: University of Alabama Press, 1963), p. 47.

A COMMENTARY ON BIBLIOGRAPHY

OUR PURPOSE in presenting this bibliographical essay is to comment briefly on important literature about the metropolis not generally mentioned elsewhere in this book. As a rule, therefore, the commentary supplements rather than duplicates the extensive footnote citations in the text. To keep it within manageable proportions and increase its usefulness, we have made a representative sampling of significant materials and have organized them under various major categories. Except in a few instances involving general treatments of subjects, single articles from periodicals have been excluded.

Two extensive bibliographies of writings on metropolitan affairs with emphasis on governmental aspects are Government Affairs Foundation, *Metropolitan Communities: A Bibliography* (Chicago: Public Administration Service, 1956) and Government Affairs Foundation and University of California (Berkeley) Bureau of Public Administration, *Metropolitan Communities: A Bibliography, Supplement: 1955–1957* (Chicago: Public Administration Service, 1960). Briefer, more recent bibliographies are Barbara J. Hudson, "The City in America," *American Review*, II (May, 1962), 142–160, and U.S. Senate Committee on Government Operations, Subcommittee on Intergovernmental Relations, *Metropolitan America* (Washington: 1964). A selected bibliography concentrating on items dealing with local government adaptation to changing urban needs is contained in Roscoe C. Martin, *Metropolis in Transition* (Washington: U.S. Housing and Home Finance Agency, September, 1963).

Various enumerations conducted by the U.S. Bureau of the Census constitute basic general sources of data. Those most relevant here are the *Census of Population* (the latest in 1960), the *Census of Housing* (1960), the *Census of Governments* (1962), the *Census of Manufactures* (1963), and the *Census of Business* (1958). *County and City Data Book* (1962) provides a convenient compilation of information assembled from these and other census publications.

Other basic general sources are *Metropolitan Area Problems: News and Digest*, released bimonthly by the Graduate School of Public Affairs, State University of New York, Albany; the sections titled "Metropolitan

Areas," "County Government," and "Citizen Action" in the *National Civic Review* (formerly the *National Municipal Review*), issued monthly, except in August, by the National Municipal League, New York; and articles and tables relating to metropolitan areas, counties, and other urban developments in the *Municipal Year Book*, published by the International City Managers' Association, Chicago. All three publications contain bibliographies.

The status of research on urbanism and metropolitanism and suggestions about further lines of investigation have been receiving increased attention. Examples are Stephen B. Sweeney and George S. Blair (eds.), *Metropolitan Analysis: Important Elements of Study and Action* (Philadelphia: University of Pennsylvania Press, 1958); Coleman Woodbury, *A Framework for Urban Studies: An Analysis of Urban-Metropolitan Development and Research Needs* (Washington: Highway Research Board, October, 1959); and Raymond Vernon and others, *The Myth and Reality of Our Urban Problems* (Cambridge: Harvard University Press, 1962). Additional illustrations are Roscoe C. Martin and Douglas Price, *The Metropolis and Its Problems* (1960); Stanley Scott, Ronald R. Royce, and Robert L. Brown, *Two Notes on Metropolitan Research* (1961); and Harvey E. Brazer, Scott Greer, and York Willbern, *Metropolitan Issues: Social, Governmental, Fiscal* (1962), edited by Guthrie S. Birkhead. Of these three publications, the first two are summaries of Syracuse University faculty seminars on metropolitan research and the third consists of background papers prepared for a similar seminar. These monographs were published by the Maxwell Graduate School of Citizenship and Public Affairs, Syracuse University, Syracuse, New York. In addition, important critiques have appeared in article form: Allan R. Richards, "Local Government Research: A Partial Evaluation," *Public Administration Review*, XIV (Autumn, 1954), 271–277; Robert Daland, "Political Science and the Study of Urbanism," *American Political Science Review*, LI (June, 1957), 491–507; Lawrence Herson, "The Lost World of Municipal Government," *American Political Science Review*, LI (June, 1957), 330–345; and William Anderson's rejoinder to Professor Herson, "Municipal Government: No Lost World," *American Political Science Review*, LI (September, 1957), 776–783.

The historical approach to urbanism is represented by such recent works as Gideon Sjoberg, *The Preindustrial City* (New York: Free Press, 1960); Lewis Mumford, *The City in History* (New York: Harcourt, Brace & World, 1961); Oscar Handlin and John Burchard (eds.), *The Historian and the City* (Cambridge: The M.I.T. Press and Harvard University Press, 1963); Blake McKelvey, *The Urbanization of America, 1860–1915* (New Brunswick: Rutgers University Press, 1963); Charles Glaab, *The American City: A Documentary History* (Homewood, Illinois: Dorsey Press, 1963); and Wilson Smith (ed.), *Cities of Our Past and Present* (New York: Wiley, 1964). Scholarly histories of individual cities include Bayrd Still, *Milwaukee : The History of a City* (Madison: The

State Historical Society of Wisconsin, 1948); Blake McKelvey's three-volume study of Rochester, New York, published by Harvard University Press, 1945–1956; and A. Theodore Brown, *The History of Kansas City to 1870* (Columbia: University of Missouri Press, 1964).

The pioneering broad analyses of metropolitan developments were Paul Studenski, *The Government of Metropolitan Areas in the United States* (New York: National Municipal League, 1930); Victor Jones, *Metropolitan Government* (Chicago: University of Chicago Press, 1942); and R. D. McKenzie, *The Metropolitan Community* (New York: McGraw-Hill, 1933). The Studenski and Jones volumes concentrated on governmental phases; the McKenzie book gave some attention to governmental matters and to certain economic considerations but it emphasized social trends. Professor Jones elaborated upon and updated specific portions of his earlier study in Part IV of Coleman Woodbury (ed.), *The Future of Cities and Urban Redevelopment* (Chicago: University of Chicago Press, 1953). The editor's chapters in Part V of this book furnish a wide and penetrating survey of some of the basic issues confronting urban communities.

Among the insightful broad studies of recent origin are Robert C. Wood, *Suburbia: Its People and Their Politics* (Boston: Houghton Mifflin, 1959); Scott Greer, *The Emerging City: Myth and Reality* (New York: Free Press, 1962) and his shorter *Governing the Metropolis* (New York: Wiley, 1962); Webb S. Fiser, *Mastery of the Metropolis* (Englewood Cliffs: Prentice-Hall, 1962); and York Willbern, *The Withering Away of the City* (University: University of Alabama Press, 1964). Broad treatments published as entire numbers of periodicals include "A Symposium on Metropolitan Regionalism: Developing Governmental Concepts," *University of Pennsylvania Law Review* (February, 1957); Martin Meyerson, Barbara Terrett, and Paul Ylvisaker (eds.), "Metropolis in Ferment," *Annals of the American Academy of Political and Social Science* (November, 1957); Thomas P. Peardon (ed.), "The Urban Problems," *Proceedings of the Academy of Political Science* (May, 1960); Lloyd Rodwin and Kevin Lynch (eds.), "The Future Metropolis," *Daedalus* (Winter, 1961); and Robert B. Mitchell (ed.), "Urban Revival: Goals and Standards," *Annals of the American Academy of Political and Social Science* (March, 1964). Books of readings containing interesting reprints are Oliver P. Williams and Charles Press (eds.), *Democracy in Urban America* (Chicago: Rand McNally, 1961); Edward C. Banfield, *Urban Government* (New York: Free Press, 1961); and C. E. Elias, Jr., James Gillies, and Svend Riemer (eds.), *Metropolis: Values in Conflict* (Belmont, California: Wadsworth, 1964). Werner Z. Hirsch (ed.), *Urban Life and Form* (New York: Holt, Rinehart and Winston, 1963) features papers by nine scholars from a variety of academic disciplines.

Also of a broad nature are the reports of the national Advisory Commission on Intergovernmental Relations (such as *Performance of*

Urban Functions: Local and Areawide, Apportionment of State Legislatures, and *Directory of Federal Statistics for Metropolitan Areas*); the publications of the Committee for Economic Development (for instance, *Guiding Metropolitan Growth,* and Robert C. Wood's *Metropolis Against Itself*); the monographs on legal problems in metropolitan areas issued by the University of Michigan Law School Legislative Research Center (*Planning and Zoning in the United States, Interstate Metropolitan Areas,* and others); and the New York Metropolitan Region Study, which although primarily oriented toward economic factors includes social studies (Oscar Handlin's *The Newcomers*) and governmental evaluations (Robert C. Wood's *1400 Governments*). The summary publication in the New York series is Raymond Vernon, *Metropolis: 1985,* published originally in 1960 by the Harvard University Press, Cambridge, and subsequently issued in paperback in 1963 by Doubleday, Garden City, New York.

Urban social dimensions are discussed in a wide variety of works including Otis Dudley Duncan and Albert J. Reiss, Jr., *Social Characteristics of Urban and Rural Communities* (New York: Wiley, 1956); Bennet M. Berger, *Working-Class Suburb: A Study of Auto Workers in Suburbia* (Berkeley and Los Angeles: University of California Press, 1960); Alvin Boskoff, *The Sociology of Urban Regions* (New York: Appleton-Century-Crofts, 1962); James M. Beshers, *Urban Social Structure* (New York: Free Press, 1962); and William A. Dobriner, *Class in Suburbia* (Englewood Cliffs: Prentice-Hall, 1963). Amos H. Hawley, *The Changing Shape of Metropolitan America: Deconcentration Since 1920* (New York: Free Press, 1956) analyzes patterns of population growth and change; and Harold M. Mayer and Clyde F. Kohn (eds.), *Readings in Urban Geography* (Chicago: University of Chicago Press, 1959) brings together a number of previously published articles on geographic concepts related to urban structure and functions.

Social problems are examined in Robert K. Merton, *Contemporary Social Problems* (New York: Harcourt, Brace & World, 1961); James Bryant Conant, *Slums and Suburbs: A Commentary on Schools in Metropolitan Areas* (New York: McGraw-Hill, 1961); Bernard Rosenberg, Israel Gerner, and F. W. Howton, *Mass Society in Crisis: Social Problems and Social Pathology* (New York: Macmillan, 1964); Robert C. Weaver, *The Urban Complex* (Garden City, New York: Doubleday, 1964); and *Converging Social Trends and Emerging Social Problems* (Washington: U.S. Department of Health, Education, and Welfare, 1964).

The economic aspects of metropolitan communities are treated in such studies as Gunnar Alexandersson, *The Industrial Structure of American Cities* (Lincoln: University of Nebraska Press, 1956); John Rannells, *The Core of the City: A Pilot Study of Changing Land Uses in Central Business Districts* (New York: Columbia University Press, 1956); Otis Dudley Duncan and others, *Metropolis and Region* (Baltimore: Johns Hopkins Press, 1960); Ruth L. Mace, *Industry and City Government* (Chapel Hill: University of North Carolina Institute of Government, 1960); Donald J. Bogue and Calvin L. Beale, *The Economic Areas of the United States* (New York: Free Press, 1961); Richard B. Andrews, *Urban Growth and Development* (New York: Simmons-Boardman, 1962); F. Stuart Chapin, Jr., and Shirley F. Weiss (eds.), *Urban Growth Dynamics in a Regional Cluster of Cities* (New York: Wiley, 1962); and Benjamin Chinitz (ed.), *City and Suburb: The Economics of Metropolitan Growth* (Englewood Cliffs: Prentice-Hall, 1964). The nature and purpose of economic base studies are examined in Charles M. Tiebout, *The Community Economic Base Study* (New York: Committee for Economic Development, December, 1962). Economic analyses of individual metropolises include John L. O'Donnell and others, *Economic and Population Base Study of the Lansing Tri-County Area* (East Lansing: Michigan State University Bureau of Business and Economic Research, 1960) and the excellent four-volume study of the Pittsburgh region, directed by Edgar M. Hoover and published by the University of Pittsburgh Press in 1963 and 1964.

There have been numerous studies of decision-making, power structures, and leadership in urban settings since the early 1950s. A series of essays on these topics is contained in Darwin Cartwright (ed.), *Studies in Social Power* (Ann Arbor: University of Michigan Press, 1959); Charles Adrian (ed.), *Social Science and Community Action* (East Lansing: Michigan State University Institute for Community Development and Services, 1960); Morris Janowitz (ed.), *Community Political Systems* (New York: Free Press, 1961); William V. D'Antonio and Howard J. Ehrlich (eds.), *Power and Democracy in America* (South Bend: University of Notre Dame Press, 1961); Bert E. Swanson (ed.), *Current Trends in Comparative Community Studies* (Kansas City, Missouri: Community Studies, Inc., 1962); and Harmon Zeigler and M. Kent Jennings (eds.), *The Electoral Process* (Englewood Cliffs: Prentice-Hall, 1964). Other relevant works, in addition to those cited in Chapter 7, are Martin Meyerson and Edward C. Banfield, *Politics, Planning, and the Public Interest* (New York: Free Press, 1957); James Q. Wilson, *Negro Politics* (New York: Free Press, 1960); Roscoe C. Martin, Frank J. Munger and others, *Decisions in Syracuse* (Bloomington: Indiana University Press, 1961); Edward C. Banfield and James Q. Wilson, *City Politics* (Cambridge: Harvard University Press and the M.I.T. Press, 1963); Carol E. Thomitz, *The Decision-Makers: The Power Structure of Dallas* (Dallas: Southern Methodist University, 1963); M. Kent Jennings, *Community Influentials: The Elites of Atlanta* (New York: Free Press, 1964); and Aaron Wildavsky, *Leadership in a Small Town* (Totowa, New Jersey: Bedminster Press, 1964). Useful reviews of the research literature concerned with decision-making, power, and leadership are Wendell Bell, Richard J. Hill, and Charles R. Wright, *Public Leadership* (San Francisco: Chandler, 1961), and Charles Press, *Main Street*

Politics: Policy-Making at the Local Level (East Lansing: Michigan State University Institute for Community Development and Services, 1962).

Studies of voting and other forms of political participation at the local level are widely scattered in articles, monographs, and sample survey reports. Robert E. Lane, *Political Life* (New York: Free Press, 1959) presents a comprehensive summary of the findings of such studies. Specialized works on this subject include Lawrence W. O'Rourke, *Voting Behavior in the Forty-Five Cities of Los Angeles County* (Los Angeles: University of California Bureau of Governmental Research, 1953); Richard A. Watson, *The Politics of Urban Change* (Kansas City, Missouri: Community Studies, Inc., 1963) which focuses on political participation in an urban redevelopment area; and Alvin Boskoff and Harmon Zeigler, *Voting Patterns in a Local Election* (Philadelphia: Lippincott, 1964).

Considerable research dealing with housing and redevelopment in urban areas has emerged in recent years. The most comprehensive works in this field are the two volumes edited by Coleman Woodbury, the first entitled *The Future of Cities and Urban Redevelopment,* and the second, *Urban Redevelopment: Problems and Practices* (Chicago: University of Chicago Press, 1953); and Martin Meyerson, Barbara Terrett, and William L. C. Wheaton, *Housing, People, and Cities* (New York: McGraw-Hill, 1962), the final and summary book of a series prepared under the sponsorship of ACTION, the national council for good cities. Other works in this substantive area include Miles L. Colean, *Renewing Our Cities* (New York: Twentieth Century Fund, 1953); Louis Winnick, *American Housing and Its Use* (New York: Wiley, 1957); Edward C. Banfield and Morton Grodzins, *Government and Housing in Metropolitan Areas* (New York: McGraw-Hill, 1958); Reuel Hamdahl, *Urban Renewal* (Washington: Scarecrow Press, 1959); R. M. Fisher, *Twenty Years of Public Housing* (New York: Harper & Row, 1959); George S. Duggar (ed.), *The New Renewal* (Berkeley: University of California Bureau of Public Administration, 1961); Thomas F. Johnson, James R. Morris, and Joseph G. Butts, *Renewing America's Cities* (Washington: Institute for Social Science Research, 1962); Kurt W. Back, *Slums, Projects, and People* (Durham: Duke University Press, 1962); Bernard J. Frieden, *The Future of Old Neighborhoods* (Cambridge: Massachusetts Institute of Technology Press, 1964); and Martin Anderson, *The Federal Bulldozer: A Critical Analysis of Urban Renewal* (Cambridge: The M.I.T. Press, 1964). The story of urban renewal in the Hyde Park-Kenwood section of Chicago is recounted in Julia Abrahamson, *A Neighborhood Finds Itself* (New York: Harper & Row, 1959). Redevelopment trends abroad are discussed in Leo Grebler, *Urban Renewal in European Countries* (Philadelphia: University of Pennsylvania Press, 1964). The politics of redevelopment is treated in Peter H. Rossi and Robert A. Dentler, *The Politics of Urban Renewal:*

The Chicago Findings (New York: Free Press, 1961), and Harold Kaplan, *Urban Renewal Politics: Slum Clearance in Newark* (New York: Columbia University Press, 1963).

The physical planning of urban and metropolitan communities is discussed in Harland Bartholomew, *Land Uses in American Cities* (Cambridge: Harvard University Press, 1955); Paul Zucker, *Town and Square* (New York: Columbia University Press, 1959); Humphrey Carver, *Cities in the Suburbs* (Toronto: University of Toronto Press, 1962); Arthur B. Gallion, *The Urban Pattern*, 2nd ed. (Princeton: Van Nostrand, 1963); and T. J. Kent, Jr., *The Urban General Plan* (San Francisco: Chandler, 1964). Harvey S. Perloff (ed.), *Planning and the Urban Community* (Pittsburgh: University of Pittsburgh Press, 1961) is a collection of perceptive essays on city planning and urbanism. Various aspects of zoning and land use control are covered in Charles M. Haar, *Land Use Planning* (Boston: Little, Brown, 1959); John Delafons, *Land Use Controls in the United States* (Cambridge: Harvard University and Massachusetts Institute of Technology Joint Center for Urban Studies, 1962); and Sidney M. Willhelm, *Urban Zoning and Land Use Theory* (New York: Free Press, 1962). Works that focus on the "new town" concept include Clarence S. Stein, *Toward New Towns for America* (New York: Reinhold, 1957), and Frederic J. Osborn and Arnold Whittick, *The New Towns: The Answer to Megalopolis* (New York: McGraw-Hill, 1963). A classic critique of urban planning in the utopian tradition is Percival and Paul Goodman, *Communitas*, 2nd ed. (New York: Vintage Books, 1960). Selective planning bibliographies are contained in Samuel Spielvogel, *A Selected Bibliography on City and Regional Planning* (Washington: Scarecrow Press, 1951), and George C. Bestor and H. R. Jones, *City Planning: A Basic Bibliography* (Sacramento: California Council of Civil Engineers and Land Surveyors, 1962). The City and Regional Planning Library of the University of California, Berkeley, issues *Urban Items*, a bibliography of materials on city problems and planning, approximately bimonthly. *Planning*, published each year by the American Society of Planning Officials, Chicago, contains selected papers from the organization's annual national conference.

Financing government in the metropolis has been the subject of various studies, most of them reported in periodical literature and monographs. Papers covering a wide range of metropolitan fiscal problems are contained in *Financing Metropolitan Government* (Princeton: Tax Institute, Inc., 1955). Several reports of the Advisory Commission on Intergovernmental Relations are pertinent, including *Local Nonproperty Taxes and the Coordinating Role of the State* (September, 1961); *Intergovernmental Cooperation in Tax Administration* (June, 1961); and *Measures of State and Local Fiscal Capacity and Tax Effort* (October, 1962). An example of a fiscal analysis of a particular metropolitan area is Seymour Sacks and William F. Hellmuth, Jr., *Financing Government in a Metropolitan Area: The Cleveland Experience* (New York: Free Press, 1961).

Specialized studies in this field include R. A. Sigafoos, *The Municipal Income Tax* (Chicago: Public Administration Service, 1955); H. F. Alderfer and R. L. Funk, *Municipal Non-Property Taxes* (Chicago: Municipal Finance Officers Association, 1956); John F. Due, *Sales Taxation* (Urbana: University of Illinois Press, 1957); Harvey E. Brazer, *City Expenditures in the United States* (New York: National Bureau of Economic Research, 1959); Raymond J. Green, *The Impact of the Central Business District on the Municipal Budget* (Washington: Urban Land Institute, 1962); and Werner Z. Hirsch's essay, "Urban Government Services and Their Financing," in *Urban Life and Form*, which was listed earlier.

In addition to the previously mentioned Studenski and Jones books, the subjects of governmental services and reorganization are considered in John C. Bollens, *The States and the Metropolitan Problem* (Chicago: Council of State Governments, 1956); *Special District Governments in the United States* (Berkeley and Los Angeles: University of California Press, 1957) by the same author; Robert G. Smith, *Public Authorities, Special Districts and Local Government* (Washington: National Association of Counties Research Foundation, 1964), which is a five-state inquiry; and Luther H. Gulick, *The Metropolitan Problem and American Ideas* (New York: Knopf, 1962). Numerous studies of services and reorganization have been made of individual metropolitan areas, many of which are summarized in Government Affairs Foundation, *Metropolitan Surveys: A Digest* (Chicago: Public Administration Service, 1958). This work also includes a helpful introductory essay by Daniel R. Grant. In recent years, the final annual number of *Metropolitan Area Problems: News and Digest* has contained a description of metropolitan surveys currently in progress. Practically all of the individual studies have been published in small editions by the sponsoring agencies and are not generally available. Among the exceptions are Leverett S. Lyon (ed.), *Governmental Problems in the Chicago Metropolitan Area* (Chicago: University of Chicago Press, 1957), and John C. Bollens (ed.), *Exploring the Metropolitan Community* (Berkeley and Los Angeles: University of California Press, 1961). The reflections of a director of a metropolitan survey are presented in James A. Norton, *The Metro Experience* (Cleveland: The Press of Western Reserve University, 1963).

The politics of attempts to reorganize the governmental system of particular metropolitan areas is receiving considerable scrutiny. The published results include Henry J. Schmandt, Paul G. Steinbicker, and George D. Wendel, *Metropolitan Reform in St. Louis* (New York: Holt, Rinehart and Winston, 1961); Edward Sofen, *The Miami Metropolitan Experiment* (Bloomington: Indiana University Press, 1963); David A. Booth, *Metropolitics: The Nashville Consolidation* (East Lansing: Michigan State University Institute for Community Development and Services, 1963); and Scott Greer, *Metropolitics: A Study of Political Culture* (New York: Wiley, 1963), which is largely concerned with Metropolitan St. Louis and to a lesser extent with the Cleveland and Miami areas. Frank S. Sengstock and others, *Consolidation: Building a Bridge Between City and Suburb* (Worcester: Heffernan Press, 1964) analyzes the 1962 consolidation attempt in the St. Louis area. The perceptive essays in Part III of Norton E. Long, *The Polity* (Chicago: Rand McNally, 1962), edited by Charles Press, are also relevant to the politics of reorganization.

Prominent illustrations of writings on intergovernmental relations and the mounting influence of the national and state governments in the metropolis are Robert H. Connery and Richard H. Leach, *The Federal Government and Metropolitan Areas* (Cambridge: Harvard University Press, 1960); W. Brooke Graves, *American Intergovernmental Relations* (New York: Scribner, 1964); *Impact of Federal Urban Development Programs on Local Government Organization and Planning* (Washington: 1964), issued by the Subcommittee on Intergovernmental Relations of the U.S. Senate Committee on Government Operations; *State Legislative Program of the Advisory Commission on Intergovernmental Relations* (Washington: 1963 and 1964); and the Council of State Governments' *State Responsibility in Urban Regional Development* (Chicago: 1962) and *Suggested State Legislation* (Chicago: issued annually).

The literature pertaining to metropolitan communities in a world setting is diversified and extensive. The United Nations and its various agencies and the International Union of Local Authorities at The Hague, Netherlands, are rich sources for both bibliographies and specialized studies. Two of the latest and most valuable bibliographical compilations are *A World of Cities*, edited by Robert Lorenz, Paul Meadows, and Warner Bloomberg, Jr., and published by the Center for Overseas Operations and Research, Maxwell Graduate School of Citizenship and Public Affairs, Syracuse University, in 1964 and *Comparative Urban Development: An Annotated Bibliography*, prepared by William Bicker, David Brown, Herbert Malakoff, and William J. Gore and issued by the Comparative Administration Group of the American Society for Public Administration, Washington, in 1965. Works that treat of local government on a world basis are William A. Robson (ed.), *Great Cities of the World: Their Government, Politics and Planning*, rev. ed. (New York: Macmillan, 1957); Samuel Humes and Eileen Martin, *The Structure of Local Governments Throughout the World* (The Hague: Martinus Nijhoff, 1961); and Harold F. Alderfer, *Local Government in Developing Countries* (New York: McGraw-Hill, 1964). Others covering specific areas include Ronald Wraith, *Local Government in West Africa* (New York: Praeger, 1964); and Fred G. Burke, *Local Government and Politics in Uganda* (Syracuse: Syracuse University Press, 1964). Recent studies with a sociological emphasis are illustrated by Takeo Yazaki, *The Japanese City* (Tokyo: Japan Publications Trading Co., 1963), and E. Gordon Ericksen, *Africa Company Town* (Dubuque: William C. Brown, 1964).

General aspects of urbanization abroad are dealt with in Francis Violich, *Cities of Latin America* (New York: Reinhold, 1944); Philip M. Hauser (ed.), *Urbanization in Asia and the Far East* (Calcutta: UNESCO Research Centre, 1958); and T. Lynn Smith, *Latin America Population Studies* (Gainesville: University of Florida Press, 1961).

Indexes

Indexes

INDEX OF NAMES [1]

[1] This is an index of personal names. The names of places and organizations appear in the Index of Subjects. The letter "n" after a page number indicates that the reference is in a footnote.

INDEX OF SUBJECTS

London County Council, 555, 558

London Transport Executive, 557

Long Branch (Ontario), 480

Los Angeles: predominant ethnic group in, 94; declining proportion of white population in, 97; weak mayor-council government in, 168; political party activity in, 204; slums in, 253; water supply of, 322; use of annexation by, 323, 404, 405; per capita public spending in, 342; municipal consolidation involving, 404

Los Angeles County (Calif.): chief administrative officer in, 162; voting in, 238; law enforcement in, 334; governmental agreements in, 381-383, 385-392; as an urban county, 386-388

Los Angeles–Long Beach SMSA: population of, 18; rapid population increase of, 18; air pollution in, 30; rankings in multidimensional typology, 75; proportion of non-whites in suburbs of, 98; gain of manufacturing employment by central cities of, 132; loss of retail trade sales by central cities in, 133; expressways in, 315; air pollution in, 328; fire protection in, 378 n.

Low-income areas, residents of, 250

Lubbock (Tex.), sizable amount of land annexed by, 412

Macon (Ga.) SMSA, defeat of city-county consolidation in, 430, 433

Madison (Wis.) SMSA, number of local governments in, 145

Maine, township managers in, 170

Manila (Philippine Islands), 553

Manpower exchange, 381-383

Manufacturing employment, losses by central cities of, 131-133

Manufacturing value added, state increases in, 116

Market mechanism, and local public services, 352-353

Market place, relation to economic model, 64

Maryland, number of metropolitan areas in, 15

Mass transit, 441, 544, 545, 546; decline of, 314; as part of balanced transportation system, 315; subsidy of, 316; aid by national government to, 317

Massachusetts: number of metropolitan areas in, 15; aid in acquiring land

for parks and recreational facilities, 336

Massachusetts Bay Transportation Authority (Boston area), 318

Master plan: components of, 279; execution a political act, 280

Mayor, and city planning, 281

Mayor-council government: organization of, 165; characteristics of, 168

Medical societies, 106

Megalopolis: characteristics of, 37-39, 582-583; implications for local government, 583, 584; effect on two-level approach to governmental reorganization, 583

Memphis (Tenn.) SMSA: voting on governmental reorganization in, 227; defeat of city-county consolidation in, 433

Merger. See City-county consolidation; Municipal consolidation; School district consolidation

Meriden (Conn.) SMSA, population of, 17

Merit system county, 161

Metropolis, different meanings of, 1-2. See also Metropolitan areas

Metropolitan age: governmental system in, 156-159; governmental adjustments in, 159-177

Metropolitan Air Pollution Control District (Boston area), 330

Metropolitan Area Council (Baltimore area), 393 n.

Metropolitan Area Problems: News and Digest, 606

Metropolitan areas, definitions of, 6-10, 32-34, 46-50. See also Metropolis

Metropolitan Community Studies (Dayton area), 455

Metropolitan councils of governments, 303, 372, 538, 589; contrasting views about, 392; number of, 392; recent origin of, 392; features of, 393; future of, 398-399

Metropolitan districts: territorial scope of, 440-441; mostly of recent origin, 441; functions of, 441; accomplishments of, 441-442; factors prompting growth of, 443-444; frequent remoteness from public of, 444; governing board composition of, 444; use of constituent-unit principle of representation in, 445-447; proposed expansion to multipurpose basis, 447-452. See also Metropolitan multipurpose districts

STANDARD METROPOLITAN STATISTICA

SOURCE: EXECUTIVE OFFICE OF THE PRESIDENT,
BUREAU OF THE BUDGET,
WASHINGTON, 1961